OUT OF THIS WORLD

Mysteries of Mind, Space and Time

CAXTON

A Macdonald Book

Material in this book previously appeared in the partwork
The Unexplained

This edition published in 1989
by Macdonald & Co (Publishers) Ltd
London & Sydney

British Library Cataloguing in Publication Data
Out of this world.
  1. Paranormal phenomena, to 1914
  I. Brookesmith, Peter, *1944–*
133'09

ISBN 0 356 17959 1

Consultants to *The Unexplained*
Professor A. J. Ellison
Dr J Allen Hynek
Brian Inglis
Colin Wilson

Printed and bound in Belgium

Macdonald & Co (Publishers) Ltd
66–73 Shoe Lane
London EC4P 4AB

CONTENTS

PART 1
APPEARANCES AND DISAPPEARANCES

Introduction

Introducing the mystery of the disappearance of the British diplomat, Benjamin Bathurst, Charles Fort (pioneer collector of accounts of strange phenomena) wrote: 'Here is the shortest story I know . . . He walked around the horses.' That was all that could be said about the moment, on 25 November 1809, when Bathurst examined the coach horses prior to resuming his journey home to England from the court of Emperor Francis at Vienna. Outside an inn in the small German town of Perleberg, and in full view of his valet and secretary, Bathurst stepped around the horses and off the face of this earth.

Ultimately, not much more can be said about the truly mysterious disappearance, or its counterpart, the inexplicable and sudden appearance, of a person or object from or into the world. Indeed, as a useful index I have often found that the probable verity of a case is in inverse proportion to the authentic details available about its crucial moment. After all, a sudden disappearance takes its essential evidence with it, and in noticing the vacuum even the keenest of observers would sooner or later begin to doubt their own eyes.

Those who witness or stumble upon an appearance are more fortunate in being able to grasp or interrogate their material evidence, although most usually, as in the celebrated case of Kaspar Hauser, the cryptic information they receive only adds to their confusion. Those who appear are usually less fortunate still, as illustrated by the following fatal example, told to the English philosopher, John Aubrey, by an acquaintance who heard of the case while in Portugal in 1655. As Aubrey records it in his *Miscellanies*, a Portuguese man was tried by the Inquisition following his unexplained appearance in that country. I say 'unexplained' because the man himself could not say why or how he came to be there. He had been about his business, in the Portuguese colony of Goa, in India, when suddenly, as far as he could tell, he was back in Portugal. What little he could say was that he must have been 'brought thither . . . in the air, in an incredible short time.' This sounds like levitation, spontaneous flight or even teleportation to our wonder-thirsty age; but in the dark age of its happening, fear was spreading over Europe as the light of reason was blotted out by the smoke from witch-burnings. The man who had survived his magical translation from India to Portugal was found guilty of consorting with the Devil, tied to a fiery stake, and given a public send-off on a longer journey from which he could never return.

In his wide-ranging study of a bewildering variety of reports of paranormal and unexplained phenomena, Fort encountered many forms of appearances and disappearances. In particular he noted the comings and goings of objects that the spiritualists call apports, but his fact gathering showed many instances in which the attributing of these mysterious journeys to the actions of discarnate entities was not only inappropriate, its 'special pleading' was also an obstacle to any more accurate understanding of what was going on. For his *Book of the Damned*, in 1919, Fort coined the less emotive term 'teleportation' to describe – not explain – the hypothetical force by which objects and people could be transported, presumably instantaneously, from one place to another, and again presumably without necessarily traversing the intervening physical distance. If teleportation existed, argued Fort, it would show up, mostly indirectly, in data about objects or people mysteriously disappearing or appearing. This exists in abundance, if looked for in the right places.

Take conventional 'missing persons' statistics, for example. We are told that in London alone, the Metropolitan Police receives on average more than fifty calls a day. In most cases the person turns up, or is traced one way or another, but an alarming seven vanish without trace in London every day. General statistics for the year 1977, cited by Paul Begg in his *Into Thin Air*, suggest that UK disappearances may reach a quarter of a million. It would not be unreasonable to believe that this figure has been exceeded, here in the mid-1980s, and that the world-wide total would be several orders larger if it were at all calculable. There are many reasons for wanting to vanish – family and marriage problems figure most highly. It seems that a few turn up in mental institutions, a greater number fall prey to drugs, crime and murder, and a large percentage, it must be assumed, have no wish to be found.

From our modern standpoint we must take into account the mental phenomenon of fugue states (loss of sense of identity) and secondary personalities, the classic example of which, recorded by the pioneering American psychologist, William James, involved the Rev. Ansel Bourne, of Rhode Island, U.S.A. On January 17, 1887, Bourne withdrew some money from a bank in Providence, paid some bills, got into a horse-drawn tram and vanished. About two months later, a man calling himself A.J. Brown, who had recently rented a small shop in Norristown, Pennsylvania, woke up in confusion, his frightened calls bringing the other people in the shared building. He did not know where he was and insisted his name was Ansel Bourne. On his return to his Rhode Island family, Bourne was weak, having lost twenty pounds in weight, and had no recollection of what he had done between stepping into the tram and waking up in Norristown. Three years later James met Bourne and under hypnosis brought forward the 'A.J. Brown' personality, complete with its memory of the missing weeks.

Recent studies have shown that similar amnesic states may be more common than is generally believed; for not only can fugue states last from several seconds to a number of years, but whereas Bourne regained his identity spontaneously, some do not, remaining lost to their wives, children and friends, even if they are accidentally discovered in their new lives. Besides the psychological pressures or conflicts which produce such dramatic hysterical dissociations of personality, similar effects can be caused by head injuries, or by other kinds of brain damage which may result variously from disease or strokes, poisoning by over-indulgence in drugs or drink, extreme fatigue, epilepsy or even schizophrenia. Any one of these might produce alternating personalities, fugue and amnesia, and become the background to an intriguing story of a disappearance or appearance. Although the mechanism of this psychological phenomenon still eludes today's witch-doctors, how much more mysterious it must have seemed to people in earlier times.

When facing the difficulty of explaining strange phenomena, it is not hard to imagine how satisfying it was to look for answers in the twilight world of witches and demons, spirits and fairies, and in the whole folklore of changelings and spirit possession. And lest we think we are superior to our medieval forebears, these themes are just as alive today in the UFO myths of abduction by aliens. Indeed, it seems that if stories of bizarre disappearances did not exist, the fertile human imagination would create – or in psycho-mythological terms, *re-create* – them. This is shown in this volume with the example of how successive variations have been published of the entirely fictitious story of a boy who vanished (his footprints in the snow stopping suddenly) on the way to a farmyard well. This was said to have taken place on Christmas Eve 1876, or 1889, or 1890, depending on which version you read.

There is an issue lurking here which has been the bane of every serious researcher into the genre of appearances and disappearances. It is that many of the writers of popular books on UFOs and Fortean mysteries in the 1960s and 70s were careless in their verification of stories, grabbing material indiscriminately from the most dubious of sources. Some even deliberately fabricated or distorted data to fit their notions. The consequence was that a great many preposterous stories went into general circulation, and it has taken many tedious hours of research to separate the fiction from any kernel of fact. The classic example of this is the legend of the vanishing regiment in the campaign at Gallipoli in 1915, and of the strange cloud that was said to have swept it away. The story was used shamelessly in later UFO books to show how cunningly alien machines can disguise themselves as they carry out their nefarious abductions of unwary earthlings. You will read the true story in this volume, but the irony is that the UFO version will undoubtedly live on.

Harder and even more time-consuming to unravel are the open-ended enigmas such as the notorious Bermuda Triangle, and the so-called 'Philadelphia Experiment' (which allegedly demonstrated the phenomena of invisibility and teleportation) because they are vast and ill-defined. In both cases the sparse facts are obscured by a heavy smokescreen of lies, rumours, omissions and distortions which has been created by unscrupulous writers to back up a web of occult and speculative science fiction posing as fact. In the case of the Bermuda Triangle there have indeed been some unexplained disappearances, but no more or less, it seems, than could be expected in any other busy shipping area, and in numbers which reflect only the large amount of traffic within an area of generally unpredictable and extreme weather and ocean conditions.

Much in the same vein is the disappearance in 1587 of the population of Roanoke, a small English colony on the coast of North Carolina, about which there has been much fantastic speculation. Paul Begg, the intrepid researcher who has battled to the heart of many of the classic mysteries described in this volume, writes herein: 'The Roanoke disappearance *is* a mystery, but only insofar as there is no absolute proof of the colonists' fate and not because of any suggestion that their disappearance was in even the slightest way paranormal or supernatural.' The same could probably be said of one of the world's favourite and more genuine mysteries: the fate of the crew of the *Mary Celeste* (not *Marie Celeste* as many books wrongly have it). We simply don't know what happened to them, and that makes it more of an authentic vanishing mystery than tales of kidnap by a marauding UFO, attack by a sea serpent, or a slip into another dimension, all of which explanations of the mystery are no more than guesswork.

It would be easy to judge all the stories in this volume, either accept or dismiss them, and place them on a spectrum ranging between fact and fiction. But to do this would be ignoring the fact that they are more than one-dimensional. Right or wrong, true or false, the incidents of appearance and disappearance described here have become part of contemporary folklore. An excellent example is the continuing phenomenon of 'phantom hitch-hikers'. Once studied only in the light of local folklore, we now know that reports of this phenomenon can be found all over the world and in every century. Folklorists have studied the genre in the hope of revealing the origin of the idea and how it travelled, but it is so universal they now accept that it has sprung up independently at different times and places. Given their evidence, some believe it therefore to be an example of a mythological archetype, whose true origin lies in the human unconscious and whose true meaning is found in the realm of psychological symbology. And here is another mystery; we also have seemingly real events to go on, with eye-witness testimony, suggesting that this particular branch of folklore is continuously and spontaneously recreated in daily life.

While Charles Fort rather jokingly proposed that, if teleportation existed, there could be many people on this earth who have come from other worlds, a more disturbing idea has originated in the ancient religious and philosophical system of Tibet, which many contemporary researchers into the paranormal are taking more seriously. It is the idea of the *tulpa*, a phantom form of a human being, indistinguishable in all respects from the real thing, but created by the power of thought and imagination alone. If tulpas do exist, some of the people in this world of ours may not be real in the same way that we think of ourselves as real; they may come and go in 'unnatural' ways which give rise to the kind of stories represented here.

In the legends of many peoples, their heroes have passed into other worlds, some permanently, ascending to celestial regions or descending into the underworld. These themes are dramatized symbolically in the shaman's trance and are thus universally familiar. As we have seen, in our materialistic age a man can simply vanish. But in the archaic world in which the shaman had a fundamental social, spiritual and psychological function, the event had a significance for all men. A man may have disappeared from mortal ken, but that only meant his spirit was beyond us in a greater life, peopled with gods and demons, wizards and elementals. It should not surprise us then, that when Colonel Percy Fawcett failed to come back from exploring the Amazon in 1925; when Flight 19 took off into oblivion on its disastrous training mission over Florida in 1945; when 'Princess Caraboo' appeared in Bristol in 1817; and Kaspar Hauser was found at the gates of Nuremburg in 1828, *ad infinitum*, whatever the facts were, the mundane event was blasted into mythological perpetuity by the human imagination.

BOB RICKARD

The mysterious disappearance of ships and aircraft in an area of the North Atlantic has led to the belief that the region is host to strange and powerful hostile forces. PAUL BEGG gives the background to the legend

MERE MENTION of the Bermuda Triangle is likely to enliven any flagging conversation and set people's spines tingling almost anywhere in the world. It has been the subject of books, novels, films, television dramas and documentaries, newspaper and magazine articles – even a board game. The Bermuda Triangle – formed by an imaginary line connecting Bermuda with Puerto Rico and the coast of Florida – is the place where scores of ships and aircraft are said to have vanished without trace. Dozens of researchers and writers are convinced that the losses are caused by some kind of force or phenomenon unknown to science.

Charles Berlitz, author of two best-sellers about the region, *The Bermuda Triangle* and *Without a trace*, has written:

Large and small boats have disappeared without leaving wreckage, as if they and their crews had been snatched into another dimension . . . in no other area have the unexplained disappearances been so numerous, so well recorded, so sudden, and attended by such unusual circumstances, some of

Above: Charles Berlitz has done most to foster the idea that disappearances in the Bermuda Triangle are the result of extraordinary happenings

Below: the island of Bermuda in the Atlantic. Is it at the centre of a whole series of sinister events?

which push the element of coincidence to the borders of impossibility.

'The number of disappearances are out of all proportion to the number of losses elsewhere,' writes Ivan T. Sanderson in *Invisible residents*. And John Wallace Spencer claims in *Limbo of the lost*: 'Tragedies connected with this region continually occur without explanation, without pattern, without warning, and without reason.'

Bermuda has had an evil reputation for generations. Its 300 or so tiny islands were discovered in 1515 by Juan de Bermúdez. Yet, despite an equitable climate, plentiful supplies of fresh food and water, and an ideal location for a mid-ocean refuge and provisioning base, the islands were shunned for almost a century after their discovery. They were feared by the tough Elizabethan sailors, Shakespeare called them 'the still-vex'd Bermoothes', and they gained an evil reputation as a place of devils. Nobody knows why. Perhaps the only reasonable explanation is that then, as now, the region was known as the home of inexplicable forces that made men and ships disappear.

According to writers on the subject, the modern catalogue of losses in the region begins in 1800 with the disappearance of the USS *Pickering*. In 1854 the British ship *Bella* disappeared en route from Rio de Janeiro to Jamaica, although she was known to have

Tales from the Bermuda Triangle

been dangerously overloaded and may simply have capsized. In 1866 the Triangle claimed the Swedish barque *Lotta* and two years later the Spanish merchantman *Viego* vanished. In 1872 the crew of the *Mary Celeste* disappeared and the vessel was found drifting between the Azores and Gibraltar (see page 76). Although this is far outside the accepted limits of the Bermuda Triangle, the *Mary Celeste* is often referred to in discussion of the subject. The British training ship *Atalanta* and her 290 cadets and crew sailed into oblivion in 1880. They were followed in 1884 by the Italian schooner *Miramon*.

It is said that in 1902 the German barque *Freya*, sailing from Manzanillo in Cuba to Punta Arenas, Chile, was found in the Triangle. Her crew had disappeared. The vessel itself was listing badly, was partly dismasted and showed every sign of having been caught in a particularly violent storm – but there had not been any storms; weather records revealed that only light airs had prevailed.

In 1918 the large collier *Cyclops* mysteriously vanished. She had carried a radio but no distress message had been received. A message *was* sent by the Japanese freighter *Raifuku Maru* in 1925 but it only intensified the mystery because the radio operator is reported as saying: 'Danger like dagger now. Come quick!' What kind of danger looks like a dagger? Was dagger the only comparison the terrified radio operator could draw to the unworldly something that threatened and eventually took his ship? Thirteen years later, in 1938, the blue skies were cloudless and the sea was still when the steamship *Anglo-Australian* radioed an 'all's well'

Above: Ivan T. Sanderson has suggested that the Bermuda Triangle is one of 12 'vile vortices' on Earth, regions where the rate of disappearance of ships and aircraft is unusually high

Below: the Bermuda Triangle is usually represented as a region touching Florida and the islands of Puerto Rico and Bermuda. But some writers extend it much further and refer to it as the 'Devil's Triangle' and 'Limbo of the Lost'

message before sailing into the Bermuda Triangle. She never emerged.

Although the Bermuda Triangle has been claiming ships since the days when Christopher Columbus sailed its waters, it did not begin to attract attention until 1945. That year five US Navy bombers – Flight 19 – vanished after sending a series of baffling and bizarre radio messages. A few years later the writer Vincent Gaddis called the region the Bermuda Triangle. There is little agreement among writers on its size and shape, and each region is given a different name such as Devil's Triangle and Limbo of the Lost. At its smallest, however, the Bermuda Triangle is the size of the United Kingdom and Eire, and at its largest it takes in about half the North Atlantic Ocean.

Charles Berlitz and other writers such as Richard Winer, John Wallace Spencer, Vincent Gaddis, John Godwin, Ivan T. Sanderson, Adi-Kent Thomas Jeffrey and Alan Landsberg maintain that the mystery of the Triangle cannot be explained by storms and other natural causes. They believe that the disappearances were caused by a phenomenon unknown to orthodox science.

Vanishing aircraft

In January 1948 the British airliner *Star Tiger* was nearing the end of a routine flight from the Azores to Bermuda when she is said to have radioed: 'Weather and performance excellent. Expect to arrive on schedule.' But the aircraft did not arrive at all. While a search was being made for survivors or wreckage, radio stations picked up a couple of faint messages purporting to be from the aircraft. It was 'as if the final message was being sent or relayed from a far greater

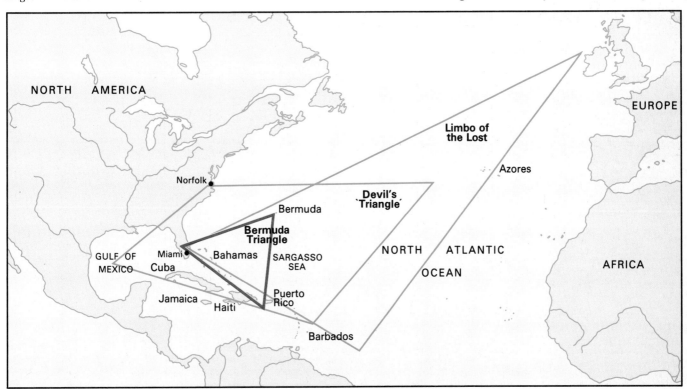

Left: the coast of Florida in 1563, as shown on a map by Lazaro Luis. Christopher Columbus travelled through the area now known as the Bermuda Triangle in the late 15th century and noted that his ship's compass acted erratically. He also recorded that a 'great flame of fire' fell into the sea

Below: an Avenger torpedo bomber of the type that vanished in December 1945 after leaving Fort Lauderdale naval air base for a brief training flight off the Florida coast. No trace of the five aircraft and 14 crew was ever found, despite an extensive search. This case, one of the most celebrated mysteries of aviation history, has been called 'the *Mary Celeste* of the sky'

Bermuda Triangle. It seemed that something prevented the satellite transmitting information to receiving stations. 'We are talking about a force we know nothing about,' Meshejian is quoted as saying.

Even more alarming is the claim that the Bermuda Triangle is not unique. The late Ivan T. Sanderson plotted the location of dozens of air and sea losses and concluded that at least 12 similar regions – he called them 'vile vortices' – encircle our globe. 'Planes, ships, and subs have, as we have stressed, been disappearing all over the world,' he wrote in his book *Invisible residents*, 'but it has to be admitted that many more are reported to have done so in these . . . areas than in any others.'

One such 'vile vortex' has long been known to lie off the coast of Japan. Called the Devil's Sea, it has been claiming small fishing craft of doubtful stability for hundreds of years. Between 1950 and 1954 no less than nine large coastal freighters went missing. The authorities were so alarmed that in 1955 they dispatched a team of scientists aboard the survey ship *Kaiyo Maru No. 5* to investigate the region. To everybody's horror the *Kaiyo Maru No. 5* and her scientists and crew inexplicably vanished. As a consequence the Japanese declared the region an official danger zone.

Unlike their Japanese counterparts the United States authorities have not declared the Bermuda Triangle a danger zone. Indeed, they deny that anything at all unusual is happening there. This official view, however, does not accord with private opinions expressed in unguarded moments. One Navy spokesman let slip: 'We know there's something strange going on out there,

distance, in space or time,' wrote Charles Berlitz.

Another airliner, a Douglas DC-3, vanished on a flight from Puerto Rico to Florida in December 1948. The pilot allegedly radioed: 'We are approaching the field . . . only fifty miles [80 kilometres] to the south. . . . We can see the lights of Miami now . . . all's well. Will stand by for landing instructions.' But when Miami replied a few minutes later she received no reply. Not another word was ever heard from the aircraft. The DC-3 had vanished over an area where the water was only 20 feet (6 metres) deep, yet search craft failed to locate any wreckage or survivors.

In June 1950 in calm seas and in good weather the Costa Rican freighter *Sandra* and her crew of 28 vanished. 'What could have happened to her? No one has the least idea,' says Adi-Kent Thomas Jeffrey.

The extent of the Triangle's range of influence startled researchers when Professor Wayne Meshejian announced that a sophisticated weather satellite operated by the National Oceanographic Administration consistently malfunctioned when over the

we've always known it, but there doesn't seem to be any reason for it at all.' And a senior intelligence officer of the Third Naval District is on record as saying: 'Nobody in the Navy sneers at this thing.' The authorities, it seems, are engaged in a cover-up to conceal their ignorance from the public.

There is little agreement about what 'this thing' in the Bermuda Triangle is. John Wallace Spencer is convinced that UFOs provide the only acceptable solution. Ships and aircraft 'are actually being taken away from our planet,' he says. Looking down instead of up, Ivan T. Sanderson suggested that a highly intelligent civilisation may have evolved on or below the sea bed and that the disappearances are connected with their periodic examination of mankind.

Other suggestions have ranged from mini black holes to openings to other dimensions where time runs quickly, slowly or not at all. That this latter theory may not be as absurd as it sounds is indicated by the experience of a young pilot named Bruce Gernon. In 1970 he was piloting his small aircraft when he flew through a strange cloud. On landing at Miami he discovered that his flight had taken half an hour less than it was possible for it to have done. Did Gernon fly into another dimension and out again? Unfortunately, his flight plan is missing and there is no way of

Above: the United States nuclear submarine *Scorpion* sank in May 1968 with the loss of her 99 crew southwest of the Azores. Although this is far outside the usual limits of the Bermuda Triangle the *Scorpion* is regularly included among its victims. A court of enquiry was unable to explain the sinking

Left: Gibbs Hill lighthouse has acted as a navigational aid on Bermuda since the 1840s. Has it also, in the years since then, been a silent witness of strange disappearances in the surrounding seas?

checking and corroborating his story.

A similar happening is said to have been experienced by the passengers and crew of an Eastern Airlines aircraft that vanished from the radar at Miami for 10 minutes. Full emergency operations were launched but then the airliner reappeared and landed safely. Nobody on board had experienced anything odd and they had no explanation for the fact that every clock and watch on board was found to be 10 minutes slow.

Charles Berlitz believes that the remains of the fabled lost continent of Atlantis have been found off Bimini in the Bahamas. Many people believe that Atlantis was the home of a technological super race and that one of their machines or weapons is still functioning, disintegrating our ships and aircraft.

'Could magnetism or some form of magnetic phenomenon be related to the strange disappearances?' asks Richard Winer, author of *The Devil's Triangle*. Few writers have failed to mention how the compass needle usually points to the magnetic north pole rather than to the actual North Pole – except, however, in the Bermuda Triangle.

The Bermuda Triangle is clearly a strange place and strange things happen there. Hundreds of ships and aircraft have inexplicably vanished without trace. They hardly ever send a distress call and wreckage is rarely found. Furthermore, as John Godwin has written in *This baffling world*, 'we find that almost monotonously fine weather conditions prevailed at the crucial times.' He goes on to ask: 'Did the lost airplanes and lost ships encounter phenomena unknown to today's science? Do the laws of nature still contain a few paragraphs not covered in our textbooks?' We shall see.

Numerous tales of people, boats and aircraft vanishing without trace have been gathered by writers about the Bermuda Triangle to support their view that something weird is happening there. But how strong is their evidence?

THE BERMUDA TRIANGLE, an area of the western Atlantic where scores of ships and aircraft have disappeared without trace, has been described as one of the greatest true-life mysteries of all time. This is not simply because ships and aircraft have vanished there, but because – according to numerous writers and researchers – the disappearances are without explanation and must be caused by some 'force' or phenomenon unknown to science.

It is a very disturbing if not highly alarming claim, and there is little reassurance in the knowledge that the chances of disappearing in the Bermuda Triangle are less than for being killed while crossing the road. Precautions can be taken against the known dangers of the highway, but not against the unknown forces of the Bermuda Triangle. Every crossing of the region is potentially fatal, rather like every pull of the trigger in Russian roulette.

Few writers agree about the precise size and shape of the Bermuda Triangle. Richard Winer thinks it is a trapezium while John Wallace Spencer sees it as a scalene triangle;

Sunk without trace

The *Cyclops*, a US Navy collier, disappeared in March 1918 after leaving Barbados for the Chesapeake Bay area of the eastern USA. The vessel, 540 feet (165 metres) long, carried a crew of about 300 and was laden with manganese ore

Ivan T. Sanderson calls it 'a sort of funny blob'.

The number of disappearances is far from alarmingly high, as some writers contend. About 150,000 boats cross the Bermuda Triangle every year and on average about 10,000 send a distress call. However, only about 100 losses are recorded annually. While 100 losses are 100 too many it is not a significant proportion of 150,000 – 0.07 per cent, in fact.

As well as being subject to all the natural hazards of the sea – such as storms, hurricanes and waterspouts – the Triangle is the home of the Gulf Stream, a fast-moving body of water that can carry an unwary or inexperienced sailor miles off course in a matter of hours and quickly disperse wreckage.

However, when all is said and done, the backbone of the Triangle legend is that catalogue of disappearances and the claim that they defy rational explanation. Charles Berlitz, the best-known of many people who have written about the area, has stated that

All ship losses are mysterious inasmuch as relatively few captains set out to lose their ships. When the fate of a ship is established, or even assumed, the mystery ceases. This has not been the case with the many ships which have disappeared in the Sargasso Sea.

It is there, or near there, that the majority of Bermuda Triangle losses have taken place, he says.

Let us now examine a random sample of

Left: disappearances in the Bermuda Triangle number about 100 annually. This reward poster drew attention to the mysterious fate of the yacht *Saba Bank*, which vanished while sailing from Nassau to Miami in April 1974

Below: the British freighter *Cyclops*, which went missing in the North Atlantic during the Second World War. It could have been torpedoed, but Charles Berlitz maintains that records show no German submarines to have been in the area when the ship disappeared

Bottom: the ss *Marine Sulphur Queen* left Beaumont, Texas, on 2 February 1963 bound for Norfolk, Virginia. She carried a cargo of molten sulphur and was last heard from on 4 February. An official investigation said the ship could have sunk because of an explosion, could have capsized in heavy seas, or its hull may have broken in two

famous case of the Richard Tichborne inheritance. This ship did not disappear without trace. Wreckage from the vessel is said to have been found six days after she had left Rio, so assuming perfect sailing conditions and maximum speed, the nearest she could have been to the Bermuda Triangle when disaster struck was some 2000 miles (3200 kilometres) away.

A similar case is that of the German barque *Freya*. She is said to have sailed from Manzanillo, Cuba, in 1902 and to have been found in the Triangle abandoned by her crew and giving every appearance of having been caught in a particularly violent storm. Weather records apparently reveal that only light airs prevailed in the region at the time. The *Freya* was, however, in an area where submarine volcanic activity had been reported at about the same time as the ship was abandoned, and it is believed that this prompted the crew to abandon ship. Whether or not this explanation is correct does not really matter because the *Freya* did not sail from Manzanillo, Cuba, but from Manzanillo, Mexico, and she was not found abandoned in the Bermuda Triangle, nor even in the Atlantic Ocean, but in the Pacific.

No hint of mystery was ever attached to either the *Bella* or the *Freya* until writers began searching for Triangle fatalities. Other ships – the *Lotta*, *Viego*, and *Miramon* or *Miramonde* – could not be traced by this writer and it is questionable whether they ever existed.

In the 19th and early 20th centuries, ships did not carry radio equipment. We cannot be certain of where they were when disaster struck or of what form the disaster took. For example, the *Atalanta* (not *Atlanta* as many authors call her) disappeared on an intended voyage of 3000 miles (4800 kilometres), only 500 miles (800 kilometres) of which were through the Bermuda Triangle. We do not know where she was when she was overwhelmed, but we do know that she had a crew of very inexperienced cadets and that severe storms swept her route.

The first radio-carrying vessel claimed by

Triangle fatalities. The British ship *Bella* is said to have vanished in 1854 on a voyage from Rio de Janeiro to Jamaica. She is known to have been overloaded and is presumed to have capsized, but author Alan Landsberg has wondered why the vessel should have had a safe voyage until she entered the deadly Triangle.

The writer of this article has been unable to identify the *Bella*. Lloyd's have a record of a ship of that name built in Liverpool in 1852, but there is no suggestion that it suffered any misfortune. The only ship corresponding with the Triangle's *Bella* is a vessel of that name that is sometimes associated with the

Berlitz's own words: 'When the fate of a ship is established, or even assumed, the mystery ceases.'

The cornerstone of the Triangle myth is the disappearance of five US Navy bombers – Flight 19 – and a sea plane, all on 5 December 1945, and this will be the subject of a future chapter. Among other aircraft to have vanished in the Bermuda Triangle were the British airliner *Star Tiger* and a Douglas DC-3, both in 1948.

The *Star Tiger*, a Tudor IV aircraft, mysteriously vanished towards the end of a flight from the Azores to Bermuda on 30 January of that year. Contrary to the Triangle legend, the last message from it was an acknowledgement of a radio bearing requested several minutes earlier and not 'Weather and performance excellent. Expect to arrive on schedule.' The weather, in fact, was anything but excellent. Cloud cover throughout the flight had prevented accurate navigation; and the aircraft had battled severe headwinds, forcing the pilot to revise

the Bermuda Triangle was the 19,000-tonne collier *Cyclops* in March 1918. As with the *Atalanta*, her route was in the path of a severe storm, winds reaching peak speeds of 84 miles per hour (135 km/h). It is quite likely that she capsized. Her top-heavy superstructure and the nature of her cargo – which may not have been properly secured – would have ensured that the *Cyclops* sank very quickly indeed.

The Japanese freighter *Raifuku Maru* is said to have vanished in 1925 after sending a strange radio message: 'Danger like dagger now. Come quick!' The message, picked up by the White Star liner *Homeric* but distorted by electrical interference, was in fact 'Now very danger. Come quick!' The *Homeric* sped to the freighter's assistance but encountered mountainous seas and saw the *Raifuku Maru* sink with all hands.

The Triangle writers say that the 355-foot (106-metre) freighter *Sandra* and her crew of 28 sailed into oblivion in calm seas and under blue skies in June 1950. About the only details they get correct are the freighter's name and nationality. The *Sandra* was 185 feet (55 metres) long, carried a crew of 11 and vanished in hurricane force winds in April 1950.

Hurricanes and storms also prevailed when the freighter *Anglo-Australian* vanished in 1938, when the yacht *Connemara IV* was abandoned in 1955, and when the *Revonoc* and its owner Harvey Conover disappeared in 1958. Similar explanations are available for the bulk of Triangle disappearances. Although it is impossible to say for certain that the *Revonoc*, for example, was engulfed by a storm, storms are known to have been responsible for maritime disasters, and the presence of a storm enables us to assume a rational explanation. At which point it is worth remembering Charles

Hurricanes and storms provide likely reasons for some of the losses in the Bermuda Triangle. The *Connemara IV* (above) was found drifting and abandoned in September 1955 off Bermuda. The crew were probably lost overboard when the yacht was caught in a hurricane. The racing yawl *Revonoc* (right) vanished between Key West and Miami in early 1958 when the Florida coast was being battered by near-hurricane-force winds

Below: A Douglas DC-3 of the type that vanished in December 1948

his estimated time of arrival and reducing the safety margin of extra fuel. The airliner disappeared at the most critical stage of her flight. She had insufficient fuel to reach any airport other than Bermuda and was forced to fly at 2000 feet (600 metres) because of the headwinds. Had anything gone wrong such as fuel exhaustion, complete electrical failure or engine breakdown the *Star Tiger* would have plummeted into the sea within seconds.

Omissions and distortions

The case of the Douglas DC-3 lost on 28 December 1948 is an example of how facts have been omitted and distorted to imply a greater mystery than exists. The aircraft, carrying 27 passengers, had left San Juan, Puerto Rico, bound for Miami, Florida. The pilot, Captain Robert Linquist, is said to have radioed that he was 50 miles (80 kilometres) from Miami, could see the lights of the city, and was standing by for landing instructions. Miami replied within minutes, but the aircraft had vanished. The water over which the aircraft was flying was only 20 feet (6 metres) deep, yet search craft failed to locate any wreckage.

The DC-3 is known to have had a defective radio (though some writers have failed to mention this), so the sudden silence does not mean that the aircraft was overcome immediately after sending the message to Miami. It also removes any mystery attached to the lack of a distress call. Furthermore, the pilot did not say he could see the lights of Miami. It seems that some writers have put these words in the pilot's mouth because he said that he was only 50 miles (80 kilometres) from Miami (from which distance the lights of the city would be visible).

However, the pilot had been compensating for a north-west wind, but the wind direction had changed during the flight and it is not known whether the pilot received notification of the fact. If not, he could have missed the Florida Peninsula and literally flown into the Gulf of Mexico. And although the depth of the sea over which the DC-3 was flying at the time of the last message is in places only 20 feet (6 metres) deep, in other areas it plunges to depths of up to 5000 feet (1520 metres). Nobody is certain where the aircraft went down.

Every air disaster is the subject of an exhaustive enquiry to establish the cause. These investigations rely largely on minute examination of wreckage. If there is no wreckage, it is virtually impossible to hazard a guess at what happened. Since none of the accepted causes of an air crash can positively be eliminated nobody can claim that some unknown phenomenon was alone responsible.

A few years ago it was claimed that the strange forces of the Bermuda Triangle reached into space. It was learned that a weather satellite malfunctioned over the Bermuda Triangle and *only* over the Triangle.

The *Star Tiger*, an aircraft of the Tudor IV type (below), went missing in 1948 on a flight from London to Havana via the Azores and Bermuda. The last message received from her gave no inkling of anything untoward

The disappearance of the *Star Tiger* has been called 'truly a modern mystery of the air'. A thorough search of the seas failed to find any trace of the aircraft or its passengers

In fact the satellite was not malfunctioning. The satellite collected visual and infra-red data on cloud cover and transmitted the information to Earth. For convenience the infra-red signal was transmitted direct while the visual signal was stored on a loop of tape for later transmission. At certain times the tape became full and had to be rewound, so no visual signal was transmitted. By pure coincidence the tape was rewinding when the satellite's orbit brought it over the Triangle.

Then there was the Eastern Airlines aircraft that is said to have disappeared from the radar for 10 minutes and landed at Miami, when every clock and watch aboard was found to be 10 minutes slow. The flight number and the date and time of this event are never given and there is no record of the incident with the FAA, Miami Airport or Eastern Airlines. In short, there is not a scrap of evidence that it ever happened.

TUDOR LOST BETWEEN AZORES AND BERMUDA

AIR-SEA RESCUE SEARCH FOR 31 ON BOARD

FROM OUR OWN CORRESPONDENT
NEW YORK, Friday.

All aircraft and ships in the vicinity of Bermuda to-day joined in the search for the British South American Airways Tudor IV., Star Tiger, which is overdue at Bermuda from the Azores.

The search was fully maintained until darkness fell, when the United States Navy recalled all its planes. American Army Flying Fortresses and Super-Fortresses, however, continued their quest during the night, assisted by two British South American Airways machines.

The Star Tiger left London on Tuesday, but was held up by bad weather in the Azores. It was due at Kindley Field, Bermuda, at 5 a.m. G.M.T. to-day.

According to New York Coast-guard H.Q. the Star Tiger was 380 miles north-east of Bermuda when its last radio message was received at 3 a.m. The pilot reported nothing unusual.

The plane, which had a crew of

SEARCH PLANE CRASHES: NINE DEAD IN ALPS

LOST DAKOTA SEEN
FROM OUR OWN CORRESPONDENT
PARIS, Friday.
While searching for the American Dakota which crashed in the

Stories about mysterious vanishings in the Bermuda Triangle and Devil's Sea have been fostered by numerous writers who have suggested fantastic explanations. So what can we believe about this legend?

New angle on the Triangle

WHEN EXAMINED CLOSELY the only mystery about the Bermuda Triangle is how it came to be believed in. Both research and reasoning leave much to be desired, as is illustrated by Ivan T. Sanderson's contention that no less than 12 'vile vortices' encircle the globe. The impression given by Sanderson and other writers is that the existence of these 'vile vortices' has been confirmed by statistical and other studies; but it would seem that Sanderson did no more than plot on a map the location of a number of air and sea disasters, concluding that those places where there had been a large number of losses were 'vile vortices'. This is about as valid as suggesting that a major motorway is a 'vile vortex' because more accidents happen there than on a remote country lane.

One such 'vile vortex', called the Devil's Sea, lies off the coast of Japan, but precisely where off the coast of Japan is something that few writers agree about. For Charles Berlitz and Vincent Gaddis it is south or south-east of Japan, between Japan and the Bonin Islands; John Godwin places it between Iwo Jima and Marcus Island; Adi-Kent Thomas Jeffrey and John Wallace Spencer put it between Japan and the Marianas; Ivan T. Sanderson locates it 250 miles (400 kilometres) south of Honshu, at about 140 degrees longitude. For Elizabeth Nichols the Devil's Sea is a triangle connecting Japan, Wake Island and Guam; for Richard Winer it is a triangle bounded by the south-east coast of Japan, the north-eastern tip of the Philippines, and Guam.

Nine large coastal freighters are said to have inexplicably vanished in the Devil's Sea between 1950 and 1954. According to Charles Berlitz the authorities undertook an 'investigation of the area in 1955. This expedition, with scientists taking data as their ship, the *Kaiyo Maru No. 5*, cruised the Devil's Sea, ended on a rather spectacular note – the survey ship suddenly vanished.' The truth of the matter is that nine fishing boats of between 62 and 192 tonnes disappeared in a 750-mile (1200-kilometre) stretch of sea between 1949 and 1953. The *Kaiyo Maru No. 5* disappeared in 1952, not in 1955, while observing the birth of an island thrust up from the sea bed by volcanic activity. The Japanese authorities have declared the region an official danger zone.

Evil doings in Atlantis?

Numerous theories have been advanced to explain the allegedly inexplicable disappearances; these range from the almost obligatory UFOs to science fiction concepts such as time travel and parallel worlds. Berlitz is of the opinion that Atlantis has been found off the coast of Bimini in the Bahamas. In the Triangle legend Atlantis is seen as the home of an antediluvian super-race, one of whose machines or weapons is still functioning somewhere on the sea bed and causing ships and aircraft to disintegrate. The earliest mention of Atlantis is to be found in an unfinished work by the Greek philosopher Plato. Plato was concerned with concepts, not history, and could weave fact with fiction without any qualms about accuracy. We have no idea whether Plato invented Atlantis or was drawing on ancient traditions, but whether or not Atlantis ever existed Plato gives no reasons for us to believe that it was a technological society. According to Plato the Atlanteans were defeated in war by the ancient Greeks.

Perhaps the most popular theory is that some kind of magnetic anomaly is causing the disappearances. Many writers point out that in the Bermuda Triangle the compass needle points to the North Pole and not to the magnetic North Pole as it does everywhere else in the world. This is not strictly true. At certain places in the world the actual North Pole and the magnetic North Pole are in a straight line, the Agonic Line, and one of those places just happens to be off the coast of Florida. As you move away from the Agonic Line so the difference in the distance between the North and magnetic North becomes greater. There is absolutely nothing mysterious about the Agonic Line. Accounts that mention compass needles gyrating wildly or otherwise acting strangely prove nothing either. Local magnetic variations can cause such behaviour and exist all over the world.

In his book *Secrets of the Bermuda Triangle* Alan Landsberg writes:

It is clear that whatever critics in the various narrow branches of science may say, something strange is unquestionably happening in the Bermuda Triangle. The world-wide interest is itself phenomenal as if the vast majority of people 'know' that there is

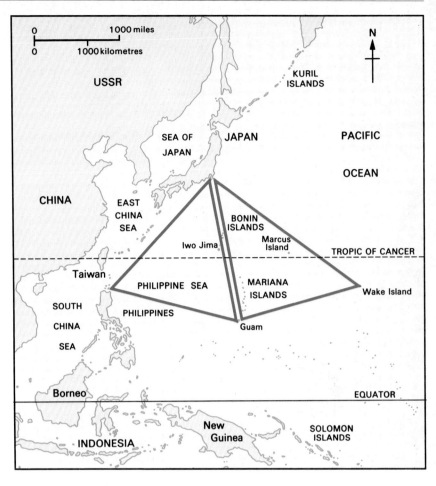

Above: the so-called Devil's Sea is one of Ivan T. Sanderson's 12 'vile vortices', areas of the globe where vanishings are said to be more frequent than elsewhere. But the location of the region is far from certain – except that it is off the coast of Japan. For Elizabeth Nichols the Devil's Sea extends eastwards to Wake Island; for Richard Winer it reaches west as far as the Philippines

Left: the *Revonoc*, a prize-winning racing yawl owned by American millionaire publisher Harvey Conover, disappeared during a trip from Key West to Miami in January 1958. Conover, his wife and two children were aboard. The Coast Guard reported that the 45-foot (14-metre) yacht had apparently been caught by near-hurricane winds in what was said to be one of the worst storms in the history of Florida

something important to be discovered there.

In effect Landsberg is invalidating expert scientific opinion by suggesting that from their position as specialists the scientific fraternity cannot take a comprehensive view of the problem. He claims to be in a far better position to comment on the Bermuda Triangle than is a scientist, because not being a scientist he is not hidebound. However, it is not critics in the narrow branches of science but the facts themselves that suggest that it is highly questionable that anything remotely strange is happening in the Triangle.

Writers about the Bermuda Triangle have a vested interest in the 'mystery' because that sells their books and earns them their money. They therefore employ many techniques to imply that a mystery exists. A great favourite is the 'as if' ploy, a minor example of which is used by Landsberg in the above quote. Charles Berlitz, perhaps the best-known of the Triangle authors, writes of how 'boats have disappeared without leaving wreckage, as if they and their crews had been snatched by another dimension'.

'Not yet' is another popular ploy. 'Scientists have not yet discovered the nature of the strange forces in the Bermuda Triangle,' which implies that scientists believe that strange forces do exist in the Triangle and are trying to find out what they are.

Sometimes Berlitz makes absurd comparisons. In *Without a trace* he says:

It has been suggested that vessels have sometimes been run down by other ships without the larger ship noticing. It was supposed that the *Revonoc* had been run over by an ocean-going freighter at night. However applicable this theory might be to sailing vessels, it would still not explain the disappearance of freighters which, if run over by other freighters, would undoubtedly be noticed.

The point here is that the theory was not intended to apply to freighters, but by connecting the two Berlitz has tried to devalue a perfectly acceptable theory for the loss of small vessels like the yacht *Revonoc*, even though the *Revonoc* disappeared in 1958 in what the *New York Times* described as 'near hurricane winds from the worst midwinter storm in the history of south Florida'.

Contrasting techniques

The jaw really does drop with disbelief when Berlitz discusses Lawrence David Kusche whose book, *The Bermuda Triangle mystery – solved*, is a crushing exposé of 50 celebrated Triangle cases. Berlitz writes that Kusche's 'approach to the subject is not influenced by any personal familiarity with the area of the Bermuda Triangle. His research techniques are characterised by a somewhat touching reliance on long-distance telephone calls as a means of investigation.' Berlitz also quotes Kusche as having said that there was nothing to be gained by going to the area to conduct research, a view that Berlitz thinks is 'a refreshing comment on investigative techniques which would immeasurably simplify the work of detectives, police, research investigators, and explorers throughout the world'. This is the extent of Berlitz's reply to Kusche's detailed criticism.

Kusche examined accident investigation reports, contemporary newspaper accounts, weather records, official documents and a wealth of important information obtained throughout the world as a result of letters and long-distance telephone calls. On the other

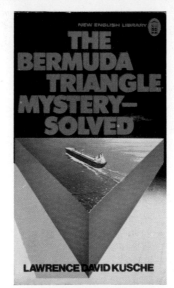

Top and above: in *The Bermuda Triangle mystery – solved* Lawrence David Kusche exposed serious factual errors in usual accounts of Bermuda Triangle disappearances

Below: the *Star Tiger* went missing in January 1948. An official enquiry remarked that 'no more baffling problem has ever been presented for investigation'

hand, had Berlitz taken the trouble to make a few telephone calls and write some letters he would not have made so many gross errors.

In *The Bermuda Triangle*, during his discussion of the disappearances of the British airliner *Star Tiger* in January 1948, Berlitz says that the last message sent by the aircraft was 'Weather and performance excellent. Expect to arrive on schedule.' No such message was ever sent at any time during the flight. The facts were fully presented in the accident investigation report (published as a government White Paper) and in press reports of the public enquiry into the matter. *Great mysteries of the air* by Ralph Barker, a book Berlitz listed in his bibliography, contains a chapter about the *Star Tiger* from which it is clear that the weather was bad when the plane went missing. Kusche's *The Bermuda Triangle mystery – solved* gives the facts again, but although Berlitz presumably read it (because he criticised its author) he repeated the 'Weather and performance excellent' story in his later book *Without a trace*.

The Bermuda Triangle is a manufactured mystery. Many readers who do not wish to believe this will argue that there is no smoke without fire. And articles critical of the alleged Triangle mysteries always provoke accusations that the author has a closed mind or is merely a professional debunker. In the introduction to her book *They dared the devil's triangle*, Adi-Kent Thomas Jeffrey implores her readers:

Let us not cover our senses with the impenetrable armour of suspicion and scepticism. Let us not don the thick helmet of closed-mindedness under the guise of so-called 'common sense' and 'reason'.

But who is being closed-minded? There is probably a great deal still to be learned about our world and the Universe in which we live, and study of unexplained phenomena may one day lead to new and exciting discoveries. But extraordinary and alarming claims for unknown forces causing the loss of ships and aircraft *must* be backed by hard, incontrovertible facts. This is not the case with the Bermuda Triangle.

As far as can be ascertained, not one of the Triangle authors has satisfactorily replied to the critics. And they have never said where certain documents can be found, or where it says that the last message from the *Star Tiger* was 'Weather and performance excellent', or why they believe the *Bella* and *Freya* were Triangle fatalities, or why the *Atalanta*, *Anglo-Australian*, *Connemara IV*, *Sandra*, *Revonoc*, and the rest were not victims of storms and hurricanes. Until they do, it is the Bermuda Triangle writers who have closed minds, not their critics.

Whatever happened to Flight 19?

The case of Flight 19 sums up the whole Bermuda Triangle myth. Triangle writers have made much of the story of the missing bombers but the popularised tale lacked one ingredient – the facts

THE DISAPPEARANCE OF FLIGHT 19 – five US Navy bombers that vanished over the Bermuda Triangle in 1945 – is the central element of the Bermuda Triangle myth. The opening sequence of the film *Close encounters of the third kind* (1977) has the aircraft being discovered, over 30 years after the disappearance, in the desert of northern Mexico, thus turning fact into fiction – or to be more accurate, turning fiction that had been made into fact back into fiction again, because the story of Flight 19 is one of the most distorted stories in the whole Bermuda Triangle myth.

According to the Triangle version of the story, the five Grumman TBM Avenger

Five US Navy bombers of the same type as Flight 19. Did it really disappear under mysterious circumstances in the Bermuda Triangle, or is there a more prosaic explanation for the tragedy?

bombers left the runway at the Naval Air Station, Fort Lauderdale, Florida, at 2 p.m. on 5 December 1945. Charles Berlitz says that the aircraft were 'on a routine training mission . . . both pilots and crews were experienced airmen'. Berlitz says that 'pilots who had flown earlier the same day reported ideal flying weather.'

At 3.45 p.m. the flight leader, Lieutenant Charles C. Taylor, radioed the control tower. 'Calling tower. This is an emergency. We seem to be off course. We cannot see land . . . repeat . . . we cannot see land.'

'What is your position?' radioed the tower.

'We're not sure of our position. We cannot be sure just where we are. We seem to be lost.'

'Assume bearing due west.'

'We don't know which way is west. Everything is wrong . . . strange. We can't be sure of just where we are. We are not sure of any direction. Even the ocean doesn't look as it should.'

Lieutenant Robert Cox, senior flight instructor at Fort Lauderdale, had been preparing to land when he overheard these messages and he thought he knew where Flight 19 was. He radioed, 'Flight 19, what is your altitude? I'll fly south and meet you.'

Taylor should have welcomed any assistance, but for a few minutes he was silent

before he cried, 'Don't come after me! They look like. . . .'

Silence. The time was now 4.30 p.m. As the last message from Flight 19 was being received a huge Martin Mariner sea plane, dispatched on a rescue mission, was nearing the bombers' last estimated position. It sent one message and then followed the bombers into oblivion. Six military aircraft had vanished in the space of a few hours!

There followed one of the largest air-sea searches in history, but not a single scrap of wreckage or debris was found. There were no survivors. Investigators were completely baffled. At the end of the long enquiry one Navy officer commented that Flight 19 and the sea plane had 'vanished as completely as if they had flown to Mars'.

To compound the mystery there is the vexing question of why Lieutenant Taylor refused help from Cox. And what did Taylor see when he cried 'They look like. . . .'? Joan Powers, widow of one of Flight 19's crew, is quoted as saying:

My own theory is that the men saw something up there over the Triangle . . . something which so frightened Lieutenant Taylor that he did not want Lieutenant Cox to jeopardise his own life; something which, possibly for national security reasons, the Navy still does not want the public to know about.

If the Bermuda Triangle version of this disappearance is correct then the case of Flight 19 must rank as the most baffling mystery in the history of aviation. But from the official report and other reliable sources it is possible to reconstruct the events of that December day and show that the Triangle account is grossly inaccurate.

The Triangle account gives the distinct

Above: Fort Lauderdale, the US Naval Air Station in Florida from where the ill-fated Flight 19 took off at 2 p.m. on 5 December 1945

Below: Lieutenant Robert Cox, senior flight instructor at Fort Lauderdale in 1945, who received the controversial last radio message from Flight 19

impression of cloudless skies and a group of experienced airmen flying a route they knew like the back of their hands; but although the weather was fine when the aircraft left Fort Lauderdale it rapidly deteriorated during the flight, and search craft later reported unsafe flying conditions and tremendous seas. With the exception of Lieutenant Taylor none of the crew was highly experienced. They had only about 300 flying hours each, only 60 of which were in TBM-type aircraft. Taylor, a combat veteran with 2509 flying hours, had recently moved to Fort Lauderdale from Miami, was unfamiliar with the area, and had never before flown the route taken by Flight 19. The flight was 'routine' only in the sense that it was an established training exercise at Fort Lauderdale. It was, in fact, a complicated navigation exercise.

The undiscover'd country

The first message from the aircraft was not received by the Fort Lauderdale tower but by Lieutenant Cox, who overheard an inter-aircraft communication in which somebody asked Captain Edward Powers what his compass read. 'I don't know where we are,' replied Powers. 'We must have got lost after that last turn.'

Lieutenant Cox radioed, 'What is your trouble?'

Taylor replied, 'Both my compasses are out. I'm trying to find Fort Lauderdale. I'm over land but it's broken. I'm sure I'm in the Keys, but I don't know how far down. . . .'

These initial communications provide the clue to Flight 19's ultimate fate. Lieutenant Taylor and, apparently, Captain Powers, the next most experienced man among the crew, believed that Flight 19 had taken a wrong turn and flown off course. The aircraft were over Great Sale Cay in the Bahamas, but Lieutenant Taylor, who had never flown over the area, was struck by the similarity between Great Sale Cay and the Florida

Keys, with which he was very familiar, having flown over them many times while stationed at Miami. Taylor could not decide whether he was to the east or west of the Florida Peninsula – over the Atlantic Ocean or the Gulf of Mexico.

Lieutenant Cox gave Taylor instructions for reaching Fort Lauderdale from the Keys and added, 'What is your altitude? I'll fly south and meet you.'

This is a statement that Triangle writers make much of, but the official report says that Taylor replied, 'I know where I am now. I'm at 2300 feet [700 metres]. Don't come after me.' There is no mention of anything looking remotely unusual.

Taylor did not know where he was, however, and he became increasingly disorientated. Many factors contributed to his disorientation: his compasses were not working, or he believed they weren't; he didn't have a clock or watch; his radio channel was subject to interference from Cuban radio stations, but the fear of losing contact with the flight deterred him from changing frequencies to the undisturbed emergency channel.

In the gathering dusk he led the aircraft first in one direction, then in another, and as dusk was replaced by the black darkness of a winter's night, the weather and the sea grew rough. At 6.30 p.m. Lieutenant Taylor, valiantly trying to keep his flight together, was heard to announce: 'All planes close up tight . . . we will have to ditch unless landfall . . . when the first plane drops to 10 gallons [45 litres] we all go down together.'

The last words heard from any of the aircraft were at 7.04 p.m. when one of the pilots was heard trying to contact Lieutenant Taylor. It is assumed that some time during the next hour the five bombers descended

A Martin Mariner sea plane of the type that set off to try to locate Flight 19 – and also apparently vanished. It left the Banana River Naval Air Station (now Patrick Air Force Base) at 7.30 p.m. and is believed to have exploded in mid-air a short time afterwards. The captain of the freighter *Gaines Mills* reported seeing an aircraft burst into flames and explode, and the commander of the USS *Solomons* confirmed that the Mariner disappeared from its radar screen at about the same time as the *Gaines Mills* saw the explosion. Yet strangely, Triangle writers persist in describing the Mariner's fate as a 'mysterious disappearance'

through the night to the turbulent sea below. Experts later testified that a TBM would sink in less than a minute.

An air search was launched almost immediately but was little more than a token gesture because the chances of spotting wreckage at night and in bad weather were slim. By daylight the sea would have dispersed wreckage beyond recognition.

The Triangle version of Flight 19 presents a set of wholly spurious radio messages and has the aircraft vanishing some two and a half hours earlier than was probably the case. As for the rescue aircraft that followed the bombers into oblivion it must be considered a separate incident.

Fire in the sky

Some books have the Martin Mariner sea plane vanishing some three hours before it had even taken off. In fact, the aircraft left the Banana River naval airfield (now Patrick Air Force Base) at 7.30 p.m., sent a routine departure message and is believed to have exploded in mid-air a short time later. Charles Berlitz refers to this explanation in his book *Without a trace*: 'The vanishing Martin Mariner,' he says, 'is conveniently explained by the fact that a flare in the night sky was observed by the crew of the *Gaines Mills*, a passing freighter.' What Berlitz considers to be a flare in the night sky was described somewhat differently by the captain of the *Gaines Mills* who reported seeing an aircraft catch fire, plummet into the sea and explode.

The commander of the USS *Solomons*, an aircraft carrier participating in the search, confirmed that it was the sea plane that had exploded. The aircraft was tracked on the *Solomons*'s air search radar from the time it left Banana River until it vanished from the screen at the same time and in the same location as the *Gaines Mills* had observed an explosion.

Nobody knows what caused the explosion, but Mariners were labelled 'flying gas

tanks' and they carried a large quantity of high-octane fuel. The fumes that gathered inside the hull could have been ignited by a spark generated by anything from an electrical fault to pieces of metal rubbing against each other.

The only mystery about Flight 19 that remains to be solved is the origin of the messages supposed to have passed between Lieutenant Taylor and the Lauderdale tower. Their earliest appearance in print is an article by Allan W. Eckert published in 1962. Eckert cannot remember his source. Charles Berlitz says that much of his information about Flight 19 came from the firsthand notes made by Commander R. H. Wirshing, then lieutenant on duty at Fort Lauderdale, but in a BBC television documentary about the Bermuda Triangle Commander Wirshing denied that he had kept firsthand notes and said that he did not arrive on duty until Flight 19 could no longer receive messages from the tower.

The case of Flight 19 is typical of the entire Bermuda Triangle myth. Facts have been distorted, there are gross errors and twisted and distorted details. It is a manufactured mystery that has developed over 40 years as one writer has taken his information from another, elaborating bits here and there, doing little original research, and perpetuating errors – each believing that his information has already been verified by somebody else. And so it goes on.

Above: the USS *Solomons*, the aircraft carrier that searched for the lost Martin Mariner – and reported its explosion

Right: map showing the Florida Keys (A), with which Lieutenant Taylor, leader of Flight 19, was familiar. He mistook Great Sale Cay (B), over which he was flying, for the Keys and became increasingly disorientated shortly before losing radio contact with ground control and presumably crashing

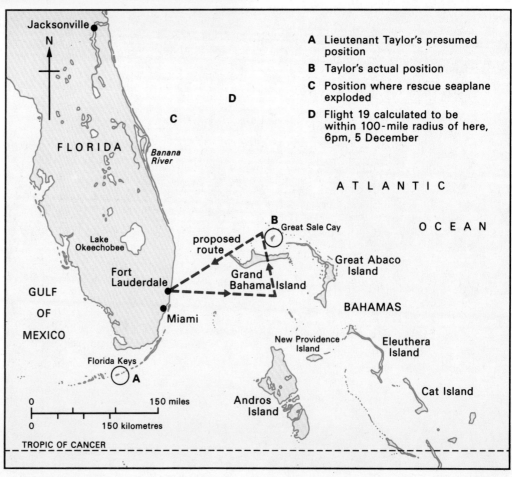

A   Lieutenant Taylor's presumed position

B   Taylor's actual position

C   Position where rescue seaplane exploded

D   Flight 19 calculated to be within 100-mile radius of here, 6pm, 5 December

Out of thin air

Murdered men with no traceable past; navigators of medieval 'cloud-ships'; mermen – PAUL BEGG discusses these, and others, who have suddenly appeared to disrupt our comfortable and ordered view of reality

THE FAINT HEARTS of some genteel young ladies hurrying about their business in the High Street, Chatham, Kent, received something of a shock on 6 January 1914. A naked man suddenly appeared in their midst and began running up and down the road. Nobody had seen a naked man in the area surrounding the High Street. Nobody had seen a man undress. The man's clothes were searched for, but could not be found. Finer sensibilities were saved from further offence when a policeman caught the man and took him to the police station. The man could tell nothing about himself and was eventually declared insane.

West Botley flyover near Oxford, England. A man was found dead – apparently having fallen from the flyover. The corpse eluded identification; the only clues were five handkerchiefs, bearing the letter 'M' – and a strip of foil containing 15 tablets of a drug that was so new that few doctors even knew it existed

In 1851, a man was found wandering in a village near Frankfurt-an-der-Oder in what is now East Germany. He could not explain how he had got there, but said that he lived in Laxaria in a country called Sakria. Neither place was or is now known to exist.

In 1975, a man in a neatly pressed pinstripe suit was found dead, apparently having fallen from the West Botley flyover near Oxford. The manufacturers' labels had been removed from his clothes and the body bore no identification. The man carried five handkerchiefs, each of which bore the initial 'M', and a thin strip of foil containing 15 tablets of a new drug called Vivalan. The drug was so new that few doctors knew of its existence and those who did had prescribed it only to women, none of whom knew who 'M' was. The identity of the man has remained a mystery. 'M', it seems, had stepped out of thin air. – presumably at some point above the A420 road – and plummeted to his death.

One day in September 1877, Mr W. H. Smith glanced at the sky over Brooklyn, New York City. He had never before seen anything in the sky except clouds, birds, and snowflakes in winter, and he probably did not expect to see anything different when he glanced heavenward on that particular day. In fact he saw 'a winged human form' and the sight so impressed and startled him that he wrote a letter to the *New York Sun* about it.

On 12 October 1976, eight-year-old Tonnlie Barefoot of Dunn, North Carolina,

linked to but separate from our own. As Evans Wentz put it in his *The fairy faith in Celtic countries* (1909): 'There never seems to have been an uncivilized tribe, a race or nation of civilized men, who have not had some form of belief in an unseen world, peopled by unseen beings.'

In the ninth century, St Agobard, Archbishop of Lyons in France, wrote in his *Liber de Grandine at Tonitruis*:

We have seen and heard many who are overwhelmed by such madness, carried away by such folly, that they believe and assert that there is a certain region called Magonia (The Magic Land), whence ships come in the clouds. . . . Certain folk have we seen, blinded by so dark a folly, who brought into an assembly four persons, three men and a woman, as having fallen from the said ships; whom they had held in bonds for certain days and then presented them before an assembled body of men, in our presence, as aforesaid, in order that they should be stoned. Howbeit, the truth prevailed, after much reasoning, and they who brought them forward were confounded.

Enemy agents

What seems to have happened is that three men and a woman were seen or were said to have been seen descending from a 'cloud-ship'. A crowd gathered and became furious when somebody claimed that the strangers were the agents of an enemy of Charlemagne and had come to destroy the crops. The four people tried in vain to vindicate themselves, saying that they were ordinary people who had until recently lived near Lyons, but that they had been taken away by men who could work miracles and who had shown them marvellous things. The peasants did not believe one word of this and were about to

saw a little man 'not much bigger than a Coke bottle' who wore black boots, blue trousers and a blue top with 'the prettiest little white tie you ever saw'. The boy insisted that he had seen the little man and became very upset when his story was not believed. But disconcertingly for adult doubters, Tonnlie was able to show where he had seen the mini-man and a search revealed a clear trail of tiny footprints.

A naked man appearing from nowhere, a man from somewhere that does not exist, a tiny man with a pretty white tie, a 'thing' with wings, an unidentified corpse with a surfeit of handkerchiefs . . . For centuries reliable, sober people have been reporting encounters with people, creatures and 'weird things' that cannot be identified and in some cases seem beyond identification. In one sense it does not matter if the cited examples of these reports are true or capable of a rational explanation. Their importance lies in the fact that they reflect a belief in a world

Above: the tiny footprints allegedly made by the little man 'not much bigger than a Coke bottle' seen by Tonnlie Barefoot (right) of Dunn, North Carolina, USA, in 1976. The tiny man wore, among other things, 'the prettiest little white tie you ever saw'. Not unnaturally perhaps, Tonnlie's story was greeted with some reservation by adults – until they found the footprints

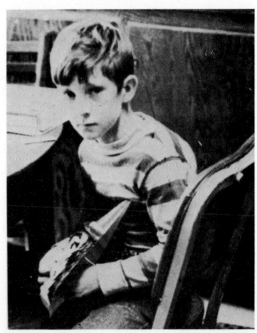

stone the four strangers when Agobard, attracted by the noise, came running to see what was going on. He listened to the opinions of both parties and then pronounced that cloud-ships did not exist, therefore the strangers could not have descended from one and were accordingly innocent of the crime of which they were accused. The peasants accepted this, which suggests that St Agobard was blessed with an enviable silver tongue, and the strangers were released to go about their business. As for Agobard, he seems to have considered the whole business to be no more than a manifestation of paganism. He wrote despairingly:

> The wretched world lies now under the tyranny of foolishness: things are believed by Christians of such absurdity as no one could aforetime induce the heathen to believe, who knew not of the creator of all.

The Magonians return

Despite Agobard's reasoning, the Magonians did not disappear but were still around 300 years later. In his *Otia Imperialia* (*c.*1211) the chronicler Gervaise of Tilbury wrote that one morning as the populace came out from mass they saw an anchor let down from a cloud-ship and accidentally become attached to a tomb. A cloud-sailor came down the rope hand over hand and freed the anchor.

> When, however, he had torn the anchor from the tomb, he was caught by those who stood around, in whose arms he gave up the ghost, stifled by the breath of our gross air even as a ship-wrecked mariner is stifled in the sea. Moreover, his fellows above, judging him to be wrecked . . . cut the cable, left their anchor, and sailed away.

Gervaise's account is even more remarkable than St Agobard's but one should beware of attaching modern interpretations to these medieval tales. In context of the period they can be less than mysterious. The Church has long been obsessed with the godlessness of mankind, and the medieval cleric was obsessed with the concept of war between the agents of God and Satan, frequently seeing evidence of the battle in the most natural of things. Nevertheless, the story is still very interesting as one of the more bizarre examples of the strange creatures that were repeatedly reported during the Middle Ages.

Writing of his own time, Gervaise makes the remarkable and perhaps startling comment that in the British Ocean (the Channel) mermaids and mermen lived in considerable number. One of the most detailed accounts of a merman is to be found in the *Chronicum Anglicarum* by Ralph of Coggeshall, a chronicler contemporary with, and possibly a friend of, Gervaise of Tilbury. Ralph writes:

> In the time of King Henry II, when Bartholomew de Glanville kept Orford Castle, it happened that the sailors

Below: the 'very frightful spectacle' that greeted the citizens of Nuremberg, Germany, at sunrise on 14 April 1561. To the medieval mind the strange and inexplicable objects – and people – that suddenly confronted them were only to be expected. It is little wonder that the belief in the 'cloud-ships' that were reported in both France and England was so widespread

there, fishing in the sea, caught a wild man in their nets. . . . He was completely naked and had the appearance of a man in all his parts. He had hair too . . . his beard was profuse and pointed, and he was exceedingly shaggy. . . .

The merman was kept under guard for several days. He eagerly ate what food was given to him, showing preference for raw fish. When taken into a church he displayed no sign of reverence or even understanding. He also insisted on sleeping when the Sun sank and waking when the Sun rose.

He would not utter any speech, or rather he could not, even when hung up by his feet and cruelly tortured. . . . Once they took him to the sea-gate and let him go into the water, after placing a triple row of strong nets in front of him. He soon made for the deep sea, and,

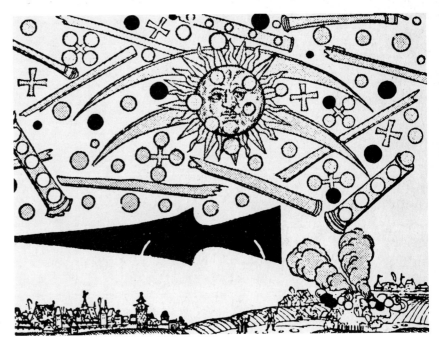

> breaking through the nets, raised himself again and again from the depths, and showed himself to those watching on the shore, often plunging into the sea, and a little later coming up, as if he were jeering at the spectators because he had escaped their nets.

For some reason, after the 'merman' had cavorted in the sea to his satisfaction, he returned to the shore and stayed with the folk of Orford for about two months before going once more into the sea, this time for ever.

> But whether he was mortal man, or a kind of fish bearing resemblance to humanity, or an evil spirit lurking in the body of a drowned man, such as we read of in the life of the blessed Audon, it is difficult to decide, all the more so because one hears so many remarkable things, and there is such a number of happenings like this.

The 16th-century chronicler Raphael Holinshed also mentions the Orford 'merman',

dating his appearance as 1197, the first year of the reign of King John.

Another bizarre story from the Middle Ages is that of the strange children who materialised at Woolpit in Suffolk. Their skin was green and they claimed to have come from 'St Martin's land', a place of perpetual twilight.

To the 20th-century mind these stories are outstanding examples, proof perhaps, of flying machines in the ninth century, of other worlds called Magonia and St Martin's land, and of a human being so well-adapted to the water that perhaps he could only be a descendant of the survivors of sunken Atlantis. But to the medieval mind such things were pretty tame, commonplace stuff compared to

Above: Orford Castle, Suffolk. Ralph of Coggeshall, the 13th-century chronicler, recorded that the fishermen of Orford had caught a merman (above right) in their nets. He was exceedingly shaggy, but otherwise he resembled a man. They placed him under guard and tortured him to make him speak, but he could not. He stayed with his captors for a total of two months before finally returning to his home under the sea

some of the many fabulous creatures that occupied the thoughts of the early Christian Church. In his *De Civitate Dei*, St Augustine of Hippo (345–430) wondered whether 'any monsterous kinds of men' were begotten by the sons of Adam. He tentatively concluded that the instance of abnormal birth supported the existence of creatures such as the Cyclops, another monster, which had its head in its breast, and Sciopodes, bizarre things that were able to run very swiftly despite the fact that they had only one leg, which could not bend. The single foot was so large that the creatures could use it to shade themselves from the Sun while they slept.

If the medieval mind could accept the reality of such fabulous creatures, it would

Left: some of the bizarre creatures discussed by St Augustine (345–430) in his *De Civitate Dei*: those with heads in their breasts, with only one eye and with only one foot. He concluded that these and other aberrations could be accounted for in terms of monstrous human births

have little difficulty in accepting Magonians, merfolk, and green children. And it is also interesting to note that, while the majority of the fabulous creatures described by people such as St Augustine have been relegated to the waste bin of discredited marvels, flying machines, merfolk and other almost human apparitions have continued to be seen throughout the ages.

One such well-documented story dates from 1955. On the night of Sunday, 21 August a 'little man' was seen approaching the Sutton family farmhouse near the small town of Kelly, to the north of Hopkinsville, Kentucky, USA. As the creature came to within 20 feet (6 metres) of the house, its arms raised, two of the Suttons shot at it. The creature somersaulted with the impact of the bullet, but it seemed otherwise unhurt and disappeared into the darkness. But there were more of them – and when the Suttons shot at them they, too, seem to feel no ill effects from the bullets that ricocheted off them – although they were knocked to the ground. The Suttons' hospitality to these 'little men', described as being about 3½ feet (1 metre) tall with large eyes and elephantine ears, consisted of shooting the contents of about four boxes of .22 shells at them.

Eventually the Suttons, frightened and alarmed by the creatures, abandoned their home and drove to the Hopkinsville police station, where they arrived in a state of excitement bordering on shock. Investigators later testified that the Suttons were genuinely agitated, that shots had been fired, and that no evidence of drinking had been found. The only conclusion that seemed possible was that the Sutton family really had seen what they claimed – but what was it?

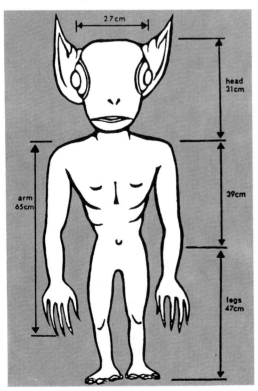

When several small goblins approached the Suttons' farm, near Hopkinsville, Kentucky, USA, on the night of 21 August 1955, they were greeted with a hail of bullets. However, the little men kept on coming, unharmed by the shooting. The Suttons panicked and drove straight to the nearest police station, where they were said to have arrived in a state of considerable shock. Later a model was made of the goblins (above) and a sketch (left) by Pauline Bowen appeared in *The humanoids* (1969). What were the goblins – creatures from another dimension? Entities from UFOs? Mass hallucinations?

It is interesting to note that strange, white, large-eyed people had previously been reported in the history of the area.

The Kelly goblin is but one of an assortment of weird and wonderful creatures that have been linked with close encounters of the third kind. But the phenomenon is much more complex than it appears at first glance. The mystery of 'appearing people', which could include ghosts and even the Loch Ness monster and the Abominable Snowman, dates as far back as written records will take us. Of course historical sightings cannot necessarily be taken as fact and more recent reports – in spite of having been made by people whose veracity we often have no reason to question – have not proved sufficiently convincing to persuade sceptics that there is a genuine phenomenon to investigate seriously. But one fact cannot be disputed; for whatever reason, thousands of people have seen, and continue to see, weird creatures that, in our reality, are not supposed to exist. Why they are seen is another question.

One-way ticket from nowhere

For centuries there have been reports of people suddenly appearing who have no known identity, or whose background is a complete mystery. Are there any explanations for these bizarre cases?

IT IS PERHAPS a telling symptom of modern society that some people can disappear and not be missed. There are dozens of accounts of people who have been found, usually dead – sometimes in strange circumstances – without any identification on their persons and without any kin or friends searching for them. While not all these people's deaths can be considered truly mysterious – at least not in the paranormal sense – sometimes the manner of their passing is so unusual that we are forced to look at the matter afresh.

For example: in November 1888 two residents of Birmingham, Alabama, USA, were murdered and their bodies were found in some woods. Nearby there was a third corpse. 'The body lies unidentified in the undertaker's rooms,' reported the *St Louis Globe Democrat*, continuing:

> No one who has seen it can remember having seen the man in life, and identification seems impossible. The dead man was evidently in good circumstances, if not wealthy, and what he could have been doing at the spot where his body was found is a mystery. Several persons who have seen the body are of the opinion that the man was a foreigner. Anyway he was an entire stranger in this vicinity, and his coming must have been as mysterious as his death.

In 1920 a naked man was found in a ploughed

Corpses that yield few clues to their identity have been found even in bureaucratic modern times, when everyone seems to be well-documented. An unknown man plummeted to his death from Kestrel House, Islington, London (left), in 1975. And corpses with no past have been discovered – amid some publicity – in Petersfield, Hampshire (right), and in Yellowham Woods (far right) and on Chesil Beach (top right) in Dorset, in the 1970s

shore near Weymouth five months later; and the third was found in Yellowham Woods, near Dorchester, in March 1975. None of the men was identified.

In 1975 a young man plummeted from the 17-storey Kestrel House in City Road, Islington, London. The man, who was not wearing a jacket or overcoat, despite it being midwinter, carried no clue to his identity beyond two bus tickets issued by Southampton Corporation and an envelope addressed to the National Savings headquarters in Glasgow. But both these potential clues led nowhere.

Inspector Robert Gibson of King's Cross police said that he could not accept that this outwardly respectable young man could have gone missing without somebody trying to find out where he was. However, when the

Unclothed Man's Death From Exposure.

From Our Special Correspondent.

PETERSFIELD, Thursday.

Who is the blue-eyed man whose nude body was found in a ploughed field at East Meon, near here, six weeks ago?

That a man could wander near to the main road between Petersfield and Winchester in a nude condition until he died in a field from exposure, aggravated by minor injuries such as cuts and abrasions, is astonishing, but that his identity and everything connected with his death should remain a mystery to-day is almost unbelievable. It is a baffling mystery.

The man's nails were manicured, the palms of his hands showed that he was not engaged in manual labour, and his features and general appearance were those of someone of a superior class. But although his photograph has been circulated north, east, south and west through the United Kingdom, the police are still without a clue, and there is no record of any missing person bearing the slightest resemblance to this man, presumably of education and good standing.

THEORIES AND SPECULATION.

There are plenty of theories. The popular one, according to my information, is that the man was brought to Peak Farm in a motor-car and was turned out to stumble along the highway presumably at about midnight, and perhaps intoxicated.

The railway runs near the ploughed field. Is it possible that he was thrown or fell from a train, his clothing having first been removed? There was a tear in the palm of one hand, cuts on the soles of the feet, bruises on the wrist and legs, and scratches on the arms. Dr. Stafford, who examined the body, believes that these injuries may have been caused by struggling through the hedges, falling over obstacles, etc.

The Coroner suggested at the inquest that the man may have been suffering from neurasthenia or shell shock—but his relatives would surely in that event have reported his disappearance or his clothes would have been found. As someone down here said to me: "When a tramp dies by the roadside he is generally in rags." This man certainly did not appear to be of the tramp class, and it seems incredible that he could have vanished from the world without being missed.

MYSTERIOUS MOTOR-CAR.

A police official who has been engaged on the case told me to-day that there was a trail through the coppice where the man had torn his way through. He had pushed his way through brambles that seem almost as formidable as a barbed-wire entanglement. No one but a madman would do such a thing.

It is possible, of course, that he was a soldier from one of the camps round here, and that he is posted as an absentee, but the inquiries have so far failed to support this suggestion.

I was told to-night of a shepherd who was watching his flocks in a field near to where the man was found, and he says that in the small hours of the morning he heard a motor-car stop and restart close by. The night was bitterly cold.

A cottager who lives not very far away also heard a car stop at about the same time.

field near Petersfield, Hampshire. Prints of the man's bare feet were traced to the road, and across the road into another field. A search of this field failed to find the man's clothing. As far as the evidence indicated, the man had appeared from nowhere, wandered aimlessly, perhaps in desperation – his body bore scratches such as would be made by bushes and hedges – until he died from exposure. That the poor fellow was unfamiliar with the area is suggested by the fact that he was only a mile (1.6 kilometres) from the nearest house. A photograph of the man was widely circulated, but nobody recognised him. 'There is no record of any missing person bearing the slightest resemblance to this man, presumably of good education and standing,' reported the London *Daily News*.

And such unidentified corpses continue to be found. On 1 December 1975, an inquest was held in Dorchester, England, into the deaths of three men. The first had been washed up on Chesil Beach, Dorset, in March 1974; the second was found on the

story of the 'Death Plunge Man' was reported in the *Sunday Express*, his body had been unidentified for a year. Said Inspector Gibson: 'Somebody somewhere must have loved him or at least known him.' Perhaps they did, but perhaps the 'somewhere' where they were was not the same 'somewhere' where we are.

These are just a few of the hundreds of examples of the unidentified and mysterious dead. Most of them can probably be explained by the fact that we live in a relatively rootless society where people easily move from place to place and can die hundreds or thousands of miles from home and friends. But this convenient idea certainly does not explain all peculiar appearances of dead men.

There are also numerous cases of so-called 'wild people' – not to be confused with people raised by animals, such as Romulus and Remus – who seem to have entered our world as if from another dimension. They are frequently unable to account for themselves and they can at best be described as total

amnesiacs. Some may subsequently be identified, but since the media soon lose interest and rarely pursue such cases it is often difficult to discover the outcome and ultimate fate of the appearer. A few, however, have become celebrities – the mysterious Count St Germain, for example, and Kaspar Hauser, who is perhaps the most famous 'appearing person' who ever lived. Kaspar was found wandering in Nuremberg in 1828, unable to say anything about himself or about how he had got there. But Kaspar was not a simple amnesiac. He said that for as long as he could remember he had been confined in a small, dimly lit room and had never seen the face of his captor. Who had held Kaspar Hauser captive, and why, has remained a mystery.

Royalty calls

Remarkable though it is, the story of Kaspar is by no means unique. Equally complex is the story of Princess Caraboo. On the evening of 3 April 1817, a girl knocked on the door of a cottage near Bristol and in an unknown language asked for food (although how the residents of the cottage knew that she was asking for food if she spoke an unknown language is as yet an unanswered question). The girl ended up standing before a magistrate, Samuel Worrell, who took her to his home. The girl's language and her equally unrecognisable writing attracted linguists from around the country, but none could understand what she was saying until one, Manuel Eyenesso, said that she was speaking in the Malay language. She was, he said, Princess Caraboo and she had been

Above left: Kaspar Hauser, perhaps the most famous of all 'appearing persons'. His strange tale of imprisonment, and the bizarre manner of his death – he was apparently murdered by an assailant who was himself a mystery – added to the enduring interest of his story

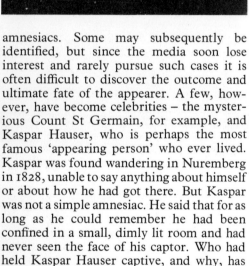

Above: a *woodwose*, one of the wild men believed to inhabit woodland Britain. There have been many reports of such people being caught by villagers, but the wild men spoke no intelligible language – which only added to the conundrum

Right: 'The Wonder of the West', or 'Princess Caraboo', who appeared at the door of an English cottage in 1817. She spoke a strange language, which was eventually identified as Malayan. However, an ordinary Englishwoman claimed her as her daughter. The truth about 'Princess Caraboo' remains obscure

kidnapped by pirates from her home in Java. After many adventures she had managed to escape from them and eventually reached England.

However, a Mrs Willcocks then arrived from the village of Witheridge in Devon and said that Princess Caraboo was her daughter Mary. Mary confessed to the deception and was entrusted to the care of Mrs Willcocks, who sent her to America, where she disappeared from the public gaze. So what of Manuel Eyenesso's fabulous story? He, it seems, was an impostor who 'translated' Mary's gibberish into a story of his own invention. Thus we have two impostors for the price of one. Or do we?

Sources differ to a considerable extent. According to one, Mrs Worrell (the wife of the magistrate) had gone to Witheridge and there located Mrs Willcocks and established Mary's identity. Moreover, it was Mrs Worrell who paid for the girl to go to America and, once there, Mary (or Princess Caraboo) did not disappear but gave exhibitions, in Philadelphia and elsewhere, of her unknown writing.

We are left, then, with two irreconcilable stories and at least two impostors. If Princess Caraboo was really Mary Willcocks, then Manuel Eyenesso must have been an impostor because he declared that she was speaking Malay, which was highly unlikely. Again, it was Eyenesso who said she was Princess Caraboo. And we have Mrs Willcocks who, if Princess Caraboo and Eyenesso were genuine, was not the mother of Mary and was therefore an impostor. And there is Mrs Worrell who, though not an impostor, may have concocted the whole Mary story simply to get the girl away from Mrs Worrell's

The Wonder of the West.

" And where did she come from ? and who can she be?
Did she fall from the sky ? did she rise from the sea ?"

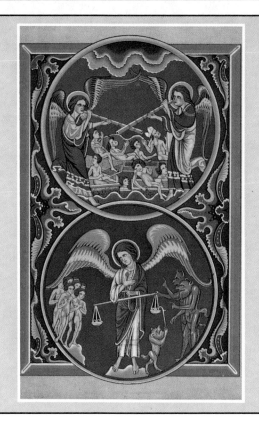

With a pinch of salt

The Bible offers many stories of mysterious 'appearing people', who are more generally known as angels. They are not always winged or bathed in a heavenly golden glow, nor do they always appear in dreams. On the contrary, they often seem solidly human in every respect. For example, take the angels who came to Abraham as he was sitting 'in the tent door in the heat of the day' and told him that his aged wife Sarah would bear a child (Genesis 18). The three angels looked like men and they behaved like men – even dining with Abraham.

Similarly the two angels who came to Lot and told him to gather his family and flee from Sodom (Genesis 19) were clearly of human form, and are repeatedly referred to as 'men'. Again, we are told that they ate, rested and took shelter with Lot, yet they were possessed of advance knowledge of the cataclysm that was about to befall the Cities of the Plain. But Lot's wife did not heed their advice not to look back on the destruction – and she was turned into a pillar of salt, which was left standing in the desert.

husband. The permutations of the Caraboo story leave the brain in a whirl.

Five 'wild men' and a 'wild girl' were found in Connecticut, USA, in January 1888. Between 1904 and 1905 ten 'wild men' were found in various parts of England. One of them is reported to have spoken a language that nobody had heard before and to have carried a book in which there was unknown and unidentified writing. Between 1920 and

Below: the High Street, Chatham, Kent, where a bewildered naked man was found wandering on 6 January 1914. He could give no account of himself and was finally declared insane and locked up in the Medway Infirmary for the rest of his life

1923 six people were found wandering in or near Romford, Essex. None could say how they had got there or tell anything about themselves.

In 1923 a naked man was seen several times at Lord Carnarvon's country estate near Newbury, Hampshire. By a striking coincidence he was first seen on 17 March, the day on which Lord Carnarvon fell ill, and was last seen on 5 April, the day Carnarvon died.

There is also the story of the naked man who, in the afternoon of Tuesday 6 January 1914, suddenly appeared in the High Street, Chatham, Kent (see page 23). The man's identity was not established and he was later declared insane and taken to Medway Infirmary.

Charles Fort, the great American collector of reports of strange happenings, commented on the Chatham naked man in his book *Lo!*:

I suspect that many persons have been put away, as insane, simply because they were gifted with uncommon insights, or had been through uncommon experiences. . . . If there have ever been instances of teleportations of human beings from somewhere else to this Earth, an examination of inmates of infirmaries and workhouses and asylums might lead to some marvelous astronomical disclosures. . . . Early in the year 1928 a man did appear in a town in New Jersey, and did tell that he had come from the planet Mars. Wherever he came from, everybody knows where he went, after telling that.

Into thin air

People, animals and ordinary household objects that vanish into thin air or appear suddenly in unlikely places – these have always been part of folklore. But, as LYNN PICKNETT points out, the disappearances continue . . .

VANISHED

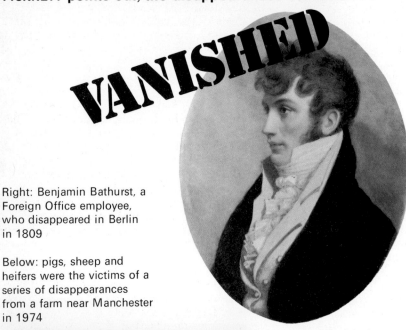

Right: Benjamin Bathurst, a Foreign Office employee, who disappeared in Berlin in 1809

Below: pigs, sheep and heifers were the victims of a series of disappearances from a farm near Manchester in 1974

VANISHED

'NOW YOU SEE HER, now you don't.' So runs the stage illusionist's traditional patter as he makes his assistant disappear. It's a skilful and enjoyable trick, this disappearing act – but even in the everyday world, far from the stage door, there have been many disappearances and strange reappearances. Only for a handful of them are there rational explanations; most of them are so extraordinary that they almost defy belief.

On 29 November 1809 Benjamin Bathurst, an employee of the British Foreign Office, was about to board a coach outside an inn near Berlin. He went to look at the horses and vanished forever.

In June 1900, Sherman Church ran into a cotton mill at Augusta Mills near Lake Michigan, USA. He never came out and could not be found again.

In 1974 pigs, sheep and heifers vanished from two farms near Manchester, England.

Weird and apparently random phenomena such as these were the province of Charles Hoy Fort, an American who published his *Book of the damned* in 1919. This – his most famous book – is a collection of well-attested stories, with a few sly hints that the natural world is one huge practical joke expressed through rains of frogs, people who disappear into nothing and people who come from nowhere. Charles Fort coined the word *teleportation* to describe the forcible removal of a person or object from one place – or even plane of existence – to another by agencies unknown and unseen. According to taste, these forces have been ascribed to God, the Devil, spirit guides, fairies and UFOs.

Sister Mary's missionary flights

Sometimes the teleportee seems to be actually in two places at once – this phenomenon is called *bilocation*. A famous case of bilocation occurred in 1620 when a young nun, Sister Mary of Agreda in Spain, embarrassed her superiors with her persistent tales of her missionary 'flights' to the Jumano Indians in Mexico; she claimed she regularly made the 2000-mile (3200-kilometre) journey. No one was prepared to take her seriously, especially as she was not missed at the convent at Agreda and she made the far-fetched claim that, during her 'flight', she noticed that the earth was round. . . . Yet the official Papal missionary assigned to the Jumano, Father Alonzo de Benevides, complained to the Pope in 1622 that the Indians had already been taught about the Catholic faith by a mysterious 'lady in blue' who had handed out rosaries, crucifixes and even a chalice – which proved to be from the convent in Agreda.

On being closely questioned by Father Benevides, Sister Mary revealed a detailed knowledge of the Indians' way of life and language and described individual members of the tribe accurately.

Like most teleportation stories, that of Sister Mary and her missionary activities seems to defy classification and analysis. The fact that she 'saw' that the earth was round indicates some kind of astral travel, yet the chalice was solid enough.

The sudden appearance of solid objects, often in sealed rooms, is called *apportation*. Apports can be literally anything, from stones or musical instruments to a dish of hot food or fresh flowers out of season.

Things that go bump . . .

Apportation seems to be a favourite diversion of poltergeists, or so-called mischievous spirits; disturbed houses often provide the setting for spectacular apports appearing from thin air. Hans Bender, Director of the Institut für Grenzgebiete der Psychologie und Psychohygenie (Institute for Border Areas of Psi) in Freiburg, West Germany, has this to say of experiences of 'things that go bump in the night':

> Stones, for instance, come into a closed room from outside a house during poltergeist attacks. Witnesses describe the stones falling from about 5 or 6 inches [12 or 15 centimetres] from the ceiling. They don't bounce, and when you touch them they are usually warm.
>
> In one case . . . in Bavaria in 1969, stones came into a closed kitchen and objects flew out of the locked house. Some little dolls came out of a closed cupboard, seemingly through the very fabric of the door, and the people saw small bottles – perfume and medicine bottles – coming from the roof of the house. Interestingly, when the bottles were seen coming from the house, they were not falling in a straight line, but in a zigzag fashion, as if they were being transported, not as if they were falling free.

This notion of apports being *carried* by an invisible force accords perfectly with the spiritualists' belief that solid objects can be dematerialised and materialised through the agency of spirits. One 'spirit guide' named White Hawk described how he does it: 'I can only explain it by saying that I speed up the atomic vibrations until the stones [or other apport] are disintegrated. Then they are brought here and I slow down the vibrations until they become solid again.'

Spiritualists often explain the inability of most mortals to see the 'other side' – which is said to interpenetrate our world in space and time – by pointing out that the material world is 'dense matter', which vibrates slowly; the spiritual plane is 'refined matter', vibrating too fast for our physical perceptions. A sudden change in atomic vibration removes objects – or people – from one plane to another or one place to another, rather like the 'beaming up' and 'beaming down' of the personnel of *Star Trek*'s starship *Enterprise*.

Vanishing people have always been part of the world's folklore – fairies, giants, spirits and, recently, UFOs have allegedly abducted

Below: Sister Mary of Agreda, who made her alleged missionary 'flights' to convert the Jumano Indians of Mexico in 1620. When the first official papal missionary visited the Jumano in 1622, he found that they had already been taught about Christianity – by a mysterious 'lady in blue'. Yet Sister Mary's fellow nuns in Agreda, Spain, testified that she had not left the convent during the time that she claimed to have been in Mexico

Bottom: Dr Hans Bender, Director of the Institute for Border Areas of Psi in Freiburg in Breisgau, West Germany. Dr Bender has made a special study of objects and people that mysteriously appear and disappear

hundreds, perhaps thousands, of people. Fairies were infamous for their trick of abducting healthy babies and leaving weak 'changelings' behind instead, and various demons of legend have been blamed for removing folk from 'before the very eyes' of their friends.

But some unfortunate people disappear without any apparent supernormal agency. These random and pointless disappearances fascinated Fort, who collected a formidable dossier of them. The victims are often typical 'men in the street', uninterested in the paranormal, on whom some practical joke seems to have been played.

The 'joke' was distinctly unfunny for a man in 1655 who was going about his business in Goa, India, when he suddenly found himself back in his birthplace, Portugal. This abrupt return home was witnessed by enough people to ensure it came to the ears of the Inquisition, who naturally – for them – assumed he was a practising sorcerer. He was tried and burnt at the stake.

In Connecticut, in January 1888, passers-by were astonished by the sudden materialisation of six people in the street. All six were suffering from concussion.

The magician vanishes

Perhaps the most ironical dematerialisation was that of the stage magician, William Neff, as related by his friend L. J. Knebel, the American broadcaster. This extraordinary happening took place at the Paramount Theatre, in New York. There were few people in the audience and Neff went into his magician's patter routinely. His friend Knebel heard none of it: he was transfixed by the gradual dematerialisation of the artist. Neff became so translucent that the stage curtains could be seen through him. Curiously, the magician seemed to be unaware of his nebulous state and continued with his patter. Gradually he became solid again, beginning with a vague outline. Confronted by Knebel with this amazing occurrence, Neff confessed it was nothing whatever to do with his act! However, he was no stranger to the phenomenon – he had once partially dematerialised during his act at Chicago, and once, 'casually', in front of his very shaken wife. One supposes that if he ever learned how to reproduce this freak happening at will, he would have become a very rich man.

Someone whose fate and fortune seem inextricably linked is the Israeli sensitive, Uri Geller. Although – as far as we know – not a teleportee, his very presence in a house provokes a flurry of apports.

Professor John Hasted, head of the department of physics at Birkbeck College, University of London, set up a test to see if the young Israeli could in any way alter the structure of a vanadium carbide crystal – chosen for its particular hardness and its rarity. It was laid on a piece of metal and enclosed in a cellulose capsule. First the professor interposed his hand between Geller and the crystal. Then as witnesses watched, Geller moved his hand, and the crystal jumped twice, 'like a jumping bean'. Apparently this was all Geller had intended to do, because Professor Hasted says 'Geller stopped concentrating and we looked at the capsule. Only half the crystal was there.' It would have been impossible for him to have broken the capsule by ordinary means.

After Geller had paid a short visit to Professor Hasted's home, solid objects began to behave unpredictably:

A small ivory ornament appeared out of thin air, not flying, but dropping to the ground from about a foot [30 centimetres] above the floor. There was also the key of a French Empire clock that teleported from one room to the next. I found it on the floor, by the kitchen door, and put it back in its proper place. . . . I walked back into the kitchen and found it lying in the same place on the floor.

Uri Geller seems to have a psychokinetic ability (power of mind over matter) that he can only partially control or predict. Ironically, it is this very lack of control that, many people consider, argues for his genuineness – anything too glib implies rehearsal or sleight of hand.

This suspicion attached itself to the feats of many famous Victorian mediums. So many of them were proved to fake their seances that any curious phenomena attached to their movement became suspect. Even the founder of Theosophy, the controversial Madame Blavatsky, was frequently suspected of sleight of hand – for example, a whole teaset conveniently fell out of the sky during a picnic and, more tellingly, her 'teleported' messages allegedly from her Master in Tibet contained whole passages from a recently published American sermon – a fact that, while it does not directly challenge the reality

Above: Uri Geller, the Israeli sensitive, whose presence causes objects to apport

Below: 'a moonlight transit of Venus' – a contemporary impression of the teleportation across London of the large Mrs Guppy in 1871

of the teleported letter, reveals the Tibetan Master as a plagiarist and on the whole not the sort of guru whose word should be taken as gospel.

Another medium whose phenomena were both spectacular and open to question was Mrs Guppy who, while still Miss Nichol, produced apports of six variegated anemones, 15 chrysanthemums and assorted other flowers at a London seance in 1867.

One of her more startling feats, however, seems to be genuine. On the evening of June 3rd 1871 Mrs Guppy, attired in her nightgown (some reports say her underwear), was sitting quietly in the breakfast room of her Highbury home, busy with the household accounts. A friend was with her, when suddenly she disappeared and appeared in a room in Lamb's Conduit Street (a few miles away) where a seance was in progress, still clutching her accounts book and in a trance. That she was as solid in Lamb's Conduit Street as in Highbury was borne out by the fact that her materialisation caused some buffeting round the seance table. There was a heavy thud on the table and one of the sitters cried out 'Good God – there is something on my head!' One sympathises; Mrs Guppy was described as 'the biggest woman in London'. She weighed over 230 lbs (100 kilograms) and, as she was something of a figure of fun, the whole story, instead of being the psychic proof of the phenomenon of teleportation so many mediums were looking for, became the biggest joke for years.

Fort, with his theory of the cosmic joke, might have pointed out that Mrs Guppy's name, size and joke reputation were precisely why it was she and not, say, Queen Victoria, who was 'selected' for this astonishing psychical demonstration . . . and why it was a stage illusionist who dematerialised 'before your very eyes'.

The famous case of the 'Mary Celeste'

On 5 December 1872 the captain of the brigantine *Dei Gratia* sighted a ship sailing so clumsily that he went to investigate. The mystery deepened as he explored the abandoned *Mary Celeste*. Although showing signs of some storm damage, she was still sea-worthy. One lifeboat had apparently been launched (rather than having been washed overboard), but there was still plenty of fresh water aboard, provisions for six months were intact and the crew's clothes – including their oilskins – were hanging

on their pegs. On one bunk a child's toys lay as if left in mid-game. Everywhere there were signs of abrupt abandonment – however, the ship's navigation instruments and some papers were missing (although the log remained). The only signs of something bizarre were two long grooves apparently etched into the wood above the waterline, blood-like stains on the deck and on the captain's sword in his deserted cabin, and a mysterious cut in the ship's rail. What really happened? Did the crew fall victim to illness, insanity, homicide, suicide or the delusion that they were sinking? Were they abducted by giant sea-creatures or spacemen, as some suggest? The theories are many, but it seems very likely that we shall never know for certain.

Who are the abductors?

What is the truth behind the phenomenon of mysterious disappearances? Who, or what, are the abductors? This chapter attempts to answer these questions and chronicles more cases of inexplicably vanishing people

PEOPLE HAVE BEEN DISAPPEARING mysteriously since the beginning of time, but the agencies blamed for abducting them have changed according to the spiritual preoccupations of the day. Gods, demons, fairies, spirits, and now UFOS show an astonishing predilection for what seems to be the random picking up and setting down – or picking up and not returning – of perfectly ordinary people.

In 1678 a Dr Moore and his three friends were touring Ireland. They put up for the night at an inn at Dromgreagh in Wicklow. Something prompted the doctor to tell his tale about how he had been abducted many times as a child by fairies, only to be rescued by the intervention of the local witch's magic. And even as he spoke the whole process went into motion again . . .

He saw a 'troop of men' come into the inn and drag him off with them. Frightening enough for him – but terrifying for the three witnesses, for all they saw was Dr Moore being pulled out of his chair and out of the room by an invisible but irresistible force. His friends made a grab at him but the force was too strong, and he vanished into the

Below: fairies abducting a human child, from a 19th-century book illustration. Folklore is full of tales of children being stolen by fairies, who leave their own fairy children – changelings – in their place

night. The innkeeper recommended they send for the local wise woman. She explained that the doctor had been abducted by the local fairies and was their prisoner in a nearby wood. She could break their hold on him, but her spell would only work for his release if he could be made to abstain from food and drink during his imprisonment. If not, he would return but would soon weaken and die. She cast her spell and they all waited.

Next morning at dawn Dr Moore came back to the inn, starving and thirsty, complaining that all the refreshments he had been offered during the night had inexplicably been dashed out of his hand. Unknown to him, the old woman's spell had been working and had finally secured his release – as morning came he had discovered he was suddenly alone near the inn.

The three witnesses attested to the story. It was published as a pamphlet and signed by one J. Cotham; a copy is now preserved in the British Museum.

Two thousand miles and nearly 300 years away, another story of abduction with witnesses reflects an entirely different preoccupation. On 5 November 1975 Travis Walton, a young forester, and his five workmates were driving to work near Snowflake, Arizona. They suddenly saw a bright light hovering over their truck. As the driver, Mike Rogers, stopped the car, Travis felt an extraordinary

compulsion to approach the light. He jumped out and rushed towards it. There was a sudden flash of light, and Travis hit the ground. Terrified, the others drove off. When they had calmed down, they returned to the same spot and instigated a thorough search that was to last for five days and cover miles of the Arizona desert and forest. Suspicion naturally fell on the five friends, but their distress seemed completely genuine and their story held up even under close questioning with the aid of a lie-detector.

Five days later, a confused and shaky Walton appeared in Heber, a small town close to Snowflake. His story tallied with that of his friends – as far as theirs went – but he added some amazing details. The beam of light had knocked him unconscious and then somehow drawn him up into a spacecraft in which he was examined by foetus-like creatures before being 'dumped' in Heber.

The 1880s saw a large number of disappearances from East London, known to this day as the 'West Ham disappearances'. One of the first victims was little Eliza Carter, who vanished from her home but later appeared in the street and spoke to some of her school friends. They tried to persuade her to

Above: Travis Walton, a young forestry worker who says he was mysteriously abducted by a UFO while driving to work near Snowflake, Arizona, USA on 5 November 1975. Five days later he reappeared, telling an amazing story of his 'flight' in the unknown craft

country station some mile and a half from my Sussex home. The train from London had arrived late, the bus had gone and no taxis were available. The rain was heavy and incessant. The time was 5.55 p.m. and I was expecting an important trunk call from overseas at 6 p.m. at home. The situation seemed desperate. To make matters worse, the station call box was out of order and some trouble on the line made access to the railway telephone impossible. In despair I sat down in the waiting room and having nothing better to do, I compared my watch with the station clock. Allowing for the fact that this is always kept two minutes in advance, I was able to confirm the fact that the exact time was 5.57 p.m. Three minutes to zero hour! What happened next I cannot say. When I came to myself I was standing in my hall at home, a good 20 minutes walk away, and the clock was striking six. My telephone call duly came through a few minutes later. Having finished my call, I awoke to the realisation that something very strange had happened. Then

go home to her family, but she said she couldn't – 'they' wouldn't let her. She was seen around West Ham for a couple of days before finally disappearing forever.

A similar case was that of Private Jerry Unwin of the US Army, who disappeared, reappeared, absented himself and appeared once more, before vanishing again on 1 August 1959.

The experience was not pleasant, and a far cry from the semi-mystical experience of the abductees portrayed in the film *Close encounters of the third kind*, but it was kin to the whole history of mysterious abductions.

The late psychic and writer Wellesley Tudor Pole recounted a strange tale of teleportation, in his book *The silent road* (1962):

On a wet and stormy night in December, 1952, I found myself at a

Above left: Eliza Carter, the 12-year-old schoolgirl who disappeared mysteriously in East London in January 1882. Her case was the first of a series of abductions that came to be known as the 'West Ham disappearances'

Above: a series of sketches showing the fate of one Amelia Jeffs, thought to be another victim of the West Ham disappearances. This time, however, there was no mystery: clues quickly led police to the discovery of the little girl's body

much to my surprise, I found that my shoes were dry and free from mud, and that my clothes showed no sign of damp or damage.

Like all such stories, there is something exasperatingly incomplete about this strange tale. Wellesley Tudor Pole has told all he can remember, but inevitably the phenomenon raises questions he cannot answer. As there were no witnesses in this case, no one will ever know how – or if – the teleportee disappeared. Did he literally vanish? Was he transported invisibly? How did he reappear? But at least one thing seems certain – what triggered off the teleporting agency seems to have been no less than the writer's own will. He was desperate to get home in time for his telephone call and his anxiety seems to have put into motion whatever natural law it is that governs the occurrence of the phenomenon.

Desire could also explain the bilocation of Sister Mary of Agreda (see page 33); intense piety and missionary zeal could have generated the unknown energies needed to transport a facsimile of herself to Mexico.

But in the annals of disappearing people there is no more controversial tale nor one stranger than the alleged 'Philadelphia experiment'. In 1943 there reportedly took place a horrifying experiment into invisibility involving a ship and its crew. This was not a psychic test, but a top-secret experiment of the United States Navy. According to Charles Berlitz and William Moore in their book *The Philadelphia experiment* (1979), the surviving witnesses to the experiment still suffer harrassment and have been repeatedly warned against discussing it by government agents.

A force field was created around the experimental ship – a destroyer – as it lay in a special berth in the Philadelphia Navy Yard. The crew could see one another normally but witnesses could only see the vague outline of both ship and men through the force field. They shimmered like a heat haze before

One of the most extraordinary disappearances ever allegedly took place in 1943, when the US Navy is reported to have carried out a horrifying experiment in invisibility, and succeeded in making a destroyer, the USS *Eldridge* (bottom), together with its crew, disappear for a few minutes from its berth in the Philadelphia Navy Yard (below). However, as most of the evidence comes from a single witness, it is impossible to judge whether the experiment took place

re-assuming normal shape and density. The effect on the crewmen involved was said to be appalling. The after-effects took various horrible forms: some of the men are said to have suffered a particularly harrowing form of spontaneous human combustion (described in an earlier volume) – bursting into flames that burned brightly for 18 days; others went mad, and yet others periodically became semi-transparent or partly invisible. Some died as a direct result of their experience.

An eyewitness claimed to have seen the entire experiment take place, and even to have thrust his arm into the force field that surged

in a counterclockwise direction around the little experimental Navy ship . . . I watched the air all around the ship . . . turn slightly darker than all the other

air . . . I saw, after a few minutes, a foggy green mist arise like a thin cloud. I think this must have been a mist of atomic particles. I watched as [it] became rapidly invisible to human eyes. And yet the precise shape of the keel and underhull of that ship remained impressed into the ocean water . . . The field had a sheet of pure electricity around it as it flowed . . . my entire body was not within that force field when it reached maximum strength density . . . and so I was not knocked down but my arm and hand was [sic] only pushed backward

The US Navy deny that the experiment took place. Yet the story is too persistent and has too much inner consistency to be dismissed entirely. If 'project invisibility' did take place, then it made scientific history – but compared to 'natural' disappearances it was clumsy and very dangerous.

The US Navy do have an interest in invisibility that can be verified, however. In September 1980 they made it known that they were experimenting with *radar* invisibility, but escaping a radar scan is a far cry from disappearing from human sight.

If it were possible to harness the 'natural force' that occasionally drags people from one place or plane of existence to another in a matter of seconds, or makes them invisible, then life as we know it would change completely. Whole armies could suddenly materialise unexpectedly in the country of their foes; spies could invisibly slip past the guards at top secret installations; criminals dematerialise when the law draws too close. . . .

Yet perhaps the clue, such as it is , lies in the very randomness of the phenomenon. Perhaps there is no natural force but, paradoxically, a random law creating freak effects for their own sake. This suggests a governing intelligence, a cosmic joker like the one who perhaps stage-manages the manifestations of the Loch Ness Monster, UFOs, bigfoot . . . and who jams the witnesses' cameras at the critical moments or contrives to discredit witnesses. So we come full circle – is the joker a god, a demon, a fairy, a spirit or a UFO?

Researcher Ivan T. Sanderson said of the UFO phenomenon, 'It cannot be all bunkum yet some of its implications are so bizarre as to be almost beyond comprehension.' This could well apply to all 'Fortean' phenomena. Those who disappear for ever – do they go to some other world, some other plane, or do they find themselves in that other unexplored region, the furthest reaches of the human mind? If abductions are ascribed to the agencies currently in vogue – put, as Fort said, 'in terms of the familiar' – then the phenomenon must be at least partly 'in the mind'. Yet the disappearances are real.

It is likely that such phenomena will remain unexplained until a comprehensive explanation for all strange phenomena can be formulated. Until then – who knows?

Apparitions, many researchers believe, exist only in the human mind. But what of the art, allegedly practised by Tibetan adepts, of making thought forms materialise so strongly that they can be seen by other people? FRANCIS KING investigates

CONDITIONS ON THE ROAD from China to Lhasa, the forbidden capital city of Tibet, were even worse than usual in the winter of 1923 to 1924. Nevertheless, small numbers of travellers, mostly pilgrims wishing to obtain spiritual merit by visiting the holy city and seeing its semi-divine ruler, the Dalai Lama, struggled onwards through the bitter winds and heavy snow. Among them was an elderly woman who appeared to be a peasant from some distant province of the god-king's empire.

The woman was poorly dressed and equipped. Her red woollen skirt and waistcoat, her quilted jacket, and her cap with its lambskin earflaps, were worn and full of holes. From her shoulder hung an ancient leather bag, black with dirt. In this were the provisions for her journey: barley meal, a piece of dried bacon, a brick of compressed tea, a tube of rancid butter, and a little salt and soda.

With her black hair coated with grease and her dark brown face, she looked like a typical peasant woman. But her hair was really white, dyed with Chinese ink, and her complexion took its colour from oil mixed with cocoa and crushed charcoal. For this Tibetan peasant woman was in reality Alexandra David-Neel, a Frenchwoman who, 30 years before, had been an opera singer of note who had been warmly congratulated by Jules Massenet for her performance in the title role of his opera *Manon*. In the intervening years

Mme David-Neel had travelled to strange places and had undergone even stranger experiences. These had included meeting a magician with the ability to cast spells to hurl flying rice cakes at his enemies, and learning the techniques of *tumo*, an occult art that enables its adepts to sit naked amid the Himalayan snows. Most extraordinary of all, she had constructed, by means of mental and psychic exercises, a *tulpa* – a phantom form born solely from the imagination, and yet so strongly vitalised by the adept's visualisation and will that it actually becomes visible to other people. A tulpa is, to put it another way, an extremely powerful example of what occultists term a thought form.

To understand the nature of the tulpa one has to appreciate that, as far as Tibetan Buddhists (and most Western occultists) are concerned, thought is far more than an intellectual function. Every thought, they believe, affects the 'mind-stuff' that permeates the world of matter in very much the same way as a stone thrown into a lake makes ripples upon the water's surface. A thought, in other words, produces a 'thought ripple'.

Usually these thought ripples have only a short life. They decay almost as soon as they are created and make no lasting impression on the mind-stuff interpenetrating the physical plane. If, however, the thought is particularly intense, the product of deep passion or fear, or if it is of long duration, the subject of much brooding and meditation, the thought ripple builds the mind-stuff into a more permanent thought form, one that has a longer and more intense life.

Tulpas and other thought forms are not considered by Tibetan Buddhists to be 'real' – but neither, according to them, is the world of matter that seemingly surrounds us. Both are illusory. As a Buddhist classic from the first century AD expresses it:

All phenomena are originally in the

Below: pilgrims approach the holy city of Lhasa, the forbidden capital of Tibet, in a photograph taken in the 1930s; this modern photograph (below right) testifies to the continuing practice of this arduous form of religious devotion. One of the most remarkable pilgrims to have undertaken this journey was Alexandra David-Neel (right, with a companion, the lama Yongden) who, in the 1920s, travelled throughout Tibet and learned many of the secrets of the Tibetan Buddhists – including the art of making thought forms materialise

The word made flesh

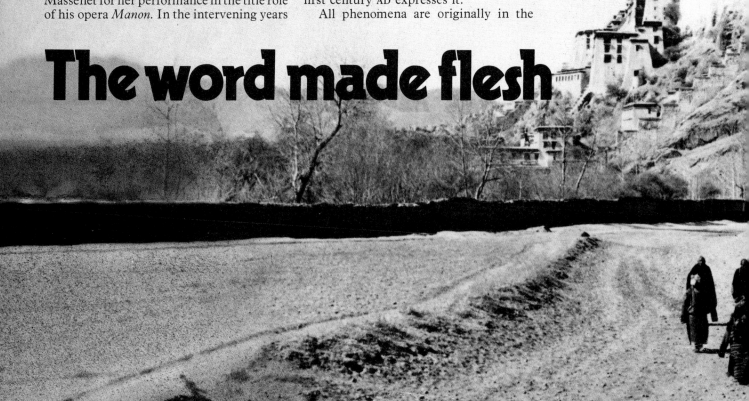

mind and have really no outward form; therefore, as there is no form, it is an error to think that anything is there. All phenomena merely arise from false notions in the mind. If the mind is independent of these false ideas, then all phenomena disappear.

If the beliefs about thought forms held by Tibetan Buddhists, by mystics and magicians, are justified, then many ghostly happenings, hauntings, and cases of localities endowed with a strong 'psychic atmosphere' are easily explained. It seems plausible, for example, that the thought forms created by the violent and passionate mental processes of a murderer, supplemented by the terror stricken emotions of a victim, could linger around the scene of the crime for months, years, or even centuries. This could produce intense depression and anxiety in those who visited the 'haunted' spot and, if the thought forms were sufficiently vivified and powerful, 'apparitions', such as a re-enactment of the crime, might be witnessed by people possessed of psychic sensitivity.

Sometimes, it is claimed by students of the occult, the 'spirits' that haunt a particular spot are tulpas, thought forms that have been deliberately created by a sorcerer for his own purposes.

The existence of extremely potent thought forms that re-enact the past would explain the worldwide reports of visitors to old battlefields 'witnessing' military encounters that took place long before. The sites of the battle of Naseby, which took place during England's 17th century Civil War, and of the 1942 commando raid on Dieppe during World War Two are among battlefields that enjoy such ghostly reputations.

A tulpa is no more than an extremely powerful thought form, no different in its essential nature from many other ghostly apparitions. Where, however, it does differ from a normal thought form is that it has come into existence, not as a result of an accident, a side effect of a mental process, but as the result of a deliberate act of will.

The word tulpa is a Tibetan one, but there are adepts in almost every part of the world who believe they are able to manufacture these beings by first drawing together and coagulating some of the mind-stuff of the Universe into a form, and then transferring to it some of their own vitality.

In Bengal, home of much Indian occultism, the technique is called *kriya shakti* ('creative power'), and is studied and practised by the adepts of Tantrism, a religio-magical system concerned with the spiritual aspects of sexuality numbering both Hindus and Buddhists among its devotees. Initiates of 'left-handed' Tantric cults – that is to say, cults in which men and women engage in ritual sexual intercourse for mystical and magical purposes – are considered particularly skilled in *kriya shakti*. This is because it is thought that the intense physical and cerebral excitement of the orgasm engenders quite exceptionally vigorous thought forms.

Many Tibetan mystical techniques originated in Bengal, particularly in Bengali Tantrism, and there is a very strong resemblance between the physical, mental and spiritual exercises used by the Tantric yogis of Bengal and the secret inner disciplines of Tibetan Buddhism. It thus seems likely that Tibetans originally derived their theories about tulpas, and their methods of creating these strange beings, from Bengali practitioners of *kriya shakti*.

Students of tulpa magic begin their training in the art of creating these thought beings

Below: a Buddhist monk with drum and incense stick. The rigorous mental and physical discipline taught by Buddhism enables some of its followers to attain paranormal powers; in her book *Initiations and initiates in Tibet* Alexandra David-Neel tells of a man (right, standing on left) who was reputed to be able to hypnotise and cause death at a distance

by adopting one of the many gods or goddesses of the Tibetan pantheon as a 'tutelary deity' – a sort of patron saint. It must be emphasised that, while Tibetan initiates regard the gods respectfully, they do not look upon them with any great admiration. For, according to Buddhist belief, although the gods have great powers and are, in a sense, 'supernatural', they are just as much slaves of illusion, just as much trapped in the wheel of birth, death, and rebirth, as the humblest peasant.

The student retires to a hermitage or other secluded place and meditates on his tutelary deity, known as a *yidam*, for many hours. He combines a contemplation of the spiritual attributes traditionally associated with the *yidam* with visualisation exercises designed to build up in the mind's eye an image of the *yidam* as it is portrayed in paintings and statues.

To keep his concentration upon the *yidam*, to ensure that in every waking moment there is a single-pointed devotion to that being, the student continually chants traditional mystic phrases associated with the deity he serves.

He also constructs the *kyilkhors* – literally circles, but actually symbolic diagrams that may be of any shape – believed sacred to his god. Sometimes he will draw these with coloured inks on paper or wood, sometimes he will engrave them on copper or silver, sometimes he will outline them on his floor with coloured powders.

The preparation of the *kyilkhors* must be undertaken with care, for the slightest deviation from the traditional pattern associated with a particular *yidam* is believed to be extremely dangerous, putting the unwary student in peril of obsession, madness, death, or a stay of thousands of years in one of the 'hells' of Tibetan cosmology.

It is interesting to compare this belief with the idea, strongly held by many Western occultists, that if a magician engaged in 'evoking a spirit to visible appearance' draws his protective magical circle incorrectly, he will be 'torn in pieces'.

Wolf at the door

In her book *Psychic self defence* (1930), the occultist Dion Fortune (left) relates how she once 'formulated a were-wolf accidentally'.

She had this alarming experience while she was brooding about her feelings of resentment against someone who had hurt her. Lying on her bed, she was thinking of the terrifying wolf-monster of Norse mythology, Fenrir, when suddenly she felt a large grey wolf materialise beside her. She was aware of its body pressing against hers.

From her reading about thought forms, she knew she must gain control of the beast immediately. So she dug her

Eventually, if the student has persisted with the prescribed exercises, he 'sees' his *yidam*, at first nebulously and briefly, but then persistently and with complete – and sometimes terrifying – clarity.

But this is only the first stage of the process. Meditation, visualisation of the *yidam*, the repetition of spells and contemplation of mystic diagrams is continued until the tulpa in the form of the *yidam* actually materialises. The devotee can feel the touch of the tulpa's feet when he lays his head upon them, he can see the creature's eye following him as he moves about, he can even conduct conversations with it.

Thoughts made visible

Eventually the tulpa may be prepared to leave the vicinity of the *kyilkhors* and accompany the devotee on journeys. If the tulpa has been fully vitalised it will by now often be visible to others besides its creator.

Alexandra David-Neel tells how she 'saw' a phantom of this sort which, curiously enough, had not yet become visible to its creator. At the time Mme David-Neel had developed a great interest in Buddhist art. One afternoon she was visited by a Tibetan painter who specialised in portraying the 'wrathful deities'; as he approached she was astonished to see behind him the misty form of one of these much feared and rather unpleasant beings. She approached the phantom and stretched out an arm towards it; she felt as if she were 'touching a soft object whose substance gave way under the slight push'.

The painter told her that he had for some weeks been engaged in magical rites calling on the god whose form she had seen, and that he had spent the entire morning painting its picture.

Intrigued by this experience, Mme David-Neel set about making a tulpa for herself. To avoid being influenced by the many Tibetan paintings and images she had seen on her travels, she decided to 'make', not a god or goddess, but a fat, jolly-looking monk whom she could visualise very clearly.

Two Tibetans dressed as gods. Tibetan Buddhists regard their gods with reverence, but believe that they are no less trapped in the cycles of birth, death and rebirth than any human being – and even attempt to make the gods materialise by a sustained effort of concentration

elbow into its hairy ribs and exclaimed, 'If you can't behave yourself, you will have to go on the floor,' and pushed it off the bed. The animal disappeared through the wall.

The story was not yet over, however, for another member of the household said she had seen the eyes of the wolf in the corner of her room. Dion Fortune realised she must destroy the creature. Summoning the beast, she saw a thin thread joining it to her. She began to imagine she was drawing the life out of the beast along this thread. The wolf faded to a formless grey mass – and ceased to exist.

She began to concentrate her mind.

She retired to a hermitage and for some months devoted every waking minute to exercises in concentration and visualisation. She began to get brief glimpses of the monk out of the corner of her eye. He became more solid and lifelike in appearance – and eventually, when she left her hermitage and started on a caravan journey, he included himself in the party, becoming clearly visible and performing actions that she had neither commanded nor consciously expected him to do. He would, for instance, walk and stop to look around him as a traveller might do; sometimes Mme David-Neel even felt his robe brush against her, and once a hand seemed to touch her shoulder.

Mme David-Neel's tulpa eventually began to develop in an unexpected and unwished for manner.

He grew leaner, his expression became malignant, he was 'troublesome and bold'. One day a herdsman who brought Mme David-Neel a present of some butter saw the tulpa in her tent – and mistook it for a real monk. It had got out of control. Her creation turned into what she called a 'day-nightmare' and she decided to get rid of it. It took her six months of concentrated effort and meditation to do so.

If this, and many similar stories told in Tibet, are to be believed, the creation of a tulpa is not a matter to be undertaken lightly. It is a fascinating example of the power of the human mind to create its own reality.

When impossible demands are made of us we say 'we can't be in two places at once' – but in 1845 a French teacher, Emilie Sagée, apparently was. Her well-witnessed bilocation was specially researched by COLIN GODMAN, who tells the story

IN 1853 THE AMERICAN WRITER Robert Dale Owen paused while in London to hear a story told by a young German woman that was to become a classic of its kind. It was the apparently well-documented story of a *doppelgänger*, the exact double that is supposed, according to legend, to stalk us all, but that stays just out of sight. The 'double' in this story – or 'fetch' as the Victorians chose to name it – stayed out of sight of its victim but nevertheless it evoked widespread terror. This 'fetch' was that of a French schoolmistress. And it was seen not only by the young woman telling the story, but by over 40 of her companions at school. Dale Owen made a note of every detail of the story, and it was soon to find a place in the annals of late 19th-century psychical research.

Julie von Güldenstubbe, the second daughter of the Baron von Güldenstubbe, was 13 in 1845 and attended a school for

Above: Robert Dale Owen (1801–1877), the American writer who helped to popularise the strange tale of Emilie Sagée

Below: a scene from the BBC's Sagée story. Emilie, played by Juliet Harmer, was seen in the school garden while her double supervised the girls in the classroom

daughters of the nobility. This exclusive school, the Pensionat von Neuwelcke, was said to be 36 miles (58 kilometres) from the port of Riga and 3½ miles (6 kilometres) from Wolmar in Livonia (now part of the USSR). Lessons were conducted in German, the language of the landowners and ruling classes. The principal, Herr Buch, a distinguished Moravian scholar, had appointed a French teacher, Mademoiselle Emilie Sagée, to the staff in 1845, and it was with her that Baroness Julie's story was concerned.

The French teacher said that she was born in Dijon 32 years before she took up her post at Neuwelcke. She was fair skinned, with chestnut hair and blue eyes, and was fairly tall and slim. The pupils described her as having a sweet and lovable nature. The superintendents at the school were entirely satisfied with her work and were impressed by her gaiety, intelligence and education.

Everything promised well for Mlle Sagée's career at Neuwelcke – but within a few weeks of her arrival she became the focus of rumour and gossip in the school. It seemed that Emilie could be – literally – in two places at once. If she was reported to be in a particular part of the school someone would contradict, saying, 'Oh no, she cannot be there; I just passed her on the stairs' or in some distant corridor. Individual pupils

Me and my shadow

repeated this sort of confusion time and time again, but the teachers dismissed the girls' stories as silly mistakes.

But naturally the most excitement was caused by the rumours that followed the first appearance of the 'double' to a number of witnesses. Mlle Sagée was giving a lesson to Julie von Güldenstubbe and 12 other girls. The subject of the lesson varied slightly with

each storyteller: for example, one suggested Emilie was energetically demonstrating a mathematical theorem on the blackboard; Julie said the lesson was French grammar. What *was* agreed on was that Emilie Sagée was standing at the blackboard with her back to the class. Suddenly, a second 'Emilie' materialised at Mlle Sagée's side. The two were exactly alike and went through the same movements, synchronising perfectly. The only difference was that the real Emilie had chalk in her hand but the fetch had none; it merely mimed the teacher's action as she wrote on the board. This story caused a great sensation at Neuwelcke, particularly as all 13 pupils in the class agreed precisely in their description of what they had seen.

A spirited imitation
In the following weeks the fetch was seen on a number of occasions. For instance it appeared at dinner, standing behind Mlle Sagée and imitating her movements as she ate. But, as in the classroom, the double's hands were empty. On these occasions the schoolgirls were not alone in seeing Emilie's fetch; the servants also reportedly saw the figure behind the chair.

One of Julie's schoolfriends was badly frightened by the fetch. Fräulein Antonie von Wrangel was in a group invited to a local rural festivity and she was getting ready in her room. Emilie was helping her to fasten her dress. There was a mirror hanging behind them and Antonie turned to catch sight of two identical mademoiselles, each

Soon after Emilie Sagée arrived at the small *pensionat* (boarding school) in 1845 the girls started spreading rumours that their new French teacher had been seen in two places at the same time. Naturally all eyes were on Mlle Sagée and the strain on her must have been extraordinary. She is said to have had moral support from Julie von Güldenstubbe (left, played by Lesley Manville)

Below: the real Emilie takes a lesson – but is soon to be joined by her double, or 'fetch', which mirrored her every move; however, only the real Emilie held chalk

doing up her dress. Startled, she fainted clean away.

However, the fetch did not always mirror Emilie Sagée's actions. Sometimes, Baroness Julie reported, it would behave quite independently. For example, the real Mlle Sagée would rise from her chair – but her double would remain seated. Antonie von Wrangel and a group of friends looked after Emilie when she was taken ill with a feverish cold. The girls took turns to read to her as she recovered in bed. Antonie was alone with her when she noticed the colour suddenly drain from Mlle Sagée's face. She was so pale she seemed about to faint, and Antonie asked if she was feeling worse. Emilie answered in a weak and trembling voice that she was not, but her frightened look alarmed Antonie. A few moments later Antonie looked up from her book to see the fetch walking up and down the room, apparently in excellent health. This time Fräulein von Wrangel remained calm and did not tell Emilie what she had seen. When she came downstairs from Mlle Sagée's room she told the others exactly what she had experienced. On that occasion there had been only one witness – but the next and most remarkable appearance of the fetch was witnessed by the whole school.

This time all 42 pupils were gathered in

Left: pupil Antonie von Wrangel (actress Lalla Ward) faints after seeing Mlle Sagée's 'fetch' in the mirror while the teacher was helping her dress. Fräulein von Wrangel had happened to glance in a mirror that was hanging behind her – and saw two Emilie Sagées, one fastening her dress, the other, perfectly synchronised, going through the motions of doing so

the school hall to do their sewing and embroidery. Four french windows opened onto a corridor leading to the large garden in front of the house. The weather was fine and the girls had a clear view of the garden, where Mlle Sagée could be clearly seen picking flowers.

The girls sat round a long table and the teacher sat at one end, supervising their work. After a little while she got up to leave them alone for some reason. Her chair did not remain empty for long however, as suddenly Mlle Sagée appeared in it. The girls turned their eyes to the garden and, sure enough, there was Emilie. Although still gathering flowers, her movements were slow and languid as though – as the girls later remarked – she had suddenly been overcome with fatigue and tiredness. All the while her fetch sat silent and motionless.

Although afraid, the girls were getting used to the strange phenomena and two of the boldest among them decided to take a closer look at the fetch. They approached the chair, determined to touch the apparition. Stretching out their hands they encountered a slight resistance in the air surrounding it, such as a thin film of muslin or crêpe-de-chine might offer.

One brave girl tried to pass between the chair and the table – and stepped right through the figure in the chair. Emilie's double did not react, however, remaining seated until, a short time later, it slowly disappeared. As before, the girls turned to the garden to watch the real Mlle Sagée again gathering flowers with her usual animation.

All 42 girls agreed on what they had witnessed and some questioned their teacher

Below: rural Latvia, the Eastern European setting for the Sagée saga

soon after. They asked how she had felt in the garden and if she had experienced anything special. Emilie answered that she had noticed the other teacher leaving the girls unattended. Emilie had had a clear view of the empty chair and recalled wishing the teacher had not left her pupils alone to waste their time and probably get up to mischief. She had wished, she added, that she could have been sitting there to keep an eye on the girls so they would get on with their work.

Over a year had passed since Emilie Sagée had arrived at Neuwelcke and the girls had

Mixed doubles

To come face to face with one's *doppelgänger*, or double, is a rare but chilling experience. The German poet Goethe (1749–1832) once met 'himself' coming towards him up a garden path; according to European folklore this should have been a sign of his imminent death, but Goethe lived for some years after his experience.

The doppelgänger, or in Victorian terms the 'fetch', is always said to be indistinguishable from the real person and is apparently solid-looking. However, much more common in the archives of psychical research is the ghostly double, or 'wraith', sometimes called the *ka* by occultists. This is believed to be attached to the physical body by an invisible cord that can stretch (left) to accommodate astral travel during sleep and that snaps at death.

Emilie Sagée's double seems to have harmed only her career, but it is said that the wraith, when disengaged from the body, can leave it prey to possession by all manner of evil spirits.

had plenty of opportunities to see and talk about the fetch – or doppelgänger as they must have called it. They noticed that there was an apparently vampiristic relationship or link between Emilie and her double. When the fetch appeared strong and clear Emilie seemed to suffer as a consequence, as though the wraith drew its power from the living woman. When she was busy and absorbed in a task she would suddenly be overcome with weakness and tiredness; at just such moments the double would be seen.

Emilie herself seems not to have seen her

Below: a music lesson is interrupted by a fresh rumour about the 'two Mlle Sagées'. In a closed community of impressionable adolescents the stories of the teacher's 'fetch' spread like wildfire until they became a craze. Discipline became difficult to maintain; in short, excellent teacher though she was, Mlle Sagée had to leave the school

fetch while at Neuwelcke but she would be instantly alerted to its presence by the reactions of the girls around her. She also came to realise that the return of her strength and energy signalled the moment that the double disappeared.

How did the school react to the events of 1845 and 1846? All the pupils, to some degree, had witnessed the phenomena; so Emilie, unwittingly, caused considerable commotion at Neuwelcke. Although she was very popular among the girls, the more timid gradually became disturbed by her presence. They told their parents, and the school directors noted with growing concern that fewer and fewer girls returned to the Pensionat at the beginning of each term.

The reasons they gave for leaving the school varied, but Herr Buch and his colleagues were left in little doubt as to the true reason for Neuwelcke's fall from favour. Buch must have been gravely tempted to dismiss Mlle Sagée, but she was, after all, a perfectly good teacher. She seemed, he realised, to be the innocent victim of something quite beyond her control. It would create a scandal to dismiss such an excellent teacher on what must have seemed like grounds of insanity – and scandals at Neuwelcke were to be avoided at all costs.

However, Julie von Güldenstubbe tells us that the school's hopes for normality were in vain. Eighteen months after Emilie Sagée had taken up her post at Neuwelcke the school rollcall of 42 had dwindled to a mere 12. Something had to be done.

Emilie Sagée was not the only 19th-century girl to have a well-witnessed double, as the archives of psychical research show. But, ask COLIN GODMAN and LINDSAY ST CLAIRE, was the evidence for these bizarre events just too good to be true? What really happened?

EIGHTEEN MONTHS after the young French teacher Emilie Sagée came to the Pensionat at Neuwelcke, in Livonia (now in the USSR), the number of pupils had dwindled from 42 in 1845 to a mere dozen. Emilie's doppelgänger, or double, was blamed for this change in fortune, and at the risk of scandal the school's directors had no choice but to dismiss Mlle Sagée.

Although her professional qualifications and conduct were beyond reproach, Emilie had to leave. As long as she remained at Neuwelcke, she was told, the school's future was at risk. Emilie's dismay is easy to imagine, and Julie von Güldenstubbe – whose

Seeing double

account forms the basis of this story – recalled Emilie exclaiming, 'Alas, this is the nineteenth time: What am I to do?'

To have been dismissed from 19 teaching posts in such a short career may seem rather improbable, but Emilie explained to her young friends that she had begun teaching in 1829, when she was barely 16. She had been dismissed each time for more or less the same reason: two 'Emilie Sagées' were one too many for every school. It would have come as little comfort to Emilie to note that things improved at Neuwelcke after she left. And within a term or two the nobility resumed sending their daughters to the Pensionat. Peace had returned to the school.

Julie did not immediately lose contact with Mlle Sagée. Although she did not see her for a while after the dismissal, she learned

Top: two of the schoolgirls at the Pensionat von Neuwelcke who were witnesses to Emilie Sagée's 'fetch', from the dramatised story made by the BBC in the 1970s for their *Leap in the dark* television series. Introduced by Colin Wilson (above), the series was well-researched – although hard facts about the Sagée case proved difficult to come by

that Emilie had gone to live with a sister-in-law who had several young children. The young Baroness went to visit her and found that the toddlers knew all about the French woman. They said they had two 'Aunt Emilies'.

Unfortunately, Emilie Sagée's recorded story ends there. Julie lost contact with her completely when her former teacher disappeared into the heartland of Russia some time in the 1850s.

What do we really know about Emilie Sagée? Apart from her unfortunate teaching record we know she claimed to be 32 years old when she arrived in Neuwelcke in 1845 and that she gave her place of birth as Dijon, France.

When the authors began researching this case in 1976 they hoped to find at least some record of an Emilie Sagée's birth in Dijon in 1813. Every available source in the town was searched, to no avail. The writer Camille Flammarion, however, had been more fortunate. In his book *Death and its mystery* (1922) he writes about Mlle Sagée and records his own search for her origins during 1895. He describes a fruitless hunt for civic records of a family named Sagée – but he did find a note of the birth of a child named 'Octavie Saget'; a 'natural' (illegitimate) child born on 3 January 1813.

Like Mlle Sagée, Octavie would, therefore, have been 32 in 1845. Flammarion ventured to suggest that Octavie and Emilie were one and the same; the change in name occasioned, perhaps, by the young teacher's shame about her illegitimacy.

Emilie's pupil, Julie von Güldenstubbe, was at Neuwelcke throughout Mlle Sagée's short stay, but she was only 13 and may well have misremembered the spelling of her teacher's name. Flammarion knew Julie and her brother, the Baron Güldenstubbe, in the 1860s. They were much the same age and he described them as totally sincere, a little mystical in inclination, but of the utmost integrity. Julie's brother had published a book in Paris in 1857 entitled *La realité des spirits et le phénomène de leur écriture directe* ('The reality of spirits and the phenomenon of their direct writing').

Camille Flammarion was born in 1842 and was a distinguished astronomer at the

Paris Observatory when he met Julie. Although a scientist, he was intrigued by the paranormal and by Julie's story.

The first account of the case was written by Robert Dale Owen. His background was very different from Flammarion's. Dale Owen was born in 1801 in Glasgow, the son of the famous social reformer, Robert Owen, who created experimental communities on both sides of the Atlantic. In old age Robert Owen's socialism gave way to Spiritualism and this had influenced Dale. After joining his father in Indiana, in the USA, Robert Dale Owen went into politics, entered Congress, supported Emancipation and became one of the chief advocates of Spiritualism in America. In 1859 he completed his book *Footfalls on the boundary of another world*; in it he included an account of his meeting with Julie, giving her version of the events surrounding Emilie Sagée.

The third source of material about Emilie Sagée is the Russian writer Alexander Aksakov. He came from an important literary family and became a distinguished physiologist at St Petersburg (now Leningrad) University. He was the same age as Julie and

Above: Dijon, France, where Mlle Sagée claimed to have been born in 1813. Yet research failed to reveal any record of her birth, although an 'Octavie Saget' – an illegitimate child – is noted in the register of births at about the right date. Could Octavie and Emilie have been one and the same?

Right: Riga, now part of Latvia. The Sagée story places the school 36 miles (58 kilometres) from here – but no 'Neuwelcke' could be found by the BBC research team

shared her interest in Spiritualism. He was to become the most important Russian parapsychologist of the last century and his book *Animismus und spiritismus*, published in Leipzig in 1890, contains the Emilie Sagée story.

As before, Julie von Güldenstubbe was credited as the source of the information, but Aksakov added a few insights of his own concerning Emilie's personality. He points out that although Emilie enjoyed good physical health, she had a nervous, excitable disposition. In itself this is not inconsistent with the schoolgirls' description of her as 'quiet and friendly', but it does suggest that she may have been under more strain than Julie and the other girls realised.

An elusive place

The school at Neuwelcke proves harder to track down than Emilie herself. All the accounts locate Neuwelcke 36 miles (58 kilometres) from Riga and $3\frac{1}{2}$ miles (6 kilometres) from Wolmar – but Wolmar, or Valmiera as it has been renamed, lies 75 miles (120 kilometres) from Riga. In itself the error may not be significant, but it does raise the question: did Neuwelcke ever exist? Unfortunately, the Latvian Legation have been unable to identify such a place. There is a farm (which has never been a school) near Valmiera called 'Jaunvelki' but that is the nearest that the Latvians can find to 'Neuwelcke' – not a very convincing link.

However, the loss of the Neuwelcke connection need not be too discouraging. Livonia itself has experienced many changes of identity over the years. The small country had long been hotly disputed by Poland, Sweden and Russia. In the 1800s Russia

ruled Livonia, but the country was still controlled by the rich German families who owned large estates there. The whole expanse of flat peatbogs, lakes and forests became the Republic of Latvia in 1918, bounded by Estonia, Lithuania, Russia and the Baltic Sea. Since 1940 Latvia has been part of the USSR.

How does the Emilie Sagée case fit into contemporary knowledge? It is possible to discount the traditional anecdotes of astral projection or out-of-the-body experiences. All such cases imply an effort of will to 'project' the subject or some sort of perception while 'out of the body'. In Emilie's case there is no evidence that she ever projected her 'fetch' of her own volition or that she recorded any sensations while 'in' her double.

For 100 years the Emilie Sagée case has attracted such labels as illusion, hallucination, mass hysteria and the like. But there is no evidence that the schoolgirls all suffered from any marked nervous disorder that may have encouraged them to hallucinate. 'Hallucinations' and 'illusions' are commonly understood to be the result of the brain misinterpreting unusual data fed into it by our senses. In other words what we see is merely a subjective interpretation of the information sent to our brain from our eyes, based largely on our personal experience – and expectation.

Optical illusions are often the result of trying to make sense of incomplete data; in fact, often a small sensory input is turned, by our ever-rational brains, into something different; it can become almost anything

Two by two

In the book *Phantasms of the living* (1886) by SPR founders Gurney, Myers and Podmore, there appear stories of other 'Emilies'.

Like Mlle Sagée, Lucy Eden could be in two places at once. In the autumn of 1845 a party of young people were staying at Cherington, a house near Shipston-on-Stour in Warwickshire, England (below). Although Lucy was 17 and her cousins much the same age, they were playing hide-and-seek. Lucy was clearly seen wearing a brown and white dress, standing under a tree in the orchard. Her cousins gave chase, and Lucy ran out into the cowyard, where, to the amazement of the others, she disappeared. But Lucy protested that she had been hiding in the wash-house with another cousin – who verified her story.

Lucy's 'fetch' appeared again in the spring of 1847 at her father's rectory at Leigh in Essex. Lucy had mumps, but she was up and about, although her face was bandaged. One morning the nursery

maid, Caroline, passed Lucy walking from the drawing room to the library. Soon after, the Edens' maid asked Caroline where Lucy was. But the library was empty. Lucy was found in her bedroom where she had been, she claimed, all morning. Caroline refused to admit she had been mistaken, having particularly noted the bandages on Lucy's face.

Lucy, like Emilie Sagée, never saw her own fetch. But Sarah Jane Hall saw *her* double in 1863 in her home, Sibberton, near Wansford (now in Cambridgeshire). One night at supper Sarah's fetch was seen standing by the sideboard. Four people saw the figure: Sarah, her husband, and a cousin and her husband. They all saw Sarah's double distinctly, and her husband said: 'It is Sarah.' But the apparition, which had looked quite real, vanished. Had Mr Hall 'suggested' the identity of the apparition to the others? If not, what had they all seen?

– as long as it fits the pattern that suits our subconscious minds (a fact exploited by stage illusionists and the theatre in general). One can imagine an old house, ill-lit with flickering candles, where shadows and reflections create convincing illusions of sinister figures; a spurious reality created from insufficient information.

Before your very eyes

The brain demands logic; it needs to 'rationalise' the data with which it is presented. This appears to be an intelligent response to confusing sights – perhaps the only way of keeping sane in many circumstances. Optical illusions such as those produced by candlelight, sunshine streaming through trees in an orchard, or a flash of white that perhaps suggested a fetch's handkerchief, go some way towards explaining illusory fetches. But neither optical illusions nor mental rationalisations explain why 42 schoolgirls at Neuwelcke consistently agreed that there were two Mlle Sagées.

However, the 'risky shift' effect noted by modern psychologists may throw some light on the Sagée case. This is based on the observation that when individuals bring their beliefs to a group discussion they often leave with much more extreme attitudes than they started with. Psychologists maintain that this is an unconscious result of the group discussion or argument, and that these polarised opinions tend to be lasting. These 'risky shifts' can occur in any group; we can speculate that the school at Neuwelcke – isolated, enclosed and something of an aristocratic hothouse – would provide an ideal propagating medium for the phenomenon.

But does this theory throw any light on the Emilie Sagée story? The evidence in its

Is seeing believing? During a severe drought a mirage of water appears behind Thomson's gazelles on the parched Sambura plains of Kenya

A 19th-century allegorical painting by G.A. Roche-grosse, illustrating the effects of human credulity. A single rumour of a paranormal being seen in the sky ends in this tangled mass of hysterical humanity

favour is tempting: we discover that events began quietly, as single rumours that circulated swiftly, building into 'a ceaseless discussion', a kind of schoolgirl craze. After a time the events began to be viewed as something genuine – and very strange. And when the events grew even more bizarre, the number of convinced witnesses in the school also grew.

This is precisely what would be expected when a 'risky shift' occurs; there was no single, striking initial event, just the slow accumulation of gossip. But group discussions seemed, true to the 'risky shift' effect, to have dramatically reinforced their belief in Emilie's doppelgänger. That is why, ironically, the schoolgirls' 'perfect agreement' about what they witnessed is less convincing than if they had disagreed, even in trivial ways, about what they saw. Perfect unanimity among witnesses is virtually unknown. Even striking incidents produce widely varying descriptions – as any police force will testify. Total unanimity is the result of either pre-arranged agreement – a hoax or deliberate perjury – or more innocent, but intense, discussion and rationalisation.

That, then, is the psychologist's view of the little evidence we possess. The truth of what happened in Livonia in 1845 will never be known. Was Emilie Sagée's doppelgänger simply the product of gossip, reinforced by hysterical group discussion, and later recorded as fact by the mystically inclined Julie von Güldenstubbe?

There seems no doubt that the girls genuinely believed that Mlle Sagée was haunted by her fetch. At the Pensionat von Neuwelcke it seems that the old adage 'seeing is believing' was turned on its head: for a few bizarre months between 1845 and 1846 'believing', for 42 young girls, became even better than 'seeing'.

Gone but not forgotten

Stories abound of people disappearing in mysterious circumstances, never to be seen again. But, argues PAUL BEGG, these tales should be examined closely: many have simpler explanations – and some are pure fiction

SOME CURIOUS, inexplicable, and sometimes very frightening things have happened in this 'ordinary' world of ours, haven't they? Just look at all the books you can buy about ghosts, ESP, the Bermuda Triangle, ancient astronauts, mysterious disappearances, big-foot, the Loch Ness monster. A whole host of things that are incredible yet indisputably true. Or are they?

It is a mistake to believe everything you read. Alas, that is a truism that can be applied less to newspapers than to books about the mysterious, the unexplained and the paranormal. Look at any display of books on these subjects and it is almost guaranteed that a great many of them will be about what Arthur C. Clarke has called 'Mysteries of the Zeroeth Kind – the mental junk food of our generation.' As he said in *Arthur C. Clarke's mysterious world* (1980):

The only mystery about *these* is that anyone ever thought they were mysterious. The classic example is the Bermuda Triangle, though this has not prevented countless writers, some of whom may even believe the rubbish they are regurgitating, repeating the

In December 1900 three lighthouse keepers vanished from the Eilean Mor lighthouse (below) off the west coast of Scotland. James Ducat, Donald McArthur and Thomas Marshall were there when Joseph Moore left for shore leave on the 6th, but when he returned on the 26th they were gone. The beacon was not working and two sets of oilskins and boots were missing. The log told how a fierce storm had raged. On the 12th, Marshall had written in the log, 'Never seen such a storm.' The final entry, on the 15th, read: '1 p.m. Storm ended. Sea calm. God is over all'

same nonsense over and over again.

In recent years, possibly because of the worldwide attention given to the Bermuda Triangle, the subject of mysterious disappearances has attracted considerable interest and a large number of truly incredible 'vanishings' have been recorded: there is the case of David Lang who vanished before the startled eyes of his family; of the 11-year-old boy who went to fetch a bucket of water from a well and vanished, leaving in the snow a trail of footprints that came to a sudden and abrupt end; of the British diplomat who walked around the heads of his horses and seemingly stepped off the face of the Earth; of an English settlement in North America that disappeared into thin air; of the three light-house keepers who vanished from Eilean Mor, off the coast of Scotland, in 1900. Case after amazing case.

James Burne Worson was a shoemaker of

Leamington Spa, Warwickshire, who boasted about his physical prowess and stamina to such a degree that one day in 1873 three of his friends decided to call his bluff and they wagered that he could not run to Coventry and back. Worson accepted the challenge and set off. He jogged down the dusty roads and his friends – Hammerson Burns, Barham Wise, and a third man whose name is not known – followed in a horse-drawn cart, watching Worson carefully for any sign that he was about to give up. Several miles had been covered in this manner when Worson suddenly stumbled. He cried out – and vanished!

This remarkable story has been told in several books, sometimes with a little elaboration, sometimes with a few details omitted, but it is always essentially the same. Rarely is a source given for the story and when one is, it always turns out to be another book about unexplained phenomena. Nobody, it seems, has tried to verify the truth of the tale. Nobody has produced a contemporary newspaper account of the disappearance or a report of the police investigation or of the

All smoke and no fire

One of the more dramatic ways in which people have been known to disappear from this life is by means of spontaneous human combustion. Apparently, 7 April 1938 saw no less than three people engulfed in flames: Willem ten Bruik, who was driving a Volkswagen near Nijmegen, Holland; John Greeley, who was at the wheel of the ss *Ulrich*, approaching Cornwall; and lorry driver George Turner, reportedly burnt to ashes in Chester, though a can of petrol was untouched beside him. Not only that, but the apparent locations of the three deaths make an isosceles triangle.

Unfortunately, Volkswagens were not made at the time, the *Ulrich* does not appear on Lloyd's register, and no George Turner died in Chester that day. The three cases seem to be the product less of fire than of an overheated imagination – in this instance belonging to author Eric Frank Russell, who reports two of them as fact.

Left: Leamington Spa in the mid 19th century. It was from here that James Burne Worson is said to have set out on his run to Coventry in 1873 before disappearing en route. Reliable facts about this story are difficult to find. Indeed, the tale has probably never been verified

Right: Labour MP Victor Grayson addresses a rally in 1906. Grayson, a rousing orator, vanished during a train journey from Liverpool to Hull in 1920. Although there were reports that he had been subsequently seen in Britain and also that he had emigrated to Australia, no final answer has yet been found to the question: what happened to Victor Grayson?

inquest. Nobody has produced any proof of any kind that Worson, Wise and Burns ever lived in Leamington Spa or, indeed, that they ever existed. The only known fact about James Burne Worson is that his death – that is assuming that he was ever born – is *not* recorded at St Catherine's House, repository of all records of births, deaths and marriages filed since 1837.

The story of James Burne Worson is just one of many celebrated cases of 'mysterious' disappearance that have never been substantiated, stories that have been circulating for so long and so widely that authors no more think of checking their veracity than an historian would bother to confirm that the battle of Hastings took place in 1066.

It is sometimes difficult to take a charitable view of the authors who perpetuate these non-mysteries. Some authors have related cases that they clearly know to be fraudulent, others have been satisfied to conduct little or no research beyond borrowing their material from somebody else, many are interested only in amazing their readers and are happy to disregard the facts completely.

The blurb to *Stranger than science* (1963) by the late American writer and broadcaster Frank Edwards says: 'The author has carried out extensive research to establish the authenticity and accuracy of all these fascinating stories.' Edwards says that if asked to cite what he believed to be the strangest case of disappearance he would 'unhesitatingly refer to a twin-engined Marine plane which crashed on the Tahoma Glacier in 1947'. Searchers apparently reached the aircraft and could

tell from the wreckage that the crew could not possibly have survived such a devastating crash, yet not one body of the 32 people who had been on board could be found. The authorities were baffled and offered a reward of $5000 for information leading to the recovery of the bodies.

In fact this aircraft crashed in 1946, not 1947, 10,000 feet (3000 metres) up the storm-shrouded west slope of the crevasse-scored South Tahoma Glacier in the state of Washington, USA. Six months later, on 18 July 1947, searchers eventually reached the crash site and found all the bodies embedded in the ice. Bad weather and dangerous rock falls made recovery too hazardous to contemplate and the corpses lie there to this day. A memorial service was held for the men on 24 August 1947.

The story of how the wreckage was found, the bodies located, and of the memorial service, was told in the *Post-Intelligencer* of

The lady vanishes

In 1937 Amelia Earhart, the celebrated aviator, disappeared in the Pacific during an intended round-the-world flight in a twin-engined Lockheed Elektra. The first woman to have flown the Atlantic solo (and in record time) began her most ambitious journey of all from Miami, accompanied by Fred Noonan, a navigator of great experience.

They headed eastward in a series of planned 'hops'. All went well enough until they left New Guinea. On 2 July at about 7.30 a.m. Earhart radioed that fuel was running low. A little over an hour later she reported her course. She was heading for Howland Island, just north of the equator and east of the Gilbert Islands. Nothing more was heard from her.

The US Navy recorded that the aircraft had been lost at sea. In *The search for Amelia Earhart*, Fred Goerner claims that Earhart was carrying out an intelligence mission, reporting on Japanese military activity, when low fuel and high winds forced her to alter course. He agrees with Admiral Chester Nimitz, former US commander in the Pacific, that the aircraft went down in the Marshall Islands, over which the Japanese held a mandate. Earhart and Noonan may then have been transported to Saipan in the Marianas, for the locals tell of two American fliers, one a woman, who arrived in 1937, were imprisoned and interrogated by the Japanese, and then executed and buried in unmarked graves.

Amelia Earhart and Fred Noonan (above) climb aboard their aircraft in Puerto Rico during their 1937 attempt to fly round the world. They disappeared somewhere between New Guinea and Howland Island (right)

Left: Colonel Percy Fawcett, who disappeared in 1925 in the Amazon jungle

Below: Ambrose Bierce, the American satirist, wrote about mysterious vanishings – and then disappeared himself. Nothing more was heard from him after he went to Mexico in 1913 as an observer with Pancho Villa's rebel army in the civil war

Bottom: South Tahoma Glacier, USA, where an aircraft crashed in 1946 with the loss of 32 lives. The bodies did not vanish, as writer Frank Edwards says; they were found six months later buried in ice

Seattle during August 1947. So much for 'extensive research to establish the authenticity and accuracy . . .'. The only mystery is how the fiction about the bodies being missing survived from 1947 to 1959 when Edwards published his book.

One dark night in November 1878, 16-year-old Charles Ashmore of Quincey, Illinois, went to fetch a pail of water from the well in the yard outside his home. After he had been gone an undue length of time his family went looking for him. In the feeble, flickering light of their lantern they saw the trail of the boy's footprints in the snow, but they came to a sudden and mysterious end halfway to the well. Charles Ashmore had inexplicably vanished. Even more mysterious, for several days Charles's mother could hear her son calling for help.

But wait. Perhaps it was 11-year-old Oliver Larch of South Bend, Indiana, who went to fetch a pail of water on Christmas Eve 1889, and vanished, leaving in the snow a clear trail of footprints, which came to an abrupt end. Or is that Oliver Lerch of the same place who vanished in the same manner on Christmas Eve 1890? Or Oliver Thomas of Rhayader, Wales, who went to fetch a bucket of water on Christmas Eve 1909 and never came back. *His* tracks in the snow ended halfway to the well. Or Charlotte Ashton, who met a similar fate on the night of 17 October 1876. Or James Settle, whose tracks came to an abrupt end in the snow of New York City. One does not have to be a particularly astute reader to detect certain similarities between these stories; perhaps all or some are derivatives of an original. But which account is the original and which, if indeed any, is true?

Ashmore, it seems, was an invention of the writer Ambrose Bierce in one of his short stories. The Oliver Lerch story (the change of year and the name from Larch to Lerch came later) is an old newspaper hoax, and its inconsistencies have been exposed several times: for example, there was no snow in South Bend, Indiana, over the Christmas period in 1890. As for the Welsh boy, Oliver Thomas, the story appears to have originated with a writer who is notorious for fictionalising events. The present author has searched the relevant copies of the *Brecon County Times*, which served the Rhayader area, and discovered that they contain no mention of an Oliver Thomas vanishing. There is also no record of a birth or death certificate for an Oliver Thomas of Rhayader to be found at St Catherine's House. From this we can conclude only that, like Ashmore and Lerch, Oliver Thomas is a figment of somebody's imagination. The same is also true of Charlotte Ashton and James Settle.

Abducted by a UFO?

Several writers have used one or more of these stories to support a particular theory. For example, in his book *Strangers from the skies* (1966), Brad Steiger tells a much-expanded story of the Oliver Thomas 'disappearance' in a chapter called 'Flying saucers and disappearing people'. Steiger does not directly state that Oliver Thomas was abducted by a UFO, but his account follows the question: '. . . have outer-space creatures been periodically plucking up earthlings for study and interrogation?'

In his book *Vanishings*, Michael Harrison speculates whether the boys' cries (Larch and Thomas are supposed to have cried out something like: 'Help! They've got me!' which has, not unnaturally, given rise to much speculation about the use of the plural) released some sort of energy that snatched the boys away. 'Had the three boys remained silent,' writes Harrison, 'there would have been no sound to activate the forces arrayed against them; forces their own fear, *as well as the paraphysical properties of lonely farmhouses*, had created.' (The italics are Harrison's.)

Michael Harrison does not explain what paraphysical properties lonely farmhouses have, but such speculation, be it ludicrous or not – and frequently it can only be politely described as imaginative – is valueless when the incidents on which it is based never happened.

If 'mystery' books – which are presented as fact – are bought for their entertainment value, readers might find their money better spent on horror fiction, in which there is certainly no shortage of suitably blood-chilling tales to set the imagination working overtime of a dark winter night.

**Stories of people who 'disappear into thin air'
abound – but disappointingly the facts, even
in some of the classic cases, do not
often bear close scrutiny**

IN 1872 THE *Mary Celeste* was found aimlessly wandering in the Atlantic. She was in remarkably good condition and well-provisioned, but her crew had apparently abandoned ship. Since no experienced sailor is ever likely to desert a seaworthy ship for a comparatively dangerous lifeboat unless his life is in severe danger, the disappearance of *Mary Celeste*'s crew is an outstanding mystery (see page 76). Over the years, however, it has been made even more mysterious by the addition of fictional details such as half-eaten breakfasts being found on the galley table and the aroma of fresh tobacco smoke lingering in the captain's cabin.

Such additions come into being for many reasons: to add to the eeriness of a story for entertainment value, for example, or, less innocently, with the deliberate intention of introducing supernatural overtones to a mystery that would otherwise be confined within the comparatively boring limitations of the natural and the known. Another much-publicised case is that of the disappearance in 1809 of the British diplomat Benjamin Bathurst (see page 32).

The Bathurst disappearance is a complex and, indeed, an impenetrable mystery yet, perhaps significantly, it is rarely expanded beyond a single, simple, and mystery-making paragraph that generally goes along the lines of: Benjamin Bathurst was about to board a coach outside an inn in (or near)

Disappearing disappearances

Berlin. He was seen to walk around the heads of the horses – and was never seen again.

The disappearance of Bathurst is far too complex to describe here in anything but the broadest outline, but it is sufficient to say that in 1809 the British government sent him on a secret mission to the Court of Austria. Earlier in the year the Austrians had suffered a demoralising defeat at the hands of Napoleon and it is generally accepted that Bathurst's mission was to dissuade Emperor Francis II from total capitulation.

Bathurst was returning from this mission with a companion when he stopped at an inn in Perleberg, a day's journey from Hamburg, where a ship was waiting to return him to England. He stayed at the inn for a few hours and at 9 p.m. he told his companion that he was going to have the horses made ready for the continuation of the journey. What happened next is disputed. According to the memoirs of his father, Bishop Bathurst, published in 1837, it was an hour before the

One of the most frequently told 'mysterious disappearance' stories is that of the British diplomat Benjamin Bathurst (above), who walked round the heads of his coach horses in the German town of Perleberg (right) in 1809 – and vanished, never to be seen again. His disappearance, however, seems less mysterious when it is known that he was on a top secret political mission at the time

companion grew alarmed by Bathurst's continued absence and made enquiries, learning that Bathurst was about to climb into his coach when something in the shadows of the entrance to the inn courtyard caught his attention and apparently compelled him to investigate. He walked into the darkness and was never seen again.

So it is most certainly a mystery, but there was almost certainly no supernatural element to the Bathurst story. Nobody actually saw Bathurst disappear into thin air. He did *not* simply walk around the heads of his horses and step off the face of the Earth. It should be remembered that Bathurst was in a precarious political position: Napoleon would have been interested in the outcome of Bathurst's discussion with Francis II, and Bathurst had made enemies at the Emperor's court who may not have wished to see a renewal of hostilities between Austria and France. Besides, there were rogues and vagabonds in Perleberg itself who would have killed Bathurst for no more than the clothes he wore. Bathurst could have met his end at the hands of any one of these. Yet the fact remains that his body was never found.

The exciting story of the 'lost colony' is another mystery that some unscrupulous authors have made more mysterious than it ever was, although this time they have done it by omitting certain details. The tale has several versions, a typical account being that given in Michael Harrison's *Vanishings*.

According to Harrison: in 1585 Sir Walter Raleigh established a settlement on Roanoke Island off the coast of present-day North Carolina. Harrison says that Raleigh left the colonists and

> returned to England for needed supplies and a reinforcement of emigrants. The date of the settlement was 1585. When Raleigh returned to Roanoke, he found no trace of the settlers; all had gone. . . . The rationalists say that, despairing of their ever seeing Raleigh again, the settlers trekked over the mainland until they were either captured by, or voluntarily made common cause with, the Mandan Indians.

Almost everything Harrison has written about the disappearance of the Roanoke settlement is wrong. Raleigh organised and part-financed the settlement, but he never visited Roanoke personally. The colony that disappeared did so in or after 1587, not 1585, and the man who returned to England for supplies was not Raleigh but one John White. He was prevented from returning to the New World for the next three years, during which time the colonists are not known to have seen another European face. From these facts alone it is not too difficult to deduce a reasonable explanation for the disappearance of the colony.

In an effort to dismiss contrary and often more prosaic solutions to these 'mysteries',

Top: Michael Harrison, author of *Vanishings* (1981) which repeats many of the popular tales of people who allegedly disappear under 'mysterious' circumstances

Above: Sir Walter Raleigh (1554–1618) who, in 1585 – according to Harrison – established a settlement on Roanoke Island, off the coast of North Carolina. Harrison says that Raleigh returned to discover that the colonists had vanished. Yet the fact is that Raleigh never visited the settlement personally

sensationalist authors employ a variety of writing techniques designed to persuade the reader that the unlikely explanation is in fact the more reasonable one. Harrison uses one of these ploys when he refers to the theory that the colonists were absorbed by the Mandan Indians. He is clearly contemptuous of those whom he calls 'rationalists', implying that the *only* rational solution ever offered is the Mandan theory. Presumably the reader is intended to conclude that this is a desperately contrived idea evoked by people who refuse even to consider a more sinister, but reasonable, solution.

The Mandan solution

In fact, rationalists would be among the first to dismiss the Mandan solution as absurd; it is highly improbable that the colonists would have attempted, let alone survived, a crossing from the Outer Banks of North Carolina to the Mandan Indians of Missouri. Moreover, it is doubtful that the Mandan solution was proposed by historians since they have had a fairly good idea of the colonists' fate for over 400 years.

Before John White left Roanoke he arranged that if the colonists abandoned the settlement they should carve the name of their destination on a stockade post and append a cross if the move was made under duress or in distress. To quote White's own words: 'one of the chiefe trees of postes at the right side of the entrance had the barke taken off, and 5 foote [1.5 metres] from the ground in fayre Capitall letters was graven CROATOAN without any crosse or signe of distresse.'

Yet much mystery has been made of this. In his *Strange people* (1966) Frank Edwards writes: 'It is possible that the word meant little or nothing to the Englishmen who found it. Or if they did recognise it as a clue to the missing colonists, perhaps they realised that they dared not follow the clue to its conclusion.' All very mystery-making – and all very untrue. White had stated quite plainly: 'I greatly joyed that I had safely found a certaine token of their safe being at Croatoan, which is the place where Manteo was borne, and the savages of the Iland our friends.'

White's joy was short-lived. He was prevented from going to Croatoan and was never able to verify that this was where the colonists went, but it is a fair conclusion that without food, surrounded on all sides by hostile Indians, and cut off from home in a new, unexplored, and equally hostile country, the settlers would have sought refuge in the one place where they were assured of friendship – Croatoan. Sad to relate, there is some evidence that suggests that the Indians of Croatoan were later massacred by the Indians of the powerful Powhatan Confederacy of the Algonkian tribes in the Virginia Tidewater.

The Roanoke disappearance *is* a mystery,

but only insofar as there is no absolute proof of the colonists' fate and not because of any suggestion that their disappearance was in even the slightest way paranormal or supernatural.

Another example of the 'manufactured mystery' is the case of the missing Norfolks (see page 68), a battalion of British soldiers who disappeared at Gallipoli in 1915 and whose fate remains unknown to this day – a mystery that considerably pales in significance when one takes into account the fact that 27,000 British and Empire troops died at Gallipoli and have no known grave. However, the story has become particularly popular in books about 'mysterious' disappearances and UFOS because a soldier named Reichardt claimed to have witnessed their fate. He says they were abducted by a cloud.

Delayed reaction

Most accounts of the Norfolk disappearance omit to mention that Reichardt told his story 50 years after the event at an old comrades' reunion – events that are not noted as particularly sober affairs – and that it contains many details that are either wrong or inconsistent with the circumstances of the genuine disappearance. Examined in the light of thoroughly documented facts, it is almost certain that Reichardt confused two separate incidents.

In recent years writers such as Lawrence Kusche, Ronald Story and Philip Klass have conducted thorough research into many fields of the unexplained and on the basis of well-researched, and fully documented, evidence have concluded that many stories such as that of the Norfolks are not supported by the facts. Of course, these conclusions do not have to be accepted, but they should not be dismissed without reason. Some authors, however, for reasons best known to themselves, refuse to accept that certain stories have been demonstrated to be untrue and they continue to repeat these tales without providing a scrap of evidence to support their reasons for having done so. It might be thought that such authors intend deliberately to mislead their readers.

In this respect, two books are noteworthy for the retelling of tales long since discredited: Charles Berlitz's *Without a trace* (1978) and Michael Harrison's *Vanishings* (1981). Charles Berlitz, for instance, repeats once more the story of the *Freya* as a Bermuda Triangle fatality, long after it had been established that the incident took place in the Pacific; and Michael Harrison, while claiming to have read most, if not all, of the books that expose so many of these tales, nevertheless presents them again as if such evidence did not exist, or could safely be ignored.

For example, Harrison dismisses the errors in Reichardt's story about the disappearing Norfolks as 'unimportant' – which they most certainly were not – and makes the

Above: a drawing of the Indian settlement Secoton by John White, the English colonist who discovered the message left by the 'missing' settlers. They quite clearly stated that they were intending to make for the village of Croatoan – yet curiously many popular accounts of the settlers' subsequent disappearance make no mention of this

Above right: a North American Indian, as painted by one of the first European settlers. The Indians at Croatoan were known to be friendly to the Roanoke settlers, but shortly after the Europeans are assumed to have arrived at Croatoan it was overrun by a hostile tribe – and there were few survivors

remarkable statement that Reichardt's story was received by 'sceptics baying for "the facts"'. It seems he expects fantastic tales to be accepted without an ounce of corroborative evidence.

The paranormal attracts frauds, cranks, and hoaxers, and it is never easy to distinguish between serious books about the paranormal and those that are sensationalist. A good rule of thumb guide is to check whether the author begins by appealing to his readers not to have a closed mind.

In the introduction to her book *They dared the Devil's Triangle*, Adi-Kent Thomas Jeffrey almost fanatically implores her readers:

> . . . let us lift our faces to the winds of mystery and not cover our senses with the impenetrable armour of suspicion and skepticism. . . . Let us not don the thick-helmet of closed-mindedness under the guise of so-called 'common sense' or 'reason'.

And in the foreword to *Vanishings* Michael Harrison similarly warns his readers against 'contemptuous scoffers' and 'authors charitably inclined to reassure the uneasy'.

But facts speak for themselves. The author of a well-researched and fully documented book has no need so to implore his readers. But the absence of facts is, of course, the essential weakness of writers who seek only to amaze and astound, and what sensationalist writers want of you, apart from your money, is your faith in what they write.

Facts and fictions

Two of the most frequently repeated of all 'mysterious disappearance' stories are those of David Lang and the airliner *Star Tiger*. But it appears that the real mystery is the extent of human credulity

DAVID LANG disappeared on 23 September 1880 in front of five witnesses – or so the story goes. This is probably the most famous case of 'vanishing' on record and the story has been told by so many authors that a list of their names would read like a *Who's who* of writers on matters paranormal. Yet not one of them has produced a scrap of evidence that David Lang ever existed.

Apparently, Lang was walking across the 40-acre (16-hectare) pasture in front of his large, vine-covered farmhouse on the 'Old Cottontown Road' near Gallatin in Sumner County, Tennessee, USA, when a buggy turned into the long drive leading to the house. It contained a friend of the family, Judge August Peck, and his brother-in-law, a man named Wade, from Akron, Ohio. Lang waved and began to retrace his steps to the house. He had gone no more than a short distance when he vanished. One moment he was there, the next he was gone. David Lang had stepped off the face of the earth. Mrs Lang, the two Lang children, Judge Peck and his brother-in-law had all seen farmer David Lang cease to exist.

Events were to become even more bizarre. About a year later the Lang children, Sarah and George, noticed that there was a ring of stunted yellow grass on the spot where David Lang had vanished. For some reason Sarah called her father's name and to her astonishment received a faint reply. Her father called for help over and over again until eventually his voice faded away for ever.

Years later Sarah Lang developed an interest in Spiritualism and, according to an article entitled 'How lost was my father' in *Fate* magazine (July 1953), which was written by Stuart Palmer but based on Sarah Lang's own testimony, she spent thousands

Below: Herbert Hoover, then US Secretary of Commerce, headed the investigation into the mysterious disappearance of the *Carroll A. Deering* (bottom). The ship had been found drifting in 1921. There was no sign of life but no evidence of bloodshed or violence. Three months later one Christopher Gray of North Carolina claimed to have found a dramatic message in a bottle that stated that the crew had been kidnapped, but Hoover dismissed it as Gray's own work. The fate of the ship

of dollars cultivating the most famous mediums, but with little success. Then someone gave her a planchette – an automatic writing device – and this awakened her own psychic abilities. In April 1929, compelled by a strange force to take up her planchette, Sarah Lang received the message: 'Together now and forever . . . after many years . . . God bless you.' Sarah compared this 'spirit' writing with an inscription written by her father on the flyleaf of a book. The writing matched. Sarah knew that at long last her father and mother were reunited in the realm beyond the grave.

Sarah Lang speaks out

The story of David Lang contains three elements, the last of which – Sarah's story as told to Stuart Palmer – would help to confirm the others, so let us examine it first.

Palmer sent his article with a covering letter to Curtis Fuller, editor of *Fate*, and by good fortune that letter remained in the magazine's files. In it Palmer says that the article is a rewrite of a story he had written years before for *Ghost*, a small magazine published in 1936 and 1937. As proof of the truth of the story, Palmer and Sarah Lang went to the trouble of signing an affidavit and having it witnessed by a notary public. Palmer concludes the *Fate* article by saying: 'a student of Clark Sellers, perhaps the nation's foremost expert in handwriting and the study of questioned documents, has said that the inscription on Miss Lang's childhood book and the planchette writing are by the same hand.'

It is worthwhile noting that neither the handwriting expert nor Palmer says that the handwriting was that of Sarah Lang's father. A researcher and writer named Robert Schadewald submitted reproductions of the handwriting in the book, the planchette writing and the signatures on the affidavit to Ann B. Hooten, a member of the prestigious American Society of Document Examiners. Miss Hooten's reply came in the form of a

five-page report in which she concluded that the result of her examination conclusively proved that the accumulated writings were from the same individual. In other words, David and Sarah Lang's handwriting is, by some strange 'coincidence', the same as Stuart Palmer's.

Hershel G. Payne, a librarian at the Public Library of Nashville and Davidson County, was intrigued by the celebrated local mystery and set out to establish as many facts about it as he could. He checked the census records for 1830, 1850 and 1880, but there was no mention of anyone named Lang or Peck. He consulted a dozen or more early histories of the area, but none of them mentioned Lang or the Lang farm. Other librarians, local newspapers and local historians all replied to his requests with the same answer: there were no documents, photographs or records of any kind attesting to Lang, Peck or the Lang farm. Mr Payne even drove down the 'Old Cottontown Road', but found nothing that could have been or may once have been the Lang farm.

Numerous writers have told this story and each has used an earlier writer as their source. The principal source since the 1960s has been Frank Edwards's book *Stranger than science*, or books that have used

To Sarah:—
On her tenth birthday,
From
her Father

together now and forever after many years God bless you

Edwards's information. Edwards does not give his source, but it could have been any one of a number of writers who cite one of two articles about the Lang 'disappearance' in *Fate*: either that written by the psychical researcher Nandor Fodor, which was published in December 1956, or Stuart Palmer's article of July 1953. Palmer, of course, was rewriting his article originally written for *Ghost*, and it is at this point that the trail to the origin of the story runs into a stone wall. On the other side of the wall the trail picks up in 1893 with the publication of *Can such things be?* by Ambrose Bierce, which features a story called 'The difficulty of crossing a

To Whom It May Concern:

I, Sarah Emma Lang, hereby affirm and depose that I have read the accompanying hitherto unpublished account of my father, David Lang's, disappearance, and that in every detail this story is true.

Signed *Sarah Emma Lang*

Witnessed by *Stuart Palmer*

Subscribed and sworn to before me this 30th day of October, 1929 *William C. Wendling*

Notary Public in and for the County of New York, State of New York.

My Commission expires March 30, 1931

The extraordinary collection of 'evidence' for the Lang case: Sarah Lang and author Stuart Palmer swore an affidavit (above) to the effect that the story of David Lang's 'disappearance' is true; and the two samples of handwriting, one taken from the flyleaf of a book (below left) and the other allegedly written from beyond the grave (below) by means of a planchette (bottom). Handwriting experts agreed that the samples were written by the same person – but further research revealed that that person was Stuart Palmer, whose article for *Fate* magazine popularised the story

field', based on the Lang case.

Bierce is believed to have taken the idea from an article in the *Cincinnati Enquirer*, but the date of publication is unknown; copies of the newspaper for the 1880s are available on microfilm, but there is no index and searches have failed to locate the relevant edition. However, the article is thought to have been written by a travelling salesman named Joe Mulhatten from Cincinnati who was delayed in Gallatin, Tennessee, by a snowstorm in 1889, and wrote the tale to pass the time and earn a few extra dollars. But where did he get the story?

The biggest lie of all

Hershel G. Payne says that in the late 1880s there were lying contests, a prize being awarded to whoever told the biggest lie. Mulhatten apparently won with his story of David Lang. However, in his book *Among the missing*, Jay Robert Nash says that the Lang story was based on a real event: the disappearance in July 1854 of Orion Williamson from his farm in Selma, Alabama. And so we are back to square one. Did Orion Williamson vanish?

The story of the search to verify the 'mystery' of David Lang serves to illustrate how such myths are born and how they develop over the years as they pass from one author to another, are occasionally elaborated, and sometimes even gain fraudulent 'corroborative evidence'. In the end the story becomes so well-accepted as fact that nobody thinks to check it, or perhaps they choose not to. For example, the Lang case crops up in *Vanishings* by Michael Harrison (1981) – despite the fact that at least one of the sources quoted gives all the information you have just read.

It is, perhaps, disappointing when such tales turn out to be no more than fiction, but some people – writers and readers alike – are so wrapped up in self-deception that they are hostile to any suggestion that these cherished whimsies are anything other than fact.

It may be argued that the truth of such

called Station VRT, and no radio message was dispatched from the aircraft at 10.30 p.m.

None of these errors is particularly important insofar as they influence either Wolfe's theories or provide any possible solutions to the airliner's fate, but it is worth considering whether any rational reader would tolerate a history book that claimed that the battle of Hastings was a fist fight between Robin Hood and Abraham Lincoln. The mistakes made by many writers of books about the unexplained are of this calibre.

Often there is no deliberate intent to deceive and errors do not always invalidate the rest of an article or book, but it is a rather

Above: in 1858, 650 highly trained French troops, sent to quell a riot in the Indo-Chinese city of Saigon, apparently disappeared only 15 miles (24 kilometres) from their destination. Did they desert *en masse*, were they taken prisoner or blown up – or was there a genuine mystery involved?

stories is irrelevant because they are read for their entertainment value, but people do honestly believe these tales or at least believe that there is some substance behind them. Children are particularly susceptible to the misconceptions promoted through sensationalist books, and teachers have frequently expressed their concern over them.

James Raymond Wolfe contributed a chapter to *The riddle of the Bermuda Triangle* edited by Martin Ebon. Wolfe is a lecturer in paranormal phenomena at Clark University in Worcester, Massachusetts, USA, and his chapter, says Ebon, was 'edited from a segment of one of his course lectures'. In other words, this is what he told his students.

Referring to the *Star Tiger*, an airliner that disappeared on a flight from the Azores to Bermuda Wolfe says: 'At 10.30 p.m. its pilot, Captain David Colby, radioed the tower at Hamilton, Bermuda. . . .' Hardly one of these 13 words is correct. The pilot was Captain Brian McMillan (Colby was the First Officer), all radio messages were sent by Robert Tuck and were not sent to the tower at Hamilton but to an Air Guard service

Above: in 1889 Malcolm Macmillan, a publisher from London and forbear of Harold Macmillan (the former British Prime Minister), vanished from the summit of Mount Hymettus in Greece. He had paused to wave to some companions, then disappeared. Careful searches of the area gave no hint as to his fate, yet the possibility remains that he could have committed suicide, his body being concealed by undergrowth

disturbing thought that parts of one's general knowledge are completely untrue. That is one of the reasons why stories such as that of David Lang have to be weeded out and set aside.

Critics of the many sensationalist books and their writers lay themselves open to the accusation of being unwilling to accept anything that lies outside the bounds of orthodoxy. But such criticism is not indicative of having a closed mind. On the contrary, it indicates having an open mind, one that is prepared to accept the possible truth that David Lang vanished before the startled eyes of his family and friends, but also a mind willing to investigate the story and try to get at the truth.

People do disappear and sometimes in the most bizarre circumstances. It remains possible that some people have stepped into another dimension or have been snatched by a UFO or fallen into a timeless void, but no matter how fascinating or frightening such possibilities might be, they remain the province of science fantasy writers until good, hard evidence can be presented to support their possible reality.

The day the Norfolks disappeared

One of the most frequently repeated stories of mysterious disappearances concerns an entire Norfolk regiment – allegedly abducted by a UFO in 1915. PAUL BEGG examines the story in the light of new evidence

THERE ARE MANY STRANGE accounts of people having been abducted by a UFO. In most cases the unfortunate victim is returned to Earth and able to tell his story, often to an incredulous audience who not unnaturally express considerable disbelief. But sometimes the victim disappears forever, his fate to remain unknown. These cases are rare because a number of witnesses are required if more prosaic explanations for the disappearance are to be dismissed. Of this latter category is the case of the vanishing Norfolks, one of the most bizarre of such incidents and accordingly featured in dozens of books about UFOs, the Bermuda Triangle, and other 'paranormal' mysteries. But is it – can it possibly be – true?

The incident allegedly took place in August 1915 during the ill-fated Gallipoli campaign. According to a statement made by three of the original witnesses, 22 members of a New Zealand field company saw a large number of British soldiers, later identified as the 'First-Fourth Norfolk Regiment', march into a strange loaf-of-bread shaped cloud that was straddling a dry creek bed. After the last man had entered, the cloud lifted and moved off *against* the wind. Not one of the soldiers was ever seen again.

The New Zealanders' story contained

Below: troops landing at Anzac Cove, Gallipoli, in 1915. Conditions were appalling; dysentery decimated the ranks and corpses lay everywhere, adding to the nightmare

some obvious errors; the First-Fourth Norfolk was not a regiment, for example, but a battalion of the Royal Norfolk Regiment. None of the errors has ever been corrected in any of the books that feature the story, which suggests that it has never been substantiated, the authors having simply copied the myth from one another.

This opinion is supported by one further and very important fact: the First-Fourth Norfolk did not disappear from Gallipoli in August 1915 or at any time or place thereafter. There is ample evidence to show that

they were in active service until the end of the year, when they were withdrawn from Gallipoli and sent to another theatre of war.

This fact would be sufficient to dispose of the New Zealanders' story of cosmic abduction as a figment of someone's imagination, but, perhaps coincidentally, it is a matter of undisputed historical fact that another battalion of the Royal Norfolk Regiment, the First-Fifth, *did* disappear at Gallipoli in August 1915, their fate never having been satisfactorily ascertained. Therefore, if the New Zealanders saw any Norfolks abducted, those Norfolks could only have been the First-Fifth. So is it possible that, bizarre though their story most certainly is, 22 members of a New Zealand field company did witness the fate of the First-Fifth Norfolk? If not, where did their story come from, and what was the First-Fifth's fate?

The twisting trail in search of some answers begins in Dereham, a small market town not far from Norwich, England. It was here, as part of the predominantly East Anglian 163rd Brigade, that the First-Fourth and First-Fifth Norfolks prepared to go to war.

They were Territorials – called 'Saturday night soldiers' by men of the regular army – but they belonged to a regiment with a long and distinguished history going back to 1685, when it was raised by King James II at the time of Monmouth's Rebellion. At that time it was called Colonel Henry Cornwall's 9th Regiment of Foot.

The Norfolks embarked for Gallipoli on 29 July 1915. The Gallipoli campaign was fought for control of the Dardanelles – the ancient Hellespont – a long, narrow channel extending some 40 miles (65 kilometres) along the Gallipoli Peninsula in Turkey and

Below: a corner of the ANZAC position. Digging in was a necessary evil in a slow-moving war, providing both shelter and cover. But the overcrowding and less than perfect sanitation, added to the heat and flies, meant a squalid death for many before they had fired a shot. It was in such chaotic conditions that the Norfolks 'disappeared'

Bottom: Turkish artillery pound the ANZACS during the advance on Tekke and Kavak Tepe

connecting the Mediterranean with the Black Sea, for which reason it had acquired strategic importance following the alliance between Turkey and Germany.

The Gallipoli Peninsula is exquisitely beautiful in spring and early summer, but from May onwards it bakes under a relentless sun and by August it is one of the most inhospitable places on Earth. It was on 10 August, at the height of the terrible summer, that the Norfolks landed at Suvla Bay and surveyed what had already become the graveyard for so many men.

Not far from the beach was a large salt lake. Dry in summer, it reflected the harsh glare of the sun. Beyond lay the battlefield, Suvla Plain, and in the distance a semicircle of bleak hills stretched from north to south,

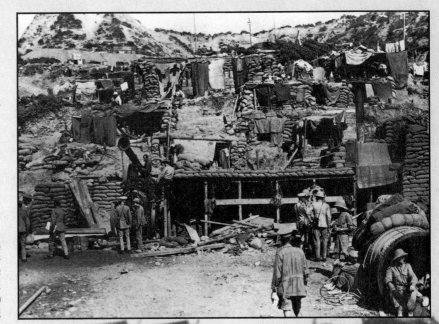

giving the plain the appearance of a giant arena. The northernmost was Kiretch Tepe, in the middle were the twin heights of Kavak Tepe and Tekke Tepe, and to the south was Sari Bair.

The Gallipoli campaign has gone down as one of the worst theatres of war in recent military history and to those Norfolks who had deluded themselves that they were off on a great adventure, the sights that met their eyes must have seemed like a nightmare vision of hell.

Conditions were appalling. The trenches were like ovens; a hot wind, pungent with the stench of death, stirred a fine dust across the plain; the food, the trenches, the latrines and the corpses were infested with a vile, bloated green fly – called the 'corpse fly' by the men because it feasted on the bodies of the dead and wounded – that spread a particularly virulent form of dysentery from which no soldier escaped and that reduced many to walking skeletons.

The troops, riddled with disease, were exhausted; corpses lay about in great numbers and it was by no means unusual to see the face or hands of a hastily buried comrade protruding from the ground; morale was low and a miasma of defeat hung heavy in the air.

The Norfolks had no experience of combat and in normal circumstances they would have been given time to acclimatise in a quiet sector, but Sir Ian Hamilton, Commander-in-Chief of the Mediterranean Expeditionary Force, believed that the only chance of wresting victory from the jaws of dreadful defeat lay in the use of his fresh forces in a major offensive.

Into the jaws of death

Hamilton envisaged a bold, sweeping attack on Tekke and Kavak Tepe and it was arranged that under cover of darkness on the night of 12 August the 54th Division (of which the Norfolks' brigade was a part) should advance to the foothills and prepare to attack at dawn the next day. However, it was believed that a cultivated area called Kuchuk Anafarta Ova, over which the night advance would take place, was held by enemy snipers and it was accordingly decided that the Norfolks' 163rd Brigade should move forward and clear the area during the afternoon of 12 August.

The advance that afternoon was a complete and utter fiasco, a prime example of the muddle and incompetence that marked the whole Gallipoli campaign. It was to begin at 4 p.m. with artillery support, but there was a delay of 45 minutes; however faulty communications prevented the artillery from being informed and they opened fire as scheduled, thereby wasting their support. The area was totally unreconnoitred, commanding officers were unfamiliar with the terrain and uncertain about their objective, most of the maps hurriedly issued at the last moment only depicted another part of the

Top: the 'glorious fallen'. The effects of delay in burial and the burning heat made identification of the corpses often impossible

Above: Major-General Sir Ian Hamilton, Commander-in-Chief of the Mediterranean Expeditionary Force, under whose command 46,000 men lost their lives – including the 267 men of the Norfolks

Peninsula, and the strength of the enemy was completely unknown.

The 163rd Brigade, with the First-Fourth Norfolk bringing up the rear, had advanced no more than about 1000 yards (900 metres) when it became obvious that a mistake had been made in trying to cross the open plain in daylight. The strength of the enemy was greater than had been supposed and the main body of the brigade encountered heavy machine-gun fire and were forced to ground. However, on the right flank the First-Fifth Norfolk encountered less stiff opposition and pressed forward.

Sir Ian Hamilton described the following events in a dispatch to Lord Kitchener, the Secretary of State for War:

In the course of the fight, creditable in all respects to the 163rd Brigade, there happened a very mysterious thing . . . Against the yielding forces of the enemy Colonel Sir H. Beauchamp, a bold, self-confident officer, eagerly pressed forward, followed by the best part of the battalion. The fighting grew hotter, and the ground became more wooded and broken. At this stage many men were wounded or grew exhausted with thirst. These found their way back to camp during the night. But the Colonel, with 16 officers and 250 men, still kept pushing forward, driving the enemy before him. . . . Nothing more was seen or heard of any of them. They charged into the forest and were lost to sight or sound. Not one of them ever came back.

Two hundred and sixty-seven men had vanished without trace!

The failure of the advance that afternoon delivered a crushing blow to Sir Ian Hamilton's hope of turning the tide of the campaign and the evacuation of Allied forces at the end of 1915 was a major defeat. The Gallipoli campaign had lasted eight and a half months and cost the lives of about 46,000 soldiers, a horrific number by any previous standards of modern warfare. In 1916 the Government appointed a Royal Commission to investigate the causes of the defeat. A heavily censored report, *The final report of the Dardanelles commission,* was released in 1917 and another in 1919. It was not until 1965 that a declassified edition was made available – a significant date as we shall see.

The fate of the First-Fifth Norfolk remained a mystery for four years when there was a further development in the story.

At the end of 1918 the British returned to

Above: a poster celebrating the Turkish victory over the invading ANZAC forces, Gallipoli, 1915

Below: Turkish troops. Knowing the terrain, used to the climate and far better organised, their victory over the ANZAC troops rapidly became inevitable

Gallipoli as the ultimate victors. A soldier of the Occupation Forces was touring the battlefield when he found a cap badge of the Royal Norfolk Regiment, and on making enquiries he learned that a Turkish farmer had removed a large number of bodies from his property and dumped them in a nearby ravine. On 23 September 1919, following the unpleasant task of recovering the bodies, an officer commanding a Graves Registration Unit triumphantly announced:

We have found the Fifth Norfolk – there were 180 in all: 122 Norfolk and a few Hants and Suffolks with 2/4th Cheshires. We could only identify two – Privates Barnaby and Carter. They were scattered over an area of about one square mile [3 square kilometres], at a distance of at least 800 yards [750 metres] behind the Turkish front line. Many of them had evidently been killed in a farm, as a local Turk, who owns the land, told us that when he came back he found the farm covered with the decomposing bodies of British soldiers which he threw into a small ravine. The whole thing quite bears out the original theory that they did not go very far on, but got mopped up one by one, all except the ones who got into the farmhouse.

'We have found the Fifth Norfolk . . . Although generally considered the last word on the fate of the First-Fifth Norfolk, it is evident that this statement was somewhat premature. Only 122 Norfolks were found, which leaves more than half the men who vanished unaccounted for. Their fate remains a mystery – unless, of course, the New Zealanders' story of the strange cloud is true.

Lost, believed kidnapped

Fifty years after the Gallipoli campaign three old soldiers came forward with a bizarre tale of a cloud kidnapping a whole regiment. The timing of their accounts shed new light on this 'mysterious' disappearance

ON 12 AUGUST 1915 the best part of the First-Fifth Battalion of the Royal Norfolk Regiment disappeared. The decomposing corpses of slightly less than half the battalion were later found, but the precise fate of the remaining troops remains a mystery. However, a solution may lie in a story which has featured in several books about UFOs and other relative phenomena. According to a statement made by three of the original witnesses, members of a New Zealand field company saw a large number of British troops abducted by a strange cloud, perhaps a UFO. The troops were identified as the First-Fourth Norfolk and the event allegedly happened on 21 August. As there is ample proof that the First-Fourth Norfolk did not disappear it seems that the New Zealanders' story is either a complete fabrication or describes the fate of another body of men, perhaps the disappearance of the First-Fifth Norfolk on 12 August.

What the New Zealanders allegedly saw is described in a statement signed by three of the original witnesses:

August 21, 1915
The following is an account of the strange incident that happened on the

Below: British troops go 'over the top' during the Gallipoli campaign, 1915. These soldiers were part of the hastily formed Naval division – basically sailors, they lacked proper training in land fighting. Other divisions deployed at Gallipoli were equally inadequately trained. The Norfolks, for example, consisted mainly of raw recruits and 'Saturday soldiers' (Territorials) whose exposure to the conditions at Gallipoli came as a brutal – and in many cases, fatal – shock

above date, which occurred in the morning during the severest and final period of fighting which took place on Hill 60, Suvla Bay, ANZAC.

The day broke clear, without a cloud in sight, as any beautiful Mediterranean day could be expected to be. The exception, however, was a number of perhaps six or eight 'loaf of bread' shaped clouds – all shaped exactly alike – which were hovering over Hill 60. It was noticed that, in spite of a four- or five-mile-an-hour [6–8 km/h] breeze from the south, these clouds did not alter their position in any shape or form, nor did they drift away under the influence of the breeze. They were hovering at an elevation of about 60 degrees as seen from our observation point 500 feet [150 metres] up. Also stationary and resting on the ground right underneath this group of clouds was a similar cloud in shape, measuring about 800 feet [245 metres] in length, 220 feet [65 metres] in height, and 200 feet [60 metres] in width. This cloud was absolutely dense, solid looking in structure, and positioned about 14 to 18 chains [900–1100 metres] from the fighting in British-held territory. All this was observed by twenty-two men of No 3 Section, No 1 Field Company, N.Z.E., including myself, from our trenches on Rhododendron Spur, approximately 2500 yards [1350 metres]

south-west of the cloud on the ground. Our vantage point was overlooking Hill 60 by about 300 feet [90 metres]. As it turned out later, this singular cloud was straddling a dry creek bed or sunken road [Kaiajik Dere] and we had a perfect view of the cloud's sides and ends as it rested on the ground. Its colour was a light grey, as was the colour of the other clouds.

A British regiment, the First-Fourth Norfolk, of several hundred men, was then noticed marching up this sunken road or creek towards Hill 60. However, when they arrived at this cloud, they marched straight into it, with no hesitation, but no one ever came out to deploy and fight at Hill 60. About an hour later, after the last of the file had disappeared into it, this cloud very unobtrusively lifted off the ground and, like any cloud or fog would, rose slowly until it joined the other similar clouds which were mentioned at the beginning of this account. On viewing them again, they all looked alike 'as peas in a pod'. All this time, the group of clouds had been hovering in the same place, but as soon as the singular cloud had risen to their level, they all moved away northwards, i.e. towards Thrace [Bulgaria]. In a matter

Above: seen from a distance the Allied camp at Walkers Ridge, Gallipoli, looks organised enough. But the truth was very different; the tents provided little shelter from the relentless heat for men already weakened by disease

of about three-quarters of an hour they had all disappeared from view.

The regiment mentioned was posted as missing or 'wiped out' and on Turkey surrendering in 1918, the first thing Britain demanded of Turkey was the return of this regiment. Turkey replied that she had neither captured this regiment, nor made contact with it, and did not know it existed. A British Regiment in 1914–18 consisted of any number between 800 and 4000 men. Those who observed this incident vouch for the fact that Turkey never captured that regiment, nor made contact with it.

We, the undersigned, although late in time, this is the 50th Jubilee of the ANZAC landing, declare that the above described incident is true in every word.

Signed by witnesses:
4/165 Sapper F. Reichardt,
 Matata, Bay of Plenty
13/416 Sapper R. Newnes
 157 King Street, Cambridge
J. L. Newman
 75 Freyberg Street, Octumoctai, Tauranga

This statement is sometimes accompanied by an extract referring to the event from an unspecified 'official history' of the Gallipoli campaign:

> They were swallowed up by an unseasonable fog. This fog reflected the sun's rays in such a way that artillery observers were dazzled by its brilliance and unable to fire in support. The two hundred and fifty men were never seen or heard from again.

The New Zealanders' statement contains several obvious errors: ANZAC was not a place at the time (although there is a faint likelihood that they were referring to an area that was invested with that name), but an acronym for Australia and New Zealand Army Corps, and the First-Fourth Norfolk was a battalion of the Royal Norfolk Regiment and not itself a regiment. It is difficult to believe that anyone familiar with the British Army or the Gallipoli campaign would have made such mistakes, which suggests that the statement may have been written by someone other than those who signed it and that signatures were provided without the statement having first been checked for accuracy.

Most important, of course, is the fact that the First-Fourth Norfolk did not disappear but were in active service throughout the Gallipoli campaign. The only Norfolks who disappeared were the First-Fifth Battalion and they disappeared on 12 August, not 21. It is perhaps possible but highly unlikely that the First-Fifth, disorientated after the fighting, wandered around Suvla Plain for nine days, but a more likely explanation for the difference of dates – assuming that the New Zealanders' story relates to the First-Fifth – is that Sapper Reichardt, who seems responsible for telling the story, confused the dates. After all 21 is the reverse of 12.

An insubstantial cloud

As for the substance of Reichardt's story, the most dilligent research has failed to locate any account of the 'kidnapping cloud' predating the signed statement (except the alleged entry in an 'official history', of which more will be said later), and the statement is not contemporary with the events it describes, having been signed at an old comrades' reunion to celebrate the 50th anniversary of the ANZAC landing, namely in 1965. One can only wonder why Mr Reichardt and his companions did not report such an unusual occurrence at the time, or at least when the mystery could not be solved later, but perhaps they feared ridicule. Whatever the reason, the story rests with the testimony of those who signed the statement.

Sapper Frederick Reichardt, a sailor, enlisted in the British Section of the New Zealand Expeditionary Force on 8 October 1914 as a member of No 3 Section, First Divisional Field Company, New Zealand Engineers. He embarked for Gallipoli on 12 April 1915.

It will be recalled that Suvla Plain is dominated by a semicircle of hills stretching from north to south, the southernmost being Sari Bair, which has three summits: Koja Cheman Tepe, Besim Tepe, and Chunuk Bair. The most practical route to the summit of Chunuk Bair is along the Rhododendron Spur, so named by the Allies because of the red flowers (not rhododendrons) that had blazed along its length during the early days of the campaign. It was from Rhododendron Spur that Reichardt claims to have seen the First-Fourth abducted.

One and a half miles (2.5 kilometres) to the north of Chunuk Bair is a small hillock called Hill 60, towards which Reichardt claims the troops were marching when abducted by the cloud. A further three miles (5 kilometres) to the north is Kuchuk Anafarta Ova, the scene of the Norfolks' advance on 12 August.

According to the *War diary* of the First Divisional Field Company, No 3 Section was

Below: a rough trench congested with walking wounded and stretcher cases after an action. Rudimentary medical attention patched up the wounded until they could be carried out to the hospital ships moored offshore. However, the heat and dust – and the ever-present 'corpse fly' – combined to produce fever and infection, which wiped out thousands of the wounded

Right. Turkish attendants look after graves in one of the 31 cemeteries maintained on the Gallipoli Peninsula by the Commonwealth War Graves Commission. Thousands of the dead, however, were never identified and many soldiers were never found

Below: a grim relic of the Gallipoli campaign – a human jawbone washed up by the Aegean Sea 50 years after the Dardanelles invasion by the Allies. Such was the carnage that the tides are still washing up fragments of the fallen and their equipment

three miles (5 kilometres) away from where the Fifth Norfolk vanished and has them marching towards enemy territory; he calls ANZAC a place; he waited 50 years before telling his story. It all weighs against believing the main substance of his story.

The only thing that will tip the scales in his favour is the reference to the event in the unspecified 'official history' of the Gallipoli campaign.

None of the official histories contains the entry cited in connection with Reichardt's story. However, in *The final report of the Dardanelles commission*, on the page facing the account of the First-Fifth's advance on 12 August, is the following:

> By some freak of nature Suvla Bay and Plain were wrapped in a strange mist on the afternoon of 21 August. This was sheer bad luck as we had reckoned on the enemy's gunners being blinded by the declining sun and upon the Turks' trenches being shown up by the evening sun with singular clearness. Actually, we could hardly see the enemy lines this afternoon, whereas to the westward targets stood out in strong relief against the luminous light.

Havoc in the afternoon

There can be no doubt that this is the extract used to support Reichardt's story. And it refers to events on 21 August 1915!

'Freak of nature', 'strange mist', 'luminous light', these are words to conjure with, but the report in fact describes an unseasonable but otherwise perfectly normal mist that descended shortly after noon on 21 August and caused havoc with what was, in terms of numbers, the greatest offensive ever launched at Gallipoli.

During that afternoon a composite ANZAC force of 3000 men attacked Hill 60. The battle would rage for a week before the Allies withdrew, leaving a corpse-strewn hillock behind them. It was in the late afternoon when, as the *Final report* says, the mist reflected the sun. The Sherwood Rangers, led by Sir John Milbanke VC, could not see the enemy, but the enemy could see the Rangers only too well and wiped them out.

It is this incident that Reichardt seems to have confused with the disappearance of the First-Fifth Norfolk to produce the story of the kidnapping cloud. Both incidents are described on facing pages in the *Final report* and significantly, the declassified edition of the report was released in 1965, the same year that Reichardt told his story. But the Norfolks' fate is still a mystery and in all probability will remain one, but it is up to you to decide how mysterious their disappearance is. People disappear in time of war. Of the 34,000 British and Empire troops who died at Gallipoli, 27,000 have no known grave. In the light of such widespread carnage, how many more 'strange disappearances' do those bald statistics hide?

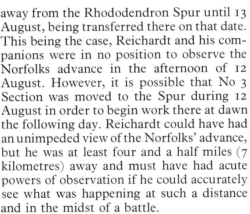

away from the Rhododendron Spur until 13 August, being transferred there on that date. This being the case, Reichardt and his companions were in no position to observe the Norfolks advance in the afternoon of 12 August. However, it is possible that No 3 Section was moved to the Spur during 12 August in order to begin work there at dawn the following day. Reichardt could have had an unimpeded view of the Norfolks' advance, but he was at least four and a half miles (7 kilometres) away and must have had acute powers of observation if he could accurately see what was happening at such a distance and in the midst of a battle.

Sadly, Reichardt's position neither proves nor disproves his story since he says that the troops were marching towards Hill 60, some three miles (5 kilometres) to the south of the scene of the Norfolks' advance. So once again the question is raised as to whether the Norfolks, disorientated, blindly wandered around Suvla Plain for up to nine days, eventually finding themselves heading for Hill 60, which was, incidentally, held by the enemy. This is possible, of course, but it seems highly unlikely that the Norfolks would not have fallen into the hands of either the Allies or the enemy.

When considering this eventuality it is impossible not to balance it against the errors in Reichardt's story: he names the wrong battalion; he calls it a regiment; he gives the date of 21 August, nine days after the First-Fifth disappeared; he says the troops were

The last of the Romanovs?

The young woman who had been fished out of a Berlin canal claimed to be the Grand Duchess Anastasia, daughter of the last tsar of Russia. Had she really survived the killing of the Imperial Romanovs? FRANK SMYTH investigates

ON THE MORNING OF 18 February 1920 the Berlin police issued a bulletin to the press:

> Yesterday evening at 9 p.m. a girl of about twenty jumped off the Bendler Bridge into the Landwehr Canal with the intention of taking her own life. She was saved by a police sergeant and admitted to the Elisabeth Hospital in Lützowstrasse. No papers or valuables of any kind were found in her possession, and she refused to make any statement about herself or her motives for attempting suicide.

As a news item it was trivial enough in a city swarming with despairing refugees, made homeless and stateless by the First World War. As an historical document, however, it may be momentous. For many authorities claim that it records the survival of a young woman who was said to have died with her family in a hail of Bolshevik bullets some 18 months before: Her Imperial Highness the Grand Duchess Anastasia Nikolayevna Romanova, daughter of Nicholas II, the last tsar of Russia.

That would-be suicide, who was known to her neighbours in the affluent university town of Charlottesville, Virginia, USA, as Anna Manahan, lived into her eighties and died in early 1984. She had married Dr John Manahan, a former professor of history at the University of Virginia, in 1967, in order to establish American citizenship. Dr Manahan, who was almost 30 years her junior, not only helped her gain citizenship but also protected her from unwelcome publicity. His very name was a shield to a great extent, for under her previous name of Anna Anderson, which she adopted in the 1920s, she became the subject of two feature films, numerous books and countless articles. She was also the focus of the longest legal case of the 20th century, which ran spasmodically from 1938 until 1970 and was still unresolved by the early 1980s.

Each of the two opposing parties in the court case is made up largely of British and German cousins of the Russian Romanov family. They have fought to establish or refute Anna's claim to be Anastasia – and feelings have run extremely high. For example, when the BBC proposed a television programme on the case in 1958, the late Lord

Below: Tsar Nicholas II, the last Imperial ruler of Russia, and his family. The Romanovs were all believed to have been killed after the Bolshevik revolution – but an amazing story of survival came to light with the sudden appearance of a young woman who said she was Anastasia (third from right), youngest of the daughters

Dr James H. Kimble, once the head of the United States Weather Bureau in New York, and author Gershom Bradford have both suggested that *Mary Celeste* was struck by a waterspout, a tornado at sea; a column of whirling wind and water that can appear without warning, last for up to an hour, and then break up as quickly as it appeared.

At first glance this theory does not seem very plausible, particularly as waterspouts are not common outside the tropics, nor is it common for ships to be struck by them. But the fact is that waterspouts are not totally restricted to the tropics: for example, in December 1920 the steamer *British Marquis* reported no less than 20 waterspouts in the English Channel.

Mr Bradford and Dr Kimble believe that a relatively small and harmless spout, narrow and travelling at an angle, could have struck the ship without doing a great deal of damage; indeed, it would have left the vessel no worse than had she encountered a storm. All this is consistent with the state of *Mary Celeste* when first sighted by the *Dei Gratia*. However, within a waterspout the barometric pressure is extremely low and, as the spout passed over the ship, the marked difference in pressure between the inside and outside of the ship could have caused the hatch covers to blow off – in the same way that a building's walls explode outward when struck by a tornado.

In this context, the method by which *Mary Celeste* was sounded may be extremely significant. This was done by dropping a rod down the pump well to measure the water in the hold, in much the same way as a motorist checks his oil with a dipstick. The drop in barometric pressure could have driven the bilge water up the pump-well, where a valve

either ignited by a spark, resulting, perhaps, from friction caused by the metal bands around the barrels rubbing together, or a naked light used during cargo inspection. Or perhaps the fumes had been mistaken for smoke and gave rise to the belief that the ship was about to be blown out of the water.

Experts have expressed the opinion that there could have been no *visible* vapour, but that an explosive mixture could have been formed. However, this would not have resulted in a minor explosion, but would have blown *Mary Celeste* into matchwood.

The most likely solution was in part offered by Oliver Deveau at the salvage hearing. He said that he thought the crew had panicked, believing that the ship was sinking. It was not an opinion that has impressed many commentators and most have dismissed it as idiotic (and Deveau himself as an idiot). But in fairness to Deveau, his comment has to be taken in context. At the hearing he was asked a straightforward question, and he answered it without elaboration. Later researchers, however, have tried to interpret his meaning.

Above: a reconstruction of one theory about the disappearance of the crew of *Mary Celeste*: they all fell overboard. The influential *Strand Magazine* heard that a reputable schoolmaster had a servant named Abel Fosdyk who claimed to have been the only survivor. Fosdyk said that Captain Briggs went mad. This may or may not be connected with the 'fact' that everyone else on board was precipitated into the sea from a flimsy play area built for the captain's daughter. Fosdyk threw no light on why no one managed to climb back on board

Right: in the 1936 film version the bosun goes mad and kills the entire crew, including himself

vessel's crew among the victims of whatever unexplained force they consider to exist in the area, imbuing that force with a singular selectivity, and in the process enlarging the Triangle so that it reaches the Azores. A superficially acceptable theory put forward by a number of rational people was that the food or drinking water was contaminated and caused the crew to hallucinate, driving them mad so that they threw themselves over the side. But Oliver Deveau and other members of the *Dei Gratia*'s crew used the food and water they found aboard *Mary Celeste* and suffered no ill effects.

The United States Consul in Gibraltar, Horatio Sprague, wrote in July 1887 that:

This case of the *Mary Celeste* is startling, since it appears to be one of those mysteries which no human ingenuity can penetrate sufficiently to account for the abandonment of this vessel and the disappearance of her master, family and crew. . . .

No solution so far offered seems to account for all the circumstances, but it is possible to list some salient facts that might provide a few clues: *Mary Celeste* was abandoned by her captain and crew; those who abandoned ship did so in the ship's yawl. This small vessel would have been overloaded and easily capsized, so the crew's fate is not wholly inexplicable. The ship was abandoned in a hurry: extra clothing was not taken nor – as far as is known – was any food or water, but the crew did not abandon ship in a complete panic, since they took the time to collect the sextant, chronometer, and the ship's papers (apart from the temporary log). Since there was no evidence that *Mary Celeste* had suffered any damage, whatever made the crew abandon her was something they feared had happened or was about to happen, but clearly never did.

The part-owner of the ship, James H. Winchester, suggested that *Mary Celeste*'s cargo of denatured alcohol gave off fumes, which collected in the hold and formed an explosive mixture. This, he speculated, was

in Keating's book was its title: the story *was* a hoax; Lee Kaye, Laurence Keating, and the *Evening Standard*'s 'special correspondent' were all one and the same person, an Irish-Liverpudlian named Laurence J. Keating. John Pemberton was a figment of Keating's fertile imagination and the photograph of 'Pemberton' was of Keating's own father.

While the majority of theories to explain the abandonment of *Mary Celeste* are generally a variation on the theme of murder – committed either by *Mary Celeste*'s own crew or by the men of *Dei Gratia* – other solutions are not uncommon and are frequently bizarre. The 1900s favoured 'monster from the depths' stories in which *Mary Celeste* was attacked by a huge hungry octopus that plucked the entire crew from the deck. Although it has its attractions for illustrators, the theory also has a number of flaws. Even if such a huge and vicious creature exists it is highly unlikely that everyone aboard *Mary Celeste* would have been on deck at the same time or that they would have obligingly stayed there as the monster plucked them off one by one. We must also assume that for some reason it craved *Mary Celeste*'s yawl, chronometer, sextant, and ship's papers.

The late Morris K. Jessup, who was involved with the alleged Philadelphia experiment (see page 60), suggested that *Mary Celeste*'s crew were abducted by a UFO. And Bermuda Triangle writers list the

Above: the alleged suicide of the *Marie Celeste*'s captain – 'Tibbs' – from an illustration of Conan Doyle's story *J. Habakuk Jephson's statement*. A gripping tale, it was taken by many to be true and popularised the misnomer *'Marie' Celeste*

Below: sea monsters have also been blamed for the tragedy

Did you ever meet one,

Voyage into the unknown

**Still-warm tea on the galley table, lifeboats all secure
– and the crew of the *Mary Celeste* had vanished.
Thanks to a deluge of fictional stories, this has become
the legend. But what really happened?**

IT DID NOT TAKE LONG for the myth surrounding the disappearance of the *Mary Celeste*'s crew to be born. Indeed, it could be argued that it began in Gibraltar in 1872 when Solly Flood tried in vain to attach guilt to Captain Morehouse and the crew of the *Dei Gratia*. But the story was seized upon by writers and journalists and soon caught the public imagination.

The first major piece of fiction about the ship was published in January 1884 by the prestigious *Cornhill Magazine*, 11 months before Gilman C. Parker deliberately burnt the ship (see box on page 83). It was a sensational short story called *J. Habakuk Jephson's statement* and it bore little resemblance to the actual facts. It was picked up by American newspapers however and published as fact, much to the outrage of Solly Flood and Horatio Sprague, the US Consul in Gibraltar, both of whom wrote letters condemning the tale.

Apart from its literary worth, *J. Habakuk Jephson's statement* is interesting for two reasons: it was one of the first literary efforts of a young English doctor named Arthur Conan Doyle, and in it *Mary Celeste* is called *Marie Celeste*, the name by which the ship is

Above: crewmen of the *Dei Gratia* sight the mystery ship *Mary Celeste*, in a painting by Gordon A. Johnson. This was commissioned in 1965 by the Atlantic Mutual Insurance Company – the original insurers of the *Mary Celeste*

now most commonly known. However, Conan Doyle was not the first to make the error – this version of the name first appears in *Lloyd's List* of 25 March 1873.

Conan Doyle's story was the first of many fictional accounts that have appeared over the years; for example, a novel based on the mystery was published as recently as 1980. Some of these tales have been presented as straight fiction, others as fictionalised fact (but nevertheless proposing a serious explanation), and quite a few have been intended to be taken as fact.

In the late 1920s *Chamber's Journal* published an article by Lee Kaye purporting to be a true account of what happened aboard *Mary Celeste* as supposedly told by a survivor named John Pemberton (one of the many 'survivors' who have popped up over the years but whose names are mysteriously absent from the crew list).

Pemberton's story was expanded to book length by Laurence J. Keating in 1929 and called *The great Mary Celeste hoax*. It was a bestseller on both sides of the Atlantic; John Pemberton rapidly became the man of the moment. Many journalists sought interviews with him, but Pemberton remained elusive until a 'special correspondent' of the London *Evening Standard* tracked him down – and obtained not only the coveted interview but a photograph as well. Both were published in the *Evening Standard* on 6 May 1929.

However, one of the few true statements

ship and loading his wife and two-year-old daughter and the seven members of crew into a small and comparatively unstable boat? Abandoning ship is a desperate measure, an act taken only when there is no alternative; yet as one of *Dei Gratia*'s crew said later, *Mary Celeste* was in a fit enough state to sail around the world. So why was she abandoned?

Under international maritime law anyone who salvages an abandoned vessel is entitled to a percentage of what the vessel and its cargo are worth. Generally such a vessel is a wreck, but *Mary Celeste*, a seaworthy ship, and her valuable cargo were worth a substantial sum, and the salvors could expect to make perhaps as much as $80,000. Captain Morehouse was not consumed by avarice, as many subsequent writers have implied, and was actually reluctant to lay claim to *Mary Celeste*. He could not really spare the men to form a skeleton crew without both vessels being undermanned and therefore at risk in the event of an emergency; but he was eventually persuaded by Deveau.

Deveau and two seamen, Augustus Anderson and Charles Lund, took only two days to restore *Mary Celeste* to order, and then the two ships set off for Gibraltar. *Dei Gratia* arrived on the evening of 12 December and *Mary Celeste* the following morning. Within two hours of dropping anchor *Mary Celeste* was placed under arrest by Thomas J. Vecchio, of the Vice-Admiralty Court.

The Attorney General for Gibraltar and Advocate General for the Queen in Her Office of Admiralty was an excitable, arrogant and pompous bureaucrat named Frederick Solly Flood; he found the abandonment of *Mary Celeste* explicable only as a result of murder and piracy. Without Solly Flood the

Oliver Deveau, first mate of the *Dei Gratia*, who, with only two other crewmen, brought the *Mary Celeste* into Gibraltar in December 1872. The British authorities refused to believe their story of how they had discovered *Mary Celeste*

Below: Captain David Reed Morehouse, master of the *Dei Gratia* (bottom). Under maritime law anyone who salvages an abandoned ship is entitled to a handsome percentage of its total worth. In the case of *Mary Celeste* this would have been considerable for she was in excellent condition and had her full complement of cargo. However, Morehouse was reluctant to lay any such claim and found it hard to spare crew to look after *Mary Celeste*. Yet some critics still maintain that Briggs and Morehouse were conspirators, who, having set up the 'disappearances', planned to split the salvage money between them – and live in luxury

Mary Celeste mystery would have probably faded into obscurity, but his accusations at the hearings in the Vice-Admiralty Court attracted worldwide publicity.

First, Flood accused *Mary Celeste*'s original crew – in their absence – of having gained access to the cargo of alcohol and having murdered Captain Briggs, his wife and child, and Mate Richardson in a drunken fury. It is a theory that has been proposed several times since, once by William A. Richard, Secretary of the Treasury of the United States, in an open letter published on the front page of the *New York Times* in 1873. The fact remains that the cargo was denatured alcohol and liable to give the drinker acute pains long before he could become intoxicated. Flood was forced to abandon his theory.

He next suggested that Briggs and Morehouse were conspirators. Briggs, said Flood, killed his crew and disposed of their bodies. He then took the lifeboat to a destination prearranged with Captain Morehouse, who in the meantime would have found *Mary Celeste* abandoned, taken her to Gibraltar and claimed the salvage reward. The two men would then meet and split their ill-gotten gains. This theory is just plausible, but there was and is no evidence that Briggs or Morehouse were villains. Moreover, Briggs was part-owner of *Mary Celeste* and his cut of the salvage money would not have been more than his investment in the vessel. Flood abandoned this idea too.

Guilty until proved innocent

His third suggestion was that Captain Morehouse and the crew of *Dei Gratia* had boarded *Mary Celeste* and savagely slaughtered all on board. Flood tried very hard to make his claim stick, but all he succeeded in doing was generating an atmosphere of suspicion in which Morehouse and his crew would be considered guilty until they could prove themselves innocent. Fortunately, the Vice-Admiralty Court denounced such a flagrant abuse of the law and cleared Morehouse and his crew of any suspicion. They granted them a salvage reward of £1700. In the opinion of many people the award should have been twice or three times as much.

Mary Celeste was returned to James H. Winchester and, under the command of Captain George W. Blatchford, she continued her voyage to Genoa and finally delivered her cargo. Winchester then sold the ship – it is rumoured at a considerable loss – and over the next 12 years the vessel changed hands no less than 17 times. None of her new owners had a good word to say about her. She lurched up and down the coast of the United States losing cargoes, sails and sailors, running aground and catching fire with depressing regularity. It seemed that *Mary Celeste*'s jinx was there to stay.

many more voyages, it was the last time anyone would see this particular crew.

On 15 November 1872, eight days after *Mary Celeste* left New York, *Dei Gratia* set off with a cargo of petroleum bound for Gibraltar. Her skipper was a Nova Scotian named David Reed Morehouse and the first mate was Oliver Deveau. Both these men and the rest of *Dei Gratia*'s crew were highly able sailors – as later events were to prove – and no 'dirt' has ever been attached to their characters except by sensationalists.

On 5 December, shortly after 1 p.m., one of the *Dei Gratia*'s crew, John Johnson, who was at the wheel, sighted a vessel about 5 miles (8 kilometres) off the port bow. Attracted by the poor state of the ship's sails and her slight 'yawing' (listing), he called the second mate, John Wright, and together they summoned Captain Morehouse. After surveying the vessel through his telescope, Morehouse gave orders to offer assistance.

At 3 p.m., having come within about 400 yards (370 metres) of the mystery ship, Morehouse hailed her several times, but, receiving no reply from her, he decided to send some men to investigate.

Oliver Deveau, with Wright and Johnson, rowed across to the distressed craft, noting as they drew closer, its name – *Mary Celeste*. Johnson was left in the boat as the other two hauled themselves over the ship's rails. The *Mary Celeste* was deserted.

Over the next hour Deveau and Wright searched *Mary Celeste* from stem to stern. The main staysail was found on the foreward house, but the foresail and upper foresail had been blown from the yards and lost. The jib, fore-topmast staysail and the fore lower topsail were set. The remaining sails were furled. Some of the running rigging was

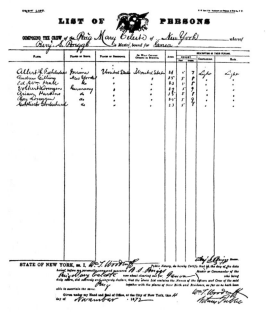

Top left: Captain Benjamin Spooner Briggs, master of the *Mary Celeste*. A puritan and abstemious New Englander, his alleged religious fanaticism has been blamed for whatever disaster hit the crew – mutiny or madness perhaps

Top right: Briggs's wife, Sarah Elizabeth who, with their two-year-old daughter Sophia Matilda, also sailed on the fatal voyage

Above: the first mate, Albert G. Richardson, who had served before under Briggs and was deemed an excellent seaman

Left: the ship's list, giving the names of those who sailed – and were doomed to vanish without trace

fouled, some had been blown away, and parts of it were hanging over the sides. The main peak halyard – a stiff rope about 100 yards (90 metres) long used to hoist the outer end of the gaff sail – was broken and most of it missing. The wheel was spinning free and the binnacle had been knocked over and broken. The main hatch to below decks was well-battened down and secure, but certain of the hatch covers had apparently been removed and were found discarded near the hatchways. There was less than a foot (30 centimetres) of water in the galley and little of the six months' store of provisions had been spoilt. There was ample fresh water.

In short, *Mary Celeste* was in a far better condition than most vessels then regularly plying the Atlantic. And, aside from some evidence that she had recently weathered a storm, she bore no clues as to why she had been so abruptly abandoned by her crew.

On a table in Captain Briggs's cabin Oliver Deveau found the temporary log. It read: 'Monday, 25th. At five o'clock made island of St Mary's bearing ESE. At eight o'clock Eastern point bore SSW six miles [3 kilometres] distant.'

In the mate's cabin Deveau found a chart showing the track of the vessel up to 24 November.

Missing from the ship were the chronometer, sextant, bill of lading, navigation book, and a small yawl, or boat, that had been lashed to the main hatch. A piece of railing running alongside had been removed to launch the boat. This at least answered the mystery of where *Mary Celeste*'s crew had gone; they had abandoned ship. But why? What possible reason could an experienced seaman like Benjamin Spooner Briggs have had for abandoning a perfectly seaworthy

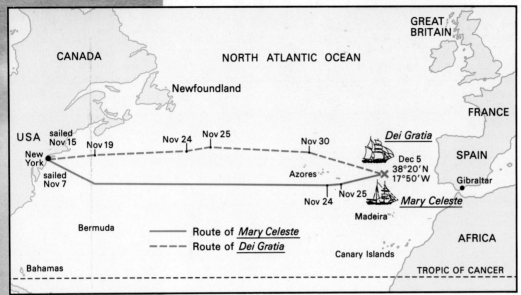

CANADA NORTH ATLANTIC OCEAN GREAT BRITAIN

Newfoundland

FRANCE

USA sailed Nov 15 Nov 19 Nov 24 Nov 25 Nov 30 *Dei Gratia* SPAIN
New York Dec 5 38°20′N 17°50′W Gibraltar
sailed Nov 7 Azores Nov 24 Nov 25 *Mary Celeste*
Bermuda Madeira AFRICA
——— Route of *Mary Celeste*
– – – Route of *Dei Gratia* Canary Islands
Bahamas TROPIC OF CANCER

Left: map showing the respective routes of the *Dei Gratia* and the *Mary Celeste* during November and December 1872. X marks the spot where the crew of the *Dei Gratia* sighted the bedraggled sailing ship, apparently becalmed and showing no sign of life

one owner to another, several of whom seem to have gone bankrupt and none of whom derived any good from their contact with the ship. She eventually passed into the hands of J.H. Winchester and Co., a consortium of New York shipowners. By this time the *Amazon* was unrecognisable as the vessel that had left the shipyards of Joshua Dewis. She had been enlarged, now flew the Stars and Stripes, and on her nameboard was *Mary Celeste*. It has been suggested that the peculiar mixture of English and French names was the result of the painter's error, the intended name being *Mary Sellers* or even perhaps *Marie Celeste*, the name, ironically, by which most people know her.

Sometime during late September or early October in 1872 *Mary Celeste* was berthed at Pier 44 in New York's East River, preparing to take on a new cargo and a fresh crew.

Benjamin Spooner Briggs

The latest captain of *Mary Celeste* was a stern, puritan New Englander named Benjamin Spooner Briggs. He was born at Wareham, Massachusetts, on 24 April 1835, the second of five sons born to Captain Nathan Briggs and his wife Sophia. It was a seafaring family; apart from his father, four of his brothers also went to sea. Two became master mariners at an early age, one of them being Benjamin Briggs, who had already commanded the schooner *Forest King*, the barque *Arthur*, and the brigantine *Sea Foam*. In later years many authors painted him as weak and ineffectual, a man whose religious beliefs had become a form of perversion, a mania, turning his strict abstinence from alcohol – which went so far as to allow none on board his ship unless it were cargo – into something akin to over-zealous morality. Briggs was in fact a man of strict beliefs and religious convictions, and although he was a teetotaller he was no monomaniac on the subject. He was described by those who knew him as always bearing 'the highest

character as a Christian and as an intelligent and active shipmaster'. He was also a shareholder in the *Mary Celeste*.

The first mate was Albert G. Richardson. A soldier in the American Civil War, he had married a niece of James H. Winchester's and had served before with Captain Briggs. He seems to have been trustworthy and competent and was held in high esteem.

Andrew Gilling was the second mate. His birthplace was given as New York but he seems to have been of Danish extraction. Again there is no reason to suspect that he was other than upright and honest.

The cook and steward, Edward William Head, hailed from Brooklyn, New York, where it is said that he was respected by all.

The remainder of the crew consisted of four seamen of German birth, about whom little is known except that two of them – both named Lorenzen – had lost all their possessions when shipwrecked prior to signing on as crewmen on *Mary Celeste*. None of these Germans appears to have been anything other than of good character.

Also making the voyage into the unknown were Captain Briggs's wife, Sarah Elizabeth – the daughter of the preacher of the Congregational Church in Marion, Massachusetts – and one of their two children, two-year-old Sophia Matilda. The elder child, their son Arthur Stanley, remained at home.

Late on Saturday, 2 November 1872 *Mary Celeste*'s cargo was loaded and made secure. She carried 1701 barrels of denatured alcohol being shipped by Meissner Ackerman and Co., merchants of New York, to H. Mascerenhas and Co., of Genoa, Italy.

Early on 5 November the Sandy Hook pilot ship towed *Mary Celeste* from Pier 44 to the lower bay off Staten Island, New York. The Atlantic was particularly stormy for the time of year and Briggs was forced to drop anchor for two days before he dared to venture out to sea on 7 November. But although *Mary Celeste* herself would make

The classic case of 'Mary Celeste'

The abrupt disappearance of *Mary Celeste*'s entire crew is one of the most fascinating mysteries of the sea. But, as PAUL BEGG points out, that was only the climax of a long history of weird misfortunes

ON 5 DECEMBER 1872 a crewman on watch on board the British ship *Dei Gratia* sighted a vessel that seemed to be in distress. Three seamen lowered the *Dei Gratia*'s small boat and rowed across to the troubled craft to offer assistance. They hauled themselves over the ship's rails and dropped onto the deck; save for the sound of the wind in the sails and the eerie creaking of the ship's timbers, there was not a sound. The seamen searched the ship from stem to stern and found her to be in excellent condition, but there was not a soul on board. Her crew had disappeared. The name of the ship was *Mary Celeste*.

The disappearance of her crew is the central element in *Mary Celeste*'s long history of misfortune. She attracted bad luck like a magnet attracts iron filings. The superstitious would call her jinxed, and *Mary Celeste*'s story is one that would make even a hard-boiled sceptic agree that the superstitious might have a point.

Mary Celeste was built in 1860, the maiden venture of a consortium of pioneer shipbuilders at the shipyards of Joshua Dewis on Spencer's Island, Nova Scotia. She was originally christened *Amazon* and was launched in 1861, the year that saw the start of the American Civil War. Tragedy struck a short while later when her first skipper, a Scot named Robert McLellan, fell ill and died. Then one John Nutting Parker assumed command and skippered the *Amazon*'s maiden voyage, but she ran into a fishing weir off Maine, received a large gash in her hull and had to go to the shipyards for repair. While she was there a fire broke out amidships, bringing Captain Parker's short-lived command to an end.

Amazon's first Atlantic crossing went without mishap until she entered the Straits of Dover and collided with a brig. The brig sank, *Amazon* again went for repairs, and her third skipper went to seek another command.

Following the necessary repairs and the appointment of a new captain, *Amazon* returned to America, and she promptly ran aground off Cow Bay, Cape Breton Island, Nova Scotia.

Amazon's history now becomes a little hazy. She was pulled off the rocks and repaired, but appears to have passed from

Right: the *Mary Celeste*, the Nova Scotian half-brig whose name is synonymous with the most bizarre kind of disappearance

Above: J. H. Winchester, one of the owners of the hapless sailing ship that eventually became the *Mary Celeste*

Below: the *Amazon*, built in 1860 in Nova Scotia. Until she became the *Mary Celeste* a few years later, her short career was 'unlucky'; but afterwards it was disastrous

jeopardy if he championed the Tsar.

But another reason for the opposition to 'Anastasia's' claims, particularly from the Germans, may well tell in her favour. While gravely ill in hospital in 1926, Anna implored a visitor, the widow of a German dignitary, to bring the Grand Duke of Hesse – her 'Uncle Ernie' as she called him – to her bedside. She said she had last seen him 'in the war, with us, at home'. To the visitor and others present this seemed impossible, for Russia and Germany had been at war and Grand Duke Ernst Ludwig had been an active German general. When this woman did visit the Grand Duke and did mention this conversation, he immediately turned cold and told her that he could not become involved. Later, despite scepticism amounting almost to scorn, 'Anastasia' made the claim again, to Herluf Zahle. 'Uncle Ernie' she said, had paid a secret visit to the Tsar in 1916 to attempt to arrange a separate peace between Russia and Germany.

Vindication for Anna Anderson came from a highly respectable source in 1953 when Crown Princess Cecile, the Kaiser's daughter-in-law, swore a formal deposition:

> If the view is still held today that such a visit never took place, I can assert from personal knowledge – the source is my late father-in-law – that this visit was already known in our circles at the time. In my opinion [Anna] showed by her statement, which I only heard about much later, strong evidence at least of her intimate knowledge of the high politics and of the most secret dealings of the Imperial family.

Since then other depositions and documents have come to light making the secret trip

Top: the house in the Bavarian Black Forest where Anna Anderson sought to escape the glare of publicity

Above: Crown Princess Cecile of Germany, whose father-in-law was Kaiser Wilhelm II, another Romanov cousin. She gave testimony favourable to Anna Anderson in 1953

almost a certainty. In view of this, the opposition of the Grand Duke and many of his close German family, who always hoped for a restoration of the German monarchy, is understandable. Proof of such an act would have been a sword in the hands of German republicans, though as Summers and Mangold have said, it seems odd that they still opposed Anna Anderson even after their hopes must have died.

In 1918 the real Anastasia was described as 'plump and pretty'. By 1922 the claimant to her name had undergone great hardship and was almost skeletal. Yet despite her physical change, many members of her 'family' recognised her as their supposedly dead 'kin'. Grand Duke Andrei, for instance, was quite convinced. The Tsar's sister Olga, who saw the real Anastasia only rarely, was partially convinced but could never make up her mind, while Prince Sigismund of Prussia, her companion in childhood, knew who she was without having seen her. When 'Anastasia' first surfaced, Sigismund was in central America, so he sent the claimant a list of personal questions that only the real Anastasia could answer correctly. Anna answered all of them accurately.

The court files amount to almost 8000 foolscap pages – but no decision as to Anastasia's identity has been made. Anna had ceased to be personally involved, and after a short period in a mental hospital she died in early 1984. She had stopped caring long ago and in 1977 – weary of the never-ending publicity – she wrote a personal letter to a press agency formally declaring that she was closing the case for good. And the question of whether she was the real Anastasia remains a puzzle of history.

74

again in 1931 and to another mental hospital. Befriended by a Romanov cousin while there, she spent the next 13 years in relative peace as the guest of many of Europe's aristocracy.

Meanwhile, a legal wrangle began in earnest in 1933. It started over who exactly was to get the Tsar's legendary fortune, allegedly distributed among banks in various countries. The only money ever actually discovered was in Germany – and was far from a fortune. But in 1937 the courts ruled that it could be divided among a named number of the Tsar's near relatives. One of the legal documents mentioned that Anastasia was 'deceased', and, scrupulously fair, the bank holding the money wrote to Anna Anderson to warn her. Her lawyers, recommended and provided by friends, found her a reluctant client. But they entered the long – and

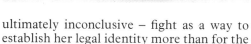

Above: Serge Lifar (right), world-famous ballet dancer, choreographer and writer, testified in the Anastasia court case in 1958

Left: Marie, Dowager Empress of Russia and grandmother of the real Anastasia. She instituted an investigation of Anna Anderson but never saw the claimant in person

Below: the Grand Duke of Hesse, one of the German relations of the Romanovs. He refused to consider the possibility that Anna Anderson was his cousin

'presumed' the death of Anastasia. The late Lord Mountbatten, his sister Princess Andrew of Greece – mother of Prince Philip – and Queen Louise of Sweden were among the likely defendants, but instead the choice fell on two German cousins from the line of Hesse. From 1957 until 1970 the case was almost continuously before the German courts and, as the journalists Anthony Summers and Tom Mangold remarked in their book *The file on the Tsar*: 'Given that there is supposedly no Romanov fortune at stake, the Tsar's relatives in exile went to extraordinary lengths to smother the Anastasia affair.'

One reason for this could well be a collective sense of guilt by royal relatives who made little if any attempt to rescue the Imperial family through diplomatic means. For example, documents exist showing that King George v quashed a tentative British plan to save his cousin Nicholas – perhaps out of concern that his position would be in

ultimately inconclusive – fight as a way to establish her legal identity more than for the inheritance.

During the Second World War Anna Anderson was trapped in Soviet Russia, undoubtedly a nightmare experience if she was who she claimed to be. After the war she became increasingly eccentric, settling as a hermit in the Black Forest in a hut bought for her, and living with an elderly female companion, a host of cats, and four ferocious wolfhounds.

But the spotlight was still on her. A German feature film, starring Lilli Palmer and dealing with 'Anastasia's' fight for recognition, was followed by the glittering Hollywood version starring Ingrid Bergman. The world's press literally beat a path through the woods to her humble door, while the fresh publicity brought a new legal turn. The Berlin Court of Appeal, on turning down her lawyers' appeal for her legal recognition, suggested that she sue those who had

persuade the outside world of it. Her 'case' has always been in the hands of others. In fact, her reaction to von Kleist's revelation was to run away from his care, and for the next five years she was in and out of hospitals – and the world's press.

One of the dozens of people who visited Anastasia – among them members of the Romanov clan – was Tatiana Botkin, daughter of the Tsar's doctor who had presumably perished with the Imperial family. Tatiana Botkin arrived determined to expose the 'impostor'. Instead, despite the nameless woman's gaunt appearance, she immediately recognised her as Anastasia.

The German authorities seemed also to be convinced. In 1926 'Anastasia' was advised to go to Switzerland for medical reasons, and the German Foreign Ministry instructed the Berlin Aliens Office to issue her with an identity card, although bureaucratically she did not exist, alluding to 'special reasons' for doing so. A senior official at the Prussian Home Office said that '. . . on the basis of police enquiries so far, the unknown woman is in all probability one and the same as the Tsar's daughter Anastasia.'

Sinister opposition

In 1925 the Tsar's mother, Dowager Empress Marie, who was living in exile at the Danish court, asked her brother Prince Valdemar of Denmark to look into the affair. He instructed Herluf Zahle, then Danish ambassador in Berlin as well as the president of the League of Nations, to conduct enquiries. After a time Zahle also became convinced that 'Anastasia' was genuine, but he found the German relatives – the Tsarina's side of the family – obstructive. Grand Duke Andrei, a senior Romanov, a trained jurist and the Tsar's cousin, also undertook an investigation. He met with the same opposition, so much so that he began to think there was something sinister behind it. Grand Duke Ernst Ludwig of Hesse, the Tsarina's brother, had told Andrei that his enquiries could be 'perilous', which prompted Andrei to write in one of his letters: '. . . it is plain to see that "they" fear something and are very disturbed, as if the investigation could uncover something embarrassing and even dangerous for them. . . .'

Certainly the Grand Duke of Hesse made a number of fumbling attempts to discredit the claimant. At the same time, one of the other cousins, Duke George of Leuchtenberg, invited her to stay at his castle in Upper Bavaria, which she did. Then in 1928 she went to New York as the guest of Princess Xenia Georgievna, the real Anastasia's second cousin. There she changed her name to Anna Anderson to escape the press ballyhoo. There she also became involved in an ill-advised court action under the irresponsible guidance of Gleb Botkin, son of the Tsar's doctor.

The repercussions sent Anna to Germany

who had lived in Moscow before the revolution, was discharged from Dalldorf. Soon after, she told a former White Russian officer that she thought she had recognised the Grand Duchess Tatiana, Anastasia's older sister, among the inmates of the mental hospital. Apparently she had not spoken to the patient calling herself Anastasia.

As a result of this conversation, a former police officer from Russian Poland, Baron Arthur von Kleist, visited the mystery woman and spent two months gaining her confidence. He then secured her release and took her into his own home. According to him, she told him – in a confidence that he quickly broke – that she was Anastasia. She recounted that she had made her escape from Russia under the protection of a soldier by the name of Alexander Tschaikowsky, who had later been killed. In a mood of black despair, she had made her own way to Berlin where she had tried to kill herself.

By July 1922 Baron von Kleist had broken the news – and 'Anastasia' entered a glare of publicity that was to surround her for the next half century. It is worthy of note that, while privately asserting her Romanov identity, the woman last known as Anna Manahan has never personally attempted to

Anna Anderson as she began her sheltered years as the wife of the American professor Dr John Manahan (standing). Gleb Botkin, son of Tsar Nicholas II's doctor and staunch supporter of Anna's right to the name of Anastasia, was a witness at the wedding in 1967. By then, Anna had been through nearly 50 years of publicity and controversy – with no resolution to the court case deliberating whether she was really the last of the Imperial Romanovs of Russia

would have prevented it from returning immediately to the hold. Although this would have been merely a temporary malfunction, the crew may not have realised it.

Suppose, then, that after the waterspout had moved on the crew were shaken and confused. Somebody went to sound the ship to see if she had suffered any underwater damage, and to his horror found that *Mary Celeste* had leaked 6 to 8 feet (2 to 2½ metres) of water in less than a minute – or so the seaman would have thought when he removed the sounding rod. Believing *Mary Celeste* to be sinking fast, Captain Briggs, perhaps panicking out of concern for his wife and daughter, gave the order to abandon ship. Perhaps this was what Oliver Deveau had meant by his cryptic statement. We shall never know, but the waterspout theory certainly seems to fit most of the reported circumstances and also explains the most baffling feature of the case: what monstrous happening threatened those aboard *Mary Celeste*, resulting in their hurried evacuation but still allowing them time in which to grab sextant, chronometer and ship's papers?

One commentator has called the case of *Mary Celeste* 'a detective-story writer's nightmare: the perfectly perplexing situation without any logical solution – a plot which can never be convincingly unravelled.'

On 16 May 1873 the *Daily Albion* of Liverpool reported that two rafts had been found by fishermen at Baudus, in Asturias, near Madrid, Spain. One of the rafts had a corpse lashed to it and was flying an American flag. The second raft bore five decomposing bodies. Curiously, the matter was not investigated, so no one will ever know who they were or what ship they belonged to. But could they have been from *Mary Celeste*?

Above: a waterspout at sea. A fast, angled one could have hit the *Mary Celeste*, causing only superficial damage and temporarily falsifying the crew's soundings. Believing that they were sinking, the crew could have panicked and abandoned ship. Although this is one of the more reasonable theories, it is unlikely that anyone will ever discover the truth

A terrible risk

In late 1884 an ageing and rather unkempt *Mary Celeste* was bought by Gilman C. Parker and loaded with freight, which he insured for $30,000. The vessel then sailed for Port-au-Prince, Haiti. But she never arrived. On 3 January 1885 *Mary Celeste* ran aground on the razor-sharp coral reef of Rochaelais Bank in the Gulf of Gonave, off the coast of Haiti.

Parker put in an insurance claim, but for some reason the insurance companies regarded it with deep suspicion and sent enquiry agents to investigate. They found that Parker had loaded the ship with rubbish – not the valuable cargo he had insured – had deliberately run *Mary Celeste* aground, unloaded the part of the cargo that he could sell, and then set *Mary Celeste* alight.

Parker was charged with barratry – fraud and/or criminal negligence by a ship's officer or crew against the owners or insurers. In those days this was a crime punishable by death. The case was heard in a federal court in Boston, but it was dropped because of a legal technicality. Gilman C. Parker, a grizzled old sea-dog who was – judging by the evidence – undoubtedly guilty of every maritime crime short of piracy, and his associates walked from the court free men. Free, that is, from the penalties of a court of law, but not from the jinx of *Mary Celeste*. In a short time Parker went bankrupt, and he died in poverty and disrepute. One of his fellow conspirators went insane and was placed in a mental institution where he ended his days. Another killed himself. In the end the jinx of *Mary Celeste* had won, having horribly ruined many lives.

PART 2
STRANGE TALENTS

Introduction

ONE OF THE REASONS why almost everyone is intrigued by the paranormal is that almost everyone has had some experience of it, no matter how slight. How many times have you had a relative – or a friend, or even a neighbour whom you may know only slightly – pop into your mind for no apparent reason, then had them telephone just a little while later – or write a letter which arrives in the next mail? This kind of thing happens often enough for most of us to suspect, at least, that something unusual is going on – that more than coincidence is at work. Yet, at the same time, most events like this are so trivial they don't stop us in our tracks either.

Some people however simply *can't* ignore their encounters with the paranormal. The things they experience are so remarkable – sometimes so disturbing – that they are forced to acknowledge that there are forces at work around them that they – along with everyone else – do not understand and often cannot control. Most people who discover that they can bend metal by means of psychokinesis, or hear the voices of the dead, or have premonitions of the future, find positive uses for their strange talents. But the way in which they first discover that talent can be something of a shock – indeed paranormality can manifest itself in its early stages quite differently from the way its energies may ultimately be used. The English psychic Matthew Manning, for instance, was first made aware of his strange talents by way of a massive outbreak of poltergeist activity that wrought havoc in his parents' house. As you can read in another volume in this series, he first channelled his psychic energy into an apparent ability to communicate with dead artists, producing some remarkable pictures as a result. Later he became adept at metal-bending, but by the early 1980s he had found his true vocation as a healer.

Others are introduced to their talents in less troubling ways, though often through a crisis or shock that triggers off an ability which may have been lying dormant until then. Psychic detective Gerard Croiset and clairaudient medium Doris Fisher Stokes discovered their abilities in this way. Tom Lethbridge, on the other hand, probably always had his remarkable capacity for dowsing, but had never had either the inclination or the opportunity to develop it until his retirement from academic life. The Scottish seer Kenneth Odhar would appear to have had his ability to see into the future all his life – though without his gift of prophecy the chances are his life would have been rather longer, and certainly not drastically curtailed in the way it was.

This inconsistency makes it all the more difficult to develop a theory as to the origins of such abilities. No less mysterious is the way in which some people's powers increase, are refined, or even change with time – or in some cases simply fade away. To some extent it is possible to suggest what kind of power is at work, in that a metal-bender like Uri Geller and a healer like Jose Arigo are both apparently using some form of psychokinesis (PK) – the ability to affect material things by mental effort alone – but to say that is really little more than saying we can put labels on *some* of the phenomena that occur. And even the labels we do have are precious little help when confronted by a medium like Doris Fisher Stokes or a – what? a magician? – such as Sai Baba.

In the case of Doris Stokes, opinion is divided between those who believe that she does exactly what she claims to do – hear the voices of the dead speaking from 'over there' – and those who believe that she is picking up, by telepathic means, information already in the mind of the person who wants to contact someone who has 'passed over'. To suggest that Doris Stokes is using telepathy does not, of course, mean that we should reject the idea that we survive bodily death: it is simply a question of what is really happening when Doris Stokes goes to work. When asked by the editorial team of this series whether she had considered the possibility that she *was*, in fact, reading the (unconscious) minds of her sitters, Doris Stokes replied that she would refuse to carry on her work if she felt she had been doing any such thing. 'That would be an invasion of privacy,' she said. 'I don't think God would allow that.' Nonetheless, the possibility remains that Doris Stokes is indeed highly telepathic, picking up memories from the mind of someone who knew the dead person. These memories are then dramatised by Mrs Stokes' own subconscious, and come to her in the form of voices. If her descriptions are anything to go by, they usually resemble the voice of the one who has passed on.

Presumably the reasons for this are two-fold. In the first place, Doris Stokes has that very strong resistance to the notion that she is invading other people's most private space – the mind. And, as you can read here, she has been utterly convinced that we *do* survive death. She cannot prevent her talent manifesting itself, and so has rationalised it in a way that has brought her, and thousands of people who have sat with her, great comfort. Even so, as we will see, such an explanation doesn't account for the remarkable way in which she first was made aware of her paranormal ability! On top of that, those of us who have seen Doris Stokes at work have no doubt that her abilities are indeed absolutely genuine – and very impressive.

There seems no reason to question the genuineness of guru Sai Baba, either. He has been investigated closely by representatives of the Society for Psychical Research, who could find no evidence of chicanery or sleight of hand – and no explanation of any other kind for Baba's production of apports. These range from holy ash, which he materialises by scooping it from the air or taking it from an empty urn, to fully formed medallions and even crucifixes (Baba reveres Christ as a prophet and redeemer). If that kind of activity can be labelled PK, it is PK of a very special kind. Mental control of physical reality is one thing: the capacity actually to *create* material objects seems to be of another order entirely. (If both phenomena seem too unlikely for comfort, it's worth remembering that every time you move a limb – walking to the kitchen because you've decided to make coffee for instance – you are proving that thought can affect the physical world. But there seems to be no simple equivalent like this to creating an apport.) It's scarcely surprising, then, that Sai Baba is regarded as a saint by many people – and not only in his own country; his following is world-wide. But while he may be a miracle man and a wise one at that, his particular kind of wisdom is little help in explaining his extraordinary feats – which set everything we thought we knew about the world on its ear. Sai Baba defeats the laws of space and time – *and* by all the evidence appears to be a reincarnation of another holy man.

This perplexing quality is common to many of the people described in these pages. To have abilities that fly in the face of common sense in just one respect would be unusual enough. But the kind of thing represented by Joan Grant, or the 'Seer of Brahan', Kenneth Odhar, involves so many problems with such fundamental concepts as time, free will, the nature of physical matter, and more besides, that any attempt to unravel the implications leaves the mind reeling not least because there seems nothing certain in the Universe if these things are true.

So it is not surprising that orthodox scientists have found it difficult to take claims for the paranormal seriously. Not only does it undermine everything they believe they have demonstrated about the nature of reality, it is simply terrifying as well. And that in turn tells us a lot about why research into the paranormal is so scarce – and why what little is done comes in for such violent attack.

Not that sometimes scientists don't have a point. Even if on those occasions it doesn't take a person with rigorous scientific training to see the flaws in the case. An instance that springs to mind is Uri Geller's remarkable claim that his powers were in the gift of some form of extra-terrestrial entities. Just why Geller should be singled out for special treatment when so many others with similar abilities were not, was not at all clear. Even supposing we accept in the first place that extra-terrestrials are hovering near our planet, ready to take a helping or hindering hand in our affairs such extravagant ideas do not help the cause of serious research into the paranormal, and they may not have been entirely Geller's own. Quite what the place of Andrej Puharich was in this affair has never been made clear, though it would seem that, even if by accident, Puharich attracts odd events and unusual behaviour. And even if Puharich is in some way a focus *himself* for paranormal events, Geller's metal-bending abilities seem real enough – and have not been explained to anyone's satisfaction, by scientists or anyone else.

Finally, there are three people in this collection whose talents were not strictly speaking paranormal, but whose activities most certainly remain unexplained. They are the Count St Germain, who appears to have wandered around Europe for many more years than one man's natural lifespan; the alchemist Fulcanelli, who seems to have discovered the art of turning base metal into gold – and if he did not, then certainly he discovered something very strange, something that had the strangest effects on him; and the necromancer John Dee who, despite almost certainly being duped by his assistant, nonetheless concocted a form of ritual magic that actually seems to work for its practitioners. Like those with paranormal capacities, these men seem to have tapped some force, power or aspect of the Universe that most people scarcely imagine, let alone glimpse; though it manifested itself in a manner quite different from the other strange talents discussed in this volume.

Perhaps one day we will know what it is that allows such people to act in the way that they do – maybe then we will all be able to develop our own strange talents. After all, every one of us has some musical potential – and can be trained to improve it. Why shouldn't the same be true, given the right way to go about it, of the paranormal?

PETER BROOKESMITH

The self-styled Count St Germain – alchemist, diplomat and adventurer – led a chequered career in the royal courts of 18th-century Europe. Some believe the enigmatic Count is still alive; FRANK SMYTH explores the myths

The man from nowhere

TOWARDS THE END of the year 1745 London was gripped by 'spy fever'. It was the year in which the Young Pretender, Prince Charles Edward Stuart, had staged his Jacobite rebellion in an attempt to regain the British throne for his father. Although the Jacobite cause had been defeated at the battle of Culloden in April, it was feared that Jacobite plotters and their French sympathisers might be in hiding in London. Foreigners, particularly Frenchmen, were prime suspects. One such man was arrested in November and accused of having pro-Stuart letters in his possession. He indignantly claimed that the correspondence had been 'planted' on him and, somewhat surprisingly, he was believed and released.

Commenting on the case in a letter to Sir Horace Mann, dated 9 December, Horace Walpole wrote:

The other day they seized an odd man who goes by the name of Count Saint-Germain. He has been here these two years, and will not tell who he is or whence, but professes that he does not go by his right name. He sings and plays on the violin wonderfully, is mad and not very sensible.

Walpole's comment sheds a tantalising and authentic light on one of the strangest characters of 18th-century high society – a man described by Count Warnstedt as 'the completest charlatan, fool, rattle-pate, windbag and swindler', and by his last patron, Prince Charles of Hesse-Cassel, as 'perhaps one of the greatest sages who ever lived. . . .'

Dazzle of diamonds

The first of the scant historical records of Count St Germain dates from about 1740, when he began to move in fashionable Viennese circles, a handsome man who appeared to be in his thirties. His clothes attracted attention in those days of brightly coloured silks and satins, for he habitually wore black, relieved only by crisp white linen at neck and wrists. The sombreness of his clothes, however, was brilliantly set off by a dazzle of diamonds on his fingers, his fob, his snuff box and his shoe buckles; according to later accounts he also carried handfuls of loose diamonds in his pockets in lieu of money.

In Vienna he met Counts Zabor and Lobkowitz, contemporary leaders of fashion, and through them the ailing French Marshal de Belle Isle, who had been taken seriously ill while campaigning in Germany. The nature of his illness is not recorded, but according to the Marshal it was Count St Germain who

Left: the only known portrait of the man who called himself the Count St Germain, an engraving made for the Marquise d'Urfé in 1783, when the Count must have been in his late sixties, and shortly before his reported death. St Germain was arrested in London as a spy some months after the defeat of the Scottish forces at Culloden in 1745 (below). He was accused of carrying letters for the Young Pretender, Charles Edward Stuart (below left), but was soon released. He then returned to Paris, where he was introduced to Louis XV by Jeanne Antoinette de Pompadour, the king's mistress (right). Sent to the Hague by Louis, St Germain lost the friendship of Giacomo Casanova (below right), who has left us some of the most revealing descriptions of the Count

cured it, and in gratitude he took him to France and set him up with apartments and a well-equipped laboratory.

The bare bones of the Count's life after his arrival in Paris are well documented, but it is the long-vanished detail that provides the lasting mystery.

The legend begins shortly after the Count's arrival in Paris. One evening, according to the pseudonymous 'Countess de B. . .' in her memoirs, *Chroniques de l'oeil de boeuf*, the Count had attended a soirée given by the aged Countess von Georgy, whose late husband had been Ambassador to Venice in the 1670s. Hearing the Count announced, the Countess said she recalled the name from her days in Venice. Had the Count's father perhaps been there at that time? No, replied the Count, but *he* had been, and well remembered the Countess as a beautiful young girl. Impossible, replied the Countess. The man she had known then was 45 at least, roughly the same age as he himself was now.

'Madame,' said the Count, smiling. 'I am very old.'

'But then you must be nearly 100 years old,' exclaimed the Countess.

'That is not impossible,' the Count replied and recounted some details that convinced the Countess, who exclaimed: 'I am already convinced. You are a most extraordinary man, a devil.'

'For pity's sake!' exclaimed the Count in a thundering voice. 'No such names!' He appeared to be seized with a cramp-like trembling in every limb, and left the room immediately.

Many such stories circulated – and were believed – in fashionable French circles during the days of the Count's early fame. He hinted, for instance, that he had known the Holy Family intimately, had been present at the marriage feast at Cana, and had 'always

known that Christ would meet a bad end.' He had been particularly fond of Anne, the mother of the Virgin Mary, and had personally proposed her canonisation at the Council of Nicaea in AD 325.

In Paris the Count soon charmed the jaded Louis XV and his mistress, Madame de Pompadour. The truth about his two-year stay in England before his arrest in 1745 may never be known, but he could well have been engaged on a secret mission; on his return to France he carried out several delicate political errands for the King.

In 1760 Louis sent Count St Germain to the Hague as his own personal representative, ostensibly to arrange a loan with Austria to help finance the Seven Years' War against England. While in Holland, the Count fell out with his erstwhile friend Casanova, also a diplomat at the Hague, who tried hard but unsuccessfully to discredit him in public. But St Germain also made a more powerful enemy. The Duc de Choiseul, Louis's Foreign Minister, discovered that the Count had been putting out feelers with a view to arranging peace between England and France. Somehow the Duke convinced Louis that Count St Germain had betrayed him, and the Count was forced to flee, first back to England and then to Holland.

For two or three years he lived in Holland under the name Count Surmont and set about raising money to build laboratories in which he made paint and dyes and tried to perfect the techniques of alchemy, 'the ennoblement of metals'. He seems to have been successful, for records show that he disappeared from Holland with 100,000 guilders – only to turn up in Belgium, this time calling himself the Marquis de Monferrat. Here, in Tournai, he set up another laboratory before vanishing again.

Over the next few years reports of the

Count's activities continued to come from various parts of Europe. In 1768 he appeared in Russia at the court of Catherine the Great. Turkey had just declared war on Russia, and it seems that his powers as a diplomat and as an insider in French politics stood him in good stead, for before long he was advising Count Alexei Orlov, head of the Russian Imperial Forces. As a reward he was made a high-ranking officer in the Russian Army, this time choosing an ironic English alias – General Welldone. At this point he could have settled down in Russia to lead an honoured and profitable life, but after the defeat of the Turks at the battle of Chesmé in 1770 he chose to go travelling again.

In 1774 he turned up in Nuremberg, seeking funds from Charles Alexander, Margrave of Brandenburg, to set up another laboratory. This time he claimed to be Prince Rákóczy, one of three brothers from Transylvania. At first the Margrave was impressed, particularly when Count Orlov visited Nuremberg on a state visit and embraced the

were lame. The Prince declared he was not a Mason, while the Count feebly replied that he was, but had forgotten all the secret signs.

In 1779 Count St Germain came to his last known resting place, at Eckenförde in Schleswig, Germany. He was an old man, probably in his late sixties, although typically he claimed to be much older. Some of his surface charm had gone, and at first he failed to make much impression on Prince Charles of Hesse-Cassel – but soon, like his predecessors, the Prince was won over.

By this time St Germain, who by all accounts had previously paid at least lip service to the Catholic Church, was openly mystical in his thinking. He told Prince Charles:

> Be the torch of the world. If your light is that only of a planet, you will be as nothing in the sight of God. I reserve for you a splendour, of which the solar glory is a shadow. You shall guide the course of the stars, and those who rule Empires shall be guided by you.

Parish records show that on 27 February 1784 Count St Germain died at Prince Charles's home on Eckenförde. He was buried locally, and his last patron erected a tombstone bearing the words:

> He who called himself the Comte de Saint-Germain and Welldone of whom there is no other information, has been buried in this church.

But was the Count dead? There is evidence that he appeared to a number of people over the years from 1784 to 1820; some occultists believe he is still alive. The mystery has lived on and deepened in the two centuries since his supposed death.

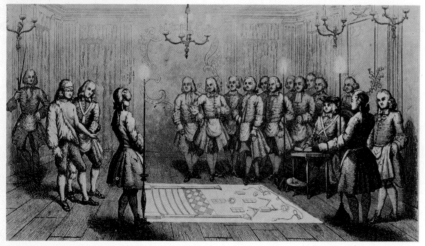

Following his exile from France, Count St Germain went to the court of Catherine the Great of Russia (top), where he soon achieved high standing as a diplomat and took the title of 'General Welldone'. Towards the end of his career he began to claim that he was a high-ranking Freemason. The illustration (above) shows the ceremony of the entered Apprentice, the first degree of masonry, in the 'Scottish' rite, in a Paris lodge during the 1740s. Laid on the floor is a 'tracing board', used to instruct the new member in the symbolism of masonry

Right: Prince Charles of Hesse-Cassel, the Count's last patron, in whose castle he died

'Prince' warmly. But on checking, the Margrave found that all three Rákóczys were indubitably dead, and that the 'Prince' was in fact Count St Germain. The Count made no attempt to deny these charges, but felt it prudent to move on, and did so in 1776.

The Duc de Choiseul claimed that St Germain had worked as a double agent for Frederick the Great during his period at the French court. If this were so, his old master preferred to forget the connection, for a letter from Count St Germain to Frederick begging for patronage was ignored. Undaunted, the Count went to Leipzig and presented himself before Prince Frederick Augustus of Brunswick, claiming to be a Freemason of the fourth grade.

This was a bold move, for Frederick Augustus was Grand Master of the Prussian Masonic Lodges – and, unaccountably, it was a move that went wrong. If he was a confidence trickster, Count St Germain in his prime had few equals at the game; his background stories generally stood up to close scrutiny. This time, however, they

Searching for St Germain

Fluent linguist, 'wonderful' musician and painter, gifted jeweller, healer – the talents of the Count St Germain seemed endless. FRANK SMYTH concludes his account of the adventurer's remarkable career

Above: '. . . intended by nature to be the king of impostors', as Casanova described him, Count St Germain claimed to know all the secrets of alchemy, including the nature of the Elixir of Life. He set up numerous laboratories in different countries in Europe; they would have looked very like this alchemist's laboratory portrayed by Pietro Longhi

THE MYSTERY surrounding the Count St Germain is deepened by the genuine uncertainty about his origins, which remains today. One account states that he was born in 1710 in San Germano, the son of a tax collector. Eliphas Levi, the 19th century occultist, claimed that St Germain was born in Lentmeritz in Bohemia, the bastard son of a noble Rosicrucian, at the end of the 17th century. The date fits, and the background would account for the Count's strong leaning towards mysticism as well as his formidable talents – even if they were not 'powers' in the paranormal sense of the word.

He had, for instance, a genuine gift for languages; it is known that he spoke fluent French, German, English, Dutch and Russian, and he claimed that he was also a master of Chinese, Hindu and Persian – although there can have been few people around with sufficient knowledge of these languages to challenge him.

Horace Walpole wrote that the Count was a 'wonderful' musician. He was also a 'wonderful' painter – although none of his canvases are known to have survived. The uniqueness of his oils seems to have lain in the fact that he could reproduce jewels which 'glittered . . . as in the life'.

There is plenty of evidence that St Germain was an expert jeweller – although not, as he claimed, that he had studied the art with the Shah of Persia. He is reported to have delighted Louis XV by repairing a flawed diamond and it may well be that he decorated his famous jewel paintings with mother-of-pearl or some such substance.

He also had an excellent knowledge of chemistry in all its branches; the many laboratories that he set up with borrowed money throughout Europe were all apparently devoted to the production of brighter and better pigments and dyes, as well as to the study of the ennoblement of metals – alchemy.

St Germain also had a reputation as a healer; besides curing the Marshal de Belle Isle, he revived a young friend of Madame de Pompadour after mushroom poisoning had almost killed her.

The Count was reputed never to eat in company – he sat and sipped mineral water

Below: St Germain claimed to have studied the art of jewellery at the court of the Shah of Persia, where he is said to have lived from 1737 to 1742. The many fantastic claims made by the Count, and the persistent stories that he was alive well into the 19th century, caused Napoleon III (below right) to set up a special commission to enquire into the matter. The findings of the commission were, however, completely destroyed in a fire at the Hotel de Ville, Paris, in 1871 (below, far right), an event that the supporters of the Count's story maintained was not an accident

while everyone around him was gorging in the self-indulgent manner of the time. This can only have added to his air of mystery. Casanova was certainly impressed:

> Instead of eating, he talked from the beginning of the meal to the end, and I followed his example in one respect as I did not eat, but listened to him with the greatest attention. It may safely be said that as a conversationalist he was unequalled.

In fact, as Colin Wilson points out in *The occult*, the Count was probably simply a vegetarian.

The real remaining mystery surrounding the legend of St Germain lies in the question of where he gained all his specialised knowledge. Again there is a simple answer: experience. The Count's 19th-century followers insisted that the knowledge was his when he first appeared at the French court in the 1740s, but it is more likely that he amassed it

during his long life; after all, he lived at least into his seventies.

Not all of St Germain's contemporaries were impressed by his talents. Casanova, who met him in the Hague when they were both on diplomatic missions there, regarded him as a charlatan, but nevertheless found him charming:

> This extraordinary man, intended by nature to be the king of impostors and quacks, would say in an easy, assured manner that he was three hundred years old, that he knew the secret of the Universal Medicine, that he possessed a mastery over nature, that he could melt diamonds, professing himself capable of forming, out of 10 or 12 small diamonds, one of the finest water . . . All this, he said, was a mere trifle to him. Notwithstanding his boastings, his bare-faced lies, and his manifold eccentricities, I cannot say I found him offensive. In spite of my knowledge of what he was and in spite of my own feelings, I thought him an astonishing man . . .

And in 1777 Count Alvensleben, Prussian Ambassador to the Court at Dresden, who knew St Germain well, wrote of him:

> He is a highly gifted man with a very alert mind, but completely without judgement, and he has only gained his singular reputation by the lowest and basest flattery of which a man is capable, as well as by his outstanding eloquence, especially if one lets oneself be carried away by the fervour and enthusiasm with which he can express himself. Inordinate vanity is the mainspring driving his whole mechanism.

Many of the stories about St Germain that gave rise to these sceptical attitudes did not actually stem from the Count himself but, as was revealed by the researches of Gustav Berthold Volz in the 1920s, from the mouth of an impostor named Gauve. Gauve was

Left: Louis XVI says farewell to his family, as the gaoler waits to lead him to the guillotine. In her diaries the Queen, Marie Antoinette, regretted that she had not paid heed to St Germain's warnings.

Below left: the famous French singer Emma Calvé autographed this photograph in 1897 to St Germain, 'the great chiromancer, who has told me many truths'.

Below right: Richard Chanfray, a Parisian claiming to be Count St Germain, photographed in 1976

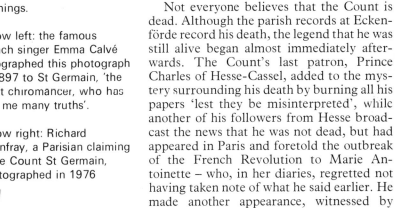

employed by St Germain's arch-enemy, the Duc de Choiseul, who, in his jealousy of the Count, would stop at nothing in his attempts to discredit him. The idea was that Gauve, who looked remarkably like the Count, should wander around society exaggerating the Count's known foibles to discredit him.

Not everyone believes that the Count is dead. Although the parish records at Eckenförde record his death, the legend that he was still alive began almost immediately afterwards. The Count's last patron, Prince Charles of Hesse-Cassel, added to the mystery surrounding his death by burning all his papers 'lest they be misinterpreted', while another of his followers from Hesse broadcast the news that he was not dead, but had appeared in Paris and foretold the outbreak of the French Revolution to Marie Antoinette – who, in her diaries, regretted not having taken note of what he said earlier. He made another appearance, witnessed by many people, at Wilhelmsbad in 1785, a year after his supposed death – accompanied, so it was said, by the magician Cagliostro, the hypnotist Anton Mesmer, and the 'unknown philosopher', Louis Claude de St Martin.

In 1789 he went to Sweden to warn King Gustavus III of danger, and visited his friend, the diarist Mademoiselle d'Adhémar – who noted that he still looked like a man of 46 – and told her that he would see her five times more. She claimed that this did, indeed, happen – 'always to my unspeakable surprise' – the last occasion being the night before the Duc de Berri's murder in 1820.

The legend lives on

The Emperor Napoleon III (1808–1873) was so intrigued by the story that he ordered a special commission to be set up to investigate the life and doings of the enigmatic Count. The commission's findings were destroyed in a disastrous fire that consumed the Hôtel de Ville in Paris in 1871 – an event that the Count's followers found impossible to ascribe to coincidence.

A few years later Madame Blavatsky's Theosophical Society announced that St Germain was one of its 'hidden masters' – immortals whose stores of secret knowledge were available to adepts for the enrichment of the world – along with such figures as Christ, Buddha, Apollonius of Tyana, Christian Rosencreutz and Francis Bacon. It is said that a group of theosophists went to Paris after its liberation from the Nazis, convinced they would meet the Count; apparently he failed to turn up.

Nevertheless, the legend of this enigmatic figure lives on. As recently as January 1972 a Parisian called Richard Chanfray appeared on French television claiming to be the Count St Germain. In front of the TV cameras, using a camping gas stove, he apparently successfully turned lead into gold. Will the Count appear again? Time only deepens the mystery of his true nature.

Croiset: the psychic detective

The Dutch clairvoyant and healer Gerard Croiset was often successful in locating missing persons – dead or alive – and frequently made the headlines for his work with the police. ROY STEMMAN outlines the life and work of this remarkable psychic

EIGHT WEEKS after his 24-year-old daughter Carol had disappeared, Professor Walter E. Sandelius was prepared to try anything to find her. Carol had disappeared from a hospital in Topeka, Kansas, USA, and although photographs of the attractive young woman had been circulated throughout the country she was still missing.

Walter Sandelius, a professor of political science at the University of Kansas, had read about the Dutch clairvoyant and healer Gerard Croiset, who had a reputation for finding missing people – dead or alive – and solving crimes with his psychic powers.

So, on 11 December 1959, with no other immediate hope of finding his daughter, he telephoned Utrecht University. He spoke to Professor Willem Tenhaeff, the parapsychologist who had spent many years studying Croiset, and arranged to call again the following day when the clairvoyant would be in Tenhaeff's office.

When he did so, Croiset told the Kansas professor: 'I see your daughter running over a large lawn and then crossing a viaduct. Now I see her at a place where there are stores, and near them a large body of water with landing stages and many small boats. I see her riding there in a lorry and in a big red car.'

'Is she still alive?' asked the anxious father.

'Yes, don't worry,' said Croiset. 'You will hear something definite at the end of six days.'

On the sixth day, as arranged with Croiset, Professor Sandelius went downstairs at 8 a.m. to telephone Tenhaeff. As he picked up the telephone he glanced towards the living room and was astonished to see his daughter sitting on the sofa! Subsequent questioning of the Dutch clairvoyant proved that he had successfully 'seen' across nearly 5000 miles (8000 kilometres) and described Carol's movements with impressive accuracy.

This is one of hundreds of such cases that were investigated and kept on file at Utrecht University. Many were described in Jackson Harrison Pollack's book, *Croiset, the clairvoyant*. But not all had such happy endings. Croiset was often the first person to break the news to relatives that a missing person was dead. Sadly in many of the cases they were children who had fallen into Holland's waterway system and drowned.

The father of five children, Croiset was

Left: Croiset using an electronic version of the Zener card experiment, designed to test the powers of precognition. Croiset's guesses were often significantly above average

Below: Croiset tells the Dutch police in 1963: 'The body is there – you can look for it.' He had located the body of a missing boy in the Vliet Canal through psychic means alone

always eager to help distraught parents whose sons or daughters had disappeared, and he refused to take any money for his psychic work.

In the case of one missing boy, Wimpje Slee, Croiset told an uncle over the telephone that he had fallen into the water and drowned, and that his body would be found near a bridge. Then, on Friday 19 April 1963, in order to get stronger impressions, he met the boy's uncle and was able to tell him that Wimpje had drowned near a small house with a slanted weather-vane. But, he added, his body was no longer there. It would be found, however, on Tuesday, between two bridges near the house described.

Newspapers in The Hague heard of the story and published Croiset's prediction the following day, enabling their readers to check for themselves. On Tuesday, 23 April – just as Croiset had foretold – Wimpje's body was discovered floating on the Vliet Canal, precisely where the clairvoyant had said it would be found. Not surprisingly, the *Haagsche Courant* headlined its story: 'Croiset proved right once more'.

Pictures of Croiset's craggy features and wiry hair frequently appeared in European and Scandinavian newspapers. He assisted the police to look for missing persons in half a dozen countries and co-operated in tests conducted by leading psychical researchers. But it was to Professor Tenhaeff that he was particularly loyal.

A star performer

Of the 47 psychics and sensitives tested by the professor, Croiset was undoubtedly the star performer. Unlike other clairvoyants who shun research work, Croiset moved to Utrecht in 1956 in order to be closer to the university and to make himself more readily available. And when grateful individuals offered him money for helping to find lost friends or relatives he always declined, saying the only 'reward' he wanted was for them to file a report of what happened with Professor Tenhaeff. As a result, the Utrecht archives must contain some of the best authenticated accounts of clairvoyance on record.

Despite the research work, however, Croiset never really knew how his psychic power functioned. He once described it as like seeing a fine powder, which formed first into dots and then lines. Out of these lines shapes and scenes would form, first in two dimensions then in three. Usually his clairvoyance was in black and white, but if a corpse was involved he would see pictures in colour.

Croiset's involvement in police investigations tends to make his popular image a distorted one. Although he was undoubtedly a brilliant psychic detective, he was hesitant about working on certain cases of murder and theft for fear that he would wrong an innocent person. For example, at the site of a murder he might describe a person in great

Professor Tenhaeff of Utrecht University and the Utrecht Chief of Police are pictured here with Gerard Croiset. They were a regular team, Croiset helping the police in their search for missing persons and Professor Tenhaeff monitoring the clairvoyant's progress. Few psychics have been as rigorously tested as Croiset

detail who was not the murderer, but an innocent passer-by. In fact, Croiset said that in 90 per cent of criminal cases he found it difficult to discover the culprit, though he was able to give police valuable clues. On the other hand, in cases of accidental disappearances it is claimed that Croiset had an 80 per cent success rate.

But it was not necessary for Croiset to wait for crimes to be committed or for people to vanish in order to prove that he possessed extra-sensory powers. Instead, Professor Tenhaeff devised a 'chair test', which was repeated with astonishing accuracy over 20 years or more. It demonstrated that Croiset could apparently see into the near future.

It worked like this: a week or more in advance of a large public meeting, Croiset would be asked to make written statements about the person who would sit in a specific seat. On the day of the meeting, individuals would be allowed to sit where they wanted (no one knowing which chair had been selected) or were given numbered tickets at random as they arrived directing them to sit in certain seats. Then Croiset's predictions would be read to the audience. Time and again, the unsuspecting person sitting in the pre-selected seat confirmed that the majority of the statements Croiset had made were correct. These would often consist of the person's sex, a physical description and details of their work, people around them, or descriptions of specific incidents in their life. Occasionally, Croiset could get no advance impressions – in which case it was usually discovered that the seat was left unoccupied on the night.

Gerard Croiset died on 20 July 1980, at the age of 71. But the records on file at Utrecht University of the world's most tested psychic will continue to intrigue and baffle scientists for many years to come.

Tom Lethbridge

Tom Lethbridge is a major figure in the world of the paranormal, but, as COLIN WILSON explains, he took many years of painstaking academic and practical research to reach his important conclusions

NO ONE WHO IS interested in the paranormal can afford to ignore Tom Lethbridge, yet when he died in a nursing home in Devon in 1971, his name was hardly known to the general public. Today, many of his admirers believe that he is the single most important name in the history of psychical research. His ideas on dowsing, life after death, ghosts, poltergeists, magic, second-sight, precognition, the nature of time, cover a wider field than those of any other psychical researcher. Moreover, they fit together into the most exciting and comprehensive theory of the 'occult' ever advanced.

These ideas were expressed in a series of small books published in the last 10 years of his life. The odd thing is that Lethbridge took no interest in psychic matters until he retired to Devon in his mid fifties. He was trained as an archaeologist and a historian, and spent most of his adult life in Cambridge as the Keeper of Anglo-Saxon Antiquities at the University Museum. But even in that respectable setting he was a maverick, and in 1957 he left Cambridge in disgust at the

Above: Tom and Mina Lethbridge were keen – and accomplished – dowsers

Below: Ladram Bay, Devon, where people felt a strong urge to jump off the cliffs

hostile reception of one of his books on archaeology. Together with his wife Mina, he moved into Hole House, an old Tudor mansion on the south coast of Devon. He meant to spend his retirement reading and digging for bits of broken pottery. In fact, the most amazing period of his eventful life was about to begin.

The person who was most responsible for this change of direction was an old 'witch' who lived next door. This white haired little old lady assured Lethbridge that she could put mild spells on people who annoyed her, and that she was able to leave her body at night and wander around the district – an ability known as 'astral projection'. Lethbridge was naturally sceptical – until something convinced him.

The witch explained to him one day how she managed to put off unwanted visitors. What she did was to draw a five pointed star – a pentagram – in her head, and then visualise it across the path of the unwanted visitor – for example, on the front gate.

Shortly afterwards, Tom was lying in bed, idly drawing pentagrams in his head, and imagining them around their beds. In the middle of the night, Mina woke up with a creepy feeling that there was somebody else in the room. At the foot of the bed, she could see a faint glow of light, which slowly faded

A seeker after truth

as she watched it. The next day, the witch came to see them. When she told them that she had 'visited' their bedroom on the previous night, and found the beds surrounded by triangles of fire, Tom's scepticism began to evaporate. Mina politely requested the old witch to stay out of their bedroom at night.

Three years later, the old lady died in peculiar circumstances. She was quarrelling with a neighbouring farmer, and told Lethbridge that she intended to put a spell on the man's cattle. By this time, Lethbridge knew enough about the 'occult' to take her seriously, and he warned her about the dangers of black magic – how it could rebound on to the witch. But the old lady ignored his advice. One morning, she was found dead in her bed in circumstances that made the police suspect murder. And the cattle of two nearby farms suddenly got foot and mouth disease. However, the farmer she wanted to 'ill wish' remained unaffected. Lethbridge was convinced that the spell had gone wrong and 'bounced back'.

The invisible world

But the old lady's death resulted – indirectly – in one of his most important insights. Passing the witch's cottage, he experienced a 'nasty feeling', a suffocating sense of depression. With a scientist's curiosity, he walked around the cottage, and noticed an interesting thing. He could step *into* the depression and then out of it again, just as if it was some kind of invisible wall.

The depression reminded Lethbridge of something that had happened when he was a teenager. He and his mother had gone for a walk in the Great Wood near Wokingham. It was a lovely morning; yet quite suddenly, both of them experienced 'a horrible feeling of gloom and depression, which crept upon us like a blanket of fog over the surface of the sea'. They hurried away, agreeing that it was something terrible and inexplicable. A few days later, the corpse of a suicide was found a few yards from the spot where they had been standing, hidden by some bushes.

About a year after the death of the witch, another strange experience gave Tom the clue he was looking for. On a damp January afternoon, he and Mina drove down to Ladram Bay to collect seaweed for her garden. As Lethbridge stepped on to the beach, he once again experienced the feeling of gloom and fear, like a blanket of fog descending upon him. Mina wandered off along the beach while Tom filled the sacks with seaweed. Suddenly she came hurrying back, saying: 'Let's go. I can't stand this place a minute longer. There's something frightful here.'

The next day, they mentioned what had happened to Mina's brother. He said he also had experienced the same kind of thing in a field near Avebury, in Wiltshire. The word 'field' made something connect in Tom's brain – he remembered that field telephones

Above: Hole Mill and Hole House in Devon. Hole Mill was the home of Lethbridge's neighbour, a 'witch' or 'wise woman' whose strange powers convinced Lethbridge that the world of the paranormal was worth investigating. Hole House became the Lethbridges' home after Tom left Cambridge in disgust at the reception of one of his books. Here he was to develop his theories on psychic phenomena until his death in 1971

often short-circuit in warm, muggy weather. 'What was the weather like?' he asked. 'Warm and damp,' said the brother.

An idea was taking shape. *Water . . .* could that be the key? It had been warm and damp in the Great Wood. It had been warm and damp on Ladram beach. The following weekend, they set out for Ladram Bay a second time. Again, as they stepped on to the beach, both walked into the same bank of depression – or 'ghoul' as Lethbridge called it. Mina led Tom to the far end of the beach, to the place she had been sitting when she had been overwhelmed by the strange feeling. Here it was so strong that it made them feel giddy – Lethbridge described it as the feeling you get when you have a high temperature and are full of drugs. On either side of them were two small streams.

Mina wandered off to look at the scenery from the top of the cliff. Suddenly, she walked into the depression again. Moreover, she had an odd feeling, as if someone – or something – was urging her to jump over. She went and fetched Tom, who agreed that the spot was just as sinister as the place down on the seashore below.

Now he needed only one more piece of the jigsaw puzzle, and he found it – but only years later. Nine years after the first known experiences of depression were felt on those cliffs a man did commit suicide there. Lethbridge wondered whether the 'ghoul' was a feeling so intense that it had become timeless and imprinted itself on the area, casting its baleful shadow on those who stood there.

Whether from the past or from the future the feelings of despair were 'recorded' on the surroundings – but how?

The key, Lethbridge believed, was water. As an archaeologist, he had always been mildly interested in dowsing and water-divining. The dowser walks along with a forked hazel twig held in his hands, and when he stands above running water, the muscles in his hands and arms convulse and the twig bends either up or down. How does it work? Professor Y. Rocard of the Sorbonne discovered that underground water produces changes in the earth's magnetic field, and this is what the dowser's muscles respond to. The water does this because it has a field of its own, which interacts with the earth's field.

Significantly, magnetic fields are the means by which sound is recorded on tape covered with iron oxide. Suppose the magnetic field of running water can also record strong emotions – which, after all, are basically electrical activities in the human brain and body? Such fields could well be strongest in damp and muggy weather.

Magnetic emotions

This would also explain why the banks of depression seem to form a kind of invisible wall. Anyone who has ever tried bringing a magnet closer and closer to an iron nail will know that the nail is suddenly 'seized' by the magnet as it enters the force field. Presumably the magnetic field of water has the same property. And if it can 'tape record' powerful emotions, then you would feel them quite suddenly, as you stepped into the field. Both Tom and Mina noticed that the ghoul on Ladram beach came to an end quite abruptly

And what about 'ghosts' – that is, things actually seen, rather than just sensed? Here again, Lethbridge was convinced that his electrical theory fitted the facts. In 1922 – when he was an undergraduate at Cambridge – he had seen a ghost in the rooms of a friend. He was just about to leave, late at night, when the door opened and a man wearing a top hat came in. Assuming he was a college porter who had come to give his friend a message, Lethbridge said goodnight, and went out. The man did not reply. The next morning, Lethbridge saw his friend, and asked casually about the identity of the man in the top hat. His friend flatly denied that anyone had come in. And when Lethbridge brooded on it, he realised that the man had not worn a porter's uniform. He wore hunting kit. Then why had he not recognised the red coat? Because it wasn't red; it was grey – a dull grey, like a black and white *photograph*. Lethbridge realised that he had seen a ghost. Moreover, his friend's rooms overlooked the river, so there was a damp atmosphere.

Tom had seen a ghost in the witch's garden, in the year before she died. He had been sitting on the hillside, looking down at the witch's house, when he noticed two women in the yard. One was the witch; the other was a tall old lady dressed in rather old-fashioned grey clothes. Later, he saw the witch and asked her about her visitor. The witch looked puzzled; then, when Lethbridge described the figure, said, 'Ah, you've seen my ghost.'

This happened in 1959, before Lethbridge had his important insight on Ladram beach. So it never entered his head that the ghost was a 'tape recording'. His first

Left: map showing the position of the ghost at Hole Mill in relation to the underground stream and its field of force. Lethbridge plotted the area 'blind' with his hazel twig. Later excavation showed this plot to be correct in every detail

Right: the 'witch's' house, Hole Mill, as seen from Hole House. This was the spot where Lethbridge saw the ghost of an old lady and experienced a curious tingling sensation when he stood over an underground stream. He later discovered that the two experiences were connected

Below: the Reverend Bishop Leonidas Polk, who intrigued Professor Joseph Buchanan in the 1840s by being able to detect brass in the dark simply by touching it with his fingers

thought was that the old lady in grey might be some kind of thought projection – in other words, a kind of television picture, caused by someone else *thinking* about the ghost, and somehow transferring the thought into his own mind. Then it struck him that ghosts are supposed to reappear on anniversaries. So he and Mina decided they would go to the same spot at the same time the following year, and see what happened.

In fact, nothing happened. They stood quietly at the same spot, on a fine, warm morning, but the old lady failed to reappear. However, both of them noticed a kind of electrical tingling feeling in the atmosphere. There was a tiny underground stream running down the lane – under a drain cover – and they felt the tingling most strongly when they stood on top of it. Tom would only realise the significance of that tingling feeling after his experience on Ladram beach. And then he decided to explore the stream and see where it led. The result confirmed his suspicions. The stream turned at right angles quite close to the witch's house. And it was directly above this stream that he had seen the old lady in grey. He had been connected to the spot by the magnetic field of the flowing water. But the witch, standing a few yards away from the underground stream, had seen nothing.

So Lethbridge had been quite mistaken to believe that his 'old lady' was some kind of television picture projected by someone else's mind, or a ghost that would return exactly a year later. It was almost certainly just another 'tape recording' – a kind of videotape recording this time – but in black and white, just like the huntsman he had seen in his friend's rooms at Cambridge.

It would be very satisfying to be able to add that he decided to investigate the apparitions, and found that a huntsman had died of apoplexy in the room in Cambridge, or that the old lady had drowned in the underground stream. No such neat, satisfactory solutions can be provided. And neither is it necessary. The huntsman had probably been a previous inhabitant of the rooms; the old lady had probably lived most of her life in Hole Mill – the witch's house. (From her clothes, Lethbridge thought she dated back to before the First World War.) But there is no earthly reason why the 'force field' of water should record only unpleasant emotions. The old lady might have been unusually happy or excited when she was 'photographed' on the field. Or perhaps she passed over the spot so often that her image finally became indelibly imprinted there.

How much evidence is there for the Lethbridge theory of ghosts and ghouls? Well, to begin with, it is worth noting that his 'tape recording' theory was by no means new. In America in the 1840s, a professor named Joseph Rhodes Buchanan was intrigued when a certain Bishop Polk told him that he could

A diagram showing the 'psyche-field' around a tree, plotted with a hazel twig. The shaded area shows the limits of the force field that can be 'picked up' by a dowser

A Hawaiian volcano erupting. In the mid 19th century William Denton gave a piece of volcanic rock to a sensitive who 'saw' a volcano exploding. This was one of the first serious experiments into psychometry – or object reading – and its results had far-reaching implications for dowsing

detect brass in the dark by touching it with his fingers; it produced an unpleasant taste in his mouth. Buchanan tested him and found it was true. He discovered that certain of his students also had the same curious ability. In fact, some of them could even detect different substances when they were wrapped up in brown paper. Buchanan decided that the nerves produce some kind of force field – he called it the 'nerve aura' – which streams out of the finger ends, and which operates like an extra sense.

A strange talent

What really puzzled him was that some of his sensitives could hold a sealed letter, and describe the person who had written it, and whether the writer was sad or happy at the time. Buchanan explained this by suggesting that all substances give off emanations (another name for a force field) on which human emotions can be recorded. He had stumbled on Lethbridge's theory just about 100 years before Lethbridge.

Buchanan's friend William Denton, a professor of geology, took the theory even further. He tried wrapping a piece of Hawaiian volcanic rock in paper and handing it to a sensitive, who immediately saw in his mind an island in the midst of blue seas, and an exploding volcano. When handed a pebble of glacial limestone, the sensitive saw it frozen in deep ice. A fragment of meteor produced a picture of the depths of space, with glittering stars. Denton was so excited by all this that he believed he had discovered a new – or forgotten – human faculty, and that one day we shall be able to look back into the past just as easily as we can now look at the stars (which may have died millions of years ago) through a telescope.

Buchanan and Denton called this strange faculty *psychometry*, and for a few years it caused considerable excitement in the scientific world. Then, with the coming of Darwin, T. H. Huxley and the rest, a more sceptical climate prevailed, and it was forgotten. Even so, Sir Oliver Lodge, the notable scientist who dared to be interested in psychical research, wrote in 1908:

> Take, for example, a haunted house . . . wherein some one room is the scene of a ghostly representation of some long past tragedy. On a psychometric hypothesis, the original tragedy has been literally *photographed* on its material surroundings, nay, even on the ether itself, by reason of the intensity of emotion felt by those who enacted it.

It may seem, then, that Lethbridge's discovery was not so remarkable after all. That would be a mistake. For it was only a part of a far more comprehensive and more important theory of the paranormal.

The master dowser

During his career as an archaeologist Tom Lethbridge discovered dowsing – 'picking up' electrical fields of objects and reacting to them. But this fascinating ability was only the beginning of an important series of experiments

ALTHOUGH TOM LETHBRIDGE had no interest in ghosts or 'ghouls' before he retired to Devon, he had always been fascinated by dowsing.

It all started in the early 1930s, when he and another archaeologist were looking for Viking graves on the island of Lundy in the Bristol Channel. They located the graves, then, having time on their hands while they waited for the boat back to the mainland, they decided to try some experiments with dowsing. Hidden under the soil of Lundy Island are seams of volcanic rock that pass up through the slate. Lethbridge decided to see if he could locate these. So he cut himself a hazel twig, allowed his friend to blindfold him, and was then led along the cliff path, the forked hazel twig held tightly in his hands. (The twig has to be held with the forks bent slightly apart, so it has a certain amount of 'spring'.) Every time he passed over a volcanic seam, the hazel fork twisted violently in his hands. His friend had an extra-sensitive

Above: Tom Lethbridge, the archaeologist who became a master dowser

Top: the island of Lundy in the Bristol Channel, where Lethbridge conducted his first experiment into dowsing. Using a forked hazel twig, he and a colleague dowsed for volcanic seams. The hazel twig located the seams by twisting violently when held over them

magnetometer, so he was able to verify that Lethbridge had accurately located every single one of the volcanic seams.

To Lethbridge, that seemed logical enough. Like running water, a volcanic seam has a faint magnetic field. Presumably he was somehow able to pick up these fields through the hazel twig, which reacted like a sensitive instrument. In one of his earlier books he wrote: 'Most people can dowse, if they know how to do it. If they cannot do it, there is probably some fault in the electrical system of their bodies.'

The garden of Lethbridge's house in Devon was full of interesting archaeological remains – some of them dating to Roman times. And, soon after moving in, Lethbridge remembered an experiment he had seen performed in the University Museum of Archaeology and Ethnology in Cambridge. Someone had asserted that a pendulum can tell whether a skull is male or female, and demonstrated this by dangling one over an ancient skull. The pendulum swung back and forth, which meant – apparently – that it was a man's skull. If it had swung round in a circle, the skull would have been female. Midwives sometimes use the same method to determine the sex of an unborn baby, dangling a wedding ring on a piece of thread over the stomach of the pregnant woman.

But how can such a method possibly work? It sounds completely absurd. Male and female skulls do not have electrical fields; and even if they did, there is no reason why one of them should make a pendulum swing back and forth, and the other make it swing in a circle.

With characteristic thoroughness, Lethbridge set out to test it for himself. His first question was: if a pendulum can somehow respond to different substances, then how does it do it? A pendulum is, after all, just a weight fixed to the end of a piece of string. It must be the unconscious mind – or possibly the muscles – of the dowser that respond. But respond to what? The answer seemed to be: to some kind of vibration. In which case, it seems a fair assumption that different lengths of the pendulum respond to different vibrations.

It was the most fruitful assumption he ever made. And he set out to test it by putting a wooden bob on the end of a long piece of string, and then winding the string round a

pencil, so he could lengthen or shorten the pendulum at will. Next, he put a piece of silver on the ground, held the pendulum over it, and then carefully began to lengthen the string. And, when he had unwound about 2 feet (60 centimetres), the pendulum suddenly began to go into a circular swing. Lethbridge measured his string. It was precisely 22 inches. (Lethbridge believed one could dowse successfully only using Imperial measurements. Feet and inches, he said, were 'natural' measurements based on the human body, whereas metric measurements were 'unnatural'. So pendulum 'rates' will be given in inches only.)

The pendulum reacts

Next, he went out into the courtyard of Hole House – which dates back to Tudor times – and walked around with his pendulum. At one place, it went into a circular swing. Lethbridge dug down carefully, and eventually located a small piece of Rhineland stoneware pottery. He tried his pendulum over it; it went into a powerful circular swing. That puzzled him greatly, until he tried his 22-inch pendulum over a piece of lead, and it also went into a circular swing. Apparently, 22 inches is the 'rate' for both silver and lead. And Rhineland pottery in the 17th century was glazed with lead.

Now very excited, Lethbridge kept the pendulum at the same length and walked round the courtyard until it went again into a circular swing. He dug down, and found a bit of lead from an Elizabethan window. So he proved that the pendulum was accurate. He tried holding the pendulum over a copper pot, and found that it reacted at $30\frac{1}{2}$ inches. He walked around the courtyard until the pendulum responded, and this time, dug up a tiny copper tube. It was very small, so evidently the pendulum was extremely sensitive.

Convinced that he had made a major discovery, Lethbridge spent days testing all kinds of different substances with his pendulum and discovered, to his delight, that every one of them had its own 'rate': glass, sulphur, iron, slate, amber – even alcohol, garlic and apples. When he held it over a bottle of Australian Burgundy, the pendulum responded at 14, 20, $25\frac{1}{2}$ and 32 inches, which Lethbridge proved to be the 'rates' for glass, vegetable matter (the label), alcohol and iron.

He even tested a truffle – that delicious fungus that is used in *foie gras*. The pendulum responded at 17 inches. Trying to locate any buried truffles, Lethbridge stood with his pendulum in one hand, while pointing his other hand around in a slow semicircle. When the 17-inch pendulum began to swing, he drew a straight line in the direction he was pointing. Then he went and stood several yards away, and repeated the experiment. Where the two lines crossed, he dug down with a trowel. He located a tiny, dark

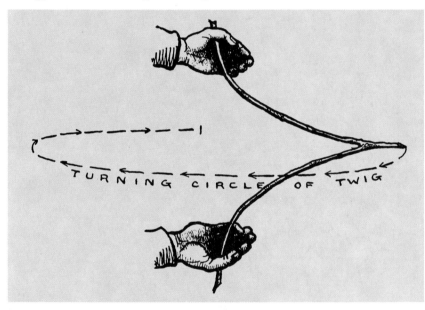

Above: the characteristic movement of a forked hazel twig when actively dowsing. Its usual – though not invariable – reaction when held over a subterranean stream, for example, is to turn in a circle from right to left

Left: the late S. J. Searles of North Cray, Kent, showing the power of the hazel twig as it pulls downwards when reacting to the presence of underground water

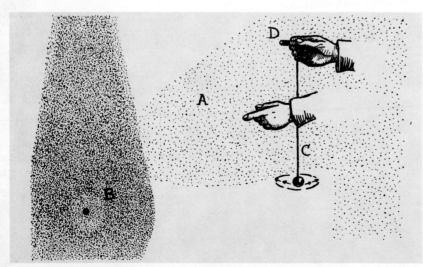

object, the size of a pea, and sent it to the Science Museum in London for identification. Incredibly, it turned out to be a rare variety of truffle.

There were still a number of minor mysteries – such as how to distinguish between lead and silver, when both react at 22 inches, or between truffles and beech wood, both of which respond to a 17-inch pendulum. Further experimentation solved that one. The number of times the pendulum gyrated was equally important. For lead, it gyrates 16 times, then goes back to its normal back-and-forth motion; for silver it gyrates 22 times. It looked as if nature had devised a simple and

Above: the corner of the courtyard at the Lethbridge home, Hole House in Devon, where dowsing revealed a number of buried objects

Below: how dowsing with a pendulum works
A. dowser's psyche-field
B. static field of object
C. pendulum – where A meets B it begins to move in a circle
D. how the pendulum length is controlled by dowser

foolproof code for identifying any substance.

And not just substances. The pendulum also responded to colours – the natural colours of flowers, for example: 22 inches for grey, 29 for yellow, 30 for green, and so on. Lethbridge found himself wondering whether the pendulum would respond to thoughts and emotions as well as substances. A simple, two-part experiment convinced him that this was so. During his last excavations near Cambridge, Lethbridge had collected a number of sling-stones from an Iron Age fort. He tried his pendulum over them, and found that they reacted at 24 inches and also at 40. He fetched a bucketful of stones from the beach and tried the pendulum over those. They failed to react at either 'rate'. Now he divided the stones into two piles, and told his wife Mina to throw half of them at a wall, while he threw the rest. He tried the pendulum again. All Mina's stones now reacted at 29 inches (the 'rate' for females), while those he had thrown reacted at 24 – like the Iron Age stones. So it looked as if the Iron Age stones had been thrown by males. But what about their reaction to a 40-inch pendulum? Could it, he wondered, be the rate for anger or death? Lethbridge set the pendulum at 40 inches and thought about something that made him angry; immediately, the pendulum began to gyrate. So it looked as if 40 was indeed the rate for anger. He later ascertained that it was also the rate for death, cold and blackness.

Now all this, admittedly, seems absurd. Yet Lethbridge repeated the experiments dozen of times, and each time he got the same result. The pendulum responded to ideas – like evolution, pride, life, danger and deceit – just as readily as to substances. Moreover Mina got the same results. And, through his experience of psychometry, Lethbridge realised that there is nothing very odd in a pendulum responding to ideas. If a 'sensitive' can hold an unopened letter, and somehow feel the emotions of the person who wrote it, then it seems reasonable to assume that human beings possess some 'sense' that registers these things just as our eyes register colours and shapes – a sixth sense perhaps? In fact, you could say that a pendulum is merely an aid to psychometry. A psychometrist – or sensitive – can pick up these vibrations directly; non-sensitive people, like Lethbridge, can only feel them indirectly through the pendulum.

After months of experiment with the pendulum, Lethbridge constructed tables of the various 'rates'; and it became clear that 40 inches was some kind of limit. Every single substance that he tested fell between zero and 40 inches. And at this point he discovered something rather odd. Sulphur reacts to a 7-inch pendulum. If he extended the pendulum to 47 inches – 40 plus 7 – it would still react to a heap of sulphur. But not when directly over the heap. It only reacted a little

to one side. The same was true of everything else he tried beyond 40 – the pendulum reacted, but a little to one side.

Forty inches is also the 'rate' for death. Was it possible, Lethbridge wondered, that when the pendulum registers beyond 40 inches, it registers a world beyond death – another dimension? He remembered an experience of being at the dentist, under anaesthetic, and finding himself outside his body – hovering up in the air, and slightly to the left – just like the 'displacement' reaction of the pendulum to the heap of sulphur.

He noticed another odd thing. Below 40 inches, there is no 'rate' for the concept of time; the pendulum simply will not respond. But when he lengthened the pendulum to 60 inches, he got a strong reaction for time. He

Lethbridge's pendulum rates

inches	
7	sulphur
10	graphite
12	carbon
13	slate, concrete
14	glass, porcelain,
15½	quartzite, flint
20	all animals, plants wood, rubber, coal, paper, bread, potatoes
22	silver, lead, salt
23½	vegetable oil, amber
24	masculinity, diamond
25½	alcohol
26½	running water
29	femininity, gold
30½	copper, brass, tin
32	iron
40	Death

?

Above: table of pendulum 'rates' as discovered by Tom Lethbridge in the course of his experiments. Through trial and error he came to realise that the pendulum reacted consistently at certain lengths to specific substances, qualities and even abstract ideas

Left and right: mended pots that had been found in fragments in the courtyard and orchard of Hole House solely through dowsing. Lethbridge dowsed them to find their ages, finally coming up with the dates he scratched on the bottoms. Lethbridge achieved a high degree of accuracy – his dates for certain standing stones, for example, were later proved to be correct by carbon dating. As he said 'It may seem absurd, but it delivers the goods'

reasoned that because 'our world' – that is, the world that registers below 40 – is in time, there is no reaction to the idea of time itself – just as you could not appreciate the speed of a river if you were drifting down at the same speed as the current. But there is a reaction to the idea of time in this 'world beyond death'. Moreover, Lethbridge found that if he lengthened the pendulum beyond 80, he got the same result all over again – as if there is yet another world – or dimension – beyond that one. And this 'third world' also has a reaction for time. But when Lethbridge lengthened the pendulum beyond 120 inches he discovered that the 'world' beyond that also had no reaction for time.

Secrets of the 'other you'

Tom Lethbridge's own explanation of this strange 'power of the pendulum' is that there is a part of the human mind – the unconscious, perhaps – that knows the answers to all questions. Unfortunately, it cannot convey these answers to the 'everyday you', the busy, conscious self that spends its time coping with practical problems. But this 'other you' *can* convey its messages via the dowsing rod or pendulum, by the simple expedient of controlling the muscles.

Lethbridge had started as a cheerfully sceptical investigator trying to understand nature's hidden codes for conveying information. His researches led him into strange,

bewildering realms where all his normal ideas seemed to be turned upside down. He compared himself to a man walking on ice, when it suddenly collapses and he finds himself floundering in freezing water. Of this sudden immersion in new ideas he said: 'From living a normal life in a three-dimensional world, I seem to have suddenly fallen through into one where there are more dimensions. The three-dimensional life goes on as usual; but one has to adjust one's thinking to the other.' He did more than adjust his thinking; he set out boldly to explore the fourth dimension – and came to highly significant conclusions.

Gateway to other worlds

Tom Lethbridge progressed from finding hidden objects through dowsing to exploring the timeless world beyond death.

IN 1962, FIVE YEARS AFTER his move to Devon, Tom Lethbridge's ideas on ghosts, 'ghouls', pendulums and dowsing rods began to crystallise into a coherent theory, which he outlined in a book called *Ghost and divining rod*. This appeared in 1963, and it aroused more interest than anything he had published so far. It deserved to be so popular, for its central theory was original, exciting and well-argued.

He suggested that nature generates fields of static electricity in certain places, particularly near running water. These 'fields' are capable of picking up and recording the thoughts and feelings of human beings and other living creatures. But human beings are also surrounded by a mild electrical field, as the researches of Harold Burr of Yale University in the United States revealed in the 1930s. So if someone goes into a room where a murder has taken place and experiences a distinctly unpleasant feeling, all that is happening is that the emotions associated with the crime (such as fear, pain and horror) are being transferred to the visitor's electrical field, in accordance with the laws of electricity. If we are feeling full of energy, excitement, misery or anger, the emotional transference may flow the other way, and our feelings will be recorded on the field.

But if human emotions can be imprinted in some way on the 'field' of running water, and picked up by a dowser, then this world we are living in is a far more strange and

Above: Tom Lethbridge cataloguing some archaeological finds

Below: Saddell Abbey, Strathclyde, Scotland – a place of curiously strong and varied atmospheres: menacing in the castle, melancholy in the abbey ruins and peaceful at the wishing well. Lethbridge believed that 'atmospheres' are powerful emotions 'recorded' in the electrical field of water

complex place than most people give it credit for. To begin with, we must be surrounded by hidden information – in the form of these 'tape recordings' – that might become accessible to all of us if we could master the art of using the dowser's pendulum.

It looks – says Lethbridge – as if human beings possess 'psyche-fields' as well as bodies. The body is simply a piece of apparatus for collecting impressions, which are then stored in the psyche-field. But in that case, there would seem to be a part of us that seeks the information. Presumably this is what religious people call the spirit. And since the information it can acquire through the pendulum may come from the remote past, or from some place on the other side of the world, then this spirit must be outside the limits of space and time.

It was this last idea that excited Lethbridge so much. His experiments with the pendulum seemed to indicate that there are other worlds beyond this one, perhaps worlds in other dimensions. Presumably we cannot see them – although they co-exist with our world – because our bodies are rather crude machines for picking up low-level vibrations. But the psyche-field – or perhaps the spirit – seems to have access to these other invisible worlds.

It also seems to have access to other times and other places. In May 1964, a BBC camera

team went to Hole House to record an interview with Lethbridge about dowsing. A young cameraman looked so dazed and startled as he got out of the car that Lethbridge asked him: 'Have you been here before?' The cameraman shook his head. 'No. But I've dreamed about it.' He asked if he could look behind the house. Pointing to a wall that Lethbridge had knocked down and rebuilt, he said: 'It wasn't like that years ago. There used to be buildings against it.' That was true – but not in Lethbridge's time. In the herb garden, the cameraman said: 'There used to be buildings there, but they were pulled down.' In his dream a voice had said, 'Now we shall be able to see the sea.' Again, it was true – but many years before, at the turn of the century. Now a row of trees blotted out the view of the sea.

The cameraman had never been in the area before, and he had no friends or relatives there who might have told him about it. Yet on five occasions he had dreamed about Hole House – as it was before he was born.

Lethbridge had always been interested in dreams, ever since he read J.W. Dunne's *An experiment with time* in the 1930s. Dunne was an aeronautics engineer, and around the turn of the century he had a number of impressive dreams of the future – for example, he dreamed accurately about the forthcoming eruption of the volcano, Mount Pelée, on Martinique. Dunne had suggested that time is like a tape or a film, which may get twisted or tangled, so that we can catch glimpses of

Above: diagram illustrating Lethbridge's theory about the creation of the world-wide belief in nymphs:
1. Aroused youth, pausing within the static field of a stream (A), vividly creates the image of a girl bathing (C) in his own static field (B). The image leaks into the weaker field (A) where it is 'recorded'.
2. Perhaps years later a passing youth with a weak psyche-field (D) comes into contact with (A) from which the image of the girl (C) leaks into his field (D). He thinks he has witnessed a supernatural being when he has really only seen the recording of a thoughtform

Right: eruption of the volcanic Mount Pelée, Martinique. J. W. Dunne, author of *An experiment with time*, had dreamed accurately of the event some time before it happened. This and other dreams convinced him that we dream regularly of future events but do not always remember these dreams

other times. He used to keep a notebook and pencil by his bed, and jot down his dreams the moment he woke up. He was convinced that we all dream about the future – probably every night of our lives – but that we forget it almost as soon as we wake up.

Lethbridge decided that if he wanted to study this mystery of dreams, he should keep a dream notebook. It was soon filled with his own vivid and idiosyncratic observations.

He became convinced that Dunne was correct in believing that we all dream of future events, but that most of these are so trivial – or so brief – that we fail to remember them. One night, he woke up dreaming about the face of a man that seemed to be looking at him out of a mirror. He was doing something with his hands, which seemed to be moving in the area of his chin. Lethbridge thought he might be shaving.

The next day, Lethbridge was driving slowly along a narrow lane; a car came round the corner, and at the wheel was the man he had seen in his dream. His face was framed by the windscreen – which Lethbridge had mistaken for a mirror – and his hands were moving in the area of his chin, on top of the steering wheel. Lethbridge was certain that he had never seen the man before.

He also noted that some of his dreams seemed to go backwards. He once dreamed of a furry snake-like object coming into his bedroom; but all the furniture in the room was reversed, as in a mirror. The snake-like object he recognised as the tail of their Siamese cat, walking backwards. A friend also told him about two 'backward dreams' she had had recently: in one, she saw a couple she knew walk backwards out of their door and drive their car backwards down a lane. In another, she saw some men walking backwards carrying a coffin, and one of them uttered the baffling sentence: 'Burnt be to

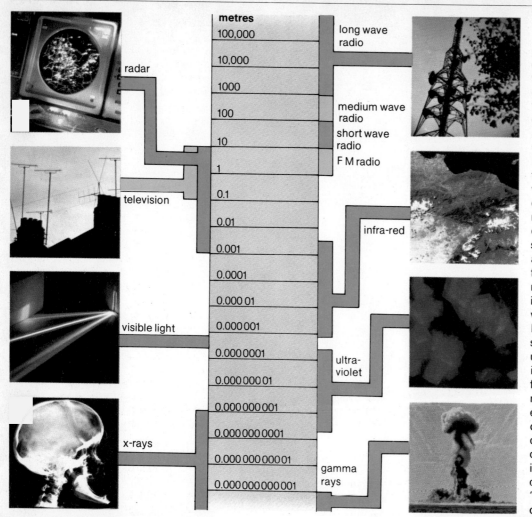

metres		
100,000		long wave radio
10,000		
1000		
100		medium wave radio
10		short wave radio
1		F M radio
0.1		
0.01		
0.001		infra-red
0.0001		
0.000 01		
0.000001	visible light	
0.0000001		
0.000 000 01		ultra-violet
0.000 000 001		
0.000 000 0001	x-rays	
0.000 000 00001		gamma rays
0.000 000 000 001		

radar

television

visible light

x-rays

Left: the spectrum of electromagnetic (EM) vibrations. EM waves consist of electric and magnetic fields vibrating with a definite frequency, each corresponding to a particular wavelength.

In order of increasing frequency and decreasing wavelength, the EM spectrum consists of: very long wave radio, used for communication with submarines; long, medium and short wave radio (used for AM broadcasting); FM radio, television and radar; infra-red (heat) radiation, which is recorded in the Earth photographs taken by survey satellites; visible light; ultraviolet light, which, while invisible, stimulates fluorescence in some materials; x-rays; and high-energy gamma rays, which occur in fallout and in cosmic rays. The progressive discovery of these waves has inspired speculations concerning unknown 'vibrations' making up our own and higher worlds

enough good woods any.' On waking up, she wrote down the sentence, read it backwards, and realised that it actually said: 'Any wood's good enough to be burnt.'

But why, Lethbridge asked, should time sometimes go backwards in dreams? The clue was provided by his pendulum, which informed him that the energy vibrations of the next level – the world beyond ours – are four times as fast as those of our world. Lethbridge speculated that during sleep, a part of us passes through this world to a higher world still. Coming back from sleep, we pass through it once again to enter our own much slower world of vibrations. The effect is like a fast train passing a slower one; although the slow train is moving forward, it appears to be going backwards.

More impressive examples of precognitive dreams came from his correspondents. One woman dreamed of the collapse of a building as the side was blown out and heard a voice say: 'Collapsed like a pack of cards.' A month later a gas explosion blew out the side of a block of flats called Ronan Point in East London, and a newspaper report used the phrase 'Collapsed like a pack of cards'. Another correspondent described a dream in which he saw a square-looking Edwardian house with many chimneys being burnt down; a few days later, Tom saw a house of

The ruined London tower block, Ronan Point. A gas explosion ripped through the building causing death and devastation. One woman dreamed precognitively of the disaster, hearing the very words of the subsequent newspaper headline 'Collapsed like a pack of cards' spoken clearly

this description being burnt down on a television newsreel.

The more he studied these puzzles, the more convinced Lethbridge became that the key to all of them is the concept of *vibrations*. Our bodies seem to be machines tuned to pick up certain vibrations. Our eyes will only register energy whose wavelength is between that of red and violet light. Shorter or longer wavelengths are invisible to us. Modern physics tells us that at the sub-atomic level matter is in a state of constant vibration.

Worlds beyond worlds

According to Lethbridge's pendulum, the 'world' beyond our world – the world that can be detected by a pendulum of more than 40 inches – consists of vibrations that are four times as fast as ours. It is all around us yet we are unable to see it, because it is beyond the range of our senses. All the objects in our world extend into this other world. Our personalities also extend into it, but we are not aware of this, because our 'everyday self' has no communication with that 'other self'. But the other self can answer questions by means of the pendulum. When Tom and Mina Lethbridge visited a circle of standing stones called the Merry Maidens, near Penzance in Cornwall, Lethbridge held a pendulum over one of the uprights and asked how old it was. As he did so, he placed one hand on the stone, and experienced something like a mild electric shock. The pendulum began to gyrate like an aeroplane propellor, and went on swinging in a wide circle for several minutes – Lethbridge counted 451 turns. Arbitrarily allowing 10 years for each turn, Lethbridge calculated that the circle dated back to 2540 BC – a result that sounds highly consistent with carbon 14 dating of other megalithic monuments like Stonehenge. His 'higher self' – outside time – had answered his question.

In 1971 Lethbridge was engaged in writing his book on dreams – *The power of the pendulum* – when he became ill and had to be taken into hospital. He was a huge man, and his enormous weight placed a strain on his heart. He died on 30 September, leaving his last book unrevised. He was 70 years old, and his life's work was by no means complete. Yet even in its unfinished state, it is one of the

The ancient circle of standing stones known as the Merry Maidens near Penzance, Cornwall. While dowsing over the stones Lethbridge experienced a mild electric shock as if the stones were some kind of battery. But, persisting with his pendulum, he was able to dowse for the age of the stones. Later, more sophisticated techniques – such as carbon 14 dating – were used to date the Merry Maidens and Lethbridge's dating was confirmed

most important and exciting contributions to parapsychology in this century.

Lethbridge's insistence on rediscovering the ancient art of dowsing also underlined his emphasis on understanding the differences between primitive and modern Man. The ancient peoples – going back to our cavemen ancestors – believed that the Universe is magical and that Earth is a living creature. They were probably natural dowsers – as the aborigines of Australia still are – and responded naturally to the forces of the earth. Their standing stones were, according to Lethbridge, intended to mark places where the earth force was most powerful and perhaps to harness it in some way now forgotten.

Modern Man has suppressed – or lost – that instinctive, intuitive contact with the forces of the Universe. He is too busy keeping together his precious civilisation. Yet he still potentially possesses that ancient power of dowsing, and could easily develop it if he really wanted to. Lethbridge set out to develop his own powers, and to explore them scientifically, and soon came to the conclusion that the dowsing rod and the pendulum are incredibly accurate. By making use of some unknown part of the mind – the unconscious or 'superconscious' – they can provide information that is inaccessible to our ordinary senses, and can tell us about realms of reality beyond the 'everyday' world of physical matter.

Lethbridge was not a spiritualist. He never paid much attention to the question of life after death or the existence of a 'spirit world'. But by pursuing his researches into these subjects with a tough-minded logic, he concluded that there are other realms of reality beyond our world, and that there are forms of energy that we do not even begin to understand. Magic, spiritualism and occultism are merely our crude attempts to understand this vast realm of hidden energies, just as alchemy was Man's earliest attempt to understand the mysteries of atomic physics.

As to the meaning of all this, Lethbridge preserves the caution of an academic. Yet in his last years he became increasingly convinced that there is a meaning in human existence, and that it is tied up with the concept of our personal evolution. For some reason, we are being *driven* to evolve.

Eileen Garrett

A thoroughly modern medium

Few Spiritualist mediums have questioned the otherworldly origin of their powers, but Eileen Garrett, one of the most gifted, had her doubts. ROY STEMMAN tells the story of this unusually objective psychic

EILEEN GARRETT has been described as 'probably the most thoroughly investigated medium of modern times'. The reason, quite apart from her exceptional psychic talents, was that she devoted most of her life to encouraging research into mediumship and its meaning, frequently offering herself as the first psychic guinea-pig in experiments.

Her powers ranged from clairvoyance and astral projection to physical mediumship. But it was as a trance medium – apparently allowing the dead to speak through her lips – that she made the greatest impact. It was in this manner that she was used as a channel for

Eileen Garrett as a young woman. Brought up against a background of sectarian strife in Ireland she soon rejected religion, and even after she became a famous medium she was frequently irritated by the dogmatic assertions of many Spiritualists. She was eager to be scientifically investigated in the hope that more could be discovered about the human psyche

communications allegedly from the captain of the British airship *R101*, Flight-Lieutenant H.C. Irwin, in 1930: a remarkable case that many still regard as among the best in providing evidence for life after death.

But Mrs Garrett was more reticent about her mediumship than others. She accepted that the content of her trance communications was paranormal in origin, but she was open-minded about 'the dead' who spoke through her. This ambiguous approach to her mediumship extended to the spirit 'controls' who worked through her, each of whom had a distinct personality. There was Uvani, who claimed to have been a soldier in India centuries ago, and Abdul Latif, a 12th-century physician from the court of Saladin, whose particular interest was healing. In the early days of her mediumship Mrs Garrett accepted them as spirit helpers, but in time she began to doubt this and believed, instead, that they might be secondary personalities produced by her own subconscious.

Split personalities?
In an attempt to find the truth Mrs Garrett willingly participated in experiments designed to compare these trance personalities with her own waking personality. The investigators spent many hours talking to Uvani and Abdul Latif – even using word association tests on the spirit controls and the medium. However, these tests were inconclusive. One investigator decided that Uvani was probably a 'split-off' personality from the medium – indeed, Uvani himself said he manipulated a split-off portion of Mrs Garrett's unconscious. Another researcher concluded that the two spirit controls were independent personalities.

Mrs Garrett's own opinion in later life, given in her autobiography *Many voices* (1968), was:

> I prefer to think of the controls as principals of the subconscious. I had, unconsciously, adopted them by name and during the years of early training respect them, but cannot explain them. . . . The controls are well aware that I have maintained an impartial, but respectful, attitude towards my own work and theirs, and so the search continues.

Later, she added, 'I have never been able wholly to accept them as the spiritual dwellers on the threshold, which they seem to believe they are.'

The mystery deepened with the surfacing of two more controls. One, named Tehotah, claimed to be an entity that personified the Logos or divine word, while Rama was said to be the personification of the life force.

Left: New York psychologist Lawrence LeShan was impressed with Mrs Garrett's psychic gifts and her analytical intelligence. He investigated her thoroughly; during one psychometry experiment LeShan was amazed when Mrs Garrett, picking up an envelope containing the target object – an ancient Babylonian tablet (below) – not only described it accurately but proceeded to give a detailed description of the secretary who had originally parcelled it up

in experiments into ESP.

New York psychologist Lawrence LeShan spent more than 500 hours questioning Mrs Garrett about her psychic abilities, then designed several experiments to test them thoroughly. One was a psychometry test in which the medium was asked to hold various objects and give her clairvoyant impressions about them.

The objects included a fossil fish, a scrap of bandage, a piece of stone from Mount Vesuvius, an old Greek coin and an ancient Babylonian clay tablet. Each was wrapped in tissue, then placed in a box that, in turn, was put inside a manila envelope and numbered. Another person then put these numbered envelopes inside larger envelopes, marking them with a different number. As a result, no one knew which object was inside which envelope.

During preparations for this experiment a secretary picked up the Babylonian tablet and examined it. Two weeks later, when LeShan conducted the experiment with Mrs Garrett 1500 miles (2400 kilometres) away in

Neither had incarnated as an individual.

Eileen Garrett was born in County Meath, in the Republic of Ireland, on 17 March 1893, the daughter of Anne Brownell and a Spaniard named Vancho. Two weeks later her mother drowned herself and a few weeks after that her father also committed suicide: the double tragedy created, apparently, by the pressures of Protestant and Catholic conflicts. As a result, Eileen was brought up by an uncle and aunt – who were Protestant, but no bigots.

A late uncle's advice

Like so many other sensitive children – and in particular natural psychics – Eileen had playmates who were invisible to others. But the most impressive paranormal experience of those early years concerned her uncle, who had been extremely kind and understanding to her. A couple of weeks after his death Eileen saw him standing before her 'looking young, erect and strong'. He said that he understood the difficulties of her present life. Then he predicted that she would go to London to study in two years – which is exactly what happened. He then vanished before she could ask any questions. It was from that moment that Eileen became interested in the question of survival of death.

In time she encountered Spiritualism and began developing her psychic gifts – particularly trance mediumship – under the guidance of James Hewat McKenzie at the British College of Psychic Science. As a result, she provided many bereaved people with impressive evidence for survival.

In 1931 the American Society for Psychical Research invited her to New York to give sittings, and she also worked with Professor William McDougall and Dr J.B. Rhine at Duke University, North Carolina,

Right: Professor William McDougall who, together with Dr J.B. Rhine, conducted experiments with Eileen Garrett at Duke University in North Carolina, USA

Left: Cecil B. de Mille, director of epic films and a notoriously tough character; nevertheless he was reduced to tears when Mrs Garrett described an old lady she 'saw' standing next to him. It was a perfect description of his dead mother

Florida, she picked up an envelope and said immediately that there was 'a woman associated with this'.

It was later found that this envelope contained the clay tablet, and Mrs Garrett's description of the woman so perfectly matched the secretary who had handled it that, according to LeShan, it would have been possible 'to pick her out of a line-up of 10,000 women'. The medium even mentioned two scars that the woman had.

During the experiments with her, LeShan learned indirectly of a man who had vanished from a mid western city in the USA. He gave Mrs Garrett, in New York, a square of cloth cut from one of the man's shirts and asked for her impressions. The medium gave a fairly accurate description of the missing man, whose appearance was, at that time, unknown to LeShan, adding that he had had a loss in his family between the ages of 13 and

Below: Eileen Garrett was a prolific writer and a dynamic personality. Here she surveys some of the books written by or about her

Below right: after Mrs Garrett's death in 1970 her daughter continued her work through the Parapsychological Foundation, which Eileen founded in 1951

15. It was discovered that his father had deserted the family when he was 14 and had not been heard of since. She also said that the man was in La Jolla, California, and it was confirmed later that he had gone there after leaving his home.

A spontaneous phenomenon of a physical kind occurred in 1931 when Mrs Garrett was lying on an operating table in hospital. Just after she succumbed to the anaesthetic, the doctors and nurses in attendance heard a voice. Her physician, who had been in India in his youth, told her later that he recognised certain definite words of command, as spoken in Hindustani. Because of the way Mrs Garrett had been prepared for the operation the doctor knew that it was quite impossible for her to utter a sound. He was so impressed by the experience that he sent a letter to various Spiritualist leaders putting the circumstances on record.

Eileen Garrett was far removed from the popular, otherworldly, image of a medium. She had a vivacious personality and a questing spirit, and in addition to her psychic work she also ran a tea room, a workers' hostel and eventually a literary magazine, *Tomorrow*, which she later changed to deal entirely with psychic matters.

She married three times, lost three sons – one at birth and two through illness. Her daughter continues her work through the Parapsychology Foundation, which Eileen Garrett founded in New York in 1951.

Eileen Garrett died at Le Piol, France, in 1970, having made an enormous personal contribution to psychical research. She had no doubt about the reality of paranormal phenomena. What she *did* doubt was the spirit hypothesis of mediumship that so many accept blindly. And by setting up the Parapsychology Foundation she ensured that the search for some understanding of the nature of psychic phenomena would continue long after her death.

Doris Stokes is, she says, a perfectly ordinary, down-to-earth person. But she has a special gift, which enables her to hear the dead speak. ROY STEMMAN looks at the life and work of the woman whose exceptional psychic powers have brought comfort to thousands of people

DORIS STOKES'S appearance on Australian television caused a sensation. The switchboard was flooded with calls, letters poured in, and Channel 9 took off *Starsky & Hutch* to make room for a second hour-long programme about this daughter of an English blacksmith.

No other personality had had such an impact on Australian viewers, yet Doris Stokes is not a superstar. She lives with her husband John in a modest London flat and regards herself as a very ordinary person. But she has an unusual gift that sets her apart from others: she is a medium who claims to be able to speak with the dead.

After being interviewed by Don Lane on his popular television variety show, Doris Stokes was invited to give messages to members of his studio audience. It is something

Doris Stokes appears on Australian television in the *Don Lane Show* (right). As a result of the programme Doris received thousands of telephone calls and hundreds of letters, and went on a whirlwind tour of Australia. She was staggered at this response from the public and told the crowds: 'I'm nothing special. Please don't get the wrong impression. I'm just the same as you are'

The medium and the message

she does regularly in Spiritualist churches in England without creating much of a stir – but for most Australian television viewers the spectacle of a woman 'speaking' to spirits was astonishing. They demanded more and Australian television was happy to oblige. 'A [psychic] star was born', her visit to Australia was extended, and soon a tour of major cities was organised during which the largest halls – including the Sydney Opera House – were packed with people eager to see her in action and perhaps receive a personal message.

What is it about Doris Stokes that created such a reaction? It is the direct and confident way in which she acts as a 'go-between', relaying names and information that she says are given to her by the dead. Much of this she hears as voices – different in accent and intonation – and so she is known as a *clairaudient*, rather than a *clairvoyant* (a medium whose impressions are visual).

In the television studio her down-to-earth, good-humoured manner ensured that there was nothing 'spooky' about her performance. She simply stood in front of her audience and waited for the voices to give her information.

'The lady over there,' she said, pointing to one of Don Lane's studio guests. 'I've got a man here called Bert.'

'That's my brother-in-law,' the woman gasped.

'He says he went over very quickly.'

'That's right.'

'Who's Wyn?'

'I'm Wyn.'

The messages she gives are usually made

up of such trivia, but the accuracy of the names and details leave her recipients in no doubt that they are witnessing a paranormal phenomenon. Guesswork alone would not explain the content of the messages. But is it really communication with the dead or is she just using extra-sensory perception (ESP)? That is something that each person has to decide for himself, just as Doris Stokes had to decide in her early days.

Her psychic gifts were apparent from an early age when she found herself describing – or predicting – things that she could not have known normally. This worried her mother, but her father – a natural psychic like his daughter – understood and did nothing to discourage her. It was not until after Doris was married and her father had died that her psychic powers grew stronger: and her experiences left her in no doubt that she was in contact with people who had died.

A visit from the dead

Her most dramatic personal experience occurred during the Second World War. Her husband was reported 'missing in action' and a medium at a local Spiritualist church in Grantham, Lincolnshire, 'confirmed' that he had been killed. Doris Stokes returned home to her baby son in a state of shock. She describes what happened next in her autobiography, *Voices in my ear*:

> Then the bedroom door flew open so sharply I thought it was mother bursting in and there stood my father. My mouth dropped open. He looked as real and as solid as he did when he was alive . . .
> 'Dad?' I whispered.
> 'I never lied to you, did I, Doll?' he asked.
> 'I don't think so,' I said.
> 'I'm not lying to you now. John is not with us and on Christmas Day you will have proof of this.' Then as I watched, he vanished.

Three days later came a letter from the War Office telling her that John was dead. But while everyone else mourned, the 'widow' refused to believe it. Her dead father was proved right, however. Just as he had predicted she learned that John was still alive, though wounded and a prisoner of war, on Christmas Day.

Doris was never trained as a medium, although she once attended a Spiritualist 'development circle' – and was appallingly embarrassed. First, she was shown into a room of 'cranky old dears clucking admiringly about a bossy medium.' They all then sat quietly, with their eyes shut, waiting for the spirit world to communicate with them. But Doris's eyes flew open again when a large lady stood up and majestically announced, in a deep voice, but still unmistakably her own, that she was 'Chief Sitting Bull'. Doris could hardly believe it – all these people taking this patent nonsense so seriously! And then

'Chief Sitting Bull' addressed some very stern words to her; she had to uncross her legs and keep her feet on the ground 'to earth the power'. Doris remarked that she was made to feel like a human light bulb and found it all quite ridiculous. She never went back.

However, she had no need for training. It soon became apparent that her special, psychic gifts could give comfort and practical help to the bereaved and the despairing. She began to give 'seances' – although that rather spooky and old-fashioned word sounds very odd in conjunction with Doris – both on public platforms and in private houses. She never promises to 'get through' to any particular person on the 'other side', but settles the audience down, confident that the spirits will eventually speak to them through her. They have very rarely let her down.

She has found that the longer a person has

Top: Tom Sutton, Doris's father. He died when Doris was a young girl, but 'visited' her twice several years later during the Second World War. On the first occasion he told her that her husband John (above) – reported missing in action – was alive and would return. The second time he warned her that her healthy infant son was soon to die. Both 'predictions' were accurate

been dead, the stronger his or her voice seems to be – those newly 'passed over' tend to sound faint. Sometimes the voices fade away altogether. She has now learned to cope with these silent phases but in her early days she was tempted to cheat. Doris Stokes must be one of the few practising mediums to admit to it.

She was young and felt very 'special' because of her strange abilities and was therefore inclined to show off. When the voices stopped, leaving her alone and unaided on a platform in front of a packed house, she was eager to heed the advice of an experienced 'circuit' medium. Get to the meetings early, he suggested, and listen in to the conversations of the audience. You're bound to pick up a few hints, names, dates and so on. People will always talk about their hopes – in this case the spirits they hope to 'hear' from through Doris. Take down some notes surreptitiously, he said, then if your voices stop abruptly you can consult them and 'fudge' the messages. That way your audience will leave happy.

Doris admits that she tried cheating in this way, twice. The first time she slipped her notes into her hymn book, hoping she would not have to use them. But gradually – in the middle of a message for a lady in the audience – the voices stopped. White-faced, Doris fumbled for her notes – but they had disappeared. Somehow, remembering bits of what she had overheard and making up the rest, she finished the 'communication' but noticed that the lady seemed a little bewildered – it was such a muddle. But the worst was yet to come.

Just as abruptly as they had departed, the voices came back. Doris managed two real messages then was aware that her spirit guide – whose name approximates to the English spelling Ramononov – had taken over and was saying 'Now we'll go back to Mrs . . .' (the lady whose message had just been faked) 'and you'll apologise to her and tell her that the last part of the message didn't came from the spirit world'.

Horrified at being faced with a public humiliation, Doris hesitated, then plunged in: 'I'm terribly sorry. I've got to tell you the last bit of your message didn't come from the spirit. That was me.'

Advice from the other side

People who seek help from mediums are mostly the grief-stricken bereaved. What raises Doris Stokes above the run-of-the-mill Spiritualist medium is her extraordinary down-to-earth attitude. To her the spirit world is as real as this one – and her firm conviction of survival after death communicates itself to her audience. Her specific and often deeply personalised messages purporting to come from the dead frequently offer urgent advice: one deeply depressed widower was told by his wife not to take the overdose he was planning. He was impressed by the fact that no one knew of his intentions except himself – that, and the anger Doris conveyed from his wife. 'Your wife is very anxious about you. She says that is not the way. You must not do it. She's waiting for you and if she's gone on she'll make sure of being there to meet you when your time comes, but you must wait until your time comes, or you will regret it.'

Many a medium could have trotted out that advice – for almost all religious people are opposed to suicide – but Doris backed this up by 'proving' the continued existence of the man's wife through conveying many personal pieces of information that only the widower and his wife could have known.

There are occasions, however, when Doris herself needs the help of psychics. One such time was when she was 33, and, her first

Below: Walter Brookes, the medium who gave Doris a message warning her of a forthcoming illness

Above: Doris 'performs' before the studio audience of Tyne Tees Television's *Friday Live* programme in December 1979

child having died, she was hoping to become pregnant again. One day she was talking to a friend, Walter Brookes, a well-known Yorkshire medium, when he suddenly asked if she had just come out of hospital. No, said Doris, who was feeling fit and well.

'Just a minute,' he said. 'This is serious. I'm afraid you're going into hospital – July I think, something to do with your right side. They'll say you're going to die, but your father wants you to write this down. It's the name of the person you must ask for. Mrs Marrow.'

That July Doris Stokes was suddenly stricken with agonising pain in her stomach. She was rushed to hospital where it was found that pregnancy had occurred in one of her Fallopian tubes. John Stokes was told there was nothing that could be done for her. She was dying.

Remembering the message from Doris's dead father, John Stokes asked the doctors if they knew a Mrs Marrow. When he learned they did and that she was a gynaecologist at a Nottingham hospital he insisted that his wife be transferred. There, under Mrs Marrow's expert care, Doris recovered. And soon she was able to resume her work as a medium, relaying messages that may well have saved the lives of others.

Following the success of her first visit to Australia, Doris returned in 1980 for an equally triumphant tour, with television and radio appearances.

Spiritualism's critics, of course, are not pleased that mediums such as Doris Stokes are allowed to demonstrate their powers to such a wide audience. But Doris is happy to be judged by the results of her work – and they speak for themselves.

Ted Serios in focus

Can thoughts really be photographed? Chicago bell-hop Ted Serios believes they can, and has produced hundreds of pictures as proof. ROY STEMMAN considers the claims made by, and for, this psychic photographer – and examines the sceptics' attempts to expose him

TED SERIOS SAT DOWN in the hotel room and pointed a Polaroid camera at his face. The flashbulb fired and Dr Jule Eisenbud immediately took the camera from him and pulled the print from the back. Instead of showing Serios's face the unmistakable image of a building appeared.

For Serios, a chain-smoking, alcoholic Chicago bell-hop, it was just another of his strange psychic photographs that he calls 'thoughtographs'. But for Dr Eisenbud, an associate professor of psychiatry at the University of Colorado Medical School, it was such an impressive demonstration of paranormal power that he went on to study Serios for several years and write a book about him.

When he flew to Chicago for the first experimental session with the hard-drinking psychic photographer in April 1964, Eisenbud was almost certain that he was about to witness 'some kind of shoddy hoax'. Because of his interest in the paranormal, Eisenbud was aware that there had been many so-called psychic photographers over the years who had been caught cheating, usually by tampering with the film. The appearance of the Polaroid camera had changed that, making it easier to control the production of such 'thoughtographic' prints as well as giving results in seconds.

Investigators who have worked with Serios supply their own film and cameras;

Right: one of the few colour 'thoughtographs' produced by Serios. He was aiming at a target picture of the Hilton hotel at Denver, but obtained this image of the Chicago Hilton instead

Below: the first picture of a 'recognisable structure' that Serios produced for researcher Dr Jule Eisenbud. It was immediately identified by one of the observers at the session as the Chicago Water Tower (below right)

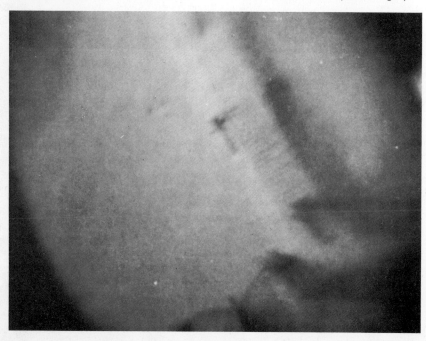

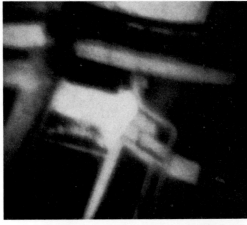

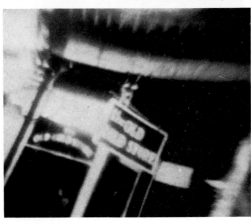

Above: one of eleven views of a shop front in Central City, Colorado, produced by Serios (left) in 1965. At that time the building was used as a tourist shop called the 'Old Wells Fargo Express Office', but several years before it was 'The Old Gold Store', no photographs of which were known to exist. In one of the pictures (top), the billing reads 'The Wld Gold Store': to create this effect fraudulently, Serios would have had to use two transparencies

from the start, and sceptics do not need to look very far to have their suspicions aroused. In his early days, Serios just looked at the camera to produce his startling pictures, but later he introduced a 'gismo', which he holds in front of the lens while concentrating. Sometimes he uses a small plastic cylinder, one end of which is covered with plain cellophane, the other with cellophane over a piece of blackened film; on other occasions he simply rolls up a piece of paper.

The purpose of the 'gismo', says Serios, is to keep his fingers from obscuring the lens. His critics, however, see it as having a far more sinister purpose. It could very easily conceal a 'gimmick' containing microfilm or transparency, they argue, and for them it is as suspicious as a conjuror's hat.

Two reporters, Charles Reynolds and David Eisendrath, constructed a small device that could be hidden in a 'gismo' and that produced similar-looking results to those of Serios. Their account, published in *Popular Photography* in October 1967, gave the sceptics the 'evidence' they needed.

Secrets of the 'gismo'

Eisenbud and other researchers, on the other hand, are satisfied that the 'gismo' contains no hidden equipment, nor does Serios slip anything inside it just before an exposure is made. They are all aware of the hidden microfilm hypothesis and have evolved an experimental protocol to overcome it. Serios is usually given the 'gismo' when he feels he can produce a paranormal print. It is then taken from him immediately and examined. It is probably in his hands for no longer than 15 seconds at a time and throughout that period it is under close scrutiny.

Serios usually wears short-sleeved shirts or strips to the waist, making it impossible for him to conceal anything close to his hands. Besides, say the researchers, they are frequently close enough to the action when Serios tells them to fire the camera that they can actually see through the 'gismo' and *know* that it contains no hidden devices.

On numerous occasions images appeared when someone else was holding the 'gismo' and the camera, and able to examine both freely. Two eminent American psychical researchers, Dr J. G. Pratt and Dr Ian Stevenson, who conducted numerous tests with Serios, have stated: 'We have ourselves observed Ted in approximately 800 trials and we have never seen him act in a suspicious way in the handling of the gismo before or after a trial.' Quite apart from the fact that Serios has never been caught with any hidden transparencies or microfilm, Dr Eisenbud argues that the very nature of the images that Serios produces rules out the 'gimmick' theory.

Serios invited investigators to bring with them target pictures concealed in envelopes, which he tried to reproduce on Polaroid film paranormally. On the first occasion that

sometimes they even take the pictures themselves, with the camera pointing at the Chicago psychic – and yet, the results that emerge are frequently very strange indeed. Not all the photographs carry images; some are unusually white while others are totally and inexplicably black, even though the room lighting and other factors remain constant. Occasionally, the image that emerges from the Polaroid covers the whole area of the print while at other times it obliterates only a portion of Serios or identifiable items in the room where the experiment is being conducted.

Can Serios really impress his thoughts on photographs? It is so unlikely that the possibility of a cunning fraud has to be looked at

116

change, says Eisenbud, must have occurred no later than 1958 and possibly earlier, and research has failed to unearth any photographs of the store in its earlier days.

But, although Serios's paranormal picture corresponds perfectly (but for the name) with the present-day store, there is a curious substitution in one picture of the letter 'W' for 'O' so that it reads 'The Wld Gold Store'. And the 'W' is exactly where it would be if 'Wells Fargo' had been spelled out.

Something similar happened with a picture that showed two storeys of a building and some slightly out-of-focus lettering that was, nevertheless, discernible. The building was ultimately acknowledged by the Royal Canadian Mounted Police as one of their Air Division hangars, but they pointed out a curious misspelling, which other observers had also noted. The words in Serios's picture read 'Air Division *Cainadain* Moun——'.

If Serios were somehow using concealed transparencies to produce his pictures then he was also having to tamper with the

Eisenbud saw Serios produce a paranormal picture, in a Chicago hotel room, the psychiatrist had taken with him two views of the Kremlin buildings, each hidden in a cardboard-backed manila envelope.

One of the images that Serios produced at this session was of a tall, thin building, which one of the witnesses immediately identified as the Chicago Water Tower – a landmark that would have been familiar to Serios. Though this seemed to be totally off target, Eisenbud was very impressed, partly because some of the images and symbols in the picture were relevant to a line of thought that was in his mind at the time.

Two years later, however, Eisenbud came across another view of the Kremlin buildings and this time Ivan's Bell Tower, which was only partly visible in one of the two target pictures, was prominent. It was only then that he realised that it has 'an easily discernible resemblance' to the Chicago Water Tower. Serios, it seems, scored a hit after all.

But stranger things have happened. In May 1965 Serios produced 11 slightly different versions of what appeared to be a plate glass store front. On two of them the name 'The Old Gold Store' is clearly visible in bold block lettering. Two years later the place was recognised as a tourist shop in Central City, Colorado, which is now the 'Old Wells Fargo Express Office'. The name

Top: the blurred lettering on this 'thoughtograph' enabled researchers to identify the building as a hangar belonging to the Air Division of the Royal Canadian Mounted Police (above). The picture bears the unmistakable stamp of Ted Serios in the misspelling 'CAINADAIN'

originals in an expert way to come up with such bizarre images. Another very clear picture showed Williams's Livery Stable, across the street from the Opera House in Central City. But there were strange distortions. The brickwork had changed: in Serios's picture it was like imbedded rock whereas the building is in fact constructed of pressed brick. Also, the windows in the paranormal print were bricked up.

Because of such pictures, in which Serios seems to be photographing the past (and distorting reality, too), Eisenbud and some fellow researchers arranged an experimental session on 27 May 1967 at the Denver Museum of Natural History where, surrounded by neolithic and paleolithic artefacts, it was hoped his powers might capture on film something that was several thousand years old.

Serios felt confident of success and began by drawing a mental impression he had received of a man lighting a fire. Strange images were recorded on several of the

Hidden in the hand?

James Randi, professional stage magician and debunker of things paranormal, is convinced that Ted Serios is a fraud and that his so-called 'thoughtographs' are produced not by the power of his mind but by the device Serios calls a 'gismo'.

A 'typical Serios gimmick', described by Randi in his book *Flim-flam! – the truth about unicorns, parapsychology and other delusions*, consists of a small magnifying lens, about ½ inch (1.2 centimetres) in diameter and with a focal length of about 1½ inches (4 centimetres), fixed to one end of a cylinder about 1½ inches (4 centimetres) long. A circle cut from a colour transparency (a 35-millimetre slide, for example) is glued to the other end of the cylinder. To avoid detection,

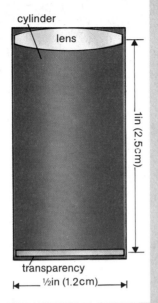

cylinder
lens
1in (2.5cm)
transparency
½in (1.2cm)

the device can be wrapped loosely in a tube of paper.

By holding the 'gismo' – lens end towards the palm – close to the lens of a Polaroid camera focused to infinity, and snapping the shutter, the image on the transparency will be thrown onto the Polaroid film. After use, Randi explains, the 'gismo' will slide easily out of the paper (to be disposed of secretly later) and the empty paper tube can be offered for inspection.

It is possible to take photographs in this way, although the pictures that result will usually be of poor quality, just as those 'taken' by Serios were. However, showing how the images *could* have been produced is very different from using such an optical device undetected in hundreds of demonstrations. And neither Randi nor any other of Ted Serios's critics has done that.

pictures, the most impressive of which shows a Neanderthal man in a crouching position. But Serios's camera lens had *not* delved into time to record this image. It was realised immediately by one witness, Professor H. Marie Wormington, of the Department of Anthropology, Colorado College, that it resembled very closely a well-known life-size model of a Neanderthal man group in the Chicago Field Museum of Natural History, postcards of which were readily available.

The final curtain

So, was Serios faking the photographs? Subsequent studies show that the man in Serios's pictures is shown at different angles and in the opinion of several professional photographers and photogrammetric engineers, these paranormal prints 'could not have been produced from a single microtransparency, but would have required at least several and perhaps eight different ones, most of which could not have been produced from a simple photographic copying of the Field Museum photograph or of a photograph taken by Ted himself.'

Soon after this session, Serios's psychic powers waned and within a year, although he continued to submit to experiments, all he could produce were 'blackies' or 'whities' without discernible images, leaving psychical researchers still baffled about just what paranormal forces had been at work to produce his astonishing pictures.

Serios had lost his powers at other times – the longest period being for two years – and it seemed to happen without warning. He said: 'It is as if a curtain comes down, ker-boom, and that's all, brother.'

But perhaps there was a warning. The last supervised full-frame thoughtograph he produced was in June 1967 . . . and it showed the image of a curtain.

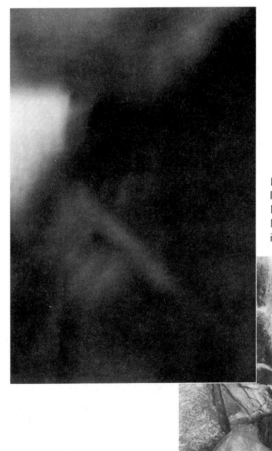

Left: Serios's version of a life-size model of a group of Neanderthals in the Field Museum of Natural History in Chicago (below)

Fulcanelli

One of the strangest stories to have emerged from the cloud of mystery that surrounds the ancient science of alchemy is that of the modern master Fulcanelli. KENNETH RAYNER JOHNSON describes what is known of this extraordinary man

The hidden face o

A. E. S. Fulcanelli

THE NAME FULCANELLI has flickered tantalisingly in and out of modern occult literature and speculation for more than half a century. Yet the identity of the 20th-century alchemist behind the pseudonym remains a complete mystery.

Today, Fulcanelli has taken on the aura almost of an alchemical 'saint' – an ageless adept of our own times, as enigmatic and fascinating as the semi-legendary Comte de St Germain.

It was in the early 1920s that the Fulcanelli legend started: Parisian occultists and alchemists began overhearing oblique and intriguing references to an actual master, alive and working secretly in their midst. These came mainly from Eugène Canseliet, an intense, slightly-built man in his early twenties who was known to be an enthusiastic researcher into alchemy. They were also bandied about by his constant companion and friend, an impoverished artist and illustrator, Jean-Julien Champagne, who was 22 years Canseliet's senior. The pair, who rented adjacent quarters on the sixth storey of a dilapidated tenement at 59 bis, rue de Rochechouart, in the Butte-Montmartre district, quickly became the focal point of a small, select circle of occultists. They were frequently seen in the city's great libraries, the Arsenal, the Sainte Geneviève, the Mazarin and the Bibliothèque Nationale, poring over rare books and manuscripts.

Those on the periphery of this informal study-group heard hints that 'the Master, Fulcanelli' was elderly, distinguished, rich, immensely learned and possibly even of aristocratic or noble lineage. He was a genuine, practising alchemist who, if he had not done so already, was on the brink of perfecting the Great Work – the manufacture of the Philosopher's Stone, which would ennoble base metals to perfection by transmutation, and the Elixir, which could prolong life indefinitely.

But who the Master really was remained a mystery. Few had apparently actually met him – except, so they claimed, Champagne and Canseliet. Sceptics began to question the fact of his existence.

Then, in the autumn of 1926, evidence of the Master's reality – or at least the reality of someone – appeared. It came in the form of a remarkable book, *Le mystère des cathédrales* ('The mystery of the cathedrals'), published in a limited luxury edition of only 300 copies, by Jean Schemit, of 45 rue Lafitte, in the Opéra district. It was subtitled 'An esoteric

The mystery of the cathedrals

In his book *Le mystère des cathédrales* Fulcanelli takes the reader on a guided and interpretative tour of many of France's finest examples of Gothic architecture, including the Cathedral of Notre Dame in Paris (below). Like many mystical commentators before him, he sees architecture as a means of passing on esoteric knowledge, encoded in the form and proportion of the building, its sculpture and stained glass.

His enthusiasm for Gothic architecture is reached via a circuitous route

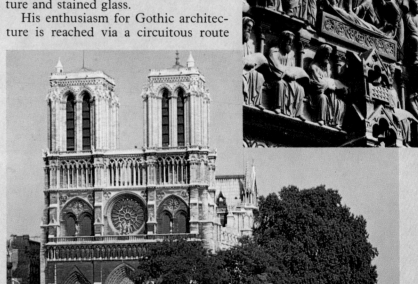

Fulcanelli

The Greek Sun-god Helios in his chariot, in a detail from a vase, and the Roman fire-god Vulcan, in a relief found at the Roman camp of Corstopitum in Northumbria. 'Fulcanelli' is a phonetic approximation of 'Vulcan' and 'Helios' – an allusion, perhaps, to the flames used to heat the mysterious substances that combine to form the Elixir of Life

Opposite page: this bracket in the mansion of Lallemant in Bourges shows a medieval adept holding the Vessel of the Great Work, in which the Elixir of Life is prepared

Above left: 59 bis, rue de Rochechouart, Paris. In this house lived Eugène Canseliet and Jean-Julien Champagne, reputedly pupils of the mysterious Fulcanelli

Below: Marguerite de France (1553–1615), who perhaps knew the secret of the Great Work. Rumour suggested Fulcanelli might be descended from her

involving a kind of punning logic. He interprets gothic art, *art gothique*, as *argot*-hique – and, he says, *argot* (cant or slang) is defined in dictionaries as 'a language peculiar to all individuals who wish to communicate their thoughts without being understood by outsiders.' And he claims that those who use this secret language are descendants of the sailors who accompanied Jason on his search for the Golden Fleece – aboard the ship *Argo*; they, he claims, 'spoke the *langue argotique* [language of the Argo] . . . while they were sailing towards the felicitous shores of Colchos . . .'

How does Fulcanelli's method work in practice? In the Portal of the Virgin of Notre Dame Cathedral (left), he sees the medallions of the sarcophagus as symbols of the seven planetary metals. (In the standard alchemical interpretation, the Sun stands for gold, Mercury for quicksilver, Saturn for lead, Venus for copper, the Moon for silver, Jupiter for tin and Mars for iron.) Taken as a whole, Fulcanelli claims, the portal gives clues as to how to transmute these metals. But Fulcanelli has not made matters too easy; the final step in interpretation is left to the alchemist. Perhaps this is just as well – for, as Fulcanelli's pupil Canseliet reveals in his introduction to the book, the '*key to the major arcanum* is given quite openly in one of the figures.'

interpretation of the hermetic symbols of the Great Work'. Its preface was by Eugène Canseliet, then aged only 26, and it contained 36 illustrations, two in colour, by the artist Champagne. The text itself was ascribed simply to Fulcanelli.

It purported to interpret the symbolism of various Gothic cathedrals and other buildings in Europe as encoded instructions of alchemical secrets, a concept only darkly hinted at by previous writers on the esoteric in art and architecture. Among occultists, it caused a minor sensation.

But even in his original preface, the young Canseliet intimated that his Master, Fulcanelli – the name is a phonetic approximation of Vulcan, the blacksmith god, and Helios, the sun-charioteer – had attained the Stone, become mystically transfigured and illuminated, and had disappeared.

He disappeared when the fatal hour struck, when the Sign was accomplished. . . . Fulcanelli is no more. But we have at least this consolation that his thought remains, warm and vital, enshrined for ever in these pages.

Perhaps understandably – especially in view of the immense scholarship and unique haunting qualities of the book – speculation about Fulcanelli's true identity ran wild within the occult fraternity.

There were suggestions that he was a surviving member of the former French royal family, the Valois. Although they were supposed to have died out in 1589 upon the demise of Henri III, it was known that members of the family had dabbled in magic and mysticism and that Marguerite de France, daughter of Henri II and wife of Henri IV of Navarre, survived until 1615. What is more, one of her many lovers was the esoterically inclined Francis Bacon (whom many still claim as an adept to this day); she was divorced in 1599 and her personal crest bore the magical pentagram, each of whose five points carried one letter of the Latin word *salus* – meaning 'health'. Could the reputedly aristocratic Fulcanelli be a descendant of the Valois, and did the Latin motto hint that some important alchemical secret of longevity had been passed on to him by the family? It was, at least, one possibility.

There were other, more or less plausible identifications. Some claimed Fulcanelli was a bookseller-occultist, Pierre Dujols, who with his wife ran a shop in the rue de Rennes in the Luxembourg district of Paris. But Dujols was already known to have been only a speculative alchemist, writing under the nom de plume of Magophon. Why should he hide behind two aliases? Another suggestion was that Fulcanelli was the writer J.H. Rosny the elder. Yet his life was too well-known to the public for this theory to find acceptance.

There were also at least three practical alchemists working in the city around the same period. They operated under the respective pseudonymns of Auriger, Faugerons and Dr Jaubert. The argument against them being Fulcanelli was much the same as that against Dujols-Magophon: why use more than one alias?

Finally, there were Eugène Canseliet and Jean-Julien Champagne, both of whom were directly connected with Fulcanelli's book, and both of whom had claimed to have known the Master personally.

The argument against Canseliet's identification as the Master was fairly straightforward: he was far too young to have acquired the erudition and knowledge so obviously and remarkably demonstrated by the text of *Le mystère des cathédrales*. And a study of his preface showed a distinct difference in style from that of the text, a difference that remains notable in Canseliet's more recent writings.

Champagne, meanwhile, seemed to some the more likely contender. He was older and more experienced, and his work as an artist

Above: Eugène Canseliet, pupil of Fulcanelli, who continues to keep the secret of the master alchemist's identity

Above: the writer J. H. Rosny the elder (1856–1940) who, many people suspected, was the figure behind the pseudonym 'Fulcanelli'

Left: Jean-Julien Champagne, artist and illustrator, and constant companion of Fulcanelli's pupil Eugène Canseliet. Champagne was a braggart and a practical joker, and his habit of trying to pass himself off as Fulcanelli added to the confusion about the true identity of the master alchemist

could have taken him around the various cathedrals, châteaux and other curious monuments whose symbolism Fulcanelli had obviously studied and interpreted in great detail as keys to the Great Work.

On the other hand, Champagne was a noted braggart, practical joker, punster and drunkard, who frequently liked to pass himself off as Fulcanelli – although his behaviour was entirely out of keeping with the traditional solemn oath of the adept to remain anonymous and let his written work speak for itself.

A vain and dangerous quest

Two examples of Champagne's wicked sense of humour suffice to show the great gap between his own way of thinking and that of the noble-minded author of *Le mystère des cathédrales*. Champagne once persuaded a gullible young follower that he should stock up a massive supply of coal to ensure that his alchemical furnace was kept constantly burning at the required temperature. The naïve youth lugged sack after sack of the fuel up to his garret until there was barely room in which to lie down and sleep. Champagne then announced to the would-be alchemist that the quest was an utterly vain and dangerous one – leaving him almost banished from his apartment by coal and, presumably, considerably out of pocket into the bargain.

The other carefully contrived prank of Champagne involved his forging a letter, purportedly from Monsieur Paul le Cour, who edited and published a periodical called *Atlantis*, to the publisher of the *Mercure de France*. In it, the fake le Cour urged the setting up of a fund by the *Mercure's* subscribers to build a monument for the victims of the fabled lost continent – a cenotaph that, since he suggested it be placed in the Sargasso Sea, would have to be unsinkable. Champagne sat back and laughed while the unsuspecting 'real' le Cour received an indignant volley from the *Mercure* publisher.

To crown all of this, Champagne's huge

appetite for absinthe and Pernod finally killed him. He died in 1932 of gangrene in his sixth-floor garret. His friend Canseliet nursed him through his long, painful and particularly unpleasant illness (Champagne's toes actually fell off). The poor artist was aged only 55.

Only three years earlier, a second work by the mysterious Fulcanelli had been published, again by Jean Schemit. It was *Les demeures philosophales* ('The dwellings of the philosophers'), which was in two volumes and double the length of the first book. Like its predecessor, it interpreted particular architectural embellishments, such as ornate ceiling panels – this time in 12th- to 15th-century mansions and châteaux – as encoded alchemical knowledge.

The appearance of this book inspired yet another theory about Fulcanelli's possible

Below: F. Jolivet Castelot, a practising 'archimist' – someone who tries to use ordinary chemical methods to transmute base metals into gold – and yet another Fulcanelli-suspect

identity. Inside the rear cover of the second volume were the armorial bearings of Dom Robert Jollivet, a 13th-century abbot of Mont-St-Michel, known to have dabbled in alchemy. This, according to the theory, implied that the name of Jollivet was intended to indicate that his modern near-namesake, F. Jolivet Castelot, was in fact Fulcanelli. Jolivet Castelot was President of the Alchemists' Society of France from around 1914 and was a member of the Ordre Kabbalistique de la Rose-Croix. Between 1896 and 1935, he had published many studies in hermeticism, alchemy and spagyrics – the art of making chemical/medical preparations using alchemical principles. But he made no secret of the fact that he was an 'archimist' rather than an alchemist – that is, a researcher who tried to effect transmutation by orthodox chemistry, rather than a more mystically inclined alchemist.

There was, however, an even stranger heraldic shield on the final page of the original edition of *Le mystère des cathédrales*.

The occult scholar Robert Ambelain who,

Is this inscription on the grave of Jean-Julien Champagne, containing clues pointing to Fulcanelli, merely a last attempt to convince people he was the mysterious alchemist?

in the 1930s, made one of the most thorough investigations into the Fulcanelli mystery was the first to draw attention to this shield. Among many other alleged clues, Ambelain pointed out that the dog-Latin motto beneath the shield was *uber campa agna*, which was a phonetic approximation of Hubert Champagne. And, he claimed, Hubert was the middle name of the artist, Jean-Julien Champagne, He also noted that the pseudonym Fulcanelli is an anagram of *l'écu finale* ('the final shield'), thus indirectly indicating the heraldic device and its motto.

Eugène Canseliet, however, has flatly denied the identification of Champagne as Fulcanelli – or of anyone else, for that matter – consistently since 1926. Hubert was not the artist's middle name, he claims – although it is, by sheer coincidence, that of his own maternal grandfather. In any case, he further asserts, the damning shield was inserted into the first edition of the book by Champagne – without the permission or knowledge of the Master, Fulcanelli, or of himself – another practical joke!

Deceptions and forgeries

Canseliet, who is Fulcanelli's sole surviving pupil and official literary executor, similarly claims that an inscription on Champagne's gravestone, along with a deliberate forgery of Fulcanelli's signature by the artist, were further attempts to deceive or mislead. The gravestone epitaph, at the cemetery of Arnouvilles-les-Gonesses, reads:

Here rests Jean-Julien Champagne
Apostolicus Hermeticae Scientiae
1877–1932

The alleged Fulcanelli signature, meanwhile, appeared in a handwritten dedication of the original edition of *Le mystère des cathédrales*, given by Champagne to an occultist named Jules Boucher. It was signed A.H.S. Fulcanelli – the same initials as those of the Latin motto on the gravestone. And in Jules Boucher's *Manual of magic*, the author's dedication is to 'my master Fulcanelli'.

Curiously enough, despite all his alleged evidence to the contrary, Ambelain reaches the conclusion that Champagne did actually achieve the Philosopher's Stone – the stone that transmutes base metals into gold and allows the manufacture of the Elixir of Life – some three years before his death.

But if Ambelain is correct, how could this explain Champagne's untimely and less than dignified death through over-indulgence in drink at the age of 55? Quite simply, it doesn't make sense.

And yet, more than one person has attested to Fulcanelli's success in transmutation and to his continued existence – even in the 1980s – which would make him more than 130 years old!

Transformation of an alchemist

At their final meeting in 1954, Canseliet reported that his master Fulcanelli seemed youthful – although he must have been over 100 years old. Had he found the secret of eternal life?

IN FRANCE THE NAME of Fulcanelli quickly found popular acceptance as the traditional pseudonym of an alchemical Master. Go to the 16th-century Château de Terre-Neuve, Vendée, even today, and there you will be shown an ornately decorated 'alchemical fireplace' – and the French guide will tell you it is the one of which Fulcanelli wrote in *Les demeures philosophales*, without even bothering to explain who Fulcanelli was . . . or is.

But to English-speaking students of occultism and alchemy, it was not until 1963 that the publication of Louis Pauwels's and Jacques Bergier's best-seller *The dawn of magic* in English ensured that Fulcanelli and his works came to be more widely known. And it was a further eight years before Fulcanelli's first masterpiece, *Le mystère des cathédrales*, was translated into English.

Each of these books provided astounding new information about Fulcanelli. The latter, for example, contained the bold assertion by Fulcanelli's disciple Eugène Canseliet that the Master had given him a minute quantity of the alchemical 'powder of projection' in 1922 – and permitted him to transmute 4 ounces (100 grams) of lead into gold. The experiment, Canseliet told Walter

Below: the noted French atomic physicist André Helbronner. In 1937 his research assistant Jacques Bergier was warned of the implications of manipulating nuclear energy by a mysterious stranger – whom he identified as Fulcanelli

Lang, who wrote the book's introduction, took place in the unlikely setting of a gasworks at Sarcelles before two witnesses: the artist Jean-Julien Champagne and a young chemist named Gaston Sauvage.

Furthermore, in a letter to Lang, Canseliet maintained that, when he had last worked with Fulcanelli, 'The Master was already a very old man but he carried his eighty years lightly. Thirty years later, I was to see him again . . . and he appeared to be a man of fifty. That is to say, he appeared to be no older than I was myself.'

Canseliet, aged 80 in 1981, has subsequently asserted that he has, on more than one occasion, kept a secret rendezvous with his Master – and that Fulcanelli is still very much alive.

Another possible appearance of the Master was reported by Pauwels and Bergier in their book. Bergier claimed that in June 1937 – eight years before the first atom-bomb test in New Mexico – he was approached by an impressive but mysterious stranger. The man asked Bergier to pass on a message to the noted physicist André Helbronner, for whom he was then working. He said he felt it his duty to warn orthodox scientists, now

Louis Pauwels (right) and Jacques Bergier (far right), whose best-selling *The dawn of magic*, published in 1963, brought the first news of Fulcanelli to English-speaking readers

that they were on the brink of being able to manipulate nuclear energy, of the danger of this new discovery. The alchemists of bygone times – and previous civilisations that had destroyed themselves – had obtained such secret knowledge. The stranger said he held out no hope that his warning would be heeded, but nonetheless felt obliged to issue it. Bergier remained convinced, right up to his death in November 1978, that the enigmatic stranger was Fulcanelli.

As a result of Bergier's experience, the American Office for Strategic Services, forerunner of the CIA, made a search for Fulcanelli when the Second World War ended in 1945. They were anxious to round up anyone who had prior knowledge of nuclear physics, to prevent their defection to hostile powers. But Fulcanelli could not be found.

Alchemy and the atom bomb
There is, however, one flaw in Bergier's story. According to his own account, the man who visited him, while speaking apparently knowledgeably about the manipulation of nuclear energy, mentioned the element plutonium. Yet this element was not isolated until February 1941, by the physicist Glenn T. Seaborg, at Berkeley, California. Furthermore, it was not actually *named* plutonium until March 1942 – five years after Bergier's alleged encounter. In fact, Element 94, as it was previously called, was almost dubbed 'plutium' – but Seaborg, as its discoverer, decided plutonium rolled more easily off the tongue.

But the fact remains that Bergier claimed that *someone* highly knowledgeable visited him at the Paris Gas Board laboratory in 1937. And he was said to have a photographic memory.

There is one further account that tells of a transmutation performed by Fulcanelli himself. It comes from a modern alchemist, now

Glenn T. Seaborg, who discovered the element plutonium in 1941. Bergier claimed that the stranger who visited him in 1937 mentioned plutonium by name – and yet this event occurred four years before the element was isolated, and five years before it was actually called plutonium

operating from Salt Lake City, Utah. He is Frater Albertus Spagyricus, born Albert Riedel in Dresden, Germany, in 1911. A former interior decorator, Frater Albertus now heads the flourishing Paracelsus College (Utah Institute of Parachemistry), formed originally as the Paracelsus Research Society in 1960. The college operates regular seminars on alchemical subjects at its headquarters and seeks to 'bring alchemy out of the Dark Ages'.

In his book *The alchemist of the Rocky Mountains* (1975), Frater Albertus claims that Fulcanelli transmuted half a pound (200 grams) of lead into gold and 4 ounces (100 grams) of silver into uranium in 1937 – the same year, it will be noted, as Bergier's meeting with the mysterious stranger. The experiment, according to Albertus, took place at the Castel de Leré, near Bourges, and was witnessed by the castle's owner, Pierre de Lesseps, along with two unnamed physicists, a chemist and geologist.

When Fulcanelli added an 'unknown substance' to the half-pound of molten lead, says Albertus, it was transmuted into the same weight in gold. Afterwards, Fulcanelli did the same with the silver, producing a like amount of uranium.

Asked what the unknown substance was, Fulcanelli 'would only mention offhandedly that it was derived from ferrous pyrite (fool's gold), a ferrous sulphide FeS_2.'

The present author wrote to Frater Albertus asking for his sources of information. But an assistant politely answered that Frater Albertus was unfortunately too busy teaching and attending to his lecture programme to be able to answer personally and in detail.

According to Frater Albertus, however, it was after the 1937 transmutation that Fulcanelli disappeared.

The only other person who has claimed to have contacted Fulcanelli in more recent

The perfect being

The aim of alchemists in attempting to complete the Great Work is not merely to enable them to change base metals into gold, or even to achieve eternal youth. For alchemists believe that every stage in the alchemical process is accompanied by a spiritual change in the person conducting the work.

The secret of the alchemical art is said to be contained in the aphoristic principle *solve et coagula*, 'dissolve and combine'. This is a fair description of the physical aspect of the alchemical process: at each stage, the various characteristics of a substance are stripped away, and a new, nobler substance is built up. In the spiritual aspect, this means a 'death' followed by a 'rebirth' into a better, purer life – a concept familiar in many religions; St Paul, for instance, exhorts the faithful to 'die to sin and live to righteousness'.

In the final stage of the Great Work, 'the King is reunited in the Fire of Love with his blessed Queen' – and the Alchemist becomes the perfect being, the Divine Androgyne, the perfect conjunction of man and woman.

times is his faithful pupil Canseliet. He has asserted that he met his Master in Spain in 1954 in highly unusual circumstances.

If Fulcanelli was, as Canseliet maintains, 80 when last they worked together in the late 1920s, it would make the Master Alchemist between 100 and 110 years old by the time of the Spanish meeting. Confirmation that Canseliet did indeed go to Spain that year was obtained by the late Gerard Heym, founder member of the Society for the Study of Alchemy and Early Chemistry and editor of *Ambix*, its journal. Heym, who was acclaimed by many as Europe's foremost occult scholar of his day, made friends with Canseliet's daughter and through her managed to take a look at his passport. It carried a Spanish entry-visa stamp for 1954.

But how Canseliet received the summons to Spain and what actually went on there is highly mysterious. Heym told the occultist Walter Lang that he gained the impression that a message was received in some paranormal way, possibly through clairvoyance. And a close friend of Canseliet, who was still engaged in alchemical research in 1981 and must remain anonymous, told the present writer: 'He has told me in detail how he met Fulcanelli in Spain – in another dimension, as it were, or rather at a point where such meetings are possible.'

Further enquiries elicited the information that Canseliet went to Seville and was met and taken by a long, circuitous route to a large mountain château. It turned out to be a secret colony of alchemists – and it was here that Canseliet had once again met his former

Frater Albertus Spagyricus, director of Paracelsus College, the Utah Institute of Parachemistry. He claims that in 1937, before three witnesses, Fulcanelli performed transmutations of lead into gold, and silver into uranium

Master in such mysterious circumstances.

But, even more peculiar to those not familiar with alchemical philosophy and its aura of mysticism, Fulcanelli appeared to have undergone a curious form of transformation. He seemed androgynous – to have characteristics of both men and women.

Canseliet has told sources close to him – he does not receive casual visitors and cannot deal with his massive mail – that Fulcanelli actually had the appearance of a woman. This kind of physical change has been reported in obscure pockets of alchemical literature as one of the side effects of taking the Elixir of Life. If the elixir is successful, the subject is said to lose all his hair, teeth and nails, then regrow them and take on younger, smoother, almost asexual facial features.

According to Gerard Heym, Canseliet returned home with only vague recollections of his experiences in Spain – almost as if, said Heym, he had been subjected to some form of hypnosis, designed to make him forget the details of what he had seen and been told.

Curiously enough, Canseliet has admitted his own failure to perfect the Third Degree of the Great Work – the manufacture of the Stone and Elixir. And, apart from being a respected author and savant on the alchemical art, he seems to have gained little personal benefit – financially or otherwise – from his long association with the mysterious Fulcanelli.

The image of perfection

Alchemists believe that, in the final stage of the Great Work, the adept himself is transformed into a 'perfect being' – half man, half woman.

A statue representing Prudence, from the tomb of François II in Nantes Cathedral. It shows the figure of a young girl – with the face of a wise old man on the back of her head. Fulcanelli believed the statue symbolised nature in all her aspects, and also the final stage of the alchemical process, in which opposites combine to produce the perfect, androgynous, being

ON HIS MYSTERIOUS VISIT to Spain in 1954, Eugène Canseliet claimed he again saw his Master, Fulcanelli – transfigured, as it seemed, by the results of his alchemical attainment. The Master appeared not only to have retrieved his youth and vitality, but was clear-skinned and effeminate – perhaps even, Canseliet said, asexual.

Absurd as this idea may sound, especially to those unversed in alchemical philosophy, there is within the deeper esoteric traditions of the Hermetic art a suggestion that with the blinding flash of illumination that heralds success comes a tremendous change in the adept, both spiritual and physical. Like the base metal that attainment of the Philosopher's Stone permits him to transmute into gold, the alchemist himself is transformed utterly. The metamorphosed adept takes the form of a perfect balance of the female and male polarities within human nature – and with it, an outward form of bisexuality or hermaphroditism, certainly in the facial features. These mysterious changes, the results of inner, profound, spiritual experiences – with equally physical, tangible effects – have been said to occur also in saints, holy men and devotional mystics in beatific states.

Could the modern alchemist Fulcanelli have undergone this transformation after attaining the Stone and Elixir and completing the Great Work?

In his second book, *Les demeures philosophales*, Fulcanelli indicates that he is not unaware of this possibility. In fact, he draws particular attention to a remarkable piece of sculpture – one of four statues that guard the tomb of François II in Nantes Cathedral. Fulcanelli calls it Prudence.

In frontal view, it depicts the figure of a beautiful young girl in a hooded cloak and floor-length gown. She seems mesmerised by her own reflection in a strange, convex mirror she holds in her left hand. In her right hand is a set of compasses – or perhaps *dividers*; throughout alchemical literature, there are frequent injunctions to separate and conjoin. And on the back of the girl's head is another face – that of a full-bearded, wise old sage, apparently deep in philosophical contemplation.

Fulcanelli compares this figure of Prudence with the god Janus, the two-faced, son of Apollo and Creusa. Enfolded within the cloak of philosophy, he says, she symbolises nature in all her aspects – both inward and outward. But beneath her exterior veil, he adds, there appears the mysterious image of ancient alchemy, 'and we are, through the attributes of the first, initiated into the secrets of the second.' He writes:

It is generally recommended to unite

A cryptic message

The penultimate chapter of Fulcanelli's book *Le mystère des cathédrales* concerns an unusual stone cross located in the village of Hendaye in the foothills of the Pyrenees. Somewhat circumspectly, Fulcanelli suggests that the monument contains encoded prophecies indicating a future cataclysm.

Fulcanelli believes that the inscription INRI, normally rendered as *Iesus Nazarenus Rex Iudeorum* ('Jesus of Nazareth, King of the Jews'), has a second

interpretation that gives the cross its true meaning: *Igne Natura Renovatur Integra*, 'by fire nature is renewed whole'. This, Fulcanelli claims, is a reference to the purifying fire that will soon consume the northern hemisphere.

He also draws attention to the strange inscription OCRUXAVES PESUNICA at the head of the cross. This can be broken up to form the phrase *O crux ave spes unica*, 'Hail, o cross, the only hope'. But the strange way in which the inscription is carved suggests that there may be a hidden message.

By an extension of what Fulcanelli calls the phonetic cabala, a retired engineer and student of Fulcanelli's cryptographic writings, Paul Mevry, has arrived at a fascinating new interpretation. OCRUXAVES PESUNICA is an anagram of the Latin phrase *Orcus ave pus e canis*, meaning 'Orcus, hail, down from the Dog'. Orcus is the Roman Lord of the Underworld – whom the ancient Egyptians knew as Osiris, the Lord of the Dead. Since the Egyptians associated Osiris with the Dog star, Sirius, could this then be some form of warning of destruction to come from the system of Sirius and its dark companion Sirius B?

And could the very location of the cross at Hendaye – similar to *end-day* – be a clue to the coming apocalypse?

'an old man, hale and vigorous, with a young and beautiful virgin.' Of these alchemical nuptials, a metallic child is born and receives the epithet of *androgyne*, because he possesses all at once the nature of sulphur, his father, and that of his mother, mercury . . . . Practically all esoteric systems of self-illumination, of raising the base human body and spirit to a higher state, at some stage emphasise the necessity – allegorically or otherwise – to attain this inner balance of the

male and female polarities. And the concept even squares with more modern psycho-analytic thinking, especially with Jungian psychology. Indeed, Jung himself devoted more than 10 years of his life to the study of alchemy and wrote several large volumes on the subject, linking its strange 'archetypal' symbolism to that of dreams, inner experiences – and psychology.

The symbolism of the Divine Androgyne is not, by any means, simply physical or sexual. Its main, inner meaning appears to

The tangled web

'The picture of the labyrinth,' Fulcanelli tells us in *Le mystère des cathédrales*, is 'emblematic of the whole labour of the Work. . . . It is there that the *thread of Ariadne* becomes necessary for him [the alchemist] if he is not to wander among the winding paths of the task, unable to extricate himself.'

He goes on to use the phonetic cabala to elucidate the symbolic value of the famous Greek legend of Ariadne, who with a thread helped Theseus to escape after he had slain the Minotaur.

'Ariane (Ariadne) is a form of *airagne*

(araignée, the spider). . . . In Spanish ñ is pronounced gn; αράχνη [pronounced arachne] (the spider) can thus be read *arahne, arahni, arahagne*. Is not our soul the spider, which weaves our own body? . . . The verb αἴρω [airo] means *to take, to seize, to draw, to attract*; whence αἴρην [airen], that which takes, seizes, attracts. Thus αἴρην is the lodestone, that virtue shut up in the body. . . .'

Fulcanelli connects, through some cunning twists of logic, the Provençal *aran, iran, airan* – iron – with the Greek αρυαν meaning both 'lodestone' and 'rising sun'. And there he leaves it – a set of tantalising word-associations, significant only for the initiated.

or, as he confided to one associate 'in another dimension, as it were'? It is mere conjecture, of course, but could he have been the subject of some form of initiation into the deeper mysteries of the Hermetic Quest? In the light of alchemical tradition, there would seem to be no other logical explanation for Canseliet's bizarre encounter.

And why should an elderly man, respected for decades as an authority on alchemy, invent such a weird and wonderful tale – at the risk of his reputation?

No one has managed to identify the historical person who hid behind the cloaked pseudonym of Fulcanelli. And M. Canseliet, if he *does* know the personality behind that name, has certainly respected the anonymity of his most unusual and erudite Master.

evoke stability, harmony, perfect balance in all possible ways. In the system of the Jewish *qabalah*, this finds beautiful religious expression in several passages of the Lesser Holy Assembly: 'When the Bride is united to the King in the excellence of the Sabbath, then are all things made one body,' and 'the beauty of the female is completed by the beauty of the male. . . . When the Mother is united to the King, the worlds receive a blessing and are found in the joy of the universe.'

How may these concepts be equated with the strange experience of Canseliet in Spain –

Above left: a Roman coin showing the two faces of Janus, Roman god of doors and archways, sometimes referred to as *divom deus*, the god of gods

Below: in the Lallement house in Bourges is a *bas-relief* of the Golden Fleece (right). Fulcanelli claimed the story was 'a complete representation of the hermetic process'

The strange histories of Joan Grant

Have we all had previous existences in many different centuries and civilisations? Joan Grant believes she has – and ROY STEMMAN recounts the fascinating story of how she has learned to trace those many other lives

JOAN GRANT HIT the public eye in 1937 with her first highly praised book, *Winged pharaoh*. It was classified as an historical novel and, like others that followed, was judged by the experts to be a very accurate account of the time it portrayed. But Joan Grant did not have to research a single detail – she recorded everything from her 'far memory' of the life she had lived as a priest-pharaoh in a previous incarnation.

Joan Grant had intimations of her other lives even as a tiny child; she told stories about who she had been 'before she was Joan' – but nobody believed her. Soon she learned that it was better to keep her stories to herself, and she told nobody else until she was a teenager. Meanwhile, she struggled to unravel her strange dreams and to understand who she was. It took a great effort to train herself to wake several times a night so she could write down the events that had just occurred in her sleep.

Joan Grant was born in 1907 of a wealthy family and lived a sheltered life of comfort and plenty. Even during the First World War she suffered little physical privation. But during that time she began to have vivid

Joan Grant, flanked by her first and best-known book and a photograph of herself as a girl. She had glimpses of other lives even as a tiny child – and Winged pharaoh told the story of one of them as a priest-ruler in ancient Egypt

war dreams in which all five senses were engaged. In fact, the smells of battlefield and hospital made her violently sick upon waking, and for weeks she tried to keep herself from sleeping by self-torture such as sitting on an icy floor or pulling hairs out. At one point during this time, when at a convent in London where she loved the nuns, she was constantly terrified for no reason. Nearly 20 years later she found out that the reason lay in a life she had lived in the 16th century.

One morning at home she came down late for breakfast after a terrible nightmare. There was a soldier with her father, and Joan said to him:

Somehow I know you will not laugh at me. Last night I was with a man called McAndrew when he was killed. I can describe the regimental badge although I cannot remember the name of the regiment, except that it was not an English one. And I can tell you the slang name of his trench.

The visitor did not laugh because he was able to identify the regiment as Canadian. Later, he wrote to Joan's father, Jack Marshall:

For heaven's sake don't laugh at the

child. I cannot attempt an explanation, but I have checked what she said. A battalion of that regiment went over the top on a night attack a few hours before she told me about it at breakfast. A private called McAndrew was among the killed. She was even correct about the local name of the front-line trench.

Joan was only nine at the time, and it was years before her father told her of this unexpected confirmation.

Marshall was a scientist who won a CBE for his work in mosquito research, on which he wrote the standard text. Many eminent men were visitors to his home. One, C.G. Lamb, was professor of engineering at Cambridge University and Joan's special favourite. They had long talks and she felt at ease with him, partly because of his great interest in psychical research.

Lamb had been a friend of Joan's grandmother, Jennie Marshall. One day while they were chatting, he told Joan that Jennie could have been a world-famous concert pianist if her husband had not stood in her way. 'Jennie gives me music lessons,' said Joan in reply, aware that any other adult would have scoffed at the claim, since Jennie was dead. 'Father knows I would never be a first-class pianist so there is no point in my having lessons, but Jennie knows I need music and she teaches me. Sometimes she plays the piano with me – music that is quite different from the ordinary tunes I have learned.'

Feeling that her grandmother was present, young Joan went to the piano and music began to flow. When she stopped, Lamb mopped his brow and remarked: 'Extraordinary. Quite extraordinary but completely evidential. What you have just played was

Top: Seacourt, the childhood home of Joan Grant at Hayling in Hampshire

Above: C.G. Lamb, professor of engineering at Cambridge University, was interested in psychical research and gave a sympathetic ear to Joan Grant's accounts of unusual occurrences. And in one instance he was able to prove from personal knowledge that her experience was paranormal

Left: Blanche and Jack Marshall, parents of Joan Grant. Through her father's wide social contacts, Joan met H.G. Wells. The author advised her to keep her 'secret life' to herself for a while – and then to write about it later

often played to me by your grandmother. . . . I have not heard it since she died.'

When Joan suggested that she may have heard her grandmother play it, or have heard it at a concert, Lamb assured her that she had not.

Only one copy of that music ever existed. It was given in manuscript to the Tsar of Russia, who sent it to your grandmother. . . . I happen to know that the manuscript of that music, together with several other manuscripts of similar value, was burned two years before you were born.

Jennie Marshall had learned that she had terminal cancer, and decided that no one else would play her music if she could not do so.

It was to the author H.G. Wells, whom she met at the age of 16, that Joan confessed all about 'the secret part of her life'. He was sympathetic, but advised her to keep it to herself until she was 'strong enough to bear being laughed at by fools'; then, when she was ready, she should write down what she knew – 'It is important that you become a writer,' said Wells.

Joan Grant broke off her first engagement because her fiancé and his family were intolerant of her belief in her dream lives. It was indeed a dream that led her to her next romance.

This dream of a man recurred over a period of time, during which she went to Switzerland for a ski-ing holiday. Alone in the hotel music room, she was playing Jennie's music on the piano when the door opened – and she looked into the eyes of the man in her dream. The stranger looked at her intently and then said, 'It really is you. I have dreamed with you for nearly two years':

dictation. Joan says she learned how to shift levels of consciousness between sleep and wakefulness so that she did not have to break the thread of events and was able to describe her dreams as she had them. This, she said, helped her to dip more easily into what she called her 'far memory'. Her far-memory dreams transcended space and time.

Another category of her dreams she called 'true dreams'. These depicted incidents that were later found to have occurred at about the time she was dreaming. In one such dream she was a sailor on a burning ship. On waking she told Leslie about it. There was enough detail to say with certainty that the ship was in the Channel, the sailor was French, and the vessel was going to Cherbourg. She thought the ship's name was *Atlantic*. Later that day, newspaper headlines declared '*Atlantique* burns in English Channel: many dead'.

Besides far-memory dreams, Joan Grant soon discovered another way of tuning into the past. At her husband's suggestion, she took up psychometry, and was able to receive vivid impressions of events or people connected with an object just by holding it in her hand for a short time.

A pharaoh's life

In 1936 the psychic was given a scarab and whenever she handled it she recalled events of what appeared to be a previous life in Egypt. In 200 sessions she dictated the story of her existence as Sekeeta, the daughter of a pharaoh and later a priest-pharaoh herself. It amounted to 120,000 words and was published as Sekeeta's 'posthumous autobiography' under the title of *Winged pharaoh*.

What makes Sekeeta's story particularly fascinating is its claim that far memory was known and developed in Egyptian times. Those who received training in it had to remember at least 10 of their own deaths, and their graduation examination required them to be shut in a tomb for four days and nights, during which they underwent seven ordeals.

Sekeeta passed the test and seems to have brought her ability into the 20th century, remembering along the way lives in Greece in the second century BC, in medieval England and 16th-century Italy, and various others in Egypt.

Has Joan Grant really lived all these lives? Do we all have such a continuous past, spanning many centuries and civilisations? Her series of far-memory books and three autobiographical volumes insist that there is much more to life than the existence we are currently experiencing.

What is equally interesting is Joan Grant's claim that our present ills and problems may well have their roots in previous incarnations – and can be cured by far-memory recall of them.

within 24 hours of meeting, Joan and Esmond decided to become engaged.

Esmond had to go to France for six months on business and they planned to marry on his return. He spent the last few days before going abroad at the Marshall home. On the last night, as Esmond was walking to his bedroom, Joan heard a voice – she believes it was her grandmother's – say softly but distinctly: 'After Esmond leaves here tomorrow you will never see him again.'

On the night before he was due to return to England, Esmond died in an accident at a Paris shooting gallery with a gun he thought was not loaded.

Another dream in which a woman told her to 'Go to Leslie' sent Joan to Leslie Grant, whom she married in 1927 at the age of 20. Now she had an ally and a helper in her husband, who willingly undertook the job of writing down her dream experiences from

An aerial view of the burning of the French ship *Atlantique* off Guernsey on 4 January 1933. Joan Grant had a precognitive dream about the disaster. In it she was a French sailor caught in a ship fire. She even named the ship as the *Atlantic* and knew it was sailing the Channel

Have we shared previous lives with those who are close to us in this life? Can learning about traumas experienced in other lives relieve emotional problems?

JOAN GRANT HAS SUFFERED some dreadful deaths. She has been burned as a witch, been killed by a spear through the eye during a joust, and has bled to death when she ordered her Roman court physician to cut her wrists.

Twice she has committed suicide and twice she has died after being bitten by snakes. During a lifetime in Egypt, when she was a man, she was bitten by an insect and died from the infection. Another life ended when she broke her neck in a diving accident.

Joan Grant believes that everyone has had similar past lives, with deaths that are just as traumatic and horrifying. The difference is that most people can no longer remember their previous incarnations, whereas she has had a 'far memory' since childhood. Moreover, she has developed it to the extent that she can recall her earlier lives in exact detail.

Joan Grant perfected the technique of 'shifting the level of consciousness' between sleeping and waking so that she could dictate her dream experiences of previous lives. Seven books of these experiences have been published as historical novels, though she calls them 'posthumous autobiographies'. In addition, she has written about her experiences and abilities in this lifetime (*Far memory*, 1956) and her therapy work with her third husband, Dr Denys Kelsey (*Many lifetimes*, 1969).

The book for which she is best-known is

Above: Ramesses II, pharaoh of Egypt over 3000 years ago. Joan Grant believes that she lived as a man during his reign, a life she described in her book *So Moses was born*

Left: vultures savaging the carcase of a dead elephant. Vultures hovering over Alec Kerr-Clarkson in a previous incarnation created a phobia about touching bird feathers in this life. He overcame this fear when Joan Grant showed him the root cause of it by 'resonating' with his earlier self and discovering what had happened

Breaking with the past

Winged pharaoh (1937). It is the story of Sekeeta, a pharaoh's daughter, who became co-ruler with her brother when her father died. Sekeeta spent 10 years in a temple learning to recall her previous lives, an ability she has brought with her into the 20th century as Joan Grant. Sekeeta eventually qualified to be both a ruler and a priest: a winged pharaoh.

In another Egyptian life nearly 1000 years later, Joan Grant was a man: Ra-ab Hotep. His life appeared in two books, *Eyes of Horus* and *Lord of the horizon*, which were published in the early 1940s. *So Moses was born* (1952) dealt with a life when Joan Grant was a male contemporary of Ramesses II.

Joan Grant was born in England in 1907. As well as several lives in Egypt, she had incarnations in other places. In the 16th century she was in Italy, having been born Carola di Ludovici on 4 May 1510. She became a singer with a troupe of strolling players and died at the age of 27. In more recent times, she was an English girl named

Lavinia who broke her back in a fall from a horse. Lavinia died in 1875.

Taken at face value, it would seem that Joan Grant has lived numerous times before her present existence. But that, she says, is too simple an interpretation. She believes that our spirits are far greater than we realise and that each of the many other personalities she can recall has a soul. At death they become part of the whole spirit again. If, for some reason, the soul fails to integrate with the spirit, it produces a ghost. Joan Grant explains: 'Joan and Sekeeta are two beads on the same necklace and the memory they share is contained in the string.'

There are still wider implications to Joan Grant's far memory. She believes that many of the people who are close to us in this life have shared our lives in previous times. Sometimes they were husbands, sometimes wives. They may have been brothers or

Below: a witch being burned at the stake in the late Middle Ages in Germany. In one of her previous lives, Joan Grant believes she died just such a horrible death

Bottom: a group of strolling players rehearsing in 18th-century England. Joan Grant recalls leading the life of a singer with a troupe like this – but in Italy 200 years previously

sisters, sons or daughters, lovers or friends. Our spirit, she asserts, is androgynous and therefore we incarnate in both male and female form. This makes for a wide range of personal relationships over time.

For example, one of the greatest influences on Joan Grant's early life was Daisy Sartorius, a family friend. It was while holding a scarab belonging to Daisy Sartorius that Joan Grant began recalling her previous life as Sekeeta, in the First Dynasty of Egypt about 3000 BC. In that existence, Joan discovered, Daisy had been her mother.

Similar connections were found between previous lives and her third husband, Dr Denys Kelsey. It was Denys Kelsey, a physician and psychiatrist, who cut the veins in Joan's wrists in Roman times on her orders, when he was also a physician. They later shared a life together as husband and wife in 18th-century England.

Dr Kelsey worked in the psychiatric wing at a military hospital in 1948. In trying to help the patients, he discovered the value of

hypnosis, at which he became adept. In addition, 'a series of cases came my way which, step by step, extended the framework of what I believed to be fact until, after four years, a session with a particular patient forced me to the intellectual certainty that in a human being there is a component which is not physical.'

Joan Grant's first book had a profound effect on Dr Denys Kelsey. He records in *Many lifetimes*: 'Before I had finished *Winged pharaoh* . . . I knew beyond any possibility of doubt, that reincarnation was a reality. . . . I would have journeyed halfway round the world to meet the author, but fortunately such a long pilgrimage proved unnecessary.' He discovered they lived only 30 miles (50 kilometres) apart. They met in 1958, and within two months 'embarked upon life together'.

Dr Kelsey had anticipated that his knowledge of hypnosis would link with Joan Grant's knowledge of reincarnation. What he did not realise, until they met, was that Joan had already worked closely with a psychiatrist during the war years and had gained a good deal of psychiatric experience. Now, working as a team, they were able to offer help to many people with a unique form of psychotherapy having its roots in past lives.

Joan Grant knew from her own experience that events in her previous incarnations, such as violent deaths, could have an effect on her present existence. On one occasion, for example, she battled unsuccessfully with herself for one hour in an attempt to pick up a slow-worm. She knew she was in no danger. But part of her was still 'resonating' to a stored memory of agonising pain in three snake-bite episodes in previous lives, two of which proved fatal.

While working in the laboratory of her

father's Mosquito Control Institute, she had often given blood meals to the mosquitoes as part of her job. She had never had any ill effects. However, on several subsequent occasions, when she had mosquito bites on her eyelid, they produced a totally disproportionate amount of swelling and suffering. The reason, she discovered, was a resonance with her previous existence as an Egyptian captain. A bite on his eyelid, though from a fly, had led to what was probably septicaemia – and death.

According to Joan Grant and Denys Kelsey, once the causes of fears and anxieties are known and understood by bringing them into normal waking consciousness, the latent energy contained in them is defused. The soul can then be properly integrated and the problem usually disappears.

With the discovery that she could resonate with other people's past lives, Joan Grant found she was able to rid individuals of their apparently irrational fears when such emotion was a throw-back to previous times.

An early case, which occurred during her second marriage, concerned a psychiatrist, Alec Kerr-Clarkson. He visited her to discuss the possibility of reincarnation research. At the end of a pleasant weekend, he was about to leave the house to catch a train back to the north of England when her then husband, Charles Beatty, offered him a brace of pheasants, tied by the neck with a loop of string. The psychiatrist, looking embarrassed, backed away and asked if they could be wrapped in a parcel. Charles insisted they would travel better unwrapped, at which point Alec Kerr-Clarkson admitted, 'But I can't touch feathers.' No sooner had he said that than Joan Grant added:

As a young woman, Joan Grant battled with herself to pick up a slow-worm, which repelled her. She later learned through her 'far memory' that this was a reaction against three very unpleasant experiences with snakes in her past lives – two of which ended in her death

The reason you can't touch feathers is because you had a death which was very similar to one of mine. You were left among the dead on a battlefield. . . . Vultures are watching you . . . six vultures. You are very badly wounded, but you can still move your arms. Every time you move, the vultures hop a little further away. But then they hop closer again. . . . Now they are so close that you can smell them . . . they are beginning to tear at your flesh.

This account caused the psychiatrist to collapse on a sofa, sweating profusely, and he needed little persuasion to stay another night. Joan Grant spent most of the night at his bedside, during which time she realised what his problem was. He had begun to recall the episode himself quite vividly. 'Why did they leave me to die alone . . . why?' he cried out. 'Every other man had a friend to cut his throat . . . why did they betray me. . . . Me!'

to find out what was troubling him.

Dr Kelsey later was startled to find his wife in a distressed state. She was obviously in acute pain and tears were rolling down her face. He soon realised that she was reliving an episode in a previous life of the young patient. She told him:

I can feel the blood clots in the tooth sockets. . . . It was bad enough during the first two days, after he pulled out all her teeth, but then the taste got worse and worse, not only dead blood but pus. Then the fever started . . . and she died on the fourth day.

It turned out that the woman concerned had had beautiful teeth that had been pulled out with nail pincers by a jealous husband. The youth had been that woman in a previous life and also had beautiful teeth in his present incarnation.

Dr Kelsey remembered that, in an early session, the troubled youth had said the anxiety problem had begun after an incident in a bar when another youth had threatened: 'I'm going to kick your teeth in!'

When told of Joan Grant's experience and the belief that he had had all his teeth wrenched out by a husband in the 19th century, the young man had no difficulty in accepting it. His anxiety disappeared instantly. Five years later, when Dr Kelsey and Joan Grant wrote about the case, it had not recurred.

Only a small number of people can be helped in this way, but Joan Grant believes that the message contained in her books will help many more. It is, very simply, to view this life – whatever its difficulties and sorrows – as just one of numerous others that will present us with challenges and opportunities to improve ourselves and help others.

It was this feeling of betrayal associated with the vultures that had created the feather phobia. Once Joan Grant was able to convince him that his comrades had not deliberately left him to a slow and painful death, having thought he was already dead, he was cured.

Using hypnosis, Dr Kelsey was able to produce similar past-life recalls in troubled patients. Joan Grant helped the therapy by resonating with the patient's experience and giving more details. Sometimes it was not even necessary for the patient to relive the experience. This happened in the case of a youth who had a severe anxiety problem. One day his parents telephoned to say he had tried to commit suicide that day. Joan Grant decided to delve into his past lives on her own

Above: Hurtwood, in Surrey, home of Daisy Sartorius. Joan Grant lived here for a number of years following a personal tragedy. During that time, she recalled her life as Sekeeta – and found out that Daisy Sartorius had been her mother then

Below: Dr Denys Kelsey, husband of Joan Grant, in his army days. The two worked in a psychiatric practice together for many years, and Kelsey still has a practice in their home at Pangbourne in Berkshire

The world of Uri Geller

Uri Geller's metal-bending magic has made him famous throughout the world. But how does he perform such baffling feats? What is the source of his remarkable power? COLIN WILSON investigates

IN THE SUMMER of 1971, the teenagers of Israel were beginning to talk about a new pop idol – not a singer or a disc jockey, but a stage magician. His name was Uri Geller, and his popularity was undoubtedly influenced by the fact that he was tall, good-looking, and only 24 years old. But the act itself was startlingly original. Who had ever heard of a 'magician' repairing broken watches by merely looking at them? Or bending spoons by gently massaging them with his finger? Or breaking metal rings without even touching them? Yet these were just a few of the 'tricks' in Geller's dazzling repertoire.

Tales of this 'magic' reached the ears of a well-known psychical researcher named Andrija Puharich, who was so intrigued that he flew from New York to Israel to investigate. On 17 August 1971, Uri Geller was performing at a discotheque in Jaffa, and it was there that Puharich went to see him.

The first thing that struck him was that Geller was a born showman; he obviously loved performing in front of an audience. Yet Puharich found most of his act disappointing. Geller began with a demonstration of mindreading. He was blindfolded, then members of the audience were asked to write words on a blackboard. It was impossible for Geller to see the board; yet he guessed correctly every time. The enthusiasm of the teenage audience showed that they found it amazing; but Puharich knew that such feats are simple if the magician has a few confederates in the audience.

But the last 'trick' impressed him more. Geller announced that he would break a ring without touching it, and a woman in the audience offered her dress ring. She was told

to show it to the audience, then hold it tightly in her hand. Geller placed his own hand above hers and held it there for a few seconds. When she opened her hand, the ring had snapped in two.

After the show, Puharich asked Geller if he would submit to a few scientific tests the next day. So far, Geller had consistently refused to be examined by 'experts'. But this time he readily agreed – to his own surprise, as he later admitted. It was a fateful decision: Geller's first step on the road to world fame.

Geller duly arrived at Puharich's apartment the next day. And his first demonstration convinced Puharich that this was genuine 'magic'. Geller placed a notepad on the table, then asked Puharich to think of three numbers. Puharich chose 4, 3 and 2:

Geller began giving demonstrations of his powers in 1968, first to groups of school children and at private parties, then to large audiences in theatres all over Israel. He said he was surprised at how well the experiments worked in front of so many people – having an audience even seemed to help

'Now turn that notepad over,' said Geller. Puharich did, and found himself looking at the figures 4, 3 and 2 – written *before* he had thought of the numbers. Geller had somehow 'influenced' him into choosing those three figures.

The point is worth remembering, for it suggests that Geller could hypnotise people by means of 'telepathy'. Yet whether this helps to explain the weird and incredible events that followed is open to debate.

At further demonstrations, Geller went on to raise the temperature of a thermometer by staring at it, move a compass needle by concentrating on it, and bend a stream of water from a tap by moving his finger close to it. Puharich's conclusion was that Uri Geller was no mere conjuror: he was a genuine psychic, with a definite power of 'mind over matter' – a faculty known as psychokinesis.

Geller admitted that he had no idea of how he came to possess these curious powers. He had become aware of them when he was little more than a baby. At the age of six, he realised he could read his mother's mind. She came back one day from a party at which she had played cards for money. Geller took one look at her, and was able to tell her precisely how much she had lost.

When he started to go to school, his stepfather gave him a watch. But it always seemed to be going wrong. One day, as Geller stared at it, the hands began to go faster and faster, until they were whirling around. It was then that he began to suspect he might be causing it. Yet he seemed to have no control over this freakish ability. One day, when he was eating soup in a restaurant, the bowl fell off the spoon. Then spoons and forks on nearby tables began to bend. Geller's parents were so worried they even thought of taking him to see a psychiatrist.

By the age of 13, he was beginning to gain some kind of control over his powers. He broke a lock on a bicycle by concentrating on it, and learned to cheat at exams by reading the minds of more diligent pupils – he said he

only had to stare at the backs of their heads to see the answers.

Puharich was intensely excited; it looked as if he had made the find of the century. Ever since the formation of the Society for Psychical Research in 1882, scientists have been studying psychics and mediums, trying to prove or disprove their claims. They have never succeeded in doing either. And the reason is mainly that most psychics claim they cannot switch their powers on and off at will. Yet Geller's powers seemed to work to order, whenever he wanted them to. If they would work in a laboratory as well as on stage, it would be one of the greatest triumphs in the history of psychical research.

At this point, events took a completely unexpected turn. On the morning of 1 December 1971 Geller was hypnotised by Puharich in the hope of uncovering clues about the origin of his powers. Puharich asked him where he was; Geller replied that he was in a cave in Cyprus – where his family had lived

American psychical researcher Andrija Puharich who investigated Uri Geller in the early 1970s. His account of his experiences with Geller was published in 1974 and made the astonishing claim that Geller was the messenger of the Nine, a group of extra-terrestrial beings who were the 'controllers of the Universe'

Interest in Geller and his paranormal powers grew rapidly and a multitude of books about him appeared in the 1970s. Geller himself is an author – his autobiography, *My story*, was published in 1975, and many of his poems, which he says seem to 'come through' him rather than being composed by him, have been set to music and recorded

when he was 13 – and that he was 'learning about people who come from space.' He added that he was not yet allowed to talk about this. Puharich regressed him further, and Geller began to speak in Hebrew – the first language he had learned. At this point he described an episode that, he said, had taken place when he was three years old. He had walked into a garden in Tel Aviv, and suddenly become aware of a shining, bowl-like object floating in the air above his head. There was a high, ringing sound in the air. As the object came closer, Uri felt himself bathed in light, and fell down in a faint.

As Geller recounted these events, Puharich and his fellow investigators were startled to hear a voice speaking from the air above their heads. Puharich described it as 'unearthly and metallic'. 'It was we who found Uri in the garden when he was three,' said the disembodied voice. 'He is our helper, sent to help man. We programmed him in the garden.' The reason, it explained, was that mankind was on the point of a world war. Uri, it implied, had been 'programmed' to avert the catastrophe.

The voice stopped speaking. When Geller woke up, he seemed to have no memory of what had happened; so Puharich played the tape back. As he listened to his voice recounting the episode in the garden, Geller looked worried. 'I can't remember any of this.' And then, as the metallic voice began to speak, Geller snatched the cassette off the recorder. As he held it in his hand, it vanished. Then Geller rushed from the room. When they found him, some time later, he seemed to be

Geller's powers began to manifest themselves when he was a small child: he found that he could read his mother's mind, affect the workings of clocks and watches simply by looking at them, and cause spoons and forks to bend or break. At first his parents were merely embarrassed by the extraordinary events that occurred, but then they became concerned that something was wrong with him, and even considered consulting a psychiatrist

confused, and there was no sign of the tape.

What had happened? The sceptical explanation is that Geller performed a little ventriloquism, then palmed the tape and made sure it 'disappeared', so that subsequent tests would not reveal the resemblance between his own voice and the 'space being' on the tape. But Puharich and the others said the voice came from above their heads, and that it sounded mechanical, as if manufactured by a computer. And even if Geller could have tricked a number of trained observers on this first occasion, it would certainly have been quite impossible on some later occasions described by Puharich. For the bodiless voice was only the first in a series of weird and inexplicable events – events that finally destroyed all Puharich's hopes of convincing the world that Geller's powers were genuine.

These events are described by Puharich in his book *Uri: a journal of the mystery of Uri Geller*. And they sound so confused and preposterous that the reader ends by doubting Puharich's common sense, then his sanity. He describes how, the following day, he recorded yet another hypnotic session with Geller, and how the 'voice' again interrupted and talked about war. Then Puharich and Geller went for a drive, taking the recorder with them, and the tape suddenly vanished into thin air. From then on, hardly a day went past without the mysterious 'entities' performing some mind-boggling trick to convince Puharich of their reality. They made the car engine stop, and then start up again. They 'teleported' Puharich's briefcase from his house in New York to his apartment in Tel Aviv. When Geller and Puharich went to an army base to entertain the troops, they were followed by a red light in the sky that was invisible to their military escort. Geller actually photographed a 'space ship' on the orders of the metallic voice.

Was it a joke? Or some kind of trickery? Puharich, at least, was convinced that no

fraud was involved. A few years before, a psychic had given him messages from some mysterious beings who called themselves the 'Nine', and who said they came from outer space. And at one of the hypnotic sessions with Geller, Puharich asked whether the voice was one of the Nine, and it answered 'Yes'. He went on to ask if the Nine were behind the UFO sightings that had been taking place since Kenneth Arnold saw the first 'flying saucer' in 1947; again the answer was 'Yes'. The voice told Puharich that the Nine were beings from another dimension, and that they lived in a star ship called *Spectra*, which was '53,069 light ages away'. They had been watching Earth for thousands of years, and had landed in South America 3000 years ago. And they would soon prove their existence by landing on planet Earth. . . .

It is easy to jeer at all this, and to condemn

Puharich for his gullibility. The simple explanation seems to be that Geller had been reading Erich von Däniken's *Chariots of the gods?* and decided to fool the naïve Puharich with this preposterous gobbledegook about space beings and star ships. Yet if Puharich's description of the various events is accurate, this is totally impossible. No doubt Geller could have palmed the cassettes, imitated the metallic voice, and faked the photograph of a UFO. But it is hard to see how he could have transported Puharich's briefcase from New York, caused the car engine to stop and start, and arranged for them to be followed by a red light that was invisible to the soldiers who were escorting them.

Could Puharich himself be telling lies? This hypothesis must also be ruled out. Puharich's aim was simply to prove that Geller possessed paranormal powers, and all he had to do was to arrange for scientific tests

A photograph taken on 4 November 1972 by Geller when travelling by jet from London to Munich. According to Geller, his camera rose into the air of its own accord and stopped in front of him, as if signalling him to take a picture. Geller could see nothing in the sky but nevertheless took several shots. When the film was developed, five frames contained images of UFOs alongside the aeroplane

of these powers – as he later did in the United States. Far from making his case more convincing or interesting, all this talk about *Spectra* and the Nine only makes it sound absurd. By writing about it, he only destroyed his own credibility.

Does this mean, then, that the Nine were genuine, and that they have really chosen Geller to be their emissary on Earth? This is equally difficult to accept – and Geller says that he himself does not accept it. Then what *does* he believe? The answer is: nothing. He declares that the events described by Puharich leave him totally bewildered, and that he has no idea of their explanation.

Geller himself was becoming rather worried by all these strange events by the beginning of 1972. Unlike Puharich, he had no desire to convince the scientific establishment of the reality of his powers; he was more interested in becoming rich and famous. And the bewildering tricks performed by the Nine seemed unlikely to bring him closer to that goal. The same thing applied to Puharich, with all his talk about scientific proof and laboratory testing. Geller must have heaved a sigh of relief when, in April 1972, Puharich flew back to New York, promising to return in a few weeks. He proceeded to finalise plans to display his psychic talents in Germany, under the guidance of a professional impressario.

A sign from the Nine

Another curious event, described in *Uri*, guaranteed that Geller was able to make this trip to Germany alone. According to Puharich, Geller went into his apartment on 1 June 1972, and found a letter from Puharich on the mat. It stated simply that Puharich was unable to leave the United States for another three months, and would join Geller later. Accordingly, Geller flew on to Rome – en route for Munich – and telephoned Puharich to ask about the delay. Puharich was amazed, and denied writing any such letter. At which point, it struck them both that the letter must be yet another 'sign' from the Nine. The 'proof' was that it had vanished from Geller's shirt-pocket while he was on the aeroplane – obviously dematerialised by the owner of the metallic voice. A simpler explanation might be that Geller had invented the letter. But then, its appearance and disappearance are no more incredible than all the other baffling events described by Puharich.

Whatever the explanation, the letter incident convinced Puharich that the Nine wanted him to remain behind in the United States, trying to convince various eminent scientists that Geller was worth investigating. Meanwhile, his volatile and unpredictable protégé flew on to Munich, to keep his first appointment with fame and fortune – or at least, with notoriety and publicity.

Under the eyes of scientists

After a successful tour of Germany it seemed that Uri Geller had at last been accepted as a genuine psychic. But in the USA he was not so well received

URI GELLER ARRIVED in Munich in June 1972, and immediately displayed that gift for publicity that would make him the most famous – and the richest – 'psychic' in the world. The tour had been arranged by an agent named Yasha Katz, who made sure that Geller was met by crowds of reporters. One of them asked him: 'What can you do that would be really astounding?' 'Suggest something,' said Geller. 'How about stopping a cable car in mid-air? After a moment's hesitation, Geller said: 'Sure, why not.' And the crowd of goggle-eyed reporters trailed behind him to the Hochfelln funicular line outside Munich.

The car left on its journey to the mountain top, and Geller concentrated hard. Nothing happened. It came down again, and still nothing happened. Then up and down again. By this time, Geller's confidence had drained away, and the reporters were losing interest. Then suddenly, to everyone's astonishment,

Geller and the cable car that halted halfway up the mountainside after he had been concentrating on stopping it. This was just one of the 'stunts' Geller performed in Germany in 1972

the cable car stopped in mid-air. The mechanic called the control centre – and was told that the main switch had suddenly flipped off. Minutes later, the reporters were scrambling to get to the nearest telephones.

Inevitably, they wanted him to do something else. Someone suggested stopping an escalator in a department store. This time, Geller's luck seemed to have run out. Up and down, up and down they went. Then, at the twentieth attempt, the escalator stopped. . . .

Not surprisingly there were sceptics who felt that the amazing feat could be explained by a large bribe to a friendly electrician. Yet Geller also impressed a German scientist, Friedbert Karger, with his ring-breaking trick. Karger held the ring tightly in his hand; Geller held his own hand above it for a few moments – and when Karger opened his hand, the ring was broken. Karger was so excited that he rang Geller's mentor, Andrija Puharich, in New York, suggesting that Geller should stay on in Germany to be thoroughly investigated by scientists. Puharich squashed that one. Geller was already booked by some of America's most eminent scientific investigators.

Geller himself was not that enthusiastic

either. He was tasting fame, and enjoying the flavour. One impressario even wanted Geller to play in a musical about 'unknown powers', and Geller loved the idea. When told about all this over the telephone, Puharich gave a heartfelt sigh, and flew to Germany. And the young celebrity was persuaded to drop his plans to become the world's first singing mystic, and accompany his distraught Svengali back to the United States.

In fact, he was not too difficult to persuade. After weeks of non-stop exposure in the German media, Geller's feats were beginning to lose their impact on the public.

One of the oddest things about the Geller story is that he failed to achieve the same instant fame in the United States that he had found in Germany. There seem to be two explanations. One is that the Americans are hardened to publicity, and tend to become sceptical at the sight of 'miracle workers'. The other is that Geller's reputation had preceded him, and he found himself faced with considerable 'sales resistance'. Tales about Puharich's new protégé had already reached the world of paranormal research in the United States – a world in which Puharich was regarded as an eminent scientific investigator. According to the rumours, Puharich had been completely 'taken in' by this Israeli 'pop-magician', even to believing that he was an emissary from outer space. There were whispers that Geller was Puharich's 'evil genius'. So when Geller arrived in New York in the autumn of 1972, he found the atmosphere distinctly chilly.

From the beginning, he was surrounded by eminent scientists – men like Ed Mitchell, the Moon astronaut, Wernher von Braun, inventor of the V-2 rocket, and the physicist Gerald Feinberg. Geller was suspicious and unhappy; yet his powers seemed to be working excellently. In von Braun's office, he performed an interesting variant on his ring-breaking, flattening the gold wedding ring

In the years since he began demonstrating his powers, Uri Geller has been seen to bend thousands of metal objects, either by stroking the metal lightly with his finger or simply by concentrating on it. In some cases the object has continued to bend after it has left his hand

Geller with John Lennon, talking about UFOs. Geller became interested in UFOs when he heard the voice of a 'space being' talking about the starship *Spectra*. After that, he claimed to have seen a 'red, disc-shaped light' that seemed to be following him, and managed to capture UFOs on film – even though he had not seen them in the sky at the time he took the photographs

that von Braun held tightly in his own hand. Then von Braun found that his calculator battery was flat, although it had been put in that morning. Geller held the calculator between his hands. And when von Braun pushed the 'on' switch, the battery was no longer dead, but the display flashed random numbers. Geller had another try, and this time the calculator worked normally. There was no way in which it could have been faked – even a conjuror cannot get at the circuitry of a sealed calculator. Von Braun concluded that Geller could produce some strange electrical currents – a reasonable and probably correct assumption.

Return of the 'space spooks'
In spite of these successes, Geller was tense and miserable. Apart from anything else, the 'space spooks' were at it again. In a room in a Washington hotel, an ashtray floated off the table, as if moved by invisible hands. Then the tape recorder began to work of its own accord. When Puharich – who was present – played the tape back, the weird metallic voice they had first heard in 1971 spoke again, explaining that the starship *Spectra* would soon be making a landing on Earth – but only for refuelling. The 'mass landing' promised in earlier interviews was evidently to come later. They also – to Puharich's surprise and irritation – told him not to start experiments with Geller for the time being, and not to tell anyone about these strange messages. When all this was over, the tape – according to Puharich – simply dissolved into thin air. Later messages that arrived through the tape recorder again insisted that Puharich should

Left: American astronaut Ed
Mitchell, who met Geller on
his first trip to the United
States in 1972. Mitchell
himself experimented with
telepathy, and was intrigued
by the so-called 'Geller
phenomenon' – so much so
that he offered to pay for
scientific investigation of
Geller's powers at the
Stanford Research Institute
(SRI) in California

'storm', his friendly black labrador dog suddenly bit Geller on the wrist. The day before this same dog had suddenly vanished from the kitchen before their eyes, and a few moments later, was seen walking towards the house from 70 yards (65 metres) away – mysteriously 'teleported' by the space men, according to Puharich, to demonstrate their power. But perhaps the dog knew better. Perhaps it knew intuitively that the real culprit was Geller himself – or rather a stranger living in Geller's unconscious mind.

A few days later, the scientific tests began. They were held at the Stanford Research Institute in California, and conducted by Dr Hal Puthoff and Russell Targ. And as soon as the tests began, Geller knew he had nothing to worry about. Most psychics find it hard to perform under laboratory conditions; Geller

scrap his plans for scientific tests. Understandably, Puharich was distraught. These beings from outer space – if that is where they came from – were wrecking his plans. Even Geller was unexpectedly sceptical; in one indignant outburst he said that he thought the 'space beings' were clowns playing practical jokes.

All this culminated in one highly significant event that Puharich dismisses in a single paragraph in his book on Geller, yet that could well provide the key to the mystery.

A psychic storm

When Puharich told Geller that he intended to ignore the 'space beings', and go ahead with the plans for scientific testing, Geller lost his temper and hurled a sugar bowl at his head. Puharich exploded in violent indignation. At that moment, an immense wind blew up outside, shaking the trees, and a grandfather clock shot across the hall and shattered into a thousand pieces. Overawed but still determined, Geller begged Puharich to forget the scientists. Puharich dug in his heels, and eventually won his point.

These incredible events – assuming that Puharich is reporting them accurately – may seem to confirm that some 'superhuman' powers were involved. Yet every paranormal researcher is aware that poltergeists can often produce equally amazing effects. And there is general agreement that poltergeists are closely connected with the unconscious minds of some human being or beings.

If the 'space beings' really existed, why should they suddenly order Puharich to drop the scientific investigations that they had earlier approved? On the other hand, if the strange manifestations originated in Uri Geller's unconscious mind, it would be perfectly understandable. He wanted to be famous and (if possible) rich, and the idea of being tested by sceptical scientists worried him. Significantly, the one project to which the 'space beings' gave the go-ahead was a film about the life of Geller.

Puharich tells how, the morning after the

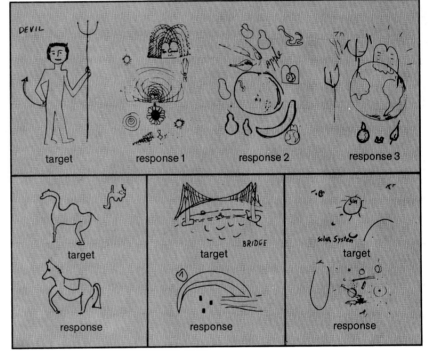

Target pictures and responses drawn by Geller during the SRI series of tests. Before each experiment Geller was isolated from the researchers in a shielded room – only then was the target chosen and a picture drawn

had no such problems. As soon as he began to concentrate on trying to bend a brass ring out of shape, the television monitor through which he was being watched began to distort, and its distortions occurred every time Geller's face distorted with concentration. Obviously, he was producing some kind of mysterious electrical effect. At the same moment, a computer on the floor below began to go wrong.

Next, Geller was tested for extra-sensory perception (ESP). Here his success was spectacular. A die was placed in a closed box and shaken; then Geller was asked to guess which side was uppermost. His guesses were right every time. Ten empty cans were placed upside down on a table, with a small object hidden under one of them; then Geller was brought into the room and asked to guess which can concealed the object. Again, his score was incredible – 12 out of 14 correct guesses. He was then asked to try to duplicate drawings sealed inside double envelopes; again and again, his response was breath-takingly accurate. Yet when 'target drawings' were selected at random from a huge pile made by many people in the building – so that the experimenters themselves had no idea of what was in the sealed envelope – Geller's score fell dramatically. This suggests that his success in the drawing experiments depends heavily upon telepathy or 'mindreading'. Yet this failed to explain the experiments with the dice, which prove genuine ESP *without* telepathy.

Challenged by the sceptics

Just as it seemed that Geller had passed his most difficult tests, and proved the genuineness of his powers, his American visit began to go badly wrong. He was asked to present himself at the offices of *Time* magazine; but the 'photographer' who made the appointment was, in fact, a professional 'magician' named Charles Reynolds. Puharich guessed that the magicians of America were plotting to 'lynch' Geller – and he was right. James Randi – one of the most celebrated illusionists since Houdini – was convinced that Geller was a fake, and was determined to expose him. Puharich was inclined to refuse to allow Geller to be tried by this kangaroo court of stage magicians; but Geller realised that his refusal would only be interpreted as guilt. So on 6 February 1973, he and Puharich presented themselves at the *Time* offices.

Geller was understandably nervous, faced with the obvious hostility of two 'magicians' and two *Time* editors. But he succeeded in demonstrating his telepathic powers by duplicating a drawing in a sealed envelope. After this, he bent a fork by stroking it lightly with his finger; the fork went on bending after he put it down. Charles Reynolds offered Geller his own apartment key – to make sure there could be no 'switching' – and Geller bent it by concentrating; again, the key continued to

Above: Russell Targ who, with Harold Puthoff, conducted the experiments on Geller at Stanford in 1972

Right: stage magician James Randi is convinced that Uri Geller is a fraud, and claims that he can duplicate every one of Geller's 'paranormal' effects. Here Randi demonstrates his own apparent control over metal: he was handcuffed and locked into a high security bank safe – and escaped in less than four minutes

bend after it had left his hand. On the whole, Geller performed very creditably, and might have been justified in expecting a favourable report. In fact, the article that appeared in *Time* a few weeks later was damning. The two magicians claimed that they could easily duplicate every one of Geller's 'tricks', and that Randi actually did so after Geller had left the office. It ended by stating – quite untruthfully – that Geller had been forced to leave Israel in disgrace after a computer expert and some psychologists had duplicated his feats and accused him of fraud.

Randi and Charles Reynolds even asserted later that they themselves had caught Geller cheating – or at least, had seen him bending the fork by pressing it against the desk. Oddly enough, this extremely important accusation is not mentioned in the *Time*

article – which seems strange in view of its determination to prove Geller a fake.

As far as the great American public was concerned, the Geller myth had now been exploded; he had been 'proved' to be a mere trickster. And since *Time* had such an immense worldwide circulation, there was little that either Geller or Puharich could do about it. By the end of March 1973, it looked as if the amazing career of Uri Geller had come to an end – a mere 18 months or so after it had begun. Yet as Puharich sat down at his desk, and wrote the opening lines of his book *Uri: a journal of the mystery of Uri Geller*, he experienced a quiet conviction that there was more to come.

What Geller experienced was more than quiet conviction; it was an outraged determination to make the sceptics eat their words.

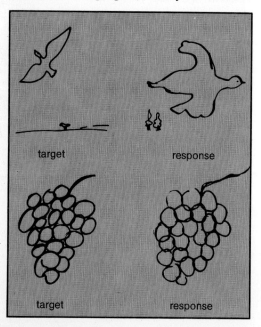

target

response

target

response

More target pictures and Geller's responses during the SRI tests. Geller's success with the 'grape' target is astonishing: he drew exactly the same number of circles as in the original drawing

The psychic superstar

Scientific investigation largely redeemed Uri Geller from accusations of fraud, but the controversy still raged.

FAME ARRIVED FOR URI GELLER on the evening of 23 November 1973 when he appeared on BBC-TV's *David Dimbleby Talk-in*. Overnight, that television programme turned Geller into the most controversial man in the British Isles.

By his own standards, the feats Geller performed that evening were not spectacular. With his eyes closed, he duplicated a drawing that had been made just before the programme and sealed in an envelope. Then he bent a fork – which Dimbleby held in his own hand – by gently stroking it. He started two broken watches by rubbing them, and caused the hands of one of them to bend upwards inside the glass. A fork on the table began to bend of its own accord. At the end of the programme, the producer came on to announce that they had received dozens of telephone calls from viewers saying that their own forks and spoons had begun to bend.

The next morning, there was probably not a single office or factory in England where Geller was not the main topic of conversation. Possibly the British are more gullible than the Americans. Or possibly, as J. B. Priestley once suggested, they are simply less accustomed to high-pressure advertising, and therefore less cynical. Not that there was any absence of cynicism after the programme. One journalist stated authoritatively

Uri Geller at the first World Congress of Sorcery in Bogotá, Colombia, in 1975. Geller was billed as the main attraction of the show, the intention of which was 'to discuss and analyse the New Dimensions of Man and Life'. Besides demonstrating his power to bend metal, Geller started 50 broken watches, including one that, its owner claimed, had not worked for 40 years

that Geller had invented a powder that could cause metal to crumble instantaneously – then had to admit this was pure speculation. The science editor of the *Sunday Times*, Brian Silcock, was also a sceptic, until he rode with Geller in a taxi to the airport, and offered his own front door key for experiment. The moment Geller began to stroke it with one finger, the key bent like melting wax.

Metal bending nationwide

The excitement in England was reported all round the world. After two false starts – in Germany and the United States – Geller had achieved what he always wanted: the instantaneous fame of a pop star. Even the Americans, who had declined to take him seriously, suddenly had second thoughts: when Geller went back there later, they made up for their former indifference and treated him like a returning hero. Meanwhile, in England, a Sunday newspaper – the *People* – organised an experiment at short notice. They announced that at noon on the Sunday following the broadcast, Geller would concentrate his powers, and try to make spoons and forks bend all over England. They asked readers to report any such phenomena. The following Sunday, they described the flood of mail and telephone calls that began soon after the appointed time; 300 spoons and forks had curled up, and over 1000 broken clocks and watches had started up again.

The British seem to have broken the 'scepticism barrier'. Only two days after his triumph on the Dimbleby programme, Geller was demonstrating his powers in

Paris; then he moved on to Scandinavia, Spain, Italy and Japan. Luck – or perhaps his guardians from outer space – continued to favour him with amazing coincidences. In Oslo, he told a reporter jokingly that his psychic powers could fuse lights – and all the street lights in Oslo fused. On a ship in the Mediterranean, Geller said he would try stopping the ship – and a few minutes later, it slowed down and stopped. (A crimped fuel line was found to be the cause.)

Back in the United States, he received the kind of attention and adulation he had hoped for the first time – and also discovered that old enemies like Charles Reynolds and James Randi had lost none of their hostility. *Time* magazine once again denounced him, and took the opportunity to pour scorn on the whole 'psychic' scene, from Kirlian photography and psychic surgery to the 'secret life of plants'. Reynolds and Randi took this belated opportunity to assert that they had seen Geller bending a fork manually against the desk in the previous *Time* interview, although they failed to explain why they had withheld this important piece of information for so long. On the other hand, the publication of the report from the Stanford Research Institute – in the influential magazine *Nature* – convinced many scientists that

Right: housewife Dora Portman of Harrow, England, was listening to a radio programme featuring Uri Geller in November 1973. Geller invited listeners to hold a piece of cutlery and try to bend it by concentration. To Mrs Portman's surprise the ladle she was using suddenly began to bend and the enamel to crack

Geller's powers were basically genuine. And the affirmative reports of various British scientists – like John Taylor and Ted Bastin – supported this view. (John Taylor, however, has since concluded that there is nothing paranormal about Geller's powers.) So instead of being merely the helpless victim of a campaign of defamation, Geller was now a figure of controversy.

Now that all the controversy has died down, and Uri Geller is merely another one of those names of the 1970s, a nine days' wonder that no longer causes wonderment, we can look back on his remarkable career,

Geller with David Dimbleby, experimenting with a key. Geller's appearance on BBC-TV's *David Dimbleby Talk-in* programme on 23 November 1973 was an outstanding success, and convinced scientists that he was worthy of serious scientific investigation

and see that Puharich was right from the beginning. What Geller really needed was to be studied by scientists, not exposed in front of television cameras. A film star or a pop singer has a firm foundation for celebrity; people all over the world are still listening to the records of Bob Dylan and Elvis Presley, or watching old movies of James Dean and Marilyn Monroe. But once you had seen Geller bend a spoon on television, there was nothing more to look forward to – except watching him bend a fork on some other programme. Geller himself was painfully aware of this: he wrote an autobiography; he wrote a novel; he made persistent attempts to star in a film about his own life. And he submitted to hundreds of scientific tests.

The essence of all this investigation is published in a remarkable volume called *The Geller papers*. It makes impressive reading, and demonstrates beyond all doubt that Geller possesses some kind of paranormal powers. Yet because he achieved his main celebrity as a 'magician' on television, Geller has suffered the fate of so many overnight celebrities, and become merely a half-remembered name.

A personal view

My own acquaintance with Geller began when he was at the height of his fame, in 1974. My agent rang me one day and asked me if I would be interested in writing a biography of Uri Geller. I said no. I had just read Puharich's book, which had been one of the major publishing disasters of the year. All his incredible stories about disembodied

voices speaking out of tape recorders, and dogs being 'teleported' down the garden, sounded too absurd to be taken seriously. A 'straight' book about Geller's psychic abilities would probably have been a best-seller; but the miracle-working inhabitants of the starship *Spectra* turned the whole thing into farce.

Geller, it seemed, had persuaded the famous impressario Robert Stigwood – producer of *Hair* and *Jesus Christ superstar* (and later of *Saturday night fever*) – to back the idea of a film about his life. First of all, someone had to write the life. When I declined, they suggested that I might like to work on a film script. And as the pay – for an underpaid student of the paranormal – was generous, I decided it might be worth looking into.

I met Geller at Robert Stigwood's offices in London. He seemed a charming and unassuming young man, whose enthusiasm seems to keep his whole personality on rather a high note. As I walked into the office he asked me: 'Are you anything to do with Spain?' I looked blank. 'Just as you walked in that door, a coin jumped out of this tray on the desk – a Spanish peseta – it made me wonder if you had anything to do with Spain.' Stigwood's personal secretary, Rae Knight, verified that this had actually happened, and I later learned to regard her with total trust. They had both been on the opposite side of the room when the coin leapt across it.

At lunch in a nearby restaurant, Geller talked non-stop, made my watch go back several hours by simply holding his hand above it (he changed the date too), bent a spoon, and broke a key I had brought along by simply rubbing it. But he insisted on taking the key to the other side of the room, where there was a radiator – he said he could gain power from metal. On the whole, I was

Author Colin Wilson with Geller in Barcelona, discussing the nature of Geller's paranormal powers. Geller told him: 'I don't know where they come from or what they mean, or why it should be me and not somebody else'

Geller undergoing one of a series of tests designed to discover whether his physical make-up is responsible for the powers of his mind

not too impressed. I knew enough about conjuring to know that the spoon bending and watch-changing could have been sleight of hand, and the fact that he had to cross the restaurant to bend a key struck me as suspicious. Yet he performed one feat that left me in no doubt of his genuineness.

What happened was this: Geller turned his back on me, so he looked out over the restaurant (I was in a corner), and asked me to do a drawing on the back of the menu card. I did a sketch of a funny monster I draw for my children. I kept glancing at Geller to make sure he wasn't peeping, or holding a mirror in his hand. Then he made me turn the menu over and cover it with my hand. He turned round again, and asked me to redraw the thing *in my mind*, and try to convey it to him. After a couple of false starts, he suddenly drew a duplicate of the 'monster' on the menu. There was no way in which he could have 'guessed' it, or that Rae Knight might have conveyed it to him – even if she had been an accomplice.

An odd coincidence

A few months later, when asked to write a short book about Geller, I travelled to Barcelona to see him – it struck me only later that his first question to me had been: 'Are you anything to do with Spain?' – an odd coincidence. Again objects fell from the air, and Geller demonstrated metal bending and mindreading. In the office of my Spanish publisher he silenced the sceptical audience by holding up a spoon by its end, and bending it by simply 'tickling' the thin part with his index finger – no kind of pressure would have been possible. He placed his foot against a radiator as he did this.

My own study of Geller has convinced me that his powers are genuine. His mindreading was particularly convincing. James Randi – who likes to call himself the 'Amazing Randi' – declared that he could easily

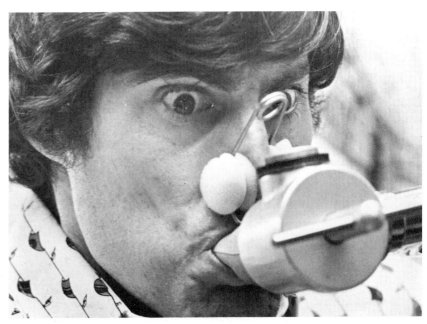

duplicate any of Geller's 'tricks'; but when I met him, he was unable to duplicate the mindreading trick – although he offered to do it for me next day (obviously when he'd had time to prepare it). But Randi *did* bend spoons by stroking them and made my watch go back several hours by rubbing it.

The film on Geller never came off, although I made several 'outline' sketches. I continued to see and correspond with Geller, on and off, for a year or so, but lost touch with him when he moved to New York. In one of his later letters to me he mentioned that he had produced a tremendous impression in Mexico, and was a frequent guest at the home of the president. He also mentioned that he had taken up 'dowsing' for metals from an aeroplane, and made a considerable success of it, working for a mining company. From the financial point of view, I gather he has no reason to complain of the way the world has treated him. And if his spoon bending has ceased to attract much attention, this is hardly surprising. From Geller's point of view, I feel it is a pity it ever did.

And what do I feel about the source of his powers? After a great deal of thought, I am still inclined to believe that Geller is an unconscious 'medium', and that he simply produces more-or-less controlled 'poltergeist' effects'. (That other remarkable psychic, Matthew Manning, whom I have also investigated, began his career as the unconscious 'focus' of a series of alarming poltergeist occurrences in his own home.) Geller told me how, at the age of three, he received a bad electric shock from his mother's sewing machine; this, I am inclined to believe, may have started the whole thing. It is surprising how often 'mediums' have had severe traumas or emotional strains in childhood.

'Unconscious mediums'

And what about the 'space men' from the starship *Spectra*? Here again, I believe that Geller's unconscious mind is the basic explanation. But I suspect there was more than that involved. In one of their mysterious 'interviews', the 'space men' told Puharich that he himself had psychic powers. I believe this to be almost certainly true. And the astounding series of events that began when Puharich and Geller got together in Tel Aviv were a kind of wild collaboration between two 'unconscious mediums'. Unlikely? I can only say that the more I have studied the evidence, the more I feel this is the case.

There is one more point. Spiritualists believe that there *are* such things as disembodied spirits, hanging around on the 'earth plane', and often getting into mischief. Such spirits may cause poltergeist effects. And the more I read the weird but inconsequential communications of the 'space beings' from *Spectra*, the more I am reminded of the confused and usually irrelevant material that emerges at so many seances.

These may not, I agree, be the correct explanations. But of one thing I am certain. There *is* something about Uri Geller that demands a deeper and more far-reaching explanation than mere trickery.

Professors John Hasted and John Taylor (above) carried out tests on Geller in 1974. Geller succeeded in bending metal strips sealed in plastic tubes (right). And he was asked to bend a brass strip taped to a letter balance so the pressure he applied could be measured. The scale read only half an ounce (15 grams), and the strip bent upwards, against the pressure of his fingers (far right)

Raising the dead, healing the sick, producing religious medals and even food out of thin air – these are some of the miracles of Sai Baba. ROY STEMMAN looks at the life and beliefs of this modern saint

A SMALL, CHUBBY FIGURE in a bright red robe and with a halo of crinkly black hair stood before a typically huge crowd eagerly awaiting him. He turned an empty hand palm down and began moving it in circles. When he turned it over it contained a gold necklace. The spectators were delighted. Satya Sai Baba had performed another miracle. The necklace is one of more than 10,000 objects he is said to have materialised in this way, including diamonds, gold rings, beads, books, religious idols and even food.

The miracles of Satya Sai Baba are so incredible that they invite disbelief. Yet the witnesses who have come forward to testify to his astonishing powers often have impeccable credentials: they include government officials, scientists and religious leaders.

His followers run into tens of thousands around the world, though the majority are in his native India which now has 3000 Sai centres to promote his teachings, and five Sai universities. Many of his devotees regard him as an *avatar* – a god incarnate. Colin Wilson describes him as a 'contemporary Hindu saint.' And others who have written about him find many parallels between his miracles and those of Christ.

When he was born on 23 November 1926, Satyanarayana Raju was a normal robust child, though he soon caused consternation by refusing to eat meat and bringing beggars

Above: Sai Baba as he is today. Significantly his robe has no pockets and only narrow wrists – there is nowhere he could hide the 'apports' he produces

Right: Sai Baba as a young man. The powers he possesses have always been special: his father even sought to have him exorcised

Man of many miracles

home so that his mother could feed them. At school he was fun-loving and popular. He would arrive early in order to conduct worship with other children, most of whom were attracted by his ability to dip his hand into an empty bag and bring out sweets, or everyday objects they had lost.

Despite these early signs that he was special, the Raju family had hopes that he would be well educated and become a government officer. Instead, a strange incident occurred when he was 13 which proved to be a turning point in his life.

While walking with friends he suddenly leapt in the air with a loud shriek, holding a toe of his right foot. Everyone thought he had been stung by a scorpion, but next day he showed no sign of pain or sickness . . . until the evening when he suddenly fell unconscious to the ground.

When he recovered consciousness next day he seemed to be another person: bursting into song, reciting poetry and quoting long passages in Sanskrit that were far beyond his knowledge.

His worried parents consulted various doctors who prescribed different remedies, and when these failed to cure Satya they arranged for the 'demon' in him to be exorcised. The young boy took it all in his stride, showing no sign of suffering despite

Left: the Hindu holy man, Sai Baba of Shirdi, who died in 1918. Satyanarayana Raju, born in 1926, 'became' Sai Baba after suffering the physical trauma of a scorpion sting when he was 13. On a visit to Shirdi he recognised the first Sai Baba's friends although he had never met them in his present life

the ghastly treatment administered to him by the exorcist.

Then, one morning while his father was at work at his store, Satya called the rest of the family together. He waved his hand in front of them and produced candy and flowers. When the neighbours heard what had happened they crowded in and Satya obliged by producing candy and flowers for them, too.

News of these 'conjuring tricks' reached his father who was so incensed that he found a stout stick and went to the house to chastise his wayward son. 'This is too much! It must stop!' he shouted when he confronted Satya. 'What are you? Tell me – a ghost, a god, or a madcap?'

Satya replied simply: 'I am Sai Baba.' Then, addressing everyone present, he continued: 'I have come to ward off your troubles; keep your houses clean and pure.'

The reply was hardly helpful. The Raju family did not know of anyone named Sai Baba, but others in the village had heard of such a person: a Hindu holy man who performed many miracles, including healing the sick with ash from a fire which he had kept burning constantly at a mosque in Shirdi. He died in 1918 but he told his followers that he would be born again. That promise, it seems, was fulfilled with the birth

Above: a holy medallion created by Sai Baba. On one side (left) is the image of Sai Baba of Shirdi, on the other (right) the AUM symbol, signifying the word of creation. Baba says 'to hear that sound one has to approach as near as possible, the core of one's being . . . the Truth is AUM'

of Satya, eight years later, but many were sceptical of his claim.

Eventually someone challenged him to prove that he really was who he claimed to be. 'Bring me those jasmine flowers,' he ordered. Then he threw them on the floor. To everyone's amazement they landed in such a way that they spelt 'Sai Baba'.

In time, Satya came face to face with devotees of Sai Baba of Shirdi and he invariably recognised them. On one occasion, he took a photograph from someone, looked at it, and named the person it pictured – though it was a man Satya had never met. He then named the man and said he was the visitor's uncle – 'your father's elder brother, and my old devotee at Shirdi'.

For many people, however, it does not matter whether Satya Sai Baba is a reincarnation or not. The miracles he now performs leave them in no doubt that he is a very special person. A recurring miracle is the materialisation of holy ash (vibhuti), sometimes scooped from the air and sprinkled into the hands of visitors, but at other times made to pour out of an empty upturned urn into which his hand has been placed.

This ash has a variety of uses. He tells many of his followers to eat it, and it is reputed to have cured many ailments.

But it is the materialisation of solid objects which stretches belief to its limit. Sceptics argue that any competent stage conjuror can make objects apparently appear from nowhere, but Sai Baba's talents – if we accept the numerous testimonies that have been made – are in a very different league. Often

he invites people to name what they would like – then plucks it out of the air, or the 'Sai Stores' as he jokingly calls the invisible dimension from which it suddenly appears.

Howard Murphet, author of Sai Baba, man of miracles, tells of an occasion when Sai Baba asked him the year of his birth and then said he would get for him an American coin minted in that year.

He began to circle his down-turned hand in the air in front of us, making perhaps half a dozen small circles, saying the while 'It's coming now . . . coming . . . here it is!' Then he closed his hand and held it before me, smiling as if enjoying my eager expectancy. When the coin dropped from his hand to mine, I noticed first that it was heavy and golden. On closer examination I found, to my delight, that it was a genuine milled American ten-dollar coin, with the year of my birth stamped beneath a profile head of the Statue of Liberty.

Among the many reports which Murphet collected for his book is one by Mrs Nagamani Pourniya, widow of a Government District Transport Officer, who told him of a visit she and a small group of followers paid to the sands of the Chitravati river with Sai Baba. Instead of plunging his hands into the sands to produce materialised objects – which is a method he frequently uses – the miracle man simply scraped away sand to reveal buried objects. These proved to be statuettes, which then slowly rose out of the sand 'as if driven up by some power beneath'.

Hard to believe? Yes, but Christians are asked to believe that Jesus Christ worked many similar miracles.

Christians who accept the raising of Lazarus should not find it difficult to believe the story of V. Radhakrishna, a 60-year-old factory owner who visited Sai Baba's Puttaparti headquarters in 1953 in the hope of finding relief from the severe gastric ulcers that were making his life a misery.

He was given a room and spent all his time

Above: three forms of *avatar* – or gods incarnate – from the Indian pantheon. Sai Baba is believed to be an avatar

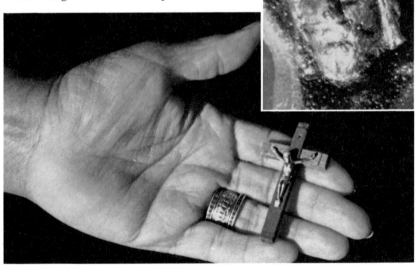

in bed, waiting for a visit from Sai Baba. When that came, the holy man made no attempt to cure him. He just laughed when Radhakrishna said he would rather die than go on suffering, and left the room without making any promises.

Eventually, the man's condition got worse and he went into a coma. When Sai Baba learned of this he said to the man's wife, 'Don't worry. Everything will be all right.' But when there was no improvement next

Above: Sai Baba often materialises crucifixes for his Christian friends

Inset: detail of a crucifix, said to show Jesus at the point of death. Sai Baba reveres Christ as a Master who came to unite all men through peace, sacrificing himself to atone for their violence and aggression

day the sick man's son-in-law sent for a male nurse who said the patient was so near death there was no hope of saving him. An hour later Radhakrishna became very cold and his family heard what they took to be the 'death rattle' in his throat. Slowly he turned blue and stiff.

When told what had happened, Sai Baba laughed. And when he visited the room to see the man's condition for himself he left without saying a word.

By the morning of the third day the body was even more corpselike: it was dark, cold and beginning to smell of decomposition. Some people advised the family to have it removed, but when Mrs Radhakrishna told Sai Baba this he replied: 'Do not listen to them, and have no fear; I am here.'

Eventually, Sai Baba went to the room again and found the family distraught. He asked them to leave and remained with the body for a few minutes. Then he opened the door and called them in. To their great relief and astonishment they found the 'dead' man conscious and smiling. Next day he was strong enough to walk and the gastric ulcers were found to be completely cured, never to return.

Such miracles are said to be the least important part of his work. He refers to his psychic phenomena as 'small items.' His mission is to attract attention to his spiritual teachings – to lead Man away from violence and hatred towards compassion and higher consciousness, and to unite many religions. He explains it this way: 'I give you what you want in order that you may want what I have come to give.' And that, he says, is to avert a nuclear holocaust.

But his incarnations as Sai Baba of Shirdi and Satya Sai Baba will not be enough to achieve that aim. He has already said he will be born again, as Prema Sai, in the 21st century in order to complete his mission.

Brahan Seer

In the 17th century, Kenneth Odhar – the prophet of the Seaforth family – was hailed as one of the greatest Highland seers ever. And, as FRANK SMYTH explains, it seems that his predictions continue to be fulfilled today

IF WE ARE to give folklore and historical legend any credence at all, the power of 'second sight' has been commonplace in the Highlands of Scotland – and in Ireland whence the Celtic people of the north came – for centuries. Until the 18th century, every glen and braeside from Lochaber to the far tip of Caithness had, it would seem, its resident 'wise' man or woman, traditionally the seventh child of a seventh child, who through the power of God or fairies inherited the gift of *taibh-searachd* – prophecy.

After the last Jacobite uprising ended with the disastrous battle of Culloden in 1746, the clans were considerably reduced in number and their remnants exiled and scattered to the West Indies, North America, and later Australia and New Zealand. But the tradition of the 'Highland seer' lived on; even today his descendants are looked upon tolerantly and with respect.

In the 19th century there was a quickening of interest in the 'romantic' Highlands. George IV encouraged the trend by appearing at Edinburgh with his portly frame wrapped in the newly invented 'Royal Stewart' tartan, a fashion followed by the Prince Consort, who went as far as to design a tartan wallpaper and carpet for Balmoral, and Sir Walter Scott had already fanned the flame with his popular historical novels.

In the wake of this 'romanticism' came the folklorists, indefatigably tramping over the heather in search of quaint tales and superstitions. One of the more respected of these

Baile-na-Cille in Uig on the Isle of Lewis, reputedly the place where Kenneth Odhar, the Brahan seer, received his precognitive powers. According to legend, he either found or was given a magic stone, and it was in this that he was able to see the future. It seems that Kenneth paid dearly for his gift, for one tale has him half-blinded, and several accounts describe him as 'cam' – one-eyed or squinting

was Andrew Lang, himself a Scotsman, an active member of the Society for Psychical Research, and the author of, among other books, *The making of religion* (1898), which dealt with examples of second sight among primitive societies. Turning to his homeland, Lang examined the evidence for and against the powers of the native seers. In a paper published in 1899, he was able to 'unblushingly confess the belief that there probably are occasional instances of second sight, that is of "premonitions"'.

However, Lang urged that all the evidence in each individual case be considered, pointing out that the strongest cases must rest on prophecies that had been recorded before their 'fulfilment', thus ruling out the possibility of romantic hindsight. Obviously, the more explicit the prediction, the more convincing its detailed fulfilment would be.

Under these terms, the posthumous claims made for Coinneach Odhar of Mackenzie, the Brahan seer, stand up to considerable scrutiny. Famous in his lifetime as the resident prophet of the mighty Seaforth family, he came to be regarded as one of the most impressive Highland seers ever when, 150 years after his death, his predictions regarding the unusual circumstances of the family's extinction came precisely true.

Coinneach – Gaelic Kenneth – was born in the parish of Uig on the Isle of Lewis around the year 1600. According to Alexander Cameron of Lochmaddy, who chronicled many of the seer's prophecies some years after his death, it was at some time during his early teens that Kenneth's powers developed. Several versions of their origins exist, all involved with the supernatural. According to one, his mother, tending her cattle in the graveyard of Baile-na-Cille near Uig, met

Prophet by appointment

the ghost of a daughter of the King of Norway, who gave her a blue stone in which Kenneth would see the future. Other accounts tell how Kenneth himself was given a white stone with a hole in it by the fairies, and it was through this that he was able to see coming events.

Whatever the source of his powers, news of them spread to Kenneth's feudal overlord, Kenneth Cabarfeidh – Staghead – Mackenzie, who in 1609 had been created first Lord Mackenzie of Kintail. The chief's stronghold was Brahan Castle, a few miles from Dingwall on the Cromarty Firth, and at his summons Kenneth Odhar went to live on the Brahan lands. Soon after Odhar's arrival the old chief died and was succeeded by his son, who was created first Earl of Seaforth in

Above: the writer and psychical researcher Andrew Lang (1844–1912), who examined the evidence for second sight in his native Scotland. He confessed to a belief in the existence of 'premonitions', saying: 'I know too many examples among persons of my acquaintance . . . to have any doubt about the matter'

Left: a *taibhsear* – seer – of the Highlands. Such figures commanded respect in the community as it was widely believed that the power of second sight was a gift from God, or inherited from the fairies

Below: the battle of Culloden, 1746, which – in one of his more memorable prophecies – the Brahan seer accurately predicted over 100 years before

for one thing, Macrae had been distinguished in the Mackenzie army in clan wars without coming to harm, and for another there had been no tribal feuding for years. Nevertheless, recorded his kinsman and contemporary the Reverend John Macrae of Dingwall, Duncan Macrae died as predicted, the victim of a misunderstanding. In 1654 General Monck led a troop of Parliamentary soldiers up to Kintail and a company of them met Macrae walking in the hills behind his house. Addressed in a language he did not understand and startled by the strange uniforms, Macrae put his hand to his broadsword and was immediately cut down: 'This was all the blood that General Monck or his soldiers, amounting to 1500 men, had drawn.'

The weeping widow

Most of the time the seer's advice was unsolicited, and his predictions were interesting only because they proved accurate. One day he announced that 'A Lochalsh woman shall weep over the grave of a Frenchman in the burying place of Lochalsh.' Frenchmen were virtually unknown north of Edinburgh, and yet within a few months the Earl of Seaforth discovered that a Lochalsh woman had married a French footman who died young; the widow had taken to weeping by his graveside every day.

Doubtless these insights into the immediate future enthralled Odhar's contemporaries, but it was his long range predictions that fascinated the likes of Andrew Lang. Odhar gained nothing from them personally, not even prestige, for their fulfilment lay far in the future, and this as much as their accuracy gives them the hallmark of genuine precognition.

One pronouncement that was marvelled at when it proved true was that in the village of Baile Mhuilinn, in the west of Sutherland, there would live a woman named Baraball n'ic Coinnich (Annabella Mackenzie) who would die of measles. In about 1860 there was a woman of that name living in the

1623; it was the first Earl's grandson who was to build Odhar's fame.

Kenneth, third Earl of Seaforth, was roughly the same age as Kenneth the poor prophet and seems to have been fascinated by him. He released the seer from his job as farm labourer on the Brahan estate and, although still lodged in a sod-roofed cottage, Odhar the Lewisman – who spoke only Gaelic – was introduced into local learned society.

He cannot have been a cheerful companion, for his predictions invariably involved bloodshed or disaster, pronounced with a dour relish. On one occasion, for instance, an elderly man, Duncan Macrae of Glenshiel, asked the seer to tell him 'by what means he would end his days'. Odhar immediately replied that he would die by the sword. Such an event seemed so unlikely that Odhar stood in danger of being discredited:

land but, said Kenneth, one day it would 'be under lock and key, and the Fairies secured within'. In the mid 19th century it became a cemetery, and today is surrounded by a fence with a locked gate.

For the Mackenzies of Fairburn, cousins of Seaforth, Odhar could see nothing but doom. Over the years he predicted gruesome fates for them, combined with financial ruin and final obliteration; eventually, Odhar said, a rowan tree would grow from a crack in Fairburn Tower, and a cow would calve in its upmost chamber. In Odhar's time the tower was new and strong, but in the 18th century, when its owners lost their lands following the Jacobite rebellion, it fell into ruin. In 1851 a cow did make its way up the narrow and precipitous stairway and calved in the top room, while a rowan tree sprang from a fissure half way up the tower wall and grew to a considerable size before dying in the summer drought of 1957.

village, but she was 95 years old and it seemed unlikely that her death would be caused by that disease; then, a few years later, Annabella died – as predicted – of measles.

In 1630 Seaforth 'lent' Odhar to a 'gentleman from Inverness', who wrote down a string of the seer's utterances. One well-authenticated pronouncement was made on the way to the gentleman's house. Crossing a bleak patch of moorland, Odhar said: 'Oh! Drummossie, thy bleak moor shall, ere many generations have passed away, be stained with the best blood of the Highlands. Glad I am that I will not see that day . . . heads will be lopped off by the score, and no mercy will be shown.' One hundred and sixteen years later the battle of Culloden was fought on that very spot.

Mystery of the moving stone

Another startling prediction concerned an 8-tonne stone that marked the boundaries of the estates of Culloden and Moray. The day would come, said Odhar, when the 'Stone of Petty' would be moved mysteriously from its position on dry land and re-erected in the sea of Petty Bay. It is a matter of record that during the stormy night of 20 February 1799 the huge stone was uprooted and ended in the sea some 250 yards (230 metres) from the shore line. No satisfactory explanation of its moving has ever been put forward.

In another of his predictions Odhar spoke of 'strings of black carriages, horseless and bridleless', which would pass through the Highlands, led by 'a fiery chariot' – a fair description of the railways of mid Victorian times. He also stated that ships with sails would pass behind the 'fairy hill' of Tomna-hurich near Inverness; they began to do so when the Caledonian Canal was opened in the 1820s. Tomnahurich itself was common

Some of the seer's accurate predictions: of the common land at Tomnahurich that became a cemetery (above) in the 19th century, he said it would be 'under lock and key and the Fairies secured within'; of the advent of the railways (right) he said 'horseless' carriages would be led by a 'chariot of fire'; and the downfall of the Fairburn Mackenzies, he rightly said, would be signalled by the birth of a calf and the sprouting of a rowan tree in the ruin of Fairburn Tower (below)

Famous last words

When the mighty Seaforth family sentenced their resident seer to death, they also condemned themselves.

POPULAR FAITH in the prophecies of Kenneth Odhar, the most distinguished of Highland seers, was strong and widespread in the mid 17th century. Many of his predictions were well-known and were passed on from generation to generation: some came true in his lifetime, others long after his death; many are still unfulfilled.

Some of Odhar's prophecies may have been helped by his natural shrewdness. The strange, sulphurous waters of Strathpeffer, a few miles north of Brahan, had been shunned by locals as poisonous for years, but Odhar claimed that

> Uninviting and disagreeable as it now is, with its thick crusted surface and unpleasant smell, the day will come when it shall be under lock and key, and crowds of pleasure and health seekers shall be seen thronging its portals, in their eagerness to get a draught of its waters.

In 1818, Strathpeffer became a fashionable spa, and the pump room, normally kept locked, is still a centre for health cures.

On the other hand, his prediction of a disastrous flood 'from a loch above Beauly', which would destroy a village in its vicinity, was unlikely in the extreme. There was no loch anywhere near Beauly, which stands at the innermost point of Beauly Firth. However, in the 20th century a dam was built across the river Conon at Torrachilty, a few

Right: the pump room at Strathpeffer mineral wells. The Brahan seer's prophecy that one day the waters would draw crowds of 'health seekers' astonished the local people, for it was popularly believed that the Devil himself washed there. However, in the late 18th century it was discovered that the waters had healing properties, and in 1818 Strathpeffer was established as a fashionable spa

Below: in 1966 heavy rain caused the hydro-electric dam at Torrachilty to overflow and this, in turn, caused the river Conon to burst its banks. The flooding created havoc in the village of Conon Bridge, destroying buildings, crops and cattle. The precise nature of this disaster had been foreseen, centuries before, by the Brahan seer

miles away from Beauly, and in 1966 it unexpectedly overflowed. The flood water killed hundreds of sheep and cattle, destroying grain, fences and buildings in the village of Conon Bridge, some 5 miles (8 kilometres) 'above Beauly'.

Odhar's end was surprisingly unforeseen, considering his gifts, but it did cause him to forecast with uncanny accuracy the end of his patron's line. Kenneth, third Earl of Seaforth, was a staunch Royalist who led a troop of his Mackenzie clansmen during the Civil Wars against Cromwell's army along the Scottish borders. After the death of Charles I he was imprisoned but, after the Restoration, was held in high esteem by Charles II, being granted extra lands and winning the hand of Isabella Mackenzie, sister of the Earl of Cromarty.

In the mid 1660s the Earl was sent to Paris by King Charles, and several months passed without Isabella receiving a letter from him. One night, Isabella asked the seer to tell her what her husband was doing. Odhar said that he saw him in a splendid room, well and happy, and 'indisposed' to return home yet. Isabella pressed him to tell her more, and the incautious prophet told her that the Earl was 'on his knees before a fair lady'.

The Countess immediately ordered the seer to be burned to death in a tar barrel as a

witch. Odhar was astonished and filled with
dismay at her reaction: he had expected
reward for his prophecies, not condemnation. But the Countess's decision was
upheld and, attended by representatives of
the Kirk, Odhar was taken to Chanonry
Point on the Moray Firth for execution.
There, he begged the ministers to write
down what he was going to say.

Speaking in his native Gaelic, he said that
he saw a Seaforth chief, the last of his house,
who would be deaf and dumb. He would
have four fair sons, all of whom he would
follow to the tomb. One of them would die on
the water. His daughter, whom the prophet
described as 'white hooded', would come
from lands to the east to live at Brahan, and
she would kill her sister. Thus all the
Seaforths would die. The seer continued:

And as a sign by which it may be known
that these things are coming to pass,
there shall be four great lairds in the
days of the last deaf and dumb Seaforth
– Gairloch, Chisholm, Grant, and
Raasay – of whom one shall be buck-
toothed, another hare-lipped, another

When Kenneth, third Earl of
Seaforth (left), patron of the
Brahan seer, was abroad on
business, his wife Isabella
(below), having had no
word from him, summoned
the seer to Brahan castle
(below left: the castle in
ruins) to give an account of
her husband. The seer told
her that he could see the Earl
with another woman, and
Isabella was furious.
Unfortunately for the seer,
she directed all her anger
against him and condemned
him to be burned as a witch

half-witted, and the fourth a
stammerer.

There would also be a laird of Tulloch, 'stag
like', who would kill four wives in succession, but the fifth would outlive him.

Odhar was executed near the modern
Chanonry Point lighthouse, by the road from
Fortrose to Fort George ferry; the place is
marked with a stone slab. But the memory –
and the implied threat – of his predictions
lived on, not least in the minds of the
Seaforth family. For the next hundred years
their fortunes fluctuated, and several of them
must have wondered if extinction were close
at hand. For their activities in the risings of
1715 the family were stripped of their titles,
but these were restored in 1726, and the
Seaforths subsequently became staunch

Hanoverians, growing richer and more
powerful by the year. The title of Earl of
Seaforth died out with its holder in 1781, but
the chieftainship passed to a second cousin
who seemed destined to bring even greater
honours to Brahan.

Francis Humberstone Mackenzie was
born in 1754 and early in his life became
member of parliament for Ross and Lord
Lieutenant of the county. During the re-
volutionary wars with France he raised a
regiment that subsequently became the
Seaforth Highlanders, and in 1797 he was
created Baron Seaforth of Kintail. In 1800 he
became Governor of Barbados, and in 1808
he was promoted to Lieutenant-General of
the army. As well as his military interest,
Seaforth was an amateur painter of great

having another 30 illegitimate offspring in Tulloch gained him the nickname 'the stag'.

Odhar's final prophecy came true within a few years of Seaforth's death. His eldest surviving daughter Mary had married Admiral Sir Samuel Hood in 1804; and when Hood died at about the same time as Seaforth while commanding the East Indian station, Mary returned home in widow's weeds to take over her father's lands: this formal dress included a white hood – so that she was both 'hooded' in fact, as Odhar had said she would be, and 'Hood' by name. One day she was driving her younger sister, the Hon. Caroline Mackenzie, through the woods by Brahan Castle when the ponies bolted and the carriage overturned; Lady Hood was merely bruised, but her sister died of her injuries.

The prophecies of the Brahan seer form a perennial guessing game for those Highlanders who know of them, for from time to time they still appear to come true – as in the case of the Conon Bridge disaster. One of the

talent, and he sponsored not only Sir Walter Scott, but also the painter Sir Thomas Lawrence and the scientist Sir Humphry Davy in their early years. He was happily married to the niece of Lord Carysfort, who bore him four sons and six daughters; altogether he presented a picture of enduring, well-established worth.

But the truth of the matter was that the prophet's predictions had begun to come true for Seaforth when he was 12 years old. In that year an outbreak of scarlet fever at his boarding school killed several of his fellow pupils and rendered Seaforth totally deaf; over the years his speech became affected, and towards the end of his life he could communicate only by making signs or writing notes.

His eldest son William Frederick died as a baby in 1786 and eight years later his second son George died at the age of six. His third son, Francis, a midshipman in the Royal Navy, was killed in his eighteenth year in a skirmish at sea – 'dying on the water', as Kenneth had foretold, in November 1813. Finally his last son, another William Frederick, the 24-year-old MP for Ross, died suddenly in August 1814. Seaforth himself died in January of the following year and was buried with his ancestors at Fortrose Cathedral. His contemporaries and neighbours, as the *Edinburgh Daily Review* pointed out in Seaforth's obituary, were the buck-toothed Sir Hector Mackenzie of Gairloch, the hare-lipped Chisholm of Chisholm, the retarded Laird Grant, and the stammering Macleod of Raasay. They also included Duncan Davidson, Laird of Tulloch, but it was to be many years before his part in the prophecy was fulfilled. When he died, Tulloch – then Lord Lieutenant of the county of Ross – had had five wives, four of whom had died in childbirth. Between them they had borne him 18 children, while his reputation for

Above: the stone at Chanonry Point, Fortrose, commemorating the 'legend of Coinneach Odhar, better known as the Brahan seer'. It was here that, in his final hour, the seer made his last prediction. 'I see far into the future,' he said, 'and I read the doom of the race of my oppressor. The long-descended line of Seaforth will, ere many generations have passed, end in extinction and sorrow. . . .' More than a century later, the Seaforth line came to an end just as the seer had foretold

Right: one of the seer's well-known proclamations concerned the depopulation of the Highlands, which began in the 18th century when many tenant farmers were evicted to make way for sheep on the land. This cartoon dates from the mid 19th century, when the problem was compounded by landowners charging high rents, forcing crofters to move south or, in many cases, emigrate

most remarkable of the seer's predictions related to the emptying of the Highlands of crofters in order to breed sheep. This came to pass with the Highland clearances of the mid 18th century. But the seer went on to say that those Highlanders driven away to far off lands as yet 'undiscovered or explored' would return to work in the Highlands in the days when the 'horrid black rains' should fall. Today, many Canadians, Texans and New Zealanders of Highland descent work in Scotland, notably in connection with off-shore oil rigs and nuclear plants and submarine sites.

Naturally, the natives are curious: do the Brahan seer's 'black rains' – *siantan dubha* – refer to North Sea oil? Or do they refer to a fall-out of a much more sinister nature?

José Arigo

Arigo: surgeon extraordinary

He operated on the dying with only a rusty knife – and cured them. ROY STEMMAN looks at the extraordinary career of the humble Brazilian who performed surgical miracles 'under spirit guidance'

A PRIEST had arrived to administer extreme unction to the dying woman. Candles were lit and relatives and friends were gathered around her bedside in the town of Congonhas do Campo, Brazil. Her death, from cancer of the uterus, was expected at any moment.

Suddenly, one of those present rushed from the room, returning moments later with a large knife from the kitchen. He ordered everyone to stand back. Then, without warning, he pulled the sheets from the woman and plunged the knife into her vagina.

After several brutal twists of the blade he removed the knife and inserted his hand into the woman, withdrawing a huge tumour the size of a grapefruit. He dropped the knife and the bloody tumour into the kitchen sink, sat down on a chair and began to sob.

A relative rushed off to fetch a doctor; the rest stood silently as if transfixed by the astonishing scene they had witnessed. The patient was unperturbed: she had felt no pain during the 'operation' and the doctor confirmed that there was no haemorrhaging or other ill-effects. He also confirmed that the growth in the kitchen sink was a uterine tumour.

The extraordinary incident proved to be a turning point in the lives of the two people concerned. The woman recovered her health

Below: Arigo performs a delicate eye operation in his back parlour. Although it is the medium who goes into a trance, the patient feels no pain – nor, it seems, any fear, despite the unhygienic surroundings, primitive lighting and the complete lack of anaesthetics

completely. And the man who performed the 'surgery', José Arigo, found himself in great demand from people whose doctors had given them up as incurable patients. Yet he could not remember 'operating' on the woman.

Later, when such startling surgery became a daily occurrence in Congonhas do Campo – Arigo's home town – it was realised that he was in a trance when he treated the sick. His patients noticed he spoke with a German accent, and this was allegedly because Dr Adolphus Fritz, who died in 1918, was said to be 'operating' through him.

On most days when Arigo's clinic opened at 7 a.m. there was already a queue of 200 people waiting. Some he would treat in a rapid and often brutal fashion, pushing them against a wall, jabbing an unsterilised knife into them, then wiping it clean on his shirt. Yet they felt no pain or fear. There was very little blood, and the wound would knit together immediately and heal within a matter of days.

Not everyone received psychic surgery. For many he would simply glance at them, diagnose their problems without asking any questions, then write a prescription rapidly. The medicines prescribed were usually well-known drugs made by leading companies, but in large doses and combinations that were surprising according to conventional

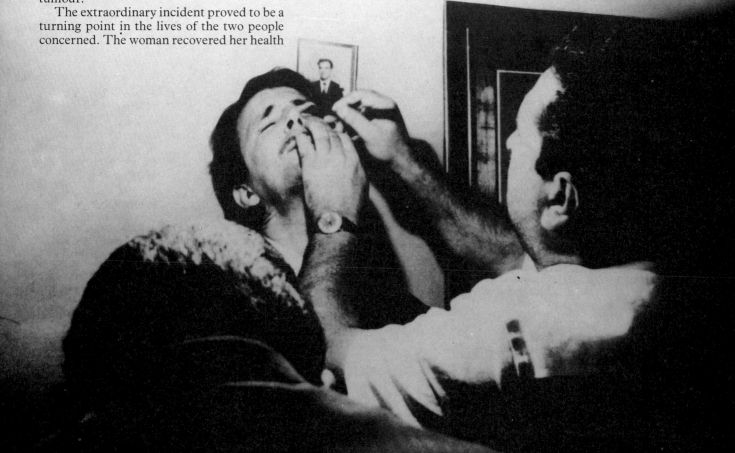

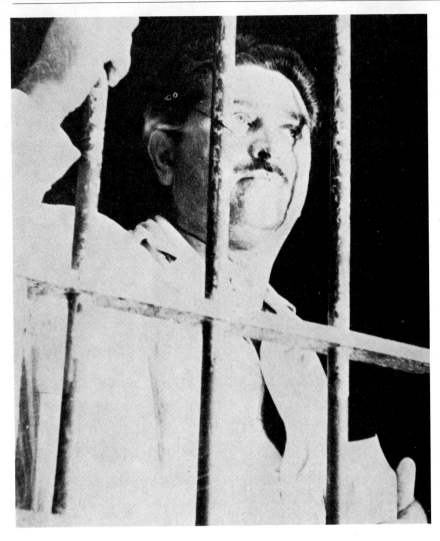

medical knowledge. Yet they cured people.

One conservative estimate suggests that he treated half a million patients in a five-year period. These included people from all walks of life: rich and poor alike, it made no difference to Arigo because he never accepted any money or gifts for his services.

During the 1950s and 1960s Arigo was a national hero in Brazil and hardly a day passed without newspapers headlining his latest healing miracles. Patients came from all over the world and he attracted the attention of Andrija Puharich, a New York researcher with a keen interest in the paranormal, who, after an initial visit, went back to Brazil with a team of doctors to investigate and film the phenomenon.

Puharich described the scene that first greeted him as 'a nightmare'. He wrote:

These people step up – they're all sick. One had a big goitre. Arigo just picked up the paring knife, cut it open, popped the goitre out, slapped it in her hand, wiped the opening with a piece of dirty cotton, and off she went. It hardly bled at all.

Puharich was able to experience Arigo's extraordinary surgery for himself. He asked the Brazilian psychic surgeon to remove a small benign tumour from his arm. Arigo did

Above: José Arigo was put in jail twice for 'practising medicine illegally', but during both periods of imprisonment his jailers secretly let him out to perform operations on the sick – as successfully as ever

so in seconds and Dr Puharich was able to take the growth, and a film record of the surgery, back to the US for analysis.

In all the years that Arigo treated the sick by psychic surgery there was never a single allegation that his unconventional treatment caused anyone any harm. Nevertheless, what he was doing was frowned upon by the authorities because Arigo had no medical qualifications, and in 1956 he was charged with practising illegal medicine.

Many people were willing to testify that Arigo had cured them of serious illnesses, but their testimonies only gave ammunition to the prosecution case. Arigo was given a prison sentence, which was reduced to eight months on appeal, and was fined. But just before he was put into prison the Brazilian president, Kubitschek, gave him a pardon.

Eight years later he was charged again. Kubitschek was no longer president and Arigo was jailed for 16 months. After seven months he was freed, pending an appeal, but eventually had to serve a further two months in prison, in 1965. During both periods, the warden allowed him out of his cell to visit the sick and operate on them.

Arigo investigated

The man who had to hear that appeal was Judge Filippe Immesi, a Roman Catholic with little knowledge of Arigo. The more he studied the case the more difficult it became for him to make a decision without seeing the astonishing psychic surgery for himself.

One day, unannounced, he visited Congonhas do Campos with a friend who was a district attorney from another part of Brazil. Despite their anonymity Arigo recognised them immediately as representatives of the law and invited them to see the 'operations' from close quarters. He knew that he was breaking the law but thought the authorities might as well satisfy themselves that fraud was not taking place.

A near-blind woman with cataracts on both eyes was one of the first patients they saw being treated, and Arigo asked the judge to hold her head. Though he felt queasy he agreed to do so. John G. Fuller, author of *Arigo: Surgeon of the rusty knife*, quotes this testimony from Judge Immesi:

I saw him pick up what looked like a pair of nail scissors. He wiped them on his sport shirt, and used no disinfectant of any kind. Then I saw him cut straight into the cornea of the patient's eye. She did not blench, although she was fully conscious. The cataract was out in a matter of seconds. The district attorney and I were speechless, amazed. Then Arigo said some kind of prayer as he held a piece of cotton in his hand. A few drops of liquid suddenly appeared on the cotton and he wiped the woman's eye with it. We saw this at close range. She was cured.

What Judge Immesi saw convinced him that

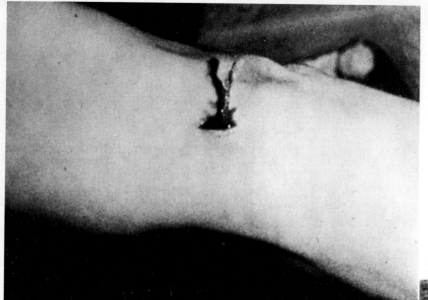

rushed to a São Paulo clinic with symptoms of intestinal obstruction. It was found that a tumour was blocking the transverse colon and a colostomy was performed.

Later she entered the Central Cancer Hospital in the same city for another operation, where it was found that the cancer had spread dramatically. Her weight had dropped by nearly half and the surgeon reported that she was totally beyond the resources of medical science.

So, as a last resort, she was taken to Arigo. Dr Madeiros accompanied the couple on the long trip to Congonhas do Campos and the dying woman had to be carried into the clinic. Being an Austrian, the husband spoke to 'Dr Fritz' in German and he replied in that language. Then Arigo glanced at the sick woman, scribbled a prescription, and said,

Arigo was a remarkable man who deserved to be the subject of scientific study. But the law was beyond doubt. What Arigo was doing was illegal and he would have to be punished – even though he was helping people. However, the judge looked for every possible excuse to reduce the sentence, with the result that Arigo was sent back to prison for just two months. While he was serving that sentence Arigo's case was under review by the Federal Supreme Court and it eventually decided to drop the charges against him. He was released on 8 November 1965.

The judge, of course, was not a medical man but he gave special attention to doctors' testimonies before reaching a verdict. And there were several who had had experience of Arigo's 'operations' and were prepared to say so in public. One of these was Dr Ary Lex, a distinguished Brazilian surgeon, a specialist in surgery of the stomach and digestive systems, lecturer at the Surgical Clinic of São Paulo University, and author of a standard textbook for Brazilian medical students.

Like Judge Immesi, Dr Lex was invited to hold a patient's head in his hands while Arigo operated. He witnessed four operations in half an hour and was satisfied that what Arigo was doing was paranormal. But he was not so impressed with the prescriptions. 'They were absolutely ridiculous,' he told author Guy Playfair. 'Some of them were for obsolete medicines which were only still being made because he prescribed them.' Some of them, he said, were also dangerous in the doses prescribed, and expensive.

However absurd the prescriptions may have seemed, their effects were frequently startling. Such a case concerned a young Polish woman whose body was riddled with cancer. She and her husband were friends of Dr José Hortencia de Madeiros, an X-ray specialist with the State Institute of Cardiology, who took a close interest in the case. The cancer was discovered when she was

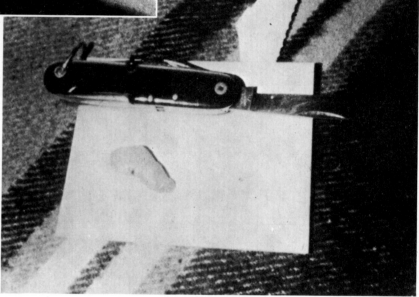

Andrija Puharich, investigator of the paranormal, paid Arigo a visit to see the 'psychic surgeon' in action. He asked Arigo to remove the benign tumour (lipoma) from his arm and Arigo immediately made a deep incision (top) in the arm, then cut out the tumour with his unsterilised penknife (above)

'You take this, and get well.'

Dr Madeiros administered the abnormal dosage of drugs prescribed and she showed signs of improvement within a week. After six weeks her weight had returned to normal. She returned to Arigo who announced that she was out of danger and gave her two more prescriptions. On a third visit to the psychic surgeon, the patient was told that she was completely healed and he advised her to 'undo the operation' – a reference to the colostomy that enabled the body's waste to be passed through the abdomen into a bag. Arrangements were made for the operation to be reversed, and when her abdomen was opened the surgeons confirmed that all signs of cancer had vanished.

Arigo was killed in a car crash in January, 1971 – having told several people that he would not see them again – and the techniques he used to cure the sick remain a mystery. Arigo himself offered no explanation except to give credit to Jesus and Dr Fritz. And when he once saw a film of himself performing operations . . . he fainted.

Margo Williams

Medium Margo Williams claims to receive, through dictation by the dead, pleas for help, which she regards as her special mission to fulfil. But, asks ROY STEMMAN, how convincing are these 'spirit' messages?

ONE BRIGHT spring morning in 1976, Margo Williams was busy in the kitchen of her home in Ventnor, Isle of Wight, when she was startled by a woman's voice saying, 'My name is Jane.'

Margo turned with alarm to see who had entered the house, but there was no one there. Immediately, however, she had an overwhelming urge to pick up a pencil and write down what her invisible guest said; but later she could make little sense of her notes.

'Jane' dictated another message two days later and she returned on over 70 further

Below: Farnham parish church in Surrey, where Margo Williams, accompanied by author Roy Stemman, received an automatically written script allegedly from the spirit of John Lacey, who was searching for his wife Ann. Later, a tablet (inset) was discovered in the church, giving the name John *Lacy* and his wife's name as Agnes

occasions, telling a little about herself each time. She was, she said, a housewife from the mid Victorian period and she had lived in a seaside town in Devon. Margo's husband Wally began researching the scripts to see if he could verify the information given by their 'spirit' guest. When Jane said her family doctor's name was Mackenzie, Wally wrote to the Wellcome Medical History Library and discovered that there had been a doctor of that name with a practice in Sidmouth, Devon, at the time Jane said she had been alive. This, said Wally, 'fitted the facts perfectly'.

By this time Jane had been joined by numerous other communicators. 'We've had people from all walks of life,' Wally explains. 'Men and women, from humble servants to the top brass of the world in different forms.

Whispers from the past

There have been civilians, military, clergy, doctors – you name it, we've had it: an ever-increasing variety. At first it was very much a Victorian thing, but the time zone has extended and we have even heard from a woman called Margaret who died just after AD 1500.'

These voices from the past are known to psychical researchers as 'drop-in' communicators because they appear without rhyme or reason – unlike the 'spirits' of seances who apparently return to speak to their relatives or friends. But if the dead really were dictating Margo Williams's scripts, why were they doing it? Or could it be that the medium was deluding herself into believing that she was in touch with the next world?

It is not easy to answer these questions on the evidence of the scripts alone. If the information they contain is proved accurate by research, then critics could rightly suggest that the medium or her husband may have acquired that information normally and presented it as 'spirit messages'. Or perhaps Margo had read the information earlier in her life and forgotten it, and it was now being dredged up by her subconscious in the form of scripts.

I first met Margo in 1978 and was impressed by her sincerity and down-to-earth attitude to the phenomena. Wally, on the other hand, seemed to over-emphasise its importance, seeing great significance in every enigmatic word or odd coincidence.

During this meeting we discussed Appuldurcombe House, a ruin near Wroxall, on the Isle of Wight. The house is not said to be haunted, but when Mrs Jenny Gibbons, a friend of the Williamses, visited the place she felt very uneasy and decided to ask Margo and Wally if they could pick up anything psychically.

Soon after arriving at the ruin, on 24 June 1978, Margo heard a woman's voice and began writing. The script is typical of those

received by the medium:

Please, please, hear me. He desired me. He said I was comely. I was but a dairymaid here. Please, please, I have waited so long, so long. Old Targett, my father. Been here for years. Please, please hear me. His tongue as sweet as honey, so pleading with me. I met him by the big clump of trees where he deflowered me.

Richard, where are you? Please help me, please, please. My baby I called Thomas. Please, please help me to find him. He cared not how I fared after he gave me some money. My pa was so upset. Please, please, I try to look for

Margo Williams receives a script in the grounds of Waverley Abbey, Surrey. The communicator claimed to be a young woman who had lived in Waverley Abbey House, a mansion nearby. Like many automatic scripts, the information given was insufficient to provide the basis for a detailed investigation

him. . . . Until I find Richard I will stay by the house for eternity. Please help me find Richard. . . . 'Ee called me Mary, where art'ee Richard? 'Ee was the only one who called me Mary. . . .

Moved by her plea, the Williamses conducted their own research to see if Mary Targett really existed. They were almost at the point of giving up when Wally discovered a book entitled *The Oglander memoirs* in which there was a chapter headed 'Ye history of ye Worsley family', written by Sir John Oglander (1595–1648). Reading through the chapter, Wally found an account of a man named Richard Worsley, who was the equivalent of governor of the island around 1550; he had produced a bastard son Thomas by a dairymaid, Mary Targett.

A spirit found

On discovering that Richard Worsley had died in 1565 and was buried on the Isle of Wight at Godshill, Wally went with Margo and Jenny Gibbons in search of his grave. And the ghost of Mary Targett apparently went with them. For, in the church, using Richard's tomb as a writing table, Margo received a final, poignant message from the ghost of Appuldurcombe House: 'I have found 'ee Richard! Thank 'ee, thank 'ee. I can go onwards. Richard I love 'ee.'

This reunion reduced the three earthly 'witnesses' to tears. Sceptics, however, would remain unimpressed. Perhaps the Williamses had concocted the whole thing, or Margo had read about Mary Targett in some other book.

During the next eight months Margo visited many other sites, taking dictation from 33 earthbound spirits, 12 of whom were subsequently identified by Wally. Several of them announced that they had been 're-leased' by the Williamses' intervention.

Here, it seemed, was something that could be put to the test. I invited Margo and her husband to visit the mainland and join me on a ghost hunt in Hampshire and Surrey – a challenge they readily accepted. I selected a number of places to visit, some of which were reputedly haunted and others that, as far as I knew, had no ghosts at all. I did not tell the Williamses where I was taking them.

We went first to the ruin of Waverley Abbey, which had been founded in 1128 by the White Monks of the Cistercian Order. Margo wandered through the remains of the abbey, then began to write furiously in her notebook; the communicator was a young woman who claimed to have lived in Waverley Abbey House.

At the parish church of Farnham, Margo received a script from one John Lacey, who was searching for his wife Ann. And while we were taking a pub lunch, at the William Cobbett in Farnham, the ghost of Sir Reginald Bloomfield 'appeared'. He revealed that he had designed the chancel of an

the wall of the church we found a stone tablet recording the death of 'Mr John Lacy' (note the different spelling) on 6 October 1766. But Margo had walked past the stone before receiving the script, so she could have seen the inscription, consciously or subconsciously. The tablet also recorded the death of Lacy's wife Agnes in 1784. Margo's script referred to the wife as Ann.

In the William Cobbett pub, Sir Reginald Bloomfield interrupted our lunch to tell us about a lady love he had visited there. He mentioned designing a church chancel. The man concerned was easy to identify, even though the spelling of his name was incorrect: it should have been Blomfield. He was a noted church architect in the Surrey and Hampshire area and his name is to be found in most reference books relating to southern England. Strange, then, that he should 'appear' in a pub. There was no way that we could verify his story. The same was true of the other communicators, who gave even fewer clues as to their identities.

Although that investigation failed to provide evidence that Margo Williams was in

unusual church some way away. 'I travelled in my carriage,' he said. 'The fair lady I had an assignation with was staying here. . . .'

I thought Farnborough Abbey in Hampshire might have a ghost or two. The bodies of Napoleon III and his wife, the Empress Eugénie, are in its vaults. The French Emperor came to England after he was deposed in 1871, dying two years later at Chislehurst in Kent. While Wally and I discussed the history of the abbey with a guide, Margo found a quiet corner where she received a script from one of her regular communicators, Captain Charles Bennett. 'There are bodies where no souls dwell now,' he told us, adding that the Empress was now living another life on earth.

Our final visit was to Mytchett Place, which is occupied by the Royal Army Medical Corps. I knew that a variety of ghostly happenings had been reported in recent times, and that Rudolph Hess, Hitler's deputy, was imprisoned there during the war, after he had parachuted into Scotland on an unsuccessful peace mission. I told Margo nothing. The communication she received was from a man who had stayed there, at an unspecified date, and had been burned after a cigar fell on his bed sheets.

Rather than visit more sites, we agreed that Margo would return to some of those already mentioned in the hope that she would receive more information, and more scripts were produced.

So had Margo Williams's scripts proved her claim that the dead were communicating with her? I had to conclude that, on this occasion, they had not.

At only two of the locations did a communicator provide a full name. 'John Lacey' dictated his message at Farnham church. On

Above: Margo in front of Waverley Abbey House

Right: Margo receives a script in the William Cobbett public house, Farnham. It was here that a Sir Reginald Bloomfield communicated; he said he had met a lady love there and that he had designed a church chancel. Sir Reginald *Blom*field was a noted architect who had lived in the area and designed many churches there. Most reference books about Surrey and Hampshire mention him, and Margo could easily have read about him – yet who is to say that this communication is not genuine?

touch with various spirits, this does not necessarily mean that the information in her scripts was not obtained paranormally. Late in 1979 Margo's psychic talents became more varied; to include healing and physical manifestations – a silver glitter appeared on her hands and body when she was 'achieving release of earthbound spirits'. Perhaps investigation of these facets of her work will provide proof of her paranormal powers.

But for the time being, the intriguing case of Margo Williams serves to show just how difficult it is at times to prove – or disprove – mediums' claims.

Coral Polge

Coral Polge has the remarkable talent of being able to draw exact likenesses of people she has never seen or known – people whose faces come to her from beyond the grave through her psychic powers. ROY STEMMAN describes an extraordinary medium

Portrait of a lady

MANY THOUSANDS of people believe they have received tangible proof of life after death. It has been given to them in the form of portraits of their loved ones, drawn by a London medium, Coral Polge.

These pencil and pastel sketches, which now adorn walls in homes around the world, often show a striking likeness to dead relatives and friends. Not only are their features recognisable but sometimes they are dressed in a characteristic style.

Psychic artist Coral Polge, wife of spiritual healer Tom Johanson, does not see the dead, nor is her hand controlled by spirits in the way that automatic writing mediums claim to receive their scripts. 'I just "feel" the people coming through,' Coral told the Spiritualist newspaper *Psychic News* in 1972. 'I know exactly what to draw without thinking about it. It's involuntary, like breathing or walking.'

In the early stages of her career Coral gleaned the information for her portraits by holding letters written to her by those anxious to discover the fate of people near to them who had died; nowadays she concentrates on personal sittings, enabling enquirers to see the sketches as she produces them. She also demonstrates her remarkable talent in public, using an overhead projector so that large audiences can witness the drawings being made.

It was during one of these public performances that Coral drew the features of an elderly man with a droopy moustache. Among those in the audience was Phyllis Timms of Salisbury, Wiltshire, who recognised the man as her grandfather, Herbert Light, who had died of cancer.

But Mrs Timms did not acknowledge the portrait immediately: she wanted 'absolute proof'. In addition to drawing likenesses of the dead, Coral Polge also picks up psychic impressions that help to confirm their identity. In this case, she announced that she felt the elderly man was related to someone in the audience in a green dress. No one responded, and Mrs Timms was not wearing green. The psychic artist was insistent, however, that green was important as a link with the man she had drawn. It then occurred to Mrs Timms that her maiden name was Green – and she raised her hand to accept the portrait.

Coral's introduction to Spiritualism came through her parents, both of whom received spiritual healing in the 1940s. Then, during a visit to Harrow Spiritualist Church, she was

Above: Coral Polge often gives public demonstrations of her skills as a psychic artist by projecting her drawing on an overhead screen while working on it. This example was made in Australia in 1980

Right: drawings made by Coral Polge compared with pictures of the subjects. She produces her sketches in a matter of minutes – which makes her ability to capture her unseen 'communicators' all the more remarkable. Sometimes the results are unexpected, as one sitter discovered. She was hoping for a portrait of former UN Secretary-General Dag Hammarskjöld, whose biography she was writing. When Coral drew a 'pretty little girl' the sitter was disappointed – until she remembered a family portrait that showed that Coral's depiction of Hammarskjöld was in fact very accurate (far right, top)

Above: Coral Polge's drawing, made at a public demonstration, of a man called Herbert Light (above right). Light's grand-daughter, who was in the audience, recognised his features immediately. But it was only after Coral had given further information – which could not have been acquired by normal means – that she acknowledged the portrait

told by a medium that she would be a psychic artist. Coral was trained as an artist at Harrow Art School, but she confesses that she was then hopeless at portraits – her particular interest was textile design; nevertheless, the medium's prediction was not met with scepticism: 'I never had any doubts this was what I had been looking for.'

Coral took her first psychic circle in 1950, and in the next two decades produced an estimated 35,000 portraits.

To begin with, many of the people she drew were spirit guides – Red Indians, nuns, wise Chinese, smiling monks – and although they pleased the sitters they did not provide definite proof of survival, for no one could positively identify the subjects as having once lived on earth. So Coral made a special effort to produce more portraits of relatives. The results can sometimes be very impressive; it is not unusual for a sitter to burst into tears as he or she sees recognisable features appear on the psychic artist's pad. 'If I never get any more evidence for as long as I live, this is enough to convince me Spiritualism is true,' one woman told Coral.

High expectations

Coral cannot produce portraits to order. 'It creates barriers when people come expecting or wanting me to draw someone in particular. I draw whoever is able to get through.' Yet people do visit her with high expectations, sometimes raised by messages from dead relatives that they have received through other mediums.

One such visitor, who went to see Coral Polge anonymously, was expecting a portrait of a 'special person'. What Coral did not know was that the woman was writing a biography of Swedish-born Dag Hammarskjöld, the former United Nations Secretary-General who died in an aeroplane crash in Africa in 1961. The woman had a keen interest in Spiritualism and had apparently received several communications from the statesman through other mediums;

Left: a drawing by Coral Polge of the celebrated opera singer Maria Malibran compared to a portrait from life (right). In this case the picture was not produced for a relative, but for another singer

Below: a portrait of a spirit guide. In the early part of her career Coral Polge often drew spirit guides, but this meant little to those who wanted to communicate with someone known to them. She then made a special effort to sense her sitters' relatives trying to 'come through'

in one of these he promised her a portrait if she visited a psychic artist.

It was therefore with some disappointment that she watched as Coral drew a pretty little girl. At first she thought the sitting was a failure, but slowly, as the portrait took shape, it began to look strangely familiar. Soon she was smiling with pleasure: Hammarskjöld *had* produced his portrait after all.

While researching her book, the woman had looked at many old family photographs. One, she recalled, showed Dag Hammarskjöld at the age of two, sitting on his mother's knee, with long hair and wearing a dress. He looks just like a pretty little girl.

From singer to singer

A portrait produced by Coral Polge also provided corroboration of spirit messages received by singer Grace Brooks. When Grace visited the psychic artist she received a portrait of a young woman with an unusual hair style. 'This is a Spanish singer named Maria,' Coral told her.

Grace had received messages from Maria through the automatic writing of a young Australian singer, Deidre Dehn, whom she met on the set of the film *Oliver!* At first, Maria had simply given Deidre her Christian name and the surname Garcia; later she supplied the name Malibran. Deidre discovered that Maria Malibran (*née* Garcia) had been a celebrated opera singer of Franco-Spanish descent. Born in Paris in 1808, she made her London début at the age of 17; she died in Manchester, aged 28, after a fall from a horse.

When Deidre Dehn returned to Australia, Grace Brooks believed her contact with Maria Malibran to be broken. But the link persisted, it seems. The drawing produced by Coral Polge is strikingly similar to a

portrait Grace found later at the British Museum.

The British medium has demonstrated her psychic art in various other European countries and in Canada and Australia. She has also made numerous television appearances. During a six-week tour of Australia in 1980 she was featured on the nationally broadcast *Don Lane Show*. On this occasion Coral was asked to draw just one portrait; she produced a picture of a young man, saying that he had three brothers and a father who was in poor health. A member of the studio audience recognised him immediately as the son of a friend; he had been killed in a car crash a year earlier.

Coral Polge also spent three weeks in Canada in 1980, during which time she gave 80 private sittings and several newspaper interviews and appeared in public twice, sharing the platform with another medium, David Young – she drawing the spirit communicators while he conveyed messages from them.

Not everyone accepts that Coral's drawings provide evidence of survival beyond the grave. Some regard them as extraordinary examples of extra-sensory perception, while sceptics dismiss them as coincidence. Not all the faces she draws are of the dead: she has occasionally produced portraits of babies before they were born. And she once did a drawing for a Norwegian television producer who was in Britain with a camera crew; he recognised the portrait immediately – it was of one member of the crew who had been unable to visit Britain at the last moment.

What does Coral Polge think of her strange gift? 'After producing so many drawings, you don't try to rationalise it,' she says. 'But I still feel a slight amazement that it has anything to do with me.'

THE UFO CASEBOOK

The UFO paradox

Only the most hardened sceptic can still pretend that UFOs do not exist. But in what way are they real? HILARY EVANS examines this vexed question – and finds that there may be more than one answer

'THEY FLEW LIKE A SAUCER would if you skipped it across the water.' This is how, on 24 June 1947, American airman Kenneth Arnold, an experienced pilot, described some unusual flying craft he had seen over the mountains of America's west coast. Newspapermen applied his phrase to the craft themselves, and the misleading label 'flying saucer' has followed the UFO ever since, like a tin can tied to a cat's tail.

This fanciful name has deepened the reluctance of professional scientists to take the UFO seriously. Only a few have taken the trouble to investigate this bizarre phenomenon, which surely qualifies as the strangest of our time. Even that phrase, 'of our time', is a subject of controversy: many people claim that the UFO has been with mankind throughout history. But the evidence they offer is meagre and their case far from proven. There seems little doubt that our earliest ancestors were considerably more advanced than has generally been supposed, but that is a long way from the theory that our planet was long ago visited by extraterrestrial voyagers.

Whether or not UFOs existed in the past, there is no doubt that UFO sightings have proliferated in astonishing numbers over the past 30 years. This fact seems to be in some way linked with man's first steps towards

exploring space, and this connection is undoubtedly an important clue in trying to explain the UFO.

Estimates of the total number of UFO sightings vary so widely as to be meaningless; more helpful figures are provided by the catalogues of reported sightings prepared by individual investigative organisations. Recently a French team catalogued more than 600 encounter cases in France alone, each vouched for by responsible investigators; how many more were not reported or investigated? In the early 1970s UFO investigators made lists of all reported landing cases for particular countries: 923 were recorded in the United States, 200 in Spain.

Are UFOs real in the sense that, say, spacecraft are real? The surest proof would be actually to get hold of one, and there are persistent rumours that certain governments, notably that of the United States, have indeed obtained a UFO, which is kept in total secrecy. However this remains mere conjecture, despite the sworn affidavits of alleged witnesses. Indeed, the whole matter of governmental involvement – or the lack of it – is a further and fascinating aspect of the UFO controversy.

In the absence of a real UFO that we can touch and examine, there is a great deal of evidence of the phenomenon in the form of a

The COMING of the SAUCERS

By Kenneth Arnold & Ray Palmer

Above: Kenneth Arnold's book, first published in 1952, was the first full study of UFOs. Arnold began collecting accounts of UFO sightings after he saw several disc-shaped objects in the sky in June 1947

mass of photographs and a handful of movies. The majority are undoubtedly fakes. Those with good credentials are so blurred, so distant or so ambiguous that they simply add a further dimension to the problem: why, if UFOs exist, and in an age when many people carry cameras with them most of the time, have we not obtained better photographic evidence?

Perhaps the strongest evidence we have is from the effects caused by UFOs on surrounding objects, particularly machinery. In November 1967 a truck and a car approaching each other on a Hampshire road in the early hours of the morning simultaneously suffered engine failure when a large egg-shaped object crossed the road between them. The police, and subsequently the Ministry of Defence, investigated the incident, but no official explanation was ever issued. Such a case may leave investigators puzzled, but it makes one thing certain: if they can cause physical effects, UFOs must be physically real.

If they are physical objects, UFOs must originate from somewhere. When the first UFOs of the current era were seen, back in the 1940s, it was assumed they came from somewhere on Earth. The Americans suspected they were a Russian secret device, perhaps developed using the expertise of German scientists captured at the end of the Second World War.

But as more reports came in it became clear that no nation on Earth could be responsible. Nor was there sufficient evidence to support other ingenious theories – that they came from the Himalayas, long a favoured source of secret wisdom, or Antarctica, where unexplored tracts of land and climatic anomalies provide a shaky foundation for speculation. Instead, ufologists began to look beyond the Earth, encouraged by the fact that our own space exploration programme was just beginning. We were starting to take an active interest in worlds beyond, and it seemed reasonable that other civilizations might have a similar interest in us.

However, although the number of potential sources of life in the Universe is virtually infinite, the probability of any civilisation being at a stage of development appropriate for space travel is very small. The fact that no solid evidence has been found for the extra-terrestrial hypothesis is discouraging. Although it is the best available explanation, it remains no more than speculation.

Messages from outer space?

Today it is recognised that the UFO poses a problem not only for the astronomer and the engineer, but also for the behavioural scientist. The psychologist confirms that an individual's response to a sighting is conditioned by his psychological make-up, while the sociologist places such responses in a wider social context and relates them to cultural patterns. The anthropologist detects parallels with myth and traditional belief, while the parapsychologist notes how frequently sightings are accompanied by such psychic manifestations as precognition and poltergeist phenomena.

This is particularly true of 'encounter' cases in which the observer claims to have had actual meetings with UFO occupants. The entities are generally described as extra-terrestrial aliens, often ambassadors from an inter-galactic power; their purpose is to examine human beings, to warn us of misuse of resources and to bring reassuring messages from some cosmic brotherhood. With only one or two such cases on record they could be dismissed as fantasy, but there are hundreds of such cases on file.

If a single one of these cases could be shown to be based on fact, the UFO problem would be established on solid foundations and serious scientific interest assured. But in every instance it remains an open question whether the incident actually occurred or is simply a fabrication – deliberate, unconscious, or perhaps induced by some external force. Hypotheses range from brainwashing by extraterrestrial invaders, to deliberate invention by the CIA.

Almost certainly, UFOs exist on both the physical and the psychological level. Somehow we have got to recognise that, although they are real, they are not what they seem. This is the paradox that lies at the heart of the UFO mystery, which we examine in the classic UFO case histories that follow.

Right: this photograph was taken at Taormina, Sicily, in 1954. Sceptics claim the 'objects' are nothing more than lenticular clouds, or even the result of lens flare

Below: a shot taken from Skylab III in 1973. The object rotated for several minutes before disappearing. UFOs have been reported by almost all astronauts

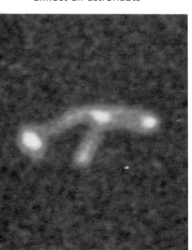

Strange encounters of many kinds

ESTABLISHED SCIENCE has always tended to view the UFO phenomenon with scepticism. In his book, *The UFO experience*, Dr J. Allen Hynek, who was astronomical consultant to Project Blue Book (the US Air Force investigation into UFOs), tells the story of an event at an evening reception held in 1968 in Victoria, British Columbia, at which a number of astronomers were present. During the evening it was announced that strange lights – possibly UFOs – had been spotted outside. Dr Hynek continues: 'The news was met by casual banter and the giggling sound that often accompanies an embarrassing situation.' And, he reports, not a single astronomer went outside to look.

Even Project Blue Book attempted to explain away every reported sighting in terms of conventional science. It soon began to earn itself a bad name because many of its explanations were impossible to believe. In 1966 the US Air Force set up a two-year research project – to investigate, in effect, its own investigations!

The Condon Report, as it was unofficially known, was published in 1969 and stated,

Unidentified flying objects have intrigued the world for decades, but objective reports by experienced investigators rarely reach the mass media. CHARLES BOWEN examines our collection of carefully authenticated cases

broadly, that since nothing valuable to science had come out of the study of UFOs, further research was not justified. This conclusion was reached despite the fact that about one in three of the 87 case histories studied by the commission remained unexplained in the report. After this the US Air Force relinquished responsibility for the monitoring of UFO reports and Project Blue Book was disbanded in December 1969. Since 1969 research has been largely left to private organisations, such as Ground Saucer Watch and Project Starlight International in the USA, and UFOIN (UFO Investigators' Network and BUFORA (British UFO Research Association) in Britain.

From UFO reports made over the past 30 years it has been observed that they occur in distinct waves, often called 'flaps'. The flaps of 1954 and 1965, when reports reached vast numbers, were particularly interesting. Featured below are two incidents from the 1954 flap. The third incident we describe, at Socorro, New Mexico, belongs to the smaller flap of 1964; it is a classic early example of an encounter involving humanoids.

What kind of sighting?

Astronomer Dr J. Allen Hynek, Director of the Centre for UFO Studies, USA. Dr Hynek has spent many years in applying the techniques of science to the study of UFOS

Dr J. Allen Hynek, while acting as a consultant to Project Blue Book, developed a system of classification of UFO 'types' which has become standard. He divided UFO reports according to the distance, greater or less than 500 feet (150 metres), at which the UFO was observed, and subdivided each of these two sections into three, giving six categories altogether.

The commonest sightings are of the 'distant' type.
Nocturnal lights Strange lights seen at a distance in the night sky, often with unusual features such as variations in the intensity of light or colour and sudden, remarkable changes of speed and direction of movement.
Daylight discs Distant objects seen against the sky during the daytime. The shapes vary considerably: cigars, spheres, eggs, ovals and pinpoints as well as discs are often reported.
Radar-visuals Distant UFOs recorded simultaneously on radar and visually with good agreement between the two reports. Dr Hynek excluded 'sightings' made solely by radar since false traces can result from a number of natural factors such as ground scatter – the signal is reflected from high ground – temperature inversions and even thick banks of cloud or flocks of birds. Radar-visual sightings are the most important

category of UFO reports as they give independent instrumental evidence of the sighting; unfortunately, they are very rare.

Reports of UFOS seen at close range are the most interesting and often spectacular; these are the famous 'close encounters'.
Close encounters of the first kind Simple observations of phenomena where there is no physical interaction between the phenomena and the environment.
Close encounters of the second kind Similar to the first kind except that physical effects on both animate and inanimate matter are observed. Vegetation may be scorched or flattened, tree branches broken, animals frightened or car headlights, engines and radios doused. In cases of electrical failure the equipment usually begins to work normally again once the UFO has disappeared.
Close encounters of the third kind 'Occupants' are reported in or around the UFO. Dr Hynek generally ruled out so-called 'contactee' cases in which the reporter claimed to have had intelligent communication with the 'occupants', arguing that such reports were almost invariably made by pseudo-religious fanatics and never by 'ostensibly sensible, rational and reputable persons.' But even these cases occasionally have to be taken seriously by scientists.

'We are not alone'

The UFO seen by Captain James Howard and the crew and passengers of BOAC Stratocruiser *Centaurus* on 29 June 1954 was not a saucer or a disc; it was, astonishingly, a shape that kept changing shape. The airliner had taken off from Idlewild, New York, bound for Newfoundland before making the Atlantic crossing to Shannon, then London.

The airliner was making its way steadily northeastwards when the radio crackled an order from ground control to 'hold' – a manoeuvre adopted when there is a hazard ahead. After half an hour's circling the skipper advised control that if he couldn't proceed he would have to return to Idlewild, as his fuel was low. After some delay permission was given to proceed and *Centaurus* went on automatic pilot at 19,000 feet (6000 metres), just below a broken layer of cloud and with a solid mass of cloud beneath it at 200 feet (60 metres). After some 20 minutes a glint of light suddenly caught Captain Howard's eye. On the port side of the aircraft he saw a large object of metallic appearance emerge from a gap in the clouds. Moving around this main shape were six much smaller objects, not unlike a screen of small destroyers escorting an enormous aircraft carrier.

A bizarre aspect of this remarkable apparition was that it seemed to be changing shape all the time. Captain Howard sketched on his knee pad the different forms he saw: they were a 'delta wing', a telephone handset, a pear. He has since said that, with its continual changes in shape, the object reminded him of a swarm of bees in flight. It was an estimated 4 miles (6 kilometres) from *Centaurus* and it maintained that position.

When Captain Howard turned to speak to his first officer, Lee Boyd, he found him already out of his seat, standing to watch the display. Captain Howard called up control:

'We are not alone.'

'We know.'

'What is it?'

'We don't know, but we've scrambled a Sabre from Goose Bay to investigate.'

'Good. Give me his frequency and I'll vector him in.'

A few minutes later the captain was in touch with the pilot of the Sabre jet fighter who, once he was in range, announced he had two images on his radar scope – one for *Centaurus* and the other, presumably, for the UFO. Then the unexpected happened: the six small objects manoeuvred into single file, bore down on the main object and appeared to merge into one end of it. Thereafter the size of the large UFO began to diminish until the Sabre's pilot announced he was overhead, at which point the object finally disappeared from the radar scope '. . . like a TV picture going off'.

Since about 1953, airline pilots have been required not to disclose to the public information about UFO sightings. In the case of *Centaurus*, however, many of the passengers had watched the display with amazement and the incident received wide press coverage. Researchers were fortunate in this, for this sighting falls into the important category of radar/visual cases. In this instance two separate radar sets were involved (at control and in the Sabre) plus visual observation by experienced pilots, air crew and some 30 or more passengers – only one of whom had a camera, and he was asleep!

'Luminous, silent and eerily still'

Nocturnal lights: Vernon, France, 23 August 1954

Vernon lies on the River Seine some 50 miles (80 kilometres) downstream from Paris; it is the point at which the Allied forces first crossed the river in pursuit of the German armies in 1944. Ten years later, and barely eight weeks after the Idlewild affair, the town was the scene of another significant event, which was witnessed by four people but received little attention in the press.

The sky was clear at 1 a.m. on 23 August 1954, with the moon in its third quarter and due to appear later that night and give only a faint light. M. Bernard Miserey had just returned home and was closing his garage door when he saw a giant cigar-shaped object hanging vertically over the north bank of the

river about 300 yards (275 metres) from him. This object, which he estimated to be some 300 feet (90 metres) long, was luminous, silent and eerily still. While the witness gaped at the phenomenon, a horizontal, disc-shaped object dropped from the bottom of the giant 'cigar', halted its free-fall, wobbled, turned a luminous red with a brilliant white halo and shot towards M. Miserey, passing silently over his house heading south-west.

This remarkable happening was repeated three times, then, after an interval, a fifth disc dropped almost to the level of the river bank before wobbling and disappearing at great speed to the north. While this last manoeuvre was under way the glow of the giant cigar began to fade and soon it was lost in darkness.

M. Miserey reported the incident to the police and was informed that two policemen on their rounds had also observed the happenings, as had an army engineer who was driving on Route Nationale 181 south-west of the town.

What was the meaning of the apparition M. Miserey saw? Was the large cigar-shaped object the 'carrier' of the smaller ones? Other UFO sightings have led many people to think this may be the case – including the Idlewild incident. The significant difference is that, whereas at Idlewild the smaller objects were assimilated by the larger one, at Vernon the small objects were ejected. But no conclusive evidence exists to establish what these objects in the sky actually are.

'Humanoids . . . and strange insignia'

Close encounter of the third kind: Socorro, New Mexico, USA, 24 April 1964

Below: Patrolman Lonnie Zamora whose close encounter is one of the best authenticated cases on record

At about 5.50 p.m. on 24 April 1964 Patrolman Lonnie Zamora of the Police Department in Socorro, New Mexico, was alone in his Pontiac giving chase to a speeding motorist who was heading out of town. Suddenly he heard a roar and at the same time saw a 'flame' in the sky, bluish and orange and strangely static as it descended some distance away. Fearful that a nearby dynamite shack might blow up, the patrolman gave up chasing the motorist and headed off over rough ground towards the point where the flame had come down.

After three attempts he forced his car to the top of a ridge and drove slowly westwards. He stopped when, suddenly, he saw a shiny, aluminium-like object below him, about 150–200 yards (140–185 metres) south of his position. Zamora said it looked like a car on end, perhaps 'turned over by some kids'. Then he saw two humanoid figures in white 'coveralls' close to the object. He estimated later that they were about 4 feet (1.2 metres) tall. One of them looked straight at him and seemed to jump. Zamora was wearing clip-on sunglasses over his prescription spectacles and couldn't distinguish any features or headgear at that distance.

The patrolman now accelerated thinking that, whoever the strangers were, they might be in need of help. The shape he'd seen was a

sort of vertical oval, and looking down he could see it was supported on girderlike legs. When the terrain became too rough for the car to go any further he radioed his headquarters to say that he was near the scene of a possible accident and would proceed on foot.

As Zamora left the car he heard two or three loud thumps, like someone hammering or slamming a door. These thumps were a second or two apart. When he was about 50 paces from the object there was a loud roar, which rose gradually in pitch. The humanoid figures were nowhere to be seen. At the same time he could see a blue and orange flame rise from the ground leaving a cloud of dust. Zamora beat a hasty retreat towards his car and as he reached it turned to see the oval shape, now horizontal, rising towards the level of the car. Frightened by the continuing roar, he ran on and dived for shelter over the edge of the ridge. When he realised the noise had ceased he raised his head from his hands and saw the UFO still in the air and moving away from him about 15 feet (4.5 metres) above the ground. It safely cleared the dynamite shack and continued to rise gradually, watched by the policeman, who was retracing his steps to the car. As he called up the radio officer he watched it accelerate away to clear a mountain range and disappear.

Zamora had seen a kind of strange insignia about 18 inches (45 centimetres) high on the side of the object and while he was waiting for his sergeant to arrive he decided to make a sketch of it.

Sergeant Sam Chavez was soon on the scene. Had he not taken a wrong turning he would have arrived in time to see the craft.

'What's the matter, Lonnie?' he asked. 'You look like you've seen the devil.'

'Maybe I have,' replied Zamora.

Zamora pointed out to Sergeant Chavez the fire that was still burning in the brush where the UFO had stood. When they descended to the site they found four separate burn marks and four depressions – all of similar shape – made, they assumed, by the legs of the landing gear. On three of the marks the dense soil had been pushed down about 2 inches (50 millimetres) and dirt had been squeezed up at the sides. The fourth pad mark, less well defined, was only 1 inch (25 millimetres) deep. When engineer W. T. Powers investigated the case he estimated that the force that produced the marks was 'equivalent to a gentle settling of at least a ton on each mark!' He also pointed out an interesting fact about the positions of the marks. Measurements show that the diagonals of a quadrilateral intersect at right angles, then the midpoints of the sides all lie on the circumference of a circle. Mr Powers noted that one of the burn marks occurred on the intersection of the diagonals and speculated that, assuming the linkage among the legs was flexible, this would mean the burn was immediately below the centre of gravity of the craft and might indicate the position of the blue and orange flame seen by Patrolman Zamora. Four small round marks were found within the quadrilateral on the side farthest from where Patrolman Zamora had stood; these were described as 'footprints'.

The Socorro incident was widely reported in the press and generated immense excitement throughout the world. The US Air Force's Project Blue Book usually ruled out UFO sightings with only one witness, but at Socorro Patrolman Zamora's story was so plausible that it was decided to carry out intensive on-the-spot investigations. This was one case in which Project Blue Book was forced to admit defeat: the apparition could

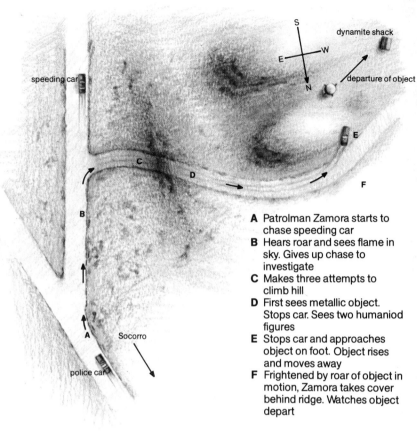

A Patrolman Zamora starts to chase speeding car
B Hears roar and sees flame in sky. Gives up chase to investigate
C Makes three attempts to climb hill
D First sees metallic object. Stops car. Sees two humaniod figures
E Stops car and approaches object on foot. Object rises and moves away
F Frightened by roar of object in motion, Zamora takes cover behind ridge. Watches object depart

not be explained as any known device or phenomenon. Dr J. Allen Hynek admitted that he was more puzzled after completing the investigation than when he had arrived in Socorro. He commented, 'Maybe there *is* a simple, natural explanation for the Socorro incident, but having made a complete study of the events, I do not think so.'

Below: one of the four impressions left by the UFO which landed at Sorocco, New Mexico on 24 April 1964. An engineer said pressure of 1 ton would have been needed to make the holes

him for 90 minutes.

Dr J. Allen Hynek is very wary of all so-called 'contactee' cases. And Allen Hendry, author of *The UFO handbook*, points out a suspicious feature of 'contactee' reports: until the late 1950s, when it was still believed that planets in our solar system were likely to be able to support intelligent life, most of the reported visitors came from Mars, Jupiter and Venus – but once scientists had proved that this was unlikely, the visitors began to hail from planets outside our own solar system.

Paul Villa's photographs have been subjected to very detailed analysis by Ground Saucer Watch Inc., a UFO organization in Phoenix, Arizona. Using advanced computer techniques, they can establish the exact shape of an

THE BEST UFO pictures usually turn out to be hoaxes; pictures of well-documented sightings are usually blurs on under- or over-exposed film.

These spectacular photographs, taken by Paul Villa in Albuquerque, New Mexico, are almost certainly fakes. The top photograph shows an object Villa claims to have seen on 18 April 1965; its three occupants, he says, talked to him. The other two pictures are views of a UFO he photographed on 16 June 1963. It contained nine beings from the constellation of Coma Berenices, who conversed with

alleged UFO, its distance from the camera, and even estimate its true size. Paul Villa's photographs failed GSW's tests: comparison between the photographic images of the UFOs and surrounding objects revealed that the alleged UFOs were in fact small objects seen at close range – not, as Villa had claimed, large ones at a distance. GSW have been known to be wrong – but ufologists the world over agree that Villa's pictures are just too *good* to be true!

Right: at about 6 p.m. on 19 November 1974, Christophe Fernandez, aged 16, was alone at home near Uzès in southern France. Suddenly he noticed a bright light outside. Forty yards (35 metres) from the house was a luminous sphere 2.5 yards (2.2 metres) wide. It was standing still on the ground or just above it.

Christophe could hear a faint 'glug-glug' sound like a bottle being emptied. On the surface of the sphere three circular shapes were moving about. Trembling, Christophe managed to photograph them.

Next, the globe rose slowly to a height of 5 or 6 yards (4 or 5 metres). A dazzlingly bright cylinder, about 1 yard (1 metre) long emerged from the underside of the sphere. Then the UFO suddenly shot upwards and out of sight

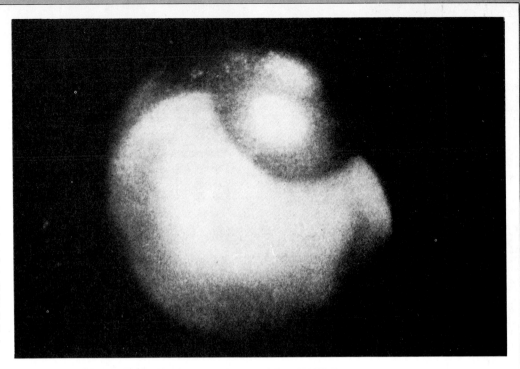

Left: 15-year-old Stephen Pratt and his mother were returning from a visit to the local fish-and-chip shop to their home in Conisbrough, Yorkshire, on the evening of 28 March 1966. At about 8.30 p.m. they saw an orange-coloured light in the twilit sky.

The light, they said, was 'throbbing'. Stephen went indoors to fetch his Instamatic camera, which was loaded with black and white film and set for 'cloudy'. Stephen took one shot of the light, which was travelling westwards.

Stephen claimed to have watched the light for 10 minutes – a long time for a UFO sighting. The film was taken to a local chemist's shop for processing, but when the negatives and prints were collected it was discovered that no print had been made of the 'UFO' negative.

Later Stephen sent his film to Granada TV asking them if they could explain the strange objects on the negative. Granada made the first prints and broadcast the photograph on 12 April 1966.

The negative did not appear to have been tampered with. The strangest feature of the story, however, is that, although Stephen told investigators he had seen only one light, the photograph shows three objects – and they appear to be solid, shaped like flying saucers, not lights.

The men from Mars

WHEN PATROLMAN Lonnie Zamora saw two small humanoids beside a UFO near Socorro, New Mexico, at about 6.50 p.m. on 24 April 1964 (previous case), he was not the first American that day to experience such an encounter. Several hundred miles away, a dairy farmer of Newark Valley, New York State, had not only seen two ufonauts emerge from their craft at about 10.00 a.m., but also claimed he had conversed with them.

'We have spoken to people before'

Close encounter of the third kind: Newark Valley, New York State, USA, 24 April 1964

At about 10.00 a.m. on 24 April 1964, farmer Gary Wilcox of Newark Valley, Tioga County, was using his manure spreader in a field to the east of his farmhouse. It was a clear, sunny day, and the ground was dry.

The field sloped up a hill, at the top of which stood an old abandoned refrigerator, half hidden by trees. Suddenly Gary saw a glint of something shining. At first he thought it was the refrigerator, but it soon dawned on him that the shining object was between him and the fridge. His curiosity aroused, Gary drove the tractor, with spreader in tow, up the slope to the top of the hill – about 800 yards (730 metres) from where he had first seen the thing.

With about 100 yards (90 metres) still to go, it occurred to him that he might be looking at a fuel tank from the wing of an aeroplane; he stopped the tractor and walked over towards the object. Then he realised that the thing was off the ground, presumably hovering, for he could not see any 'undercarriage'. As he drew closer to it he could see that it was 'bigger than a car in length . . . shaped something like an egg . . . no seams or rivets. . . .' He estimated later that it was 20 feet (6 metres) long, 4 feet (1.2 metres) high and 15 feet (4.5 metres) wide. He 'thumped it and kicked it . . . it felt like metallic canvas.'

While Gary was carrying out this rough examination, two 4 feet (1.2 metre) tall 'men' came out from under the object, each carrying a tray about 1 foot (30 centimetres) square, 'filled with alfalfa, with roots, soil, leaves and brush'. They walked towards Gary and stopped a couple of yards away.

The farmer said that at first he thought 'it was some kind of a trick . . . a sort of candid camera gag', and he laughed. Amusement turned to surprise when he heard one of the beings speak: 'Don't be alarmed, we have spoken to people before.'

The voice did not sound like one Gary could find words to describe; he could understand what the being said, yet could not tell whether it was speaking in English or not.

Gary said the little 'men' were standing one behind the other. They wore white, metallic-looking overalls without seams, stitching or pockets, and no features of their

took off gently towards the north, with no blasting, no heat, and no more noise.

The farmer drove home, telephoned his mother and told her what had happened. He then milked his cows, did a few other jobs, and, at 4.30 p.m., he drove up the hill with a bag of fertiliser, which he left at the site of the landing. The next morning, it was gone.

News of the incident spread, and reached the ears of a neighbour, Miss Priscilla Baldwin, who interviewed Gary, alerted the local newspaper, and reported the matter to the Tioga County sheriff. The police investigation was carried out on 1 May 1964, and Gary made a statement to Sheriff Paul J. Taylor and Officer George Williams.

In 1968 a well-known psychiatrist, Berthold Eric Schwarz MD, visited the area and conducted a thorough investigation of the case, with psychiatric study of the witness. In addition Dr Schwarz interviewed many of the farmer's family, friends and neighbours

bodies were visible. They had arms and legs, but he could not see hands or feet. When the creatures raised their arms, he could see wrinkles where the elbows would be. The farmer could not see faces – eyes, ears, noses, mouths or hair. The voice that addressed him seemed to be coming 'from about them rather than from either of them'.

The conversation continued: 'We are from what you know as the planet Mars.' They asked Gary what he was doing; when he explained, they showed great interest in manure and, when he told them about it, in artificial fertiliser too. Gary said he would get them a bag of fertiliser, whereupon they told him they were 'travelling this hemisphere'. When Gary asked if he should go, the 'spokesman' added that they could only come to Earth every two years, and included a warning that people should not be sent out into space. It seems that Gary asked if he could go back with them, but his request was declined because of the thinness of their atmosphere. The ufonauts also mentioned that astronauts John Glenn and Virgil ('Gus') Grissom, and two Russian cosmonauts, would die within a year, due to exposure in space.

Further revelations were that they were learning about our organic materials because of the 'rocky structure of Mars', and that they did not fly near our cities because the fumes and air pollution affected the flight of their spacecraft.

Gary Wilcox said that no attempt was made to harm him, and that they carried no visible weapons. He also said that their voices stayed at the same pitch throughout, and that they did most of the talking. Then, with a warning that Gary should not mention the encounter, the two mysterious humanoids walked back under their ship, ducking down as they went, and disappeared. The craft made a noise like a car engine idling, then

and, from all of these interviews and the psychiatric examination, it appears that Gary Wilson is a very normal, 'truthful person with no emotional illness, and that his experience was "real" even though the interpretation of his encounter is a complicated and uncertain matter.' In his report, prepared exclusively for *Flying Saucer Review*, Dr Schwarz revealed that Gary had never had any other UFO experiences, either before or since his encounter on 24 April 1964.

As for the alleged prophecy, this was not fulfilled as stated. But on 27 January 1967 Virgil Grissom, together with Ed White and Roger Chaffee, died in a fire in an Apollo spacecraft that was being tested at Cape Kennedy. And on 23 April 1967, three years almost to the day after Gary Wilcox's encounter, the Russian Vladimir Komarov was killed when his capsule parachutes failed to open after re-entry into the atmosphere.

Tantalising evidence: The New Zealand UFO film

LATE IN THE EVENING of 30 December 1978 an Argosy freight plane set off from Wellington, New Zealand. Its skipper was Captain Bill Startup, who had 23 years' flying experience behind him, and the co-pilot was Bob Guard. On board was an Australian TV crew from Channel 0-10 Network: reporter Quentin Fogarty, cameraman David Crockett and his wife, sound recordist Ngaire Crockett. Their purpose was to try to film UFOS, for there had been reports of 'unknowns' during the preceding weeks in the region of Cook Strait, which separates New Zealand's North and South Islands. They were spectacularly successful in the quest. So successful that, after the story had appeared in hundreds of newspapers and clips from the films had been shown repeatedly on television around the world – the BBC, for instance, gave it pride of place on the main evening news – critics and droves of debunkers lined up to try to explain what the television crew had seen, in terms ranging from the sublimely astronomical to the ridiculously absurd.

'Bright lights over the ocean'

Radar-visual: Blenheim, New Zealand, 30 December 1978

This spinning, luminous sphere was filmed by a New Zealand television crew on the night of 30 December 1978. The crew made two flights, looking for UFOs, on the same night – and, incredibly, saw them both times

The Argosy had crossed Cook Strait and was flying over the Pacific Ocean off the northeast coast of South Island when the excitement began. The television crew was down by the loading bay filming 'intros' with Quentin Fogarty when Captain Startup called over the intercom for them to hurry to the flight deck; the pilots had seen some strange objects in the sky. According to Dave Crockett, they had already checked with Wellington air traffic control for radar confirmation of their visual sighting.

Quentin Fogarty stated that when he reached the flight deck he saw a row of five bright lights. Large and brilliant, although a long way off, they were seen to pulsate, growing from pinpoint size to the size of a large balloon full of glowing light. The sequence was repeated, the objects appearing above the street lights of the town of Kaikoura, but between the aircraft and the ground.

Dave Crockett, who was wearing headphones, received a call from Wellington control warning the pilots that an unknown target was following the Argosy. Captain Startup put his plane into a 360-degree turn to look for the unidentified object but the passengers and crew saw nothing. Control however, was insistent: 'Sierra Alpha Eagle . . . you have a target in formation with you . . . target has increased in size.' This time lights were seen outside the plane, but because of interference from the navigation lights of the plane, Crockett was unable to film. So First Officer Bob Guard switched off the navigation lights – and everyone saw a big, bright light. The plane was now back on automatic pilot, so Bob Guard gave up his seat for Crockett, who obtained a clear shot

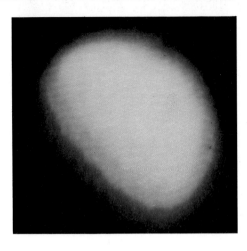

moonlight via cabbage leaves'. A more reasonable explanation was that the films showed a planet – but which one? One newspaper claimed it was Venus (left), another said it was Jupiter (right). But even the quickest glance at the planets themselves show these explanations to be unlikely. The *Daily Telegraph*, surprisingly, printed a strong condemnation of the Venus theory: 'The scientist who suggested that all [the television crew] were seeing was Venus on a particularly bright night can . . . be safely consigned to Bedlam.'

Rogue planets?

For a time it was thought that the New Zealand films might provide solid scientific evidence for UFOs.

Faced with this possibility, scientists were quick to react by putting forward a whole range of alternative explanations of what the object in the films might be. Some of their theories were wildly implausible – one even claimed the television crew had seen 'reflections from

Right and far right: two stills from the New Zealand television crew's film. The presence of the strange objects was confirmed by Wellington air traffic control, who saw their traces on their radarscopes

Below: Captain Bill Startup, pilot of the aircraft from which the UFO film was taken

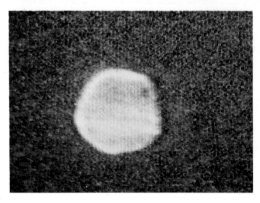

of the object with his hand-held camera. Dave Crockett has since explained that this changing of seats with the camera running was responsible for the violent shake seen at that point in the movie film.

After this, Bill Startup put the plane into another 360-degree turn. They then lost sight of the UFO, although Wellington control said its echo was still on the radar scope.

It should be noted that, although there was no room for a camera tripod to be mounted on the flight deck, the unidentified object stayed steady enough for David Crockett to be able to keep it dead centre in his camera viewfinder for more than 30 seconds.

As the plane approached Christchurch, the fuel gauge went into a spin, but the captain said that this occasionally happened and was not necessarily caused by interference by the UFO. At this point they were

tuning in on the UFO off Banks Peninsula and were out of touch with Wellington control. Christchurch control had the object on its radar scope but later, when Captain Startup and American investigating scientist Dr Bruce Maccabee asked to see the radar tapes, the Christchurch supervisor replied that they had been 'wiped' clean as part of routine procedure.

The Argosy landed at Christchurch and journalist Dennis Grant joined the team in place of Dave Crockett's wife Ngaire. They left on the return flight to Blenheim at about 2.15 a.m. on 31 December 1978.

Early in this flight the observers saw two more strange objects. Through the camera lens Crockett saw what he described as a sphere with lateral lines around it. This object focused itself as Crockett watched through his camera – without adjusting the lens. He said the sphere was spinning. Significantly, one of the objects swayed on the Argosy's weather radar continuously for some 4 minutes. Later, as the aircraft approached Blenheim, they all saw two pulsating lights, one of which suddenly fell in a blurred streak for about 1000 feet (300 metres) before pulling up short in a series of jerky movements.

True or false?

Were the objects 'flying saucers'? Many alternative explanations were put forward: the film depicted a 'top secret American military remote-control drone vehicle', plasma or ball lightning, a hoax, meteorites, 'helicopters operating illegally at night', mutton birds, lights on Japanese squid boats, 'reflections from moonlight via cabbage leaves' (at Kaikoura), while Patrick Moore hedged his bets with a guess of 'a reflection, a balloon or an unscheduled aircraft.'

One newspaper claimed the film showed the planet Venus, out of focus because it was filmed with a hand-held camera. Another offered Jupiter as a candidate; an amateur astronomer had enhanced the light values of the film by putting through a line-scan analyser and had identified four small points of light that could be taken to correspond to the positions of the four largest moons of Jupiter. Venus and Jupiter appeared in

completely. They definitely moved, varying between 50 and 100 knots (92.5 km/h and 185 km/h). I certainly couldn't identify them as anything. It's pretty inconclusive. They were purely the sort of radar echoes that constantly pop up. It is not unusual to get strange echoes appearing on what we call primary radar. They usually amount to nothing at all.

Nevertheless, the Royal New Zealand Air Force was concerned enough about the incident to put a Skyhawk jet fighter on full alert to intercept any other UFOs that might appear in the area. By the end of January, however, the fuss had died down and the New Zealand Defence Ministry stated that the radar images were 'spurious returns' and the unidentified objects 'atmospheric phenomena'.

What is the truth of the New Zealand affair? The film appears to be genuine; computer enhancement has not proved it to be a fake. It seems almost too good to be true that a television crew that had set out with the deliberate intention of filming 'flying saucers' should come up with such spectacular results; and yet it has to be assumed that the objects they saw were real enough to those who beheld them – and were not mere hallucinations. The case remains on file, a fascinating question mark.

Below: this unique frame from the New Zealand film seems to show the UFO performing an extraordinary feat of aerobatics – looping the loop in 1/24 of a second. An alternative explanation for this typical UFO behaviour: the hand-held camera was jogged

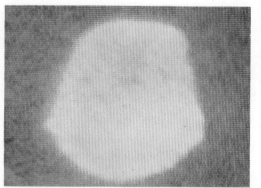

With the navigation lights of the aircraft switched off, the television crew was able to obtain this film of one of the objects. It pulsated from a pinpoint to the size of 'a large balloon'

different regions of the sky; because the television crew were so vague about the position of the lights relative to the aircraft as they were filming them, it was impossible to make a positive identification.

One of the most exciting aspects of the incident is that it appears to offer independent instrumental evidence of the sighting both on film and radar. But even here there are problems. Although both ground radar and the Argosy's own radar picked up unidentified traces, the number of UFOs the television crew claimed to have seen – about eight – conflicts with the 11 reported by ground radar. And the crew actually filmed only one object. The radar controller at Wellington, Ken Bigham, was dismissive about the whole affair:

I managed to plot three of the echoes for 20 minutes or so before they faded

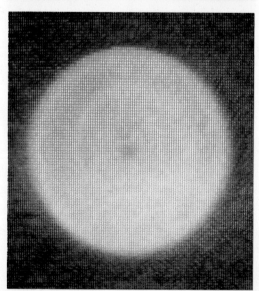

Silently, out of the night sky

SCIENTISTS GENERALLY consider UFOS that give responses on radar scopes the most reliable for their purposes. The first sighting described below took place at Caselle Airport in Turin, Italy, and is one of the most well-documented radar–visual sightings on record, while the second, at Ivinghoe, Bedfordshire, had only one witness, but its authenticity is vouched for by his sheer terror.

One of the most spectacular UFO waves lasted for five months in the winter of 1973 to 1974. It was heralded by the impressive sighting at Turin in November 1973—an event of profound significance for the science of ufology. It attracted the attention of Jean-Claude Bourret, a top reporter from the French radio station France-Inter, who broadcast a series of programmes about UFOS culminating in a startling and important interview with the then Minister of Defence, Monsieur Robert Galley.

The Ivinghoe incident, which took place 11 years earlier in 1962, shows a fascinating aspect common to many UFO reports—electromagnetic effects on electrical and mechanical equipment such as car radios.

'Sudden vast jumps to and fro'

Radar-visual: Caselle airport, Turin, Italy, 30 November 1973

On 30 November 1973 Riccardo Marano was preparing to land his Piper Navajo at Caselle Airport when he was advised by control that there was an unidentified object at a height of about 4000 feet (1200 metres) above the runway, close to where he was due to land. Control had the object on its radar screens and gave Marano permission to approach it to see what it was. As he neared his target, control reported that it was moving and was heading for the Suza Valley. Accordingly, Marano changed course to follow it – and suddenly control announced that the target had disappeared from its radar.

At that moment Marano received a message from another aircraft: the UFO was behind him at about 12,000 feet (3600 metres). Marano's Navajo was then flying at about 10,000 feet (3000 metres). He began to turn – and saw in front of him what appeared to be a bright white luminous sphere, which was emitting light of all colours of the spectrum. The light pulsated from bright to dim, but never went out completely. As he closed on the UFO, Marano reported that it was 'flying in a most irregular fashion, making fantastic lateral deviations and sudden vast

jumps to and fro'. Taking advantage of a moment when the object was below him, Marano put his plane into a dive, accelerating to a speed of over 250 mph (400 km/h) – but he could not catch up with the UFO. When he gave up the chase, it was heading southeastwards. He estimated its speed at about 550 mph (900 km/h).

Two other pilots confirmed the presence of the object. They were Comandante Tranquillo, who had just taken off in his Alitalia DC-9, and Comandante Mezzalani, who was bringing his Alitalia DC-9 in from Paris. Comandante Tranquillo advised control that he dared not approach the 'shining object giving out flashes' and thereupon adjusted his course.

Comandante Mezzalani observed the object as he was touching down. He said it was large and bright, yet dimmer than a star or an artificial satellite.

There was another very reliable witness, none other than the commander of the neighbouring Caselle military airfield, Colonello Rustichelli, who stated that he had observed the UFO on his radar screen. It was, he said, something solid, which lit up like an aircraft on his radar, giving the same sort of return as would a DC-9. He said it looked like a star, but when he got it on his radar it stayed firm. Soon afterwards it headed off westwards.

A curious event, which may or may not be

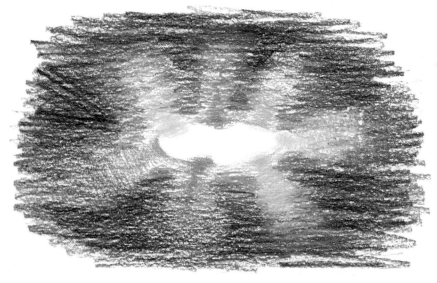

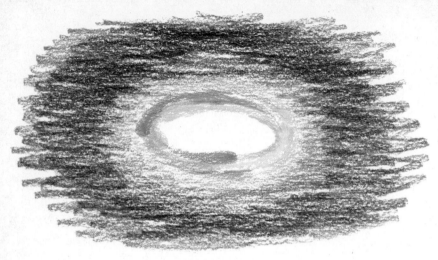

connected with the UFO sightings described above, took place earlier on the same evening. At 5.00 p.m. Signor Franco Contin, an amateur photographer, saw an extremely bright object in the sky. At first he thought it was a star, but when he saw it begin to move about, he realised it must be something else. A slightly misshapen luminous globe, it was white at first and then suddenly turned deep orange. Signor Contin fetched his camera and took a total of eight photographs. These show an enormous object, oval in shape and brightly luminous.

The Turin sighting was remarkable not only because it was followed by a world-wide wave of UFO reports, but also because it attracted the attention of two very important people. The first of these was M. Jean-Claude Bourret of the French radio and television service ORTF, chief reporter of the radio station France-Inter, who was so impressed by the report of the sighting that he made a series of 39 radio programmes devoted to UFO research, which were broadcast between January 1973 and March 1974.

The other person whose interest was aroused by the Turin incident was Monsieur Robert Galley, Minister of Defence for France, who granted an exclusive interview to M. Bourret, which was broadcast on 21 February 1974.

This interview was of immense importance for the science of ufology – for in it a serving Minister of Defence admitted, not only that UFOs exist, but also that in 1954 his government had set up a secret section devoted to their study within the Ministry of Defence. M. Galley spoke of the massive nature of the UFO phenomenon, of the many detailed eyewitness reports he had read and of the volume of reports received from the Air Force in the early days of the project – in which, he said, 'the general agreement was quite disturbing'. Since 1970, UFO research in France has been in the hands of the *Centre National d'Etudes Spatiales* (The national centre for space studies), which evaluates reports of UFO sightings from both the Air Force and the Gendarmerie. Unfortunately, however, the French UFO group has no contact with international military groups.

M. Galley also admitted that 'it is certain that there are things that we do not understand and that are at present relatively inexplicable. I will indeed say that it is undeniable that there are things today that have not been explained or that have been incorrectly explained'.

This startling interview was immediately given wide coverage in the French papers, including *France-Soir, Le Parisien Libéré, L'Aurore* and *Le Figaro* and all the big provincial papers. It was soon reported in German, Spanish, Swiss, Italian, Brazilian and American newspapers – but not in the British press, or on radio or television. In his English translation of Jean-Claude Bourret's book *The crack in the universe* Gordon Creighton describes his unsuccessful attempts to convince the BBC that the interview was important enough to warrant a mention on one of its radio science programmes. He suggests that the scant and biased reporting of the UFO phenomenon by the British media may be the result of an official debunking attitude on the part of the authorities. Their methods are different from those used in the USA; indeed, says Mr Creighton,

> quieter and more subtle techniques of ridicule and denigration, plus, no doubt, the occasional discreet telephone call to the newspaper that has offended by printing a serious looking UFO report, have yielded far better results than the CIA's methods.

This scepticism on the part of the authorities no doubt accounts for the fact that very little serious scientific research is carried out into UFOs in Britain. Amateur UFO societies can do little more than monitor sightings. Suppression of information can only be harmful to research, and it is disturbing to think there may be many UFO sightings we simply never hear about.

Below: Monsieur Robert Galley in his historic interview with reporter Jean-Claude Bourret of the French radio station France-Inter on 21 February 1974. M. Galley admitted that the French government had been secretly studying UFOs for 20 years

'Like a halo round the moon'

Close encounter of the second kind: Ivinghoe, Bedfordshire, England, 9 February 1962

Mr Ronald Wildman, a delivery driver for the Vauxhall Motor Company, left his home in Luton, Bedfordshire, at 3.00 a.m. on 9 February 1962 to drive a new estate car from the factory to Swansea. He had passed Dunstable, and was on the Ivinghoe road approaching a set of crossroads at Tringford, when he saw an oval-shaped object ahead of him on the road. It was white with black markings at regular intervals around the perimeter. It appeared to be 20 to 30 feet (6 to 10 metres) above the road, and was at least 40 feet (12 metres) wide. Mr Wildman drove straight towards the object, but when he was 20 yards (18 metres) from it the power of the car's engine began to fade until he was going at just 20 mph (30 km/h). Putting his foot flat down on the accelerator did not help; neither did changing down through the gears. Mr Wildman noticed, however, that his headlights stayed on. For some 200 yards (180 metres) as he drove down the road, the UFO stayed about 20 feet (6 metres) ahead of, and above, him.

Suddenly a white haze appeared around the perimeter of the object – it was 'like a halo round the moon', said Mr Wildman – and it veered off to the right at high speed. As it went, it brushed particles of frost from the trees onto the windscreen of the Vauxhall.

In an interview, Mr Wildman recalled that his headlights were reflected from the object when it was closest to the road, and in his opinion this showed it was solid.

After the UFO had disappeared, the car's engine returned to normal working and the witness, by now panic-stricken, drove as hard as he could to Aylesbury where he reported the affair to the police. They noted the distraught condition of the driver.

The credibility of sightings with only one witness rests on the trustworthiness of the person concerned. Mr Wildman's report was checked by three investigators from *Flying Saucer Review*, who were extremely impressed by Mr Wildman's obvious sincerity. They were convinced his sighting had been genuine, not a hallucination.

Interference with electrical equipment such as televisions, car radios and headlights is a common feature of UFO reports. It has been suggested that this phenomenon may result from electromagnetic fields created by UFOs along their surfaces in order to minimise the effects of air resistance. Whatever the cause, this phenomenon can be one of the most frightening aspects of a UFO incident.

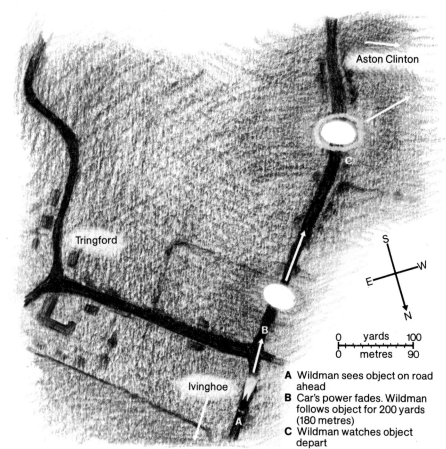

Aston Clinton

Tringford

Ivinghoe

A Wildman sees object on road ahead
B Car's power fades. Wildman follows object for 200 yards (180 metres)
C Wildman watches object depart

Terror by night

DESPITE MANY people's scepticism about the existence and reported sightings of UFOs, some accounts are so vivid and detailed as to merit serious discussion. There are elements of the case of the Moreno family that inevitably keep alive the search for an explanation, in particular the length of time that members of the family were able to observe and what they had described they had seen invading their ranch.

'The figures were undoubtedly humanoid'

Close encounter of the third kind: Trancas, Argentina, 21 October 1963

At 7 p.m. on 21 October 1963 there was a breakdown of the private power plant of the Moreno family at their Santa Teresa Ranch, 2 miles (3 kilometres) from the small town of Trancas in the Tucumán province of Argentina. Since there was no light, the family retired to bed early, at about 8 p.m.; 21-year-old Señora Yolié de Valle Moreno (her maiden name is used at her request) stayed awake to feed her baby son.

Suddenly the maid, Dora Martina Guzman, 15, knocked on Yolié's door,

went outside the house to see for themselves. At first they could see nothing, but as they ventured further away from the house they saw, apparently on the railway line to the east, two bright, disc-shaped objects linked by a shining tube; Yolié described it as 'something like a small train, intensely illuminated'. A number of silhouettes – the sisters estimated about 40 – were moving about inside the tube. The figures were undoubtedly humanoid and the witnesses thought at first that there must have been a

crying that she was frightened. Yolié put this down to the loneliness of the place and took no notice. But moments later Dora Martina was back – there were strange lights outside the house, for which she could see no cause. She explained that every time she went outside the house the whole farmyard was suddenly lit up for a few seconds. This could not have been lightning; there was no thunderstorm brewing, and there were only a few clouds in the sky.

Yolié and her sister Yolanda got up and

derailment on the line, or some sort of sabotage.

The sisters decided to go closer and investigate. They returned to the house for warm clothing, and Dora Martina fetched her Colt .38 pistol, which she kept as a safeguard for when she was alone in the house. Yolié woke her other sister Argentina, and asked her to listen for her baby. When Argentina heard what Yolié and Yolanda proposed to do she warned them of the dangers of guerillas and saboteurs and then, being curious, ventured outside to see for herself. She let out a terrified scream, shouting that there were strange machines near the house. As she ran away from them she fell over a pile of bricks that was lying in the yard.

Yolié, Yolanda and Dora Martina continued investigating; as they walked round the southern side of the house they could see a pale greenish light ahead of them near the front gate of the farm. They thought this must be from the headlights of the truck driven by one of the farm employees and Dora Martina ran forward to open the gate for it. As she ran ahead, Yolié shone her flashlight at the green light.

Instantly a disc-shaped, domed object was

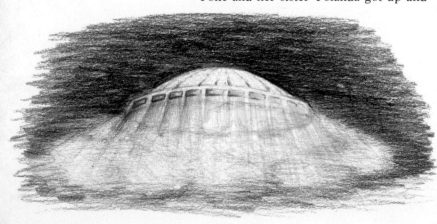

revealed, hanging in mid-air in front of them. It had six brightly lit windows and was some 30 feet (9 metres) wide; metallic in appearance, it had a number of sections that were joined together with rivets at the seams. The dome was also metallic, but it was darker and had no rivets. The object was rocking gently to and fro.

Suddenly a multicoloured band began to rotate inside the windows and a whitish mist thickened around the object, which emitted a faint hum. The witnesses became aware of a sulphurous smell.

The three women took in all these details in less than 30 seconds. Then, without warning, a tongue of flame shot from the object, hit Dora Martina and hurled her and the two sisters to the ground. At the same time three more discs along the railway lit up, making six in all.

By now the parents, who had been woken by the sound of falling bricks, were watching the object nearest the house from the window of Argentina's room, which faced eastwards. As the band inside the craft rotated faster and faster, they watched while the disc gradually became enveloped in the white mist until all that could be seen was an orange-coloured cloud. A 'tube' of light emerged from the top of the object and probed the features of the house, as if conducting a careful scrutiny. Double 'tubes' of light probed forward from three of the objects on the railway line – one pair focused on a hen house, another on a tractor shed, and the third on a neighbour's house. The ends of these 'solid' light beams or tubes edged forwards slowly, penetrating a fence as they went.

It took a few minutes for the beams to cover the distance of 200 yards (180 metres) from the railway line to the shed, and they finally stopped about 6 feet (2 metres) from the front of the shed. The beams were perfectly cylindrical, about 10 feet (3 metres) wide. There were no shadows anywhere.

Recklessly, Yolié thrust her arm into one of the beams; she had been thinking that the beam might be a jet of water that had somehow been concentrated into a parallel-sided beam. What she felt, however, was a powerful sensation of heat – but there was no effect on her skin.

Yolié ran indoors. There, the temperature had risen from 60°F (16°C) to a stifling 104°F (40°C). The air was filled with a sulphurous smell and everyone felt burning, prickling sensations in their skin. Yolié's mother was praying, and Argentina and Yolanda were pleading with their father not to go outside.

The house was lit up as bright as day. Nobody was able to explain where the light was coming from; none of the witnesses noticed whether the light from the discs was passing through the walls of the house, though this is a possible 'explanation'.

The light had a powerful effect on the household animals. The Morenos owned three very fierce dogs and noticed that, whenever the light fell on the animals, they immediately became quiet and listless. When, occasionally, the beams fluctuated, the dogs seemed to come to life.

Next, the object closest to the house swung its tubular beam of light in the direction of Trancas. The beam advanced slowly for some 10 or 15 minutes until Yolié estimated it had reached the outskirts of Trancas; then, amazingly, it switched the tube in a U-turn back towards the house. Next it slowly withdrew the tube of light – which was, like the others, about 10 feet (3 metres) wide – until it vanished completely,

A Witnesses first see objects
B Large object becomes illuminated. Witnesses hurled to ground

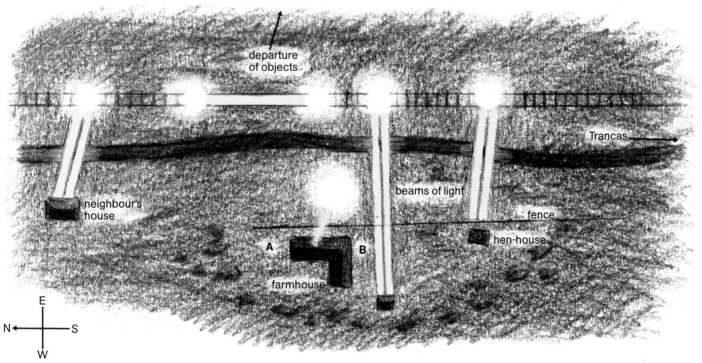

departure of objects

Trancas

beams of light

neighbour's house

fence

hen-house

A

B

farmhouse

E
N — S
W

there was a strong smell of sulphur. The cloud did not disperse until four hours later. A journalist who visited the family the next day said that the heat and the smell of sulphur inside the house were still quite striking.

Underneath the spot where the object had hovered the Morenos found, forming a perfect cone 3 feet (1 metre) high, a pile of small white balls half an inch (1 centimetre) in diameter. Next day they found similar little balls on the railway line.

The balls were found to disintegrate under gentle pressure. They were later analysed in the laboratories of the Institute of Chemical Engineering in the University of Tucumán and found to contain 96.48 per cent calcium carbonate and 3.51 per cent potassium carbonate.

An enquiry into the events at the Morenos' farmstead was quickly mounted by the local police. It was found that a Señor Jose Acosta and an entire family named Huanca had seen the strange illumination on the railway embankment, while a Señor Francisco Tropiano had seen the six discs flying across the sky at about 10.15 p.m., about the time the Morenos' ordeal had ended.

What was the purpose of this extraordinary siege of the lonely Argentinian ranch? It seems the alien pilots of the craft were conducting some kind of investigation – but what did they hope to find? Another possibility is that they were simply carrying out repairs to their craft. The light beams appear to have been used to discourage onlookers from approaching the craft. Whatever the purpose of the unknown pilots' visit, it seems they did not wish the Morenos any harm.

and then moved towards the other objects on the railway line. Finally all six objects rose and flew off at low altitude in an easterly direction towards a mountain range, the Sierra de Medina.

The time from the beginning of the sighting was then about 40 or 45 minutes. For more than half an hour after the objects had disappeared, the horizon was tinged with an orange glow. Once the Morenos had recovered from their shock, they ventured out into the garden. The cloud produced by the object that had been nearest to the house was still hanging in the air. It was very thick and

Aliens in the dark

THE UFO PHENOMENON often seems to veer into the realms of the psychic – indeed, some researchers believe UFOs to be from another dimension altogether. However, this view must be considerably modified when one comes across cases in which UFOs show up on radar screens, make deep marks in railway sleepers, or leave calcined stones behind as they did in these cases from England, France and Spain.

'Something is buzzing our airfield'

Radar-visual: Bentwaters, near Ipswich, England, 13 August 1956

THE NIGHT OF 13 August 1956 was a busy one for RAF and USAF air controllers and radar operators in East Anglia. Although some of the many inexplicable radar traces they obtained were probably spurious, others were undoubtedly from unknown objects. The sighting described here was stated by the USAF Condon Report as 'the most puzzling and unusual case in the radio-visual files'.

The main events began at 10.55 p.m. at RAF Bentwaters, near Ipswich, a station leased to the United States Air Force. A Ground Controlled Approach (GCA) radar

had been alerted by ground control, looked down and saw the fuzzy light flash between his aircraft and the ground. The UFO was heading towards Lakenheath, another RAF aerodrome leased to the USAF, and immediate warning was given.

For the record, there was no mention of a sonic boom at Bentwaters. Ground observers at Lakenheath saw the light approach, stop dead, and then move swiftly out of sight to the east. Some time after that two white lights were seen; they joined up and disappeared in formation.

Observers and radar operators of the

operator picked up a fast-moving target 30 miles (50 kilometres) to the east, heading in from the sea at a speed of 2000 to 4000 miles per hour (3200 to 6440 km/h). It passed directly over Bentwaters and sped away until it disappeared from the scope 30 miles (50 kilometres) to the west. This overflight was not just a radar observation, however; a tower operator on the ground looking up saw a light 'blurred out by its high speed', while the pilot of a USAF C-47 aircraft flying over Bentwaters at 4000 feet (1200 metres), who

Lakenheath GCA and radar traffic control centre scopes testified to having recorded objects travelling at terrific speeds, stopping, and changing course instantaneously. After some hesitation the Americans at Lakenheath put through a call to the RAF.

The RAF Chief Controller at Bentwaters remembers USAF at Lakenheath telephoning to say something was 'buzzing' their airfield circuit. He scrambled a Venom night fighter from RAF Waterbeach, and his interception controller, with a team of three highly

few seconds, and in the space of one or two sweeps on the scopes, the object appeared behind the fighter. The pilot called out 'Lost contact, more help,' and he was told that the target was now behind him.

Meanwhile the chief controller scrambled another Venom fighter. The American witnesses said the UFO 'flipped over' and got behind the RAF fighter, which then manoeuvred to try to get behind the UFO. This information was given to the USAF-sponsored study of the UFO phenomenon under Dr E. U. Condon at Colorado University. Until the Condon Report was published in January 1969 the case had remained secret. A detailed study was carried out by Dr James McDonald, an upper atmosphere physicist at Arizona University. This was a sighting the Condon Report could not dismiss; indeed, it had to admit that 'the apparently rational, intelligent behavior of the UFO suggests a mechanical device of unknown origin as the most probable explanation.'

trained personnel, took over. The Venom was vectored onto the UFO and the pilot, who was accompanied by a navigator, called out 'Contact' when he could see it, and 'Judy' when the navigator had the target fairly and squarely on the fighter's own radar scope. The Venom closed on the target but after a

'Two very odd creatures'

Close encounter of the third kind: Quarouble, near Valenciennes, France, 10 September 1954

The small French village of Quarouble, not far from Valenciennes close to the Belgian border, was shaken by the events of the night of 10 September 1954.

At about 10.30 p.m., 34-year-old Monsieur Marius Dewilde was sitting reading in the kitchen of his little house. His wife and son were already in bed. The house was situated among woods and fields just under a mile from the village. There was a fenced garden in front of the house, and to one side of this there ran a National Coal Mines railway track between St Amand-les-Eaux and the giant Blanc Misseron steel works where M. Dewilde was employed.

Suddenly his dog started to bark and howl and, thinking there was a prowler or smuggler outside the house, M. Dewilde took his flashlight and ventured out into the darkness. He was instantly aware of an ill-defined shape to his left, on or near the railway line; he thought it might be a farmer's truck. Then, as his dog came up to him, cringing on her belly, he heard a sound to his right. He swung round, and his torch beam fell on two very odd creatures, each just over 3 feet (1 metre) tall and wearing what appeared to be a diver's suit. M. Dewilde said they seemed to

be shuffling along on very short legs. He noticed that they had very broad shoulders, but no arms and that they wore huge helmets. They were heading for the dark shape he had seen on the railway line.

Recovering from his initial surprise, the tough, taciturn steel worker ran to the garden gate with the intention of cutting off the interlopers from the path. He was about 2 yards (2 metres) from them when a blinding beam of light, the colour of magnesium flares, issued from an opening in the side of the dark shape. The beam struck him and he was stopped dead in his tracks, unable to move or shout; it was as though he were paralysed, he said. With a sense of horror he watched the two creatures pass within a yard (1 metre) of him, and on towards the still indistinguishable shape.

Suddenly the light went out and, recovering the use of his muscles, M. Dewilde set off after the small creatures. All he saw, however, was what appeared to be a door closing in the side of the object, which then rose slowly from the ground like a helicopter. There was a whistling noise, and M. Dewilde saw steam clouding up from beneath the contraption. After rising about 30 yards (30 metres) the craft – if that is what it was – set off towards the east, climbing and glowing red as it went.

Shocked, and in a highly agitated state, M. Dewilde woke up his wife, then ran off to the police station in the village. The policemen on duty thought he was out of his mind and sent him on his way. But he contrived to get access to the Commissioner who, after listening to his semi-coherent account, realised that this man – by now in a state of incontinence – was neither joking nor mad.

A detailed enquiry was set up by the regular police, the air gendarmerie and the

Territorial Security Department. They were convinced that the witness was not lying. They were convinced, too, that the object

could not have been a helicopter (carrying contraband for example) because of the mass of telephone wires overhead which would have prevented a landing.

It was suggested by one journalist that M. Dewilde was suffering from the effects of a head wound, and had had an hallucination, but this theory was untenable in view of the discovery of marks, sharply and deeply cut, in the iron-hard wood of the railway sleepers where M. Dewilde said the object had stood. A railway engineer calculated that it would have taken a weight of 30 tons (30 tonnes) to have made the marks. It would have taken great heat to have produced the burnt and calcined ballast stones found between the affected sleepers, and this would have called for an extremely powerful hallucination!

'As big as a jumbo-jet'

Radar-visual: Valencia, Spain, 11 November 1979

On Sunday evening, 11 November 1979, a Supercaravelle of the Spanish airline TAE, on a charter flight from Salzburg to Tenerife, put down unexpectedly at Valencia in Spain. The flight had been four hours late in starting, and this extra delay was almost the last straw for the tourists on board the aeroplane. Fortunately, most of them were unaware of what had gone on outside – 24,000 feet (7000 metres) above the Mediterranean.

The incident began after the aeroplane had passed over Ibiza. In an interview with newsman Juan J. Benítez, the skipper, Commandante Lerdo de Tejada, said that a few minutes before 11 p.m. he was requested by Air Control in Barcelona to tune in to radio frequency 121.5 megahertz, an emergency wavelength. He picked up the hiss of the carrier wave but received no instructions. Before the captain could query this he saw two powerful red lights at the 'nine o'clock' position (to the left, or port side).

Commandante Tejada thought there was only one 'thing' carrying two lights. This object bore down on them at great speed,

coming up on their left, and a little behind them. He added:

When we saw them first they were at about 10 miles [16 kilometres]. Then they made towards us and literally 'played' with us at about half-a-mile [1 kilometre] . . . the object was moving upwards and downwards at will, all around us, and performing movements that would be quite impossible for any conventional machine to execute.

According to the captain the object seemed to be as big as a jumbo-jet. Finally, he said, the speed and closeness of this monstrous object were such that he was forced to perform a 'break' – a sharp turn to avoid possible collision – about 60 miles (100 kilometres) from Valencia. Air Control in Barcelona were informed that unidentified traffic was close by, and that the UFO had stayed near to the aircraft for eight minutes. After the 'break' the UFO followed the jet for another 30 miles (50 kilometres).

The controls and instruments of the Supercaravelle were not affected during the emergency. The automatic pilot did, in fact, fail – but that, said the captain, was not due to the UFO. Finally Manises Airport at Valencia was contacted and permission was requested to make an emergency landing, The Supercaravelle touched down a few minutes before midnight.

Señor Morlan, director of the airport, his traffic controller and other personnel confirmed seeing an extraordinary object with red lights over the airport.

Señor Benítez also found that there had been a vigorous response to the alert by the Spanish Air Force as military radars had picked up unidentified targets in the precise area where the TAE airliner was flying. The unidentified echoes persisted and two F-1 fighters were scrambled from Los Llanos five minutes after the Supercaravelle had landed. It is understood that visual contact was made – and that one of the fighters was subjected to a number of close approaches by the UFO.

Above: this photograph was taken by a coastguard, R. Alpert, at 9.35 a.m. on 16 July 1952 from the control tower at Salem Air Base in Massachusetts, USA. The objects were reported to be moving at great speed. They appear much brighter in the photograph than they actually were because the aperture of the camera was set for the brightness of the surrounding landscape and consequently the UFOs themselves are over-exposed.

But is the photograph genuine? The images are unlikely to have been caused by lens flares, as these almost always appear in straight lines. But it is reported that the picture was taken through a laboratory window – and sceptics have suggested that the objects could actually be reflections of lights inside the laboratory. Photographic experts, however, point out that reflected lights are rarely as opaque as these.

Right: this picture, published here for the first time, was taken by London photographer Anwar Hussein in the Spanish Pyrenees in July 1978. After finishing filming one day, he found he had left one of his lenses at the top of a mountain. The next morning, about 9 o'clock, he returned to look for it. Mr Hussein found the lens and took some pictures; his camera was set on motor-drive. At the time he noticed nothing unusual – except the brightness of the light and the uncanny quietness. Back in London, he sent the film to be developed – and received a worried telephone call from the lab, who pointed out the 'object' on the film and thought it must be a fault that had appeared during developing. On examination, however, the emulsion was found to be undamaged. This is typical of many of the best UFO pictures, which are often of objects that go unnoticed at the time of filming.

Above and left: early in January 1958 a survey ship of the Brazilian Navy, the *Almirante Saldanha*, set off from Rio de Janeiro bound for the rocky island of Trindade, where the Navy had an oceanographic station. Among those on board was Almiro Barauna, a specialist in underwater photography.

Just before the ship was due to set sail on the return journey at 12.15 p.m. on 16 January 1958, a retired Air Force officer, Captain Viegas, who was on deck with other officers and technicians, called to Barauna that there was a bright object in the sky. Barauna located it and watched the moving object until it was silhouetted against some cloud. Then he shot two photographs. The UFO then disappeared behind the main peak of the island for a few seconds. When it reappeared it was flying in the opposite direction. Barauna took a third photograph, then a fourth and fifth, but these last two were wasted shots because the photographer was jostled by the other people aboard the ship, who were by now extremely excited. The UFO appeared briefly to halt its passage away from the

island, and Barauna took his last picture of the object as it moved swiftly away.

The photographer said the object was silent, dark grey in colour, and was apparently surrounded by a greenish vapour or mist.

Barauna developed his film on board ship in the presence of the skipper, Commander Bacellar. (As there was no photographic paper on board, prints were made when the ship had returned to Rio.) Barauna said that in the urgency and excitement of the sighting, he did not think to check the settings of his camera and the pictures were consequently over-exposed.

Back in Rio de Janeiro, the Brazilian Navy examined the negatives. They found them to be genuine, and any possibility of a hoax was eliminated. Based on Barauna's account, the naval authorities set up a mock re-run of the incident, and were able to compute the speed of the object as about 550 to 600 mph (900 to 1000 km/h). The diameter of the Saturn-shaped UFO was estimated at around 40 yards (37 metres). At least 100 people had seen the UFO — and the photographs seem to be unimpeachable.

Grand UFO spectaculars

ONE RECURRENT FEATURE of UFO reports is the seeming pointlessness of the incidents – lights that hover in the skies, 'buzz' aircraft or frighten small groups of witnesses, all to no apparent purpose. Here we describe two extraordinary UFO events. The first is from the Canary Islands, where a UFO appeared before large numbers of people at a distance, as well as treating three terrified witnesses to a close-up display involving the humanoid 'pilots' of the craft. The second story comes from Lot-et-Garonne in south-west France, where a UFO appeared silently above a field in which a farmer was working one night, frightening him half out of his wits – and then simply, and silently, disappeared.

'Two enormous beings'

Close encounter of the third kind: Canary Islands, Spain, 22 June 1976

On the evening of 22 June 1976 an extremely active UFO visited the Canary Islands. It was witnessed by many people, and a number of reports found their way into the Spanish press. There the matter would, no doubt, have rested but – in a surprise turn of events – the Spanish Air Ministry released documentation on 12 UFO incidents to journalist Juan José Benítez of the Bilbao newspaper *La Gaceta del Norte*. One of the cases listed in their dossier was the extraordinary Canary Islands spectacular.

Some interesting facts emerged. A report by a doctor on the island of Gran Canaria had already achieved international publicity, and apparently the events had been confirmed by a Spanish warship and by photographs taken by a private citizen (later impounded to be examined by the authorities).

At 9.27 p.m. on 22 June 1976 the Captain, an ensign and several crewmen of the Spanish Navy corvette *Atrevida* spotted the UFO off the south-eastern coast of the island of Fuerteventura. They saw a light, part yellowish and part blue, moving across the sea towards them, gaining altitude. They thought at first that they were watching an aeroplane with its landing lights on, but then rapidly revised that opinion when the light stopped suddenly and was abruptly extinguished, only to be replaced by a rotating beam of light shining downwards. Two minutes later the light took the form of a great halo that lasted for some 40 minutes, lighting up both land and sea. The original yellow-bluish light now reappeared, splitting into two parts, the bluish part remaining within the halo while the upper part began to climb in an irregular spiral before vanishing in the direction of the neighbouring island of Gran Canaria. It took only three minutes to get there, reaching the astonishing speed, over 85 nautical miles (158 kilometres), of some 1900 miles per hour (3060 km/h).

There were a number of witnesses to the UFO in the northern part of Gran Canaria but the one with the best story to tell was the local doctor, Don Francisco-Julio Padrón León. He had been called out by a young man, Santiago del Pino, to attend his sick mother. The doctor and the young man were travelling in a taxi driven by Francisco Estévez, which had just negotiated a bend in the road at a place called Las Rosas (between Gàldar and

Agaete in the north-western corner of the island). Suddenly they found themselves confronted by a giant sphere hanging a few yards from the ground. The sphere was outlined in a pale greyish-blue. Almost instantly the radio in the taxi cut out and the three witnesses shivered as they felt a surging wave of cold.

The taxi driver had stopped his vehicle. He was trembling with cold as all three men watched two enormous beings apparently inside the sphere (which was the size of a two-storey house and quite transparent – the stars behind it could be seen quite clearly). There were panels of instruments on a kind of platform inside the sphere.

The two ufonauts seemed to be clad in tight-fitting clothing in a deep shade of red and wore black helmets. No features were described in the witnesses' statements, but the creatures were seen in profile. They stood facing one another on either side of an instrument console, manipulating levers and switches with hands that were enclosed in black cones. Dr Padrón was particularly impressed by the disproportionate size of the backs of their heads.

Suddenly the taxi driver took it into his head to switch on the spotlight. At that instant the sphere began to rise until the watchers could see a transparent tube inside it that emitted a blue gas or liquid. This gradually filled the sphere, which expanded until it was as big as a 30-storey building although the beings and their console panels remained the same size.

Greatly alarmed, the driver turned the car and back-tracked to some nearby houses where a family who lived in one of them told

the doctor that their television had blacked out. The witnesses joined the family in the house and, as they watched the extraordinary object from the windows, they saw the blue 'gas' stop swirling inside the sphere. Then the object emitted a high-pitched whistle and flashed away in the direction of Tenerife, changing as it went to a 'spindle' shape surrounded by a halo.

It is now known that Dr Padrón was instructed by the Spanish Air Ministry investigators not to speak about his experience. Consequently details of his statements were not known until the dossier was handed over

to Senor Benítez. However, a sketchy outline of the story had leaked out before the restriction was applied. Some newspapers carried the story about a large spherical object that had been seen with control panels and 'pilots' visible inside, hovering over an onion field where part of the crop was destroyed. The destruction of a circular area about 33 yards (30 metres) in diameter was confirmed in the Ministry file.

The UFO was next seen by hundreds of people in Puerto de la Cruz as it passed over the island of Tenerife, then by the crew and passengers of a ferry plying between Tenerife and La Palma – while many inhabitants of the outlying islands of Gomera and Hierro telephoned newspaper offices and local radio stations about their sightings of the object.

The Ministry's dossier contained a report that the object had been detected and followed on radar along with prints from photographs of the UFO taken from the southern part of Gran Canaria. The photographer had been located by the police and his film had been impounded until the release of the dossier some months later.

The doctor's testimony gives the impression that he witnessed a truly unique UFO 'display'. But as ever, the question remains: was it an exhibition of remote control?

Over the years there has been a great deal of speculation about the nature of the objects seen by UFO witnesses. Are UFOs, in fact, some kind of projection from the controllers of the phenomenon? And if so, who – or what – are these controllers, and why will they not show themselves to us? What is the message they are trying to give us?

'All around . . . was bathed in light'

Close encounter of the first kind: Lot-et-Garonne, France, 13–14 November 1971

The weather in Lot-et-Garonne in southwestern France, 56 miles (90 kilometres) east of the city of Bordeaux, on the night of Saturday, 13 November 1971, was miserable. The sky was overcast and there was a drizzling rain. Nevertheless farmer Angelo Cellot was out working, ploughing a field that adjoined the minor road between his house and that of his brothers. Monsieur Cellot's tractor was fitted with headlights and a movable spotlight – for he was accustomed to working late into the night.

At about 1.50 a.m. he suddenly became aware of a light that he first thought was from another farmer's tractor. However, as he turned his tractor at the road's edge and proceeded in the opposite direction towards the stream at the northern boundary, he realised the light was in the air, and moving along the stream towards his field. He thought it was a helicopter, but as he turned again towards the road he realised the object had changed direction and was following him up the field, preceded by a red light. The UFO, hovering at an estimated altitude of 130 feet (40 metres), had five bright lights underneath it, so bright that when he trained the spotlight onto it Angelo could not distinguish any shape behind them.

The farmer had reached the end of the furrow close to the road when he realised the aerial intruder was directly overhead. All around him was bathed in light from the five beams, and now puzzled concern gave way to fear. He saw that the UFO was descending and was already only 50 to 70 feet (15 to 20 metres) above him. Fear changed to panic. Angelo deserted his tractor, leaving the engine running and headlights on, and dashed away towards his brother Jean's house to raise the alarm. He had covered about 30 yards (30 metres) when he looked back and saw the UFO climbing and heading away to the north. So he ran back, and switched off lights and engine. It was only then that he realised the object had been completely silent. As Angelo watched he saw, to his relief, the UFO slowly disappear from sight beyond a low ridge.

Thoroughly shaken, and with no wish to finish his job, the farmer put the tractor in its barn and went to bed at 2 a.m.

This important story eventually reached the newspaper *La Dépêche du Midi*, and thence the French investigatory group GEPA, for whom Colonel Pierre Berton interviewed Angelo Cellot. He was accompanied at the interview by two officers of the Gendarmerie, and later made an official report.

As in many other reports the predominant feature of this UFO sighting is *light*; glowing light, opalescent light, haloes of light, coloured light, revolving light, beams of light, and the mysterious *solid* beams of light. But here the similarity ends; the 'light shows' display a bewildering variety. How should we make sense of it?

The Rex Heflin photographs

UFO sightings are generally worth taking seriously if they satisfy two criteria: they are made by reliable witnesses and supported by some form of independent evidence. Yet here is a report that presents the serious investigator with an unsatisfactory number of loose ends – even though it was made by a responsible highway official and comes armed with what are, if they are authentic, some of the best UFO pictures ever taken.

'Too controversial'

Daylight disc: Santa Ana, California, USA, 3 August 1965

Right: photograph 1 (see map overleaf), taken by Rex Heflin of the UFO he saw near Santa Ana, California, USA. The photographs were taken with a Polaroid camera through the windscreen of the truck in which Heflin was sitting at the time of the sighting

One of the most impressive sets of photographs of an alleged UFO is that taken by Mr Rex Heflin at 12.38 p.m. (Daylight Saving Time) on 3 August 1965, on the Myford Road near the Santa Ana Freeway outside Los Angeles in California, USA. Heflin, who had been a police officer for four years, was working for the Orange County Highways Department at the time when he took the photographs.

In his report of the sighting, Heflin stated that, at about 11.30 on the morning of 3 August, his truck was standing facing north-north-east at the side of Myford Road, within sight of the junction of the Santa Ana Freeway. He was attempting to make contact on his two-way radio with the road maintenance superintendent, to report that tree limbs were obscuring the view of a railroad crossing sign, when the radio went dead.

All at once he caught sight of what he thought, at first, was an aircraft, approaching from the left (north-north-west) – but, seconds later, he realised it was a disc with a domed top.

He reached for his Polaroid Model 101 camera, which was standard equipment for Orange County Road Department officials, and took his first photograph, through the windscreen of his truck.

Heflin claimed that the object moved slowly in an arc over the road, and to the right of his truck. He took his second picture, again through the windscreen. He took the third picture just before the UFO, which had

Right: photograph 2. The object had now moved across Myford Road, and changed direction abruptly before photograph 3 was taken

Below: photograph 3. Heflin took this picture just before the UFO, which had wobbled once or twice, gained altitude and moved beyond the Santa Ana Freeway (marked by telegraph wires in the photograph) to the north-west

suddenly 'wobbled' once or twice, gained altitude and accelerated in a wide arc beyond the Freeway towards the north-west. When asked whether the bottom of the UFO appeared to have any markings, openings or evidence of landing gear, Heflin replied:

No! The only thing I saw on the bottom of the craft was a white beam of light emitting from the centre and sweeping in a circle to the outer edge of the craft. The movement of the beam was similar to the sweep of a radar scope beam.

Suddenly the craft was gone, leaving a ring of smoke, or vapour, in the air. Heflin said he drove up the road and stopped near the ring, jumped from his cab, and photographed the ring before it disappeared.

The witness returned to his truck and found that his radio was working again. The same afternoon, after duty, he returned to the office and showed his colleagues his UFO photographs. During the first few days after the sighting, comments the Condon report, Heflin allowed many of his friends to make copies of his pictures; 'time passed and apparently more copies of the pictures were made and handed out to various friends of friends, until most of Santa Ana was saturated with the UFO pictures.'

One of Heflin's friends, having first obtained his permission, sent copies of the photographs to *Life* magazine. According to the Condon commission report they were rejected as being 'too controversial' – even though they were 'the best that *Life* had seen so far.'

News of Heflin's sighting came to the attention of the local newspaper, the *Santa Ana Register*, which tracked Heflin down and invited him to show them the photographs. These created great interest, and enlargements were made – and 'cropped' – for printing; the first picture appeared in an

article in the *Santa Ana Register* on 20 September 1965.

Needless to say, Rex Heflin came under a great deal of pressure to supply copies of his photographs to interested groups and investigators, but curiously enough he was unable to supply any *original* prints. He claimed that the negatives from which the *Register* had made its prints were made from the original Polaroid prints, and that he himself had been present while the film was being processed – but the newspaper insisted that its prints were from Polaroid *copies*.

From this point a whole new mystery blew up around the affair, for Heflin claimed that he had handed over the original prints to a man with impressive credentials who had claimed to come from North American Air Defense (NORAD). Unfortunately Heflin did not ask for a receipt for his photographs, and he claims they were never returned to him. Months later NORAD denied having had anything to do with the incident and, according to the *Orlando Sentinel*, a Florida newspaper, among others, Colonel George P. Freeman, the Pentagon spokesman for Project Blue Book, stated that similar 'mystery men' in a number of States, claiming to represent NORAD and various other government agencies, were confronting and 'silencing' witnesses of UFOs.

A general air of confusion and speculation surrounded the Heflin photographs. Then, in April 1969, new light was thrown on the subject when aerospace engineer John R. Gray, who had formerly worked on the Apollo space programme, published a study in *Flying Saucer Review* that gave considerable support to Rex Heflin's claims.

Working from an uncropped enlargement of the first photograph – which showed, on the road, the shadow of the telegraph (utility) pole 26 feet (8 metres) from the camera

A Heflin sees object; takes
   photographs 1, 2 and 3
B Heflin takes photograph 4

photograph 4

N

to Santa Ana

B

Santa Ana Freeway

photograph 1

photograph 3

photograph 2

Myford Road

A

0   200 metres
0   200 yards

Below: photograph 4. After
Heflin had taken photograph
3, the object suddenly
disappeared, leaving only a
ring of black smoke

metres) from the camera position.

Mr Gray worked out that, if the object had been 6 feet (1.8 metres) wide, its altitude would have been 28.7 feet (8.7 metres). At this altitude, the object would have cast a shadow on the road that would have been visible in the photograph. Heflin himself had estimated the diameter of the object to be 30 feet (9 metres); if this were so, Mr Gray estimated the horizontal distance of the camera from the alleged UFO to be 723 feet (220 metres) and its altitude to be 134.5 feet (40 metres). These figures were fairly close to Heflin's estimates; he thought the object was half a mile (800 metres) away, flying at an altitude of about 150 feet (45 metres).

While many people believe the Heflin photographs to be genuine pictures of a UFO, others have suggested that the whole affair is probably a hoax. The story has a number of curious features and some small inconsistencies. And it is unfortunate, and some people think suspicious, that the original photographs have not survived.

The American UFO organisation Ground Saucer Watch has subjected Rex Heflin's photographs to rigorous computer analyses – and has concluded that they are probably fakes. However it is only fair to mention that GSW has been wrong in the past.

The incident was investigated by Dr W. Hartmann of the Condon Commission. He concluded that the case was of 'little probative value': the photographs contained 'no geometric or physical data that permit a determination of distance or size independent of the witness's testimony.' Dr Hartmann also commented that he had been able to simulate the first three photographs by 'suspending a model by a thread attached to a rod resting on the roof of a truck and photographing it.' Although, as he says himself, this does not *prove* the Heflin pictures are fakes, it certainly detracts from their value as evidence for the existence of UFOs.

position – he calculated the elevation and the azimuth of the sun at the time of the sighting to be 72°46′ and 162°51′ respectively. Using these figures, he was able to establish that the true time of the sighting was 12.38 p.m., Daylight Saving Time; Heflin, who had no watch, had estimated the time at 11.30 a.m. Mr Gray also pointed out that, because the alleged UFO cast no shadow on the road, its diameter could not lie within the range of $10\frac{1}{2}$ inches (27 centimetres) to 6 feet (1.8 metres).

This statement was based upon calculations of possible altitude and distance of the object from the camera. For instance, if the diameter of the object were 6 feet (1.8 metres), the distance from the camera would have been 143.1 feet (43.6 metres). For comparison, the vertical, white irrigation pipe that can be seen on the left-hand side of the road in the photograph was 245 feet (75

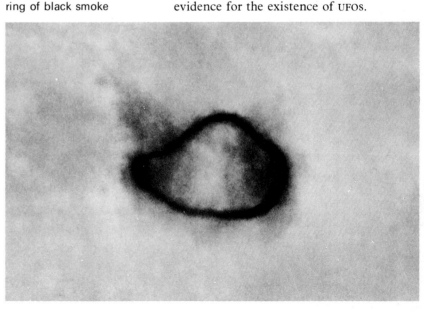

Radar echoes and angel hai

In 1957 an unidentified object accompanied a US Air Force aircraft for over 800 miles (1300 kilometres) on a military manoeuvre, and was traced all the way on radar. Was it scrutinising the aircraft? Or was it simply making its presence known? Three years earlier a rural district of south-western France was treated to two identical UFO displays. These spectaculars, though apparently pointless, seemed nevertheless to be trying to convey some kind of message. But were they? And if so, what was it?

'Bigger than a house'

**Radar-visual:
south-eastern United States,
19 September 1957**

Right: an RB-47 photo-reconnaissance aircraft

Below: how directions are given in the air. The aircraft lies at the centre of an imaginary clock, so an object 90° to the right of the aircraft is 'at 3 o'clock'

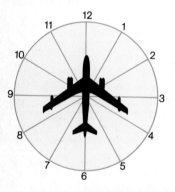

Major L. D. Chase was skipper of an RB-47 aircraft that took off from Forbes Air Force Base, Topeka, Kansas, on a training flight on the night of 19 September 1957. The RB-47 was a photo-reconnaissance version of the six-jet Boeing B-47 bomber. It was also equipped for electronic counter-measures (ECM), including location of enemy ground-based radar units, and identification of the systems employed, such as carrier frequency, pulse rate and width, scan speed and bearing.

The mission of 19 September involved gunnery exercises and navigation over the Gulf of Mexico, and an ECM exercise over the southern central United States. In addition to the skipper, there were a co-pilot, a navigator and three officers manning the three ECM monitors on board. Number 1 monitor was a direction-finding system with antennae on permanent mountings on the wing-tips. Number 2 monitor employed back-to-back antennae spinning in a housing beneath the rear fuselage of the plane, and the signals from this array were processed in a radar receiver and a pulse analyser. Number 3 monitor was not involved in the night's extraordinary events.

On the return trip from the Gulf of Mexico, the RB-47 crossed the Mississippi coastline near Gulfport and headed for Jackson, Mississippi, where the ECM exercise was to begin, at more than 30,000 feet (9000 metres) and at a speed of 500 knots (900 km/h). It was then that Captain McClure on No 2 monitor picked up an unexpected signal. The radar-scope was showing a signal at 5 o'clock, which meant a signal source behind them to starboard and out over the sea. Captain McClure assumed that the traces from the two antennae of the monitor had somehow switched and that the signal must actually be coming from a ground radar unit in Louisiana, at the 11 o'clock position. Indeed, the signal he was receiving checked out at a frequency of 2800 megahertz, a band commonly used for search radars. The lobe continued to show a 'blip' moving upscope to 4 o'clock, then to 3 o'clock and so on, but when it passed 12 o'clock and continued downscope, Captain McClure realised that the signal must be correct. But what could it be coming from?

The RB-47 changed course at Jackson and headed westwards towards Fort Worth and Dallas. Suddenly the pilots saw a white light in front of them; the crew was warned to expect evasive action, but before anything could happen the light hurtled across from left to right in front of the aeroplane.

Captain McClure heard the pilots discussing the light over the intercom, and told them of the signal that had puzzled him earlier. He then tuned No 2 monitor to 2800

reading of an unknown signal source, which was circling the RB-47 in flight!

The UFO now moved forward, detected as it did so by both the GCI at Carswell and the No 2 monitor on the aeroplane, and when it reached the 12 o'clock position both pilots could actually see it, glowing red and 'bigger than a house.'

Between Fort Worth and Dallas, the UFO changed course, and Major Chase obtained permission to follow it. He immediately found that the aircraft was closing on the object – which was simultaneously reported by GCI to be stationary. At that point, the light blinked out and the traces of the unknown object disappeared from the radar-scopes. Major Chase put the RB-47 into a left turn, and the light suddenly reappeared at a lower level – probably about 15,000 feet (4500 metres) – and its trace returned to the radar-scopes. The skipper was given permission to dive his aircraft towards the object, and he took it down to 20,000 feet (6000 metres) before the light blinked out again, and the signal on the radar at GCI at Carswell disappeared.

The RB-47 now climbed to 25,000 feet (7600 metres) and headed for Oklahoma; its fuel was running low. Once again, according to Carswell GCI, the UFO re-appeared and followed 10 miles (16 kilometres) behind the aeroplane, into southern Oklahoma, where it finally disappeared. In all this, the UFO had stayed with the aircraft for more than an hour, during which time a distance of more than 800 miles (1250 kilometres) was covered.

The incident was immediately investigated by officers from White Sands Missile Base, from Kirtland Air Force Base, and from Project Blue Book at Wright Patterson Air Force Base. Dr J. Allen Hynek was also present. But, despite the efforts of all the experts, two questions remain unsolved: was the unidentified object under intelligent control? And if so, who was controlling it?

kilohertz, and instantly picked up a strong signal at the 2 o'clock position. The signal did not move downscope; this showed that the source maintained a constant position relative to the aircraft.

After the RB-47 had been 'escorted' by the UFO for more than 100 miles (160 kilometres), the skipper called up Carswell Air Force Base, where a Ground Control Intercept (GCI) radar was in operation. Number 1 monitor had by now confirmed the existence of a target at the 2 o'clock position. Carswell came back with the information that there was another aircraft 10 miles (16 kilometres) from the RB-47 at 2 o'clock.

Captain McClure thereupon realised that the blip that had puzzled him had been a true

'Threads of the Virgin'

Daylight disc: Oloron-Sainte-Marie, France, 17 October 1952; Gaillac, France, 27 October 1952

At lunch-time on Friday 17 October 1952, a strange object appeared in the clear blue sky over Oloron-Sainte-Marie and nearby villages in the south-west of France. The headmaster of the lycée in Oloron-Sainte-Marie was at home at the time; looking out to the northern side of the town from his dining-room window, he saw a solitary cloud crossing the sky at an estimated altitude of 6500 to 9800 feet (2000 to 3000 metres). There was nothing unusual about this; but above the cloud, and travelling at the same speed, was an object shaped like a cylinder, white in colour, and not luminous, tilted at an angle of 45°. The upper part of this cylinder was leaning in the direction in which it was moving – towards the south-west – and puffs of white smoke, or cloud, seemed to be detaching themselves from the top. Ahead of

the cylinder, and travelling in the same direction, were some 30 small objects that looked like balls of smoke.

Looking through his binoculars, the headmaster could see that each of these smaller objects consisted of a red central sphere, encircled by a yellow-hued ring inclined at such an angle that it hid much of the lower part of the sphere. Indeed, the objects appeared to be domed saucers, and they were moving about in pairs in swift zig-zag flight, with each pair linked by what looked like an electric arc.

A sort of side-phenomenon now became visible. The smaller objects left long trails of a threadlike substance, which detached itself and floated slowly earthwards. The threads festooned themselves about roofs, trees and walls, street lamps, telephone wires, cables and so on. The material – which the villagers immediately named 'threads of the Virgin' – looked like strands of nylon, or finely-spun wool. When touched it became gelatinous, then vaporised and disappeared.

This phenomenon within a phenomenon, which is rare indeed, is known in English-speaking circles as 'angel hair'.

Sceptics were stumped by the 'show' at Oloron-Sainte-Marie: since so many people over a wide area had seen the same thing, it could hardly be dismissed as an hallucination. However, genuine 'threads of the Virgin' are left by spiders, and it was suggested that the festoons of filigree-like thread had been left by millions of migrating spiders. This explanation, however, did not account for the fact that, unlike spider threads, the 'angel hair' at Oloron-Sainte-Marie disintegrated within a few minutes.

The furore had almost died down when, on 27 October, at least 100 residents of Gaillac, also in south-west France – including two NCOs of the Gendarmerie – saw a repeat performance of the events at Oloron-Sainte-Marie. The time was 5 p.m., and the only difference reported between the phenomena was that there were 20 small saucers, which came much closer to the ground during their zig-zag manoeuvres, their minimum altitude being about 1300 feet (400 metres). On this occasion, the witnesses likened the falling threads to glass wool. The 'angel hair' was still falling and slowly vaporising long after the cylinder and saucers had passed out of sight to the south-east.

What was the purpose of the twin UFO

Below right: 'angel hair' similar to that found after the Oloron-Sainte-Marie and Gaillac sightings. The filigree-like strands became gelatinous, disintegrated and vaporised within a few minutes

displays at Oloron-Sainte-Marie and Gaillac? Nothing quite like them has ever been seen again. It is tempting to think that these spectaculars were put on for the benefit of humans by whatever it is that controls the UFO phenomenon – perhaps as a kind of announcement of the period of intense UFO activity that began in 1954.

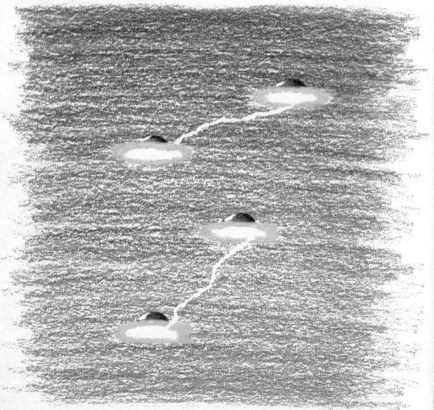

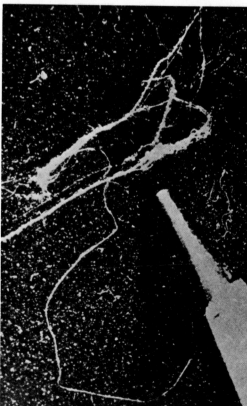

Encounters in the air

ONLY RARELY do we hear of UFO sightings involving airmen, especially military ones, for the good reason that governments have no wish to foster the notion that national defence is in the hands of eccentrics. But another view may be taken of such sightings: that the very reliability of the witnesses should speak for the reality of the phenomenon. Yet governments persist in maintaining a public silence – while, at the same time, taking careful note of unusual or inexplicable events in the air.

'Surprise turned to horror'

Close encounter of the first kind: Southend-on-Sea, Essex, England 14 October 1954

On 14 October 1954, Flight-Lieutenant James R. Salandin, flying a Meteor twin-jet fighter plane, narrowly avoided collision with an unidentified flying object over Southend-on-Sea, Essex.

What happened next was told to Derek Dempster, the then editor of *Flying Saucer Review*, and the story appeared in the very first issue of the magazine. (Derek Dempster was himself an ex-RAF pilot and knew how

Above: a Gloster Meteor Mark 8 fighter. From 1950 to 1958 this aircraft was the main daylight interceptor used by the RAF. Flight-Lieutenant James Salandin flew one as part of a nationwide air defence network designed – in the days before intercontinental ballistic missiles – to prevent enemy bombers reaching British targets

pilots value their professional reputation. Sensation seeking is not their style.)

Jimmy Salandin was one of the 'weekend' pilots of No. 604 County of Middlesex Squadron, Royal Auxiliary Air Force. He had reported for duty at North Weald, Essex, on the afternoon of 14 October, and at 4.15 p.m. took off in his Meteor Mark 8 jet. Climbing southwards into a blue and cloudless sky he soon observed two other Meteors flying in formation high above him and leaving long vapour trails. Flight-Lieutenant Salandin watched the passage of the two aircraft while occasionally checking his instruments.

He had reached 16,000 feet (4880 metres) over the outlying districts of Southend, when to his surprise he saw two circular objects, travelling in the opposite direction to the Meteors, hurtle between them. One of the objects was silvery in colour, the other gold. Salandin watched them until they disappeared, at the '9 o'clock high' position – to his port, or left, side.

After checking his own instruments he turned his gaze to the air in front of him. His surprise turned to horror – for he saw a

silvery object streaking straight towards him.

For a few split seconds he saw a thing that 'had a bun-shaped top, a flange like two saucers in the middle, and a bun underneath . . . it could not have been far off because it overlapped the windscreen'. (Derek Dempster noted that a Meteor's 37-foot [11-metre] wing span just fills the windscreen at 150 yards [140 metres].) The flying saucer, which was travelling at tremendous speed, avoided a head-on collision at the very last second by suddenly swerving off past the jet on its port side.

Badly shaken, the Flight-Lieutenant flew around quietly for 10 minutes or so to regain his composure, and reported his experience to ground control. He was annoyed, too, when he realised later that his camera – standard equipment on combat aircraft – had been loaded all the time. With everything happening so quickly he didn't have time to press the button. A valuable opportunity to gather evidence for ufology had been missed.

'Coming for me right now'

Close encounter of the second kind: Bass Strait, Australia 21 October 1978

Below: a Cessna 182 like the one flown by Frederick Valentich. A best-seller in its class, the 182 is renowned as a rugged, reliable workhorse

When a Cessna 182 light aircraft, owned by Southern Air Services of Moorabbin, in Melbourne, Australia, went missing on the evening of Saturday, 21 October 1978, when flying over Bass Strait, emergency measures were set in motion; light aircraft and a marine reconnaissance plane began a search. It seemed straightforward enough – a tragic accident. The passage of time would fill in the details . . . But within 24 hours that situation had begun to change when the words 'unidentified flying object' were whispered here and there in connection with the incident. And in another 12 hours the Australian press was scrambling to print the story with banner headlines on Monday, 23 October. The sensational account swept from continent to continent; for example it was featured in a breakfast-time radio news flash that same day in Philadelphia, USA.

The lone pilot was Frederick Valentich, aged 20, of Avondale Heights, Melbourne. He had held an unrestricted flying licence for only nine months but was considered a competent pilot and was held in high esteem by his colleagues. He had been flying to King

Island, midway between Cape Otway, Victoria, and Tasmania, where he was to collect crayfish for the officers' mess of the Air Training Corps – of which he was an instructor – but it was primarily an excuse for him to log up some night-flying time. (Although he had made the trip several times in daylight, this was the first time he had flown it after dark.) It was his intention to be back in Melbourne by 10.00 p.m.

Valentich took off in the Cessna at 6.19 p.m. and flew over Cape Otway, where there is a lighthouse, at about 7.00 p.m. There was a north-westerly breeze and visibility was excellent. At 7.06 p.m. he contacted ground control at Melbourne Flight Service. Parts of the Flight Service transcript of the ensuing conversation appeared in Australian newspapers, including the *Sun* and the *Australian*, on the morning of 23 October:

7.06 p.m.
Pilot: Is there any known traffic in my area below 5000 feet [1500 metres].
Flight Service Unit: Negative. No known traffic.
Pilot: Seems to be a large aircraft below 5000 feet [1500 metres].
FSU: What type of aircraft?
Pilot: I cannot confirm. It has four bright lights that appear to be landing lights . . . aircraft has just passed over me, about 1000 feet [300 metres] above.
FSU: Is large aircraft confirmed?
Pilot: Affirmative, at speed it is travelling.

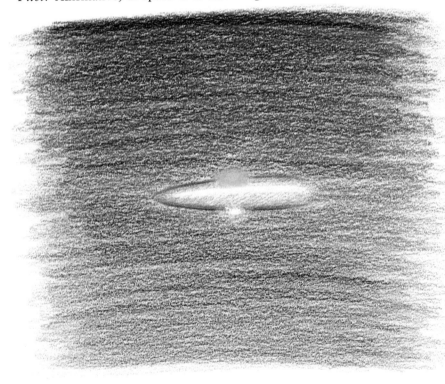

Are there any RAAF aircraft in the vicinity?
FSU: Negative.

7.08 p.m.
Pilot: Melbourne, it's approaching from due east of me. It seems to be playing some sort of game. Flying at speed I can't estimate.
FSU: What is your altitude?
Pilot: 4500 feet [1400 metres].

7.09 p.m.
FSU: Can you confirm you cannot identify the aircraft?
Pilot: Affirmative. It's not an aircraft. It's . . . (Break in transmission)
FSU: Can you describe aircraft?
Pilot: It's flying past. It has a long shape. Cannot identify more than that . . . coming for me right now. It seems to be stationary. I'm orbiting and the thing is orbiting on top of me. It has a green light and a sort of metallic light on the outside.

Valentich then told ground control that the object seemed to have vanished. Control followed by advising him that there were no military aircraft in the area.

7.12 p.m.
Pilot: Engine is rough-idling and coughing.
FSU: What are your intentions?
Pilot: Proceeding King Island . . . unknown aircraft now on top of me.
FSU: Acknowledge.
There followed a long 'metallic' noise, and thereafter contact with the Cessna was lost.

When the plane failed to arrive at King Island at the expected time of 7.28 p.m. the visual and radio search began. The Cessna had been equipped with the standard life jacket and a radio survival beacon, but no sound was ever traced from it. An RAAF Orion from Edinburgh, South Australia, conducted its 'tracking crawl' on 22 and 23 October; and reported only an oil-slick north of King Island.

Borrowed by the aliens?
There were several attempts to explain away the alleged UFO connection. It was suggested that the pilot might have become disorientated and had managed to invert his aircraft so that the lights he saw, and thought were those of the UFO, were in fact reflections of his own aircraft's lights on the sea, or were perhaps from the lighthouses at Cape Otway or King Island. Experienced pilots stated publicly, however, that such an explanation was as extraordinary as the reported UFO encounter, for there was the recorded six-minute radio conversation during which the lights were mentioned more than once, and that type of aircraft could only be flown for about 30 seconds upside down before the engine would stop from fuel starvation.

From interviews on 23 October it seemed that the pilot's father sought solace from flying saucer 'enthusiasts' and their theories. Mr Guido Valentich stated that his son was a 'believer' in UFOs, and had 'read a lot on the subject'. He was even reported as believing that his son had been 'borrowed by interplanetary visitors' – a hope that was preferable to the thought that he had lost his son in the depths of the sea.

Australian investigator Bill Chalker, writing in *Flying Saucer Review*, pointed out that Frederick Valentich was a person who 'lived for flying' and was hardly likely to have made wild claims that would have affected his professional reputation as a pilot and his chances of promotion.

So possible explanations are that he did encounter a UFO and in his final excitement and turmoil crashed, without trace, into the sea; that he collided with a UFO with the same result; or that he perpetrated a hoax. Concluded Chalker: 'This [last hypothesis] must be a consideration if Frederick Valentich turns up alive and well, but as time passes the possibility becomes increasingly less likely.'

At about 7.45 p.m. on 11 May 1950 at his farm close by the Salmon River Highway, about 10 miles south-west of McMinnville, Oregon. Paul Trent and his wife claimed they saw a UFO – and took a photograph of it which has still not been proved a fake.

Mrs Trent was in the yard on the south side of the house feeding the rabbits when she saw, to the north-east, moving westwards, a disc-shaped object. She called her husband, who was inside the house. When he realised the unusual nature of the object in the sky, Mr Trent ran to his car for his camera, but his wife remembered that he had left it in the house and hurried to fetch it. The camera already had a partly used film in it.

The object was tilted up a little as it approached, and appeared bright and silvery; it made no noise, and the Trents saw no smoke or vapour. Mr Trent took a picture (*above*) and wound on ready for the next frame, moving to the right to keep the object in the view-

finder, and taking a second shot some 30 seconds after the first. Mrs Trent said the object seemed to be gliding, with no rotating or undulating motion. It moved off westwards and 'dimly vanished'.

The couple said there was a 'breeze' as the object tilted before flying overhead. Mr Trent estimated its diameter as 20 or 30 feet (6 or 9 metres).

A few days later, when he had used up the remaining frames, Mr Trent had the film developed locally. He mentioned the incident to only a few friends. He did not seek publicity, telling his friends he didn't want to be 'in trouble with the government'. However, a reporter from the local *McMinnville Telephone Reg-*

ister heard of the sighting from two of Mr Trent's friends; he followed it up and found the precious negatives on the floor of the Trents' house, under a writing desk where the Trent children had been playing with them! The *Telephone Register's* story appeared on 8 June 1950. On 9 and 10 June newspapers in Portland, Oregon, and in Los Angeles ran the story, and *Life* magazine carried the photographs a week later.

None of this publicity had been sought by the Trents. When, 17 years after the sighting, they were visited by an investigator from the US Air Force-sponsored Colorado University Commission of Enquiry (whose findings were

later published as the Condon Report) he found them completely unchanged by their experience, well liked locally and known as reliable.

The McMinnville UFO (above left) is remarkable for its similarity to an object (above right) seen and photographed from an aeroplane by a French Air Marshal near Rouen, France, in March 1954.

After submitting the photographs to rigorous scientific examination the Condon investigation was forced to admit they might be genuine. The official report concluded: 'This is one of the few UFO reports in which all factors investigated, geometric, psychological and physical appear to be consistent.'

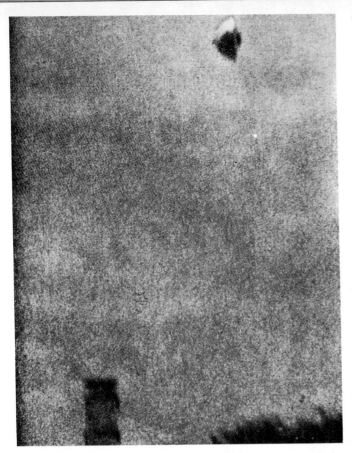

One warm, clear afternoon in early April 1966, Mr Brown (he wishes his real name to remain secret) was in his garden in Balwyn, near Melbourne, Australia, when it suddenly 'lit up' and he saw in the sky a bright object, shaped like a mushroom (left), about 20 to 35 feet (6 to 10 metres) in diameter. It was about 150 feet (50 metres) from the ground and seemed to float down towards him, spinning through a 180° angle on its vertical axis, 'during which time I photographed it'. It then shot off northwards at high speed. A carpenter working in the house witnessed the object and saw Brown photograph it.

Mr Brown is a qualified engineer, director of a large family business, and is a respected citizen of Balwyn. It is difficult to believe he would perpetrate a hoax. And yet an American UFO organisation, Ground Saucer Watch Inc., of Phoenix, Arizona, has recently cast doubt on the authenticity of the photograph. Using computer techniques to analyse the photograph, GSW has claimed it is a fake. And yet GSW has often been wrong in the past. Who is right? It is a question that is impossible to answer.

A promotional photograph of a B-57 aeroplane in flight (below) found its way into a set of UFO photographs offered for sale by NICAP (National Investigations Committee on Aerial Phenomena). An unknown object appeared in the top right-hand corner of the photograph. According to UFO investigator Robert Schmidt, the object 'appeared to be streamlined, and to have dark "ports" on its lower periphery.'

Schmidt wrote to the manufacturers, the Martin Aircraft Company, asking for a bigger enlargement (inset left) from the NICAP file. When questioned about the picture, the company replied that the unexplained image had been caused by a tear, a rub or an abrasion. Analysis, however, subsequently showed that in the original negative the emulsion grain extended over the area of the unknown object; a tear or rub would have destroyed the grain.

The Martin Company also said they had filmed another 'fly-by' to see if the same effect could be obtained again – a strange thing to do if, as they claimed, the original image had been caused by a flaw in the film.

Sightings and side effects

THE 'REALITY' OF UFOS – whether they are 'nuts and bolts' craft, or some vision-like projection – is the subject of hot debate. But witnesses and participants in close encounters frequently report physical side-effects such as violent headaches, fits of weeping, and buzzing in the ears. In the cases that follow, zoo animals stampede and soldiers are paralysed in Malagasy while an Argentinian girl weeps for days after a UFO passes by – so just how 'unreal' can such alien craft actually be?

'A luminous green ball'

Close encounter of the second kind: Tananarive, Madagascar, August 1954

One of the most spectacular of all 'light in the sky' UFO fly-overs took place over the city of Tananarive, capital of Madagascar (now Malagasy) one day in August 1954.

Edmond Campagnac, head of Technical Services of Air France, was waiting with a group of people outside the Air France office on the Avenue de la Libération for the arrival of the air mail from Paris.

Suddenly Monsieur Campagnac saw a luminous green ball in the sky. It was descending, almost vertically, like a meteorite. Other people followed his gaze, and the object was seen to disappear behind mountains to the south of the city.

The time was 5.45 p.m. and dusk was approaching, although the setting Sun was still visible. While the group waited outside the Air France office, they were joined by scores of others on the streets as people began their journeys home from work.

The witnesses were still watching when an object of the same colour as that seen seconds earlier appeared over the hills near the old Queen's Palace, this time 'flying' horizontally and at a slower speed. The UFO curved past the government buildings, still appearing like a green ball. Soon it was descending even lower, almost to roof-top height, and heading along the eastern side of the Avenue de la Libération, just above the building opposite the Air France office.

As the light drew level with the group, they saw that it was in fact *two* objects. A lentil-shaped device was leading the way, and this was described as having the colour of an 'electric-green luminous gas'. Following some 100 feet (30 metres) behind was a metallic-looking cylindrical object, about 130 feet (40 metres) in length. While described by some as a 'cigar', others said it looked more like the fuselage of the contemporary Constellation aircraft shorn of fins, elevators, wings and engines. The surface of the cylinder reflected the dying rays of the sun, while behind it there splayed a plume of orange-red flame. Estimates of the speed of the objects were in the region of 300 km/h (185 miles per hour).

People stopped and gazed in amazement at the phenomenon, so much so that a pall of quietness hung over the city. The giant cigar and its lenticular companion were completely silent. Then there was another shock for the observers for, as the objects passed over the buildings, all the electric lights were extinguished, coming on again only after the objects had passed.

The strange aerial duo continued over the city towards Tananarive airport, then swung away to the west. Before passing from sight they skimmed over a zoological park where the animals, which were normally quite undisturbed by aircraft flying into and out of the airport, went into a panic and stampeded through fences. It was several hours before soldiers and police could round them up.

Not surprisingly there was a great furore in Tananarive over this invasion of Madagascan airspace, and an official enquiry was set up by General Fleurquin, the Air Force Commandant. This was conducted by Father Coze, director of the Tananarive Observatory. Father Coze had been at the observatory at the time of the incident and had himself witnessed the passage of the UFOs. He estimated that at least 20,000 people had seen the objects, and he and his helpers questioned more than 5000 witnesses. It is not known what happened to his report of this remarkable encounter. If it ever reached France, it certainly failed to arouse interest. Details were known only to a handful of French researchers in the early 1960s,

and to *Flying Saucer Review* in 1966, which received an account from Monsieur René Fouéré of the *Groupement d'Etude de Phénomènes Aeriens* (GEPA). But not a hint of the affair was known to the French public until 1974, when M. Jean-Claude Bourret broadcast his famous series of programmes on Radio France-Inter, transcripts of which appeared in his book *The crack in the Universe*, published in 1977.

'A shining egg'

Close encounter of the second kind: Malagasy Republic, May 1967

In May 1967 there was said to be another alarming close encounter in Malagasy. But it took 10 years before news of the incident reached *Flying Saucer Review* from the French research group *Lumières dans la nuit*. On this occasion, the reason for the delay was that the witnesses were 23 soldiers, their officer and four NCOs of the French Foreign Legion, and they were forbidden to discuss the affair. The eventual informant was a legionnaire named Wolff.

Wolff's platoon, which was on a reconnaissance exercise, had halted at noon in a clearing in the bush country. The troops were eating lunch when they all saw a bright metallic object resembling a 'shining egg' descend rapidly like a falling leaf, accompanied by a piercing, whistling sound, then thump into the ground. All the soldiers were 'paralysed' and, seemingly immediately, saw the object take off. But when watches were checked, the time was 3.15 p.m., which meant that three hours had passed.

M. Wolff claimed that the object was about 23 feet (7 metres) high and 10 to 13 feet (3 to 4 metres) wide at the widest part. It rose slowly at first, and then vanished at high speed, as though 'sucked up into the sky'. It left three marks in the ground that looked as if they had been made by legs, and a 10-foot (3-metre) deep crater, at the bottom of which was a sort of vitrified ring of coloured crystals.

None of the witnesses could recall what had happened during the missing hours, but for two days afterwards they all had violent headaches, with constant 'beating' in the region of the temples and a continual buzzing sound in the ears.

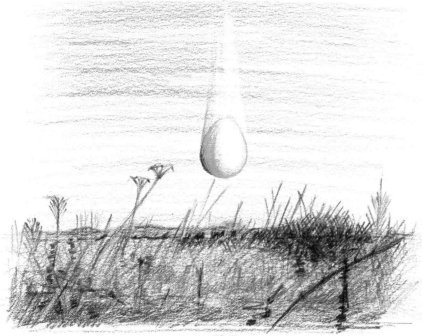

'An impression of goodness and kindness'

Close encounter of the third kind: Córdoba, Argentina, June 1968

The Motel La Cuesta is a well-appointed roadhouse, situated on Highway 20 that connects the town of Villa Carlos Paz, in the province of Córdoba, with eastern Argentina. The small country town is 500 miles (800 kilometres) to the west of Buenos Aires.

The motel's proprietor, Señor Pedro Pretzel, 39, lived at the motel with his wife and his 19-year-old daughter, Maria Eladia.

On the night of 13 June 1968, at about 12.50 a.m., Señor Pretzel was walking home when he saw, some 55 yards (50 metres) beyond the motel – and apparently on the highway – an object that he could not identify. It had two bright red lights, but could not be a car because it projected beams of peculiar intensity at the motel. This 'machine' was in view for only a few seconds. Puzzled and alarmed, Señor Pretzel ran to his motel and found Maria Eladia lying in a dead faint close to the kitchen door. After she had been revived she had a bizarre tale to tell.

Only a few minutes earlier she had said goodnight to her fiancé and had escorted some guests to the door; then she returned to the kitchen. Suddenly she noticed that the lobby was flooded with light. As she had just switched the lights off, she went to investigate. She was horrified to find herself face-to-face with a 'man' some 6 feet (2 metres) tall, dressed in a kind of diver's suit that had shiny, sky-blue scales. He was fair-haired, and was holding up his left hand, on the palm of which a sky-blue ball, or sphere, was moving about.

Maria said there was a huge ring on the fourth finger of the creature's right hand, which he moved up and down constantly in front of her. She was overcome by lethargy, as though strength was being drained from her. Light came from the creature's fingertips and feet and it seemed to Maria that the lethargic feeling was strongest when the light was pointed directly at her. But apart from this he showed no signs of aggression. Indeed, Maria remembers an impression of 'goodness and kindness' emanating from the being who, she added, smiled throughout the encounter. She said he also seemed to be trying to communicate with her, for, although his lips did not move, she could hear an unintelligible mumble that sounded 'like Chinese'.

After a few minutes – during which Maria stood transfixed in the presence of the humanoid – he walked, with slow, precise movements, to the side door, which was open. He went out and the door closed of its own accord. It was at that moment that Maria lost consciousness. Shortly afterwards her father discovered her on the floor.

Señor Pretzel reported the incident to the police, who promised to investigate it. As for Maria, she became extremely nervous and was subject to fits of weeping for some days after the affair.

Did Maria Eladia Pretzel witness a projected image – that of a 'man' in her kitchen – that was emitted from the UFO her father had seen on the nearby highway? If she had been witness to such a phenomenon, then it is possible that her father came on the scene just as the image was about to be withdrawn. Could the 'humanoid' have been a hologram transmitted by laser beams and projected against, say, the glass of the lobby window? (The intense beams of light seemed to have been emitted by the UFO, and it was presumably this light that first attracted Maria's attention.)

But however the strange and alarming effects were produced the questions remain: Why? And by whom?

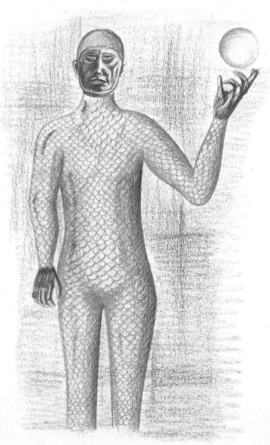

A meeting in Mendoza

FROM TIME TO TIME a bizarre UFO encounter is reported in which the witness, thanks either to his spontaneity or to his personal reaction, conveys an impression of credibility. Interest builds up around the case, only to be dashed by a confession that the whole thing has been a hoax. This can be so sudden that investigators into the case should consider whether undue pressure has been brought to bear on the witness to prompt such a recantation.

The strange experience of Fernando José Villegas and Juan Carlos Peccinetti of Mendoza in Argentina, is a case in point. Their immediate reactions to the nightmarish events that they claimed overtook them on 1 September 1968 certainly did not convey the impression that they were joking, yet in a matter of days they had 'confessed' that the story was false. How far was their retraction influenced by the fact that, at the time, the Mendoza authorities were threatening legal action against anyone reporting a UFO incident?

'Do not fear, do not fear'

Close encounter of the third kind: Mendoza, Argentina, 1 September 1968

At 3.30 a.m. on 1 September 1968, Juan Carlos Peccinetti and Fernando José Villegas, cashiers at a casino in Mendoza, Argentina, left work and set off for home in Villegas's vintage Chevrolet. They had just reached an unlighted part of the calle Nequén, near the junction with the calle Laprida, when the car suddenly stopped and the headlights went out. Villegas got out of the car to look under the bonnet.

At 4 a.m. soldiers on duty at the General Espejo Military College were startled when two young men burst into the guardroom in a state of shock, babbling that they had seen a flying saucer close to the ground. They claimed to have encountered five small beings, who communicated with them in a strange manner, took blood samples from their fingers, left inscriptions on their car, then returned to the flying saucer along a beam of light. The saucer then took off vertically at high speed and disappeared.

The soldiers insisted that the casino men should go to the Lagomagiore Hospital, which they did; the police were called in soon afterwards. The media were quickly on the trail and reports of the strange encounter appeared in *Los Principios* (2 September 1968), *Gente y la Actualidad* (5 September) and *La Crónica* (9 September). This is what is stated to have happened:

When Villegas got out of the car he cried out: 'Look, Skinny', and thereupon found himself unable to move. The same happened to Peccinetti as he scrambled out – the word 'paralysed' was used in the reports – and he found later that his watch had stopped at 3.42 a.m. (Villegas had no watch.) They found themselves facing three small beings, and two more were standing near a circular 'machine', some 13 feet (4 metres) across and 5 feet (1.5 metres) high, which was floating in

Right: Fernando José Villegas and Juan Carlos Peccinetti (far right), the two casino cashiers who felt obliged to confess that their reported encounter with ufonauts was a hoax. There were two versions of their retraction: one was that the cashiers themselves were the hoaxers; the other that someone else was responsible

These curious scratches on the side of Villegas's vintage Chevrolet were allegedly made by a humanoid with a device like a soldering iron

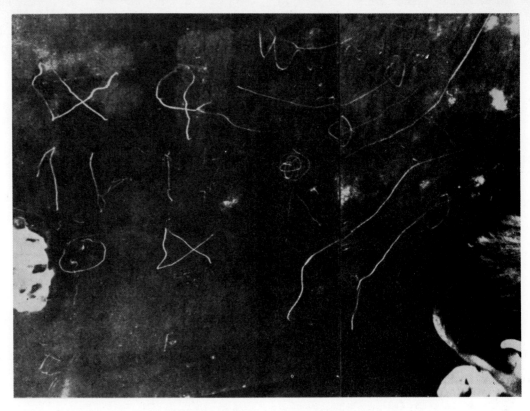

An investigator examines the inscriptions on the windscreen of the car

the air about 4 feet (1.2 metres) above a patch of the waste ground at 2333 calle Nequén. A beam of light was directed from the object towards the ground at an angle of about 45°.

The beings were said to be about 5 feet (1.5 metres) tall, and looked like humans but had unusually large heads, which were hairless. They were wearing boiler suits, and approached the alarmed cashiers 'gently and quietly', crossing a ditch 'as though by a bridge'. Both witnesses told how they heard – as though by the tiny earplugs from pocket transistor radios – a voice in Spanish saying repeatedly: 'Do not fear, do not fear.' Villegas also alleged that they had received a message in the same way; the gist of it was that the entities had just made three journeys around the Sun, studying the customs and languages of the inhabitants of the system; '. . . the Sun benignly nurtures the system: were it not so then the solar system would not exist. . . . Mathematics is the universal language.'

While this lecture proceeded, another of the entities was using an instrument like a soldering iron to make inscriptions on the doors, windscreen and running boards of the vintage car. There were bright sparks from the device, but when the car was examined later no burn marks were found.

A circular screen then appeared near the hovering object, and on it the two men saw a series of pictures. The first was a scene of a waterfall in lush countryside; the second showed a mushroom-shaped cloud, and the third the waterfall again, but neither water nor lushness. After this, said the witnesses, their left hands were taken by hands that felt no different from those of humans, and their fingers were pricked three times. The beings then retreated to their craft, ascending to it by way of the light beam. Then there was the sound of an explosion and, surrounded by intense light, the object rose into the sky and disappeared.

From the college guardroom, Peccinetti and Villegas went to the Lagomagiore Hospital, where they were examined. The report on them stated: 'Picture of psychomotor

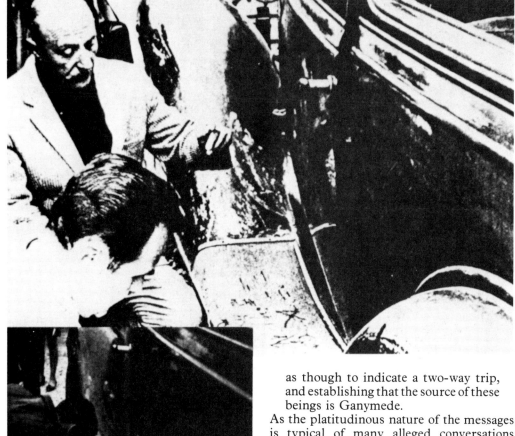

According to the proposal
put forward by the Mendoza
Centre for Space Research,
the inscriptions on the car
show that the entities
encountered by Villegas and
Peccinetti came from
Ganymede, one of the
moons of Jupiter

excitation and three small punctures on the flesh parts of the index and middle fingers of the left hand. Identical in both of them.'

Further tests were carried out at the Central Hospital, and the men were found to be sane and rational. The cashiers were kept apart for two days, during which time their stories tallied impressively.

The Chevrolet was impounded by the police and radioactivity tests on it revealed nothing abnormal. As for the inscriptions on the car, linguistics expert Gordon Creighton wrote to *Flying Saucer Review* that they seemed childishly unsystematic. The Mendoza Centre for Space Research, however, suggested that:

The sketch done by the humanoids represents two solar systems, the Earth's system, consisting of Mercury, Venus and Earth, and the Jupiter system, containing the planets Io, Europa and Ganymede. Between Ganymede and Earth there are two parallel lines,

as though to indicate a two-way trip, and establishing that the source of these beings is Ganymede.

As the platitudinous nature of the messages is typical of many alleged conversations with extra-terrestrials, Creighton's view of the script seems preferable. It is possible that the two cashiers did have a very real experience, triggered off by an object that was capable (perhaps electromagnetically, or by laser technology) of stopping the car; perhaps that object projected images for them to see, and hear, of entities, messages and cataclysmic warnings, and induced them unwittingly to scratch crude symbols on their car, and to prick their fingers.

There were some reports of possibly corroborating events – unknown at the time to the two witnesses, the college guards and the staff at the hospitals where the witnesses were examined. Staff at the Mendoza railway station had reported a sudden and total blackout of the lighting system at about 3.40 a.m., while at 3.45 a.m. Senora Maria Spinelli telephoned the police from her home in Dorrego, about 4 miles (6 kilometres) from the site of the encounter, to report that a strange luminous object was flying around very low overhead.

By 7 September 1968 notices began to appear in the Argentine press to the effect that 'the authorities have issued a communiqué that the spreading of saucer rumours is an offence penalized by law . . . that the penal code contemplates prison terms for people indulging in spreading unwarranted fear . . .' The authorities referred to were those of the Mendoza province; within days Peccinetti and Villegas took the easy way out and recanted.

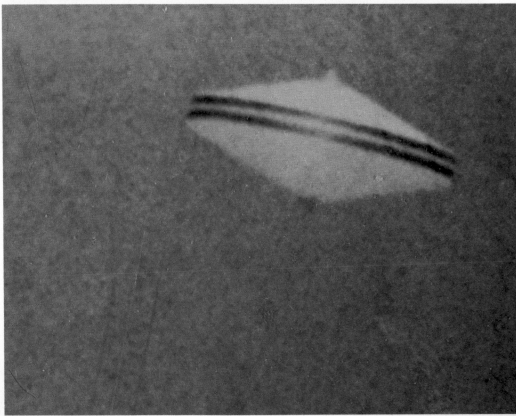

Above: 'long object with hump on back' photographed over Bear Mountain in New York State by an anonymous witness on 18 December 1966. The sighting was reported to the US Air Force's Project Blue Book who took possession of the two photographs and a negative and interviewed the witness exhaustively. Although their own technicians could find no evidence of fraud the file was nevertheless labelled 'Hoax'. Doctor J. Allen Hynek wrote to Major Hector Quintanilla (then Chief of Project Blue Book) saying: . . . the lack of satisfactory explanation of the unidentified object does not constitute sufficient reason to declare [it] a hoax. . . . My recommendation is . . . that the evaluation be changed from hoax to unidentified. Despite this recommendation the 'Hoax' label remained. Why did the Air Force want to discredit the witness?

Below and below left: two frames from a film said to be of 'an approaching UFO', taken by Daniel W. Fry during May 1964 near his home in Merlin, Oregon, using a Bell and Howell movie camera. The UFO, described by Fry as 'spinning like a top during flight', was by no means the first he claimed to have encountered. It was, according to him, in 1950 that he witnessed his first 'saucer' landing, and during the next four years he became a contactee of 'the Space People'. They allegedly told him that they are the descendants of a lost super-race from Earth who survived a nuclear holocaust over 30,000 years ago and fled to live on Mars. Later they abandoned Mars and now live exclusively in their spacecraft. Fry is said to have taken a lie detector test on live television about his alleged contactee experiences and 'flunked it flat'.

Above right and right: another 'Martian spacecraft' photographed by Daniel W. Fry, also using a 16-millimetre Bell and Howell movie camera. The time is May 1965 and the place Joshua Tree, California. This craft is also described as 'spinning like a top' in the sky. Fry, an ex-employee of the Aerojet General Corporation (where he was 'in charge of installation of instruments for missile control and guidance'), is considered to be the most technically orientated of modern contactees. Sceptics may point out, however, that his uniquely technical background might provide him with opportunities to produce fake photographs of a high standard, but there is no conclusive evidence that these are fakes.

Two electrifying experiences

ONE OF THE CURIOSITIES of the history of UFOS is the clustering of UFO activity in which several incidents occur within a small locality only a few days apart. Sometimes the events are similar; sometimes – as in this pair of close encounters in south-east England – they appear to be linked only by place and time. But always there is a strange inconclusiveness about them, something that suggests that, if only we could find the missing link, we could understand what it is they are trying to tell us.

'About as big as a gasometer'

Close encounter of the second kind: Langenhoe, Essex, England, 14 September 1965

Early one Sunday morning – 14 September 1965 – at about one o'clock, an engineer named Paul Green, aged 29, was riding his motorcycle southwards along the B1025 road, which runs between Colchester and West Mersea in Essex. He had been visiting his fiancée, and was on his way home. The motorcycle was going well, purring along at some 40 miles per hour (70 km/h).

He had just passed through the village of Langenhoe, and was up to Pete Tye Common, when he overtook a rider on a motor scooter. A minute or so later he was approaching Langenhoe Hall when he heard a high-pitched humming noise away to his left – the east. As the noise became louder he looked up, expecting to see an approaching aeroplane, but saw only a small point of blue light about 5 miles (8 kilometres) away to the east, approximately over Brightlingsea.

As Paul Green watched the light winking, then growing brighter and flashing, he realised it was moving in his direction. Rapidly it became larger, and at the same time the humming became louder and louder. When the object was over Langenhoe Marsh he became uneasily aware that his motorcycle engine was coughing and spluttering, and after it had 'missed' several times, the engine stopped dead and the lights went off. At that point the flashing blue light was just over a mile (just under 2 kilometres) away, to the east of the road. Watching intently Paul now saw, within the extreme brightness of the light, an enormous object that resembled the upper half of a large spinning top – 'about as big as a gasometer' – with a dome on the upper part. The fierce blue flashes came from inside this dome. By now the object had stopped moving in his direction and, instead, was descending slowly, and at one stage tilting its underside towards him. The outer rim of this carried round objects spaced equidistantly so that it gave the impression of a 'luminous ball-race'.

Paul Green dismounted and took a few

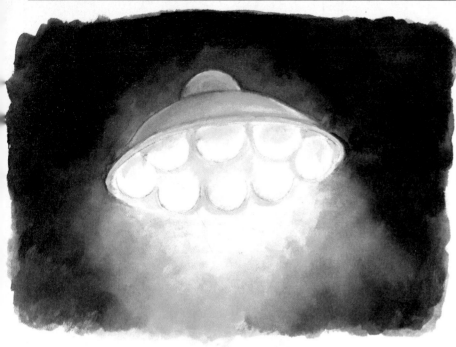

and felt as though there were a band tightening around it. With a great effort I made myself move, and I grasped the bike and tried to start it.' In the end he managed to push it along, finally achieving a bump start, mounted and drove home as quickly as he could. After a short distance a line of tall hedges hid the 'thing' from him, but he could still see the blue glow in the sky.

It was unfortunate that the witness was so terrified by his encounter and the painful physiological effects that he never thought of speaking to the young man on the scooter; it meant that a chance of obtaining corroborative evidence was missed.

Paul Green arrived home at 2 a.m., and took the unusual course of awakening his invalid mother; he needed to tell someone of his experience. Next day his hair and clothes were so charged with static electricity that they crackled continually.

Two weeks after his frightening experience, Paul Green was interviewed for *Flying Saucer Review* by Dr Bernard Finch, one of its regular investigators. Dr Finch was convinced that Paul's story was true, and added that 'he described symptoms which can only be ascribed to the effects of a very powerful magnetic field on the human body.' He went on to speculate that, if this field were strong enough, it could produce a kind of light 'as yet unknown to our science'.

There is an interesting postscript to the story. A few days after the incident, Paul was discussing his experience with a friend who lived at nearby Shrub End, some 5 miles (8 kilometres) north-west of Langenhoe. He told Paul that, around the time Paul saw the UFO, he was at home when suddenly his dog started to bark. He opened the door to let the dog out – and saw a large blue light passing rapidly by in the sky directly overhead; it was travelling towards the north-west.

involuntary steps towards the object, quickly coming to an unsteady halt. He later said, 'I felt spellbound and unable to move or speak, just as if I had become paralysed. The flashing blue light became so intense that it was painful, and it appeared to fluctuate in rhythm with my heart beat and hit against my chest. I felt myself tingling all over, rather like the electric shock one gets when handling an electrified cattle fence.'

At last the humming died down and the UFO descended towards the farmhouses at Wick. It was about then that the scooter that Paul had overtaken came coughing and spluttering to a halt. The rider, a young lad in a leather jacket, dismounted and stood looking at the flashing light as if transfixed. But Paul had no time to speak to him.

Paul reported: 'My head began to throb,

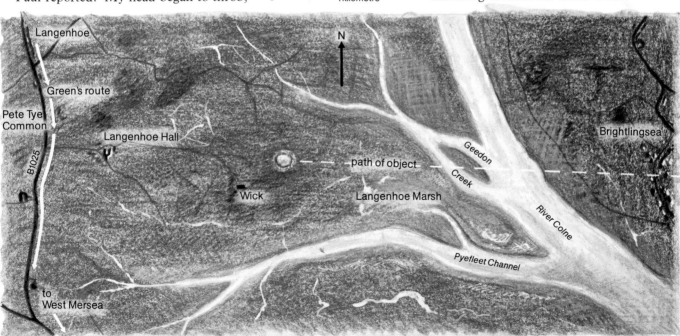

'A man in the flames'

Close encounter of the third kind: Felixstowe, Suffolk, England, 20 September 1965

Six days later, and about 20 miles (30 kilometres) from the scene of the Langenhoe close encounter of the second kind, a strange incident was reported. It may well have been a close encounter of the third kind.

Geoffrey Maskey, aged 25, had stopped his car in a Felixstowe lane known as Walton Avenue. With him were two friends, Michael Johnson and Mavis Fordyce. It was 10.30 p.m. when, without saying a word, Michael suddenly opened his door, got out and disappeared into the night. The others had been waiting for him for a few minutes when they heard a high-pitched humming noise.

Mavis was alarmed, and Geoff looked out of the car window to try to spot the source of the noise; he saw an orange-coloured, oval-shaped object some 6 feet (2 metres) in length, and about 100 feet (30 metres) above the lane. The orange glow lit up everything nearby.

The object then disappeared behind trees, with the humming noise still very much in evidence. Geoff called Michael's name and, when there was no response, reversed along the lane and called again. Suddenly Michael came stumbling through a hedge clutching his neck and his eyes; he staggered away from the car. The others thought he was having a game with them until he collapsed in the road. Geoff went over to him and found he was unconscious. They got him into the car

and took him to Felixstowe Hospital.

Michael regained consciousness at the hospital, but did not recognise his companions. The doctor who examined him diagnosed severe shock. There were burn marks on the back of his neck, and a bump below his right ear. As a precaution Michael was transferred to Ipswich Hospital, and Geoff Maskey was not allowed to see him again until he was discharged next afternoon. Michael spoke then about a force that seemed to pull him from the car, and of 'a man in the flames pointing at him.'

The remarkable thing about this incident was that if indeed there had been 'a force' capable of pulling a man from a car (or, more likely, a mental compulsion, or enticement, to leave the car) then it was remarkably selective; neither Mavis nor Geoff felt its influence in any way.

This incident merited a brief news report in the *Ipswich Evening Star* of 21 September 1965. According to that newspaper the Felixstowe Hospital doctors spoke jocularly of 'Martians' and seemed – not surprisingly – to consider that the explanation given by Mr Maskey and Miss Fordyce was a tall story. It was suggested they had mistaken the flame from the local Propane Gas Plant flare-stack for a UFO. This the witnesses denied with vehemence.

Bearing in mind the Langenhoe sighting, it seems likely that there *was* something strange in the Felixstowe lane. But what?

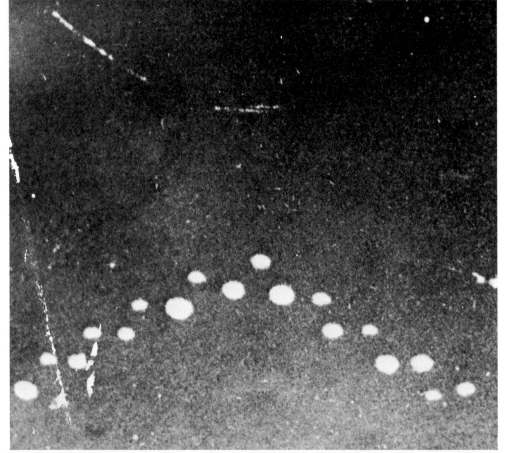

Above: this impressive photograph was taken during the Gemini XII space mission on 12 November 1966. Analysis has shown that the UFO that appears on the right of the picture is a distant object – but the NASA Photo Evaluation Lab claims this is actually rubbish that has been discarded from the Gemini XII spacecraft itself.

Left: at about 9.10 p.m. on 25 August 1951 a group of five professors and a postgraduate student were relaxing outside the house of Professor W. I. Robinson in Lubbock, Texas. Suddenly they saw a formation of bright lights flying rapidly across the sky. The professors estimated their speed at around 1800 miles per hour (2900 km/h) at a height of about one mile (1 5 kilometres) Sceptics claim that the lights were nothing more than reflections from the bellies of flying ducks - but if so they would have been flying at more than 125 miles per hour (200 km/h) - which is far too fast for ducks¹

The fishermen's tale

THE PASCAGOULA close encounter is one of the classics of UFO literature – deservedly so, if the story told by the witnesses is true. But is it? The case is typical of many UFO reports: there are few witnesses – in this case, the bulk of the information comes from one man, as the second witness lost consciousness at the beginning of the incident – and no reliable corroborative evidence. In such circumstances, even when sophisticated techniques such as lie detector tests and regressive hypnosis are used, only the personal integrity of the witnesses can guarantee their story.

'A very terrifying experience'

Close encounter of the third kind: Pascagoula, Mississippi, USA, 11 October 1973

The six-month period from October 1973 to March 1974 was a remarkable one for UFO reports. It was, in fact, one of the major 'flaps' and it visited, in particular, the United States, north-west Europe, Italy and Spain. One of the outstanding reports of that period in the USA came from Pascagoula, county town of Jackson County in the state of Mississippi. This town, whose population is just under 30,000, is situated at the south of the Pascagoula River on the coast of the Gulf of Mexico, about 100 miles (160 kilometres) to the east of New Orleans.

There were two witnesses, both of whom worked locally at the Walker Shipyard, Charles E. Hickson (45), a foreman, and Calvin R. Parker Jr (18), who allege that, on 11 October 1973, they experienced a close encounter with a UFO and its occupants, and abduction, while fishing from the pier of the Shaupeter shipyard on the Pascagoula River.

The time was about 9 p.m. when Hickson turned to get fresh bait. He says it was then that he heard a 'zipping' noise. Looking up,

he saw an elongated, oval, bluish-grey craft – in a later interview he was to refer to it as 'a spacecraft' – which had very bright, flashing, 'blue-looking' lights. This object was hovering some 2 feet (60 centimetres) off the ground, and when the next move came the witness was a trifle puzzled, for he said: 'It seemed to open up, but really there wasn't a door there at all . . . and three creatures came *floating out* towards us. I was so scared I couldn't believe it was happening.'

The creatures were said to be pale, 'ghost-like', and about 5 feet (1.5 metres) tall. Their skin seemed to be wrinkled, and was a greyish colour, while in place of hands they had 'crab-like claws' or pincers. According to the witness's first report, these entities may have had slits for eyes, but he did not see them. They did have two small cone-shaped ears and a small pointed nose, with a hole below in the place of a mouth. They approached the two flabbergasted fishermen, floating just off the ground without moving their legs. A buzzing noise was heard from

Calvin Parker, who was 19 years old at the time of the close encounter at Pascagoula. He apparently fainted when one of the humanoids touched him, and remained unconscious throughout the incident. It was reported that he later suffered a nervous breakdown

one of them and, said Hickson, 'they were on us before we knew it.' The older man was paralysed with fear, and Parker passed out when, apparently, he was touched by one of the creatures.

Meanwhile two of the entities lifted Charlie Hickson from the ground, and they glided motionless into the craft. Hickson claims he had lost all sensation of feeling and weight. He was taken into a very brightly lit room – which, however, had no visible light fixtures. His friend was apparently taken into another room by the third entity. Hickson says he was

placed in a reclining position and suspended in such a way that he did not touch any part of the craft. His limbs were completely paralysed; only his eyes were free to move. An instrument that looked like a big eye floated freely backwards and forwards about 9 inches (25 centimetres) above his body, and the creatures turned him so that all parts of his body came under the instrument's scrutiny. After some time Hickson was guided back outside the craft and was 'floated', together with Parker, back to his position on the pier, landing upright on his feet. He says he was so weak-kneed that he fell over.

Calvin Parker was unconscious throughout the incident, so all the evidence comes from Charlie Hickson. In his first interview, he said the UFO was about 10 feet (3 metres) wide, and something like 8 feet (2.5 metres) high. When it left, he said, it was gone from sight in less than a second. The occupants were like robots; they 'acted like they had a specific thing to do, and they did it. They didn't try to communicate with us. . . . I know now that they didn't intend to hurt us physically, but I feared they were going to take us away. I would like to emphasise that they didn't mean us any harm.'

That statement was made in an interview with the *Mississippi Press* a week after the incident. On the day of the encounter, Hickson and Parker had called at the *Press*'s offices, and found them closed; they then went to the sheriff's office, at 11 p.m., to make a report. Richard W. Heiden gave details of what took place in a report to *Flying Saucer Review*. Sheriff Fred Diamond and Captain Glen Ryder interrogated the witnesses, doing everything they knew to break the stories, but to no avail. Ryder commented, 'If they were lying to me they should be in Hollywood.' The interviews were taped. Then the two officers left the witnesses alone and unaware that the recorder was still running. They spoke agitatedly about their experience, and Calvin Parker was so emotionally overcome that he started praying when Hickson left the room. The sheriff was convinced the two fishermen were telling the truth.

Next morning, Friday 12 October, detective Tom Huntley from the sheriff's office drove Hickson and Parker to Keesler Air Force Base at Biloxi, Mississippi, where they were checked for radiation. There was no evidence of contamination. While there they gave details of their experience to the head of intelligence at the base, who 'acted as though he'd heard it all before!'

On Sunday, 14 October, the witnesses were interviewed in Pascagoula by Dr J. Allen Hynek of Northwestern University, Evanston, Illinois, former civil scientific consultant on UFO reports to the US Air Force and a Consultant Editor to *The Unexplained*, and Dr James Harder of the University of California, Berkeley. Dr Harder hypnotised the men individually, regressing them to the time of the experience. They each relived the terror of the occasion to such an extent that Dr Harder said: 'The experience they underwent was indeed a real one. A very strong feeling of terror is practically impossible to

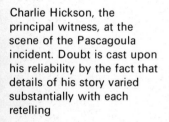

Charlie Hickson, the principal witness, at the scene of the Pascagoula incident. Doubt is cast upon his reliability by the fact that details of his story varied substantially with each retelling

fake under hypnosis.' Dr Hynek was more reserved: 'There is no question in my mind that these men have had a very terrifying experience.'

On 30 October, Hickson – but not Parker, who was apparently undergoing a nervous breakdown – underwent a polygraph examination (lie detector test) at the Pendleton Detective Agency in New Orleans. It was reported that the polygraph operator, one

that possibly corroborate the evidence. Although no one but Hickson and Parker saw the UFO – despite the fact that the incident happened close to Highway 90, a busy road – many owners of television sets in the Pascagoula area reported interference.

On the same day, 11 October, 450 miles (700 kilometres) away near Hartwell, Georgia, a former Methodist minister was driving along when he saw a UFO land on the road in front of him. He also saw silver-suited, white-haired occupants.

On the same night, Police Chief Greenhaw of Falkville, Alabama, was telephoned by a woman who claimed that a 'spaceship' had landed in a field near her house. He raced to the location, armed with a Polaroid camera. There was nothing at the alleged site, but Greenhaw said he was confronted by a silver-suited creature on a side road. He took four Polaroid shots – which show a creature seemingly dressed in aluminium foil obligingly turned to face the camera. The entity apparently bolted, and Greenhaw gave chase in his patrol car, but failed to catch up with it – an inconclusive end to what seems to be a tall story.

Above: Dr James Harder (left) and Dr J. Allen Hynek – a Consultant Editor to *The Unexplained* – interviewing Charlie Hickson and Calvin Parker shortly after their alleged abduction. Dr Harder hypnotically regressed the men to the time of their experience, and both scientists later agreed that the witnesses had had some very terrifying experience – although they were unable to say what it might have been

Right: a 'UFO entity' photographed with a Polaroid camera by Police Chief Jeff Greenhaw at Falkville, Alabama, on the night of the Pascagoula encounter. The entity reportedly bolted, and Greenhaw drove after it in his patrol car – but did not succeed in catching it

Scott Glasgow, was forced to admit after $2\frac{1}{2}$ hours of exhaustive tests that Hickson was telling the truth.

If this is true, it was a very strange remark for a polygraph operator to make. Polygraph tests are not sufficient to establish that a subject is lying; and any polygraph operator would have been well aware of this. In his book *UFOs explained*, Philip J. Klass claims that his own investigations have shown that Scott Glasgow was not, in fact, qualified as a polygraph operator. So it seems that, in spite of the newspaper publicity given to the fact that Hickson's story stood up to the lie detector test, it must remain inconclusive.

Hickson's experiences brought him considerable publicity; he appeared on television shows and even wrote a book. But unfortunately, his story often changed in the telling. Originally, for instance, he claimed that the UFO was some 10 feet (3 metres) long; in subsequent interviews, he said it was 20 or 30 feet (7 or 10 metres) long – quite a difference.

Hickson's descriptions of the alien creatures also varied on different occasions. In his original account, Hickson claimed they had two small cone-like ears, possibly slits where the eyes should have been, and a small sharp nose with a hole below it. Later, again on a television show, he said there were no eyes and that the hole below the nose was a slit. And more than a month after the incident, he disclosed for the first time that the light inside the spacecraft had been so bright that he had suffered severe eye injury, which had persisted for about three days.

These discrepancies, of course, tend to cast doubt upon the entire story – although they do not disprove it. But there are reports

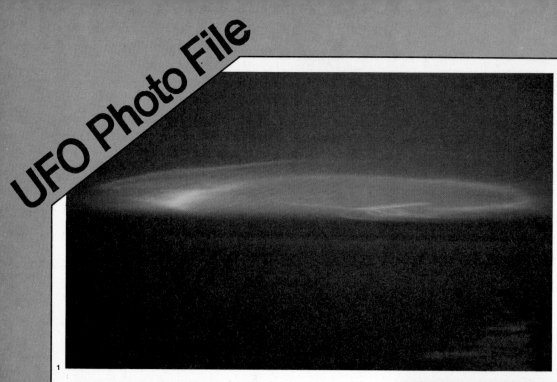

1

2

3

On the evening of 5 March 1979 Antonio Gonzales Llopis, aged 26, was taking photographs of the island of Gran Canaria in the Canary Islands when suddenly he noticed a strange, swirling light in the sky over the sea. A moment later a huge, dark object hurtled out of the sea straight up into the sky, surmounting a ball of fire (1, 2 and 3). Llopis pointed his camera at the object, checked its setting and continued to take pictures throughout the sighting, which he estimated lasted about three minutes – later verified by several other witnesses.

The brilliant light surrounding the dark object effectively obscured any detail, but it seemed to accelerate rapidly, shooting 'through' the pattern of lights in the sky. After the object had disappeared a bright trail and a golden cloud illuminated the sky for half an hour (4 and 5). Thousands of people on Gran Canaria reported the incident and many of them took photographs. Some of these found their way into the files of the Spanish government, which is, however, increasingly sympathetic to serious UFO investigation.

4

5

Right: bright lights seen near the major airport of Barajas, 6 miles (10 kilometres) from Madrid, Spain, one night in December 1979. An estimated 10 lights appeared suddenly over Madrid, executed a brief aerial ballet then sped off in the direction of Barajas, where this photograph was taken. UFOs seem to be fascinated with airports and aircraft, naval bases and ships, nuclear power stations and military establishments of all kinds. Believers in the extra-terrestrial hypothesis claim that the UFOs are aliens showing an interest in the hardware of our technology to compare our progress with theirs. More down-to-earth observers suggest that UFOs are in fact secret weapons accidentally seen while undergoing trials in the vicinity of the military bases from which they came.

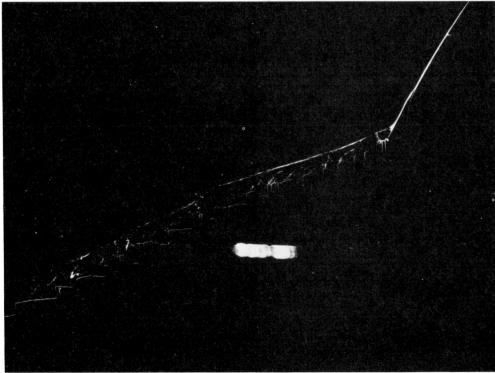

Left: photograph of a UFO seen near Lakeville, Connecticut, USA, on the night of 23 January 1967, and taken by a 17-year-old pupil from a local boys' boarding school. This was only one of the many sightings of 'bright lights moving erratically' reported over a four-month period, mainly by boys from the school, although one teacher and a 12-year-old boy who lived nearby added their testimony. Condon Report officers Ayer and Wadsworth investigated and studied the student's picture. The boy described the UFO as 'a bright point of light that blinked or pulsated regularly'. He said it 'pulsated twice' then disappeared behind Indian Mountain. The investigators left the case open – but could the UFOs have been secret weapons undergoing night trials? Or were they really 'nuts and bolts' alien spacecraft?

A logic of their own

ONE OF THE MOST curious categories in the UFO files consists of isolated reports of UFOs landing on rivers or lakes and siphoning up considerable quantities of water. We report on two cases, widely separated in both space and time: the first is from Japan in 1973, the second from northern Italy in 1952. In both instances, the amount of water taken on board by the UFOs suggests that it is not intended merely for scientific analysis – yet what else can it be used for? Are we to believe that UFOs are powered or cooled by water, or that their occupants need water for drinking or cooking?

Our third case is one of the weirdest ever to have been reported in Japan. Although it must be classified as a close encounter of the third kind, no UFO was observed during the incident. If some alien entities can survive without spacecraft, why are others so apparently vulnerable that they require regular supplies of water? The reports simply do not add up to a coherent picture of the perplexing UFO phenomenon.

'Infinite menace'

Close encounter of the third kind: Tomakomai, Hokkaido, Japan, July 1973

In 1975 *Flying Saucer Review* received an exciting account of one of the occasional sightings of UFOs taking on water. It came from a Japanese UFO investigator, Jun-Ichi Takanashi of Osaka; shadowy humanoid beings were also said to have been observed. The event took place at Tomakomai, a small industrial town on the southern coast of Hokkaido, the northernmost island of Japan, in July 1973. The eyewitness was Masaaki Kudou, a university student, then aged 20. He was home on vacation, and had taken a temporary job as a night security guard at a timber yard.

After patrolling the premises in his car, Mr Kudou returned to the prescribed place from which he could observe the premises –

and the waters of the bay beyond – and settled back to listen to his radio, light a cigarette, and relax. It was a still night, with the stars clearly visible. Suddenly he saw a streak of light flash across the sky, a spectacular 'shooting star' that suddenly stopped in its tracks, vanished, and reappeared. Remaining stationary, the light now expanded and contracted alternately at high speed, growing until it reached the apparent size of a baseball held at arm's length. It darted about in all directions within a few degrees of arc, and Mr Kudou found himself dizzily trying to follow its gyrations. As it began to descend spirally towards the sea the young student felt a surge of alarm, especially when the light halted near a distant cement works, and began to direct a beam of intermittent pulses of green light towards the north. Next, the object continued its descent towards the sea, this time sweeping in an arc until it was in a position much closer to the student observer. It halted its descent at about 70 feet (20 metres) from the sea, and the student saw a transparent tube emerge and lower itself towards the water. A soft *min-min-min-min* noise could be heard as this was happening, and the pitch of the noise lowered as the tube descended. When the tube touched the water its lower edge glowed, and it seemed that water was being sucked up into the object above.

Masaaki Kudou wondered if he were dreaming or, failing that, if his imagination were playing tricks with him. He lowered his gaze for a minute or so; when he looked again the water-suction operation was over, and the tube had been withdrawn from the water. No sooner had he registered this fact than the hovering UFO began to move towards him with what seemed to be infinite menace; he feared he was about to be attacked, and probably killed.

The object moved into a position some 160 feet (50 metres) above Kudou's car, and he, by leaning forwards and looking up, could keep it in view. He says its surface was as smooth as a table-tennis ball and, emitting its own glow, appeared to be white. Around his car everything was lit up as though by daylight, and he says he saw what appeared to be windows around the diameter of the spherical object. In the middle of one of these there was a shadowy human-shaped figure, while to the right there were two smaller shapes in another of the windows, but Kudou could not see whether or not these were similar to the first. All this, plus a sudden feeling that he was bound hand and foot, was too much for the witness, who rocked his head in his hands, with his chin on the steering wheel, moaning to himself.

Nevertheless, he still felt an urge to look upwards and, straining to do this, Kudou saw in the sky above the car three or four newly arrived glowing objects, similar in all respects to the first one. There was also a large, dark brown object, in silhouette, which looked like 'three gasoline drums connected together lengthwise' and which hovered noiselessly.

Suddenly the whole phenomenal spectacle came to an end. The glowing spheres swiftly manoeuvred into position whence they disappeared into one end of the large 'gasoline can' objects, and this in turn shot off to the north rather like a shooting star. The witness sat motionless, numb all over. He slowly became aware that his car radio was giving forth meaningless sounds, and that he himself was suffering from a severe headache. He was later able to estimate that the terrifying incident had lasted for about 12 minutes in all.

'They want to do me harm'

Close encounter of the third kind: Lucca, Italy, 25 July 1952

At 3 a.m. on 25 July 1952, a keen fisherman named Carlo Rossi was walking alongside the River Serchio, opposite San Pietro a Vico in Lucca, northern Italy, when he was puzzled by the appearance of an unusual light from an unseen position on the river below. Climbing the high embankment, he looked down to see a huge circular craft bearing a transparent cupola on top, and a shallow turret underneath from which three legs protruded, supporting the body of the craft above the water. There was also a ladder, and a long tube by which, apparently, the craft was taking in water. Suddenly a port opened in the upper part of the turret, and Carlo saw a 'human' figure look out. This figure pointed at the fisherman, who scrambled down the embankment. A green ray passed over his head, and he threw himself down. Looking up, seconds later, he saw the craft rise above the embankment and move off at high speed towards Viareggio.

Rossi was badly shaken by the incident – but something that happened a few weeks later worried him much more. To the outsider, the incident seems trivial – although it is a classic example of an MIB encounter: a strange man approached Rossi and offered him, Rossi said, a 'bad' cigarette. Rossi was terrified; he used later to say, 'I wonder if they want to do me harm, maybe, because of the thing I saw in the river?'

The circumstances of Rossi's subsequent death seem to lend substance to his suspicion. He was riding home on his bicycle one day when he was knocked down by a car. The driver was never identified.

'Alarm turned to terror'

Close encounter of the third kind: Sayama City, Saitama Prefecture, Japan, 3 October 1978

Right: Mr Hideichi Amano, victim of the Sayama encounter, recounts his experience on the television programme *11 P.M.*

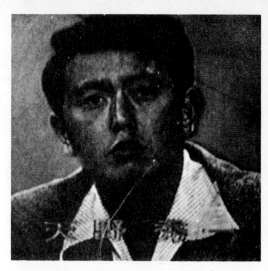

Mr Hideichi Amano, who owns and runs a snack bar in Sayama City, Saitama Prefecture, Japan, is also a keen radio 'ham'. Jun-Ichi Takanashi investigated Mr Amano's alarming experience after seeing him on the television programme *11 P.M.*

The encounter occurred on the evening of 3 October 1978, when Amano, using his mobile unit radio car, drove up a mountain outside Sayama City at about 8.30 p.m. with his two-year-old daughter Juri. He made the trip so that he could get unrestricted radio transmission and reception for a conversation with his brother, who lives in a distant part of the country. When their hook-up was finished, and a few other local calls had been made, Hideichi Amano was about to drive back down the mountain when the interior of the car became very bright, a light ten times brighter than was normal was coming from the fluorescent tube he had fitted inside the car. He observed that this light was confined to the car's interior; none, he said, was passing through the windows! Moments earlier Juri had been standing on the passenger seat beside him, but now her father was aghast to see the child lying on the seat, and foaming at the mouth. At the same instant he became aware of a round patch of orange light that was beamed through the windscreen and onto his stomach, and he saw that this was coming from a point in the sky. And then alarm turned to terror when he sensed something metallic being pressed against his right temple.

Hideichi Amano glanced sideways and saw an unearthly humanoid creature standing there with a pipe-like device in its mouth, and it was this that was being pressed against his head. From the tube came an incessant babble, as from a tape being played too fast.

The witness said the creature had a round face, but no neck, two sharply pointed ears, two small, motionless eyes that glowed bluish-white, and a triangular depression on its forehead. The mouth was clamped round the pipe, and no nose could be seen. While the babble continued Mr Amano says he found it difficult to move, and his mind became 'vague'. The terrified radio ham tried to start the car to flee the place, but there was no response from the engine, and the lights would not work, either. Then, after four or five minutes, the creature began to dim out and slowly vanished. The orange light disappeared, the interior lighting returned to normal, and other equipment that had been switched on now began to function. When the headlights returned Mr Amano switched the starter and got an instant response. Still in a confused state he roared away down the hill, and it was only when he reached the lower slopes that he remembered little Juri's condition. He stopped and, fortunately, the child stood up and said: 'I want a drink of water, papa.'

The witness decided to report the experience to the police, but they only poked fun at him, so he went home and retired to bed, still suffering a severe headache.

Researchers for the *11 P.M.* programme heard of the affair and eventually arranged for Mr Amano to be questioned under hypnosis in front of the cameras. One piece of information retrieved was that the creature was alleged to have told him to return to the meeting place at a certain time – which, to avoid a stampede by the curious, was not revealed to the viewers. Jun-Ichi Takanashi seemed to have little faith in the regression session because the 'hypnotist's insistence on more information was far too severe'; he suspected that the idea of a second meeting with the humanoid was a creation of the witness's subconscious mind. The fact that no second meeting was ever reported seems to lend weight to this. Yet, despite his reservations, Takanashi considered the encounter, as originally reported, to be 'the strangest ever to have taken place in Japan.'

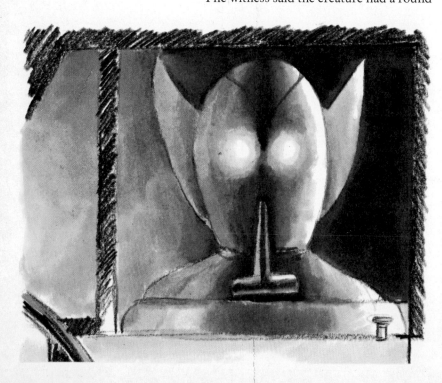

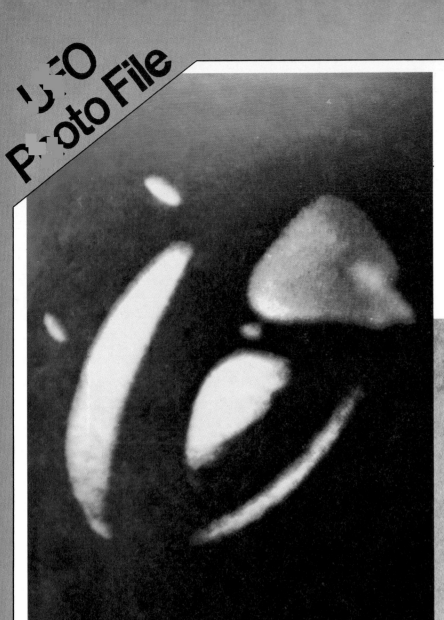

Left: this, one of the rare photographs of a nocturnal UFO to show more than an indeterminate blur of light, was taken by a 14-year-old paper-boy in Tulsa, Oklahoma, USA, on 2 August 1965. The object was observed by many witnesses, who stated that the tricoloured lights changed slowly to a uniform blue-green. The Condon Committee confirmed that the photograph represented a large object seen against a background of sky – and that the dark stripes between the bright patches were neither space nor sky, but some kind of structure, part of the UFO itself. With characteristic caution, the US Air Force concluded that the photograph represented either a genuine UFO – or a tricoloured Christmas tree light! The UFO organisation Ground Saucer Watch, on the other hand, considers it strong UFO evidence.

Right: at about 9.00 a.m. one day in September 1957 this strange, ring-shaped object was seen in the sky over Fort Belvoir, Virginia, USA. It 'seemed solid', very black with no reflection. It seemed to be about 60 feet (18 metres) in diameter. The ring gradually became engulfed in black smoke and finally disappeared. The Condon Committee identified the sighting as 'an atomic bomb simulation demonstration of the type commonly carried out at Fort Belvoir at this period'.

Left: a still from a film taken by Ralph Mayher in Miami, Florida, USA, on 29 July 1952. Using computer techniques to analyse the photograph, the UFO organisation Ground Saucer Watch has established that it is probably genuine and that it shows an object 30 to 40 feet (9 to 12 metres) long. Mr Mayher reported that its speed appeared to be less than that of a falling meteorite as it shot away over the ocean.

Puzzled by his sighting, Mr Mayher turned his film over to the US Air Force for investigation. It was never returned to him. Many people see the incident as part of a deliberate campaign on the part of the US authorities to suppress evidence for the existence of UFOs. Luckily, Mr Mayher had foreseen the possibility of his film getting 'lost': before handing it over to the USAF, he carefully snipped off the first few frames. This is one of them.

The closest encounter ever

ONE OF THE EARLIEST reports of an alleged abduction by humanoids was kept secret for over three years because it was deemed too 'wild' by those who first interviewed the abductee. And in the early reports the witness was known only as 'A.V.B.' to preserve his anonymity.

This amazing case first became known when the victim wrote to João Martins, a Brazilian journalist, and his medical friend Dr Olavo T. Fontes towards the end of 1957. Apparently, the man with the strange story was a young farmer who lived near the small town of São Francisco de Sales in Minas Gerais, Brazil. Intrigued, Martins and Fontes sent the farmer financial aid to make the long journey to Rio de Janeiro, where the investigation began on 22 February 1958 in Dr Fontes's consulting room.

The story that unfolded was, the investigators felt, so astonishing that they decided to 'keep it on ice' in case a similar incident occurred that might corroborate any of the details. And they feared that if the account became widely known there would be a rash of 'copycat' cases, which would end up invalidating this story. But a few details did leak out – fortunately in the right direction, for the outline of the tale reached the ears of Dr Walter Buhler in 1961, and he began to make his own detailed investigation.

The Buhler report eventually appeared as a newsletter and this, translated by Gordon Creighton and supplemented with editorial comments, appeared in *Flying Saucer Review* in January 1965. Very soon after, João Martin's account was published in the Spanish language edition – not the Portuguese as might have been expected – of the Brazilian magazine *O Cruzeiro*. Finally the full case, including the results of various detailed clinical reports, was included in *The humanoids*, a collection of accounts of encounters with UFO occupants, in 1969. At last the story that had been thought too 'wild' to be made known to the public was in print, and 'A.V.B.' was revealed to be 23-year-old Antônio Villas Boas.

'I am going to bear our child'

Close encounter of the third kind: São Francisco de Sales, Brazil, 15 October 1957

Antônio Villas Boas: his remarkable experience was at first concealed by UFO researchers because they considered it too wild

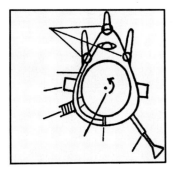

These sketches of the UFO were made by Villas Boas in February 1958 (above) for Dr Olavo Fontes, and in July 1961 (below) for Drs Buhler and Aquino of the Brazilian Society for the Study of Flying Saucers

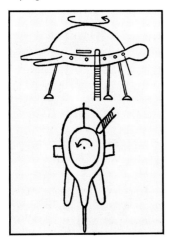

The actual abduction of Antônio Villas Boas was heralded by two unusual events. The first took place on 5 October 1957 when he and his brother were retiring to bed at about 11 p.m. after a party. From their bedroom window they saw an unidentified light in the farmyard below. It moved up onto the roof of their house, and together they watched it shine through the slats of the shutters and the gaps in the tiles (there being no ceiling proper) before it departed.

The second strange incident occurred on 14 October at about 9.30 p.m. when the Villas Boas brothers were out ploughing with their tractor. They suddenly saw a dazzling light, 'big and round', about 100 yards (90 metres) above one end of the field. Antônio went over for a closer look, but – as if playing games with him – the light moved swiftly to the other end of the field, a manoeuvre it repeated the two or three times the young farmer tried to get a closer look at it. Then the light abruptly vanished.

The following night, 15 October, Antônio was out in the field again, ploughing alone by the light of his headlamps. Suddenly, at about 1 a.m., he became aware of a 'large red star' that seemed to be descending towards the end of the field. As it came nearer he saw that it was in fact a luminous egg-shaped object. The UFO's approach brought it right overhead, about 50 yards (45 metres) above the tractor. The whole field became as bright as if it were broad daylight.

Villas Boas sat in his cab transfixed with fear as the object landed about 15 yards (15 metres) in front of him. He saw a rounded object with a distinct rim that was apparently clustered with purple lights. A huge round headlamp on the side facing him seemed to be producing the 'daylight' effect. There was a revolving cupola on top, and as he watched, fascinated, he saw three shafts – or 'legs' – emerge and reach for the ground. At this the terrified farmer started to drive off but after a short distance the engine stopped, despite the fact that it had been running smoothly. Villas Boas found he count not restart it and in a panic he leapt from the cab and set off across the heavily ploughed field. The deep ruts proved a handicap to his escape and he had gone only a few paces when someone grabbed his arm. As he turned, he was astonished to see a strangely garbed individual whose helmeted head reached only to Villas Boas's shoulder. He hit out at his assailant, who was knocked flying, but he was quickly grabbed by three other humanoids who lifted him from the ground as he struggled and shouted. He later said:

> I noticed that as they were dragging me towards the machine my speech seemed to arouse their surprise or curiosity, for they stopped and peered attentively at my face as I spoke, though without loosening their grip on me. This relieved me a little as to their intentions, but I still did not stop struggling. . . .

He was carried to the craft. A ladder descended from a door, and his captors hoisted him up this with great difficulty – especially as he tried to resist by hanging on to a kind of handrail. But in the end they succeeded.

Once inside the machine Villas Boas found himself in a square room with metallic walls, brightly lit by small, high lamps. He was set down on his feet, and became aware that there were five small beings, two of whom held him firmly. One signalled that he should be taken through to an adjoining room, which was larger, and oval in shape, with a metal column that reached from floor to ceiling, together with a table and some swivel chairs set to one side.

A 'conversation' ensued between his captors, who made sounds like dog barks:

> Those sounds were so totally different from anything I had heard until now. They were slow barks and yelps, neither very clear nor very hoarse, some longer, some shorter, at times containing several different sounds all at once, and at other times ending in a quaver. But they were simply sounds, animal barks, and nothing could be distinguished that could be taken as the sound of a syllable or word of a foreign language. Not a thing! To me it sounded alike, so that I am unable to retain a word of it . . . I still shudder when I think of those sounds. I can't reproduce them . . . my voice just isn't made for that.

Handled by humanoids

This strange communication ceased abruptly, when all five set about him, stripping him of his clothing while he shouted and struggled – but to no avail. (Apparently they stopped to peer at him whenever he yelled, and, strangely, although they seemed to be using force, at no time did they hurt him.)

The beings were all dressed in tight-fitting grey overalls and large, broad helmets reinforced with bands of metal at back and front. There were apertures through which Villas Boas could see light-coloured eyes. Three tubes emerged from the top of each helmet, the central one running down the back and entering the clothing in line with the spine; the other two curved away to enter the clothes, one beneath each armpit. The sleeves ended in thick gloves, which seemed difficult to bend at the fingers. The trouser part fitted closely over seat, thighs and lower legs, and the footwear seemed an integral part of this section, the soles being very thick – perhaps as much as 2 inches (5 centimetres). On his chest each being had a kind of breastplate or 'shield' 'about the size of a slice of pineapple', which reflected light, and the shield was joined to a belt at the waist by a strip of laminated metal.

The naked and shivering farmer – it was a

Below: Villas Boas's impression of the inscription above a door in the humanoids' craft. In the statement he made to Dr Fontes, Villas Boas said it was 'a sort of luminous inscription – or something similar – traced out in red symbols which, owing to the effect of the light, seemed to stand out about 2 inches (5 centimetres) in front of the metal of the door. This inscription was the only thing of its kind that I saw in the machine. The signs were scrawls completely different from what we know as lettering'

pumped up and down. The alarmed Villas Boas watched the chalice fill with what was presumably his own blood. The creatures then left him alone. He sat on a soft couch contemplating the nightmarish situation in which he found himself.

Suddenly he smelt a strange odour, which made him feel sick. He examined the walls and saw metallic tubes at just below ceiling level. Grey smoke was coming through perforations in the tubes. Villas Boas rushed to a corner of the room and vomited, and after that he felt a little less frightened. Moments later there was a noise at the door, which opened to reveal a woman standing there. As Villas Boas gaped, the woman walked towards him. Flabbergasted, he realised she was as naked as he was.

The woman, said Villas Boas, was more beautiful than anyone he had met before. She was shorter than he, her head reaching only to his shoulder – he is 5 feet 5 inches (1.6 metres). Her hair was smooth, and very fair, almost white, and as though bleached. Parted in the centre, it reached halfway down her neck, with ends curling inwards. Her eyes were large, blue and elongated, 'slanted outwards'. Her small nose was straight, neither pointed nor turned up. She had high cheekbones, but – as Villas Boas discovered – they were soft and fleshy to the touch. Her face was wide, but narrowed to a markedly

chilly night outside, and no warmer in the craft – stood there quaking and 'worried to death'. He wondered what on earth was going to happen to him. One of the little creatures approached him with what seemed to be a sort of wet sponge, which he rubbed all over Villas Boas's skin. He said: 'The liquid was as clear as water, but quite thick, and without smell. I thought it was some sort of oil, but was wrong, for my skin did not become greasy or oily.'

He was now led to another door, which had an inscription in red over it. He tried to memorise this, although it meant nothing to him, being written in unknown characters. In yet another room one of the beings approached with a sort of chalice from which dangled two flexible tubes; one of these, with a capped end like a child's suction 'arrow', was fixed to his chin, while the other tube was

pointed chin. Her lips were thin, the mouth being almost like a slit. The ears were normal, but small.

The door closed, and Villas Boas found himself alone with this woman, whose slim body was the most beautiful he had ever seen. She had high, well-separated breasts. Her waist was slender, her hips wide and her thighs large, while her feet were small and her hands long and narrow. He saw too that the hair in her armpits, and her pubic hair, was blood red. He smelt no perfume on her, 'apart from the feminine odour'.

She approached the farmer and rubbed her head against his (presumably by standing on tip-toe). Her body felt as though glued to his, and she made it quite clear what she wanted. His excitement welled up. The sexual act was normal – as was the one that followed – but then she tired, and refused further advances.

Villas Boas recalled that she never kissed him, but once gently bit him on his chin. Although she never spoke, she grunted, and that 'nearly spoiled everything, giving the disagreeable impression that I was with an animal'.

When she was called away by one of the other beings, she turned to Villas Boas, pointed to her belly, and then pointed to the sky. These gestures instilled a great fear in Antônio – a fear that was with him still, four

Villas Boas was examined by Dr Fontes in February 1958, four months after the alleged abduction. The symptoms he described suggested 'radiation poisoning or exposure to radiation', but it was too late for this diagnosis to be confirmed

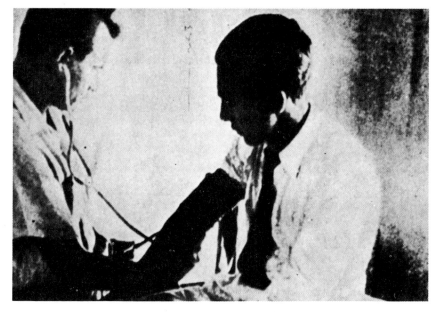

years after the event – for he interpreted them as meaning she would return to take him away. Dr Fontes later calmed him by suggesting that she meant: 'I am going to bear our child, yours and mine, there on my home planet.' This led to speculation by the farmer that all they wanted was 'a good stallion' to improve their stock.

Then Villas Boas was told to get dressed, after which he says he was taken on a conducted tour round the craft; during this he tried to steal an instrument for a

keepsake, only to be rebuffed, angrily, by one of the crew. Eventually, he was invited to go down the ladder, and back onto solid ground. From there he watched the ladder retract, while the metal legs and the lights began to glow. The craft rose into the air with its cupola turning at great speed. With lights flashing it listed slightly to one side, then suddenly shot off like a bullet.

It was by then 5.30 a.m. and the abductee's adventure had lasted over four hours.

He returned home hungry, and weakened by his spell of vomiting. He slept through to 4.30 p.m. and awoke feeling perfectly normal. But when he fell asleep again he slept badly, and woke up shouting after dreaming of the incident. Next day he was troubled by nausea and a violent headache. When that left him his eyes began to burn. Unusual wounds, with infections, appeared on parts of his body. When they dried up they left round, purplish scars.

Mysterious scars

When Dr Fontes examined Villas Boas, he observed two small patches, one on each side of the chin. He described these as 'scars of some superficial lesion with associated subcutaneous haemorrhage'. Several other mysterious scars on his body were also noted.

In a letter to *Flying Saucer Review* Dr Fontes suggested that the symptoms described pointed to radiation poisoning, or exposure to radiation. Wrote Dr Fontes: 'Unfortunately he came to me too late for the blood examinations that could have confirmed such a possibility beyond doubt.'

On 10 October 1971 João Martins was at last officially cleared to write about the case for the Brazilian public. His account appeared in the Rio de Janeiro Sunday review *Domingo Illustrado*. His abridged account concluded with a statement that:

A.V.B. was subjected by us [Martins, Dr Fontes, and a *military officer* – whose presence was not revealed in the earlier reports] to the most sophisticated methods of interrogation, without falling into any contradictions. He resisted every trap we set to test whether he was seeking notoriety or money. A medical examination . . . revealed a state of completely normal physical and mental equilibrium. His reputation in the region where he lives was that of an honest, serious, hardworking man.

Martins also revealed that the interrogation at times bordered on harsh and cruel treatment, just short of physical violence, but Villas Boas never veered from his original story in any detail. The journalist concluded: 'If this story be true, it may well be that, somewhere out there in the Universe, there is a strange child . . . that maybe is being prepared to return here. Where does fantasy end? Where does reality begin?'

UFOs over water

AN INTERESTING subspecies of UFO reports describes cases in which the objects have emerged from or disappeared into water – most often the sea. One such famous, and well-documented, instance is the extraordinary series of photographs previously examined which were taken in the Canary Islands. Some writers have even suggested that there are enormous UFO 'bases' hidden under the world's oceans. In the absence of any concrete evidence, however, it seems best to leave this speculation where it belongs, in the realm of science fiction.

All the cases that follow occurred, intriguingly, within 200 miles (320 kilometres) of each other along the Brazilian coast south of Rio de Janeiro (see map), though they were all well-separated in time. All involved several witnesses and what appear to be indubitably 'nuts and bolts' craft. Only the Santos case seems amenable to a conventional explanation: but if it represents a stray rocket, aircraft pod, or satellite debris, why were the authorities unable to locate the wreckage at the site of the crash?

'A motor boat striking the water'

Close encounter of the third kind: Rio de Janeiro, Brazil, 27 June 1970

On Sunday, 27 June 1970 Senhor Aristeu Machado and his five daughters were playing a game on the verandah of their home, 318 Avenida Niemeyer, Rio de Janeiro, from which they could look out over the road below to the South Atlantic Ocean beyond. With them was their friend and neighbour Senhor João Aguiar, an official of the Brazilian Federal Police.

Dona Maria Nazaré, who was preparing lunch in the kitchen, called out to check the time: it was 11.38 a.m. About two minutes after that Senhor Aguiar happened to look out over the sea, and quickly drew the attention of the others to 'a motor boat striking the water'. As this object descended it threw up spray on all sides.

The game and lunch were quickly forgotten for, as the family and their guest watched the 'motor boat' they could see two 'bathers' aboard the craft, who seemed to be signalling with their arms. In a statement to Dr Walter Buhler, who investigated the case, Aguiar said there were definitely two persons on board and that they were wearing 'shining

Above: the Avenida Niemeyer, which runs northeast along the coast into the suburbs of Leblon and Ipanema near Rio de Janeiro. The Machados' house stands above it to the left of the picture

Right: Senhor Aristeu Machado and his wife on the verandah from which they watched the UFO and subsequent events in the sea

clothing, and something on their heads'. The craft was a greyish metallic colour; it seemed to be between 15 and 20 feet (5 and 6 metres) in length and had a transparent cupola. One strange feature was noted: at no time did the object make the 'bobbing' movement associated with a boat on a swell.

Sr Aguiar ran down to the nearby Mar Hotel, and telephoned the Harbour Police; they promised to send help to the occupants of the 'motor boat', who were presumably involved in a mishap offshore. Aguiar then

returned to the house and rejoined the Machados on their verandah. He had been away from the house for about 30 minutes.

Shortly after Aguiar returned, the object – which was now seen to be disc-shaped – took off; it had been on the surface for 40 to 45 minutes. It skimmed the water for some 300 yards (280 metres), throwing off a wave from the bows at it went, then lifted from the sea and made off quickly towards the south-east. It was then that the witnesses realised it was not a motor boat, but rather an object that looked like a *flying saucer*. A hexagonal-shaped appendage retracted into the underside of the main body, and a number of lights on the appendage flashed, in sequence, green, yellow, red.

Once airborne, the object appeared to be transparent rather than aluminium-coloured, and Dona Maria Nazaré said she clearly saw two entities sitting inside. There was little traffic noise from the road at that time, but the witnesses could hear no sound from the object.

On the sea where the UFO had originally rested, the witnesses saw a white hoop-shaped object 'about the size of a trunk or chest', according to Dona Maria Nazaré. Suddenly the hoop sank, then it reappeared and a yellow oval-shaped section separated from it. This, it was estimated, was some 16 inches (40 centimetres) across with about 8 inches (20 centimetres) projecting above the surface of the water. It remained stationary for about three minutes, then began to move towards the shore, with its longer axis directed at the witnesses. A green flange at the rear of the object separated from the main body and followed it at a distance of about a yard (1 metre). After 15 minutes the yellow oval was about 130 yards (120 metres) from the shore, when it made a right-angled turn to its left and headed for the beach at Gávea – a movement directly opposed to the maritime current in the area at the time.

The white hoop disappeared several times, but when it came back into view it was still pursuing its direct course for Gávea Beach, as though it were going to link up once again with the yellow object.

Meanwhile the police launch from Fort Copacabana had arrived at the spot where the UFO had remained stationary, having come into view about 20 minutes after João Aguiar made his telephone call. So it seems likely that the crew must have seen the UFO take off. At roughly the position where the hoop had been left the launch stopped and the police hauled on board a red cylindrical object. They then made off at speed towards their base.

No statement was made by the police regarding what they saw or found. And, although an account of the incident appeared in the newspaper *Diário de Notícias* on 28 June 1970, no other witnesses came forward to confirm the sighting.

'Like beads in a necklace'

Close encounter of the second kind: near Curitiba, Brazil, 10 January 1958

On 10 January 1958 Captain Chrysólogo Rocha was sitting with his wife in the porch of a house overlooking the sea near Curitiba, and was surprised to see an unfamiliar 'island'. He had his binoculars with him, and when he had focused on the island he was amazed to see that it was growing in size. He cried out to people inside the house, and very soon eight of them joined the couple on the porch to witness the strange phenomenon.

The object seemed to consist of two parts, one in the sea and the other suspended above it. Then, without warning, both parts sank out of sight; soon afterwards a steamer hove in sight and passed very near the point where the objects were last seen. Fifteen minutes later, when the ship had gone, the 10 observers saw the objects rise once again from the sea. Now they could see that the upper section was attached to the lower one by a number of shafts or tubes, which were quite bright. Up and down the shafts, small objects 'like beads in a necklace' passed in disorderly fashion. This second display lasted for a few minutes, then the sections closed up, and the whole thing started to sink, eventually disappearing beneath the waves.

One of the witnesses, the wife of another army officer, telephoned the Forte dos Andrades barracks at Guarajá, and the air force base was alerted. An aeroplane was scrambled to investigate, but it arrived on the scene after the objects had disappeared.

'The water was boiling up'

Close encounter of the second kind: Santos, Brazil, 31 October 1963

On 31 October 1963 eight-year-old Rute de Souza was playing near her home in Iguapé, south-west of Santos, when she heard a roaring noise that was growing rapidly louder. Looking round, she saw a silvery object coming down out of the sky, heading towards the nearby Peropava River. After passing over the house the UFO collided with the top of a palm tree and began to twist, turn and wobble in the air. Then Rute saw it fall into the river close to the far bank.

The child turned to run home, and met her mother who, alarmed by the noise, was running towards the river. Then followed Rute's uncle, Raul de Souza, who had been working about 100 yards (90 metres) from the house. The three of them stood transfixed as they watched the surface of the river: at the spot where the object had sunk the water was 'boiling up'. This was followed by an eruption of muddy water, then one of mud.

Rute was not the only witness. On the far bank a number of fishermen had watched the spectacle. One of them, a Japanese gentleman named Tetsuo Ioshigawa, gave descriptions of the incident to official investigators and reporters. The object, shaped like a 'wash basin', was estimated to have been about 25 feet (7.5 metres) in diameter; it had been no more than 20 feet (6 metres) off the ground when it hit the palm tree. The general assumption was that the object was in difficulties after the collision.

The authorities also assumed that a wrecked 'flying saucer' was embedded in the muddy bottom of the river, but divers could find nothing in the 15 feet (5 metres) of water. Finally engineers searched the area with mine detectors, but they too failed to locate the object.

Speculating about the incident in the *Bulletin* of the Aerial Phenomena Research Organisation (APRO), Jim and Coral Lorenzon wrote that the reported size of the UFO suggested it could have carried a crew, and if so, then repairs may have been effected that would have enabled the craft to escape.

Not dreaming and not mad

UFOLOGISTS OFTEN LAMENT the fact that so few UFO sightings are made by people with 'trained minds' – by which they mean scientists and engineers. But this is not really surprising, since the 'trained mind' of a witness is likely to reveal prejudices that discourage him from reporting an extraordinary experience and encourage him to explain it away. On the other hand, unsophisticated observers, unacquainted with the UFO controversy, are often impressive witnesses, telling their story without embroidering it. The sightings of classic 'flying saucers' described here may have more value by virtue of coming from people of little formal education or technical training.

'Dwarf-like creatures with pumpkin-shaped heads'

Close encounter of the third kind: Valensole, France, 1 July 1965

Just after 5 a.m. on 1 July 1965, Maurice Masse, a 41-year-old lavender grower, set to work in his fields situated on the Valensole plateau in the Basses Alpes of south-eastern France. At about 5.45 a.m. he stopped to have a cigarette, parking his tractor by a hillock at the end of a small vineyard that lay along the northern side of the field.

Suddenly he heard a shrill whistling noise and glanced round the hillock, fully expecting to see a helicopter; instead, he saw a dull-coloured object the size of a Renault Dauphine car, shaped like a rugby football, with a cupola on top. It was standing on six metallic legs, and there was also a central support, which appeared to be stuck into the ground. Close to the 'machine' Masse saw two boys, about eight years old, bending over a lavender plant.

Masse crossed the vineyard and approached the boys, believing them to be the 'vandals' who had picked young shoots from a number of his lavender plants on several occasions during the preceding month. Then, to his surprise, he saw that he was not

approaching boys at all, but two dwarf-like creatures with large bald heads. He was about 15 feet (5 metres) from the beings when one of them turned and pointed a pencil-like instrument at him. Immediately he was stopped in his tracks, unable to move any part of his body. (In the first reports of the case it was stated that the witness was 'paralysed', but UFO investigator Aimé Michel suggested the term *immobilised*, perhaps by some form of hypnotic suggestion.)

According to Masse's description, the creatures were less than 4 feet (1.2 metres) tall, and were wearing close-fitting grey-green overalls. They had huge pumpkin-shaped heads, but no hair – only smooth white skin. Their cheeks were wide and fleshy, narrowing to very pointed chins; the eyes were large and slanting. The witness did not mention their noses, but he did describe the mouths, which were like thin slits and opened to form lipless holes. It is rare in close encounters for humanoids to be reported as having their heads uncovered outside the craft, as in this case.

The creatures appeared to communicate

with each other, but not with their mouths, for inarticulate sounds seemed to come from their mid-body regions. The hapless lavender grower thought they were mocking him, although he admitted that their glances were not hostile; indeed, he never had the impression he was face to face with monsters. Masse has never disclosed what took place during the rest of the time he was immobilised, 15 feet (5 metres) from the beings.

After a few minutes the creatures returned to their machine, moving in a remarkable manner: 'falling and rising in space like bubbles in a bottle without apparent support . . . sliding along bands of light . . .' to enter the object through a sliding door. The witness said he could see them looking at him from inside the craft. Suddenly there was a thump from the central support, which retracted, the six legs began to whirl, and the machine floated away at an angle of 45°, making a shrill whistling sound. At 65 feet (20 metres) it just disappeared, although traces of its passage in the direction of Manosque were found on lavender plants for more than 100 yards (90 metres). (These plants withered, then recovered and grew taller and finer than those nearby.)

The farmer grew alarmed as the invisible bonds that held him failed to relax their grip, but after 15 minutes he slowly regained the use of his limbs. He could see marks left by some of the legs of the craft, and almost liquid mud around the hole where the central support had entered the ground. (There had been no rain in the area for several weeks.)

Masse ran down to Valensole, on the outskirts of which is the Café des sports. The proprietor, a friend, was just opening for the day, and Masse, shaken and as white as a

Maurice Masse, owner of vast lavender fields in south-eastern France, stands on the area where a UFO stood while he watched, unable to move. Only weeds grew in this patch of land after the incident

sheet, told him part of his story. The café owner pressed Masse for further details of what had happened, but the farmer refused to say any more because he feared the rest of his story would not be believed. His friend advised him to report the incident to the gendarmes, but Masse would not. So the café proprietor rushed to the field, saw the marks and returned to tell Masse's story.

That evening Masse took his 18-year-old daughter to see the landing site; they saw that only four of the craft's legs had left marks on the ground, and that the mud around the central hole had set like concrete.

The world's reaction

Soon after Masse's experience was made public he was questioned by the chief of the local gendarmerie. Crowds of sightseers visited the field, and Valensole was flooded with representatives of the press, radio and television. On 4 July, overwhelmed with interviews and questions, Masse collapsed, seized with an insuperable desire to sleep. Aimé Michel reported that he would have slept 24 hours a day had his wife not awakened him to make him eat.

The initial private investigation was conducted by a local magistrate, who handed his report to *Flying Saucer Review* in October 1965. He said that Masse had prevented his daughter approaching too close to the hole for he feared she might suffer some harmful effect from it; indeed, he was worried about possible genetic effects it might have on himself. In the end he filled the hole, which was shaped like an inverted funnel.

Aimé Michel interviewed the witness twice at Valensole in 1965, and found him anxious and distressed, still worried about possible effects on his health. During his second visit, Michel showed Masse a photograph of a model based on Lonnie Zamora's description of the UFO he had seen at Socorro, New Mexico in the spring of 1964. Masse was staggered that someone should have photographed *his* machine; but when told that it had been seen in the USA by a policeman he sighed with relief: 'You see then that I wasn't dreaming, and that I'm not mad.'

Two years later UFO investigators visited Maurice Masse again and he took them to see the landing site. It was 10 feet (3 metres) in diameter, and distinguishable because lavender plants around the perimeter were withered, and only weeds grew in the inner area – despite the fact that it had been ploughed and replanted.

Although Masse had recovered from his experience, he was anxious to avoid any more publicity. In an endeavour to hide the location of the landing site he trimmed the mass of weeds to the shape of lavender plants. Eventually, he tore up the vineyard, ploughed the lavender field and sowed it all with wheat.

'A disc surrounded with a ring of coloured lights'

Close encounter of the third kind: Puente de Herrera, Valladolid, Spain, 15 August 1970

In 1974 *Flying Saucer Review* received a report from the Charles Fort Group of Valladolid in Spain, who had investigated a UFO sighting that had been made some years earlier. The witness was a 22-year-old woman, a domestic employee in the house of a farmer at Puente de Herrera, close by the river Duero, south of Valladolid. The young woman's name was withheld, at her request, as she had had no primary education, and was illiterate. We shall refer to her simply as the 'señorita'.

On the night of 15 August 1970 the señorita had been watching television when she heard a piercing whistling noise. At the same time the television picture was suddenly blotted out by a mass of lines. Playing with the controls had no effect, so she switched off the set and went to the front door of the house.

The señorita was astounded to see a weird object with various lights standing on the drive. And nearby there stood a very strange-looking 'man' who seemed to be surveying a crop of alfalfa in an adjacent field. Very scared, the young woman went back inside the house and shut the door. Then the whistling sound began again but, when she went to look out of the window of her room, both machine and 'man' had gone.

The señorita told only her boyfriend of her experience at the time. Members of her family became aware of it only in March 1972 when, after her brother-in-law had made some observation about UFOs, she told them about what she had seen. It was her brother-in-law who passed the information to the Charles Fort Group.

During the investigation that followed, J.

Macías and his fellow researchers learned that the period of time between the onset of the whistling noise and the witness first looking out of the window was about 5 minutes. The whistling noise persisted while she was peering through the door, but seemed a little less intense. She had switched off the porch lights as she usually did between 10.30 and 11.00 p.m., so she felt nobody could have seen her when she opened the door.

The UFO, which was balanced on several 'feet' on the road surface, was about 12 feet (4 metres) wide and 8 feet (2.5 metres) high. The upper part consisted of a hemispherical cupola, which seemed to be made of crystal. On top of this a bluish-white light revolved erratically, the light dimming whenever it slowed down. The cupola was supported by a disc surrounded with a ring of coloured lights that changed constantly from white to purple and then yellow.

The occupant of the craft was about 5 feet 10 inches (1.8 metres) tall and was dressed in a dark, tight-fitting garment and a helmet. Around his ankles and wrists there were glowing white 'bracelets' and in the middle of his belt was a square 'buckle' of similar iridescent material. The señorita was not sure about the colour of his skin, and could not see any hair. She said the 'man' seemed to be interested in the alfalfa, and walked towards it with unusually long strides.

A persistent afterglow

According to the witness, physical vestiges of the craft were left at the landing site, for when she went to the window of her room she saw a soft glow where the object had been standing. Intrigued by this, she inspected the ground. On the surface of the road there were black footprints, similar to those made by ordinary shoes, the heel mark narrower than that of the sole. The marks must have been seen by everybody coming to the house, but the señorita told no one of her experience at the time and therefore did not draw attention to them. While they remained, however, the area where the UFO had landed continued to glow at night.

The investigators considered that the señorita's illiteracy added to the authenticity of her account on the grounds that she could hardly have fabricated a story of such complexity. After speaking with members of her family they realised that their knowledge of other UFO encounters was insufficient for her to have picked up such detailed data from them. Furthermore, there seemed to be no motivation for a hoax, for it was only by chance that she mentioned her experience to her brother-in-law 18 months after the event. Other members of the family later told the investigators that after their first interview with the señorita she had wept hysterically and rounded on her brother-in-law for having given away her secret.

UFOs can kill

EVER SINCE the post-war wave of UFO sightings began, a debate has raged among ufologists as to whether or not the objects seen in the sky are hostile.

Some researchers cling to the belief that a surveillance of this planet is being carried out by extra-terrestrial explorers. Others take this a step further and proclaim that 'space beings' come to the Earth to warn Man of the evil of his ways. Yet others believe that the extra-terrestrials – or meta-terrestrials, if one holds the theory that they are denizens of 'parallel universes' – are engaged in a struggle for possession of the human race, and that they have no interest in human welfare.

Still other investigators claim that UFOs are psychically caused phenomena, while others counter by suggesting that UFOs may cause manifestations of psychic phenomena. Lastly, there are those who have come to the conclusion that UFOs are mere products of the witnesses' imaginations.

On the whole, however, UFO researchers assume that they are dealing with a benign phenomenon. If human beings occasionally suffer harm from UFOs, they believe, it is either an unintended consequence of UFO activity that had no malicious purpose, or it was a purely defensive response.

In the cases discussed here, human witnesses of UFOs suffered temporary or permanent injury – and in one case, death. In two of them the injured people could be held guilty of provoking the trouble. Nonetheless, these incidents invoke the spectre first raised by H.G. Wells in *War of the worlds* – of attack on mankind by alien beings.

'An eerie orange light'

Close encounter of the second kind: São Vicente, São Paulo, Brazil, 4 November 1957

The Brazilian coastal fort of Itaipu is situated at São Vicente, close to the port of Santos in the state of São Paulo. To the two sentries patrolling the gun emplacements in the small hours of 4 November 1957, everything seemed quiet. Nothing warned them that within a few minutes they were to be put through a nightmarish ordeal that still lacks an explanation.

At 2 a.m. the sentries spotted a 'bright star' that suddenly appeared above the horizon over the Atlantic. It grew larger and the soldiers realised that it was approaching them at high speed. They were astonished by this glowing object, which they thought was an aeroplane, but they gave no thought to sounding the alarm.

In a few seconds the UFO, travelling silently, reached a point high above the fort and halted. Then it floated down until it had stopped motionless some 150 feet (50 metres) above the highest gun turret, bathing the ground between the turrets with an eerie orange light. The object appeared to be circular and was, in the soldiers' words, about the size of a 'big Douglas' (meaning, presumably, a Douglas DC-6). The sentries could now hear a gentle humming noise that seemed to be associated with it.

Without warning, a wave of searing heat suddenly engulfed the men. Fire seemed to be burning all over their uniforms, while the humming intensified.

One sentry staggered, dazed, and then fell unconscious to the ground. His comrade managed to stumble into a relatively sheltered spot beneath one of the guns. But once there his mind seemed to give way: he was seized by horror and rent the air with blood-curdling screams.

His terrible cries awakened the rest of the garrison, but within seconds the power supply cut off, lights went out and equipment failed. An officer tried to start the emergency generator, but that too failed. Meanwhile, the horrifying screams continued and confusion turned to panic in the dark subterranean corridors.

Suddenly, the lights returned. The officers and men who were first to get into the open were in time to see a great orange light climbing away vertically, before shooting off at high speed. The last of the soldiers to arrive found those who had preceded them examining the unconscious sentry while the other was still crouched in hiding and crying hysterically.

In the sick bay both men were found to have 'first- and deep second-degree burns – mostly on areas that had been protected by clothes'. The sentry who had retained consciousness was in deep nervous shock and many hours were to pass before he could talk.

The fort's electric clocks had stopped at 2.03 a.m., which suggested that the whole nightmare experience had lasted no more than about four minutes.

Later that morning the colonel in command of Fort Itaipu issued orders forbidding the communication of the incident to anyone. Intelligence officers were quickly at work conducting an investigation, and a report was sent to army headquarters. Some days later officers from the US military mission arrived, together with Brazilian Air Force officers. Meanwhile, the sentries were flown to Rio de Janeiro and admitted to the Army Central Hospital, where a security net was promptly drawn around them.

Three weeks later, an officer from the fort who was interested in UFO reports sought out Dr Olavo Fontes, who was involved in the investigation of the famous Antônio Villas Boas case examined earlier. The officer had been present at the fort during the incident and, once he was satisfied that his name would never be divulged, he gave Fontes full details of the case. Dr Fontes approached medical colleagues at the hospital, who confirmed that two soldiers were being treated for severe burns, but would tell him nothing more about their case.

Without further corroboration, Dr Fontes could not publish an account. So the case lingered in the files until mid 1959, when, by chance, the doctor met three other officers who in the course of conversation confirmed what had happened. Thanks to the unauthorised disclosures of the officers who talked to Dr Fontes, the world has some knowledge, tantalisingly incomplete though it is, of a UFO's unwelcome visit to Fort Itaipu on that terrifying night.

'Like an upturned wash basin'

Close encounter of the third kind: Pilar de Goiás, Brazil, 13 August 1967

Illiterate, simple, honest, trustworthy and reserved – this was how Inácio de Souza, a 41-year-old Brazilian ranch worker, was described by his employer. He was to meet a tragic end, apparently as a result of an encounter with a UFO in which, gripped by fear, he resorted to violence, and was repaid in kind.

On 13 August 1967, at about 4 p.m., de Souza and his wife Luiza, the parents of five children, were returning to the ranch after a shopping trip on foot to the nearest village. The ranch was near Pilar de Goiás, some 150 miles (240 kilometres) from Brasilia, the country's capital. The couple had almost reached the first building on the ranch when they saw three 'people' apparently playing on the landing strip. (The ranch owner, a well-known and extremely wealthy man, possessed several aircraft.) De Souza thought the trespassers were naked, but his

wife said they were wearing skin-tight yellow clothes. At the same time the intruders seemed to see the couple, and started to approach them.

It was then that de Souza spotted a strange aircraft at the end of the runway. It was either on or just above the ground, and looked like an upturned wash basin. The ranch hand suddenly became very frightened, unslung his .44 carbine, took aim and fired a shot at the nearest figure.

Almost immediately a beam of green light was emitted by the strange craft. It hit de Souza on the head and shoulder, and he fell to the ground. As his wife ran to his assistance she saw the three 'persons' enter the craft, which thereupon took off vertically at high speed, and with a noise like the humming of bees.

During the following few days, de Souza complained of numbness and tingling of the body, of headaches, and of severe nausea. On the third day he developed continuous tremors of the hands and head. The rancher was informed of the incident on that day, and he flew his sick employee to Goiânia, more than 180 miles (300 kilometres) away, where he was examined by a doctor.

'Burns' were discovered on his head and trunk, in the shape of perfect circles 6 inches (15 centimetres) across. The doctor thought they could be a rash produced by a poisonous plant. When he laboured this theory the rancher told him de Souza's story of the encounter with the UFO and its occupants. The surprised doctor proposed some tests of de Souza's faeces, urine and blood, prescribed an unguent for the 'burns' and expressed his opinion that de Souza had suffered an hallucination and that he had already contracted some disease. He made no

secret of the fact that he had no time for flying saucer stories, that he did not believe de Souza and that the whole affair should be hushed up.

The sick man and his employer stayed on in Goiânia for five days while investigation and treatment continued. When de Souza was discharged the illness had been diagnosed as leukaemia. The prognosis was poor: he was expected to live no more than 60 days. And he did indeed waste away quickly, covered with white and yellowish-white blotches. He died on 11 October 1967.

Did alien action kill the ranch worker?

The doctor in Goiânia might have wished to suppress de Souza's story because he feared the panic that such a disturbing tale could cause. This could have been the motive behind his 'hallucination' theory, which will not bear much examination. If de Souza did have an hallucination, then his wife shared it – unless she dutifully lied about her experience out of loyalty to him. And if there was a joint hallucination, then there must have been some agency responsible for causing it – an agency whose nature is as mysterious as the strange 'aircraft' and 'people' that the couple thought they saw.

'It's blinded me!'

Close encounter of the second kind: Itatiánia, Rio de Janeiro, Brazil, 30 August 1970

Brazil seems to have had more than its share of UFO incidents in which witnesses have suffered injury or even death. Only a few years after Inácio de Souza's disastrous experience, another Brazilian came to harm in a brief and terrifying encounter with a mysterious object. The victim on this occasion was Almiro Martins de Freitas, a security watchman who was on duty at the time.

The incident occurred at 9.30 p.m. on 30 August 1970. De Freitas, a married man with three children, was working for the Special Internal Security Patrol Service on the Funil Dam at Itatiánia, in the state of Rio de Janeiro. On this evening he was out on patrol, inspecting the area for which he was responsible. Heavy rain had just fallen and the ground was wet. He had almost come to the end of his beat when he saw a hump-shaped mass on a mound, displaying a row of multicoloured lights. Orange, red and blue were among the colours of the light that the object was emitting.

De Freitas felt uneasy but he overcame his first instinctive urge to retreat as fast as possible. He began to move cautiously towards the object. Even when he had come to a distance of about 50 feet (15 metres) from the object, its shape was still unclear to him in the darkness.

At this point an intense noise assailed his ears. It was like the sound of a jet engine, and it deafened him. Startled, he drew his revolver and started firing towards the lights. After his second shot there was a dazzling flash from the object, seemingly aimed at the security guard. De Freitas was blinded. He fired a third shot wildly, and then a wave of heat engulfed him. He found that he was immobilised.

Shortly afterwards another watchman and a passing motorist arrived at the spot. They found a surreal scene. De Freitas was standing stiffly by a mound of earth, brandishing his revolver and shouting warnings to them: 'Don't look! Beware the flash! It's blinded me!' The two newcomers contrived to carry the stricken man to the car. After a while he began to recover his ability to move, but he did not recover his sight.

A significant fact supporting de Freitas's account was noticed at the scene of the incident. At the place where he had seen the multicoloured lights there was a circular area of dry ground, despite the downpour that had soaked the ground elsewhere.

From Itatiánia the security guard was taken to a hospital in the city of Guanabara, where psychiatrists and ophthalmologists subjected him to psychological and physical examination. These tests showed that, physiologically, the patient was perfectly normal. His blindness, the investigators decided, had been brought about by shock. De Freitas became noticeably disturbed whenever he talked about the experience.

On 3 September the incident found its way into a number of Brazilian newspapers. At the time of these reports, although a full three days had elapsed, de Freitas had still not recovered his vision.

From this point the investigations were taken over by the government's security authorities, with a major role being played by the department assigned to study UFOs. Civilian UFO researchers who attempted to find out more about the case found that the official investigation was being handled with an air of secrecy. Evidently the Brazilian government took seriously this latest incident in the string of violent events involving UFOs intruding into its national territory.

Sick with fear

ONE OF THE MORE CURIOUS aspects of the UFO phenomenon is the way in which certain individuals are sometimes singled out for more than one visitation. A notorious example is the astronomer George Adamski; another, more credible, is the experience of Maureen Puddy of Victoria, Australia, who had two close encounters in three weeks in July 1952. Our first story concerns another such 'repeater', who experienced UFO sightings and related phenomena for nearly 20 years, culminating in a terrifying encounter on a lonely road in southern France.

Our second story is a close encounter of the second kind – with a difference. In addition to the interference with electrical equipment that has come to be regarded as normal in UFO sightings, there were some more unusual side effects: after the sighting, the witness noticed that the front of her car, which had been dirty, was as clean as if it had just been washed, and her hair, which had recently been treated with a permanent wave, went completely straight!

'Blinded by the fierce light'

Close encounter of the second kind: Noé, Haut-Garonne, France, 29 August 1975

It was 10.45 p.m. on 29 August 1975 and Monsieur R. Cyrus – a former gendarme turned businessman, aged 48 – was driving along departmental route D10 from Longages to a point south of Noé where the road joins Route Nationale 125. It is a country district, deep in the Haut-Garonne department of south-western France. The sky was clear, the weather was mild, and a light south-east wind was blowing. Under a bright Moon, he had travelled about three-quarters of the way along the road when he observed, in a field to the right of the road, an aluminium-coloured machine. When, a second or two later, the car was almost level with this object, the underpart became illuminated with a phosphorescent glow, and it floated in the air, at bonnet height, towards the front of the car.

M. Cyrus rammed on the brakes just as the object tilted back to present its underside to the driver. At that moment the luminosity increased enormously and, blinded by the fierce light, M. Cyrus threw up his arms to protect his head and eyes. His car swerved off the road and ended up in a shallow ditch. Even as that happened the UFO shot straight up and hovered, a bright point of light in the sky, directly above the car. All this took place in the space of five seconds or so, and there was no sound whatever from the UFO.

M. Cyrus sat motionless, getting out of his car only when, about a minute later, a passing motorist stopped nearby and came over to open the door for him. 'I thought your car was exploding,' he said.

The former gendarme stood shocked and unsteady, touching himself 'to see if he were still alive'. Then he muttered: 'Good heavens – is this it?'

Meanwhile the light of the UFO, high above, was fluctuating in intensity, and had taken on a reddish tinge. M. Cyrus stood where he was, watching the phenomenon for some 15 minutes. A compact beam shone down from the object, illuminating the car but

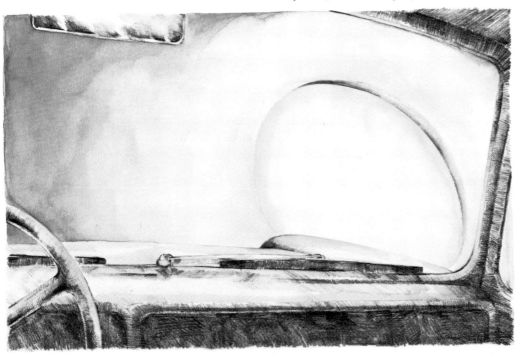

not the surrounding area.

By now a number of people had arrived on the scene, and the consensus of opinion was that M. Cyrus should report the matter immediately to the gendarmerie, but he declared – something that puzzled him later – 'You all know me; I'll go to the gendarmerie tomorrow. Now I'm off home!' His wife said that when he arrived home he was distraught.

When questioned later the witness said he could not recall having been 'paralysed' by the UFO's presence, but he did remember that his throat was all 'jammed up', and he was unable to utter a sound until the other motorist opened the door. There were other physiological effects: after the encounter, the witness experienced bouts of sleepiness, even when driving; whenever he stopped doing anything he found himself falling asleep. His eyesight, too, was briefly affected: when awakening on the two mornings following his experience, he had black spots before the eyes, but these gradually faded.

Surprisingly, there were no signs of burns

or scratches, or changes of colour on the car after the event. There was another unusual feature about the sighting: the engine did not stall during the event, and the lights continued to work normally throughout.

Attempts were made by investigators to locate landing marks or other traces of the UFO, but nothing was found. Aerial photographs also failed to reveal anything.

It was unfortunate that, although the motorist who approached M. Cyrus after the sighting presumably made a report to the gendarmes, and spoke to the investigators, he declined to make a statement, and refused to allow his name to be mentioned. There were two other independent but vague reports of lights in the sky, and of one in a field some distance from the road.

During the course of their investigation for the French UFO organisation *Lumières dans la nuit*, the researchers – a M. Cattiau and his colleagues – greatly assisted by the good-natured collaboration of M. Cyrus, unearthed the remarkable fact that M. Cyrus appeared to be one of the group of witnesses known as 'repeaters': he had had at least three earlier UFO experiences.

In 1957 he was at a vineyard at Quillan in Aude during the grape harvest, when he saw, at about 8.30 one evening, two orange-coloured, cigar-shaped objects some 200 yards (180 metres) away. They were hovering over rows of vines while a cart passed below, its driver apparently oblivious to what was happening. M. Cyrus called other vineyard workers from their dinner who, when they saw the intruders, began to run towards them, whereupon the objects departed silently.

Again, near midnight one day in the autumn of 1974, M. Cyrus was driving with his wife from Noé to Muret when they saw a strange object to their left looking like flashes of light. These were suddenly succeeded by a huge orange sphere that illuminated the countryside, and kept pace with their car for about 5 miles (8 kilometres). When they arrived at the village of Ox they were able to compare the size of the sphere with that of the church, and the sphere appeared enormous. Then, as they passed, a nearby transformer appeared to explode; it was confirmed next day that the circuit breaker had tripped during the night for some unknown reason.

Twice in 1975, a few weeks before the encounter of 29 August, M. Cyrus stated that he had heard guttural voices speaking in an unidentifiable language on his car radio – each time when he had the radio switched off! While this is not strictly within the UFO realm, one is forced to wonder whether or not M. Cyrus is a deep-trance subject, or perhaps possesses a degree of clairvoyance – in which case something could well have been 'beamed in' on him, setting him up for the big encounter of 29 August. It would answer many a question if we knew *why*.

'Glowing orange and silver'

Close encounter of the second kind: Launceston, Tasmania, Australia, 22 September 1974

Late on the afternoon of 22 September 1974 a woman who wishes to be known only as Mrs W. arrived at the junction of the Diddleum and Tayene Plains roads, around 30 miles (50 kilometres) north-east of Launceston, Tasmania, Australia. It was raining, and the mountains were shrouded in mist, as she parked her car around 200 yards (180 metres) from the junction and waited for the arrival of the relative she was due to pick up. Because there was a steep bank to the left of the road, she parked her car on the other side to ensure that any of the heavy log trucks that frequently used the narrow road would see the vehicle clearly.

Over the car radio, she heard that the time was 5.20 p.m. Suddenly the radio developed a high-pitched whine and the whole landscape lit up, the bright light flooding the inside of the car. She leaned over to switch off the radio – and, looking up through the windscreen, saw a glowing orange and silver object moving between two trees and coming downhill towards her. It was about the size of a large car, moving slowly 50 to 60 feet (15 to 18 metres) above the ground, and dropping steadily towards the road.

Not surprisingly, Mrs W. panicked. She started the car and began to reverse up the road, away from the UFO. The object went on approaching until it was at the level of the fence at the side of the road, and hovered

over the middle of the road about 30 to 35 yards (25 to 30 metres) from Mrs W.'s car. It was domed on top, although it was difficult to make out its shape because of the intense orange-yellow light it emitted; Mrs W. could not estimate its size. Beneath the dome, the UFO was silver-grey in colour. There was a wide band on which there could have been portholes, and six to eight horizontal bands below it, decreasing in diameter; their width was about 5 feet (1.5 metres) in all. At the bottom of the object was a small revolving disc, and below this what appeared to be a box or tube, which protruded from the base a short way.

After reversing about 100 yards (90 metres), Mrs W. accidentally backed the car over the edge of the road, and the wheels stuck fast. The UFO now stopped in front of the witness. It then dipped to the right and moved away to the south-west over a valley beside the road. It then rose vertically upwards, fairly fast, and was lost from Mrs W.'s field of vision. The entire sighting had lasted 3 to 4 minutes.

Mrs W. jumped out of her car and ran all the way to her house, which was about a mile (1.6 kilometres) away. She had the feeling that she was being watched, and kept looking up to see if the UFO was following her; she did not, however, see anything. When she arrived home, her husband and son went out to inspect the car. They could see nothing unusual.

The next day, however, when the car was towed home, it was noticed that the front of the car was exceptionally clean, although the rest of it was as dirty as it had been before the encounter. Previously, there had been cat footprints all over the bonnet – and yet this part of the car was as clean as if it had been given a good polish. Neither Mrs W. nor her husband believed that the rain of the previous day could have cleaned the front of the car while leaving the back dirty.

For some days after her terrifying experience, Mrs W. was ill with nervous tension – a kind of state of shock. Her hair, which had been newly treated with a permanent wave, turned straight after her encounter.

Mr and Mrs W. claimed that the car radio was in perfect working order before the UFO sighting; afterwards, it was reported that it suffered from distortion. This, of course, is a common phenomenon in close encounters with UFOs.

Mrs W. initially reported the sighting to the Royal Australian Air Force (RAAF), who could not supply any explanation – they ruled out such things as weather balloons, aircraft, helicopters and meteorological phenomena. The case was investigated by the northern representative of the Tasmanian UFO Investigation Centre, and subsequently reported to *Flying Saucer Review* by W.K. Roberts.

A UFO comes to town

PHOTOGRAPHS OUGHT TO BE good evidence of a UFO sighting, but they are not always so. Sometimes, for example, a UFO can appear on a picture when the photographer did not actually see one. Sometimes, too, the object appears different on the photograph from the way that the observer remembers seeing it.

So the evidence from even genuine pictures is often ambiguous.

In this case, the photographer remembered the UFO as different from the picture. And, after all, if the UFO was in such a highly populated area as south London, why was there only one witness?

'Strange shadow effects'

Close encounter of the first kind: Streatham, London, 15 December 1966

Sightings of true UFOs over London are a rarity. Many reports are made, but these often prove to be misidentifications of lights in the sky. This is hardly surprising considering the great volume of aircraft flying over the city on the way in or out of Heathrow airport. There are also many other aircraft flying over at great height and, at night, satellites that reflect the rays of a Sun already well below the western horizon. Few who report sightings in fact fulfil the condition of having seen a UFO at close range – near enough to be classified as a close encounter of the first kind.

One sighting towards the end of 1966, however, may have fulfilled this condition – and the report was reinforced by photographs. These photographs seem to show remarkable changes in the shape of the images, and the changes cannot be due entirely to changes of aspect of the photographed object.

The day of the sighting was Thursday, 15 December 1966. It was one of the shortest days of the year: the Sun set at 3.53 p.m. The weather was unpleasant – misty, dull and damp, with drizzle, rain and low cloud – and maximum visibility was 2 miles (3 kilometres).

At approximately 2.30 that afternoon, Anthony Russell was standing by the open window of his flat in Lewin Road, Streatham, south-west London. Lewin Road is at the southern end of Streatham High Road and just west of Streatham Common. The window by which Russell stood faces approximately north-north-west. A keen photographer, he was testing for resolution two new 2 × converters for his Zenith 3N single lens reflex camera (focal length 135 millimetres increased to 270 millimetres by one converter). During the testing, Russell was aiming the camera at the gable of a house on the far side of Lewin Road, about 28 yards (26 metres) from the lens. The camera was loaded with 35-millimetre Gratispool colour film.

Suddenly Russell became aware of an

This is the first photograph taken by Anthony Russell of a UFO that he sighted from his flat window. There is a hint of an efflux from the base of the object on the right. The bar seen on the gable of the house across the road supports a chimney that is off camera

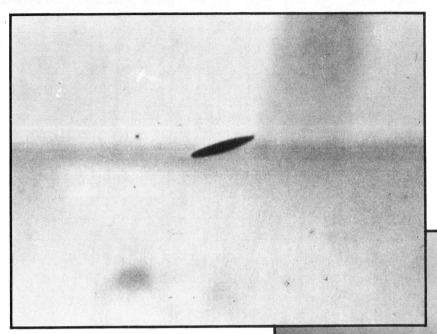

well. A fourth – the last to be taken – revealed a dim shape that had little definition. Russell was puzzled by the object's apparent changes of shape because he did not recall seeing such changes. He recalled seeing only changes of aspect of the UFO.

It is reasonable to assume that the eight blank frames were due to the speedy rolling on of the film between shots in the witness's excitement, occasioned by an incident that lasted two minutes at most. Here is a reconstruction of those two minutes:

After the initial swift descent and abrupt halt of the UFO, Russell took his first two shots. He used the single converter that he

object in the sky falling suddenly, stopping dead, and then drifting slowly earthwards with a pendulum-like motion. Amazed at first, but rapidly collecting his wits about him, he 'slapped the camera to infinity' and began snapping. He thought he got 12 photographs. The last two shots were taken as the object moved away, at first slowly and then at much greater speed.

The witness had had limited contact with UFO literature before in as much as his father had designed a cover for the book *Flying saucers have landed* (1953) by George Adamski and Desmond Leslie. Russell did not think much of the book and, after meeting Adamski, thought even less of the subject. But his scepticism received a jolt as he stood photographing the strange object in the sky.

Russell left the rest of the film in the camera so that he could take photographs at Christmas and sent it away for processing after the holiday period. In the meantime he told a few friends what had happened. They were inclined to laugh off the incident, but he felt it was worth investigating. He did not wish for the publicity a newspaper might have brought him, but he was not sure who would be genuinely interested. Fearing he would get short shrift from established bodies such as the Royal Astronomical Society or the Royal Aeronautical Society, he looked through the telephone directory under the word 'flying' and so happened on *Flying Saucer Review*. He wrote to the magazine, explaining what he expected to be found on his pictures when the film was returned, and the magazine arranged for R.H.B. Winder, an engineer, and Gordon Creighton to help in an investigation once the pictures were available for study.

From the start of the investigation there was a measure of disappointment for the witness, for only 3 of the 12 frames came out

Top: the second photograph shows the UFO edge-on, which emphasises its disc shape. The expert who examined the photographs for fraud could not explain the strange shadow effects on this shot

Above: the third photograph caught the UFO in a slanted position, perhaps in the ascent since it was taken just before the object sped away. When enlarged, the picture revealed a marked efflux to the left

had been testing, set at 1/125 second (f/5.6). He then hurried away from the window and fitted the second (Panagar) converter. With a focal length now of 540 millimetres, he set the exposure at 1/25 second (f/11). Returning to the window, he saw the object 'stand on end' and present its full circular shape to him before turning through 90° about a vertical axis until it was edge on. The UFO then started to move to his right. During all that period, Russell shot only two successful snaps, though he could not have known this at the time. It was during the moment of movement to the right that the third good picture was captured. Then the fourth followed as the UFO accelerated away. By the time Russell reset the camera for the next shot, the object had gone.

After investigation, the researchers handed the transparencies to *Flying Saucer Review*'s photographic consultant, Percy Hennell. After examining them he made plate negatives from the first three. He stated that they were 'genuine photographs of an object in the air, and, in the case of the first, some distance beyond the house opposite the position where the photographer stood'. He could detect no signs of the transparencies

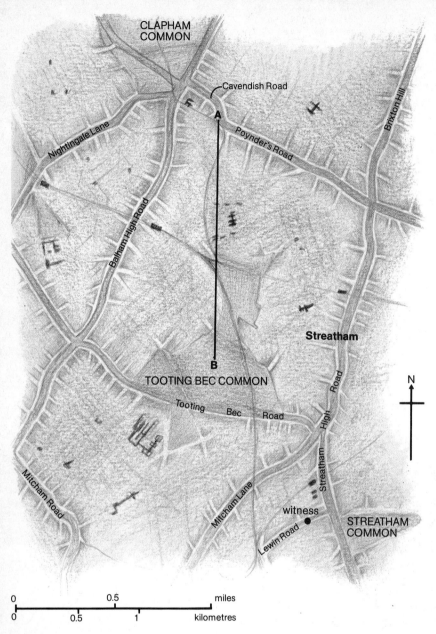

seen when the image had been enlarged and viewed on a projector.

Winder pointed out that the silhouetted image of the UFO on the first photograph bore a remarkable similarity to the shape drawn by Police Constable Colin Perks after his sighting of a UFO at Wilmslow, Cheshire, on 7 January 1966, at 4.10 a.m. Constable Perks was checking the back door of a shop when he heard a high-pitched whine. He turned and looked over the car park behind the shops, which was east. There he saw a solid-looking object – stationary – some 35 feet (10 metres) above the grass of the meadow beyond the car park. It was about 100 yards (90 metres) from him. Perks said the UFO's upper surfaces glowed steadily with a greenish-grey colour, a glow that did not hide the definite shape of the object. He said the lines in his sketch 'represented rounded, but fairly sharp changes in the profile, matched by shading in the glow'. Nowhere could he see openings like portholes or doors. His estimate of a diameter of 30 feet (9 metres) for the base was based on a mental comparison with a 30-foot (9-metre) long bus. After about five seconds the object moved off east-south-east with no change of sound. Then it disappeared.

Russell's other photographs brought no further comparisons to mind. In the second picture there are strange shadow effects, particularly one that slants away in the '7 o'clock' position. Hennell could offer no explanation for this.

The third photograph seems to have been blurred either by the motion of the object – it was beginning to move away – or by camera shake. An efflux effect is also noticeable to the left of the object. This in fact was quite pronounced when the picture was enlarged.

Judging from Russell's position and the 2-mile (3-kilometre) visibility limit, the object appears to have been somewhere on a line from the sighting point via Tooting Bec

having been tampered with. Later the transparencies were projected onto a 12-foot (3.5-metre) square screen. Close inspection revealed nothing untoward.

The investigators ascertained that the object was not luminous, and that it was virtually impossible for the witness to distinguish any colour owing to the fact that it was being viewed as a dark object against a light background. Russell merely suggested it might have been maroon.

The first photograph shows the gable of the house opposite Russell's flat with a near-horizontal bar to the right that acts as a support for a chimney that is off camera. Winder estimated that the bar would have been at an angle of elevation of 10° from the lens of the camera. Russell thought the object might have been anything up to a mile (1.6 kilometres) away. In the photograph there is a hint of an efflux streaming to the right from the base of the UFO – a feature more clearly

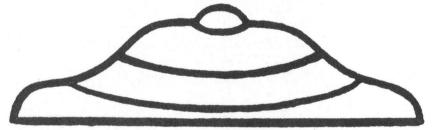

Top: map of the area in which Russell spotted the UFO over Streatham. The object appears to have been somewhere along line A–B

Above: a drawing made by PC Colin Perks of the UFO he saw in Cheshire about a year before Russell's sighting. The two reports were strikingly similar

Common to Cavendish Road.

A contact at Heathrow airport told the investigators that the object was not observed on the radar screens, but it is possible that it missed the radar sweep by virtue of its plummeting fall in between sweeps.

The Ministry of Defence (Air) was asked about weather balloons on 15 December 1966. The answer was that four were released in south and south-west England earlier than the sighting, but that they would not have migrated to the London area.

PART 4

SURVIVAL OF DEATH

Introduction

'IT'S A FUNNY OLD WORLD,' said the great American comedian W.C. Fields, and added wryly, 'You're lucky to get out of it alive.' But of course the one thing we know for certain about life on this funny old world is that it ends in death – *our* death. And the thought of what, if anything, may greet us on the other side of that final curtain has occupied people's minds since time immemorial. Even Neanderthal man seems to have had some idea of an afterlife, and every major religion contains a belief in some kind of existence after death.

Today, perhaps more people than ever are intrigued by the question of whether we survive death in some form or other, if only because relatively few people have the comfort and certainty of religious belief to sustain them. In such a climate of doubt, it is not surprising that people have begun to look for something more like scientific evidence concerning survival – one way or other – than faith alone can provide. It is a curious fact that as religious belief began to decline in the West, so interest in psychical research began to grow. And one of the most persistent claims of psychics and mediums has been that they have been able to make contact with the souls of those who have 'passed over to the other side'. So far, the nearest we can get to a scientific approach to the question remains dependent on the evidence provided by psychics.

On the surface, it would appear perfectly logical that psychic activity should be the royal road to contact with the afterlife. For psychic activity confounds the idea that the world is limited to its physical dimensions – and suggests that even these may be far stranger than we can imagine, leaping as it does outside the normal constraints of time and space. And if we survive death, we must do so in some form that is similarly separate from our limited human bodies – for they most surely do not survive. The soul, however, is not completely divorced from the physical plane, since it is both expressed and perceived by physical means – through the medium of the body. In the same way, psychic events seem to exist on another level from physical ones, but it goes without saying that they are connected with the physical world, since we, as physical selves, can become aware of them and also because they contain *information* about the physical world (in the form of telepathy, precognition and so on) just as frequently as they purport to tell us about the life hereafter. Given these parallels between the idea of the soul and the nature of psychic events, it ought to follow that the one is an aspect of the other – or that it is something like the soul that controls or conducts psychic activity. So if the soul exists beyond the veil of death, it seems likely that we could get or stay in touch with it by psychic means.

The only question that remains is whether the evidence for survival (while undoubtedly acquired by means we understand only very imperfectly) really *is* that, or if it could be no more than a manifestation of humanity's most profound hope. This book brings together some major pieces of that evidence and tries to assess it objectively.

Certainly one of the major problems concerning the validity of the evidence is what might be termed the 'noise to signal' ratio – that is, the amount of false or misleading information that gets into communications purporting to come from the dead, as opposed to what appears to be the genuine article. But there is no reason to suppose that communication from the 'other side' is easy. The most complete statement on that subject came from the shade of Professor Frederic Myers who, frustrated at the difficulty of making himself understood, complained: 'The nearest simile I can find to express the difficulty of sending a message – is that I appear to be standing behind a sheet of frosted glass which blurs sight and deadens sound – dictating feebly to a reluctant and somewhat obtuse secretary.' This may explain another facet of communications across the great divide between living and dead: the extraordinary triviality of many of the messages. Perhaps least satisfactory – though as yet there is still no conventional explanation for them – in this respect are the 'voices' appearing on recording tape that seem to be uttered by dead people.

On the other hand, a general pattern of what happens to the soul, personality or identity after death does emerge from the mass of information that has come through to us with the help of mediums. And an extraordinary picture it is, a far cry from the traditional Christian view of birth, life, death and consequent punishment or reward in the hereafter. Instead, the nature of the hereafter is initially dependent on the *character* rather than the actions of the individual, since the 'world' he inhabits immediately after death seems to be one that he is given the opportunity to create. This can be the same in effect as heaven or hell, since the indications are that a mean-spirited person will be able to create only dreary, miserable surroundings on this 'ideo-plastic' plane (meaning created through ideas alone), while someone of a sunny and generous disposition will create a landscape appropriately happy and harmonious. The purpose of this is not merely to reward or punish, however: it is to teach.

For example, consider the case of the grossly materialistic character, whose earthly life has been spent in the pursuit of riches, Rolls-Royces and riotous living, but who has done no especial good or evil, and who has generally acted with good intentions. He will almost certainly populate his ideo-plastic plane with only the ease, luxury and sensual pleasures he sought before. While this may seem like some people's idea of paradise, its essentially self-serving nature will in time dawn on this individual, causing him to seek the spiritual dimension he so clearly lacks. Something similar will occur with the person of more obviously anti-social tendencies, so that in due course the whole purpose of existence will be

PART 4
SURVIVAL OF DEATH

made apparent. This is revealed in several stages in the afterlife, and part of the process of achieving spiritual perfection involves another spell – or perhaps many spells – in an earthly life (re-incarnation).

The ideo-plastic plane can thus be seen as something nearer a purgatory experience – though of a rather different kind from the Roman Catholic Christian notion of purgatory – than a simple, and single, judgement on an earthly life. And the other major difference from Christian teaching is that life is not itself the only chance for the soul to prove its worth. Any morality that stems from this view of existence – on either side of death – must of course be a much more complex matter than our traditional morality (which is complex enough).

It has to be objected, however, that this picture of the afterlife is remarkably optimistic, despite its complexity and subtlety. And it has to be said that there are few human beings who are prepared either to contemplate an eternity of hellfire with equanimity or to live comfortably with the proposition that life is ultimately meaningless, a kind of biological accident occurring in a cosmic and moral void. And it has to be pointed out that the fascination with the nature of the afterlife – and the concurrent desire to prove the existence of life after death – have both taken root and flourished only since the decline of organised religion in the West. In other words, if there *is* no purpose to life, we have found it necessary to *invent* a purpose, and our inventions match the times in which we live. The 'evidence' presented by paranormal means for survival of death may be, in short, no more than a rationalisation of our need to inject meaning into our lives.

This makes some of the evidence peculiarly interesting, especially that which offers to demonstrate the reality of re-incarnation. While this has been accepted doctrine in numerous Eastern religions, it has never gone down well with Christians, presumably because it can be used to escape from a sense of responsibility for one's acts. But the technique of hypnosis has produced some apparently remarkable results in probing people's minds for unconscious memories of past lives, and has probably done more than anything else in the last few decades to raise the possibility of reincarnation in the West.

More than this, the technique – known as regressive hypnosis – has also proved valuable as a form of psychotherapy. For example, a girl who had an irrational and apparently causeless fear of water was discovered under hypnosis to have had her previous life ended by drowning. Once this was pointed out to her, the fear of water disappeared. These cases are surely a strong indication of the truth of the belief in reincarnation. Unfortunately this

isn't the case: the girl may have expunged her fear by finding a focus for it, however spurious, and so divorcing herself from it; once that was done, it lost its potency.

The human mind is, after all, the most creative instrument on Earth, and those of us who remember our dreams know that we *all* have the capacity to create epic stories and great dramas that our waking selves would – so to speak – never dream of. Hypnosis seems to be able to break down the barriers between our rational, conscious side and the intuitive side that surfaces in such activities as dreaming and creating works of art. And it is possible that another little-understood capacity of the individual mind – the ability to fragment into multiple personalities – may have a bearing on what occurs under regressive hypnosis. Are we, far from reliving former lives, exploring alternative but deeply suppressed personalities of our own, only dressing them up in a historical setting (perhaps to keep them from taking over in the here and now)? This would certainly explain why some of the lives described by hypnotic subjects are not simply escapist fantasies, or delusions of grandeur, but include tedious and uneventful memories as well. On the other hand, this very feature of the evidence would argue for the reality of reincarnation too. In any event, we are left with much that is bewildering and inexplicable about the human mind.

The very best evidence for the survival of the human personality after death is probably provided by the documents that have become known as the 'cross-correspondences' held by the Society for Psychical Research (SPR) in London. These involved a number of the founder members of the SPR both before and after their deaths; the peculiar feature of the communications is the tendency to pose riddles or make puns (in Classical languages as often as not) that amount to a code – one that can be broken only by reference to communications by other members of the group to different mediums. This elaborate – and deliberate – attempt to establish the reality of survival has been sadly neglected by popular writers on the subject, and receives a long-deserved summary here.

This introduction has touched only briefly on the questions that lie beyond our natural human desire to remain, in some sense, alive and sentient. What are we to make of other evidence, such as that from those remarkable people who appear to be in touch with the spirits of dead artists – and are reproducing paintings, poetry and pieces of music by some of the greatest names in those fields? How should we view the bizarre history of the Fox sisters, who founded Spiritualism? We can only invite you to read these pieces of evidence for yourself, as part of a debate that must intrigue us all until our dying day.

PETER BROOKESMITH

Death of a dream

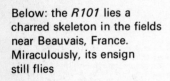

The world was stunned when the vaunted *R101* airship crashed in flames in 1930. And the sequel was no less startling: the ship's dead captain had made contact with a famous medium. EDWARD HORTON sets the scene

Below: the *R101* lies a charred skeleton in the fields near Beauvais, France. Miraculously, its ensign still flies

Right: within two days of the disaster, medium Eileen Garrett was 'speaking' to the *R101*'s dead captain

EUGENE RABOUILLE, a 57-year-old poacher, was distracted from his task of setting rabbit snares by the sound of engines overhead. He looked up into the rain-soaked night and saw a confused image of bright lights and an enormous shape illuminated by those lights. It was very low in the sky, moving slowly and falling steadily – and it was heading his way. On it came, the drone of the engines getting louder as it approached, and as Rabouille stood rooted to the spot the gigantic object suddenly pitched forward, corrected itself, and then slid almost gently into the side of a small hill about 100 yards (90 metres) from where he stood. The next moment he found himself stretched out on the ground, stunned by shock waves, deafened by noise, blinded by light.

A wall of flames shot hundreds of feet into the air, and as Rabouille picked himself up he could hear through the fire's roar terrible screams, and see in the middle of the inferno human figures rushing about, alive yet for a moment or two, but irretrievably lost. Rabouille put his hands to his eyes to shield them from the heat, and from the searing vision. Then he turned and fled. It was just after 2 a.m. on 5 October 1930.

What Rabouille had witnessed were the final moments of the British airship *R101*, and of the 48 passengers and crew who perished that rainy night near the town of Beauvais, in northern France. He had also seen the event that would crush instantly and irrevocably British faith in the whole idea of rigid airships, would spark off bitter and

lasting recriminations – and would provide the backdrop to one of the most curious episodes in the annals of psychic phenomena.

For within two days of the *R101*'s sickening destruction, no less a medium than Mrs Eileen Garrett was apparently in touch with the skipper of the enormous craft, Flight-Lieutenant H. Carmichael Irwin. Not only that, but it turned out that another airman had foretold the end of the *R101* – also from beyond the grave. And three weeks after the calamity Mrs Garrett was in contact again, this time in front of different witnesses, with the airship's dead captain.

Public fascination with these revelations was intense – naturally, as no one knew what had happened during the last few hours on board. The evidence produced by Mrs Garrett was therefore crucial not only for those who may have wanted to add ammunition to their case for survival after death, but to a question of immediate practical import. To gauge how the psychic evidence adds to both debates it is first necessary to review, in detail, the sad tale of the *R101*'s development.

In 1924 the British government had decided that the interests of a worldwide empire could be well served by the construction of a fleet of large passenger airships. Now the traditional way of going about such an enterprise would have been simply to place an order for a prototype with some suitable private firm. However, this was Britain's first Labour government, and there was strong pressure from within its ranks to give a practical demonstration of the merits of state enterprise. In the best spirit of British compromise (or fudging) the decision was reached that two airships should be built simultaneously, one by the Air Ministry

Top: the *R100* at rest after her successful flight to Montreal in July 1930

Above: Barnes Wallis, whose genius contributed so much to the success of the *R100*

Left: the *R101*, the largest airship built at that time, basks in floodlights at her mooring at Cardington. The hangar that housed her there was the biggest building in the British Empire

itself and the other by a Vickers subsidiary, the Airship Guarantee Company.

The specifications and standards of performance laid down for the two airships were more or less identical, and they were impressive – far in advance of any existing airship, more sophisticated even than the future *Graf Zeppelin*. They would be by a huge margin the largest airships the world had seen – kept aloft by 5 million cubic feet (140,000 cubic metres) of hydrogen. This would give them a gross lift of 150 tonnes, and with a stipulated maximum weight of 90 tonnes for the airships themselves (unloaded) they would provide a 'useful' lift of 60 tonnes – again far in advance of anything to date.

What this amounted to was a specification for a pair of airships that could transport 100 fare-paying passengers in considerable luxury to the four corners of the globe, and do so at the respectable cruising speed of 63 miles per hour (100 km/h). Altogether a grand vision, and it was by no means as fanciful as it may look in retrospect.

The Vickers team set up shop in a disused hangar at Howden, Yorkshire, and over the next five years put together an airship of the highest quality, the *R100*. They accomplished their formidable task in relative peace and quiet, away from the glare of publicity and political meddling. Meanwhile, the Air Ministry team resurrected the wartime airship base at Cardington, near Bedford. And there, unlike their rivals, they found themselves as goldfish in a bowl. How great a factor this was in the final débâcle is a matter for speculation, but what finally emerged in a blaze of public anticipation was a majestic flying coffin – the much-vaunted *R101*.

The first in the sorry catalogue of mistakes made at Cardington was probably the worst. Because of the competitive element it was

the conventional petrol type. This should have been weighed against a rather more significant disadvantage of the new diesel engines: they were far too heavy. The Howden team too experimented with diesel, saw quickly that they were too heavy and reverted to proven Rolls-Royce Condor engines. Such pragmatism was out of the question at Cardington. Considerable publicity had been given to the new diesels and they would stay, overweight or not.

The huge gasbags inside the rigid metal frame (16 of them in all) were held in place by an elaborate system of wiring. But the wiring was such that the bags continually rubbed against the girders and rivets of the framework itself. As bad, or worse even, when the airship rolled (a natural enough occurrence) the valves in the gasbags opened slightly, which meant there was an ever-present risk of highly flammable hydrogen wafting around outside the gasbags but still inside the body of the airship.

decided not to pool information with Howden. The design and construction of such advanced airships were bound to throw up problems both theoretical and practical. Original thinking would be at a premium – and there was not a lot of it in the world of British airship design in the 1920s. What the Air Ministry did – deliberately – was to dilute what little there was.

Vickers was in the enviable position of having a truly outstanding designer for the *R100* – Barnes Wallis, who was even then an acknowledged inventive genius and would later become a living legend. During the five years it took to build the two airships Wallis repeatedly suggested collaboration, but his appeals fell on deaf ears. It was almost as though the Cardington men thought they had nothing to learn from others.

Take the engines, for example. Early on it was decided in favour of a newly designed diesel type because it was marginally safer (from the standpoint of accidental fire) than

In a desperate attempt to make the *R101* effective, the enormous structure of the doomed craft is split in two to take in an extra gasbag

From bad to worse
The hurried solutions to these fundamental problems were bizarre – comical even, were it not for the dreadful outcome. There were only two ways of getting more lift: reduce the weight of the airship or increase the volume of hydrogen. The former was difficult to do to any significant degree (without scrapping the diesel engines) but the latter gave scope to fevered imaginations. Why not simply chop the airship in two and stick an extra bay in the middle? And surely there was an easy way of squeezing more hydrogen into the existing gasbags. Simply loosen the wiring to allow them to expand a little more (and chafe a little more as well). And so on. If the gasbags showed an annoying tendency to puncture themselves on bits of the framework, track down the offending projections and stick a pad over them (some 4000 pads were fitted).

The immediate results (like the final result) of this kind of folly were roughly what

Captain Hinchliffe's prediction

Even while the *R101* was stumbling toward completion, there were psychic portents of catastrophe. On 13 March 1928 a dashing war hero, Captain W. R. Hinchliffe, accompanied by heiress Elsie Mackay, took off from Cranwell aerodrome in eastern England in an attempt to fly the Atlantic. They were never seen again.

Then on 31 March, one Mrs Beatrice Earl was startled by a message that came through on her ouija board: HINCHLIFFE TELL MY WIFE I WANT TO SPEAK TO HER.

Through Conan Doyle, Mrs Earl passed the message to the aviator's

widow, Emilie, who in turn agreed to let Eileen Garrett (whom Mrs Earl knew) try to contact her dead husband. (He, incidentally, had once called Spiritualism 'total nonsense'.)

In the sessions that followed Hinchliffe's spirit became deeply concerned about the *R101*: 'I want to say something about the new airship. . . . the vessel will not stand the strain.' He pleaded that his old friend Squadron-Leader Johnston, the *R101*'s navigator, be told. But the men at Cardington were unmoved.

His last message was received as the *R101* headed for France: STORMS RISING. NOTHING BUT A MIRACLE CAN SAVE THEM. But by then, Eileen Garrett had begun to have visions of an airship in flames . . .

one might have expected. The 'new' *R101* was hauled out of the hangar to her mooring mast under perfectly tolerable weather conditions. At once, a gaping hole 140 feet (33 metres) long appeared along the top, where the fabric had merely given way. It was taped up. So was another, smaller tear that appeared the next day.

In defence of the beleaguered men at Cardington it should be said that they were working under intolerable pressure. In July 1930 the unheralded *R100*, having completed her trials successfully, flew to Montreal and back again a fortnight later. It was rumoured that only the more successful of the two airships would serve as a prototype for future development. To the rattled men at Cardington it was now vital that the *R101* demonstrate her superiority quickly. The destination for the maiden flight was India, a longer and more glamorous voyage than the *R100*'s to Montreal, and guaranteed to put Cardington back in the limelight.

Calendar of woe

So we come to the final grim chapter, and to the man who must bear most of the blame for the fiasco that cost his and many other lives: the Air Minister himself, Lord Thomson of Cardington. His devotion to the *R101* project bordered on the fanatical (his choice of title when elevated to the peerage provides a pointer). He combined this passion with unslakable ambition. His sights were set on becoming the next Viceroy of India, and by happy coincidence there was an Imperial Conference in London starting in late October. How better to draw attention to his claim than by descending on the conference fresh from a round trip to the Subcontinent aboard his beloved *R101*?

A September departure was impossible (Thomson accepted this but with ill-disguised resentment). Early October was the latest departure date that would get him to India and back in time to fulfil any of his commitments at the conference. The airship

Above: Lord Thomson of Cardington, whose driving ambition to get the *R101* into the air served only to hasten its end – and his own death

Below: the press immediately latched on to the strange aftermath of the disaster

Bottom: spectators are dwarfed by the burnt-out wreckage of the 777-foot (237-metre) long airship

must be ready by the fourth of the month because 'I have made my plans accordingly.'

Aside from the fact that the airship was unfit for such a voyage (or for a Sunday excursion) there was another hitch. It was essential to have a Certificate of Airworthiness, which could only be issued after the successful completion of exhaustive trials. But a temporary certificate was wangled, with the droll proviso that final speed trials be completed during the journey itself.

At 6.36 p.m. on 4 October the awesomely beautiful silver craft (for she was that) struggled away from her mooring mast. And it was a real struggle. Four tonnes of water (half the ballast) had to be jettisoned in those first moments, just to get airborne. Pitching and rolling, the airship that was in Lord Thomson's immortal words 'as safe as a house, except for the millionth chance' crossed low over the lights of London an hour and a half later, with one of the five engines already out of commission. At 8.21 Cardington received the laconic message: 'Over London. All well. Moderate rain.'

The last message

At 9.35 she reached the Channel at Hastings, still flying low and experiencing worse weather – hard rain and a strong south-westerly wind. Two hours later she crossed the French coast near Dieppe. At midnight Cardington received its final wireless message. After reporting the *R101*'s position as 15 miles (24 kilometres) south of Abbeville the message ended on a cosy note: 'After an excellent supper our distinguished passengers smoked a final cigar, and having sighted the French coast have now gone to bed to rest after the excitement of their leave-taking. All essential services are functioning satisfactorily. The crew have settled down to a watch-keeping routine.'

What seemed to pass unnoticed aboard the airship was her low altitude. It did not go unnoticed by some observers on the ground, one of whom was alarmed to see the gigantic craft flying overhead at an estimated 300 feet (90 metres), less than half her own length. That was about 1 a.m., and he judged her to be moving in the direction of Beauvais.

Morning Post

R101: REMARKABLE SEANCE

ONE PENNY

R101: the dead captain speaks

What exactly had brought the *R101* to its fiery end? The official inquiry could only guess – but it ignored some extraordinary evidence. For the ship's dead captain had 'come through' at an astonishing seance . . .

REPORTS OF THE CALAMITY that had befallen the *R101* began trickling into London and Cardington during the small hours of Sunday morning, 5 October 1930. At first they were guarded: even as late as 5.30 a.m. Reuters in Paris would go no further than say that 'alarm' had been caused by an 'unconfirmed report that the airship has blown up'. But this was quickly followed by the death knell: *R101* HAS EXPLODED IN FLAMES ONLY SIX SAVED.

The parallel with the sinking of the *Titanic* was inescapable – a vessel of heroic proportions, the largest and most advanced thing of its kind, safe 'but for the millionth chance' and yet hideously fated on her very first voyage. Public grief was unrestrained on both sides of the Channel.

But even in the midst of that grief some starkly insistent questions cried out for answers: how had it happened? Whose fault? A special Court of Inquiry was set for 28 October, amid angry rumours that its unspoken function would be to whitewash the Air Ministry in general and the dead Lord Thomson in particular.

As far as getting at the truth about the flight itself, and particularly what happened during those final minutes, there was a peculiar difficulty. Fate had been awkward in its selection of survivors. All the passengers were dead; so were all the officers. The only survivors were six lucky crewmen, none of whom was in the main control car (which was crushed) and none of whom was in a position therefore to know precisely how it was that the mighty *R101* kept her rendezvous with that small hillside outside Beauvais. Put

Above: the *R101* cruises over the outskirts of London during her first test flight on 15 October 1929. Thousands of sightseers had crowded Cardington to see her take to the air

Right: the captain of the *R101*, Flight-Lieutenant H. Carmichael Irwin. Would the testimony of 'his' spirit voice have helped the Court of Inquiry that investigated the tragedy?

together, their recollections of the final moments added little of importance to what Eugene Rabouille had seen from the ground.

The Court of Inquiry, sitting under the distinguished statesman Sir John Simon, delivered its verdict in April 1931. As the immediate cause of the crash the Court settled for a sudden loss of gas in one of the forward gasbags; this, if the airship were dangerously low to begin with (as she undoubtedly was) and taken in conjunction with a sudden downdraught (which was plausible) would certainly spell disaster. It was as good a guess as any.

It may well be, however, that what the Court did *not* consider in evidence was of greater significance than what it *did*. There was considerable testimony that, had it been given credence, shed a much clearer light on the disaster, and, because of its nature, on issues of vastly greater significance. It was testimony of an extraordinary kind from an extraordinary source – the dead captain of the airship.

On the afternoon of the Tuesday following the crash, four oddly assorted characters assembled at the National Laboratory of Psychical Research in West London. Harry Price, who had set up the laboratory a few years earlier, was a singular man: wealthy, mercurial, an amateur magician, a passionate investigator of psychic phenomena. And, what was of great importance in the light of what was to follow, he was a savage foe of Spiritualist hokum, whether of the deliberately fraudulent variety (which as a magician he was perfectly equipped to expose) or of the innocent type (in which genuine paranormal experiences such as telepathy were wrongly ascribed to 'voices from beyond').

One of Price's guests that day was the celebrated medium Eileen Garrett, a woman of unimpeachable integrity, whose paranormal faculties continually astonished her as much as they did those who witnessed them. Despite the fact that in trances she frequently delivered weirdly plausible messages purporting to come from beyond the grave, she refused to classify herself as a Spiritualist. And she backed up her modest mystification about her strange powers with a disarming eagerness to expose them to the most searching examinations that could be devised by the Harry Prices of this world.

The other principal guest was an Australian journalist, Ian Coster, whom Price had persuaded to sit in on what promised to be a potentially fascinating seance. Sir Arthur Conan Doyle had died a few months earlier. He and Price had wrangled for years, Conan Doyle huffy about Price's acerbic views on Spiritualism, Price discerning a credulity verging on dottiness in the celebrated author.

Conan Doyle had vowed to prove his point in the only way possible, and Price had

Above: Harry Price, who arranged the seance at which Flight-Lieutenant Irwin's 'spirit' was first heard

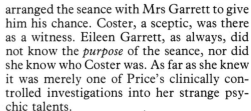

Below: the bodies of those killed in the disaster lie in state in flag-draped coffins, in Westminster Hall, London. Public reaction to the crash was intense: the French provided full military honours before the bodies were brought across the Channel by two Royal Navy destroyers. An estimated half million Londoners watched the funeral procession; world leaders from Hitler to the Pope sent condolences

arranged the seance with Mrs Garrett to give him his chance. Coster, a sceptic, was there as a witness. Eileen Garrett, as always, did not know the *purpose* of the seance, nor did she know who Coster was. As far as she knew it was merely one of Price's clinically controlled investigations into her strange psychic talents.

The three of them, along with a skilled shorthand writer, settled down in the darkened room, and Mrs Garrett quickly slipped into a trance. Soon she began to speak, not in her own voice but that of her regular 'control', one Uvani. He had first manifested himself years before and claimed to be an ancient Oriental whose purpose in establishing himself as a link between Mrs Garrett and departed spirits was to prove the existence of life after death. Sometimes he would relay messages in his own voice (deep, measured cadences, formal); at other times he would stand aside, as it were, and allow the spirit to communicate directly.

The uninvited spirit

Today, after announcing his presence, Uvani gave Price a few snippets of information from a dead German friend (of whom, incidentally, he was certain Eileen Garrett was perfectly ignorant), but nothing that excited him. And no Conan Doyle. Then suddenly Eileen Garrett snapped to attention, extremely agitated, tears rolling down her cheeks. Uvani's voice took on a terrible broken urgency as it spelled out the name IRVING or IRWIN. (Flight-Lieutenant H. Carmichael Irwin had captained the *R101*.) Then Uvani's voice was replaced by another, speaking in the first person and doing so in rapid staccato bursts:

'The whole bulk of the dirigible was entirely and absolutely too much for her engine capacity. Engines too heavy. It was this that made me on five occasions have to scuttle back to safety. Useful lift too small.'

The voice kept rising and falling, hysteria barely controlled, the speed of delivery that of a machine gun. Price and Coster sat riveted as a torrent of technical jargon began to tumble from the lips of Eileen Garrett.

'Gross lift computed badly. Inform control panel. And this idea of new elevators totally mad. Elevator jammed. Oil pipe plugged. This exorbitant scheme of carbon and hydrogen is entirely and absolutely wrong.'

There was more, much more, all delivered fiercely at incredible pace: '. . . never reached cruising altitude. Same in trials. Too short trials. No one knew the ship properly. Airscrews too small. Fuel injection bad and air pump failed. Cooling system bad. Bore capacity bad . . . Five occasions I have had to scuttle back – three times before starting.

'Not satisfied with feed . . . Weather bad for long flight. Fabric all water-logged and ship's nose down. Impossible to rise. Cannot trim . . . Almost scraped the roofs at Achy. At inquiry to be held later it will be found that the superstructure of the envelope contained no resilience . . . The added middle section was entirely wrong . . . too heavy . . . too much overweighted for the capacity of the engines.'

The monologue petered out at last, and Uvani came back to ring down the curtain on this portion of the astonishing seance. (In fact Conan Doyle did 'come through', but that is another story.)

Three weeks later, on the eve of the Inquiry, there began a sequel to this mystifying occurrence that was every bit as strange. Major Oliver Villiers, a much decorated survivor of aerial scraps over the Western Front, was badly shaken by the *R101* catastrophe. He had lost many friends in the crash, in particular Sir Sefton Brancker, Director of Civil Aviation and Villiers's direct superior at the Air Ministry. Indeed he had driven Brancker to the airship on the day of departure.

Villiers was entertaining a house-guest who had an interest in Spiritualism, and late one night, when his guest and the rest of the household had gone to bed, he suddenly had an overwhelming impression that Irwin was in the room with him (the two men knew each other well). Then he heard, mentally, Irwin cry out to him: 'For God's sake let me talk to you. It's all so ghastly. I must speak to you. I must.' The lament was repeated, then: 'We're all bloody murderers. For God's sake

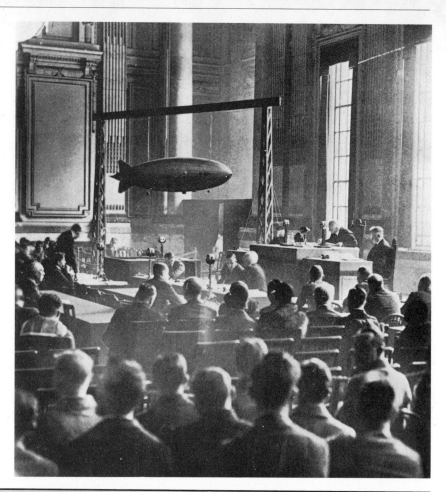

The last few minutes

None of the survivors seemed to know what had caused the *R101* to dive into the ground. One had just dozed off in his bunk when he was jolted awake by the chief coxwain rushing by shouting 'We're down lads! We're down!' Another was relaxing over a drink in the specially sealed-off smoking lounge when he felt the airship dip, dip again – and erupt into flame. Two more, in separate engine cars, were no better informed.

Engine man Joe Binks, however, had glanced out of a window only two minutes before the end, and was terrified to see the spire of Beauvais cathedral, 'almost close enough to touch'. He shouted to engineer Bell, the sixth survivor, when the floor seemed to drop away, then the ship lurched. At the same moment a message was coming through from the main control car: SLOW. Then a few moments' silence. And then the holocaust.

The Air Ministry clamped down on any news of the crash, yet in the first seance two days later 'Irwin' described how he had failed to achieve cruising height: 'Fabric all waterlogged and ship's nose down . . .'

Three survivors stand near the wreck

help me to speak with you.' In the morning Villiers recounted this most disturbing experience to his guest, who promptly arranged a session with Eileen Garrett.

The first of several seances was held on 31 October and it, like its successors, took a significantly different form from the Price-Coster episode. Rather than merely listen to Irwin, Villiers conversed freely with him through Mrs Garrett. Moreover, while in the first seance Irwin came through alone, in later seances he was joined by several of his colleagues and even by Sir Sefton Brancker.

Villiers was not served by shorthand, but he claimed the gift of total recall, which in conjunction with notes hastily scribbled during the 'conversations' convinced him that the transcripts he made were virtually dead accurate. They make absorbing reading, and a short extract from the first one will give their flavour:

Villiers: Now try to tell me all that happened on Saturday and Sunday.
Irwin: She was too heavy by several tons. Too amateurish in construction. Envelope and girders not of sufficiently sound material.
Villiers: Wait a minute, old boy. Let's start at the beginning.
Irwin: Well, during the afternoon before starting, I noticed that the gas indicator was going up and down, which showed there was a leakage or escape which I could not stop or rectify any time around the valves.

Villiers: Try to explain a bit more. I don't quite understand.
Irwin: The goldbeater skins are too porous, and not strong enough. And the constant movement of the gasbags, acting like bellows, is constantly causing internal pressure of the gas, which causes a leakage, of the valves. I told the chief engineer of this. I then knew we were almost doomed. Then later on, the meteorological charts came in, and Scottie and Johnnie (fellow officers) and I had a consultation. Owing to the trouble of the gas, we knew that our only chance was to leave on the scheduled time. The weather forcast was no good. But we decided that we might cross the Channel and tie up at Le Bourget before the bad weather came. We three were absolutely scared stiff. And Scottie said to us – look here, we are in for it – but for God's sake, let's smile like damned Cheshire cats as we go on board, and leave England with a clean pair of heels.

Price and Villiers did not know one another, nor were they aware of each other's seances with Eileen Garrett. They arrived independently at the conclusion that the 'evidence' they had should be placed before Sir John Simon (Price also informed the Air Ministry). Neither the Court of Inquiry nor the Ministry was prepared to accept that these unusual happenings contributed to an understanding of the *R101* tragedy.

What was it that caused medium Eileen Garrett to pour out a flood of information about the crashed *R101*? Did the airship's dead captain really 'come through'? And just how accurate were the technical details that he gave?

THE R101 AFFAIR is a classic of its kind for two reasons. First, the messages purporting to come from Captain Irwin contained information about a matter of widespread general interest, and this information was couched in technical language. Everyone wanted to know what had happened to cause the catastrophe, and many were in a position to have informed opinions. Moreover, the official verdict of the Inquiry was not particularly convincing – composed as it was of a fair bit of speculation wrapped up in careful qualifications (necessarily, since there was not much hard evidence to go on). Someone really well informed about airships in general and the *R101* project in particular just might come to the conclusion that where Irwin's post-mortem account conflicts with the official verdict, 'his' has more the ring of truth. This could not by itself be conclusive, but it would be undeniably strong circumstantial evidence for spiritual survival.

Second, and as important as the contents of the messages, there is little to raise the question of spiritualism's chronic bugbear – the suspicion of deliberate fraud. There can be no field of investigation where the personal integrity of those 'on trial' looms larger, and therefore comes under closer scrutiny. Eileen Garrett went to her grave with an unblemished reputation. Further, the Price-Coster seance was held in circumstances

The credibility of Eileen Garrett (above) is central to the *R101* mystery. She had been in touch with the 'spirit' of the aviator Hinchliffe, who uttered warnings about the airship; had had visions of an airship in flames; and received messages from the 'spirits' of those on board the *R101* – seen here on its initial test flight in October 1929 cruising over St Paul's London

controlled by a world-famous detective of fraudulent mediumship. To arrange a hoax, even had he wanted to, Price would have needed to enlist as fellow-conspirators Mrs Garrett and Major Villiers, a distinguished and honourable man – and indeed several others who add weight to the assertion that there was no trickery involved.

With fraud out of the way, then, the question turns on whether the information purporting to come from the dead Irwin is of such a nature that it could have come *only* from him. Put another way, is there any possible means by which the information that came *out of* Mrs Garrett could have got *into* Mrs Garrett other than by her being in contact, through Uvani, with Irwin's spirit? If not, the case for the survival of the spirit is made – a simple conclusion, but one with profound implications.

Everything hangs on the details of the messages, therefore, and it is to them that we now turn. The case for accepting the voice as being the true Irwin has been presented in considerable detail by John G. Fuller in his book *The airmen who would not die* (1979); it runs as follows.

None of those present knew anything at all about the complexities of airship design or the business of flying one, and therefore it is impossible that such startlingly specific statements as those made by 'Irwin' – at wild

Did the spirits really speak?

speed in what was to those present a language as foreign as it is to the lay reader today – could have been dredged from the conscious or unconscious mind of any of them. That rules out straightforward telepathy.

One of 'Irwin's' statements was not only highly technical, it referred to something that would not be known outside the inner sanctum intimately involved with the airship (the new hydrogen-carbon fuel mix). Another, the reference to Achy ('almost scraped the roofs at Achy'), is just as bewildering. Price tried to find Achy in conventional atlases and maps without success. But when he tracked down a large-scale railway map of the Beauvais area (a map as detailed as the charts Irwin would have had in the control car) he found it; a tiny hamlet on the railway line a few miles north of Beauvais. Where could such a snippet of information have come from, if not from Irwin?

Finally, Price had the transcript examined, clause by clause, by an expert from Cardington (who volunteered for the job). This Will Charlton, and apparently other old Cardington hands, professed themselves astonished at the technical grasp displayed therein, and by the likelihood of Irwin's account in its essentials. Charlton reckoned that *no one* but Irwin could have been the source of this information – information that explained clearly what had happened during the fateful voyage as against the speculative account in the official report.

As far as it goes this sounds pretty convincing. But it begins to fray at the edges somewhat when it is realised that in Charlton, Price had not found an expert at all; rather a convinced Spiritualist whose claim to airship expertise rested on the shaky ground of his having been in charge of stores nd supplies at Cardington. In a review of Fuller's book for *Alpha* magazine in 1980, Archie Jarman, credited by Fuller with knowing more about the subject than any living person, draws attention to some glaring examples of Charlton's ignorance, and they are certainly of such a nature as to discredit him as an expert. For example, during the Price-Coster sitting 'Irwin' made a reference to '*SL8*'. Price had no idea what it meant, and it remained for Charlton to come up with the answer: 'The *SL8* has been verified as the number of a German airship – SL standing for Shuttle Lanz.' To track down this morsel of information Charlton had had to comb through the entire record of German airships.

Experts and amateurs

Now far from being impressive (an expert having to go to considerable lengths to discover the meaning of a reference so obcure that it could emanate only from an even greater expert such as Irwin), it is utterly damning. The *SL* stands for *Schütte Lanz* (*Schütte*, not 'Shuttle' or 'Shutte' as Fuller variously has it), the Zeppelin people's German rival in airship development before the First World War, and one of whose airships was shot down in flames in a celebrated action during an airship raid on England in 1916 (a mere 14 years before). Yet Charlton, the expert, had no idea what *SL8* referred to. It is not good enough, and Fuller makes it worse by driving home the point with a sledge-hammer: 'Charlton and his colleagues of Cardington had been strongly impressed with the reference to *SL8*. No one on the staff of Cardington could confirm this designation and number until they had looked it up in the complete records of German airships.'

Further, when Jarman was compiling a report on the affair in the early 1960s he

Eugene Rabouille, the poacher who saw the *R101* plough into the ground near Beauvais. The official inquiry into the disaster seemed, to many, to add little to his account of the great airship's final moments. The question remains: how much light does the 'spirit evidence' shed on the reasons why the *R101* crashed when she did?

solicited the opinions of two real experts: Wing-Commander Booth, who had captained the *R100* on the Montreal flight; and Wing-Commander Cave-Brown-Cave, who had been intimately involved in the *R101*'s construction.

Booth spoke for both when he replied: 'I have read the description of the Price-Irwin seance with great care and am of the opinion that the messages received do not assist in any way in determining why the airship *R101* crashed. . . .' Cave-Brown-Cave ended with the crushing comment '. . . the observations of Mr Charlton should be totally disregarded.'

Booth's verdict on the Villiers material was even harsher: 'I am in complete disagreement with almost every paragraph . . . the conversations are completely out of character, the atmosphere at Cardington is completely wrong, and the technical and handling explanation could not possibly have been messages from anyone with airship experience.' This latter is surely true. Just to take one example: in the passage quoted previously (see page 15), 'Irwin' complains about the gas indicator going up and down. Booth's trenchant reply was: 'No such instruments were fitted.'

That technical inaccuracy is bad enough but it is mild in comparison to what the officers are said to have had in mind from the moment they set off from Cardington. They supposedly knew the airship was a dud and that they had no chance of reaching their destination. But they thought they might just creep across the Channel and tie up at Le Bourget. There were only four places on Earth with the facilities to cope with such an immense airship, and Le Bourget assuredly was not one of them.

When all was lost

Then after they crossed the Channel, according to 'Irwin' they 'knew all was lost'. So what did they do? Press on into a brutal headwind hoping to make Le Bourget (knowing all was lost), 'and try at all costs some kind of landing'. An emergency landing? Like the one they made outside Beauvais? No sane person would attempt any such thing, especially when there was an obvious alternative.

If the Captain and his close colleagues really *were* terrified about the way things were going, all they had to do was turn around and with the wind at their backs limp home to the safety of Cardington. Sane men do not accept *certain* death (and commit dozens of their fellows to the same fate) rather than admit that they have been defeated by an impossible task.

Returning to the Price-Coster sitting, Mr Jarman's view is that nothing whatever occurred during the seance that cannot be put down to Mrs Garrett's own subconscious and her telepathic powers. Take Achy, for instance, at first sight so inexplicable. Not really, according to Jarman, who knew Mrs Garrett well. Apparently she frequently motored from Calais to Paris. Achy is on that road, vividly signposted. Could not Mrs Garrett have retained the name subconsciously? Since it is more than likely that the *R101* did *not* pass directly over Achy, what else are we to believe?

And while Eileen Garrett certainly knew nothing to speak of about the technicalities of airships, the *R101* was much on her mind even *before* the crash. For she had already had visions of an airship disaster, and had discussed her fears at length with none other than Sir Sefton Brancker 10 days before the accident.

The supposedly secret nature of some of the technical information provided by 'Irwin' can also be explained. The fact is that the design and construction of the *R101* (fuel mix and all) was conducted in about as much secrecy as surrounded the building of Concorde. Anyone who cared to could have amassed immense technical detail about her during those long years of building simply by

reading the newspapers. And of course the papers were full of it during the interval between the crash and the seance (Villiers had even longer to become steeped in the events that had overwhelmed his friends). As for the savage indictments of the airship that form the burden of all the seances, the Cardington follies had been notorious all along, brought to the fore, naturally, by the disaster.

Coster was a journalist, reasons Mr Jarman, and as such would be pretty well up on all this, and if we accept that Eileen Garrett had telepathic gifts we need look no further. That is a perfectly reasonable explanation, if one there be, for what Jarman himself admits is a 'mystery'.

Perhaps the final word should be left to Harry Price. In his letter to Sir John Simon, which is, incidentally, couched in the language of a disinterested research scientist, he states that he does not believe that it was the 'spirit' of Irwin present at the seance. Then he goes on: 'I must also state that I am convinced that the psychic was not consciously cheating. It is likewise improbable that one woman in a thousand would be capable of delivering, as she did, an account of the flight of an airship. . . . Where such information comes from is a problem that has baffled the world for 2000 years.'

Above: Sir Sefton Brancker, who discussed the problems of the *R101* with Eileen Garrett just before the crash

Left: the giant airship is manoeuvred by its ground crew prior to its last flight

Below: the stark, burnt-out remains of the *R101* offered no clues to the precise cause of the disaster

What happens after death?

The one great certainty for everyone is death. Yet how many of us consider – let alone prepare for – this major trauma? DAVID CHRISTIE-MURRAY discusses reasons for believing in an afterlife

WHAT HAPPENS WHEN WE DIE? Nothing? Complete bliss – 'eternal life'? Or a vague, insubstantial something?

Materialists and atheists would answer 'nothing'. For them life is a purely biological process; when the body dies the personality dies with it, just as electricity stops being generated when a battery fails. To such people life cannot 'go somewhere else'.

These rationalists frequently point out that the age-old belief in an afterlife is merely a reflection of Man's terror of death, of personal oblivion. Throughout history he has either avoided the unthinkable or surrounded it with ritual and a childish optimism. The materialist believes this to be craven and intellectually dishonest – we ought to face 'the facts' – after all, it is true to

The plains of heaven by the English painter John Martin, 1853. Hosts of the blessed rejoice in a dramatic landscape worthy of the mid-Victorian Romantic poets. These angels, some of them winged, play the traditional harp

say that the one fact of life is death.

What of the concept of 'eternal life'? Nearly all religionists have preached that we survive bodily death – in one form or another. It is probably true to say that the more sophisticated the religion, the more certainly it envisages *some* form of 'life everlasting' for some deathless element of the individual, whether in a kind of paradise or amid the torments of hell.

If the materialist is correct, no further enquiry need be made. If the religionists are correct, then it surely behoves each individual to look to his or her salvation. But in the context of religion, belief in the afterlife must remain a matter of faith, and only the experience of our own death can prove us right or wrong.

But what if neither of these rigid concepts is correct? What if something – some life-spark, vestige of the human personality – survives and enters a new kind of existence, not as a form of reward or punishment, but merely obeying a natural law? Today many

Far left: a reconstruction of the Fox family's historic home in Hydesville, New York, where the modern Spiritualist movement was born

Left: the Fox sisters, Margaretta, Catherine and Leah, from a daguerreotype taken in 1852. The strange rappings and table turnings in their home were taken by many to be the long-awaited proof of communications from the dead

psychical researchers feel that the balance of evidence suggests that 'something' does survive, not necessarily for very long after death, nor necessarily the whole personality. According to them, parts of an individual's memory-system and personality traits sometimes seem to survive for a time, enabling his disembodied self to be recognised by the living who knew him, but later perhaps to disintegrate forever.

The objective analysis of purported evidence for human survival is a major concern of the Society for Psychical Research (SPR), founded in London in 1882. But the founding of the SPR would probably never have happened but for events of a generation earlier, which themselves might never have happened but for the emancipation of Man's thought that began in the Renaissance.

Closed minds, closed ranks

As the horizons of knowledge expanded, the materialist position strengthened and by the mid 19th century a 'thinker' was generally reckoned to be someone who had freed himself from the trammels of 'superstition'. Religionists, feeling themselves under attack, tended to close their minds to facts that undermined their position, ironically adopting much the same attitude that some scientists take today when confronted with overwhelming evidence for certain paranormal events ('We don't believe in it, therefore it isn't true').

In the light of such hard rationalism, a faith with results that could be demonstrated was sought after. So when poltergeist activity occurred at the Fox family home in the small town of Hydesville, New York in 1848, the public was tremendously excited. Here at last was 'proof' of the survival of the spirit; an antidote to the bleakness of materialism. Spiritualism was born and has become a significant movement in the western world.

Spiritualists believe that their faith demonstrates incontrovertibly the existence of a life after death. They point to seances where, it is said, spirits move heavy tables, play musical instruments and introduce apports; where dead relatives and friends speak recognisably in their own voices of events known only to themselves and one or more of the sitters, and sometimes even materialise in their own appearances before them.

But scientists refused to investigate seance-room phenomena, while Spiritualists – and fundamentalist Christians – took refuge (though not as allies) in simple faith that regarded scientific discoveries as due to Devil-inspired cleverness.

It was in this climate of extremes that the SPR was founded. The founder members were a group of British intellectuals who objected to the entrenched positions of 'believers' and 'sceptics' and who felt that the objective assessment of unusual phenomena was long overdue. The material collected by the British SPR and similar societies in other countries provides the strongest clues for the serious enquirer into the question 'What happens when we die?'

The huge body of material collected since 1882 may be categorised as follows: phantasms; communications through mediums; cross-correspondences; 'drop-in' communicators; 'welcoming' phantasms seen by the dying; experiences of patients during 'clinical death'; out-of-the-body experiences; cipher and combination lock tests; appearance pacts; evidence for reincarnation; electronic voice phenomena.

Phantasms The SPR's first great achievement was a census of hallucinations. Seventeen thousand replies to a questionnaire about the prevalence of hallucinatory experiences were collected, and of these – after all possible explanations were exhausted – about 8 per cent remained as apparently genuine experiences of phantasms. These

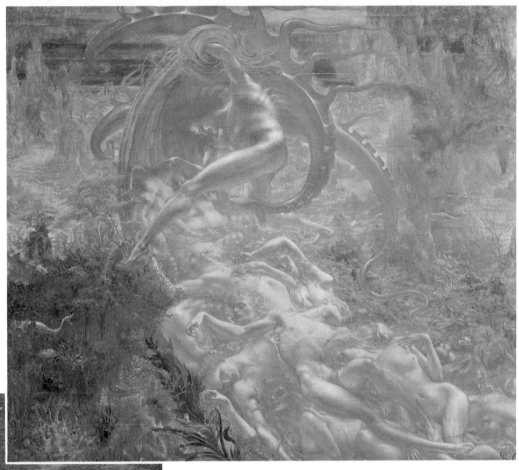

Left: *The treasures of Satan* by the late-19th-century French symbolist Jean Delville. Satan, flame-coloured as a sign of lust and of his fiery destruction of souls through degradations of the flesh, crushes his victims beneath him. Monstrous 'wings' of serpents flail about the. tormented sinners

Below left: burial of the dead is not universal. Here a Red Indian brave visits the rotting corpses of members of his tribe. They have been exposed to the elements and birds of prey, on a hill set apart for the purpose. Their spirits were believed to spend eternity in the Happy Hunting Ground

were critically examined by the leading members of the SPR and upon the findings were based two volumes, *Apparitions of the living* and *Human personality and its survival of physical death*. Listed in the former were several apparitions of people said to have appeared up to 12 hours after their deaths. At the time the researchers felt that these might be due to thought transference from the newly dead individual to his living contacts, delayed perhaps until conditions were right for it to appear. Even so, a number of these cases would now still be classified as evidence of – at least temporary – survival.

Most parapsychologists who accept the evidence of phantasms at all agree that thought transference – which includes thoughts, feelings, and images both visual and auditory, and would today be classified as extra-sensory perception (ESP) – is a faculty of some human minds and could be used to explain phantasms of the living. It also seems to be confirmed by some individuals' claims that they 'think' themselves into paying 'astral visits' – travelling while out-of-the-body – to acquaintances. The claimants not only 'see' the rooms into which they project themselves mentally but report accurately such features as changes of furniture, of which their conscious selves were ignorant. Furthermore, they are often seen by the friends they 'visit' and are sometimes also accurately described by strangers.

However, some 6 or 7 per cent of the apparitions recorded in the SPR survey appeared too long after death for them to be explained as delayed telepathic communications. This small number of cases remained after all other explanations – hoaxing, exaggeration, mistaken identity, dreaming and so on – had been examined and found inadequate.

The cases that were classified as genuine apparitions or phantasms of the dead showed certain common features. In some, the apparition conveyed information previously unknown to the percipient. In others it showed a clearly defined purpose. In yet others it resembled a dead person unknown to the percipient who later recognised him from a portrait or photograph, or from some characteristic of the deceased unknown to him at the time. Sometimes different people at different times – independently of each other – saw the same apparition.

Some psychical researchers think that only those cases in which the apparitions indicate a specific purpose for their manifestation can be taken as significant evidence of survival and even then perhaps only as evidence of temporary survival. It could well be that, as a memory survives the event remembered, so a thought or anxiety to communicate something urgently to the living might continue to exist after the thinker's death until its purpose was fulfilled; then it, too, might die.

Since the early days of the SPR many astute

will communicate through the planchette board, like 'Patience Worth' (see page 48), or through automatic script (see page 52), or draw in the style of recognised masters (see page 42), or compose in the manner of famous musicians (see page 38).

Another type of sensitive is the 'direct voice' medium, who does not, as a rule, go into a trance and from whose vicinity voices of both sexes and different kinds speak in various accents, and sometimes other, identifiable languages.

Communications from these sources vary enormously in quality. Much of it is trivial and curiously materialistic. It was a frequent gibe in the early days of Spiritualism that spirits seemed to spend their afterlife smoking cigars and drinking whisky. Yet this, and other similar 'materialistic' evidence would support the teachings of some Eastern religions that an early stage after death involves passing through a realm of illusion where the ego may indulge in anything and everything it wants.

Other communications, however, are of high ethical and literary standard. Yet frequently when challenged to give an unequivocal description of what awaits us on the other side of life, communicators reply (perhaps not unreasonably) that the spirit existence is indescribable. But some rare spirits are more forthcoming, and an uncannily consistent picture of the afterlife

minds have studied and recorded evidence of survival provided by such apparitions. Some have believed that we live on, others not. It is safe to say that none of the researchers involved has been convinced of survival on the evidence of apparitions alone.

Communications through mediums. While phantasms were being investigated by the SPR so, too, were the activities of mediums – or, as they are better named, sensitives. These are people (more often women than men) who have unusual psychic talents, which they display in various ways. According to their specific gifts they are generally classified into 'mental' and 'physical' sensitives.

A 'mental' sensitive may go into a trance, in which a 'control' ('controlling spirit' or 'spirit guide') speaks through her, frequently in a voice entirely different from her own, and occasionally even giving her a different appearance, so that a European woman may temporarily take on the likeness and voice of, say, a Chinese man.

Through the sensitive the control may introduce other alleged spirits, recognisable by voice, gesture, or the nature of the private information they give to one of the sitters at the seance. Such so-called spirits may seem extremely convincing, though it must be said that those who want to believe will believe anyway. However, sensitives often have striking gifts of clairaudience, clairvoyance and other qualities of ESP. Sometimes they

Above: the 'Viking' galley is burned at the climax of the annual Up Helly A festival at Lerwick in the Shetland Isles, Scotland. The ancient Viking funerals combined cremation with dramatic spectacle, the dead being placed in a burial ship, which was set alight as it was pushed out to sea. It must have seemed to the mourners on the shore that the journey to Valhalla (the Viking heaven) was a very real one

Right: Peruvian Incas bury a chief, preparing him for an afterlife just as stylish and prosperous as his earthly life. Like many other pagan peoples, they buried food, treasure and weapons with their dead, believing the artefacts to be necessary for the dead to survive in the next world in the manner to which they were accustomed

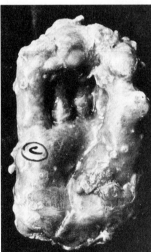

Very popular at Edwardian seances was the moulding of 'spirit' hands in paraffin wax (above); they were believed to dematerialise, leaving the moulds unbroken. But Harry Houdini, the great escape artist and scourge of fraudulent mediums, proved that it was a relatively easy trick to learn (top left)

Top right: an elaborate, pagoda-like cremation tower on the island of Bali

emerges through their communications.

'Physical' mediums are those in whose presence, whether they go into trances or not, physical phenomena occur. These may include loud raps from the seance table or from various points around the room; sometimes they seem to be in an intelligent code as if trying to convey some message. Also common are telekinetic phenomena (solid objects moving as if handled by an invisible person); levitation, of the sensitive and of objects; the playing of musical instruments by unseen hands, and actual materialisation of spirit forms.

Sadly, in the short history of Spiritualism, many of these phenomena have been faked, but there still remain many cases of genuine physical mediumship that defy 'rational' explanation. Many tests have been set up to try to trap the frauds, and, to a lesser extent, to determine the extent of the phenomena. One such was the provision of a dish of warm wax at a physical seance; the materialised 'spirit' hand dipped itself into the wax, which rapidly set. The hand dematerialised, leaving the mould unbroken.

But even such demonstrations of paranormal effects do not prove survival of death in themselves. The material accumulated by the SPR contains, so many researchers believe, far stronger evidence.

How can we possibly know if we survive death? Must it remain, as most people believe, a mystery?

'The undiscover'd

THE SOCIETY for Psychical Research (SPR) was fortunate enough in its early days to be able to call upon the services of highly intelligent, well-educated sensitives with open minds, whose names are still household words among psychical researchers: Mrs Piper, Mrs Thompson, Mrs 'Willett' (a pseudonym for Mrs Coombe-Tennant), Mrs Leonard, Mrs Garrett, among others.

Some of these were 'physical' mediums but most 'mental' – which may be significant, for physical mediums have become progressively rarer as methods of investigation have become more sophisticated. Cynics may leap to the conclusion that the likelihood of being caught as a fraud is so great these days that few dare attempt 'physical' mediumship. But an alternative view is that the very act of setting up the elaborate apparatus necessary for the investigation may inhibit the delicate, barely understood mechanism that produces the phenomena. There also seems occasionally to be an 'experimenter effect' whereby sceptical and even merely objective experimenters may have a dampening effect on the activities of the seance room.

Although the SPR's team of mediums produced some very convincing results, members of the Society were divided over the major question of proof of the afterlife. But they did agree that thought transference – including the communication of thoughts, feelings, images, sounds, even scents – had been proved beyond reasonable doubt. And although more than three decades were to pass before J. B. Rhine's work shifted the emphasis from psychical research (the scientific study of the paranormal) to parapsychology (treating psychic phenomena as expressions of little-known mental activity), extra-sensory perception, psychokinesis and general (super) ESP were already being taken as alternative explanations for the mediums' 'proof' of survival.

It is alleged that ESP explains all uncannily accurate information a medium might give a sitter, purporting to come from a dead relative. For by ESP a human mind can – almost literally – 'pick the brains' of others, without being conscious of doing so. And PK – 'mind over matter' – is the mysterious force exerted by certain gifted minds over inanimate objects. This would explain the so-called 'spirit' table turnings, rappings and so on in terms of a natural, if rare, function of the human mind. And the theory of general or super ESP is that some human minds can glean information not only from other human minds but also from any written,

Above: a soul being ferried across the river of death – the Styx – in the 16th-century painting by Joachim Patinir. It reveals a blend of Classical and Christian beliefs: the Styx and its irascible ferryman, Charon, were believed by the ancient Greeks to carry the dead to their appointed place for eternity. The dead were buried with coins in their mouths so that they could pay the ferryman. Failure to pay resulted in damnation. However the Christian conceptions of purgatory, paradise and hell are shown on either side of the dread river

country'

Left: Persephone and Pluto, in a detail from a Greek vase. Pluto was the ruler of Hades, or the realm of the underworld, believed by the Greeks to be a real geographical location that the dead souls reached through caves. It was a shadowy and sinister abode but not a place of active judgement or punishment. However, at a popular level there was a widespread suspicion that Hades was a much more fearsome place

printed or other kind of record (including presumably, microfilm), arrange it and produce it as a coherent account. Such a concept, if true, destroys any chance of proving survival as a fact, for any message from a deceased person – no matter how accurate or how personal the information given – could theoretically be the result of GESP. Put in Theosophical terms, this store of the sum of human knowledge is called the 'Akashic records' (Book of Life) and certain sensitive people have long been believed to have access to its 'files'. So it could be that, in some unknown way, the cross-referencing necessary for a medium to produce a convincing story of someone's life on Earth has already been done.

There are two other major arguments against evidence for survival as provided by mediums. The first is that a sensitive's so-called 'control' or 'spirit guide' may be no more than an example of the dissociated or multiple personalities that are occasionally discovered by psychiatrists. These seem to be personalities apparently formed by the splitting off of some mental processes from the mainstream of consciousness. If these 'other selves' come to the surface, they can take over completely and the condition becomes a serious illness. (There have been cases where over a dozen completely distinct personalities have inhabited the same body, either taking over in turns or fighting among themselves for possession.) And such manifestations have sometimes happened unexpectedly when apparently normal people have been hypnotised. So perhaps a sensitive, by her very nature, may be more susceptible to the development of secondary personalities than more down-to-earth, or openly sceptical, people.

The versatile forger

Add to this another extraordinary power of the human mind – *mythopoeia*. This is the extraordinary ability to create myths or detailed stories that are strikingly convincing and frequently surface during hypnotic regression as 'past lives'. It can also result in subconscious forgery, enabling some sensitives to imitate the voices, mannerisms, handwriting and even the style of musical composition or drawing of the (sometimes famous) dead. All this may be at second hand, drawn from the minds of others. Mythopoeia may also be responsible for the ability of people in trances to sing or pour out dramatically a flood of unintelligible language, known as 'speaking in tongues'. It is a theory that provides an alternative explanation for the many bizarre phenomena that have been taken as 'proof' of survival.

Cross-correspondences The deaths of the SPR's founder members, notably that of F. W. H. Myers in 1901, were followed by a new phenomenon, that of the 'cross-correspondences' from spiritualists. These were fragmentary messages received at different

group of dead SPR members. Although to a certain extent GESP could account for much of the material of the cross-correspondences, many researchers believe that they are the best evidence yet of survival. But even so, all they do is attempt to convince us, in as many ingenious ways as possible, of the continued existence of certain individuals. (The dead Myers is alleged to have found the effort of communication trying, and 'endlessly presenting my credentials' frustrating in the extreme.) But even assuming its authenticity, this massive, painstaking experiment tells us little of what happens when we die except that we retain something of our earthly habits of thought and some traits of personality.

'Drop-in' communicators Some seances have been interrupted by 'drop-in' spirits who are unknown to anyone present, yet who give information about themselves that is later discovered to be substantially correct. Again, this phenomenon can be explained by GESP, but why should a sensitive pick up information about someone in whom no one present has any interest?

'Welcoming' phantoms Witnesses of the dying often report that dead friends and relatives are apparently seen by them just before death

times and places through two or more sensitives unconnected with each other. The messages, often apparently nonsensical taken separately, made perfect sense when fitted together. The compiling of the cross-correspondences took over 30 years. The timing of their beginning, coinciding as it did with the deaths of those whose main preoccupation in life had been to understand the mysteries of death, seems to many investigators to prove beyond doubt who was behind the experiment. It seemed as if the founders of the SPR had a meeting beyond the grave and said, 'Any normal message we send will be ascribed to thought transference. Let us devise a method of communication that will not be open to such an interpretation.'

Certainly no messages easily ascribable to thought transference had ever been communicated in fragments to different mediums before. And the subject matter of the messages – poetry and erudite classical allusions – was highly characteristic of the

Above left: a soul farming in the Elysian fields. The ancient Egyptians believed the afterlife to be very similar to earthly life but more pleasurable

Above: funerary model of bakery and brewery slaves from an ancient Egyptian tomb. The model slaves were believed to assume real duties in the afterlife in the service of the master in whose tomb they were put

– coming to welcome them to the 'other side'. Perhaps these are hallucinations, a mechanism of nature to ease the passing from life. But this does not explain the cases where the dying have exclaimed at the 'visit' of a relative whose own death was unknown to them.

Clinical death Since the 1960s research has been carried out into the experiences of people who have clinically 'died' – often on the operating table – and who have come back to life. They nearly all report approximately similar experiences, whether they had previously believed in survival or not. They were conscious of leaving their

Right: an early 15th-century view of heaven as a peaceful garden. In days when life was short (and youth and beauty tragically brief), and Man very much at the mercy of the raw elements, an eternal period of relaxation in beautiful surroundings had an obvious, emotive appeal. Here the garden of heaven is shown peopled with young, healthy and attractive souls – among them a winged angel. They relax in each other's company, reading, picking choice fruits, playing musical instruments, and holding pleasant conversations. They are all dressed in the finest and most fashionable clothes. The wall suggests the exclusivity of heaven – and a sense of security after the fears of life

bodies and passing through a dark tunnel with a light at the end. When they emerged from the tunnel they were met by a radiant figure, often too bright to be seen clearly. This being they identified differently, according to their religious 'vocabulary'; for the Westerner he is usually taken to be Christ. They may also be aware of the presence of dead friends or relatives, and are filled with tremendous peace and joy. Yet they are told that their time has not yet come and they have to return. With the greatest unwillingness they re-enter their body. Significantly, people who have had this experience are never afraid of death again, seeing it as something to look forward to.

Out-of-the-body-experiences Another mass of evidence that we exist apart from our physical bodies concerns out-of-the-body-experiences which are sometimes referred to as OOBES. Many people have had the curious experience of finding themselves hovering over their sleeping – or uncon-

Above: the medieval hell was a place of brutal torment, believed to be both 'physical' and spiritual. Although sophisticated theologians of the day argued that the real anguish of hell was the knowledge that one was eternally denied the presence of God, most ordinary people believed that hell was the proverbial fiery pit. Paradoxically, it was for them a world in which the physical pain of lingering tortures was the only sort of punishment, although it was admitted that one no longer had a physical body. Sinners suffered tortures of the most sadistic nature without any hope of mercy or cessation of their pain

scious – bodies: frequently this happens in moments of crisis; during accidents, torture, or while undergoing an operation. Some people later astonish surgeons and nurses by telling them exactly what they had done and said while carrying out the operation. A few claim to be able to leave their bodies at will: and this, to them, is certain proof that they exist apart from their bodies and that this aspect of them will survive bodily death.

Ciphers and combination-lock tests A few tests have been arranged by the living so that, after their deaths, they might prove their continued existence by revealing, through mediums or friends, the solutions to puzzles. So far, none of these has been successful, though the number of the tests arranged may be too small to be significant.

Appearance pacts Lovers or friends have made pacts that the one who died first should appear to the other, perhaps under certain specific circumstances. Allegedly they have done so. But grief frequently produces hallucinations of the deceased – indeed, it seems part of the natural mourning process, acting as a comfort. Such appearances can also be categorised as crisis apparitions or similar dramatic manifestations of ESP.

Reincarnation Evidence for reincarnation not only indicates that we survive and are reborn (perhaps many times), but also offers clues as to why we are born at all. Hypnotic regression into 'past lives'; some children's spontaneous memories of being someone else; the 'far memory' of some adults; some *déjà vu* experiences; all these, though amenable to other explanations, point to reincarnation as

a possibility. Many people believe that we must submit to a string of different earthly lives until we have achieved near perfection of soul, then we become gods or progress on a purely spiritual plane of existence. Some think that not everyone is reincarnated but that we do not understand the rules governing the selection process involved.

Dr Ian Stevenson of the University of Virginia in the United States has made a detailed and scholarly investigation into the evidence for reincarnation. He has amassed hundreds of cases of alleged 'past lives' and came to the conclusion that 'a rational man . . . can believe in reincarnation on the basis of evidence.' However, for the majority of people such a belief will remain a matter of faith alone.

Electronic voice phenomena Since the 1960s tape recorders have allegedly been picking up voices of the dead. The phenomenon was discovered in this century by Jurgenson and Raudive and has since become something of a cult. However, all that can be said of it so far is that, whatever the source of the voices, they do not add to our information about the afterlife.

Despite the fast-growing interest in the paranormal and psychical research, it is true to say that the majority of believers in survival of the spirit belong to a religion, and

Above left: Buddha sits in the midst of the blessed. Stylised lotus flowers (symbols of enlightenment), peacocks, pagodas, elegant shrubs and a decorative pool are reminiscent of the Christian conception of heaven as a garden

Above right: this ancient Chinese painting depicts the Buddhist seventh hell, where the souls of the condemned are chased by ferocious dogs and devils into a deadly river

Far right: this illustration from Raphael's *The Astrologer of the 19th Century* shows a necromancer conjuring up a bloody spirit from the protection of his magic circle.

for them, a belief in the afterlife is entirely a matter of faith.

And this faith goes back a very long way; the oldest known burial customs show that ancient Man believed in survival. Even today, primitive religions take survival of bodily death for granted.

The world's more sophisticated religions, however, differ widely in their concept of Man's ultimate goal. Hindus and Buddhists teach that we escape from the miseries of earthly incarnations into a mystical and blissful unity with Brahma, the Supreme Principle, or entry into Nirvana, in which the self is lost in the infinite.

In the ancient world Greeks, Romans and Hebrews believed the spirit departed to an unsatisfactory existence in a shadowy Hades or *sheol*. Later Jews accepted the concept of the resurrection of the righteous to companionship with the patriarchs, but even today Judaism does not teach a certain doctrine of eternal life for everyone.

From ancient Egypt and Zoroastrianism the idea of judgement descended to Judaism, Christianity and Mohammedanism, with consequent doctrines of rewards and punishments, heaven, purgatory, limbo and hell.

But believer or atheist, philosopher or materialist, each one of us must die. And only then will we find out the truth for certain.

The journey of the soul

Do the souls of the dead live on? Do they go to heaven, hell, purgatory – or to some other, as yet unknown, plane of existence? And if they do continue to exist, how do we know about their experiences? PAUL BEARD surveys the evidence for the afterlife

EVEN AMONG PEOPLE who believe in some kind of an afterlife, alleged communications from the 'other side' are frequently regarded with suspicion. Perhaps it is natural to ascribe such accounts to the result of wishful thinking or unjustified hopes and fears (see page 19). For this reason most people are unaware of the enormous amount of material purporting to describe the next world from people *who are now there*. But if, for a moment, we suspend our disbelief, what emerges from this material is not only evidence for an afterlife but an amazingly consistent description of what it is like to be dead.

Obviously these accounts cannot be checked, and examining them in an open, unprejudiced way is not easy. The basic issue is one of testimony: who are the witnesses – the communicators and the living people who receive their messages?

Bearing witness

Although there are many 'communicators' and just as many 'mediums' or sensitives, not all bear the marks of good witnesses. If the dead speak to us at all, their task cannot be easy; but this does not mean that we should feel obliged to accept any communication no matter how garbled or trivial. We are entitled to listen to only the best – the most balanced, consistent and rational – accounts. In England the Society for Psychical Research (SPR) and the College for Psychic Studies have accrued a vast amount of material, which seems to emanate from intelligent and honest sources, that has been given to reputable mediums over the past 100 years or so. In the end we ourselves have to judge the communications on their own merits and on the responses they awaken in us. But a good witness is worthy of a good listener. So what do the majority of these accounts tell us?

If we do indeed survive death, then by definition the surviving part of us must already be present within us during our life on earth. The first feature of the accounts is that we do indeed take with us the same memory bank, and the same emotions and mental concepts that we had before death. We start from where we left off. But which of us survives: the tired elderly man, or the one in vigorous prime, or even the one full of illusory youthful ideals? The answer, judging by the mass of evidence, points to our having available the private, inward contents of *all* these various 'past selves'; we can reside in them temporarily, or hold on to one aspect or the other. All these imperfect selves have made us what we are; we are said to meet them all in turn again after death, in order to understand them as they really were, and profit by re-experiencing them.

A good witness is Mrs Winifred Coombe-Tennant, known in psychic circles as 'Mrs Willett'. In life she was one of the first English women JPs and a delegate to the League of Nations. She also took part as a non-professional sensitive in the cross-correspondences, which form a highlight in the multiplicity of evidence collected by the SPR (see page 58). After her death, medium Geraldine Cummins received an enormous amount of material (in the form of automatic writing) purporting to come from the discarnate Mrs Coombe-Tennant. Much of this describes the afterlife as she had experienced it. Of the 'many selves' enigma she says:

> A human being consists of a number of selves or aspects with a primary self, the total of a sum in arithmetic. . . . We only become unified in spirit on the higher level.

Dying, it seems, is not the absolute event most people fear; largely, it appears to be a state of altered consciousness. Evidence points to it being harder after death to get rid of the old earthly self than we had supposed. The same personal limitations continue until we resolve them. Death does not in itself change us; it gives us a different kind of opportunity to change ourselves.

In the seventh heaven

In spiritualistic communications, life after death is often described as a progress through seven spheres, each of a more rarified and spiritually invigorating nature than the last. The seven spheres – or mansions, or staging posts – basically represent levels of consciousness, and any of these levels is reached only by a widening and deepening of the moral nature. One is helped by teachers of superior moral stature who have progressed, so to speak, beyond the scope of recent arrivals, but who adapt themselves temporarily to make themselves understood. After death one must realise that life continues as a process of learning.

The great majority of communicators describe the death process itself as one of peacefulness and freedom from pain, even if, during the last hours, the physical body had shown every outward appearance of distress. Communicators often say this apparent pain

Left: *The garden of earthly delights* by Hieronymus Bosch. He saw the average man's ideal world as totally physical – and, ultimately, totally degrading

Below: the traditional Christian belief in a day of reckoning, as portrayed in Fra Angelico's *The day of judgement*

Bottom: T.E. Lawrence, better known as 'Lawrence of Arabia', who died in 1935. In life a brilliant yet difficult man, he was obliged to confront certain unappealing aspects of his character – 'the monk and the prig' – in the afterlife, in order to progress to higher planes

did not register with them. They say death is a gradual withdrawing, often accompanied by alternating periods of sleep or unconsciousness. Then they describe 'waking up' and being greeted by those they had deeply loved who had died previously – and also by others, familiar or not yet familiar, who will be found to know them intimately, even their secret selves. These are not angels sitting in judgement, but more highly developed spirits. Frequently an encounter with them is found to be disturbing. As one newly dead doctor of divinity is purported to have said of such a meeting:

He evidently regarded my whole life on earth – which hitherto I have thought of as being so important – as mere preparation, a preliminary to the real work I have to do here. That has been one of the greatest surprises.

Experiences are, apparently, by no means uniform, and naturally enough are partly determined by old patterns of behaviour and thinking. This first plane of experience is exactly – and literally – what you make of it. According to all communicators, the imagination is supreme; just by thinking of something it appears. Some have given this plane the term 'ideo-plastic', meaning creation through ideas alone. Some create around them past environments of home and possessions that they are unwilling to relinquish. The important key to understanding this plane is that matter is now reported to be of a finer texture, highly malleable to thought. Some, who had not believed in an afterlife, even fail to recognise they are dead. They feel they must be in a vivid dream.

But willing pupils in this environment – called the *summerland*, says the posthumous Frederic Myers – can create what they most desired on earth. But this is not 'heaven' as more enlightened communicators hasten to point out. Summerland in time shows that these 'dreams' are after all not wise enough, nor spiritual enough; they are gradually found to be too selfish and materialistic. People may find that they are seeking little more than a kind of perpetual summer holiday. Yet many accounts stress that the purpose of summerland is to enable its inhabitants to find that much of what they thought valuable is valueless.

But what sort of world does a man find around himself, if his life has been devoted to selfish gain, or if he has fallen prey to crime and violence? The habits of his mind remain the same and so, as in life, he finds he can contribute very little to his after-death environment. His self-absorption has cut him off from being able to enjoy any wider, disinterested feelings, which make up true companionship. As in the summerland his environment reflects himself – and his poverty of soul assumes an awful 'reality'. Many accounts tell of darkness, mist, bare earth and a hovel to live in. This is *winterland*.

In his continuing selfishness such a spirit often feels anger and indignation for his lot. Neither he nor others in that condition can please one another, for all are equally selfish. More unfortunately, he often treats with contempt those who enter his world from

The prophet Mohammad journeys to the seven heavens, as depicted in an early 16th-century Persian painting. The idea that the afterlife is a continuing process, involving the soul's ascent through various stages of enlightenment, is a belief common to many different religions

their own superior realms of freedom, who wish to help and teach him how to change. But frequently such a person is said to stop his ears, much as he often stopped them in life to the promptings of his conscience.

Yet it would be hard to find a man who is totally degraded, and each of these unfortunates who finds himself in winterland is there for only as long as he refuses to listen to the other, higher part of himself. Those who try to help him are really looking for this better self, however deeply overlaid. It is stressed that these individuals are not being 'punished'; their suffering stems only from their own nature as they have created it; and it is fully in their power to regenerate it. They can discover and build on their latent qualities, just as can those who find themselves in the summerland. And just as summerland is not 'heaven', neither is winterland 'hell'. Both states exist because of the individual's inner self. When he becomes more spiritual they are transcended.

Those who have outgrown the summerland state pass on to the *first heaven*. Here selfless ideals can be developed in a life shared with those who also wish to serve others. Its joys are not passive, however; they are certainly to be enjoyed, yet used strenuously to obtain growth of spiritual stature. But this level of consciousness is superior to that of the summerland. The soul is shown, step by step, its nature as it was when on earth. This self-knowledge includes the revelation and re-evaluation of all faults, errors and blindnesses – many of them, even at this stage, hard to accept. Faults easy to excuse on earth, or to hide from oneself, now show up in their true shape.

As others see us

This process is usually named the *judgement*. It is widely reported by communicators that the judgement is not made by God (as in the popular idea of 'the day of judgement'), nor by some superior being sitting in condemnation, but is in some way self-induced. To see, and then to have to condemn oneself, is painful, the more so since many faults now revealed were formerly unsuspected. The posthumous T.E. Lawrence is said to have recognised the monk and the prig in himself, which had led him to reject women's values, and brought about what he now says is a travesty of the man he could have been. The judgement shows what one has made of oneself, and it is more often than not a painful experience. But once recognised these faults can be transcended, creating a different self.

The judgement usually extends over a considerable period of experiences and adjustments; it also of course includes recognition of those qualities and actions that are worthy – in this sense life in the first heaven is part of the judgement. Though judgement is carried out by oneself, loving companions are there to explain, support and give guidance for necessary corrective steps. W. V. Blewett, a former agricultural scientist, is believed to have said, 'Here we receive absolute justice, such as can never be possible on earth.'

Motive is shown to be paramount. Hence one's actions are shown as they really were, not as one preferred to think them; and whatever joy or suffering they brought about in others is now exactly felt and experienced oneself. This can be very painful without the deadening effect of the physical body, in the same way that emotions felt in dreams – love, fear, disgust – are sharply defined as if suddenly in focus, whereas the same emotions felt in our everyday lives are muffled by the demands and stimuli of the outside world. Here there is no 'outside world' – it is all 'inside', all experienced with the awful, or beautiful, clarity of dreaming.

From what we can piece together, the various 'stages' of the afterlife can be experienced one after the other – and most frequently are – but sometimes the discarnate spirit can work at several tasks at the

Above: a Hindu statue of an *apsaras*, who is believed to gratify men's sexual desires in paradise. Most ancient religions – with the exception of puritan Christianity – imagine paradise, or heaven, to comprise endless feasting, drinking, idleness and sex in scented gardens. The indications are that the first stage of the afterlife is indeed a place where one's dreams come true

Left: William Blake's illustration for Robert Blair's *The grave*, 1813, showing the newly freed spirit rising from the shrouded corpse, keys in hand, to open the way to a blissful future

same time or go from one to the other alternately. There seems to be no rigid plan to which every person must adhere; as on earth, all people are individuals with different needs, and these are allowed for.

But most communicators express difficulty in conveying to us that their surroundings, seemingly much as on earth, are actually part of a wonderful mental world, and are much more malleable to thought than dense earth matter. All is permeated by the thoughts, feelings and beliefs of those at a common level of consciousness. The mental-emotional environment to which one belongs is not isolated, however; it is also influenced or 'played upon' by the consciousness of

those at higher levels, in a way that is as sustaining and invigorating as sunlight.

How far and how much we can see is, as always, bounded by our own limited consciousness; being played upon from higher levels is aimed at helping us gradually to enlarge our vision, somewhat in the way we learn on earth from a teacher's entire personality and not merely from the facts he passes on. But exactly what is learned on this plane is difficult for us to imagine. It can hardly be of a mechanical or practical nature for physical objects no longer exist. And it is unlikely, in the circumstances, to entail philosophical discussion about the 'nature of life'. Learning must be confined to lessons of a moral or spiritual nature, as indeed many communicators describe. But such a formidable course of study begins only when the student is ready – and eager – for it.

Each succeeding level is shut off from us until we are in a fit state to appreciate it. It is possible that some souls never rise above the 'summer holiday' plane of the summerland. It seems more likely, however, that everyone progresses to higher planes, but at his or her own pace.

These events – life in the summerland, winterland, the first heaven, and the process of the judgement – form what is meant by the 'astral' or 'desire' world of consciousness. Each man now begins to learn that it is necessary to leave this plane behind, to shed it in order to win the freedom to dwell in the most spiritual parts of himself.

Surrender of the self

The experience that many believe now awaits him is known as the *second death*. Each must now gradually become as willing to yield up his present values as, in very many cases, he was ready in the end to shed his earthly body on death. His desires in the astral world, however much they have included love of others, good fellowship and companionship, have also, as he now begins to see with certainty, really largely centred upon himself. Even when he loved others, much of this was for his own emotional satisfaction. Now in the second death he sheds all he has valued; his achievements and all the things he has won in the desire world (of which earth too is a part) have now to be given up. His gifts no longer exist for him but for the glory of God. Conan Doyle, in describing his own posthumous experience, calls this transition 'terrible and marvellous', adding that 'there are no trimmings on a man after the second death.' Yet this traumatic experience prepares the student, shorn of his most dearly held pretensions, for the next stage in his progress. Through this he can begin to find his 'true self'; a larger, more complete being – one, he discovers, for which he has always been searching.

The purpose of death

Far from resting in peace, it is claimed that the dead lead a strenuous and purposeful existence; in fact that they are more 'alive' than we are.

IF DEATH IS NOT the end of man's personality, but rather the beginning of a sort of 'pilgrim's progress' as many psychical researchers claim, then what are the stages of this adventure? The discarnate spirit, after meeting the loved ones who had died before him, lives first in summerland or winterland (see page 31), both of which he creates from his own habits of thought, good or bad. These are both on the *ideo-plastic* plane and seem to serve to break him of his earthly preoccupations and make him yearn for the benefits of higher, more spiritual faculties. But he must first undergo the judgement and the second death, processes that hold a mirror up to the person he was, mercilessly stripping him of his illusions about himself and making him realise — by momentarily *becoming* other people in his life — what his actions and words had done to them.

Through experiencing the shattering but

Above: the Hindu deity Vishnu reincarnates for the second time – as a turtle. Belief in the transmigration of souls, or reincarnation as man or animal, is still common in the East. But, according to the alleged evidence for the afterlife, man is always reincarnated as another human being

Right: the ninth hell as described in Dante's *Inferno* and illustrated by Gustave Doré. In this wasteland of ice and desolation, the damned soul is frozen forever, unless he confesses his sins to the superior souls who visit him

ultimately rewarding process of the second death the spirit 'earns' his entry into the *second heaven*. What has been shed in the trauma is only, he discovers, his outer self, his personality, which had seemed so essential in his earth life. Personality is derived from the Latin *persona*, meaning 'actor's mask'; having cast this away during the second death he can emerge as his real, 'undivided self'.

The purpose of the second heaven is, apparently, to enable the questing spirit to grow and develop. The process takes place in what many accounts call 'the great silence'. During this period one's former identity dissolves away and one experiences a sense of great peace. One no longer knows who or where one is, but this is not in any way distressing, any more than it is 'distressing' for a butterfly to undergo the natural process of emerging from its cocoon.

Kinship of the spirit

At this point the spirit loses contact with all those he had known during his earth life. This is a temporary phase but apparently essential if he is to concentrate his energies on coping with the new, immeasurably broader landscape he now faces. There are now highly significant meetings with others, men and women with whom one feels a deep spiritual link and an intimate familiarity. This is reported as being like meeting old friends on earth with whom one has shared profound experiences. However, the spirits on this plane, although they are indeed old friends, belong to relationships formed over many lifetimes. And this one fact is central to the understanding of the whole nature of the afterlife. With those friends from long ago the spirit relives ancient memories, memories to which his immediately previous personality had no access. Together the members of the reunion relive past events they had shared, and as they do so they begin to see a distinct purpose and meaning emerge

experienced before, or perhaps at last the spirit has overcome a lengthy pattern of mistakes. Frances Banks said, 'It is still a continuation, a sequel. There is a definite continuing thread.'

This enrichment of the soul through the revelations of the past is the first step in the process of reassessment carried on in the second heaven. There are two other, equally important steps.

The first involves advice from wiser beings on how to deal with one's future earth life. The second step clarifies the true nature of the spirit's relationship with his peers, those 'old friends' with whom he has just been reunited. He now realises that they are all bound together for all eternity, united with the same overall purpose. Together they form part of a highly important unit known as a *group soul*. It is said that to be with its members is to feel a deep spiritual homecoming.

The members of an earth family may be spiritually close or they may simply be genetically linked – effectively strangers on

Most ancient cultures believed in a supernatural deity whose sole task was to preside over the dead. Part custodian and part judge, he is usually shown as a terrible figure, such as Yamantaka, Tibetan lord of the dead (above) or the Totonac god of ancient Mexico, Mictlantecuhtli (right)

from the apparently disparate and fragmentary personalities they had been in the past. Each soul has been reincarnated many times.

They now see that their lives are in no way arbitrary; they form part of a pattern and purpose that are still being worked out. Each is slowly awakening towards recognition of, and participating in, what is named his *causal self*. This carries within it the seeds of each former life but also contains hints of what is to come in future incarnations. The second heaven is both retrospective and prospective; a plane of insight into both past and future. As the posthumous Frances Banks, a former Anglican nun, is claimed to have said, it is 'the initial stage of a journey into light, during which the surviving entity is gradually reunited with the whole soul.' And now he sees his past earth life in its true perspective; not, as he perhaps thought as he was actually living it, that it was the 'be all and end all', but that it was only a tiny fragment of a much larger prospect.

The past life is only the latest chapter in a long book, the 'story' of which can stretch back over many earth centuries. As the spirit begins to witness the unfolding panorama of his lives he will inevitably realise that much in his past life was the direct consequence of actions from other, previous incarnations. Nothing is meaningless – now at last he knows the answer to the question every person asks at some point: 'Why me?'

There are many incarnations for most spirits, for almost everyone needs many chances to learn all the necessary lessons. All the opportunities will be there over the centuries for everyone. Not everyone will profit by his experience or learn at the same rate but there are many chances to put right mistakes made or opportunities lost. Perhaps the failures of the last life are similar to those

The statue of Justice that stands above the Old Bailey, Britain's foremost criminal court. The scales and the sword she carries represent the two aspects of justice: mercy and retribution. Absolute justice, however, is said to be found only in the afterlife – where motives are seen for what they really were in life. During the judgement the soul suffers the pain and humiliation he once inflicted on others. He learns for himself – the hard way – the effects of his every word and deed. But his kindnesses are also relived and rewarded

any deeper level. Their spiritual 'family' is elsewhere. Such people are said to be the true foundlings. But in the afterlife there are no such random or loose ties; the group soul comprises only members who are totally committed to their particular long-term spiritual assignment under the leadership of one who can perhaps best be called an elder brother. The individual members of each group are responsible to each other – and to the world – in order to fulfil the special task assigned them when their group was created.

Life goes on

If these narratives that claim to describe conditions in the afterlife – and, indeed, the purpose of life itself – are true, then our individual lives on earth can be seen in proper perspective, as part of a much greater plan. And although these accounts seem basically in harmony with the conventional Christian belief in purgatory, hell and heaven, the approximately similar states exist, not as final punishments or rewards for a single earth life, but as stages in a continuing education. Each has to redeem those parts of himself that are bound by the chains of his own creation. Even in the second heaven the processes of self-cleansing and selfless service continue. Here the spirit learns that there are further states of bliss, but these are too intense for it yet.

It becomes plain that life on earth and life between incarnations simply provide different opportunities of 'growing up'. Each spirit will pass from hard work to refreshment and from refreshment to further tasks – and although on the planes beyond the surroundings are said to be more pleasant than on earth, basically the work is just as strenuous. It takes enormous effort for each spirit to make any lasting progress, but he is not alone and can expect the kind of help, advice and inspiration that would have been impossible on earth. Encouraged and inspired, the individual can progress towards his own ultimate maturity.

The destiny of each soul will be fulfilled, say the communicators, only when that of the

The man who would be king

Death is said to be 'the great leveller' and nowhere is this shown more clearly than in *A Tudor story* by the late Canon W. S. Pakenham-Walsh. This purports to tell the tale of the Canon's relationship – through several mediums – with various members of the Tudor court from the early 1920s to his death at the age of 92 in 1960. Pakenham-Walsh found that his main spiritual mission was to aid Henry VIII himself, who was angry, lost and clinging pathetically to a crown he no longer possessed, and could therefore make no progress in the afterlife.

One medium had to remind 'Henry' that he was king no longer. He was furious, saying 'I am a king. I carry royal birth and death in my hands. . . . A king does not commit acts for which he is sorry.'

The Canon enlisted the help of the 'spirits' of Anne Boleyn and Elizabeth I among others, while also praying for the King's soul himself. For a time Henry vacillated between apparent repentance and humility and outbursts of regal temperament. The breakthrough came when he was allowed to meet his sons – including the baby who had been stillborn, now grown up. Henry's last communication was: 'Know that Henry, once King of England, did repent.'

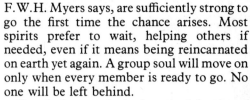

F.W.H. Myers says, are sufficiently strong to go the first time the chance arises. Most spirits prefer to wait, helping others if needed, even if it means being reincarnated on earth yet again. A group soul will move on only when every member is ready to go. No one will be left behind.

People frequently deplore the injustice of 'life', meaning their earthly existence. But if the accounts of the afterlife summarised above are substantially true, then there is such a thing as absolute justice, there is cause for hope, there is free will and ever-expanding consciousness. The narratives purporting to come from people in the after-life can be examined by anyone – religious beliefs and pious hopes aside – as evidence. Perhaps the last words of Mary, Queen of Scots, 'In my end is my beginning', express the literal truth for everyone.

group soul is completed. This may take aeons. There are many group souls, said to range from comparatively few members to many hundreds. Frequently a person's inner urge on earth is a reflection of the quest of his group soul, his equivalent of the Holy Grail. Everyone retains his free will to depart from the group soul's set path, but the promptings of his own inner nature will, it is believed, eventually lead him back to it.

During his stay in the second heaven the spirit learns from the 'replay' of his past lives to discover his true potential and what steps he should take to fulfil it. Strengthened by the insight and love of his companions he is now ready for a yet further expansion of his consciousness, which takes place in the *third heaven*. This is, however, too intense an experience for many spirits to endure for very long, although it is open to them for precisely as long as they can endure. Although almost impossible for us to under-stand, communicators tell us that in the third heaven a spirit comes to the limits of his consciousness. After a brief glimpse of this plane he finds he cannot go further into it than his nature allows. Faced with his limita-tions he has no choice but to return to earth.

Other lives, other worlds

However, if his next incarnation goes well and he grows spiritually as a result, he will find that he can then proceed deeper into the third heaven. This in turn will enable him to make more of his succeeding earth life, for it is in the third heaven that the true nature of the group soul's task unfolds as consciousness expands in the individual members.

But what happens when a person has little more to learn from earth? Most accounts agree that a choice awaits him. He can take a leap into the great unknown, leaving this planet and its successive incarnations alto-gether, and begin again somewhere else. Com-munications are vague on this point, but they do seem to imply a new cycle of physical lives on another planet. Few, the posthumous

Above: a bark painting by the Australian Aborigine artist Bunia, showing the afterlife

Right: an early 15th-century representation of St Peter receiving three souls at the gates of heaven. In the traditional Christian view, admission to heaven was in itself a kind of judgement, although the dreadful day of judgement was still to come

Below: a wall painting at Tepantitla, Mexico, dating back more than 1000 years. It is believed to show the rain god's paradise

The latest works of Beethoven, Brahms and Liszt

Many sensitives claim to receive works of art from long-dead artists – composers, authors, painters. But, asks LYNN PICKNETT, are these works truly from beyond the grave, or do they come from the subconscious mind?

BEETHOVEN IS STILL WORKING on his 10th Symphony. This extraordinary concept – that musicians and other creative beings can still produce works of art years, even centuries, after their death – is as natural as breathing to many spiritualists and psychics.

The best known of the mediums who claim to be amanuenses for long-dead composers is London housewife Rosemary Brown, who acts almost as an agent for Liszt, Beethoven, Brahms, Debussy, Chopin, Schubert and, more recently, Stravinsky. She is an unassuming, middle-aged lady with only a rudimentary musical background and she is the first to acknowledge that the works 'dictated' to her are beyond her everyday musical capacity. Mrs Brown sees herself merely as the humble scribe and friend of the late composers – the ultimate polish must come from the professionals in performance.

The idea of survival beyond death is not, however, strange to this Balham housewife. As a young girl she had visions of an elderly man who told her repeatedly that he and other great composers would befriend her and teach her their wonderful music. It

Above left: Rosemary Brown being filmed by an American television company in October 1980. During the filming Rosemary 'wrote' *Mazurka in D flat* (above), which she claims was inspired by Chopin (above right)

Left: Beethoven contacted Rosemary Brown in 1964; he told her he was no longer deaf and could once again enjoy listening to music

Right: Franz Liszt, who first appeared to Rosemary Brown when she was a young girl. He told her that, when she grew up, he and other composers would contact her and teach her their music.

far beyond her conscious capacity or even her conscious knowledge. During the writing sessions Mrs Brown chats familiarly with her unseen guests, so sincerely and normally that it is difficult to be embarrassed, despite the bizarre circumstances. Pen poised over the music sheets, she listens. 'I see . . .', she says to Franz Liszt, 'these two bars go here . . . no, I see, I'm sorry. No, you're going too fast for me. If you could just repeat . . .' With pauses for checking and some conversation with the composer, she writes down the work far faster than most musicians could possibly compose.

Sometimes communications are interrupted as she gently chides Liszt for becoming so excited that he speaks volubly in German or French. Chopin occasionally forgets himself and speaks to her in his native Polish – which she writes down phonetically and has translated by a Polish friend.

So are these posthumous works recognisably those of Liszt, Chopin, Beethoven,

Below right: American composer and conductor Leonard Bernstein. Rosemary Brown sought an interview with Bernstein on the advice of her 'spirits'. He was most impressed with the music Rosemary showed him

was only many years later, when she was a widow concerned mainly with the struggle of bringing up two children on very limited means, that she saw a picture of Franz Liszt (1811–1886) and recognised him as her ghostly friend.

In 1964 she was contacted by other great composers – including Beethoven and Chopin – and her life work began in earnest: taking down their 'unfinished symphonies' and sharing her belief that there is no death – the great musicians are still producing.

The pieces transmitted to her are no mere outlines: they are full compositions, mainly for the piano but some for full orchestras. Mrs Brown says the music is already composed when it is communicated to her: the musicians simply dictate it as fast as she can write it down.

Indeed, observers of the process are amazed at the speed with which Rosemary Brown writes the music – and the standard is

Brahms? Concert pianist Hephzibah Menuhin said 'I look at these manuscripts with immense respect. Each piece is distinctly in the composer's style.' Leonard Bernstein and his wife entertained Mrs Brown in their London hotel suite and were very impressed both by her sincerity and by the music she took to them purportedly from the long-dead composers. British composer Richard Rodney Bennett said: 'A lot of people can improvise, but you couldn't fake music like this without years of training. I couldn't have faked some of the Beethoven myself.'

Since that memorable breakthrough in 1964 Mrs Brown has also, she says, been contacted by dead artists, poets, playwrights, philosophers and scientists. Vincent van Gogh (1853–1890) has communicated his current works through her; at first in charcoal ('because that's all I had') and then in oils. Debussy has chosen to paint through Mrs Brown, rather than compose because his artistic interests have changed since he has 'passed over'.

Bertrand Russell, philosopher, has had to reconsider his atheism and disbelief in a life after death, for, as Rosemary Brown points out, he is very much 'alive' these days and wants to pass on the message of hope in eternal life. Albert Einstein also communicates, patiently explaining any difficult jargon or concepts, reinforcing the belief in further planes of existence.

Sceptics point out that the music alleged to come from the minds of the great composers is less than their best, being often reminiscent of their earliest, rather than their mature, works. This, says Mrs Brown, is not the point. Her first introduction to Franz Liszt was 'more than a musical breakthrough.' The late Sir Donald Tovey is believed to have explained the motivation behind the communications in this posthumous statement:

In communicating through music and conversation, an organized group of musicians, who have departed from

Rosemary Brown's contacts are not confined to the field of music: Van Gogh inspired this drawing (right) in 1975, and Debussy (below), now more interested in visual art, also paints 'through' her. She was contacted by Albert Einstein (bottom) in 1967, and by Bertrand Russell (below left) in 1973

your world, are attempting to establish a precept for humanity, i.e., that physical death is a transition from one state of consciousness to another wherein one retains one's individuality . . . We are not transmitting music to Rosemary Brown simply for the sake of offering possible pleasure in listening thereto; it is the implications relevant to this phenomenon which we hope will stimulate sensible and sensitive interest and stir many who are intelligent and impartial to consider and explore the unknown of man's mind and psyche. When man has plumbed the mysterious depths of his veiled consciousness, he will then be able to soar to correspondingly greater heights.

Mrs Brown has many friends and admirers outside the spiritualist circle, notably among distinguished musicians, writers and broadcasters. Whatever the source of her mysterious music, this modest and religious lady inspires respect and affection, so obvious is her sincerity.

She is, however, not unique in her musical communications. The British concert pianist, John Lill, also claims an other-worldly inspiration for his playing. This winner of the prestigious Tchaikovsky Piano Competition had a tough beginning, playing the piano in pubs in London's East End. As he says 'I don't go around like a crazed fellow with my head in the air . . . [I'm] neither a nutter nor some quaint loony falling around in a state of trance.' But, as he added thoughtfully, 'because something is rare it doesn't mean that it doesn't exist.'

The 'something' began for him when he was practising in the Moscow Conservatoire

Right: concert pianist John Lill is convinced that he has had spiritual help in his career. He believes that Beethoven watched him practising for the Tchaikovsky Piano Competition in Moscow, and has since held several conversations with him. And Beethoven has dedicated a piece of his own music to him – the *Sonata in E Minor* communicated to Rosemary Brown in 1972

Below: Clifford Enticknap, who has written an oratorio entitled *Beyond the veil* 'under the inspiration' of G. F. Handel (bottom)

for the Tchaikovsky Piano Competition. He became aware of a figure watching him – someone wearing unusual clothes. He believes he was being observed by Beethoven, who has since held many conversations with him. However John Lill does not consider himself a special case. This sort of direct inspiration, he says, is available to everyone who achieves a certain frame of mind:

'It is very difficult to conceive inspiration unless it is something you receive. I don't see it as something from within a person. When I go on stage I close my mind to what I have learnt and open it fully in the expectation that inspiration will be received.'

But sometimes it is difficult to achieve this state of mind 'if it's a particularly muggy day, or the acoustics are dry. Even the attitude of the audience makes a difference. A quiet mind is essential.'

Inspiration, says Lill, is an infinite thing: 'music begins where words leave off – where music leaves off the "force" begins'.

The composer of, among other magnificent works, the *Messiah* is still 'writing' grand oratorios through his medium Clifford Enticknap, an Englishman who has always been obsessed with Handel and Handelian music. Handel taught him music in another incarnation, says Enticknap, and their relationship as master and pupil dates back to the time of Atlantis where Handel was a great teacher known as Joseph Arkos. Yet before that the soul we know as Handel lived on Jupiter, the planet of music, together with all the souls we know as the great musicians (and some we may never know for they will not be incarnated on Earth).

In his personality as 'the master Handel', the musician communicated to Enticknap a

four-and-a-half-hour long oratorio entitled *Beyond the veil*; a 73-minute excerpt of this has been recorded by the London Symphony Orchestra and the Handelian Foundation Choir and is available on tape through the Handelian Foundation as 'proof' of Handel's survival beyond death.

In BBC-TV's programme *Spirits from the past*, shown on 12 August 1980, snatches from the oratorio were played over scenes of Mr Enticknap playing the organ in Handel's favourite English church. Television critics found little fault with the music – which did indeed sound to the untutored ear to be very similar to Handel's more familiar works – but the words provoked widespread ridicule. One critic compared them with the unfortunate poetry of William McGonagall (1805–1902) whose poetic sincerity was matched only by his total lack of talent and sheer genius in juxtaposing the risible with the pathetic. (Another critic went so far as to exclaim: 'Fame at last for McGonagall – he's teamed up with Handel beyond the veil!')

However, mediums warn against judging spirit communications in a state of flippant scepticism. As John Lill says of the difficulties the spirits have in 'getting through': 'It's all to do with cleaning a window, and some windows are cleaner than others.'

If, as many serious researchers into the paranormal have believed, the music does not in fact come from the minds of deceased musicians, then where does it come from? Certainly not from the conscious mind of Mrs Brown, who obviously struggles to keep up with the dictation.

Some psychics believe that our deeper inspirations are culled from the 'Akashic records' or 'Book of life', wherein lies all knowledge. In certain states of mind, and in some especially sensitive people, this hidden knowledge becomes available to the human consciousness. Mrs Brown could well be one of these specially receptive people and the music she believes comes from Chopin or Beethoven may come instead from this 'pool' of musical knowledge. Because of her personal humility her conscious mind may dramatise her method of receiving the music as direct dictation from the masters.

The late Mrs Rosalind Heywood, researcher into the paranormal and author of *The sixth sense*, has another suggestion. Mrs Brown is, she guesses, 'the type of sensitive whom frustration, often artistic, drives to the automatic production of material beyond their conscious capacity.'

To those who believe in the omniscience of the human subconscious the compositions given to the world by Mrs Brown and others like her raise more questions than they answer. But it is all so beautifully simple to the mediums – there is no death and genius is eternal.

A gallery of psychic art

Does artistic genius die with the artist – or does it survive, to find expression through the hands of living sensitives?

PABLO PICASSO, who died in April 1973, produced several drawings in both pen-and-ink and colour, three months afterwards. Perhaps it would be more accurate to say that Picasso-style drawings were transmitted through British psychic Matthew Manning, who had been trying to 'get through' to Picasso. While concentrating on him he had found his hand being controlled – apparently by the spirit of Picasso, or whatever signed itself 'Picasso' on the drawing.

Psychic art presents many of the same questions to the psychical researcher that are posed by the prize-winning literature of Patience Worth (see page 48) or Beethoven's 1980 symphony. Is the painting, poetry or music, believed by many to be

Above: the style is unmistakably Aubrey Beardsley's but this pen-and-ink drawing was produced through the hands of English psychic Matthew Manning

Above right: a posthumous Picasso. Matthew Manning remarked on the 'energy and impatience' of the artist. Picasso was one of the few artists who chose to use colour

evidence of the artists' survival beyond the grave, merely an exhibition of the medium's own repressed creativity, finally finding expression? Or is it really as simple as the psychics would have us believe – that the world's great musicians, writers and artists are 'proving' their continued existence by carrying on their arts through selected 'sensitives'?

But some examples of 'automatic' or psychic art are impressive, both in their own right and, more significantly, as examples of the styles of the great painters. Some collections of psychic art are also impressive in their diversity of style and their sheer quantity.

It was Matthew Manning's enormous collection of sketches, paintings and drawings,

Above right: a Manning Monet. The style seems to be consistent with that of the great French Impressionist

Right: when this sketch of a hanged man began to take shape Matthew felt physically ill and wanted to stop the drawing, but his (anonymous) communicator compelled him to finish it

produced psychically by him as a teenager in the early 1970s, that convinced his publisher that he was a very special young man.

Matthew Manning's intelligent, articulate and objective approach to all the strange phenomena in his life makes fascinating reading. In his first book, *The link*, he discusses his method of 'contacting' dead artists. He simply sat quietly with a pad and pen in his hand and concentrated on the artist. He never went into a trance and was always aware of everything going on around him. Almost immediately the pen would begin to move, usually starting in the centre of the page and finally filling the page with what seemed like a well-planned work of art. Almost always the result was recognisably in the style of the artist he had been concentrating on – sometimes it was even signed. Occasionally, although bearing a strong resemblance to the style of the artist he had wanted to 'get through' to, the pictures were not signed. It seemed to Mr Manning that some other discarnate artist, perhaps even a pupil of the greater one, had intervened.

The communicators showed very distinct personalities. 'No other communicator tires me out as much as Picasso does,' said Mr Manning. 'After only a few minutes, the time it takes him to do one drawing, I feel worn out and cannot continue for at least 24 hours . . .' When Picasso first came through in 1973, Matthew Manning says his hand was 'moved with excessive force' and two of his finer pen-nibs were snapped. When the drawing suddenly stopped, completed, and Matthew looked at the picture objectively he could see that it 'was unmistakably in Picasso's style; it was bold and strong.'

Also, Pablo Picasso was one of the few

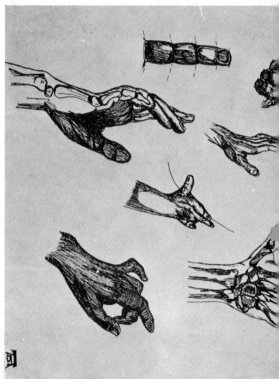

— were any mistakes made and covered over. It took between one and two hours to produce a finished work, whereas most living artists would take perhaps six or eight hours to produce a painting of similar size and complexity – and then not necessarily of the same high quality. More time would also have been spent in planning and sketching.

But one psychic artist has produced new 'old masters' at the rate of 21 in 75 minutes. In March 1978 the Brazilian Luiz Gasparetto appeared on BBC-TV's *Nationwide*

communicators who was not confused about using colour – he directed Matthew Manning's hand to pick out certain felt-tipped pens from a box of mixed colours. Most of his other discarnate artists used pen-and-ink.

Among the signed works in his collection are drawings recognisably in the styles of Arthur Rackham, Paul Klee, Leonardo da Vinci, Albrecht Dürer, Aubrey Beardsley, Beatrix Potter, Pablo Picasso, Keble Martin and the Elizabethan miniaturist Isaac Oliver.

Sometimes a finished picture would be very similar to a famous work by that particular artist. Matthew Manning often recognised them as 'copies' but occasionally the remarkable similarities had to be pointed out to him. A virtual reproduction of Beardsley's famous *Salome*, for example, took place under his eyes as he concentrated on Beardsley. But what value did these copies have – except to prove perhaps that the artist was alive and his style unchanged? Were they meant, in fact, to establish his identity?

The 'new' work came at an incredible speed. There was no preliminary sketching, nor – except in the case of Aubrey Beardsley

Above: four centuries after his death Isaac Oliver, the Elizabethan miniaturist, executed and signed such detailed – and typical – work via Matthew Manning

Albrecht Dürer (1471–1528), inventor of engraving and true son of the Renaissance, was another of Matthew Manning's alleged communicators. The rhinoceros (above right) and the study of human hands (right) – 'transmitted through' Matthew Manning – are characteristic of Dürer's minute observation and the scope of his interests

RHINOCERVS

Right: a crayon drawing by Brazilian trance artist Luiz Antonio Gasparetto in the style of Henri de Toulouse-Lautrec (1864–1901). Whereas most of Luiz's paintings take only a few minutes to complete, this one took several hours. The drawing was made in 1978 while the medium was living in London, studying English

Spiritualist medium Coral Polge presented this psychic sketch of 'a little girl' (right) to a sitter. In fact 'she' bears a striking resemblance to Dag Hammarskjöld when young (far right): the sitter was researching for a book about him at the time

Two of Luiz Gasparetto's **crayon** drawings in distinctly **different styles:** one very reminiscent of Modigliani's style (below) and a charming study (below right) that is actually signed 'Renoir'

and was seen by millions to go into a trance and produce 21 pictures – sometimes working with both hands simultaneously on two separate pictures, sometimes producing perfect paintings, but executing them upside down – and all so fast that many viewers believed the BBC had accelerated the film. And the results were apparently 'new' Renoirs, Cézannes and Picassos.

Senhor Gasparetto found working under the harsh studio lights very trying, because he normally paints – in a trance – in the dark or, at the most, in a very weak light. As he is also a psychologist by profession, he views what he produces with some objectivity. But, although familiar with others who write or

Sometimes painted with both hands simultaneously, sometimes with his toes and almost always within a few minutes, Luiz Gasparetto's trance-paintings bear striking resemblances to the works of famous, dead artists. Often the 'spirit' paintings are signed, such as this typical Van Gogh (right) – signed 'Vincent' – and this slightly unusual Picasso (far right). Others need no signature; the style is sufficient. Who else could have painted this closely-observed portrait of a *demi-mondaine* (below) but ɔulouse-Lautrec?

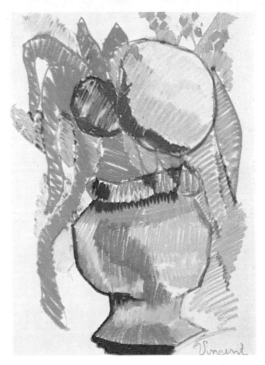

paint by psychic means, he says: 'I've never seen anyone else who can draw with both hands in the dark – in 30 different styles.' In a state of normal consciousness he says he cannot paint at all.

The Brazilian says he sees, senses and talks to all the great artists who 'come through'. Interestingly, in view of Matthew Manning's experience, Senhor Gasparetto said: 'Picasso sometimes used to be violent. If anyone whispered he would throw the paper away.'

Luiz Gasparetto travels extensively with journalist and fellow Spiritist Elsie Dubugras, giving demonstrations of psychic painting. After each session the paintings are auctioned and the proceeds go to charity.

Although Senhor Gasparetto is still producing vast numbers of psychic paintings, Matthew Manning has done little automatic art or writing since adolescence. At first he did it because he found it quelled the poltergeist activity that seemed always to surround him, but now the power, whatever it is, has been harnessed for healing.

There are some mediums, such as Frank Leah, Coral Polge and Margaret Bevan, who have produced drawings of the spirits who come to comfort the bereaved; in many cases these 'spirit portraits' of loved ones are startling likenesses.

Researchers and sceptics alike have come up with theories of repressed creativity, or even a secondary personality, to account for the strange phenomenon of psychic art. Perhaps we will never know how or why it happens, but out of all the vast array of paranormal phenomena this threatens no one – and often produces works of great beauty.

The riddle of Patience Worth

The ouija board has picked up many strange messages from the spirit world, but when 'Patience Worth' came through she produced literature of remarkably high quality.

On January 30, 1925, Patience Worth gave the following inscription for "Hope Trueblood"—

"Ye see I hae witched thee by strummin' the tenderest chord in womankind, the mither-chord. Ye see I hae witched thee by a wee lassie who lived laughin' through woein' . . . This be the acst o' life—Pennin' 'wit aneath the cowl o' sorrow."

HOPE TRUEBLOOD

"A Mid-Victorian Novel by a Pre-Victorian Writer"

By PATIENCE WORTH

Edited by CASPER S. YOST

Hope Trueblood differs materially from the previous productions of Patience Worth. In this she abandons her archaic dialect and constructs her story in standard English of the present day, free from grammatical irregularities. Modern in its language, the story is relatively modern in its time, which is about the middle of the nineteenth century—"a mid-Victorian novel by a pre-Victorian writer."

It is a simple tale of life in an English village, the autobiography of Hope Trueblood, born in that village without the knowledge of a father and suffering the tortures which that stain applies to a sensitive soul in a narrow community. One gets but a glimpse of Hope's mother, but the sweetness of her personality is a dominating influence throughout the story. It is filled with a delightful mingling of humor and pathos, and it has the quality of apparent reality that is so remarkable in "The Sorry Tale." A tantalising mystery holds the reader in suspense to the end of the tale. There are vivid sketches of scenes, and there is much characteristic beauty of thought and of diction.

Patience Worth Publishing Co., Inc.
81 Tiffany Place,   Brooklyn, New York City.

TELKA

An Idyl of Medieval England

By
PATIENCE WORTH

AUTHOR OF "THE SORRY TALE," "HOPE TRUEBLOOD," "LIGHT FROM BEYOND" (SELECTED POEMS), "PATIENCE WORTH" (WITH SPIRIT PORTRAIT), "THE POT UPON THE WHEEL," ETC.

Edited with a Preface by
HERMAN BEHR

NEW YORK
PATIENCE WORTH PUBLISHING CO., INC.
1928
LONDON

TWO RESPECTABLE LADIES placed their hands lightly on the ouija board and waited – humbly hoping for some message from recently deceased relatives. It was May 1913, the town was St Louis in the southern state of Missouri, and the two ladies were a Mrs Hutchings and her friend, Mrs Pearl Curran.

The pointer of the ouija board began to move, apparently struggling to spell out a certain name. 'Pat-C, Pat-C, Pat-C . . .' it insisted, while the ladies turned the name over in their minds in bewilderment. Mrs Curran's husband John, who was also in the room, suggested that it might be a deceased Irishman. Come to think of it, Mr Curran went on (with perhaps just a hint of a twinkle in his eye), he had once known a Pat McQuillan. Immediately, the late Mr McQuillan seemed to take over the board for a time, cursing mildly to give plausibility t the character of a 'vivid Hibernian'.

However, Mr Curran, contemptuous of what he saw as the ladies' gullibility, had invented Pat McQuillan and was naturally amused to see his fictitious Irishman swear at them. But 'Pat-C', once unhindered by the pranks of Mr Curran, was to come through again – and establish herself as one of the most prolific post-mortem authors in the remarkable history of 'automatic writing'.

On 22 June 'Pat' returned and spelt out a pretty but obscure paragraph: 'Oh, why let sorrow steel thy heart? Thy bosom is but its foster-mother, the world its cradle and the loving home its grave.' Not the utterance of an imaginary Irishman this time, but it proved to be an auspicious beginning to a lengthy and, indeed, celebrated partnership between Mrs Curran and the unknown 'writer'. Pat announced herself quite clearly on 8 July, when 'the board seemed to possess unusual strength', as 'Patience Worth'.

At first Patience Worth was reluctant to give any information about herself or her past life on Earth – or, indeed, her present situation (a common enough phenomenon in the seance room). She merely contented herself with spelling out such quaint advice as: 'Thine own barley corn may weevil, but thee'lt crib thy neighbour's and sack his shelling.' Mrs Curran, fascinated by the phenomenon, was nevertheless bewildered by these rustic sayings and often spoke sharply to Patience, requesting understandable English and a clearer 'message'.

Eventually Patience Worth told how she had been born in Dorset in the 17th century. She had been raised as a good Quaker girl, humbly working in the fields and busying herself with domestic chores, until her family emigrated to America. Not long afterwards, Patience was killed by Indians.

A clearer picture was hard to come by, for

Above: American Indians attacking European settlers in the 17th century. Patience Worth claimed she had been born in Dorset in the 17th century, emigrated as a Quaker to the New World, and been killed by Indians. But if questioned further about her earthly life she was consistently reticent

Patience apparently enjoyed her life on Earth so little that she could hardly bring herself to recall it. Perhaps such a short and unfulfilling life was not worth remembering, especially as – now she had 'found' Mrs Curran – she had an opportunity to make up for lost time.

From 1913 until Mrs Curran's death in 1938 Patience Worth 'dictated' a colossal number of words, mostly of a quality that can fairly be described as 'literary'. Some of this output was in the quaint English that she had first used, some was in a more modern, readable style. Her speed was enormous: one evening she produced 22 poems. In five years she 'wrote' 1,600,000 words through the mediumship of Mrs Curran.

Psychic bestseller

If sheer volume of words were the most remarkable aspect of this case, we might never have heard about it. Yet more staggering were the variety and quality of what Patience Worth wrote. She composed poems, novels and plays. One of her full-length novels, *Hope Trueblood*, was published in England under the name 'Patience Worth', with no explanation of the bizarre circumstances surrounding its composition. It won acclaim from the totally unsuspecting critics and public alike.

Hope Trueblood was a highly emotional tale of the life and trials of an illegitimate child, set in Victorian England. The *Sheffield Independent* commented favourably: 'Patience Worth must command a wide field of readers by the sheer excellence of *Hope Trueblood*, which contains sufficient high-grade characters, splendidly fashioned, to stock half a dozen novels.' The *Yorkshire Post*, a little more ambiguously, remarked that 'the writer, whose first work this is, harks back to the time in which the Brontës wrote, in order to portray in a form so exactly

Opposite: Mrs Pearl Curran, Patience Worth's amanuensis, who died in 1938. Though 'Patience's' books won critical acclaim, Mrs Curran's own literary abilities were negligible and her education limited. (She thought Tennyson's famous poem was called *The lady of Charlotte*, for example.) It seems impossible that Mrs Curran could have deliberately invented the ghostly Patience – but there is no evidence to show that Patience ever existed on Earth as she claimed

appropriate the biography of a brat. . . .'

Patience's epic 'Golden Age' poem *Telka* contained 60,000 words and made astonishingly accurate use of Middle English phraseology. Her book *The sorry tale* told in 325,000 words the story of a contemporary of Christ whose life ran parallel to his and who ended by being crucified beside him as one of the thieves. *The sorry tale* was written extremely rapidly – in an evening's work of only two hours, Patience Worth could produce an average of 3000 words. In addition, no research was necessary. The details of social, domestic and political life in ancient Palestine and Rome, and the language and customs of Greeks, Arabians, Romans and several sects of Jews are rich and convincing. They could have been set down only by a highly knowledgeable scholar who had specialised in the history of the Middle East of 2000 years ago.

This could not have been Mrs Curran. She had been to Sunday School and that was the limit of her knowledge of the Bible lands.

Lavendar and lace

A purple sky; twilight,
Silver-fringed of tremorous stars;
Cloud rifts, tattered, as old lace,
And a shuttling moon – wan-faced,
 seeking.

Twilight, and garden shadows;
The liquid note of some late songster;
And the scent of lavendar and rue,
Like memory of the day aclinging!

PATIENCE WORTH, 12 January 1926

(*'Lavendar' was Patience's own spelling*)

She was not fond of reading and had finished her school education at about 15 years of age. She had never been abroad and, indeed, had rarely left St Louis. Until the appearance of Patience Worth she had concentrated her energies on being a housewife and an amateur singer of some talent. She knew little poetry and the verses she composed as an adolescent were no worse – but certainly no better – than those of any other girl of her age and background. One such work, entitled *The secret tear*, was written when she was 15. It began (with her own spelling reproduced):

 I heard a voice whisper 'go out and pray'
 See how in the garden the fairies did play
 So out I went in the fresh summer air
 I spied a sweet rose and she was
  passingley fair
 But she hung her fair head, and her
  bright carmean cheek
 Could not have been equaled so far as
  you'de seek

This is not the sort of juvenilia one would expect from the pen that was later to 'write' works described by the psychical researcher

Henry Holt as 'very close to masterpieces'. One might make out a case for Mrs Curran being a late developer but this seems unlikely in view of the sheer volume of literature produced through her that was of better than passable quality.

Naturally enough, 'Patience Worth' was intensively investigated by psychical researchers as well as academics. In 1929 Walter Franklin Prince, the Executive Research Officer of the Boston Society for Psychical Research, wrote a book, *The case of Patience Worth*, in which he detailed the investigations to which Mrs Curran had been subjected.

Prince, together with Charles E. Cory of Washington University, one Caspar S. Yost and other members of the Society, searched Mrs Curran's house for books of esoteric knowledge that could have been incorporated, consciously or unconsciously, into such works as *The sorry tale*. They found none. They also noted that the few books of poetry in the Currans' meagre library were unthumbed, and in one the pages were uncut. (Mrs Curran firmly believed that Tennyson's famous poem *The lady of Shalott* was called *The lady of Charlotte*.)

The investigators tested Mrs Curran's ability to write in her own persona by asking her to produce short stories and poetry. These reveal a style that might be expected from a housewife unused to putting her thoughts on paper. Her personality shows through sufficiently to make any connection with the serious Quaker attitudes of Patience Worth seem positively ridiculous.

Other incidents concerning communications from Patience reveal significant gaps in Mrs Curran's education and reading. For

Above: a ouija board in action. This is similar to the one used, at first out of idle curiosity, by Mrs Curran in 1913. The letters of the alphabet, the numbers 1 to 10, and the words 'yes' and 'no' are inscribed on the board. The pointer is mounted on castors and one or more of the 'sitters' places a hand lightly on it. Questions are asked of the 'spirits' and almost every time the pointer moves – as if directed by an invisible force – and spells out messages. Although proper ouija boards are not much used these days, many people use an impromptu version with the letters, numbers and words on pieces of paper arranged in a circle on a table, and with an upturned glass acting as the pointer

The poet from the shadows

A phantom? Weel enough,
Prove thee thyself to me!
I say, behold, here I be,
Buskins, kirtle, cap and petty-skirts,
And much tongue!
Weel, what hast thou to prove thee? This was Patience Worth's verse entitled 'Patience Worth', a wry comment on her unique status as the genius of the ouija board – the 'phantom' behind the poetry, plays and novels written through Mrs Curran which won major critical acclaim on both sides of the Atlantic.

Among numerous literary works she produced poems, plays and *The sorry tale* – an enormous novel of 300,000 words 'dictated' every evening over a two year period. This massive work (concerning the fate of another child born in Bethlehem on the same night as Jesus) revealed scholarly knowledge of Biblical lands and customs way above

that of the medium. Professors of literature, poets, journalists and churchmen hailed the work as 'the Gospel according to Patience Worth', and gushingly complimented its ghostly author on its brilliance. But not everyone agreed. Some reviewers commented that they found her writing to be 'feverish, high-flown and terribly prolix'. Other reviewers compromised uneasily: 'but it is a wonderful book, well worth wrestling with, and the marvel is, who wrote it?'

For many people the mystery of its authorship was the book's main attraction, while others were prejudiced against it for the same reason, thinking it 'spooky' and distasteful. But Patience Worth – whoever she was –, was compared to the Brontës, Keats, Browning, Milton and even Shakespeare. She was often invited to literary receptions, but sent her regrets.

example, a Roman Catholic archbishop in the St Louis area had been preaching that if spirits returned after death, they were 'emissaries of the Evil One'. Mrs Curran asked Patience her views on the subject:

At once Patience had this to say: 'I say me, who became apparent before the Maid? Who became a vision before Bernadette? No less than the Mother; yet they have lifted up their voices saying the dead are in his [the devil's] keeping.' This last about the dead gave us the clue to what she referred, though we had no idea of what she meant by the rest. Looking up the matter the next day we found that Bernadette Soubirous was the Maid of Lourdes. . . .

Subtle impostor?

A fraud would readily acknowledge the need to look up a reference transmitted by a 'spirit' – ah, the reader would think, Mrs Curran had not even heard of Bernadette of Lourdes. But surely Patience's reference to 'the Maid' was not to 'the Maid of Lourdes' but to *the* Maid – Joan of Arc. Surely two visionary women, not one, were being cited to prove that 'spirits' were not always 'emissaries of the Evil One'. If Mrs Curran pretended to miss this point, she was a very subtle impostor.

But who was Patience Worth? Was she really a Quaker woman who emigrated from her native Dorset 300 years before to die a spinster in America? She has not been traced. But her quaint English has been analysed by linguists and apparently she used perfectly the language and idiom of her place and day. The linguists drew attention to the spelling of certain words that were spoken very differently in the 17th century than they are now. For example, 'boy' was pronounced *bwy*, 'with' and 'give' were *wi'* and *gi'e*.

But even assuming that Miss Worth had existed and returned to pour out her literary talent – denied fulfilment in life – to Mrs Curran, how could an uneducated Quaker girl know of the customs of ancient Jewish sects detailed in *The sorry tale*?

Did she perhaps gain this extensive knowledge after her death, at a kind of postmortem university? Some Spiritualists would take this view. Other groups believe such knowledge is plucked from the 'Akashic records' (see page 41): in this case, either by Patience Worth, by Mrs Curran's subconscious mind or – who knows? – by both.

Celebrity brought recognition from public bodies. The States Capitol Commission of Missouri, which wished to decorate the walls of the new State House with inscriptions by local literary figures, called on Patience Worth, through Mrs Curran, to supply a short piece. It was to be no more than 120 letters long. Patience immediately produced, as fast as Mrs Curran could write:

'Tis the grain of God that be within thy hands. Cast nay grain awhither. Even

A daughter of the dead

If Patience had been a frustrated writer she remedied that easily through Mrs Curran. But her maternal instinct had also been frustrated, so Mrs Curran received her most bizarre instructions: that she should adopt a baby girl whom she would 'share' with the long-dead Patience. Patience gave Mrs Curran a description of this as yet unborn child: it must have red hair, blue eyes and be of Anglo-Scottish descent.

The Currans found a recently widowed pregnant woman who agreed that they could adopt her child if she happened to die in childbirth. She did indeed die and the child – fitting Patience's description exactly – became known as Patience Worth Wee Curran.

The child grew up, supervised by the ghostly Patience (who insisted on her wearing quaint Quaker-girl clothes) and later moved to California where she married twice. In 1938 Mrs Curran died and Patience fell silent forever. But in 1943, at the age of 27 and in good health, Patience Wee had a premonition of her approaching death. She began to lose weight and a very mild heart ailment was diagnosed. Then, just before Christmas, 1943, she died in her sleep. Many believed that her ghostly 'mother' had come for her own.

Above: Dr Walter Franklin Prince (1863–1934) an ex-Methodist minister and psychical researcher. He was particularly interested in the case of Patience Worth, believing it to be one of the most important psychic case histories of all time

the chaff is His, and the dust thy brother's.

Counting spaces, punctuation marks and letters, this adds up to 120 characters precisely.

The ouija board was soon found to be too slow and clumsy as a means for taking down Patience's dictation. Mrs Curran began automatic writing proper. This involves resting a pen or pencil, held lightly in the hand, on a piece of paper. If one is so gifted, the pen will begin to write of its own accord. But soon even this method became too restrictive for the prolific outpourings of Patience Worth, who began instead to communicate directly with Mrs Curran's mind. She 'spoke' her poetry through Mrs Curran, who at the same time witnessed beautiful, atmospheric visions. Mr Curran took down Mrs Curran's/Patience Worth's utterances in longhand, and they were then typed.

Patience admitted to having burning literary ambition – and also acknowledged that in some way she might be a messenger of God. Perhaps she was suggesting that the mysterious phenomenon she was causing could guide people to God and a belief in eternal things. She wrote: 'I weave not, nay but neath these hands shall such a word set up, that Earth shall burn with wonder,'

The art of automatic writing

Only very rarely does automatic writing produce anything like literature. When a genius of Shakespeare's stature 'comes through', the results are bound to be fascinating.

AUTOMATIC WRITING is still a matter of intense interest among psychologists and parapsychologists alike. Not all occurrences of automatic script are as difficult to explain away as the remarkable case of Patience Worth (see page 48). A leading British psychical researcher and scientist, Professor Arthur Ellison, has said: 'I expect a third of the population of England could produce some form of automatic writing – but the results would be mostly gibberish.'

Anyone can try an experiment by resting a pen lightly on a blank page, diverting their attention from it and letting the pen do what it will. It used to be assumed that automatic script must be the product of discarnate entities, desperate to communicate and grateful for the opportunity to take command of a pen. The only question in believers' minds was: 'Is the communicator an Earth-bound spirit or a spirit sent by God?' But the scribbles produced in automatic writing can reveal a great deal, if not about the spirit world, then certainly about the subconscious mind of the pen-holder.

In the first three decades of the 20th century automatic writing was in fact used as a tool in diagnosing and treating mental

Above: William Shakespeare and his contemporaries. In 1947 a medium named Hester Dowden allegedly communicated with Shakespeare (seated centre) and other Elizabethans through automatic writing. She was told that the plays attributed to Shakespeare were in fact a group effort. Among the contributors were Francis Beaumont (standing third from left), John Fletcher (seated third from left) and Francis Bacon (seated at the end of the table)

disturbances. Dr Anita Mühl was a pioneer of this particular method of encouraging patients to express spontaneously their hidden conflicts.

The beginner in automatic writing may have to be very patient (and suffer writer's cramp before a single word has been written), for it can take hours before the pen begins to move, seemingly of its own accord. Some people never achieve automatic writing; many get meaningless squiggles or jumbles of letters; but a very few get coherent, intelligent and apparently purposeful messages, sometimes in handwriting distinctly different from their own.

An ex-clergyman, William Stainton Moses, was a medium in the latter part of the 19th century who 'specialised' in automatic script, although he could produce these automatisms only while in a self-induced trance. From 1872 to 1883 he filled 24 notebooks with trance-inspired writings, mingled with 'spirit writings', some signed. (Mendelssohn allegedly appended his signature to a page of Moses's script.)

If one takes a sceptical view, certain 19th-century religious works were not directly dictated by angels or by God, as alleged, but were the result of automatic writing by the 'prophets'. *The book of Mormon*, for example, was purportedly dictated by an angel called Moroni to a New York State farm boy, Joseph Smith, in 1827. It was written in a style similar, but inferior, to that of the King James Bible. It is not necessary to believe that Joseph Smith was a liar to doubt that *The book of Mormon* is the word of God.

One early case of automatic writing that is still considered unique is that which involved William T. Stead, a leading British Spiritualist of the late 19th century, and a certain friend who communicated with him automatically through his pen. What is remarkable about this particular case is that the friend was alive at the time. The story goes as follows in Stead's own words:

A friend of mine . . . was to lunch with me on the Wednesday if she had returned to town. On the Monday afternoon I wished to know about this, so taking up my pen I asked the lady mentally if she had returned home. My hand wrote as follows: 'I am sorry to say that I have had the most unpleasant experience, which I am almost ashamed to tell you. I left Haslemere at 2.27 p.m. in a second-class compartment in which there were two women and a man. At Godalming the women got out and I was left alone with the man. He came over and sat by me. I was alarmed and pushed him away. He would not move, however, and tried to kiss me. I was furious and there was a struggle, during which I seized his umbrella and struck him with it repeatedly, but it broke, and I was afraid I would get the worst of it, when the train stopped some distance from Guildford. The man took fright, left me before the train reached the station, jumped out and took to his heels. I was extremely agitated, but I kept the umbrella.'

Stead dashed off a sympathetic note to the lady, explaining the reasons for his solicitude, and – being a thorough investigator – asked her to call, bringing with her the broken umbrella as evidence. She replied in some perturbation, saying she had intended

Above: American psychical researcher Dr J.B. Rhine, who believed that most automatic writings can be explained as the spontaneous expression of subconscious conflicts

Below left: William Stainton Moses, a 19th-century medium who claimed to have received numerous messages from the spirit world through automatic writing. One of his scripts (below), dated 1874, was 'signed' by Mendelssohn – who died in 1847

Below right: Edward de Vere, 17th Earl of Oxford. According to medium Hester Dowden, Oxford wrote the lyrical and romantic passages of 'Shakespeare's' plays, and was the author of most of the sonnets

never to mention the incident to anyone. However, she added, one point in his account of her misadventure was wrong – the umbrella was hers, not her assailant's.

A great American psychical researcher of modern times, Dr J. B. Rhine, was inclined to dismiss automatic writings as spontaneous 'motor automatisms' or, as previously hinted, the outward expression of subconscious conflicts, obsessions or repressions. There seems little doubt that he and his likeminded colleagues are right in this appraisal of much automatic writing. But Dr Rhine admitted that some cases – that of Patience Worth, for example – are not so easily dismissed.

A provocative case of automatic writing occurred in 1947, through the mediumship of Hester Dowden, who had for many years been famous for the automatic scripts that she produced, even when blindfolded. Percy Allen, an author, sat with her while she held written 'conversations', allegedly with Elizabethan dramatists. As a result of these seances Mr Allen believed he discovered the answer to the tantalising question 'Who was Shakespeare?' Was he really Francis Bacon? Lord Oxford? Or perhaps was William Shakespeare just William Shakespeare?

Mrs Dowden claimed she received written information on the matter from those three gentlemen, and also from other Elizabethans involved in the writing or staging of plays. Mrs Dowden's communicators explained that the 'Shakespeare' plays were a group effort. Shakespeare and Lord Oxford were the principal contributors, while Beaumont and Fletcher, famous as the authors of many other plays, occasionally provided additional material. Bacon acted as a kind of stern script editor.

Each did what he was good at: Shakespeare created many of the stronger characters, both comic and tragic, such as Iago and Falstaff,

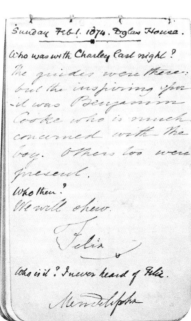

and he had a talent for dramatic construction, which the others willingly used. Lord Oxford, on the other hand, created the 'honeyed Shakespeare' by writing the lyrical and romantic passages.

Mrs Dowden was similarly informed that it was Lord Oxford who penned the majority of the sonnets. He also 'dictated' three new ones to her.

Bacon reiterated time and again to Mrs Dowden that the body of literature that the world knows as Shakespeare's was a group effort. Will of Stratford himself allegedly told Mrs Dowden:

> I was quick at knowing what would be effective on stage. I would find a plot (*Hamlet* was one), consult with Oxford, and form a skeleton edifice, which he would furnish and people, as befitted the subject . . . I was the *skeleton* of the body that wrote the plays. The flesh and blood was *not* mine, but I was *always* in the production.

Of course, automatic literature may be a dramatisation of a deep or repressed creativity, finding expression through a means we can so far only guess at. After all, many writers and artists over the centuries have 'listened' to their 'muse'. Often whole plots, scenes or minutely observed characters have 'come unbidden' to writers, dramatists, poets. Often, when Charles Dickens was dozing in his armchair, a wealth of characters would appear before him 'as it were, begging to be set down on paper'. Samuel Taylor Coleridge dreamed the whole of his poem *Kubla Khan* and would have written it all down for posterity had not someone known to history only as 'a person from Porlock' called casually and put most of it out of his mind forever. Mary Shelley dreamed *Frankenstein*, Robert Louis Stevenson came to rely on his dreams for his stories, including

Above: a 19th-century engraving entitled 'Charles Dickens's legacy to England'. Dickens said that many of his characters simply appeared before him while he was dozing, almost as if they had a life of their own

the allegorical Dr Jekyll and Mr Hyde. When such a writer as Charles Dickens says a tale 'wrote itself', however, we can only assume he did *not* mean his pen shot across the paper inscribing, of its own accord, *Oliver Twist*. Inspiration is in practice very different from the process of automatic writing.

Somewhere between the two, perhaps, lay the strange case of Patrick Branwell Brontë. He was an unfortunate and unsympathetic character, famous mainly for his inability to hold liquor and laudanum, or to cope with sharing an isolated house on the moors with his eccentric sisters Charlotte, Emily and Anne. He had literary pretensions, which came to nothing. However, during one of his brief periods of humble employment (as a railway clerk) he discovered that he could compile the week's railway accounts with one hand, while his other, quite independently, began to scrawl. First the name of his beloved dead sister, Maria, appeared; then came other fragments – some prose, some poetry. He later claimed to have written an alternative version of *Wuthering Heights* by pure coincidence at the same time as Emily was writing a book of the same name.

However, this was the second version of the incident. He had previously stolen the opening chapter of Emily's book and read it to his cronies as his own work. It was only when he was disbelieved that he came up with the 'alternative version' account.

Left: Mary Wollstonecraft Shelley (1797-1851), creator of *Frankenstein*, one of the most famous 'horror' stories. The plot of the novel came to her in a dream

Literature of the dead

Can novels, poems and plays be 'written' by the dead? This chapter describes some notable cases of automatic writing

THERE APPEAR TO BE fashions in paranormal phenomena as in other aspects of life, and automatic writing seemed to have fallen from grace for a period, whether as an attempt to communicate with the dead or even as a party trick. Yet automatic scripts are being produced in vast quantities today. Possibly the world's most important and prolific psychic writer has largely escaped attention in Europe and America because he is a Brazilian, writing in Portuguese that is sometimes extremely erudite and technical.

Francisco Candido ('Chico') Xavier, now in his seventies, is certainly one of Brazil's most popular figures, devoting his life to

Above: 'Chico' Xavier, Brazil's foremost Spiritist writer, at one of his public automatic writing sessions

Inset: the frontispiece of *Parnassus from beyond the tomb* – allegedly written by no less than 56 dead poets

helping the poor and producing edifying, entertaining and highly profitable best-sellers. He does not accept any money for these books, nor any credit. For, he says, he did not write them – discarnate Brazilian authors did.

For the past 50 years Xavier has spent at least five hours a day letting dead authors write through him. He has often given over his precious spare time for the spirits to use, for until his retirement in 1961 he also had a full-time (but humble) job in local government offices.

Best-sellers from beyond

One of 'his' best-sellers is a volume of poetry called *Parnassus from beyond the tomb*. It contains 259 poems (taking up 421 pages) in markedly differing styles, and is signed by 56 of the leading literary figures of the Portuguese-speaking world – all of whom are dead. The poems deal with many subjects – love, the hypocrisy of the priesthood, the nature of human evolution–and some contain jokes One is a simple declaration of the poet's identity, entitled *Ego sum* (Latin for 'I am'). Translated by Guy Lyon Playfair, author of *The flying cow* and expert on Brazilian Spiritism, it reads: 'I am who I am. Therefore it would be extremely unjust if I did not declare myself; if I lied, or deceived you in anonymity, since I am Augusto.' And the poem is signed 'Augusto dos Anjos', a famous deceased Brazilian poet.

But nothing so far described offers anything like proof that the automatic scripts of Chico Xavier are not either conscious or unconscious frauds (although one would think a conscious impostor would eagerly accept the millions of dollars his books have made over the years).

It is true that Xavier is not entirely illiterate – he had an elementary school education (which, as Mr Playfair wryly points out, can be very elementary indeed in Brazil). But the vocabulary he uses is far above the heads of even educated people – he says he often cannot understand a word of it! This applies to the massive work *Nosso lar* (*Our home*), which totals no less than 2459 pages and was purportedly dictated to Xavier by the discarnate doctor Andre Luiz, a pioneer in tropical medicine. It is in fact a novel in nine books with a very simple plot – the hero dies at the beginning of the first book and the subsequent action takes place in the next world ('our home'). This, says Dr Luiz, is not the paradise that the priests tell of, but is much like our life on Earth. 'Death is merely a change of clothing,' he warns and adds that the hereafter is 'the paradise or hell we ourselves have created.' We have a noble purpose, even the humblest of us, says Luiz:

'We are sons of God and heirs to the centuries, conquering values from experience to experience and millennium to millennium.' Reincarnation, we are told, does take place but the rules governing it are much more complex than many living people, even those who believe in it, can guess at.

This massive sequence of novels discourses at great length on a variety of medical and technological subjects, discussing in detail, for example, the fertilisation of the human egg and the slow processes of evolution on Earth. On 2 February 1958 Xavier took down a lengthy passage containing this sort of phraseology:

> The existent hiatus, as noted by Hugo de Vries, in the development of mutationism was bridged by the activities of the Servants of Earthly Organogenesis, who submitted the *Leptothrix* family to profound alterations . . .

Hugo de Vries was a Dutch botanist famous for his work on the laws of heredity – a fact not very likely to be taught at a Brazilian elementary school at the beginning of the 20th century. (Once Xavier had complained to Augusto dos Anjos that he couldn't understand what he was 'writing'. 'Look,' came the reply, 'I'm going to write what I can, for your head can't really cope!')

The spirits dictate

By the mid 1970s he had produced 130 books, all bearing on their title page the phrase 'dictated by the spirit of . . .'. More than 400 discarnate authors are said to have written posthumous works through him, and they are certainly selling better, using Xavier as their 'agent', than they did in life. *Our home* alone had sold more than 150,000 copies by late 1980.

One of his more remarkable achievements – which some consider final 'proof' that dead writers are still working through him – was a bizarre incidence of co-authorship, very reminiscent of the case of the 'cross-correspondences' (see page 58). *Evolution in two worlds* was psychically written by Xavier, in the small town of Pedro Leopoldo, a chapter a time – but *alternate* chapters, making no consecutive sense at all – and by Dr Waldo Vieira, who 'wrote' the interim chapters hundreds of miles away. But it was only when Xavier had finished his pile of disjointed and apparently unfinished chapters that his spirit guide told him to contact Dr Vieira. Of course then the whole project made sense. This was the first of 17 books they were to write in this way. As Guy Lyon Playfair points out, frequently one of Dr Vieira's chapters – written without any knowledge of the previous chapter 'written' by Xavier – takes up the story precisely where the other left off.

Now an old and frail man – nearly sightless in one eye – Xavier spends his days helping at the welfare centre 'his' royalties have financed, writing down spirit messages

THE DIVINE ADVENTURE
IONA: BY SUNDOWN SHORES
STUDIES IN SPIRITUAL HISTORY
BY FIONA MACLEOD

LONDON: CHAPMAN AND HALL, LTD.
1900
Second Edition

Top: the Scottish poet and occultist William Sharp, who had a secondary personality known as Fiona Macleod. Both personalities wrote, but quite differently. Their work was published separately, as Sharp had no sense that Macleod's writing was his own

Above: the frontispiece of *The divine adventure* by Fiona Macleod, a mystical work about the Scottish Isle of Iona, published in 1900

for individuals who need advice, signing books, shaking hands, handing out roses, greeting each new face as if he had been anticipating that very meeting with the utmost pleasure. His 'automatic' writing is often done in public, for perhaps three hours at a time, for anyone to watch. (He writes, said an observer, as if his hand were driven by a battery.) He types up his own psychically produced scripts, answers his own letters (usually over 200 a day, many seeking advice or prayers from him, others simply consisting of fan mail), and attends public Spiritist meetings.

He is widely regarded as a saint – even, by some of his followers, as the reincarnation of St Francis of Assisi. But he has his detractors, and his enemies. The Roman Catholic Church in Brazil believes him to be evil, even possessed by the Devil, and one leading Brazilian Jesuit has taken as his mission in life the utter destruction of Chico Xavier's reputation.

Europeans tend to discount even such well-attested cases as this when they occur in distant and exotic places like Brazil. Yet automatic writing flourishes in Europe today. The young British psychic Matthew Manning, although an accomplished automatic writer in the traditional way, has found that 'spirits' have taken it on themselves to do the writing. Notable amongst them is Robert Webbe, who built and lived in the Mannings' Cambridgeshire home in the 17th century and haunted it for some years. Over 300 names and short phrases in differing styles of handwriting have appeared on Matthew Manning's bedroom wall. After each session of spirit graffiti a blunted pencil would be found on his bed, although during the time of the writings no member of the family had been in the room, or even, on many of the occasions, in the house.

In Scotland a publishing company has been set up devoted entirely to the works of a particular spirit writer – or rather, a pair of authors making up a double personality. One half of the double is William Sharp, a Scot and self-styled poet and occultist, who died at Il Castello di Maniace, in Sicily, in 1905, aged 50. Above his grave close to Mount Etna there is an Iona cross, bearing two epitaphs. One says:

> Farewell to the known and exhausted
> Welcome to the unknown and illimitable.

The other, more obscurely says:

> Love is more great than we conceive, and Death is the keeper of unknown redemptions. F. M.

So who was 'F.M.'? These are the initials of Fiona Macleod, his *alter ego*, his feminine side personified, whose name and works had inspired the 'Celtic renaissance' in late 19th-century Scotland.

The Paisley project

Dual, or even multiple, personalities are not unknown in the annals of psychiatric medicine. But what is so significant about 'Wilfion' (Sharp's own collective name for his two selves) is that he/she is allegedly communicating thoughts and poetic works from beyond the grave.

From the early days of 1970 an American expert on William Sharp, Konrad Hopkins, began to receive psychic scripts from many discarnate souls – including one 'George Windsor', better known perhaps as King George VI – but mainly from Sharp himself. In 1974 Hopkins met a Dutch sensitive called Ronald van Roekel and shortly afterwards they began a publishing venture in Paisley, Scotland, called Wilfion Books.

Meanwhile in Ventnor, Isle of Wight, a lady called Margo Williams was discovering her long-hidden gifts as a medium. By summer 1980 Margo had received more than 4000 psychic scripts, purporting to be dictated by more than 360 discarnate persons. The first was her spirit guide, Jane, and the second was someone called William Sharp.

The deceased Scottish poet clairaudiently informed Konrad Hopkins of the Margo Williams connection. A correspondence between the medium and the directors of Wilfion books sprang up and soon arrangements were under way for *The Wilfion scripts* – the Wilfion writings received through Mrs Williams – to be published in Paisley.

There are 92 verses and some prose that make up *The Wilfion scripts*. The verses are, on the whole, short, childish (some would say child-like) and bad. The introduction to the

Above: King George VI, who, as 'George Windsor' is said to have communicated posthumously with the American medium Konrad Hopkins. Hopkins was one of the partners who published *The Wilfion scripts*

Above right: Margo Williams, the medium whose many automatic scripts include poems from 'Wilfion'

verses, by Hopkins and van Roekel, includes this curiously obscure apology for the low quality of the poetry:

> Sharp . . . admits that the verse is bad because he is trying to reach a confession of a truly horrific sight which he either saw himself or relived through his ability to pick up sensations at stone circles and it then haunted him the rest of his life.

But Mrs Williams generously ascribes Wilfion 'a masterly economy of words'. On 12 December 1976 William Sharp dictated this through her:

> Observes scenes from the past
> Which impress and will last
> Scenes which survive throughout ages
> Make interesting reading on pages.

And, perhaps shrewdly summing up the feelings of many of his latest readers, Sharp had this to write on 19 January 1977:

> What a joke
> I can cloak
> Sharp by name
> But be same.
> Macleod be known by
> Until day I die,
> Write tales so strange
> Over a wide range
> Celtic verse
> Sounds much worse
> From intelligent being
> Little folk to be seeing,
> What a joke,
> Make men choke
> With laughter loud
> About Macleod.

In the jargon of parapsychology all these bizarre effects could be the products of 'telepathic psychokinesis', 'motor automatisms', 'repressed psychosexual creativity'. But is this not disguising the fact that we just don't know what is behind them?

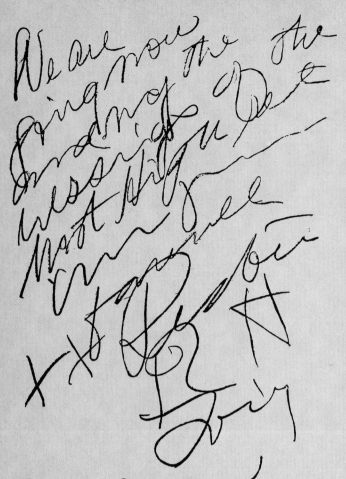

Survival: teasing out the truth

Did a group of dedicated psychical researchers plan – after their deaths – to send evidence of their survival to certain chosen mediums? LYNN PICKNETT describes a controversial series of 'communications'

AN ARDENT AND VOCIFEROUS believer in the afterlife, Frederic Myers, classical scholar and founder member of the Society for Psychical Research (SPR), wished passionately to communicate his belief to others. Judging by an impressive body of evidence, he never desired it more than after his death in 1901. For the following 30 years the SPR collected and collated over 2000 automatic scripts purporting to be transmitted from Myers and other deceased members of the Society through the mediumship of several ladies. They seem to have been specifically designed to prove to the living the reality of the afterlife.

What have become known as the 'cross-correspondences' do indeed indicate that here there was some kind of intelligent communication between the living and the dead – arranged in such a way as to confound critics. Whoever thought it up, on this or the other side of the veil, was very ingenious.

Apart from Myers the purported spirit communicators were Edmund Gurney (died 1888) and Professor Henry Sidgwick (died 1900). The mediums included 'Mrs Holland'

(pseudonym of Mrs Alice Fleming), who lived in India and was the sister of Rudyard Kipling; 'Mrs Willett' (pseudonym of Mrs Coombe-Tennant), who lived in London; Mrs A. W. Verrall, a teacher of Classics at Cambridge University; her daughter, Helen (later Mrs W. H. Salter); and the famous trance medium Mrs Leonora Piper, of Boston, Massachusetts.

A bold and complex plan

The purpose and plan of the cross-correspondences are bold yet complex, sometimes almost beyond belief. But it is this complexity that gives them their unique air of authenticity. The plan, as far as it can be understood, is this:

After Myers's death, he and his deceased colleagues from the SPR worked out a system by which fragments of automatic script, meaningless in themselves, would be transmitted through different mediums in widely separated parts of the world. When brought together they would prove to make sense. To make the situation more difficult these fragments would be in Greek or Latin, or contain

Above: Frederic Myers, a respected founder member of Britain's Society for Psychical Research, apparently tried to prove his survival after death to his living friends and colleagues. He supposedly sent messages through various mediums, in widely separated parts of the world, by means of automatic writing, which he had studied intensively in life. The fragment above is in a hand markedly different from the normal script of the medium who produced it, Mrs Leonora Piper

allusions – sometimes fragmentary in themselves – to classical works. In Myers's words as dictated to Mrs Verrall: 'Record the bits and when fitted they will make the whole . . . I will give the words between you neither alone can read but together they will give the clue he wants.'

The erudition of the classical references was beyond the scope of most of the mediums, except the Verralls, showing that the scripts were not the products of their own minds. The fact that the fragments were unintelligible to the mediums themselves would rule out the possibility of joint telepathic composition by them.

It seems that Myers thought of this plan once he had the ultimate personal proof of the afterlife. None of the thoughts he recorded during his earthly life even hints at this scheme. But at least he knew how to set about proving his point: as an ex-president of the SPR he knew which mediums were genuine and competent automatic 'scribes'.

In many cases the various automatists – in England, India and the United States – were instructed to send their apparently meaningless scripts to certain investigators, whose addresses were supplied by the communicators. Each piece of automatic script was to be carefully dated and, if possible, witnessed.

An example of what H. F. Saltmarsh, in *Evidence of personal survival*, calls a 'simple'

cross-correspondence is as follows. Mrs Piper, in America, heard in a trance state a word she first took to be *sanatos*. She then corrected herself (she was speaking her impressions out loud to be written down) to *tanatos*. That was on 17 April 1907. Later in the month the word came through as *thanatos* and on another occasion was repeated three times. On 7 May the whole phrase 'I want to say *thanatos*' 'came through' Mrs Piper. She did not recognise the word as the Greek for 'death'.

Meanwhile, on 16 April 1907, Mrs Holland in India received a curious opening phrase in her automatic script: 'Maurice Morris Mors. And with that the shadow of death fell on his limbs.' The two names seemed to be an attempt to get to the word *mors* – Latin for death.

The fire of life

Yet again, on 29 April 1907, Mrs Verrall in Cambridge received this cryptic communication: 'Warmed both hands before the fire of life. It fades and I am ready to depart.' Then her hand drew what she took to be the Greek capital letter delta (a triangle). Next came these disjointed phrases: 'Give lilies with full hands [in Latin] . . . Come away, Come away, *Pallida mors* [Latin, meaning 'pale death'].'

There are several allusions to death here:

Below: Mrs Leonora Piper was one of the most celebrated mediums of modern times. Several of the distinguished researchers who studied her, including Myers, allegedly communicated through her after their deaths

Hope, star and Browning

Above: Robert Browning, whose poems include *The pied piper of Hamelin*

One of the most famous of the cross-correspondences has been labelled the 'hope, star and Browning' case. In January 1907 one of the communicators (unidentified) proposed – through Mrs Verrall – an experiment: 'An anagram would be better. Tell him that – rats, star, tars and so on . . . .'

A few days later Mrs Verrall received a script beginning:

Aster [Latin for 'star'] *Teras* [Greek, meaning 'wonder' or 'sign'] . . . The very wings of her. A WINGED DESIRE . . . the hope that leaves the earth for the sky – *Abt Vogler* . . .

Mrs Verrall recognised these as fragments from poems of Robert Browning: *Abt Vogler* and *The ring and the book*: Within a week Mrs Verrall's daughter Helen produced an automatic script that included drawings of a bird, star and crescent moon, and verbal references to songbirds.

On 11 February Mrs Piper had a sitting with Mr Piddington. Myers 'came through' and said he had previously communicated something of interest to Mrs Verrall. 'I referred to Hope and Browning . . . I also said Star.'

The investigators noted that 'hope' had been emphasised by the very fact that in the quotation it had been substituted for another word; the quotation should have read 'the passion that left the ground . . .' and not 'the hope that leaves . . .'. Mrs Verrall, who knew her Browning, had remarked after reading through her script, 'I wondered why the silly thing said "hope".'

There was now a clear correspondence between the 'hope, star and Browning' reference of Mrs Piper and the texts of the elder and younger Verrall ladies. Mrs Verrall told her daughter that there had been such a correspondence but, in order not to influence her script, referred not to 'hope, star and Browning' but to 'virtue, Mars (the planet) and Keats'. Two days later Miss Verrall produced another script that included the phrase 'a star above it all rats everywhere in Hamelin town'. This was a clear reference to the poem *The pied piper of Hamelin* – written by Browning.

Frederick Myers had an extensive knowledge of the works of Browning and had always expressed a sympathy with many of his ideals. So perhaps it was natural that his disembodied mind should turn to his old literary favourites when trying to prove his continued existence.

critic has pointed out that the hereafter, judging by the communications of the cross-correspondences, seems to be peopled solely with upper-class Edwardians with a solid classical education and a background of SPR membership. But if the next world were to be more or less a continuation of this one, without the hindrance of physical bodies, then what could be more natural than choosing one's ex-friends and colleagues for an enormous, epoch-making venture? One does not take someone with no head for heights on an Everest expedition.

To suspend disbelief for one moment: it seems that Myers was passionately trying to 'get through', using some means that could actually constitute *proof*. On 12 January 1904 Myers had written (through Mrs Holland in India): 'If it were possible for the soul to die back into earth life again I should die from sheer yearning to reach you to tell you that all that we imagined is not half wonderful enough for the truth . . . .' Through Mrs Piper in the United States he wrote: 'I am trying with all the forces . . . together to prove that I am Myers.' And again, through the Indian connection, he wrote: 'Oh, I am feeble with eagerness – how can I best be identified?'

Sceptical challenges

The whole subject of the cross-correspondences has been analysed and is still the focus of much research. On the evidence of the examples given above there will be many sceptics who will suggest that the whole business was a kind of genteel collusion, perhaps arranged by Myers and his SPR colleagues before their deaths. Or, if conscious fraud seems unlikely, perhaps this series of bizarre word-games was the result of telepathy among the mediums – and the relationship between the two Verrall ladies was surely too close for them to keep secrets from each other. The classical words and allusions came mainly through the mediumship of the women with a classical education – they were almost totally absent in the case of Mrs Willett and Mrs Piper, who did not have this background.

Then there is the fact that the 'Myers' of, say, the Piper scripts, sounds entirely different from that of, say, the Willett scripts. And although the handwriting differed from the women's own hands, it was not actually that of Myers himself.

However, it seemed that Myers and his friends were determined to nip in the bud any such sceptical 'explanations'. In life they had known and challenged both frauds and cynics – they knew what to expect. So, marshalling their spirit forces, they began a barrage of fragmentary and intellectual cross-corresponding communications, spanning continents and decades.

apparently Mrs Verrall had always seen delta as a symbol for death; the 'lilies' quotation is a distortion of a passage in the *Aeneid*, where the early death of Marcellus is foretold; and 'Come away . . .' is from the Shakespearean song in *Twelfth night* that begins: 'Come away, come away, death.' (The first passage, 'Warmed both hands . . .', is a slightly altered quotation from a poem by Walter Savage Landor.)

So three automatists, in three countries and in three languages, received both straightforward and allusive references to the subject of death.

Mr Saltmarsh explains how more complex cross-correspondences might work by giving this hypothetical example: Suppose that the topic chosen was 'Time'. Automatist A might start the ball rolling by a quotation from the hymn 'Like an ever-rolling stream'. Automatist B might follow on with a quotation from *Alice in Wonderland* dealing with the discussion concerning Time at the Mad Hatter's tea-table, e.g. 'He won't stand beating' or 'We quarrelled last March – just before he went mad, you know' and then, Automatist C gives the clue with 'Time and Tide wait for no man'. . . . Most of the actual cases are far more subtle and it was not until after much research that the connections were discovered. It is probable that even now a good many have been overlooked.

This scholarly jigsaw puzzle may seem at first glance to be a post-mortem game of intellectual snobbery. In fact, more than one

The end of the experiment

Were the cross-correspondences really an ingenious plot designed deliberately to deceive psychical researchers? Or did they, as some would claim, provide the ultimate proof of post-mortem survival?

SINCE THE DEATH in 1901 of F.W.H. Myers, founder member of the Society of Psychical Research, his discarnate spirit – it is widely believed – has communicated many times through the mediumship of living people. In the first quarter of the 20th century the deceased Myers was most active, together with dead friends, in the case of the 'cross-correspondences'.

Over 2000 examples of automatic writing purporting to have come from Myers, Henry Sidgwick, Edmund Gurney and, later, from A.W. Verrall were transmitted through a large number of mediums over a period of 30 years. The scripts took the form of fragmentary literary and classical allusions – clues to a highly complex puzzle, intended by its very erudition to prove the existence of the purported communicators, all of whom had been literary or classical scholars in life. The fragments delivered to various mediums at different times made sense only when taken together, and usually meant little or nothing to the mediums taking them down.

'The sea that moaned in pain'

One of the simpler cross-correspondences was the Roden Noel case. On 7 March 1906 in Cambridge, Mrs Verrall, one of the mediums most heavily used by 'Myers', took down in automatic writing some lines of verse, allegedly from Myers, which began with the words 'Tintagel and the sea that moaned in pain'. The lines meant nothing in particular to Mrs Verrall but her investigator, Miss Johnson of the SPR, thought it reminiscent of a poem by the Cornishman Roden Noel, called *Tintadgel*. Even when Miss Johnson pointed this out to her, Mrs Verrall could not remember having read the poem or even knowing of its existence.

Four days later, in India, Mrs Holland (pseudonym of Rudyard Kipling's sister, Mrs Alice Fleming) received this automatic script: 'This is for A.W. Ask him what the date May 26th, 1894, meant to him – to me – and to F.W.H.M. I do not think they will find it hard to recall, but if so – let them ask Nora.'

The date given is that of the death of Roden Noel. 'A.W.' refers to Dr Verrall and 'F.W.H.M.' to Myers, both of whom were acquainted with Noel. 'Nora' was the widow of Henry Sidgwick, who had been much closer to the poet. But Mrs Holland had not discovered any of these pertinent facts when on 14 March 1906 – one week after the

Henry Sidgwick (below) and Edmund Gurney (below right). Most of the scripts from 'them' containing classical references 'came through' those mediums who had knowledge of Latin and Greek – Mrs Verrall, for example, was a lecturer in Classics at Newnham College, Cambridge (bottom). It may be that the mediums were deliberately chosen because they had such knowledge. Or perhaps the communications stemmed from the mediums' own subconscious minds

English communication, and much too soon to have received any hints from Mrs Verrall or Miss Johnson – she received this script: 'Eighteen, 15, 4, 5, 14. Fourteen, 15, 5, 12. Not to be taken as they stand. See Rev. [the book of Revelation] 13, 18, but only the central eight words, not the whole passage.'

Mrs Holland tried to make sense of the references but found it hopeless. However, when the script was sent to England, Miss Johnson seized the clue of 'the central eight words', which are 'for it is the number of a man'. The numbers cited in the script, when taken as the letters of the alphabet, translate as 'Roden Noel'.

Noel was referred to again in a script from Mrs Holland on 21 March and mentioned in one from Mrs Verrall, in England, on 26 March. On 28 March Mrs Holland's automatic writing included his name spelled out in full with descriptions of his native Cornwall and a muddled description of himself.

A complex case that took years to understand was that of the Medici tombs. It began

in November 1906, through Mrs Holland. Her scripts were full of oblique or unexplained references to evening, morning and dawn, and death, sleep and shadows. In Cambridge on 21 January 1907 Mrs Verrall received the words 'laurel' and 'laurel wreath' repeatedly. Then on 26 February yet another medium, the American Mrs Piper, said out loud (normally she only muttered indistinctly, when coming out of her trances): 'Morehead – laurel for laurel . . . I say I gave her that for laurel. Goodbye.'

Mrs Piper then had a vision of a Negro sitting in place of Mr Piddington, one of the investigators for the SPR, who was with her. She rubbed her hands together and said: 'Dead . . . well, I think it was something about laurel wreaths.' The next day Mrs Piper received: 'I gave Mrs V. laurel wreaths' in her script.

On 17 March Helen Verrall in Cambridge received: 'Alexander's tomb . . . laurel

Above: Mrs Leonora Piper, famous trance medium of Boston, USA, who was involved in a complex case of cross-correspondences that took place between 1906 and 1910. Several mediums 'received' a series of references to shadow, death, sleep, evening, morning, dawn, meditation, Alexander and laurels. Only two years after the last communication did SPR investigators realise that the references pointed to the tombs of the Medici family in Florence. On that of Lorenzo, Duke of Urbino (right), which also contains the body of Alessandro ('Alexander') de Medici, are statues representing Dawn, Twilight and Meditation; the tomb of Giuliano, Duke of Nemours (left) bears figures representing Day and Night. The laurel was an emblem of the Medici family

wreaths, are emblem laurels for the victor's brow.'

Ten days later, in India, Mrs Holland's script included: 'Darkness, light and shadow, Alexander Moor's head.'

A year and a half later, two rarely used mediums – known as 'the Macs' – received: 'Dig a grave among the laurels.'

It was two years before the topic was again referred to by the communicator. This time it was a London medium, Mrs Willett (pseudonym of Mrs Coombe-Tennant), who received: 'Laurentian tombs, Dawn and Twilight.'

A month later, on 8 July 1910, Mrs Piper in the United States spoke the words: 'Meditation, sleeping dead, laurels' when coming out of her trance.

Yet another two years passed before the investigators of the SPR discovered the meaning of the allusions: they referred to the

Above: Helen Verrall (later Mrs W. H. Slater), one of the automatists concerned; she was also a researcher for the SPR

tombs of the Medici family, who were wealthy and powerful in Florence in the 15th and 16th centuries. On the sepulchre of Lorenzo, Duke of Urbino, are statues representing Meditation, Dawn and Twilight. On the tomb of another Medici, Giuliano, are two statues representing Day and Night.

Lorenzo's tomb also holds the body of Alessandro ('Alexander') de Medici, who was murdered; it is, therefore, as much 'Alexander's tomb' as 'Lorenzo's'. Alexander was of mixed blood and in his portraits has clearly Negroid features: truly 'Alexander, Moor's head'.

Helen Verrall had heard of the tombs, but had never visited them and had no detailed knowledge of them. She, like the others, had taken 'Alexander's tomb' to refer to that of Alexander the Great.

But, perhaps significantly, Mrs Holland did know the tombs well. And in one of her previous scripts there were references to Diamond Island, where the new Lodge-Muirhead wireless system was being tested (an experiment in which she was personally very interested). The wireless connection was linked with the tombs references by a striking pun – the fact that one of the wireless pioneers was called Dr Alexander Muirhead (Alexander Moor's head). Yet in the same script was a quotation from *Othello* that reinforced the 'Moor' connection.

So was this witty allusion created by Mrs Holland's subconscious? Knowing the tombs so well, did she perhaps unwittingly make up that particular example of a cross-correspondence? The alternative view is that the communicator deliberately chose mediums whose minds contained relevant material. Communicating through mediums was said to be extraordinarily difficult. The 'Myers' persona had this to say about the problems of communicating from 'the other side' through Mrs Holland:

The nearest simile I can find to express

the difficulty of sending a message – is that I appear to be standing behind a sheet of frosted glass which blurs sight and deadens sound – dictating feebly to a reluctant and somewhat obtuse secretary.

One of those involved in the cross-correspondences was (it seemed) to find out for himself about the reality of the 'frosted glass' simile. On 18 June 1912 Dr A.W. Verrall, husband of Mrs Verrall, died. Six weeks later Mrs Willett received his first post-mortem communication, drawing its allusions from Christina Rossetti, Dante and the humorous magazine *Punch*. His further communications contained family jokes and extremely convoluted classical references. In combination, they proved beyond doubt, according to his 'oldest and dearest friend', the Reverend M.A. Bayfield, that they were from Verrall himself. One of his scripts ends with the wry note: 'This sort of thing is more difficult to do than it looked.'

Fragments and allusions

Most of the 2000 scripts that make up the cross-correspondences are far too complicated to examine here. H.F. Saltmarsh says in his *Evidence of personal survival*:

> The fragmentary, enigmatic and allusive nature of these communications is intentional, and their obscurity is due not solely to the deficiencies of the investigators.

Saltmarsh suggested experiments that, while they could not prove the Myers group's post-mortem existence, will demonstrate the difficulties of cheating and of constructing cross-correspondences deliberately.

> Begin by choosing a book by an author you know well, and a quotation or subject from it. Then from the same book or another book by the same author pick out a quotation that alludes to the subject without directly mentioning it. Give the two quotations to someone who acts as investigator, and who must try to work out what the connection between them is. It is remarkably difficult, especially if the author's works are unknown to the investigator. Huge leaps in comprehension will have to be made.

When investigating Mrs Willett's 'Myers' scripts, Sir Oliver Lodge remarked:

> The way in which these allusions are combined or put together, and their connection with each other indicated, is the striking thing – it seems to me as much beyond the capacity of Mrs Willett as it would be beyond my own capacity. I believe that if the matter is seriously studied, and if Mrs Willett's assertions concerning her conscious knowledge and supraliminal procedure are believed, this will be the opinion of critics also; they will realize, as I do, that we are tapping the reminiscences not of an ordinarily educated person but of a scholar – no matter how

Two of the investigators for the SPR: Eleanor Sidgwick (above), the widow of Henry Sidgwick, and Sir Oliver Lodge (below). The investigators studied each script as it was produced, comparing it with those from other automatists to find any cross-correspondences between them

fragmentary and confused some of the reproductions are.

Saltmarsh's second experiment concerns the improbability that chance could produce cross-correspondences between independent scripts. Simply take a familiar book and open it at random. Eyes shut, point to a passage randomly. Repeat this with another book and attempt to find a cross-correspondence between the extracts.

Despite the impressive weight of scholarly allusions, puns and quotations communicated, many modern psychical researchers regard the cross-correspondences as 'not proven'. Sceptics point out that all the people involved, including the 'investigators', were either members of the SPR or of the same social circle. They could have been in collusion. When reminded that deliberate fraud would have involved cheating on a grand scale (and over 30 years), the sceptics reply that, nevertheless, once begun, it could hardly be exposed.

The clues stop coming

When the last of the SPR's founder-members died, the cross-correspondences stopped, having accumulated to form a huge volume of scripts that any interested party can study at leisure. Cynics want to know why Myers and his group have ceased to communicate their tortuous messages. It may be because there is no one left to receive them, no medium who is – perhaps literally – on their 'wavelength'. Mediumship seems no longer to be practised in classically educated, upper middle-class circles, and there must be few automatic writers who would even recognise Greek characters or apparently nonsensical quotations jumbled together.

It is possible that subconscious telepathy took place among a group of persons, in different parts of the world and over many years. That in itself would be worth investigating. The only other explanation is that there is a life after death – at least for Edwardian gentlemen given to intellectual puns and anagrams – and that, under certain circumstances, the dead may demonstrate their existence to the living.

Although the complex cross-correspondences no longer appear, Myers is apparently still in communication. On 2 April 1972 the young English psychic Matthew Manning received this automatic script, signed 'F. Myers':

> You should not really indulge in this unless you know what you are doing. I did a lot of work on automatic writing when I was alive and I could never work it out. No-one alive will ever work out the whole secret of life after death. It pivots on so many things – personality – condition of the mental and physical bodies. Carry on trying though because you could soon be close to the secret. If you find it no-one will believe you anyway.

Knock, knock–who's there?

The strange rappings in the home of the Fox family caused a sensation throughout America – for, as HILARY EVANS explains, many people regarded them as proof that the living could communicate with the dead

WHAT HAPPENED TO Margaretta Fox and her sisters, if it was truly what it purported to be, should have been quite simply the greatest single event in human history. Conclusive proof that we can communicate with the spirits of the dead – which presupposes that the dead exist in spirit form to be communicated with – would mean that thousands of years of speculation were over; death would be positively established as being not the end of life, but a transfer of existence to another and superior plane; our stay on earth could henceforward be regarded confidently, not as a short-lived biological incident, but as part of a continuing process. This, and nothing less than this, seemed to have been established by what occurred in a small wooden house in the village of Hydesville in the state of New York on 31 March 1848. It was this 'breakthrough' that was to mark the beginning of the modern Spiritualist movement, whose adherents were to swell to millions throughout the world in the decades that followed.

There were seven Fox children in all, but only three were actively concerned in the events: Leah, aged 34 in 1848, Margaretta, aged 14, and Catherine, aged 12. The definitive account of the epoch-making incident was supplied by their mother, Margaret, in a

Below right: Catherine Fox who, together with her sister Margaretta (centre right), became the focus for paranormal rappings. These, the girls claimed, said that they had been chosen for the task of convincing the world of a life after death. When the girls travelled to Rochester to stay with their elder sister Leah (far right), the noises travelled with them and even manifested on board the steamer in the course of their journey

Below: the Fox family home in Hydesville, New York state, as depicted in a 1930s postcard. The original building was destroyed by fire; today an exact replica, built in the 1950s, stands on the site

sworn statement four days later, countersigned as accurate by her husband. She told how the house in which they were temporarily living had been disturbed by unaccountable shakings of the walls and furniture, by the sound of footsteps and knockings on the walls and doors. The family had 'concluded that the house must be haunted by some unhappy restless spirit'.

Tired by the disturbances, the family went to bed early on the night of Friday, 31 March. Margaretta and Catherine – the only two children still living with their parents – were frightened by the noises and had left their own room to sleep in another bed in

their parents' room. No doubt it was the reassuring presence of their mother and father that encouraged the girls to respond so cheekily when the sounds recommenced:

> The children heard the rapping and tried to make similar sounds by snapping their fingers. My youngest child, Cathie, said 'Mr Splitfoot, do as I do!', clapping her hands. The sound instantly followed with the same number of raps. When she stopped the sound ceased for a short time. Then Margaretta said, in sport, 'No, do just as I do. Count one, two, three, four,' striking one hand against the other at the same time; and the raps came as before. She was afraid to repeat them. . . .

From this they proceeded gradually to more elaborate questions, using an alphabetical code by means of which it was established

The Fox sisters' parents, Margaret (below) and John (bottom), documented the events of 31 March 1848 – the first day on which the rappings were heard. While they did not believe in 'haunted houses', they came to the conclusion that the noise emanated from a 'restless spirit', which in due course announced that it was a pedlar (above) who had been murdered in the house five years earlier

that the rappings were done by a spirit; eventually the entity identified himself as a pedlar, aged 31, who claimed to have been murdered in that very house, and his remains buried in the cellar.

Neighbours were called in to verify the proceedings; they too heard the raps, put questions of their own and received answers. Next day other visitors came and, in the evening, urged by the spirit, some men started digging in the cellar to see if the story could be substantiated; unfortunately the hole filled with water and the attempt had to be abandoned. Later reports suggest that parts of a body were indeed found, but Mrs Fox does not mention this in her statement of 4 April. She claims that when the noises commenced again on the Saturday evening there were some 300 people present who heard them: there were no noises on Sunday but they began again on Monday and were continuing when she made her statement on the Tuesday.

For the Fox family, then and there, it seemed to be simply a case of haunting. Stories in which the dead return to earth in order to pass messages or warnings to the living have been told throughout history; but in this instance a new element had been added – a two-way conversation between the living and the dead. Others perceived the significance of this and appreciated its implications: as a subsequent historian of the Spiritualist movement, Emma Hardinge Britten, observed, it implied that

> not only the supposed murdered pedlar, but hosts of spirits, good and bad, high and low, could, under certain conditions not understood, and impossible for mortals to comprehend, communicate with earth; that such communication was produced through the forces of spiritual and human magnetism, in chemical affinity; that the varieties of magnetism in different individuals afforded 'medium power' to some, and denied it to others.

Such subtleties were not at first realised, but

it was clear that the Fox sisters were in some way specially gifted to receive these communications: the raps occurred only in their presence, and furthermore occurred wherever they went. When, their lives disrupted by the publicity given to their experiences, the girls and their mother left Hydesville to stay with their sister Leah in Rochester, the rappings travelled with them. And although others were soon to discover that they, too, had some of this 'medium power', the spirits themselves confirmed that the Fox girls were specially endowed. Repeatedly, the messages insisted: 'You have been chosen to go before the world to convince the sceptical of the great truth of immortality.'

Had such messages come out of the blue to young and ignorant schoolgirls in a rural community, it might indeed have been convincing evidence that beings on another plane of existence were seeking to establish communication with us on·earth. But the situation was not so simple, for such notions were current in the America of the 1840s.

In the previous century there had been some who considered the newly discovered mesmerism not as an altered mental state that could be accounted for in human terms, but as a process designed to enable communication with the spirits. The controversy had raged ever since. Two years before the happenings at Hydesville, a commentator noted that 'the newspapers and magazines are teeming with slashing discussions upon the subject of magnetism and clairvoyance.'

That commentator was Andrew Jackson Davis, a semi-literate American mystic and psychic, who while in a trance state churned out volume after volume of turgid revelations about life, the Universe, and everything. The fact that his account is full of errors somewhat dents his credibility, but at the time many accepted his heralding of a new era:

It is a truth that spirits commune with

Above: Emma Hardinge Britten, a medium and author of *Modern American Spiritualism* (above right: the title page of the first edition). She helped to establish the new 'religion' in Britain

one another while one is in the body and the other in the higher sphere, and this, too, when the person in the body is unconscious of the influx, and hence cannot be convinced of the fact; and this truth will ere long present itself in the form of a living demonstration, and the world will hail with delight the ushering in of that era when the interiors of men will be opened, and the spiritual communication will be established such as is now being enjoyed by the inhabitants of Mars, Jupiter, and Saturn.

Dawn of a new era

Given such utterances, it is not surprising that Davis is often seen as the John the Baptist of the Spiritualist movement. His writings inculcated a mood of expectancy in America, and they explain why the public was so quick to seize on the events at Hydesville as signs of a new age.

Matters advanced with extraordinary rapidity. While staying with their sister Leah at Rochester, the girls were instructed by the spirits to hire the largest hall in the town and give a demonstration of their powers: they did on 14 November 1848. Now at last the whole matter was out in the open; and it was quickly apparent that public opinion was sharply divided between enthusiastic adherents, who had been awaiting just such a revelation, and no less determined sceptics who saw these manifestations as imposture at best, at worst as the work of the Devil. this

Feelings ran frighteningly high. The girls were widely ridiculed, frequently physically attacked: attempts were even made on their lives. When a committee investigated the phenomena and could find no evidence of trickery, its findings were discounted and a second, tougher committee appointed: when this, too, reported that it could detect no imposture, the girls' opponents were only made yet angrier. It became impossible for the Fox sisters to lead normal lives. They left Rochester for Troy, then for the state capital at Albany, and finally for New York, which they reached in June 1850.

The three sisters took New York by storm. The newspaper reporters descended on them, and on the whole treated them kindly; one account admitted:

We saw none that we could suspect of collusion. . . . We came away utterly disbelieving in all supernatural agency, and at the same time unable to say how any human means could be used without detection.

While it is true that investigative procedures were primitive by present-day standards, it must be accepted that the New Yorkers who sat with the Fox sisters were not eager to be made fools of; hundreds of sitters went determined to be the ones who revealed to the world how the imposture was carried out

– and emerged, if not persuaded that the message of the spirits was genuine, at least that the phenomena defied normal explanation. Horace Greeley, editor of the *Tribune* and one of the most influential men in the country, was persuaded of the girls' integrity and became their valiant champion.

By now other mediums were emerging in emulation of the Fox sisters, but none challenged their pre-eminence. The phenomena developed from rapped questions and answers to automatic writing and spoken utterances, culminating in direct voice communication in which the mediums were 'taken over' by the alleged entities. All kinds of physical phenomena accompanied the messages – movement of furniture, teleportation of objects, levitation of sitters or the medium herself, all kinds of noises and a wide variety of luminous phenomena. Time and time again the sisters were tested, perhaps most strictly when, while visiting England, Kate Fox submitted herself to the

Right: a caricature of Horace Greeley, influential statesman and editor of the *New York Tribune*, from *Vanity Fair* (1872). Greeley gave valuable support to the Fox sisters. He came to believe that the phenomena were genuine, but retained an open mind as to their nature

Below: Andrew Jackson Davis, American mystic and psychic. He had no doubt that it was possible to communicate with the dead (left: an illustration depicting Davis himself receiving information from a 'spirit'), and in the early 1840s he stated that a demonstration of this fact would soon be given. To many Americans, Davis's prediction was fulfilled in 1848, when the Fox sisters' manifestations began, and he was acclaimed as the prophet of Spiritualism

Left: monuments to the Fox sisters and Spiritualism: the obelisk at Rochester (above) where, on 14 November 1848, the girls gave the first public demonstration of their remarkable powers; and the interior of the family home at Hydesville (below), which was turned into a museum

investigations of William Crookes. He vouched for her with persuasive insistence:

For several months I enjoyed almost unlimited opportunity of testing the various phenomena occurring in the presence of this lady, and I especially examined the phenomena of these sounds. . . . It seems only necessary for her to place her hand on any substance for loud thuds to be heard in it, like a triple pulsation, sometimes loud enough to be heard several rooms off. I have heard . . . these sounds proceeding from the floor, walls, &c., when the medium's hands and feet were held – when she was standing on a chair – when she was suspended in a swing from the ceiling – when she was enclosed in a wire cage – and when she had fallen fainting on a sofa. . . . I have tested them in every way that I could devise, until there has been no escape from the conviction that they were true objective occurrences not produced by trickery or mechanical means.

But not everyone was so thoroughly convinced. From the outset, there had been sceptics who had claimed that the sisters were playing tricks. They had never succeeded in substantiating these claims, and their proposed explanations were generally ridiculously inadequate to account for the phenomena. But their claims were to receive unexpected support, first from the girls' family, then from the mediums themselves.

THE MISSES FOX.

Our readers, believers and non-believers in Spiritualism, will thank us for presenting them portraits of the "original rappers," the Misses Fox, of Rochester, who have made so much noise in the world. The likenesses are from a daguerreotype by Meade Brothers, of New York, and are therefore reliable. Since the origin of the rapping excitement in Rochester, in 1849, mysterious demonstrations of the nature of those of which the Misses Fox were the media have been signalized all over the world; they have given rise to books, pamphlets and newspapers without number, and the believers in their spiritual origin are numbered now by hundreds of thousands. The phenomena exhibited by the media are so curious, that learned and scientific men have felt it their duty to investigate them, and various are the theories by which they are sought to be accounted for. One of the most elaborate works on the subject is that by Professor Mahan. Prof. Faraday, of England, has also given the subject his attention, and honored it with his theory. Congress has been memorialized to appoint a committee of investigation; but as yet our legislators have not seen fit to devote their time to spiritualism. Of the ladies, whose portraits we present, it may be sufficient to remark, that no imposture has been found upon them; and that committees composed of the cutest Yankees, both male and female, have failed to discover any secret machinery or fixtures, by which the sounds heard from and about them might have been produced.

THE SISTERS FOX, THE ORIGINAL SPIRIT RAPPERS.

Confessions and confusions

When the Fox sisters admitted to fraud, the sceptics had a field day. But then the confessions were withdrawn. What is the truth about the acclaimed founders of Spiritualism?

THREE YEARS AFTER the epoch-making events at the Fox family home in Hydesville, USA, on 17 April 1851, a shattering statement was made at Arcadia, New York state, by a Mrs Norman Culver. She was a relative by marriage of the Fox girls, her husband's sister being the wife of their brother David.

She stated that for about two years she had been

> a very sincere believer in the rappings; but something which I saw when I was visiting the girls made me suspect that they were deceiving. I resolved to satisfy myself in some way; and some time afterwards I made a proposition to

Margaretta and Catherine Fox, the 'discoverers' of Spiritualism. To many, the girls' experiences signalled the dawning of a new era, in which the living could communicate at will with the dead. Others, however, saw the girls simply as clever tricksters and were determined to expose them; but, despite numerous tests and investigations, the sisters were never detected in a hoax

Catherine to assist her in producing the manifestations.

She claimed that Catherine welcomed her offer, and proceeded to demonstrate how the tricks were worked:

> The raps are produced with the toes. All the toes are used. After nearly a week's practice, with Catherine showing me how, I could produce them perfectly myself. At first it was very hard work to do it. Catherine told me to warm my feet, she said that she sometimes had to warm her feet three or four times in the course of an evening. . . . I have sometimes produced 150 raps in succession.

Such a statement, coming from so authoritative a source, cannot be lightly set aside, particularly as she demonstrated her ability to produce raps. It is impossible for us today to determine what motivated Mrs Culver's revelation. It may have been simple love of the truth, or there may have been some jealousy to inspire the statement. On the face of it, her revelations seem inadequate to account for *all* the phenomena associated with the Fox sisters; but they do show how *some* of them could have been effected. Clearly, trickery cannot be ruled out as a possible partial explanation.

At the same time, it is a fact that the sisters were tested and investigated time and time again, and that never once were they detected in flagrant imposture. As their champion, *Tribune* editor Horace Greeley, pointed out, it was indeed likely that many of their feats could be reproduced by stage magicians, but these were accomplished performers and the girls had none of their skills or training. Greeley was impressed as much by the Fox sisters' failures as by their successes:

> A juggler can do nearly as well at one time as another; but I have known the most eminent mediums spend a long evening in trying to evoke the spiritual phenomena, without a gleam of success. I have known this to occur when they were particularly anxious to astound and convince those who were present. . . .

'An absolute falsehood'

But the logic of their defenders and the favourable findings of investigators were forgotten when, on 24 September 1888, Margaretta (now Mrs Kane) told a reporter from the *New York Herald* that she intended to reveal that their mediumship had been a fraud from start to finish. Her younger sister Catherine (now Mrs Jencken) arrived from England to support her. On 21 October a huge crowd gathered in the New York

Although Leah, the eldest of the Fox sisters, had not been involved in the original rappings at Hydesville, she was the first of the three to become a professional medium and, in the 1850s, held many private seances in the parlour of her New York home (right). She also co-operated in a wide variety of experiments, convincing the investigators that the sounds she created had nothing to do with the physical body and that 'the medium has no more power over the sounds than the investigators have'

In 1851 a group of researchers came up with an explanation for the rappings: when the Fox sisters' legs were held, the noises stopped; therefore the girls must be 'popping' their knee joints. Sceptics seized on this as proof of the mediums' deception – but still they could not account for the variety of noises or the levitation of tables that occurred at many of the seances

Academy of Music to hear the confession:

> I am here tonight as one of the founders of Spiritualism to denounce it as an absolute falsehood from beginning to end, as the flimsiest of superstitions, the most wicked blasphemy known to the world.

The *New York Herald* described the reaction:

> There was a dead silence. Everybody in the great audience knew that they were looking upon the woman who is principally responsible for Spiritualism, its foundress, high-priestess and demonstrator. She stood upon a little pine-table with nothing on her feet but stockings. As she remained motionless loud, distinct rappings were heard, now in the flies, now behind the scenes, now in the gallery . . . Mrs Kane became excited. She clapped her hands, danced about and cried: 'It's a fraud! Spiritualism is a fraud from beginning to end! It's all a trick! There's no truth in it!' A whirlwind of applause followed.

It should have been the death-blow to the movement for whose birth Margaretta had been responsible. But though perhaps a majority of those present were convinced, others were not; and their reservations were justified just over a year later when first Catherine and then Margaretta took back their confessions. Margaretta told a reporter from *The Celestial City*, a New York Spiritualist paper:

> Would to God that I could undo the

injustice I did the cause of Spiritualism when, under the strong psychological influence of persons inimical to it, I gave expression to utterances that had no foundation in fact.

She insisted that the charges she had made against Spiritualism had been 'false in every particular'. She refused to say who had put pressure on her, but mentioned that 'persons high in the Catholic Church did their best to have me enter a convent.' She had in fact been converted to the Catholic faith soon after the death of her husband, whom she had married at the age of 16 and lived with only briefly.

She also blamed her sister Leah, accusing her of having drawn Catherine and herself into the career of mediumship. It may well be the case that Leah encouraged her younger sisters, and perhaps, as the most practical and far-sighted of the family, she had taken upon herself the decision to commit the three of them to a course of life that could not but put great social and

Right: the Swedish singer Jenny Lind who, after attending a seance held by the Fox sisters, was convinced that the mediums were genuine

Below: Margaretta's husband, the Arctic explorer Elisha Kent Kane. His letters and verses contained many references to his wife's 'deceit' and implored, 'Do avoid spirits.' After Kane's death in 1857, Margaretta agreed to the publication of this damning evidence, thereby implying that she had – as accused – been guilty of cheating

emotional stress on them all. But never at any previous time had there been any sign that this was resented by her sisters, nor that she was eager where they were reluctant.

What, then, was the truth behind the confessions made and withdrawn? Certainly one fact must be faced: if Margaretta could produce trick raps on the stage in demonstration of her ability to cheat, there is a strong presumption that those tricks had been used in the course of her mediumship – for why otherwise would she have developed the necessary skill?

The suggestion that she cheated, at least some of the time, is confirmed from an unexpected source: her husband. The eminent Arctic explorer Elisha Kent Kane had fallen in love with Margaretta when she was only 13; for three years, against his family's opposition, he courted and helped her, finally marrying her – only to die shortly afterwards, of illness, away from her in Cuba. Distracted by grief, Margaretta published the letters and verses he had written to her during those years: they contain abundant evidence that he believed her to cheat. 'Oh Maggie,' he wrote in one letter, 'are you never tired of this weary, weary sameness of continual deceit?' And in another, 'Do avoid "spirits". I cannot bear to think of you as engaged in a course of wickedness and deception.' His verses echo the same sentiments:

Then the maiden sat and wept,
Her hand upon her brow;
So long this secret have I kept,
I can't forswear it now.
It festers in my bosom,
It cankers in my heart,
Thrice cursed is the slave fast chained
To a deceitful art.

The fact that Margaretta allowed such incriminating documents to be published suggests that she was conscious of having used trickery; but if we accept the account she presented in 1888, of total deceit from start to finish, we find ourselves faced with almost as many difficulties as if we accept all as genuine. One of the many eminent sitters with the Fox sisters was the singer Jenny Lind, who perceptively distinguished between the physical and the mental phenomena: 'If it were possible for you to make these sounds, I know it is impossible for you to answer the questions I have had answered this evening.'

Reporters at the ready

Dozens of testimonials survive, recorded at the time by sitters who were convinced – often despite their previous scepticism – of the Fox sisters' psychic ability. If some visitors erred by excessive gullibility, others surely made up for it by implacable scepticism; and at all times there were reporters on hand, eager to seize on anything the least suspicious. All who investigated in hope of exposing the mediums as frauds came away frustrated.

This is not to say that the sisters' manifestations were accepted for what they purported to be. There were many, like Horace Greeley, who admitted the genuineness of the phenomena as phenomena, but retained an open mind as to their nature:

Whatever may be the origin or cause of the 'rappings', the ladies in whose presence they occur do not make them. We tested this thoroughly and to our entire satisfaction. . . . The ladies say they are informed that this is but the beginning of a new era, in which spirits clothed in the flesh are to be more closely and palpably connected with those who have put on immortality; that the manifestations have already appeared in many other families, and are destined to be diffused and rendered clearer, until all who will may communicate freely with their friends who have shuffled off this mortal coil. Of all this we know nothing, and shall guess nothing; but if we were simply to print the questions we asked and the answers we received, during a two-hours uninterrupted conference with the 'rappers', we should be accused of having done so expressly to sustain the theory which regards these manifestations as the utterances of departed spirits.

It seems not merely charitable but reasonable to attribute the 'confessions' of the two younger sisters to the strains of their personal predicament. Both had been schoolgirls when the events started, and throughout the early years; both had been swept from a rural obscurity to a prominent position in one of the world's greatest cities. The tragic end of Margaretta's story-book love affair would have unbalanced a girl far less precariously situated; she took to drink

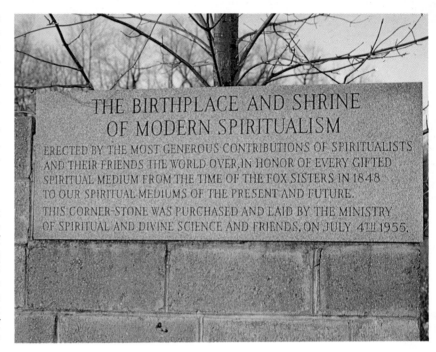

The cornerstone of a shrine to modern Spiritualism, which stands at the rear of the replica of the Fox cottage in Hydesville, USA. The building of the shrine started in 1955, but it was left uncompleted

and drugs, as did her sister Catherine before her own marriage to the lawyer Henry Jencken; though this brought her two children, it was also terminated by his abrupt and early death.

In these circumstances, and perhaps influenced by the enemies of Spiritualism, it would not be surprising if the two sisters, neither of them notably intelligent at the best of times (Crookes was scathing about Catherine's intellectual limitations), reached a state of confusion in which the truth and the falsehood of their careers became inextricably confounded.

In 1904, when all the Fox sisters were dead, a wall of their old home at Hydesville collapsed: among the debris exposed there were found the remains of a body. Whose body it had been, it was impossible to determine: but it is a curious confirmation of the 'messages' that had been given to the Fox sisters half a century before. From this it does not necessarily follow that the information came from the spirit of the dead man, but it would demonstrate that the Fox sisters' careers were, at the very least, founded in truth.

Whether, as time went on and the pressure on them to produce phenomena to order increased, the Fox sisters 'helped out the spirits' by resorting to trickery, must be a matter for individual judgement; the girls were never detected in imposture, and the evidence for it is only circumstantial. But the presumption is there: and it is hard to believe that the Fox sisters could have been induced to make confessions that were totally false, without the least shade of guilt to provide a lever for those who sought to persuade them to confess. In its confusion of truth and falsehood, in its baffling ambiguity, the career of the Fox sisters seems to be a paradigm of Spiritualism itself.

THOMAS ALVA EDISON was one of the greatest practical scientists of the 19th century. His achievements included the perfection of the 'duplex' telegraph, the invention of the phonograph and the introduction into the United States of the first electric light. In 1882 his generating station brought electric street lighting to New York for the first time, and 12 years later his moving picture show, which he called his 'kinetoscope parlour', was opened in the city.

Despite these solid successes, however, an interview he gave to the *Scientific American* in 1920 caused concern among his contemporaries, some of whom must have thought that the 73-year-old inventor had lapsed into senility. What he proposed, in the issue of 30 October, was no less than an instrument for communicating with the dead:

> If our personality survives, then it is strictly logical and scientific to assume that it retains memory, intellect and other faculties and knowledge that we acquire on this earth. Therefore if personality exists after what we call death, it is reasonable to conclude that those who leave this earth would like to communicate with those they have left here. . . I am inclined to believe that our personality hereafter will be able to affect matter. If this reasoning be correct, then, if we can evolve an instrument so delicate as to be affected, or moved, or manipulated . . . by our personality as it survives in the next life, such an instrument, when made available, ought to record something.

Edison worked on the development of such an instrument, but was unsuccessful. However in the opinion of many modern scientific researchers, his views were apparently vindicated in the summer of 1959.

At that time a celebrated Swedish painter, musician and film producer named Friedrich Jürgenson took his battery operated tape recorder out into a remote part of the countryside near his villa in order to record birdsong. Playing the tapes back later, Jürgenson found not only bird sounds but faint human voices, speaking in Swedish and Norwegian and discussing nocturnal birdsong. Despite the 'coincidence' of subject matter, Jürgenson first thought that he had picked up a stray radio transmission. On repeating the experiment, however, he heard further voices, this time addressing him personally and claiming to be dead relatives and friends of his. Over the next few years, working from his home at Mölnbo, near Stockholm, Jürgenson amassed the evidence that he was to present in his book *Voices from the Universe* in 1964. This proved sufficiently convincing to attract the attention of the eminent German psychologist Professor Hans Bender, director of the Government-funded parapsychological research unit at the University of Freiburg, who in turn set up a team of distinguished

The ghosts in the machine

Has the modern tape recorder provided evidence of survival after death? Thousands of voices – purporting to be those of the dead – have been recorded and there is no rational explanation for their origin. What are we to make of them? FRANK SMYTH investigates

scientists to repeat the experiments and analyse the results.

Their findings can be summarised as follows: that under differing conditions and circumstances a factory-clean tape, run through an ordinary tape-recording head in an otherwise silent environment, will contain human voices speaking recognisable words when played back; that the origin of these voices is apparently inexplicable in the light of present day science; and that the voices themselves are objective in that they yield prints in the same way as normal voices, and register as visible oscillograph impulses on videotape recordings.

The implications of these 'voices from nowhere' are enormous. Dr Bender himself is reported to consider them of more importance to humanity than nuclear physics;

Above: Thomas Alva Edison (1847–1931), inventor of the phonograph and the electric light bulb. In 1920 he worked on the development of a device that would, he believed, make possible a form of telepathic contact with the dead

An ordinary cassette tape recorder can be used to record 'electronic voices' but, generally speaking, the better the equipment, the more satisfactory the results. Machines with volume, tone and level controls make the task of deciphering the voices on playback much easier, and a good set of headphones is essential.

Experts agree that the hours between sunset and sunrise are the best time for experiments. Most researchers prefer to work in a quiet room, although a portable tape recorder in a quiet place in the countryside can yield good results, as Jürgenson proved.

Raudive recommended that the date and time should be spoken into the microphone before each session, followed by an invitation to the voices to speak. Each recording session should be no longer than two minutes, as intense concentration is needed in listening to the

Recording the voices yourself

playback of the voices.

Three basic recording methods are most likely to be of use. With the first, the tape recorder is simply switched to 'record', then questions are asked aloud and noted on paper.

With the second method, preliminary announcements are made through a microphone which is then unplugged and a radio attached to the recorder instead. The radio is tuned between frequencies, to a band of 'white noise', and the recording level is set mid-way between maximum and minimum.

The third method involves the use of a diode receiver, a small crystal set that is plugged into the microphone socket of the tape recorder. The recording level is set at maximum. According to Raudive, diode recording gives the best results, the voices being slower, clearer and more natural.

Right: Friedrich Jürgenson (seated), the discoverer of the voice phenomenon, with Professor Hans Bender. Together with a team of scientists, Professor Bender studied the voices received by Jürgenson and conducted exhaustive experiments with his own recordings

at the very least, he concluded in a paper for *Parapsychology Review*, the 'paranormal origin of the phenomena is highly probable.'

Other scientists besides Dr Bender were to become fascinated by Jürgenson's odd discovery. Dr Konstantin Raudive, former professor of psychology at the Universities of Uppsala and Riga, was living in Bad Krozingen, Germany, when he heard of the Jürgenson-Bender experiments in 1965. A former student of Carl Jung, Dr Raudive had been forced to flee from his native Latvia when it was invaded and annexed by the Soviet Union in 1945. Since then he had become well known as a writer on experimental psychology.

Dr Raudive too, began recording tests on the mysterious voices with conspicuous success, and between 1965 and his death in 1974,

in partnership with physicist Dr Alex Schneider of St Gallen, Switzerland, and Theodor Rudolph, a specialist in high frequency electronic engineering, he made over 100,000 tapes under stringent laboratory conditions. An exhaustive analysis of his work was published in Germany in the late 1960s under the title *The inaudible made audible*; this caught the attention of British publisher Colin Smythe, who later brought out an English language edition entitled *Breakthrough*.

Peter Bander, who wrote the preface to the book, later gave an account of how he first heard a strange voice on tape; this nicely illustrates 'what happens' as a rule, and also points out the objective nature of the phenomenon. Colin Smythe had bought a new tape and had followed Dr Raudive's instructions on how to 'contact' the voices. A certain rhythm resembling a human voice had been recorded, but it was unintelligible to Mr Smythe. Peter Bander played the relevant portion of tape over two or three times, and suddenly became aware of what the voice was saying. It was a woman's, and it said '*Mach die Tür mal auf*' – German for 'Open the door'. Mr Bander immediately recognised the voice as that of his dead mother – he had been in the habit of conducting his correspondence with her by tape recording for several years before she died. And the comment was apt: his colleagues often chided him for being unsociable by shutting his office door.

Startled, Mr Bander asked two people who did not speak German to listen to the tape and write down what they heard phonetically. Their versions matched what he had heard exactly: Peter Bander was convinced of the authenticity of the voices.

Since the publication of *Breakthrough* in 1971 serious research has begun in all parts of the world. The interest of two very different bodies reflects the spiritual and temporal

Right: Dr Konstantin Raudive with the 'goniometer', an instrument that was designed for him by Theodor Rudolph of Telefunken to record 'spirit' voices

Below: the Right Reverend Monsignor Stephen O'Connor (right), Vicar General and Principal Roman Catholic Chaplain to the Royal Navy, listening to a voice recorded by Dr Raudive (left). The voice seemed to be that of a young naval officer who had committed suicide two years earlier

Right: Pope Paul VI who, in 1969, decorated Friedrich Jürgenson with the Commander's Cross of the Order of St Gregory the Great. The Catholic Church has never expressed an official opinion on the nature of the mysterious voices, but Jürgenson has said that he found 'a sympathetic ear' for the phenomenon in the Vatican

aspects of the voices. The Vatican has shown a great deal of 'off the record' awareness of the phenomena, and a number of distinguished Catholic priest-scientists have conducted experiments of their own. Pre-eminent among the first of these researchers was the late Professor Gebhard Frei, an internationally recognised expert in the fields of depth psychology, parapsychology and anthropology. Dr Frei was the cousin of the late Pope Paul VI, the pontiff who, in 1969, decorated Freidrich Jürgenson with the Commander's Cross of the Order of St Gregory the Great, ostensibly for documentary film work about the Vatican. But Jürgenson told Peter Bander in August 1971 that he had found 'a sympathetic ear for the voice phenomenon in the Vatican'.

The interest of the National Aeronautics and Space Administration (NASA) came to light in the late 1960s when two American engineers from Cape Kennedy visited Dr Raudive at Bad Krozingen. The visitors examined Dr Raudive's experiments minutely, and asked many 'unusually pertinent questions' as well as making helpful comments. They refused, unfortunately, to give the scientist any indication of what relevance the voice phenomena might have to America's space programme. But as Dr Raudive reasoned: if he could achieve clear and regular results on his relatively simple equipment, how much more likely was it that the sophisticated recorders carried in space craft should pick up the voices? From whatever source they spring, Jürgenson's voices from the Universe represent a whole new field in the study of the paranormal.

Whispers of immortality

How can we explain the mysterious voices that appear on tape from no apparent material source? Can they truly be the voices of the surviving dead as many people believe or do they somehow emanate from those present at the recording sessions?

WHEN FRIEDRICH JÜRGENSON taped his first mysterious voices in 1959, he was using an ordinary portable reel to reel tape recorder with a microphone attached to the instrument by a lead. Subsequent researchers have used two other basic methods with great success: the radio and the diode. In the former, an ordinary radio is attached to the tape recorder's microphone socket and tuned to a point between stations that produces rushing sounds, known as 'white noise'. In the latter a diode – a rectifying device that allows current to pass in one direction only – is plugged into the microphone socket. The diode used by Konstantin Raudive was an ordinary crystal set – the 'cat's whisker' of early radio days. From a technical point of view the aerial used with his diode was only a couple of inches long – totally impractical for receiving any clear 'normal' radio signal.

While these simple techniques have provided results quite sufficient to convince most amateur researchers, it was obvious from the outset that the world of science would require much more sophisticated tests

Below: the first of the two controlled experiments set up in 1971 by Colin Smythe, under the supervision of Pye Records Ltd, before committing his company to publishing Dr Raudive's book *Breakthrough* in the English language. Among those present were (from left to right): Dr Raudive, Peter Bander (a director of Colin Smythe Ltd and author of the preface to *Breakthrough*), Ken Attwood and Ray Prickett (Pye's chief recording engineers) and Sir Robert Mayer (chairman of Colin Smythe Ltd). Over 200 voices appeared on the tape during the 18 minute recording session

before admitting that the paranormal might be behind Jürgenson's curious phenomena.

Accordingly, in 1971 Colin Smythe set up two carefully controlled experiments before committing his company to publishing Konstantin Raudive's book in English. The first of these was on 24 March at Gerrard's Cross, Buckinghamshire, under the supervision of Pye Records Ltd and the company's two chief recording engineers, Ray Prickett and Kenneth Attwood.

All the equipment was provided by Pye, and included instruments to block out freak pick-ups from radio stations and high and low frequency transmitters, as well as specially protected tapes. A bank of four tape recorders was synchronised so that one recording was made through a microphone, giving a true account of any normal noises in the room, and a sophisticated diode was also fitted, with a recording indicator attached. The audience, which included Dr Raudive, Colin Smythe, Peter Bander and the chairman of Colin Smythe Ltd, Sir Robert Mayer, was assured by the two engineers that this machinery should render any recording through the diode impossible.

The tapes rolled for 18 minutes, during which time the recording indicator attached to the diode flickered constantly, although Ray Prickett, monitoring on headphones, could hear nothing. The playback, said Mr

Prickett, was 'astounding'. Over 200 voices appeared on the tape, 27 of which were so clear that they were intelligible to everyone present. Sir Robert Mayer in particular was startled to recognise the voice of his old friend the late Artur Schnabel, a celebrated concert pianist. An unidentified voice referred to Dr Raudive as 'Kosti' – his childhood nickname.

The second experiment was conducted three days later on 27 March, at the Enfield laboratories of Belling & Lee, using a radio-frequency screen laboratory that excludes any type of electromagnetic radiation. The experiment was supervised by Peter Hale, Britain's leading expert in electronic screen suppression; he was assisted by Ralph Lovelock, a top physicist and electronics engineer. Again, clear voices appeared on the screened-off tapes.

Peter Hale's response was frank. 'The result of last Friday's experiment . . . is such that I cannot explain it in normal physical terms,' he wrote to Colin Smythe. Ralph Lovelock concurred with this view.

So the objective reality of the voices – whatever their cause – was established to the satisfaction of highly respectable scientists. But what was the nature of the voices? What sort of thing did they say?

Most experimenters report that the voices speak in a curious rhythm, at first alien to the ear. But once the listener has picked up the 'tempo', the phrases and short sentences become readily understandable. The voices speak as if they are racing against time, as if, as one researcher put it, 'either their time "on the air" is limited, or their energy is giving out.' The actual language used seems to depend upon the native tongue of the person to whom the message is addressed: both Peter Bander and Sir Robert Mayer had German origins, and the voices spoke to them in German. Dr Raudive was multilingual, and when he was present the voices often used several languages.

'The sentence construction', Raudive explained, 'obeys rules that differ radically from those of ordinary speech and, although the voices seem to speak in the same way as we do, the anatomy of their "speech apparatus" must be different from our own.'

Dr Raudive, like Jürgenson, was a devout Catholic, and it was perhaps natural that his prime interest should be in establishing that the voices were truly those of the surviving dead. He evolved a system of communicating with them, a kind of electronic 'ouija' or 'table-turning' technique, asking questions aloud and inviting the 'spirits' to reply. Unfortunately the answers were short and rarely very informative. Repeatedly, the voices appeared to avoid direct questions and insisted on being taken at 'face value'. 'Please believe; I am.' 'We are.' 'The dead live.' 'I am alive Konstantin.'

A note of surprise is often detected in the voices as they 'come through', almost as if the

Above: the late Artur Schnabel, composer and concert pianist, who was a close friend of Sir Robert Mayer. When listening to the playback of the recording made during the Pye experiment, Sir Robert was astonished to hear Schnabel's voice on the tape. As a result of the experiment, Sir Robert agreed to go ahead with the publication of Dr Raudive's book. He said: 'If the chief engineers of Pye are baffled, I don't see why we should not present this remarkable discovery to the general public'

earthly attempt to contact them has aroused them from some sort of daze. Reporter Harald Bergestam investigated the state of Swedish research for *Fate* magazine's March 1973 issue. He wrote: 'We heard a man's voice saying clearly "I am living" and he repeated this. The second time his voice was filled with excitement and happiness. We understood that he had just come to realise that although he had died he still lived.'

To the Catholic Dr Raudive, the most important messages seemed to confirm both the existence of Christ and the Church's doctrine of purgatory. Many voices asked for prayers, and assured the experimenter that they could be helped by prayer. Others said: 'Jesus wandered here in loneliness.' 'Here is Christ, here are the priests.' One voice asked: 'Great Lord, remember Raudive!'

When Dr Raudive asked if the speakers could communicate through the tape recorder at will, one voice replied: 'On the Heavenly Father; the will of man is limited.'

On the other hand some messages appear to refer to the Devil, saying: 'Pray! I am in the power of the evil one.' 'The devil exists.'

Puzzlingly, a number of voices express earthly concerns, asking for cigarettes and drink, talking of the 'officialdom' that exists on their plane, and commenting on the clothing of the experimenters – perhaps an indication that they can 'see' as well as speak to their interlocutors.

When the living intrude

An interesting sequence was recorded during an experiment conducted by Friedrich Jürgenson with Professor Hans Bender in July 1971. Jürgenson was at home awaiting the arrival of Professor Bender and his team, which included a girl named Gisela. He had been recording, and when he played back the tape a German voice said: '*Sie kommen bald. Zahnarzt. Zahnarzt.*' ('They will come soon. Dentist. Dentist.')

When the Bender group arrived, Jürgenson was told that Gisela had suffered severe toothache at about the time he had recorded the voice. As it chanced, Jürgenson's wife was a dentist, and arrangements were made for Gisela to attend her surgery while the group continued with their experiments. Some time later, a woman's voice on the tape said '*Peng!*' – a German interjection used like 'Bingo!' to show that something has been accomplished. The voice sounded like that of Gisela and came through at just the time when Gisela's tooth was being extracted.

The incidents surrounding Gisela's toothache closely resemble the phenomenon known to psychical researchers as a crisis apparition. Expressed simply, a crisis apparition occurs when one person, the 'receiver', suddenly becomes aware that another person, the 'transmitter', is undergoing a crisis – pain, shock, emotion – even though the 'transmitter' is some distance away. The most common examples of such phenomena

he was the only person in the room who knew the name.

To agnostic parapsychologists, the theory of TPK is perhaps more acceptable than the 'voices from the dead' alternative, and may explain such discrepancies as the inconsequential nature of some of the phrases recorded: odd words and half-wrought phrases form and dissolve continually in the subconscious mind, after all, and might be projected onto tape if involuntary TPK is involved.

But even granting TPK as the explanation, could not Edison and Raudive still be correct? May not the surviving dead be able to use such preternatural ability with conscious direction?

As holder of the Perrot-Warwick postgraduate studentship for psychical research at Trinity College, Cambridge, David Ellis

occur in times of war, when a mother, for instance, may report seeing or hearing her son at the moment he is wounded – often at the moment of his death. The theory is that the pain and shock trigger off involuntary telepathic contact between son and mother. If Gisela's pain was sharp enough, and the relief of the pain intense enough, she may have projected her emotions telepathically; but for those emotions to affect a machine another factor would have to be involved: psychokinesis, known as PK.

PK is the affecting of physical objects through 'the power of the mind' alone. If telepathy was responsible for Gisela's voice appearing on Jürgenson's tape, it must have been strong enough to affect the recording head of the machine. Thus 'PK at a distance' or 'telepsychokinesis' (TPK) was involved.

Although he has issued no formal pronouncement, Professor Bender inclines to the theory that TPK is behind most of the mystery voice phenomena. He feels that the voices may be PK emanating from the people present at a recording session; he points out that the voices that spoke to Raudive addressed him only in the languages with which he was familiar, and that American experimenters, for instance, tend to receive voices that speak with American accents.

He also quotes an incident that occurred during one of his own recording sessions. All the participants were wearing throat microphones attached to a separate tape recorder so that involuntary whispering could be monitored, and an engineer was taking oscillograph readings – visual voice recordings of everything heard on tape.

During the session, the name of a friend, Brigette Rasmus, came into Bender's mind. On playback, the tape contained the word 'Rasmus'; but the voice was not noticeably female. Bender was certain that it was not Brigette's, who was in any case alive and well in Germany, and both the throat-mike monitors and the oscillograph readings showed that he did not whisper the word. Yet

Russian author Valery Tarsis was present at one of Dr Raudive's recording sessions in 1967 when the voice of his old friend Boris Pasternak (above), author of *Dr Zhivago*, 'came through'. Pasternak, who died in 1960, commented on Tarsis's escape from the Soviet Union in 1966, on the book Tarsis was then working on, and on Pasternak's friend Olga. Perhaps both Tarsis and Pasternak could derive comfort from the fact that one of their old tormentors, Joseph Stalin (right), appeared to be getting his just deserts on the 'other side': another of Dr Raudive's tapes yields the words: 'Stalin. Terribly hot here'

devoted two years between 1970 and 1972 to the scientific analysis of the voice phenomena. Subsequently he announced that, in half a dozen cases at least, he believed that Dr Raudive may have confused a Russian broadcast on Radio Luxembourg with his paranormal voices, but hastened to add that most of his 100,000 tapes were inexplicable in normal terms.

On 2 September 1974, Konstantin Raudive died at his home in Bad Krozingen. On 16 November, *Psychic News* carried a short report of a voice phenomenon experiment conducted at a conference on the paranormal in Germany some 10 days after his death. An American researcher set up a recorder and microphone, and subsequently the 130 delegates heard a voice, which many of them claimed to recognise as that of Raudive. Unfortunately the dead professor was no more specific than his painstakingly recorded voices had been, merely 'making apparent reference to "other techniques"'.

'We have no other details,' explained a spokesman for *Psychic News*. 'It is what we call a "question mark story".'

Other voices, other lives

It has long been known that under hypnosis some people regress to what appears to be a previous life. They not only assume another personality, but, as DAVID CHRISTIE-MURRAY shows, they can describe details from the past that are completely unknown to them outside of the trance state

HYPNOTIC REGRESSION into alleged previous lives is one of the most exciting and fascinating of psychic phenomena – and one of the most frustrating. During the past 20 years it has been brought to the attention of the general public every so often by programmes on radio and television, articles in the press and books written either by hypnotists themselves or by collaborators working with them.

Morey Bernstein's *The search for Bridey Murphy*, published in 1965, is still remembered if the small talk veers towards the occult; Arnall Bloxham's tapes, featured on radio and television programmes, and given a longer life by Jeffrey Iverson's *More lives than one?*, are widely known. Recently, Peter Moss has collaborated with Joe Keeton, prodigious in his expenditure of hypnotic man-hours, in the book *Encounters with the past*, which describes recordings of extracts from sessions with chosen subjects.

It is not generally realised that hypnotic regression into previous lives is not a recent discovery and has, in fact, been studied for nearly a century. The work of pioneers in this field, much of it lost because it was done long before the advent of the tape-recorder, is nevertheless valuable to students of reincarnation, whether they believe in it or not.

Travelling back in time

Part of the fascination of hypnotic regression lies in the very frustration that it engenders. Its revelations are both positive and negative,

some bolstering the faith of reincarnationists and puzzling sceptics, others bewildering believers and encouraging doubt. Regression is positive in that the dramatisations of former existences are vividly portrayed far beyond the acting abilities of subjects in their waking condition, so that observers repeatedly say: 'If this be acting, neither an Olivier or a Bernhardt could better it.'

Positive, too, is the consistency with which many subjects, regressed repeatedly to the same historical period, take up the previous life, so that the same personality, outlook and intonation of speech appear without effort or hesitation. The same incidents and facts are remembered even when trick questions are introduced to try to trap the speakers. This happens even when years separate the sessions.

Regression is positive in two further ways. The first is that obscure historical facts, apparently completely unknown beforehand to either hypnotist or subject and confirmed only after considerable research, are revealed in reply to general questions. An example of this is shown by one of Joe Keeton's subjects, Ann Dowling, an ordinary housewife who, during over 60 hours of regression, became Sarah Williams, an orphan living a life of utter squalor in a Liverpool slum in the first half of the 19th century.

When asked what was happening in Liverpool in 1850, Ann Dowling mentioned the visit of a foreign singer whose name had 'summat to do wi' a bird'. Research showed

Hypnotherapist Joe Keeton (top) has conducted more than 8000 regressions. One of his subjects, Ann Dowling (above), went back over 100 years and became Sarah Williams, who lived in Liverpool in the 1850s (top right). Among the facts recalled by Mrs Dowling was the visit of Swedish singer Jenny Lind (below)

that Jenny Lind, the 'Swedish Nightingale', on her way from Sweden to America, sang for two nights in Liverpool's Philharmonic Hall in August 1850.

The second positive aspect of hypnotic regression is found in the tiny details of past usage that slip naturally into the subject's conversation while reliving the past life. These details *might* have been picked up by the subject in his present lifetime and held in his subconscious memory, but they are unlikely to have been formally taught or known to people of ordinary education.

David Lowe, a member of the Society for Psychical Research, lectures about a woman whom he has regressed into a number of lives, some of them in different generations of the same family (an unusual feature), illustrating his talks with copious tape-recordings of her conversations in previous existences.

During a 17th-century regression, David Lowe asked the woman how a certain word containing a 'w' was spelt. Her spontaneous answer was 'double v' – the common pronunciation of the letter at that time. This

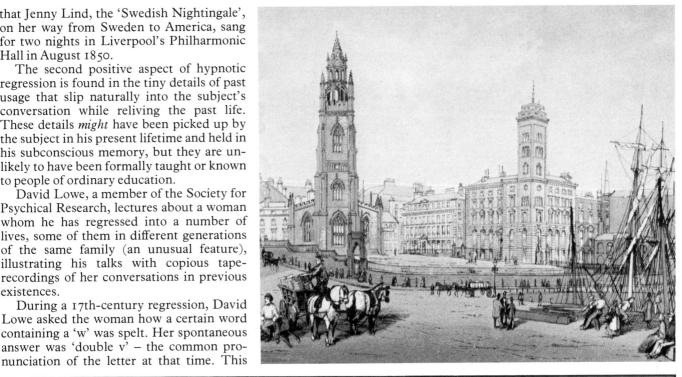

The belief in reincarnation

The belief in reincarnation – that man's soul is reborn over and over again in another body or form – stretches far back into the past. The doctrine appears in primitive religions such as those of the Indian tribes of Assam, Nagas and Lushais, who believed that after death the soul took the form of an insect. The Bakongs of Borneo believed that their dead were reincarnated into the bearcats that frequented their raised coffins. The Kikuyu women of Kenya often worship at a place 'inhabited' by their ancestral souls in the belief that to become pregnant they must be entered by an ancestral soul.

According to Buddhist and Hindu thought man or the soul is reborn in accordance with merits acquired during his previous lifetime. But some sects of Hinduism hold that a man does not necessarily assume a human form in the next life. If he has been involved with vice or crime it is possible he may return as a cactus, toad, lizard, or even as poison ivy! The Buddhists believe that man is made up of elements: body, sensation, perception, impulse, emotion and consciousness, which fall apart at death. The individual, as such, ceases to exist and a new individual life begins according to the quality of the previous life, until at last achieving perfection and nirvana – eternal bliss.

Although reincarnation is not mentioned in Western texts until the late Greek and Latin writers, the idea dates back to at least the 6th century BC. It appears in the Orphic writings, which

Tibetans believe that their spiritual leader, the Dalai Lama, is the reincarnation of a previous Dalai Lama whose soul enters the body of a child born at the precise moment of his death

appear to have played a great part in the thought of Pythagorus. He believed that the soul had 'fallen' into a bodily existence and would have to reincarnate itself through other forms to be set free. He himself claimed to have had previous existences including one as a soldier in a Trojan war.

Plato was greatly influenced by the Orphico-Pythagorean views and mentions reincarnation in his concluding part of the *Republic*. The soul, according to Plato, is immortal, the number of souls fixed, and reincarnation regularly occurs. Although discarded by Aristotle and other Stoic views, Plato's derivation was taken up by later schools of thought such as the Neoplatonists. Within the Christian church the belief was held by certain Gnostic sects during the first century AD and by the Manichaeans in the fourth and fifth centuries. But the idea was repudiated by eminent theologians at the time, and in AD 553, the Emperor Justinian condemned reincarnation, at the Second Council of Constantinople, as heresy.

Today the Westerner does have some difficulty in identifying with the Eastern idea of reincarnation. Most Western religious denominations share the view that the individual retains individuality after death, and finds the idea of returning as an animal or plant distinctly foreign. In 1917 the Roman Catholic Church denounced the idea as heresy.

Most adherents of reincarnation are now claiming the evidence from regressive hypnosis as proof for their case.

trivial detail was more telling to some listeners than all the researched dates and genealogies that substantiated the woman's story, remarkable as these were. When asked if she were engaged (to be married), the subject failed to understand the modern expression, but later talked happily of her recent betrothal.

Fact or fiction

The negative side of hypnotic regression is nevertheless considerable. There are many anachronisms, occasional historical howlers, instances of extraordinary ignorance and, with some subjects, inconsistencies (although much rarer than, and more balanced by, the consistencies).

One 19th-century character mentioned her 'boyfriend' in the modern sense of someone with a sexual love-interest in her. Another, regressed to the early 1830s and asked who ruled England, replied 'Queen Victoria', although four years of William IV's reign had still to run and Victoria's accession could not have been known for certain.

A common difficulty in substantiating historical facts is the scarcity of records of ordinary folk before the 19th century. Even when subjects mention landowners and comparatively important people, there is often no record of their existence in local archives. It is therefore sometimes extremely difficult to separate fact from fiction, especially as there may be a great deal of 'role-playing', the incubation in the subconscious mind of an imaginary personality around a nucleus of fact read in a history book or a novel.

Origins of modern hypnosis

Hypnosis is still so misunderstood and thought of as occult in the minds of many that it is as well to describe its place in modern thought.

Modern hypnosis began with Franz Mesmer, an Austrian physician who became a fashionable figure of Parisian society in the 18th century. He mistakenly believed that human beings emitted a force that could be transferred to objects such as iron rods. He 'magnetised' the rods by stroking them, then placed them in tubs filled with water in which his patients immersed their legs. Many and various were the ills allegedly cured by this method.

The extravagance of Mesmeric theory and its claims, together with the undertones of occultism that went with them, aroused intense opposition; and throughout the 19th century, serious investigators into hypnosis, and the few medical men bold enough to experiment with its use, met the kind of hostility once reserved for witches.

The Society for Psychical Research, which was founded in Britain in 1882, set up a committee to investigate hypnosis that continued to exist until a few years ago. Its findings, however, were not easily communicated to the general public and the phenomena it showed to be genuine were remarkable enough to maintain hypnotism's occult reputation, in spite of the Society's careful, objective and scholarly approach. But the therapeutic value of hypnosis was slowly established, especially in the treatment of psychological disorders.

After much investigation, it was discovered that subjects under hypnosis could be told either to *remember* what had happened on, say, their fifth birthday, or to *be* five years old again and to relive the day.

In the latter case, subjects would be led back to that day, write as they wrote at that age, relive the opening of their presents and each incident of the birthday party. They would have no knowledge of anything that happened after their fifth birthday until led forward by the hypnotist. It was as if all the layers of experience from five years old onwards had completely disappeared. The first man to attempt this age regression is said

The founder of modern hypnosis, Franz Anton Mesmer, believed that people emitted a force that could be transferred to iron rods. Parisians of all classes flocked to his salon in the 18th century where they sat round a large wooden tub called a *baquet*. This was filled with water, iron filings and bottles of 'magnetised' water. Projecting from the tub were iron rods, which patients held against their afflicted parts

to have been a Spaniard, Fernando Colavida, in 1887.

Further discoveries led to the investigation of pre-birth experiences in the womb and within a few years Dr Mortis Stark was studying the possibility of actually regressing subjects to a life before the present. At about the same time, in 1911, a Frenchman, Colonel Albert de Rochas, published an account of regressions that he had collected over several years.

A therapeutic role

The method employed in hypnotic regression is simple. After hypnotising the subject, the operator takes him back step by step to the beginning of his present life, then into the womb, and then instructs him to go back and back until he comes to some experience that he can describe. This is sometimes an 'existence' in the intermission between death ding a former life and birth beginning the present, sometimes experience of the former life itself, the period and circumstances of which the hypnotist can elicit by careful questioning.

The process is not merely used for interest's sake or to prove reincarnation – it can be therapeutic. Neuroses and other psychological disorders may be caused by traumas, the existence of which has been caused by shocks or other experiences in childhood or youth apparently too horrible for the conscious mind to face. To cure the neurosis, the trauma must be discovered and faced by the patient, and hypnosis is one technique able to dig it out.

By an extension of the process, neuroses and phobias may be caused by traumas experienced in alleged former lives that are revealed under hypnosis. Thus, one woman's terrible fear of water was caused by her having been bound with chains as a galley-slave in a previous existence, thrown into a river and eaten alive by crocodiles. A man terrified of descending in lifts had been a Chinese general who had accidentally fallen to his death from a great height. A young American girl about to dive from a high board was suddenly paralysed with fear after a moving bystander had been reflected in the water. Hypnosis revealed the hideous end of a former life in which she had been a girl in Florida who, just as she was jumping into the water, had seen the shadow of the alligator that was to devour her moving below the surface.

Whether or not these are memories of genuine previous experiences, they are convincing to many who have them. Much of the investigation into this particular aspect of hypnosis challenges the sceptics to find an explanation other than that of reincarnation. There *are* alternative explanations, which will be presented in future chapters.

Ten more lives to remember

Madame J, a soldier's wife and mother of one child, was delicate in health and as a girl had 'hated history'. She was regressed by Colonel de Rochas to 10 previous lives, some extremely detailed.

In the first she died at eight months. She then lived as a girl named Irisée in the country of the Imondo near Trieste. She next became a man, Esius, aged 40, who was planning to kill Emperor Probus in revenge for taking his daughter, Florina.

The fourth life was that of Carlomée, a Frankish warrior chieftain captured by Attila at Châlons-sur-Marne in AD 449. Abbess Martha followed, born in AD 923, who tyrannised young girls in a Vincennes convent as late as 1010. The Abbess was succeeded by Mariette Martin, aged 18 in 1300, daughter of a man who worked for the king – 'le beau Philippe'.

Madame J. then became Michel Berry, who was killed at the age of 22 in 1515 at the Battle of Marignano. This life was extremely detailed, Michel's career developing from his learning the art of fencing at 10, through his life as a page at the courts at Versailles and the Sorbonne and sundry love affairs to his presence aged 20 at the Battle of Guinegatte in Normandy.

Top: Colonel Albert de Rochas caused a sensation in 1911 with an account of hypnotic regression

Centre: the Emperor Probus, who was hated by Esius, the third personality in Madame J's previous lives

Above: the Battle of Marignano, in which Michel Berry died

After an eighth life as a wife and mother aged 30 in 1702, Madame J again became a man, Jules Robert. Jules was aged 38 in 1776 and a 'bad' worker in marble. Nevertheless one of his sculptures reached the Vatican.

Jules Robert reincarnated as Marguerite Duchesne, born in 1835, daughter of a grocer in the rue de la Caserne, Briançon. She went to school in the rue de la Gargouille. Research showed that the school existed, but there had never been a grocer Duchesne in the rue de la Caserne. Otherwise Madame J's description of places was accurate.

The case for Bridey Murphy

Have our lives been shaped not only by experiences and impressions gained since birth, but also by those from some other, previous existence?

IN 1956 AND 1957, Emile Franckel conducted a series of live experiments for a Los Angeles television programme called *Adventures in Hypnotism*. Franckel's aim was to bring to the public's attention the possibility that individuals under hypnosis can relive previous lives. His attitude was sceptical: he believed that recollections of previous lives arose from promptings from the hypnotist or deep subconscious memory. Some of the experiences he was able to draw from his subjects, however, seemed unaccountable by this explanation. Since the hypnotist did not know his subjects, he could scarcely have induced their responses except by a series of coincidences too remarkable to be statistically acceptable as mere chance.

Yet Franckel was right to have remained sceptical. For although some of the results were so remarkable as to seem almost miraculous, hypnosis is a mental state that almost anyone may experience given the right circumstances and which almost everyone can produce in at least some subjects – provided, of course, that he has mastered a few simple techniques – techniques that should never be used merely as a party game nor for exhibition purposes, nor by anyone who is unaware of its dangers. This does not mean that hypnosis is fully understood by the medical profession. The following cases illustrate some of the areas where our knowledge is still inadequate in explaining regression into previous lives under hypnosis.

We assume that the human personality consists of potentialities derived from a combination of factors – parents' genes, plus, perhaps, racial memories and other elements. If reincarnation is ever to be established as fact, these 'other elements' will include memories of previous lives.

What appears to happen under hypnosis is that the layers of experience we have all acquired during our lives – experiences that have pushed our memory of previous existences deep into the subconscious – comes to the surface. When the hypnotist suggests, for example, to a 30-year-old subject: 'It is now 1970. You are now 20—you are waking up on your 20th birthday. Tell me where you are, what is happening', the subject's life and development of the past 10 years are as if they had never been.

Practising hypnotists know that no two subjects ever behave exactly alike, for all human beings are unique in some way, and with many subjects there seems to be a 'shadow' personality—a fantasy personality

Below: King Richard II (1367–1400) and courtiers at Conway Castle, Wales. In 1906 a clergyman's daughter claimed, while under hypnosis, to have lived a previous life in the court of Richard II and to have known his mother, the 'Fair Maid of Kent'

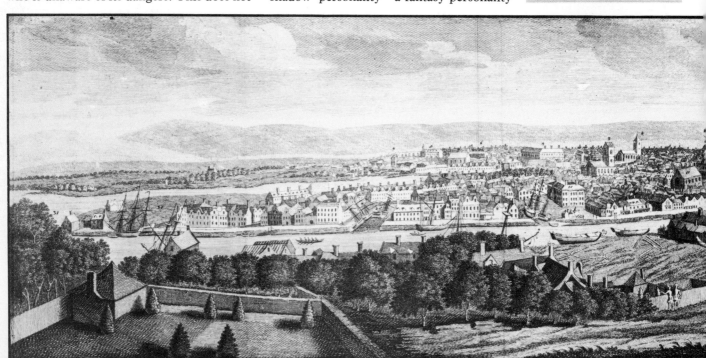

that is only revealed sometimes in dreams or under hypnosis. And, the suggestion is, it is this 'fantasy personality' that is revealed, not recollection of a previous life.

How are we to distinguish between what may be mere fantasy and a true account of a previous life? As early as 1906 the Society for Psychical Research reported the case of an unnamed clergyman's daughter who, under hypnosis, recounted her life during the reign of Richard II. In that life she was no great lady herself – despite the claim by cynics that *all* cases of regression imagine themselves to be famous people – but an acquaintance of Maud, Countess of Salisbury, her friend Blanche Poynings, née Mowbray, and Richard's mother, 'Fair Maid of Kent'.

In this case, almost every historical fact stated under hypnosis was found to be true, as were details of the dress and food described by the girl. Moreover, she had no recollection of ever having read about either the period or the people.

Some early psychical researchers into hypnotic phenomena awoke their subjects and placed their hands on a planchette board, usually screened from the subjects' view, and proceeded to interrogate them. The planchette – it is claimed – wrote down true answers to the questions from knowledge in the subjects' subconscious minds. Under these conditions the girl revealed that she had just read an historical romance in which every person and fact, except for some minor details, had appeared, though she had devised a new setting for them.

If all cases were as straightforward as this, there would be no need for further investigation, and believers in reincarnation would have to look elsewhere for evidence. How complicated the majority of cases are, however, is shown by the celebrated case of

Bridey Murphy. This is no more remarkable than a hundred other cases of hypnotic regression, but was brought to the public's attention by a heated debate in a number of American newspapers and a film shown widely in English-speaking countries.

In a number of sessions from November 1952 to October 1953, Morey Bernstein, an amateur American hypnotist, regressed Mrs Virginia Tighe to a life in early 19th-century Ireland. Mrs Tighe, 29 years old at the time, a native of Madison, Wisconsin, and resident in Chicago from the age of three until her marriage, had never visited Ireland, nor had much to do with Irish people (she

Right: Morey Bernstein, the American hypnotist, and Mrs Virginia Tighe. The account given by Mrs Tighe of her 'previous life' as 'Bridey Murphy' led Morey Bernstein to become a firm believer in reincarnation

Below: a view of Cork as it was in the mid-18th century. It was here that Mrs Tighe claimed she had previously been born as 'Bridey Murphy' in 1798

Right: kissing the Blarney Stone in the manner described by Mrs Tighe. Today, all one does is to lie on the back, hold on to two bars attached to the wall, lower the head and kiss the underside of the Stone. The earlier method, used at the time of 'Bridey Murphy', would not have been known by Mrs Tighe without her having done a great deal of research

Below: to counter the claim that he had in some way rigged his experiments, Morey Bernstein hypnotised Mrs Tighe only in the presence of two witnesses

Bottom: uillean pipes of the type 'Bridey Murphy' claims were played at her funeral in Cork in 1864

strongly denied allegations to the contrary, and the evidence supports her denials). Under hypnosis she began to speak with an Irish accent, said she was Bridget (Bridey) Murphy, daughter of Duncan and Kathleen Murphy, Protestants living at the Meadows, Cork. Her brother Duncan, born in 1796, married Aimée, daughter of Mrs Strayne, who was mistress of a day school attended by Bridey when she was 15.

In about 1818 she married a Catholic, Brian MacCarthy, whose relatives she named, and they travelled by carriage to Belfast through places she named but whose existence has never been found on any map.

The couple worshipped at Father John Gorman's St Theresa's Church. They shopped at stores that Bridey named, using coins correctly described for the period. In addition, Bridey produced a number of Irish words when asked, using some as they were used then, though their meaning had changed since: 'slip', for example, referring to a child's pinafore, not petticoat – the more common modern word. Bridey Murphy had read some Irish mythology, knew some Irish songs and was a good dancer of Irish jigs. At the end of one sitting, Mrs Tighe, aroused from her trance, yet not fully conscious,

KISSING THE BLARNEY STONE.

danced 'The Morning Jig', ending her performance with a stylised yawn. Her description of another dance was confirmed in detail by a lady whose parents had danced it. Another telling detail was that she described the correct procedure for kissing the Blarney Stone used in Bridey's day.

Bridey's story was investigated by the American magazine *Empire*. William Barker was commissioned by the magazine to spend three weeks in Ireland checking the facts 'Bridey' had given. His visit resulted in a 19,000-word report. Barker's account is typical of regression cases. Some facts were confirmed, others unconfirmed, others proved incorrect. Memories of insignificant detail proved true, while Bridey displayed total ignorance of other important events. Confirmation of facts proved impossible

in many instances. There was no possibility, for example, of confirming dates of birth, marriages and deaths, as no records were kept in Cork until 1864 and if the Murphy family kept records in a family Bible, a customary procedure, its whereabouts are not known. No information could be discovered concerning St Theresa's Church or Father Gorman in Belfast, but the two shops mentioned by Bridey, Carrigan and Farr, had both existed. Bridey had said that uillean pipes had been played at her funeral and these were found to have been customarily used at funerals because of their soft tone.

So the neutral enquirer is left puzzled. Where did Mrs Tighe learn about uillean pipes, kissing the Blarney Stone and the names of shops in Belfast whose existence was only confirmed after painstaking research? Why should she have created a vivid picture of life in Ireland at the beginning of the 19th century, if this was simply a creation of some part of her subconscious? From where did she – along with many other regressed subjects with no pretence at acting ability – draw the talent to dramatise so effectively a life in another age and another country?

Yet, if reincarnation is a fact, why should trivialities be remembered and great emotional experiences that one would have expected to have contributed to one's development in this life, be forgotten or go unmentioned? The questions are as bewildering as they are intriguing.

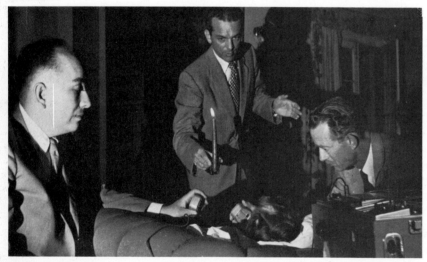

PART 5

CREATURES FROM ELSEWHERE

Introduction

THERE ARE TWO ANIMALS that are not to be found in any zoo but that must be known to almost everyone in the Western world: the Loch Ness monster and the bigfoot (or yeti, as it's known in the Himalayas). But how many people have heard of the flying black batwoman of Vietnam, the *peiste* of the Irish loughs, or know the full story of the Minnesota Iceman? You will learn of all these things in this book – and consider too whether that creature of legend, the werewolf, may not still be alive and well in Europe today.

But we are presenting here something more besides: that is not merely a collection of spine chilling tales and outlandish stories – though many reports of 'unknown' animals are far from reassuring and often very bizarre indeed. What these chapters offer are careful examinations of the reports and photographs of the creatures, informed speculations about their nature and origins, and, where appropriate, a discussion of the *kind* of reality such weird entities may inhabit. For in dealing with some of the more extraordinary of these reports, made by reliable witnesses with no apparent desire for notoriety or profit, there often appears to be no alternative explanation for the events described than some kind of parallel reality, some other dimension, from which these creatures inexplicably and elusively emerge, if ever so briefly, into the light of our world.

Legends of the Loch
That possibility does seem rather remote, however, when we are dealing with our two most famous examples. Certainly, it's true that the first reports from Scotland of something very strange swimming about in Loch Ness first filtered out only in the 1930s, following the cutting of a new road alongside the long, gloomy stretch of water. But for a hundred years or more before that, the local people had known that *something* was there. (And they were in no doubt either that there was something very peculiar lurking in the waters of 1000-feet-deep Loch Morar, 40 miles or so away to the west. But the shy denizens of that water have never had the flocks of passing strangers, publicity seekers, charlatans or even plain scientists to draw attention to them in the way that the tenants of Loch Ness have.) And, as ever, the likelihood of getting to the bottom of the mystery in Loch Ness was long kept at bay by an irritating trickle of spurious photographs of such things as posts with socks hanging off them, as well as honestly mistaken photographs of standing waves, wakes of long-passed boats, or drifting logs. Few serious investigators would go near the place, leaving it prey to cranks and the merely curious.

It wasn't simply the odour of bad publicity that kept away the biologists and ecologists who should have been there all the time, however. There were practical reasons too: Loch Ness is a vast stretch of water, and it is impossible to see very far into it because of the peat that stains it. Not until the development of sophisticated forms of sonar during the 1960s was it possible to employ a really effective method of detection in the loch. One of the more imaginative notions for tracking Nessie involved using trained dolphins to home in on a sonar contact and have them photograph it!

But even if the means had been available earlier, would the scientific establishment have taken up the challenge? Probably not, if only because in this century scientists have displayed a depressing tendency to imagine that, having mapped the globe and spread himself into all its corners, modern man has discovered all its wonders. (With a similar extravagance of closed mind, the then director of the US Patent Office in 1899 urged President McKinley to close it forthwith, on the principle that 'Everything that can be invented has been invented.') It seemed ridiculous that an undiscovered and unnamed animal could have been sitting in the civilised world's back yard and have gone unnoticed so long. Embarrassed, and nervous of the more eccentric devotees of the loch's mysterious inhabitants, scientists became as shy as any monster of the deep.

But when they do venture near the loch, even the most respected of scientists can come away with egg on his face. The famous naturalist Sir Peter Scott may have been a little over-enthusiastic in his interpretation of 'monster' photographs taken in Loch Ness, but that did not prevent him forging ahead to give the ostensible animal a scientific name – *Nessiteras rhombopteryx*. Spend a little time rearranging the letters of this honest attempt to label Nessie and you will find they also spell the words 'monster hoax by Sir Peter S'.

Nonetheless, serious and disciplined research into whatever dwells in Loch Ness is well under way in the 1980s. Not as much, unfortunately, can be said for the world's other star monster, the bigfoot, sasquatch or yeti.

Abominable mystery
Once again the evidence from local folklore is extremely strong and remarkably consistent, whether it comes from the Himalayas, the Canadian Rockies or deep in the United States. There really does seem to be some kind of man-like beast shambling around in the shadows of civilisation. Or perhaps there are several kinds: for reports come in from all over the globe, from the wastes of Siberia and the chill peaks of Nepal to the suburbs of America. It seems reasonable to suppose that there may be regional variations of the hairy man-beast. So much, however, must remain speculation, for not one of the creatures has been captured or shot. (Remembering the fate of some rare species whose last surviving examples were shot simply to be stuffed and displayed in museums, perhaps we should be grateful that none have yet been hunted down, for all the loss to human knowledge.)

That simple fact must lead the honest observer to wonder

if something else has been at work on the imaginations of those who have met or found traces of the bigfoot. In most cases we can usually dismiss the chances of deliberate hoaxing, if only because so many witnesses seem genuinely disturbed by their encounter – some to the extent of declaring they wished it had never happened, others being hurt or astonished at the amount of mockery and disbelief to which they have been subjected.

That leaves us with the possibility that the sightings or the traces were evidence of something else – something more familiar. Certainly it's hard to be sure that large footprint-like dents in the snow high in the mountains are actually footprints. A mountain goat will make quite tiny prints that melt somewhat in the sun to form large plate-like depressions, which then re-freeze to give the impression that an unusually heavy animal has trampled by. And while it is possible that in the wilderness areas of the United States a hungry bear may be mistaken for something more like a human being at night or in shadow, in the fastnesses of Asia there is an even odder risk.

Part of the training for certain religious sects' involves sending adepts out into the more remote (and unpleasant) parts of the mountains. Skilled in techniques of meditation and bodily control these extraordinary men can remain in these extreme conditions, without very much clothing and with no food at all, for days at a time. And having no desire to be disturbed in their contemplation, they will do their best to stay out of sight of mountaineers or other kinds of passer-by – meanwhile leaving mysterious footprints behind them, or tantalising glimpses of themselves as they slip away amid the snow and ice and rocks. How many of these shy and ascetic men have been mistaken for weird unearthly creatures – the 'abominable snowmen' of legend – it is impossible to say. But it is certainly possible that such cases of mistaken identity *have* occurred.

What, on the other hand, of the famous and controversial film that was shot of a bigfoot in 1967? There are certainly some rather odd features about it, not least (to the determined sceptic at least) the fact that it was a dedicated bigfoot-hunter who shot the movie. (People don't howl with derision when someone comes up with the antidote to some grim disease, for which they may have been searching for years, but the assumption generally is that the evidence gathered by seekers after the strange is somehow invalid since their motives are self-serving in the first place). One possibility is not often mentioned in connection with this case: that it was not Roger Patterson who was the hoaxer, but the bigfoot. Or rather someone who, aware of Patterson's interest in this kind of big game, dressed in a gorilla suit and gave him a run for his money. On the other hand, he might just have got some footage of the real thing.

Perhaps oddest of all the tales that surround bigfeet are those concerning their involvement with UFOs: occasionally the mysterious man-beasts appear at the same time as weird lights in the night and sometimes have strange psychological effects on the witnesses.

Winged things and werewolves

This may be some form of hallucination, or it may be some intrusion from a completely unexplained 'parallel reality', but it does make a connection, perhaps, with some of the more astounding stories of mysterious *flying* creatures, some of which bear no relation at all to conventional bird life – and precious little even to the wildest stretches of the human imagination. Whether these come from another dimension, or are just possibly material creations of the human mind that occur only in certain rare circumstances, or are something else altogether, one can only speculate. And it is after all no less possible that, if the lakes of Scotland, Ireland and North America are harbouring strange forms of marine life, the more remote areas of the country may be hiding the nests of equally peculiar winged creatures.

The thought that material reality as we understand it may occasionally become plastic, may be putty in the hands of the mind, does seem particularly appropriate when we ponder the bizarre and frightening history of the werewolf. Reported by the ancient Greeks thousands of years ago, and still heard of from time to time in the modern era, the werewolf phenomenon is one of the most gruesome and most perplexing of all unexplained animal manifestations. *Is* it a delusion? A superstition that is fostered by ignorance, tradition and fear? Or is there some interaction here between the mind and body that can bring such creatures into being, a curse to themselves and their victims alike?

These questions are all raised by the reports that follow in these pages – questions in their way no less strange than the animals that inspire them.

PETER BROOKESMITH

Everyone has heard tales of the 'abominable snowman' – or yeti – of the Himalayas. But sightings of mysterious animals, neither man nor beast, have been reported from all over the world: from North America, China, Australia, Africa, the wastes of Siberia and the Amazon jungle. JANET and COLIN BORD sift the evidence, and present he case for the reality of these elusive creatures

'WILD MEN OF THE WOODS' are common figures in folklore throughout the world. In medieval Britain they were known as 'wood-woses' or 'woodhouses', and can be seen depicted in carvings in East Anglian churches. Though it is tempting to dismiss wood-woses as colourful figments of the rural imagination, a recent stream of reports of sightings from the North American continent of 'man-beasts' up to 8 feet (2.4 metres) tall – make these not so easy to ignore.

Bigfoot – or sasquatch, to give it the Indian name that is used in the province of British Columbia in Canada – makes the headlines so frequently nowadays that similar sightings in more distant or less publicity-conscious parts of the world tend to be overlooked. Yet from time to time reports emerge from the Himalayas, traditionally thought of as the home of the yeti or abominable snowman, of strange footprints in the snow or, less frequently, distant sightings of what is taken to be the yeti itself. In 1974, a Nepalese girl guarding a herd of yaks 14,000

Man, myth or monster?

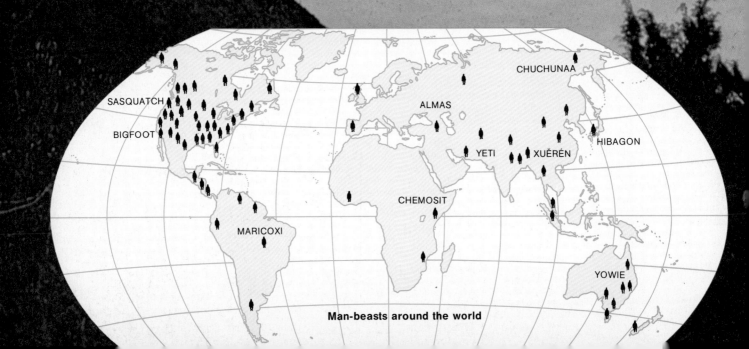

Man-beasts around the world

feet (4250 metres) up in the mountains near Mount Everest was attacked by a yeti and in 1978 Lord and Lady Hunt, revisiting Nepal to commemorate the 1953 ascent of Everest, saw and photographed large tracks in the snow around their huts.

Much has been written about the yeti over the years, although the number of actual sightings has been fairly small. In contrast, very little has been written about sightings of 'wild men' or 'man-beasts' in China, but from what has been published it seems they are fairly active in some remote areas. In the mid-1970s strange encounters with unknown creatures were reported from Hopeh and Shansi provinces – forested, mountainous country in northern China.

Particularly dramatic was the report made by 33-year-old Pang Gensheng, a commune leader, in June 1977. Pang was chopping wood in the Taibai Mountains of central Shansi province when he saw a 'hairy man':

It came closer and closer. I got scared and kept retreating until my back was against a stone cliff and I couldn't go any further. The hairy man came up to 7 or 8 feet [2.1 or 2.4 metres], and then to about 5 feet [1.5 metres] from me. I raised my axe, ready to fight for my life. We stood like that, neither of us moving, for more than an hour. Then I groped for a stone and threw it at him. It hit him in the chest. He uttered several howls and rubbed the spot with his left hand. Then he turned left and leaned against a tree, then walked away slowly toward the bottom of the gully. He kept making a mumbling sound.

The 'man' was about 7 feet (2.1 metres) tall, with a sloping forehead and deep-set black eyes. His jaw jutted out, and he had broad front teeth. Dark brown hair hung long and loose over his shoulders, and his body and face were covered with short hair. His long arms reached below his knees, and he walked upright with his legs wide apart.

Researchers at the Institute of Palaeo-anthropology and Vertebrate Palaeontology

Background picture: the Himalayas, home of the yeti, or abominable snowman

Below left: a footprint, allegedly of a yeti, found near Menlung Base of the 1951 Himalayan expedition. It is regarded as the best piece of photographic evidence for the existence of the yeti

Below right: in February 1980, a Polish climber took this photograph on Mount Everest at 16,000 feet (4800 metres). The footprint measures 14 inches (36 centimetres) long and 7 inches (17 centimetres) wide

of the 'wild men'. These mountains are a north-westerly extension of the Himalayas. In the summer of 1979 a Soviet expedition there found footprints $13\frac{1}{2}$ inches (34.3 centimetres) long and $6\frac{1}{2}$ inches (16.5 centimetres) wide at the toes, but no one actually saw who or what made them.

'Man-beasts' have also been seen in Siberia, in the inhospitable northern territory of the Soviet Union. In the early 1960s a hunter living near the River Ob saw two such creatures when they came out of the forest one evening, while he was walking with his dogs. The dogs ran off in terror, but were not harmed. Dogs are usually frightened by these unknown monsters; in America bigfeet seem to dislike dogs and have been known to injure or even kill them. The Siberian hunter noted that the wild men were covered with dark hair, had long arms and turned their feet outwards when walking. Their eyes glowed dark red – yet another characteristic that indicates a similarity with bigfeet.

In the 1920s, a chuchunaa (a name meaning 'outcast' given to the man-beast in the Yakutiya region of eastern Siberia) was seen by villagers out berry-picking.

It was also picking berries and stuffing them into its mouth with both hands. On catching sight of us, he stood up to his full height. He was very tall and lean, over 2 metres [over 6 feet], they say Barefoot and dressed in deerskin, he had very long arms and a mop of unkempt hair. His face was as big as a human's. His forehead was small and

of the Chinese Academy of Sciences have been investigating such reports, but so far have not been able to solve the riddle of the 'wild man'. Even so, it it significant that the detailed description given by Pang Gensheng is similar to those given by witnesses elsewhere in the world. And the creature's behaviour is quite typical.

Footprints in the snow

Research and investigation have also been undertaken in the Soviet Union, where Dr Jeanna Kofman has been on the trail of the so-called 'almas' in the Caucasus Mountains since 1955. She has received many eye-witness reports and has personally interviewed about 4000 people.

One of them was 39-year-old Mukhamed Tomakov, a farm manager, who in 1946 caught an almas in a mountain hut at Getmish. The creature was man-like, but covered with hair, and ran on all fours, standing on its hind legs whenever it stopped. (Sometimes, but not often, American bigfeet have been seen running on all fours.) Once the creature was safely inside the hut, Tomakov latched the door and went to get a rope. When he returned the door was open and the hut empty.

The Pamir Mountains on the southern border of the Soviet Union are another haunt

Above: the carved figure of a woodwose in the porch of Peasenhall Church, Suffolk. Woodwoses, or 'wild men of the woods', are said to have inhabited England in the Middle Ages, but they have apparently become extinct with the gradual spread of towns and villages

Right: a line of footprints said to have been made by a yeti. An alternative explanation, however, is that they were made by a mountain goat. The sun then melted the snow around the hoof marks, enlarging them

protruded over his eyes like the peak of a cap. His chin was large and broad, far bigger than a human's. Other than being a little taller, he was very much like a human. The next moment he ran away. He ran very fast, leaping high after every third step.

In America, too, bigfeet have been seen eating berries, and there have even been occasional reports of them actually wearing clothing.

'X' marks the spot

All continents still have some areas of wilderness, jungles or forested mountains that are rarely penetrated by outsiders. (Europe has the smallest area of uncivilised territory, which may explain why man-beast reports are almost non-existent there.) Vast tracts of unexplored land may conceal all manner of unknown creatures, not just wild men or man-beasts. In the East, man-beasts have been reported in Malaysia, where there is still plenty of jungle to conceal anything that wishes to stay hidden. Of course, the more remote the country, the less likely outsiders are to hear about unexpected encounters with these unknown life forms, unless expeditions are mounted with the intention of tracking them down.

This explains why we have only fragmentary data from South America and Africa. Yet what we do hear suggests there is plenty of activity. In 1978 Jacqueline Roumeguere Eberhardt of the Centre Nationale de la Recherche Scientifique in Paris published information on her research into the African man-beast, which she has somewhat unimaginatively named 'X'. At that time she had 31 accounts of sightings in 11 Kenyan forests, and she was able to identify four separate types of 'X'. One native was captured and carefully examined by an 'X' before being pushed away in the direction of his home.

Reports sometimes surface from far less promising areas. Our western image of Japan as a small, industrial nation leaves little room for remote uninhabited country able to support a population of man-beasts. Yet in the early 1970s there were several sightings of the Hibagon (as the beast became known) on Mount Hiba near Hiroshima. Farmer Albert Kubo saw this 5-foot (1.5-metre), big-eyed, smelly creature in 1974 when he was out in his rice fields spreading fertiliser. It was standing on a path, and Mr Kubo began to approach it before he realised what it was.

He said: 'I was petrified, but the stench was what really got me. He must have bathed in a septic tank and dried off with cow dung. I nearly passed out. Luckily enough, though, I managed to turn and run before it realised I was there. I ran 5 miles (8 kilometres) straight home without ever looking back over my shoulder.' The strong smell of many North American bigfeet is often described by witnesses in equally graphic terms.

The continent of Australia has many thousands of square miles of territory rarely visited by man and, as might be expected, it too has its man-beast. The Aborigines, who were apparently well aware of its existence,

Is this the yeti?

One of the most popular explanations of the yeti's origins is that it is descended from the giant ape *Gigantopithecus*, whose fossilised remains have been found in India and China. Examination of the fossils indicates that *Gigantopithecus* lived between 12 million and 500,000 years ago. Also during this period, the Himalayas were rising by as much as 8000 to 10,000 feet (2500 to 3000 metres). Because of this increase in height of the mountains, many species of animals, including the yeti's ancestor, may have become isolated.

Some experts argue that though the yeti's footprints have been discovered above the snowline (a bare terrain that is unable to support a large mammal) its present home is actually lower down in the forested valleys. Here, vegetation is dense, fog is common and there are few human inhabitants to disturb the yeti. But, as a result of seasonal changes, they must sometimes cross the high snow passes to reach nearby valleys – and leave those telltale footprints.

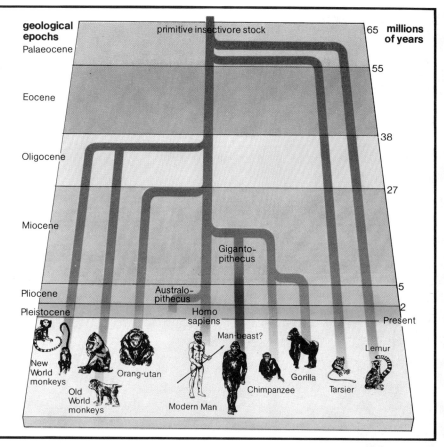

gave it many different names, but today it is usually called the yowie. Sightings have been regularly reported, especially in New South Wales and Queensland, since the late 18th century. On 3 October 1894 a boy named Johnnie McWilliams saw one while he was riding from his home at Snowball to the Jinden Post Office in New South Wales.

'A big man covered with long hair' suddenly appeared from behind a tree and seems to have been as surprised at the encounter as was the young Johnnie, for he ran off across open country, knocking his foot against a log and crying out in pain. He kept looking back as he ran, until he went out of sight over a low hill. The 'man' was over 6 feet (1.8 metres) tall and heavily built.

Joseph and William Webb, preparing to camp out one night at the turn of the century in the ranges of Brindabella, New South Wales, had a rather more dramatic encounter with a yowie. They heard a 'deep guttural bellowing' and noises, as if something was crashing through the scrub. According to John Gale, founder and editor of *The Queanbeyan Age*, writing in his book *An Alpine excursion* (1903):

Next moment a thing appeared walking erect, though they saw only its head and shoulders. It was hirsute, so much of the creature as was visible, and its head was set so deep between its shoulders that it was scarcely perceptible. It was approaching towards their camp. Now it was in full view, and was of the stature of a man. moving with long strides and a heavy tramp. It was challenged: 'Who are you? Speak, or we'll fire'. Not an intelligible word came in response; only the guttural bellowing. Aim was taken; the crack of a rifle rang out along the gully; but the

thing, if hit, was not disabled; for at the sound of the shot it turned and fled.

That the men saw no evidence of the bullet having struck its target does not necessarily mean that they missed. There is some evidence from North America that ordinary guns are useless against the hairy giants, either because they are not powerful enough, or for some stranger reason.

Australian yowie researcher Rex Gilroy has collected more than 3000 sighting reports and, as in North America, there was a big increase in reports during the 1970s. A particularly close sighting, where the witness was able to get a good look at a yowie of 7 feet (2.1 metres), was reported by a National Parks worker in the Springbrook area of Queensland in March 1978. Hearing a grunting sound, he thought a pig was loose and went into the forest to look for it.

Then something made me look up and there, about 12 feet [3.7 metres] in front of me, was this big black hairy man-thing. It looked more like a gorilla than anything. It had huge hands and one of them was wrapped round a sapling.

It had a flat, black shiny face, with two big yellow eyes and a hole for a mouth. It just stared at me and I stared back. I was so numb I couldn't even raise the axe I had in my hand. We seemed to stand there staring at each other for about 10 minutes before it suddenly gave off a foul smell that made me vomit – then it just made off sideways and disappeared.

Both its appearance and behaviour suggest that the yowie is a close cousin to the North American bigfoot.

Left: music teacher Richard Brown stands beside the fence near The Dalles, Oregon, where he saw a bigfoot in 1971. He followed the bigfoot's movements through the telescopic sights of his rifle

Below: Igor Bourtsev, a Russian 'snowman' hunter, holding a cast of a footprint found on 21 August 1979 in the Gissar Range of the Pamir-Alai Mountains, Tadzhikistan, in central Asia. The footprint, believed to have been made by an almas, measures 13.5 inches (34 centimetres) long and 6.5 inches (16 centimetres) wide at the toes. It is very nearly the same size as 'yeti' footprints found in the Himalayas

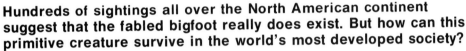

On the Bigfoot trail

Hundreds of sightings all over the North American continent suggest that the fabled bigfoot really does exist. But how can this primitive creature survive in the world's most developed society?

Above and over: Five stills from the only cine film ever taken of a bigfoot at Bluff Creek, California, in 1967. Rigorous analysis has not proved the film to be a fake – but sceptics still insist that the creature is a large actor dressed in animal skins. Casts (below) were taken of footprints found in the area after the sighting

RELIABLE REPORTS OF 'man-beasts' on the North American continent have been traced as far back as the 1830s. We have to rely on old newspaper accounts for our data before 1900, but determined researchers have found some intriguing descriptions of beasts very similar to those reported today. For example, in 1851 a local newspaper carried the story of two hunters in Greene County, Arkansas, who saw a herd of cattle being chased by 'an animal bearing the unmistakable likeness of humanity'.

> He was of gigantic stature, the body being covered with hair and the head with long locks that fairly enveloped the neck and shoulders. The 'wild man', after looking at them deliberately for a short time, turned and ran away with great speed, leaping 12 to 14 feet [3.6 to 4.3 metres] at a time. His footprints measured 13 inches [33 centimetres] each.

The newspaper reporter added that the beast was thought to be 'a survivor of the earthquake disaster which desolated that region in 1811'. In nearly all these early reports the man-beasts are referred to as 'wild men', the assumption being that they must be humans who have taken to the woods and in so doing somehow developed a thick coat of body hair. Modern evolutionary theory, however, suggests that this is unlikely.

The location of the 1851 sighting in Arkansas shows that bigfoot reports are not confined to the north-western states (northern California, Oregon and Washington) and British Columbia, where so many originate. Although these areas, with their vast tracts of forested mountains, have produced more reports than other regions, bigfeet or their footprints have been seen in nearly all the American states and Canadian provinces. Florida, far away from what is thought of as traditional bigfoot territory, has been particularly rich in sightings of the similar 'skunk ape' in recent years.

Many reports simply describe a man-beast, seen briefly in wooded country. But there are enough detailed reports for trends and characteristics to be apparent. Bigfeet seem to be timid, not wishing to get too close to humans. However, they also have a streak of curiosity and sometimes come close to people camping in the woods at night, look through their belongings, and occasionally also rock their camper or car. This behaviour, and early reports of the destruction of mineral prospectors' camps, may suggest a wish to frighten intruders away.

Bigfeet have also been seen wandering near rural houses and settlements, possibly attracted by the easy availability of food in such places. But despite their frightening appearance and the provocative behaviour of their discoverers, (whose reaction is frequently to shoot first and ask questions afterwards), bigfeet are not aggressive towards humans. Reports of injuries caused by them are rare.

As the 20th century progressed and more people became aware of bigfeet, so more reports came in concerning old as well as

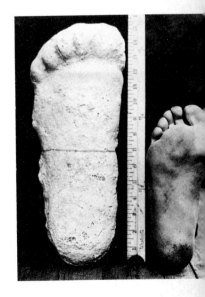

recent sightings, until in the 1960s and 1970s there was a vast number of reports on file. Although this was obviously due in part to the greater publicity, did it also mean that bigfeet were being seen more frequently? Since their habitat must gradually be shrinking as civilisation advances, it would be reasonable to expect their numbers to be declining. Perhaps it is this very pressure on living space that forces them to visit settlements for food and this might explain the increased number of reported sightings.

The *Bigfoot casebook* records nearly 1000 sightings in the past 150 years and this collection of cases is by no means complete. If, as has been estimated, only about one tenth of all sightings are ever reported, then there may have been as many as 10,000 sightings during that period. There are also many other reports of large, human-like footprints being found, usually in mud, snow or sand where they show up well, and it is usually assumed that a bigfoot left these tracks, even when the creature has not been

a very large man-like creature about 6½ or 7 feet [2 or 2.1 metres] tall came into view.

It was walking on its hind legs, was covered with dark hair, had a bearded face and large chest and so far as I could see was not wearing clothes of any kind. Startled, I let out a yell of alarm and the creature instantly turned and ran off into the woods, still on its hind legs. I told some of my co-workers about it and some laughed but others said they, too, had seen it. No one had an explanation for it and no name was given to it, but all agreed that it was a large ape-like something and that it also resembled a very large man.

Kidnapped by a man-beast

Another bigfoot report, dating from 1924, describes what, if it is true, is the most dramatic bigfoot encounter on record. Albert Ostman claims to have been kidnapped by a bigfoot and held captive for several days

Top: prospector Albert Ostman claimed to have been held captive by a bigfoot family in British Columbia in 1924

seen. Sometimes researchers investigating reports also find hair and faeces that are suspected to be a bigfoot's, but analyses done on these substances are usually irritatingly inconclusive.

A selection of a few of the many sightings reported this century will give a clear picture of bigfoot and his behaviour. In 1969 Albert M. Fletcher wrote about his encounter 50 years before, when he was a lumber-camp worker in Washington.

In the fall of 1917 when I was 17 years old I was working for a lumber camp on the Cowlitz River in the state of Washington. One moonlit evening I was walking down a logging road en route to a dance when I had the uneasy feeling that something was following close behind me. I kept looking over my shoulder but could not see anything. When I came to a bend in the road I ducked behind a tree and waited to see what it was. Almost immediately

before he managed to escape. The kidnap took place near Toba Inlet in British Columbia, when Ostman was prospecting and camping in the mountains. An 8-foot (2.4-metres) bigfoot picked him up in his sleeping bag one night and carried him across country for what seemed to the hot and cramped captive like three hours.

It was still dark when they arrived at their destination, but when it got light Ostman saw there were four bigfeet, male and female adults and male and female children. During his captivity Ostman was able to study the family's way of life, and to ponder his best method of escape. All attempts were blocked by the 'old man', as Ostman called him, whose mere size was an imposing deterrent. Ostman had his rifle with him but was loth to cause the creatures any injury, since they had not harmed him. He finally escaped by feeding the 'old man' a huge quantity of snuff and thereby incapacitating him. While the bigfoot rushed to find some water, Ostman grabbed his belongings and ran for his life.

Encounters in which the witness is able to get a long, close look at the creature are the most interesting; a perceptive and unflurried witness can add greatly to our knowledge of the creature. One of the best reports of this kind was made by William Roe, who saw a bigfoot on Mica Mountain in British Columbia in October 1955.

Roe was hidden in a bush, so the bigfoot, a female about 6 feet (1.8 metres) tall and 3 feet (1 metre) wide and weighing around 300 pounds (135 kilograms), came towards him unaware she was being watched. When the bigfoot was 20 feet (6 metres) away, she squatted by the bush Roe was hiding in.

He later wrote a careful description of the bigfoot's head, face and hair, of the shape of her body and the way she walked. He wondered briefly if he had unknowingly stepped into a film set and was looking at a made-up actor, but soon discarded that idea. His report continues:

> Finally, the wild thing must have got my scent, for it looked directly at me through an opening in the bush. A look of amazement crossed its face. It looked so comical at that moment I had to grin. Still in a crouched position, it backed up three or four short steps, then straightened up to its full height and started to walk rapidly back the way it had come. For a moment it watched me over its shoulder as it went, not exactly afraid, but as though it wanted no contact with anything strange.

Roe considered shooting what would be a unique specimen, and even raised his rifle. But he could not fire. 'Although I have called the creature "it", I felt now that it was a human being and I knew I would never forgive myself if I killed it.'

Human or animal? The witnesses are not sure, and neither are the researchers. 'If only we had a corpse to examine,' they cry. But those who feel that the priority is to kill a bigfoot and thus prove its existence once and for all are opposed by those who feel equally strongly that the creature should be left in peace. What gives man the right to commit murder simply to satisfy his curiosity?

A few reports suggest that someone with enough patience and nerve might even be able to make friends with a bigfoot. In the autumn of 1966 a couple living near Lower Bank in New Jersey found footprints 17 inches (43 centimetres) long outside their house, and saw a face peering in at a window over 7 feet (2.1 metres) high. They regularly left vegetable scraps for the bigfoot, which it ate, but one night they left nothing and their visitor showed its annoyance by throwing a dustbin against the wall. A shot fired into the air failed to deter it, so the man fired *at* the bigfoot, which ran away and did not return.

Thirty feet (9-metres) of wobbly 16-millimetre colour film shook the bigfoot-hunting world in 1967, and the questions posed by the film still have not been answered to everyone's satisfaction. Behind the camera was bigfoot-hunter Roger Patterson, who in October that year was riding through the remote forests of the Bluff Creek area of northern California with Bob Gimlin, on the lookout for signs of bigfeet. Their horses reared in fright when they suddenly came across a female bigfoot squatting beside a creek. Patterson leapt down, grabbed his camera and began to run after the retreating figure, filming as he went. Before the bigfoot was lost to sight among the trees, it turned to look back at the men. The famous strip of film has been analysed many times since 1967, but although no one has been able to prove it a hoax, scientists remain suspicious.

This may be due to natural caution, or the curious argument that 'Bigfoot can't exist, therefore it doesn't'. Meanwhile this creature continues to appear regularly in North America, to alarm but not hurt the witnesses who are invariably taken by surprise, and to puzzle all who ponder its presence.

Bigfoot hunter Rene Dahinden stands beside a statue of a bigfoot, sculpted by Jim McClarin, at Willow Creek, California. The figure, modelled on descriptions of bigfeet seen in the area, is 8 feet (2.4 metres) tall, 41 inches (1.04 metres) wide at the shoulder and has feet measuring 18 by 10 inches (46 by 25 centimetres)

Creatures from the void?

however, can never be taken at face value: size, for instance, is easily mistaken under conditions of stress.

Sometimes, however, an accurate calculation of height can be made. In April 1979, 16-year-old Tim Meissner saw a bigfoot twice in three days near his rural home in British Columbia. The first time, while fishing with friends at Dunn Lake near Barriere, he heard a high-pitched screech and saw on the lake's far shore a bigfoot with its arms raised. It ran away as the youths went to investigate. Hidden under branches and moss they found a deer with a broken neck.

Two days later, Tim Meissner returned with four friends, armed with a gun. They split up to search for the bigfoot. By an astonishing stroke of luck, Meissner saw it again. His first reaction was to shoot at the tall, black, hairy creature with glaring bright eyes and shoulders 4 feet (1.2 metres) wide. He seems to have hit it, since it went down on one knee, but then it got up and ran away at great speed. When Tim saw the bigfoot it was about 50 yards (45 metres) away, standing beside a tree. Later he returned to the tree and was able to estimate that the creature he had seen was about 9 feet (2.7 metres) tall.

The mystery deepens

Some bigfeet smell revolting. During a flurry of sightings around Little Eagle, South Dakota, in the autumn of 1977, one witness reported: 'It was like a stink of a dead person, long dead. It stayed in the air for maybe 10 to 15 minutes afterwards.' But by no means all bigfeet smell bad. It has been suggested, for example, that they can release the smell at will, perhaps to ensure that people keep their distance. Another strange feature is that some bigfeet have exceptionally large eyes which seem, uncannily, to glow. They are

Some man-beasts seem to be impervious to bullets, while others appear to be able to vanish at will. What are these strange and terrifying creatures?

THE BIGFOOT RIDDLE is not an easy one to solve. It is not simply a question of ascertaining whether or not the creature exists and, if it does, whether it is human or animal. Some reports, especially the more recent ones, have features that seem to deepen the mystery.

The average height of a bigfoot seems to be between 6 and 7 feet (1.8 and 2.1 metres), though much smaller ones are sometimes reported; these could be youngsters. However, much taller ones are occasionally reported. A 15-foot (4.5-metre) creature was seen by a USAF Staff Sergeant and two friends while they were camping at Belt Creek Canyon, Montana, in August 1977. They shot at it, but turned tail and drove away in their cars when it began to run towards them. Reports of fleeting sightings of this sort,

Above: an alleged yeti scalp belonging to the Buddhist Pangboche monastery in the Himalayas of Nepal. Despite all the efforts of hunters, no unquestionably genuine yeti remains have been made available for research

Right: 16-year-old Tim Meissner (left) estimates the height of a bigfoot he saw and shot at near his home in British Columbia, Canada, in April 1979. The creature, about 9 feet (2.7 metres) tall, was standing beside this tree when Tim saw it

usually red, but sometimes yellow or green.

The footprint evidence is also puzzling. Five-toed prints are most commonly found, resembling large human feet. But sometimes the prints appear to have only two toes, or three, four or sometimes six. Perhaps this anomaly is explicable in terms of over-eager investigators misinterpreting less than perfect footprints.

A significant number of reports, many of them made by experienced huntsmen, tell of a disturbing phenomenon: some bigfeet are apparently completely unharmed by bullets.

There seem to be three possible explanations: the guns used are just not powerful

number of other cases in which UFOS and bigfeet are reported as having been seen at the same time and in the same area. Coincidence? Or are they both part of the same phenomenon?

Another strange case involving a UFO took place on a farm near Greensburg, Pennsylvania, on the evening of 25 October 1973. When a large, bright red luminous ball was seen to come down in a field a 22-year-old farmer's son, pseudonym Stephen, went to investigate. He and two 10-year-old boys he took with him saw the shining object on or close to the ground. They also saw, near the ball, two tall, ape-like creatures with green

Left: these bones are claimed by the monks of Pangboche monastery to be the skeletal hand of a yeti. Although the hand seems small in comparison with the scalp (opposite), the remains can be taken as evidence to support the theory that the yeti is a form of ape – the hands of many ape species are relatively small

enough to tackle such a creature, or the witness in his excitement did not aim properly (although some shots were fired from very close range) – or bigfeet are not made of flesh and blood.

Bigfeet and UFOS?

If the theory that bigfeet are not composed of flesh and blood sounds incredible, there is some even more extraordinary evidence that tends to support it: the claim that some bigfeet are apparently able to disappear or dematerialise. A Pennsylvanian woman, confronted by one on her doorstep one night in February 1974, shot into its middle from a distance of 6 feet (1.8 metres). She was astounded to see it disappear in a flash of light! Other eye-witnesses have reported signs of insubstantiality in the bigfeet they have seen.

In the Pennsylvania case the witness's son-in-law, who came to help on hearing the shot, saw other bigfeet at the edge of nearby woods. He also saw a bright red flashing light hovering over the woods. There are a

glowing eyes and long, dark hair. The creatures began to approach them.

Stephen fired over their heads, but they kept walking towards the witnesses. So he fired three rounds straight into the largest creature, which raised its hand. The UFO disappeared and the bigfeet turned and slowly walked into the nearby woods.

Investigators were immediately called in, and although they saw neither UFO nor bigfeet, they found a glowing area where the UFO had been. Stephen subsequently went into a trance.

Rival killers

Bigfoot cases with such bizarre details are by no means widespread. They are generally reported in states far away from the traditional bigfoot territory in the north west of the continent. Some of the veteran bigfoot hunters and investigators are sceptical of apparent paranormal cases, possibly feeling that they do not wish to become involved in fringe eccentricities.

Those hunters who feel it is now their

life's work to convince the world of the existence of the bigfoot have a hard task for, despite the mass of data, few professional scientists or anthropologists will give their work a second glance. Certainly, if a bigfoot corpse was obtained, their case would, of course, be incontrovertible. Consequently there is rivalry – even open hostility – among those hunters who compete to be first to capture or kill one. So far they have been totally unsuccessful.

Even the rare cases of killed or captured man-beasts have not resulted in any corpses being made available for study. In 1917 Swiss geologist Francois de Loys shot a 5-foot (1.5-metre) animal on the borders of Columbia and Venezuela, which zoologist Dr Bernard Heuvelmans believes may have been an unknown type of spider monkey.

Of many reports from the USSR, the most recent tells of a man-beast captured and later killed in the mountains near Buinaksk in Daghestan. A Soviet army officer, Colonel Karapetyan, saw the creature while it was still alive and later remembered it vividly:

Above: this 'man-beast' was shot by Swiss geologist Francois de Loys on the borders of Columbia and Venezuela in 1917. It is now thought it may have been a kind of spider monkey

Above right: a drawing of the hairy man-beast captured and killed near Buinaksk in Daghestan, USSR, in 1941. The creature was seen alive by Colonel V. S. Karapetyan (right) but was never made available for scientific research

I can still see the creature as it stood before me, a male, naked and bare-footed. And it was doubtlessly a man, because its entire shape was human. The chest, back, and shoulders, however, were covered with shaggy hair of a dark brown colour . . . his height was above average – about 180 centimetres [6 feet]. He stood before me like a giant, his mighty chest thrust forward. . . His eyes told me nothing. They were dull and empty – the eyes of an animal. And he seemed to me like an animal and nothing more . . . this was no disguised person, but a wild man of some kind.

In December 1968 came a report from Minnesota, USA, of a bigfoot corpse frozen in a block of ice, Dr Heuvelmans and biologist Ivan T. Sanderson saw it and, despite the difficulties of examination, were convinced that the ice contained the fresh corpse of a hitherto unknown form of hominid. For various complex reasons, however, the corpse was never made available for proper examination.

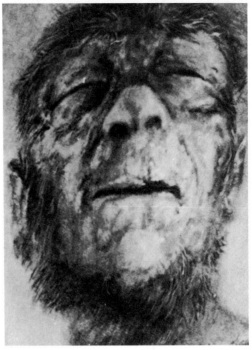

There are several reasons why, despite the number of sightings, hunters are not able simply to go into the forest and kill a bigfoot. Bigfeet are reputed to possess intimate knowledge of the terrain they inhabit such that they can travel through it far quicker than a man and remain completely concealed. Given these alleged characteristics the prospect for the hunter of capturing or killing one remains remote.

Most of the time, all the intrepid bigfoot hunter can do is interview witnesses, examine footprints, and collect newspaper reports. Such work, carried out by dedicated enthusiasts all over the North American continent, has resulted in an accumulation of data and many intriguing theories about the nature of bigfeet – and indeed all man-beasts. Nevertheless, without high-quality photographs, a corpse or a skeleton, or even part of one, all that scientists can do is speculate about possible explanations.

Man, beast . . . or hologram?

All we know for certain is that large, human-like footprints have been found in large numbers in remote areas – and not all of them are likely to be fakes – and that well over 1000 people in North America alone have reported seeing tall, hairy man-beasts. The various theories that have been put forward to explain these facts apply equally well to man-beasts seen all over the world.

On the negative side, it has been suggested that all man-beast reports are hoaxes. This seems unlikely. Another suggestion is that people may be misidentifying known animals under poor viewing conditions. This explanation could account for some of the sightings, but by no means all of them. Yet another view is that it is simply a case of hallucination. People who have seen too many horror films have had hallucinations –

and claim to have seen something that simply is not there. May not man-beast sightings be a similar case? Such a theory does not, however, account for the footprints, which appear to be real enough.

A more sympathetic view is that the man-beasts may be some form of giant ape or perhaps an early form of man-like ape, *Gigantopithecus.* This seems possible, even likely in some parts of the world. Alternatively, man-beasts may really be men, pre-historic survivals that have managed to stay concealed against all the odds.

Some people have argued that man-beasts are some kind of paranormal phenomenon. They may come into being when certain types of energy are available (electrical, nuclear or psychic, for example). Bigfeet have sometimes been reported near energy sources. An even more remote possibility is that man-beasts come from UFOs, for reasons as yet unknown. Against this, it has been pointed out that if UFOs and man-beasts are both paranormal phenomena, they are just as likely to have been formed in the same way – which may explain why they sometimes appear close together in time and space. Finally, man-beasts could be holograms, three-dimensional images projected from space by an unknown intelligence. If so, who or what is doing it – and why?

Investigators differ in their interpretations of the data, and perhaps no one explanation can account for all the reported sightings. It is most likely that the term 'man-beasts' covers a wide range of phenomena that, for unknown reasons, appear – or seem to appear – in similar guises. Whatever the truth may be, the man-beast phenomenon is an extraordinary and complex one that requires a great deal more research before any firm conclusions can be drawn.

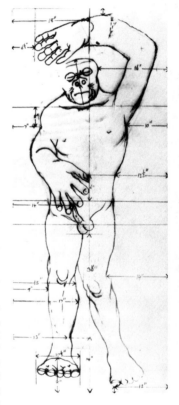

Left and below: sketches by biologist Ivan T. Sanderson of 'Bozo', a hairy man-beast seen frozen in a block of ice in Minnesota, USA, in December 1968. The owner apparently later replaced the corpse with a model – leaving only the evidence of Sanderson and zoologist Dr Bernard Heuvelmans, who had seen the original body, to prove it had ever existed

Weird Winged Creatures

Age-old myths tell of great birds that preyed upon human beings. Ornithologists scoff at the idea that such creatures exist in reality but, as JANET and COLIN BORD explain, some people think they have encountered such monsters – and some have felt the strength of their claws

IN TIPPAH COUNTY, MISSOURI, USA, a teacher had this tragic story to tell in 1878:

> A sad casualty occurred at my school a few days ago. The eagles have been very troublesome in the neighbourhood for some time past, carrying off pigs, lambs, etc. No one thought that they would attempt to prey upon children; but on Thursday, at recess, the little boys were out some distance from the house, playing marbles, when their sport was interrupted by a large eagle sweeping down and picking up little Jemmie Kenney, a boy of eight years, and flying away with him. The children cried out, and when I got out of the

Monsters on the wing

house the eagle was so high that I could just hear the child screaming. The alarm was given, and from screaming and shouting in the air, etc., the eagle was induced to drop his victim; but his talons had been buried in him so deeply, and the fall was so great, that he was killed. . . .

This is not the only case of a child being carried away by an eagle. In 1838, in the mountains of Switzerland, a five-year-old girl called Marie Delex was snatched away from her friends. She was not carried to the bird's nest – a search party found two eaglets there, with heaps of goat and sheep bones, but no sign of her. It was not until two months had passed that a shepherd found her mutilated corpse, lying on a rock.

Svanhild Hantvigsen, a Norwegian, claims that when she was three years old, in 1932, she was seized by an eagle and carried to its nest. She was rescued by some people who had noticed the eagle's strange behaviour and she was lucky enough to escape without a scratch, though her dress was torn.

Such attacks are frightening, but not mysterious. Sometimes, however, there are reports of a different kind – of monstrous winged creatures that do not seem to fit the description of any bird known to ornithology. Sometimes they seem most like giant flying creatures that became extinct millions of years ago. And sometimes, as we shall see in a later article, they seem half human.

The largest living bird known to science is

the wandering albatross, which is seen only in the southern oceans and has the largest known wingspan – 11 feet (3.3 metres). Very close to it in size is the Andean condor, with a 10-foot (3-metre) wingspan. The Californian condor's wings span 9 feet (2.7 metres) – but it is thought that today less than 40 of these birds survive.

Left: five-year-old Marie Delex was borne away by a large bird in 1838. Local people assumed it was an eagle – yet scientists believe eagles are capable of lifting nothing heavier than a fawn or goat kid

Below left: Svanhild Hantvigsen displays the torn dress that she was wearing in 1932 when an eagle swooped on her and carried her to its nest. The arrival of rescuers saved her from the fate suffered by Marie Delex nearly 100 years before

Below: the dog belonging to Peter Swadley, a bear hunter, attempted to fight off an eagle that attacked his master in West Virginia, USA, in 1895. The dog was carried off, while Swadley was left badly injured

Even a condor would look tiny, however, alongside the teratorn, a bird that became extinct about 10,000 years ago. It is thought to have been the largest bird that has ever lived on Earth, having a length of 11 feet (3.3 metres), a wingspan of 25 feet (7.5 metres), and a weight of 160 to 170 pounds (72 to 76 kilograms). Fossils have been found in Argentina, Mexico and the southern United States; some of them are thought to be 5 to 8 million years old.

Huge birds figure in mythology. The Illini Indians painted a picture of a monstrous bird, the *piasa* or 'bird that devours men', on a rock face overlooking a river near Alton in Illinois. They used to fire bows or guns at the picture as they passed by in their canoes. The painting was seen by missionary explorers in the 17th century, before the rock face was destroyed. In the 1970s a new *piasa* design, following the traditional one, was repainted at Norman's Landing.

According to the Illini, the *piasa* is scaly, with a long tail, horns and red eyes. It can be seen once a year, at dawn on the first day of autumn, as it emerges from the river to pick a cave for the winter. But despite vigils by

students on bluffs above the Mississippi River, no one has seen the dreaded *piasa* in recent years.

However, some Indians claim to see another huge creature, the thunderbird, today. According to James Red Sky, an Ojibwa Indian from the Thunder Bay region of Ontario, Canada: 'We saw a thunderbird a few summers ago. A huge bird it was; a lot bigger than planes you see go by today. It didn't flap its wings. Not even once. It was white on the underside, black on top.'

Modern reports of giant birds in the USA began in the late 19th century. At Dent's Run, Pennsylvania, in 1882, one Fred Murray saw a flock of birds that, he said, looked like giant buzzards, with wingspans of more than 16 feet (5 metres).

In February 1895 the disappearance of 10-year-old Landy Junkins in Webster County, West Virginia, was ascribed to a giant bird. Landy was sent by her mother to a neighbour's house, but never arrived. A search party found her tracks in the snow: they left the path and went a few feet into a field. There, a number of tracks were crowded together, as if she had turned round and

Above: a carved human face peers out from a mask of a thunderbird, made by Haida Indians of the American north-west coast. The Haida believe that a human spirit can take on a thunderbird's form: this is symbolised by the closing of the mask's jaws

Above right: the *piasa*, a gigantic legendary bird, was shown in these rock paintings, which formerly existed near Alton, Illinois, USA. The bird terrorised the Illini Indians until the great chief Ouatogo offered himself as bait, while 20 warriors hid nearby. The bird was killed by their arrows, while Ouatogo was unharmed. The paintings commemorated the event

round, perhaps trying to avoid something. No trace of Landy was ever found.

An incident a few days later suggested what had happened to her. A bear hunter, Peter Swadley, was attacked by a massive bird, which swooped down and dug its talons in his back. Swadley was saved from death by his dog, which made for the bird. The bird turned its attention to the dog, ripping open its stomach with one stroke of its claws before flying off with the unfortunate animal. A deputy sheriff and his son also saw the giant 'eagle', which captured a fawn while they were in the forest hunting deer. They said the bird had a wingspan of 15 to 18 feet (4.5 to 5.5 metres), and a body as large as a man's.

The same monster was also thought to be responsible for the strange disappearance of a sheep from a locked shed. One morning,

Hanse Hardrick found one sheep missing, with a hole in the shed roof showing how it had been extracted.

Some eagle – able to carry away a fawn, a hunting dog, a sheep and a 10-year-old girl, and make a bold attempt to carry off a fully grown man!

Around 1940, in Pennsylvania, an author and local historian, Robert Lyman, was in the Black Forest near Coudersport, when he saw a brownish bird standing in the middle of a road. It stood 3 to 4 feet (about 1 metre) tall and had a short neck and short legs. When it flew off, Mr Lyman saw that its narrow wings, when extended, reached across the road – a span of 20 to 25 feet (6 to 7.5 metres). He wondered how such a big bird could fly through dense trees so easily.

In 1947 farmers around Ramore in Ontario, Canada, were experiencing problems with a giant black bird that was attacking their livestock. It had a hooked beak, huge talons, and yellow eyes 'the size of silver dollars'. A few months later an outbreak of sightings of big birds occurred in Illinois. 'There's a bird outside as big as a B-29!' gasped 12-year-old James Trares as he rushed indoors to his mother. That was in January 1948, and James was the first to report seeing the monster. He lived in Glendale, Illinois, and the bird he saw, wings flapping as it flew over, was grey-green in colour.

A former army colonel, Walter Siegmund, saw something similar on 4 April. He estimated that it was 4000 feet (1200 metres) up, and from his military experience he was quite convinced that 'it could only be a bird of some tremendous size.'

More sightings followed, including some over St Louis, Missouri. Several witnesses at first believed they were seeing an aeroplane because of its size – until it began to flap its wings and to perform bird-like manoeuvres. Policemen and flying instructors were among

Above: the magnificent bald eagle of North America. Fish are its favourite prey, but it has been blamed for attacks on small animals and children

Right: the Californian condor, hideous when at rest, is majestic in flight, gliding effortlessly for long distances. One of the world's rarest birds, it can attain 9 feet (2.7 metres) in wingspan. It attacks living animals, though like other vultures it feeds mainly on carrion

Right: the imagined abduction of an Alpine peasant woman's child by an eagle. The artist entitled this picture, published in 1900, *The robber of the skies*

Left: one of the rarer hazards of the American West: in 1870 a golden eagle attacked a woman rider near the track of the Pacific Railroad and was beaten off only after severely wounding her

the witnesses. The last sighting seems to have been on 30 April 1948. Charles Dunn could hardly believe his eyes when he saw a bird 'about the size of a Piper Cub plane', flying at about 3000 feet (900 metres) and flapping its wings.

Little more was seen of monster birds for nearly two decades, although in 1957 a huge bird with a wingspan of 25 to 30 feet (7.5 to 9 metres) was seen flying at about 500 feet (150 metres) over Renovo, Pennsylvania. In 1966 there were reports from Utah, West Virginia, Ohio and Kentucky, only some of which could be explained as sightings of rare known species.

Then, in 1975, during an outbreak of mysterious deaths of animals in Puerto Rico, large birds resembling whitish condors or vultures were seen. On 26 March Juan Muñiz Feliciano, a workman, was attacked by 'a terrible greyish creature with lots of feathers, a long thick neck, bigger than a goose'.

At the end of July 1977, a big bird was seen trying to steal a young pig weighing 50 to 60 pounds (22 to 27 kilograms) near Delava, Illinois. The bird had a companion. Both resembled Californian condors and had 8-foot (2.5-metre) wingspans. But an ecologist at the University of Illinois commented that condors are rare, almost to the point of extinction, could not lift such a weight and

Right: 10-year-old Marlon Lowe, victim of an attack by a large bird in 1977, with his mother, whose cry startled the bird into dropping the boy. The incident occurred in Illinois, home of the legends of the *piasa*

Below: Juan Muñiz Feliciano, a Puerto Rican workman, fights off an attack by a 'terrible greyish creature' one night in 1975. At about this time, farm animals were being killed and mutilated in a manner reminiscent of cattle mutilation cases on the American mainland

anyway feed on dead animals, not live ones.

What was it, then, that tried to abduct 10-year-old Marlon Lowe from the garden of his home at Lawndale, Illinois, on 25 July? That bird, too, was accompanied by another, and the near-tragedy took place only a few days before the abortive pig-stealing, and 10 miles (16 kilometres) away. Marlon was playing hide-and-seek when at 8.10 p.m. one of the birds snatched him off the ground. Fortunately his mother was at hand. She saw Marlon's feet dangling in the air and screamed, and the bird dropped the boy before he had been lifted very high. Mrs Lowe was only 10 feet (3 metres) away from the birds, and afterwards recalled: 'I'll always remember how that huge thing was bending its white ringed neck, and seemed to be trying to peck at Marlon, as it was flying away.' She described the birds as 'very black' except for the white rings around their necks, which were 18 inches (45 centimetres) long. They had hooked bills 6 inches (15 centimetres) long, and a wingspan of at least 8 feet (2.5 metres). She estimated they would have stood 4½ feet (1.3 metres) tall had they landed. Six people watched the birds fly off towards Kickapoo Creek where there is heavy underbrush and thick tree cover.

But for the bird's being startled by Mrs Lowe's screams, Marlon would probably have suffered the same fate as Marie Delex, Jemmie Kenney and Landy Junkins. As it was, the Lowes suffered in other ways. They were harassed by people leaving dead birds on the front porch, and by unpleasant notes and telephone calls. At school Marlon, nicknamed 'Bird Boy', had literally to fight off the taunts of his fellows. His red hair turned grey, and for a year the frightened boy refused to go out after night had fallen.

The flying creature 'as big as a man' that attacked Armando Grimaldo in Texas, USA, in 1976, Featherless, beakless and with large red eyes, it swooped on him from above. When he had made his escape he found that his clothes had been torn, though he was uninjured. This incident was the most terrifying of a wave of sightings in Texas early that year

Flight across time?

Terrified witnesses have told of winged creatures that strikingly resembled pterodactyls, supposedly extinct for over 60 million years

AN AMAZING REPORT in a learned journal, *The Zoologist* for July 1868, describes what the writer had seen earlier the same year at Copiapó, in Chile:

> Yesterday, at about five o'clock in the afternoon, when the daily labours in this mine were over, and all the workmen were together awaiting their supper, we saw coming through the air . . . a gigantic bird, which at first we took for one of the clouds then partially darkening the atmosphere, supposing it to have been separated from the rest by the wind. Its course was from north-west to south-east; its flight rapid and in a straight line. As it was passing a short distance above our heads we could mark the strange formation of its body. Its immense wings were clothed with a grayish plumage, its monstrous head was like that of a locust, its eyes were wide open and shone like burning coals; it seemed to be covered with something resembling the thick and stout bristles of a boar, while on its body, elongated like that of a serpent, we could only see brilliant scales, which clashed together with a metallic sound as the strange animal turned its body in its flight.

In some ways this report resembles those of the aeroplane-sized birds seen over Illinois, USA, in the spring of 1948. But the Chilean workmen were closer to their 'bird' when they saw it and were able afterwards to describe its rather strange appearance. Was it really a bird, or could it have been a flying reptile?

Perhaps this was nothing more than a journalistic hoax, as the 'thunderbird' reportedly killed near Tombstone, Arizona, in 1890 is strongly suspected to be. The details came from an article in the Tombstone *Epitaph* for 26 April 1890. What supposedly happened is briefly told. Two ranchers, riding in the desert, chased a winged monster 'resembling a huge alligator with an extremely elongated tail and an immense pair of wings', which was apparently exhausted. They got near enough to kill it with gunfire, and then set about measuring it. It was about 92 feet (28 metres) long, with a wingspan of some 160 feet (49 metres). The wings and body were without hair or feathers, and the jaw was full of sharp teeth. The whole Tombstone saga is complicated by the fact that a thunderbird was supposed to have been killed in the same area in 1886. There are researchers who claim to have seen a photograph of it, but so far no one has been able to locate this elusive picture. No one seems to know what happened to the corpse of the thunderbird, if it ever existed. Several good stories published in American newspapers during the second half of the 19th century have since been found to be tall tales, and this may be another.

If the Copiapó and Tombstone 'birds' really existed, they sound more like prehistoric monsters than the birds we are familiar with today. Some years earlier, in the 1850s, a French newspaper reported that a living pterodactyl had been discovered by men blasting rock at Culmont in Haute-Marne, France. The huge, hideous creature emerged from a cavity in the rock, and it looked like a bat the size of a large goose. It was black in colour, and its wingspan was about 10 feet (3 metres). Unfortunately, present-day researchers have been unable to find any supporting evidence for this story.

Nineteenth-century pterodactyl reports are admittedly unreliable, but the 20th century has produced some puzzling American accounts that are less easily dismissed. The earliest 20th-century reports concern an enigmatic monster, the so-called 'Jersey devil'.

In January 1909 this weird 'thing' terrorised the state of New Jersey. Its lair was

Right: pterodactyls appeared about 150 million years ago, and so were contemporary with the dinosaurs. They lived in flocks in coastal areas. Their jaws were equipped with powerful teeth, though they lived only on fish and insects. For 85 million years they flourished, and then supposedly died out – yet they fit many modern descriptions of strange flying creatures

Below: an enormous 'bird' seen by workmen at Copiapó, Chile, in 1868. The animal was a curious hybrid, since its wings were covered with feathers, while its body was covered with scales, which the watchers on the ground could hear clashing with a metallic sound

supposed to be somewhere in the Pine Barrens, an isolated area in the south-east of the state. All manner of strange phenomena were attributed to the Jersey devil over the years, but the events we are describing concern sightings of a strange winged monster and the footprints it left behind.

Antics of the Jersey devil

The events began in January 1909, when the Jersey devil was reported in at least 30 towns. One of the earliest sightings was on Sunday 17 January at Bristol, Pennsylvania, close to the New Jersey border. At 2 a.m., John McOwen heard strange noises and got out of bed. He said: 'I looked from the window and was astonished to see a large creature standing on the banks of the canal. It looked something like an eagle . . . and it hopped along the tow-path.' Patrolman James Sackville also saw it in Bristol that night. He reported that it was winged and hopped like a bird, but had strange features and a horrible scream. Sackville ran towards it, and fired his revolver at it as it flew off. A third Bristol sighting early that same morning was made by the postmaster, E. W. Minster, who saw the Jersey devil flying over the Delaware River. The large crane-like bird seemed to be glowing, and it got close enough for Minster to see many details:

Its head resembled that of a ram, with curled horns, and its long thick neck was thrust forward in flight. It had long thin wings and short legs, the front legs shorter than the hind. Again, it uttered its mournful and awful call – a combination of a squawk and a whistle.

Bristol residents next morning found the

Jersey devil's footprints in the snow: they resembled hoofprints.

During the following week, the Jersey devil seemed to be everywhere, and its presence caused panic in the state. Farmers set steel traps and hunters followed the hoofprints. The scene must have looked like the present-day 'flaps' that occur when sightings of a bigfoot are publicised in any area, leading to an influx of photographers and hunters, with resulting chaos. But the Jersey devil seemed indifferent to the furore. On Tuesday 19 January, in the early hours, Mr and Mrs Nelson Evans of Gloucester City, New Jersey, were treated to a close-up view of the monster dancing on their shed roof for 10 minutes. Said Mr Evans later:

It was about three feet and a half [1 metre] high, with a head like a collie dog and a face like a horse. It had a long neck, wings about two feet [60 centimetres] long, and its back legs were like those of a crane, and it had horse's hooves. It walked on its back legs and held up two short front legs with paws on them. It didn't use the front legs at all while we were watching. My wife and I were scared, I tell you, but I managed to open the window and say 'Shoo!' and it turned around, barked at me, and flew away.

Other witnesses mentioned that it had skin like an alligator's and some thought it was nearer 6 feet (1.8 metres) high.

The last sightings seem to have been on Friday 22 January, after which the Jersey devil disappeared as suddenly as it had arrived. Many facetious explanations were proposed: that it was a 'jabberwock', the 'missing link', or an 'asertoraksidimundiakins'. Mass hysteria was also put forward as an explanation.

Common-sense explanations

Experts who took the witnesses more seriously speculated that they had seen birds: an 'invasion' of scrow-foot ducks was suggested. So, too, was a sand hill crane: with a wingspan of 80 inches (2 metres), a length of 48 inches (1.2 metres), and a 'chilling whoop for a voice', this bird was once common in New Jersey, but is now supposedly confined to remote areas of the deep South. It was also suggested that the witnesses had seen a 'prehistoric remnant'. The hoofprints were ascribed to hoaxing or to the melting and refreezing of human footprints (a possible explanation of some prints, though not those seen in inaccessible places). Which explanation you choose for the incredible events that took place between 17 and 22 January 1909 is likely to depend on your faith in the reliability of eyewitness testimony.

As we come nearer to the present day, witnesses of giant birds begin to 'identify' them as pterodactyls, a trend that may reflect increased public knowledge about prehistoric creatures. In May 1961 a businessman

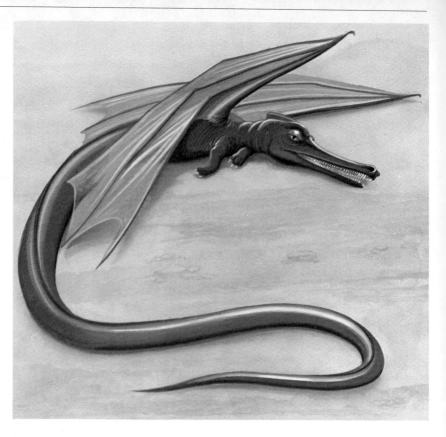

In 1890 two ranchers in Arizona, USA, allegedly killed a winged monster with their Winchester rifles. The creature was colossal – over 92 feet (28 metres) long. It attacked the two men with its formidable teeth before it died. A local newspaper, the Tombstone *Epitaph*, gave a long and detailed account, but no follow-up stories appeared and no confirming evidence survives

flying a small plane over the Hudson River Valley was buzzed by a huge bird, which scarcely seemed to move its wings. He reported that it was 'a damned big bird, bigger than an eagle . . . it looked more like a pterodactyl out of the prehistoric ages.'

In the early 1960s, a couple driving at night through Trinity Forest in California saw what they thought at first was a plane in trouble, but then decided it must be a bird. It was flying at tree-top height, and seemed to have a wingspan of about 14 feet (4 metres). The couple could not discern any detail, since the 'bird' was only a silhouette to them as it flew across the road ahead, and then up a gulch towards a mine. They decided that it had looked something like a pterodactyl. Later they learned that friends of theirs had made a similar sighting in the same area and that they too had identified the 'bird' as a pterodactyl.

Early in 1976 strange reports began to emerge from Texas of sightings of creatures resembling weird birds or prehistoric flying reptiles. As usual, there were numerous 'logical' explanations for what the witnesses claimed to have seen, but the explanations rarely fitted the facts. The first sighting was made on 1 January at Harlingen by Jackie Davis (14 years old) and Tracey Lawson (11 years old). They saw a 'bird' 5 feet (1.5 metres) tall, with 'shoulders' 3 feet (90 centimetres) wide. It was black in colour with big, dark-red eyes, a bald head and a face like a gorilla's, with a sharp beak 6 inches (15 centimetres) long. Next day their parents investigated and found five tracks, which had three toes and were 8 inches (20 centimetres) across and 1½ inches (4 centimetres) deep. A man weighing 170 pounds (76.5 kilograms) was unable to make an equally deep impression in the hard ground.

A week later, on 7 January, Alvérico Guajardo saw what might have been the same bird. He had gone outside to investigate after something had hit his trailer home at Brownsville. He switched on the headlights of his station wagon and they illuminated 'something from another planet'. The creature, 4 feet (1.2 metres) long, stared at the terrified man with blazing red eyes. Guajardo saw black feathers, a beak 2 to 4 feet (60 to 80 centimetres) long, and bat-like wings. It made a horrible noise as it backed away from the lights. Guajardo finally escaped into a neighbour's house. The newspaper reporter who interviewed Guajardo the next day said he was still terrified.

Among other sightings in the state, Armando Grimaldo's experience was the most frightening. He was actually attacked by the 'bird' during the evening of 14 January as he sat in his mother-in-law's backyard at Raymondville. As he looked round to investigate a noise like the flapping of bat-like wings and a 'funny kind of whistling', he was grabbed from above by 'something with big claws'. He fled and, looking back, saw a 'bird' as big as a man, with a wingspan of between 10 and 12 feet (3 and 3.5 metres). It had a face like a bat or a monkey, big red eyes, *no* beak, and dark leathery skin, without feathers.

A big black bird with a bat-like face seen near Brownsville by Libby and Deany Ford was identified by them as a pteranodon (a

Left: the Jersey devil as portrayed by a newspaper artist in 1909. There is a whimsical air to the drawing and its headline, 'the New Jersey "what-is-it"', but the sketch closely follows the verbal account of Mr and Mrs Evans, two of the many people who saw the monster. They described it as 'dancing' on their shed

Below: the sand hill crane, of imposing size and possessing a loud, penetrating cry, was invoked to explain some of the sightings of the Jersey devil that occurred in large numbers in 1909

Below: the pteranodon, related to the pterodactyl, was the largest flying creature known to science. Witnesses of mystery 'birds' often identify what they saw as a pteranodon

type of pterodactyl). On 24 February three elementary-schoolteachers driving near San Antonio also saw what they believed to be a pteranodon. As it swooped low over their cars, its shadow covered the road. They estimated its wingspan as between 15 and 20 feet (4.5 and 6 metres). Mrs Patricia Bryant said it was as big as a Piper Cub plane and that she 'could see the skeleton of this bird through the skin or feathers or whatever, and it stood out black against the background of grey feathers'. David Rendon commented that the 'bird' glided rather than flew and that it had huge bony wings like a bat's.

The most prosaic explanation for all these reports is that the witnesses were simply overawed by sightings of rare native birds. But does the pteranodon identification deserve to be taken seriously? These flying reptiles are supposed to have been extinct for 64 million years. Pterosaurs once lived in Texas and their fossils have been found there. Is it possible that any could have survived? Or – most fantastic suggestion of all – was the structure of time disrupted? Could animals living in past eras suddenly have materialised into the present day?

Half man, half bird

Time and again, terrifying winged humanoids have been glimpsed, on the ground or in flight, by reliable witnesses

TALES OF HUGE BIRDS carrying off children are terrifyingly credible. The sightings of creatures resembling latter-day pterodactyls strain the powers of belief much more. But the cases we now describe would be dismissed by most people as utterly unbelievable: fantastic stories of man-like beings with wings. Yet they are told by ordinary, sincere people.

In the United States, on 18 September 1877, a winged human being was seen over Brooklyn, New York. Few details are available, but a similar figure was seen in September 1880, not far away at Coney Island. It was described in the *New York Times*, none too seriously, as 'a man with bat's wings and improved frog's legs'.

Sightings of winged humanoids seem to be more widely distributed around the globe than those of giant birds and supposed

In West Virginia, USA, a winged figure as big as a small aircraft blocked the road in front of a car in the early 1960s. It took off 'straight up' – a seemingly impossible feat for a creature of such a size. This may have been the first sighting of the Mothman, which was to be seen frequently in the state five years later

pterodactyls. The next report comes from Vladivostok, in the far eastern USSR. On 11 July 1908 a man walking in the Sikhote Alin mountains saw what looked like a man's footprint on the path ahead. His dog began to act strangely, and something could be heard trampling among the bushes. After several minutes of standing and listening, the walker, V.K. Arsenyev, threw a stone towards the unseen creature, whereupon he heard the sound of wings beating and saw something 'large and dark' fly away over the river. Unfortunately he could make out no details because of fog. Later, when Mr Arsenyev told local people what had happened, they identified the creature as 'a man who could fly in the air', well-known to hunters in the area.

A Brazilian couple, the Reals, had a closer view of 'their' winged people. Early in the 1950s they were walking one night in a wood near the sea at Pelotas in the state of Rio

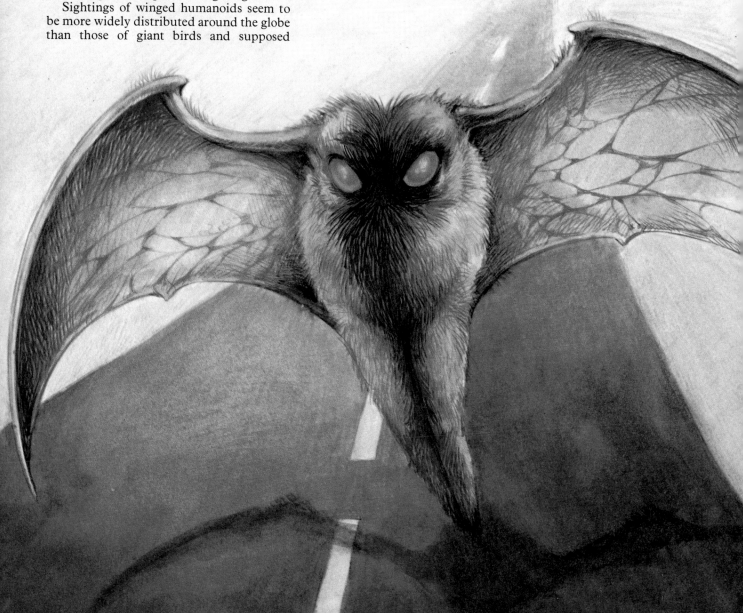

Grande do Sul when they noticed two gigantic 'birds' in the trees. As they got nearer, the 'birds' came down to the ground, and the amazed pair saw that the creatures were about 6 feet (1.8 metres) tall and looked human. They were crouching on the ground as if observing the Reals. Luiz do Rosário Real wished to approach them more closely, but his wife insisted that they return home.

A strange report describing an even closer sighting comes from Houston, Texas, USA. The night of 18 June 1953 was hot; three neighbours were sitting out on the front porch of an apartment house in the small hours. Mrs Hilda Walker said later:

> We were just talking idly, when I looked up and about twenty-five feet [7.5 metres] away I saw a huge shadow across the lawn. I thought at first it was the magnified reflection of a big moth caught in a nearby street light. Then the shadow seemed to bounce upward into a pecan tree. . . . I could see him plain and could see he had big wings folded at his shoulders. There was a dim gray light all around him.

The shadow was also seen by Howard Phillips and Judy Meyers, and they described it as 'the figure of a man with wings like a bat. He was dressed in gray or black tight-fitting clothes. He stood there for about 30 seconds, swaying on the branch of the old pecan tree. Suddenly the light began to fade out slowly.' They agreed also that he was about 6½ feet (2 metres) tall and wore a black cape, tight trousers and quarter-length boots.

As the light faded, the figure seemed to melt away, and the three heard a loud swooshing noise over the houses and saw a white flash. All were adamant that they had seen this inexplicable apparition.

First sighting of Mothman?

Not quite so clearly visible, but still definitely man-shaped, was the figure standing in the middle of the road ahead of a woman driving her father along Route 2 in the Chief Cornstalk Hunting Grounds of West Virginia, USA, in 1960 or 1961. As they got closer, the driver slowed the car. The two apprehensive witnesses saw that the grey figure was much larger than a man. The driver later reported what happened next:

> A pair of wings unfolded from its back and they practically filled the whole road. It almost looked like a small airplane. Then it took off straight up . . . disappearing out of sight in seconds. We were both terrified. I stepped on the gas and raced out of there. We talked it over and decided not to tell anybody about it. Who would believe us anyway?

Who indeed? Although she did not know it, she was possibly the first witness of a winged being later nicknamed 'Mothman', which in late 1966 plagued an area of West Virginia called Point Pleasant. First to see it at that

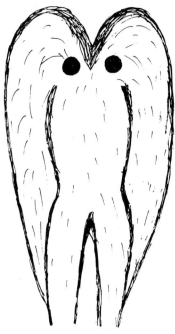

Above: Mothman was said to lack any visible arms or head, to have luminous red eyes and huge wings, and to be bigger than a man

Below: a 'birdwoman' flew so close to three marines in Vietnam that they could hear her wings flapping

time were two young local couples, Mr and Mrs Roger Scarberry and Mr and Mrs Steve Mallette. Late on the night of 15 November they were driving through the 'TNT area' where there was an abandoned wartime explosives factory. As they passed an old generator plant, they saw in the darkness two bright red circles, which looked like eyes. As the circles moved, the couples saw a man-shaped figure, between 6 and 7 feet (1.8 and 2 metres) tall, greyish in colour and with big folded wings; it was shuffling along on two legs.

Roger, who was driving, quickly turned the car in the direction of safety and they drove off at speed. But they saw the creature, or another similar one, standing near the road and as they went past it spread its bat-like wings and began to follow them. Even though they accelerated to 100 miles per hour (160 km/h), the 'bird' kept pace with them – without flapping its wings. Mrs Mallette could hear it squeaking 'like a big mouse'. When they reported their experience at the sheriff's office, the deputy could see they were scared and he drove straight to the TNT area, but saw nothing strange.

The story was publicised and Point Pleasant immediately became a focus of attention for monster-hunters. Armed men searched the TNT area but did not find their prey. However, Mothman was still around: on the evening of 16 November he appeared to Mrs

Mawnan "Bird-Man" based on sketch by June Melling, witnessed and drawn 17/4/76.

Birdman monster. Seen on 3rd July, quite late at night but not quite dark. Red eyes. Black mouth. It was very big with great big wings and black claws. Feathers grey.
B. Perry 4th July 1976.

I saw this monster bird last night. It stood like a man then it flew up through the trees. It is as big as a man. Its eyes are red and shine brightly.
Sally Chapman 4/7/76.

Marcella Bennett who was visiting friends living in the TNT area. She was sitting in the parked car when she noticed a figure in the darkness. 'It seemed as if it had been lying down. It rose up slowly from the ground. A big gray thing. Bigger than a man, with terrible glowing red eyes.' Like the two couples on the previous night, Mrs Bennett seemed hypnotised by Mothman's red eyes. As she stood there staring at it, she and her baby daughter were grabbed by a friend and dragged into the house.

During the following days, numerous people saw Mothman – or believed they did. How many of the sightings were caused by the 'contagion' of news stories, we shall never know. The writer John Keel went to the Point Pleasant area to investigate at first hand. From the many reports he collected, he established that Mothman was between 5 and 7 feet (1·5 and 2 metres) tall, grey or

Drawings made by three young witnesses of the Cornish Owlman, with their own descriptions. The resemblance between the sighting of 3 July and the one made three months earlier is striking

brown in colour and man-shaped but without any arms or head. It had luminous bright red eyes where a man's shoulders would be. The wings were folded back when not in use, and the wingspread was about 10 feet (3 metres). The majority of sightings were made in November and December 1966; then Mothman was gone.

Three marines on guard duty near Da Nang in South Vietnam, in July or August 1969, got a closer view of the extraordinary entity that flew over them in the early hours of the morning. The story was later told by one of them, Earl Morrison:

All of a sudden – I don't know why – we all three looked out there in the sky and we saw this figure coming toward us. It had a kind of glow and we couldn't make out what it was at first. It started coming toward us, real slowly. All of a sudden we saw what looked like wings, like a bat's, only it was gigantic compared to what a regular bat would be. After it got close enough so we could see what it was, it looked like a woman. A naked woman. She was black. Her skin was black, her body was black, the wings were black, everything was black. But it glowed. It glowed in the night – kind of a greenish cast to it.

The three saw her long enough to notice that she had arms, hands and fingers, but that these were joined to her wings. They just stood and watched as she flew overhead, a couple of yards above them.

The Cornish Owlman

Sometimes, as in this report, the sightings have been single ones, the mysterious winged entity afterwards disappearing as if it never existed. And sometimes, as in West Virginia in 1966, there have been repeated sightings in a small area, but still without any real clues emerging as to the nature of the apparition. Perhaps the strangest series of reports of 'winged things' are those concerning the 'Owlman', seen in Cornwall, England, in 1976 and again in 1978. The Owlman's territory was very small – the area around Mawnan Church on the south coast.

He was first seen on 17 April 1976, hovering over the church tower, by June Melling (12 years old) and her sister Vicky (9 years old). June described and drew a feathered birdman. Nearly three months passed before the second sighting, made on 3 July. Again the witnesses were young girls: 14-year-old Sally Chapman and Barbara Perry. They were camping in the woods and at about 10 p.m. they realised that they were not alone. They heard a strange hissing noise, and then saw a figure standing not far away among the pine trees. Sally described what they saw:

It was like a big owl with pointed ears, as big as a man. The eyes were red and glowing. At first, I thought it was someone dressed up, playing a joke, trying to scare us. I laughed at it, we both did, then it went up in the air and we both screamed. When it went up, you could see its feet were like pincers.

Barbara added: 'It's true. It was horrible, a nasty owl-face with big ears and big red eyes. It was covered in grey feathers. The claws on its feet were black. It just flew straight up and disappeared in the treetops.'

The next day, 4 July, yet another young girl, Jane Greenwood, along with her sister, saw the Owlman. Jane described what they saw in a letter to the local paper:

It was Sunday morning and the place was in the trees near Mawnan Church, above the rocky beach. It was in the trees standing like a full-grown man, but the legs bent backwards like a bird's. It saw us and quickly jumped up and rose straight up through the trees.

My sister and I saw it very clearly

The Owlman sightings took place in an area of ancient significance: near Mawnan Church, which was built inside a prehistoric earthwork (below). Sally Chapman and Barbara Perry encountered the creature in nearby woods (bottom)

before it rose up. It has red slanting eyes and a very large mouth. The feathers are silvery grey and so are his body and legs. The feet are like big, black crab's claws.

We were frightened at the time. It was so strange, like something in a horror film. After the thing went up there was crackling sounds in the tree tops for ages.

Later that day we spoke to some people at the camp-site, who said they had seen the Morgawr Monster on Saturday, when they were swimming with face masks and snorkels in the river, below where we saw the bird man. They saw it underwater, and said it was enormous and shaped like a lizard.

Our mother thinks we made it all up just because we read about these things, but that is not true. We really saw the bird man, though it could have been somebody playing a trick in very good costume and make-up.

But how could it rise up like that? If we imagined it, then we both imagined the same thing at the same time.

The 'Morgawr Monster' she refers to is a sea monster that was also putting in regular appearances in Falmouth Bay during 1976. UFOs were seen in the area too – Falmouth Bay was the best place to be in 1976 if you longed for a strange experience.

After July 1976 the Owlman apparently did not reappear until June 1978. Early that month a 16-year-old girl saw 'a monster, like a devil, flying up through the trees near old Mawnan Church.' On 2 August three young French girls also saw him near the church. They were frightened by something 'very big, like a great big furry bird'. It was white with a 'gaping mouth and big round eyes'.

Why should strange events occur together at certain points on the globe? If some form of energy, known or unknown, is involved in the genesis of these strange happenings, it would seem that it tends to focus or concentrate in limited areas at specific times. The result is an upsurge in sightings of monsters and UFOs, and an increase in strange happenings of all kinds.

Doubtless there will be waves of sightings of weird winged creatures again. But, as with UFOs and the bigfoot, it seems very unlikely that we shall acquire unambiguous physical traces of the things seen – we cannot count on having a corpse to study. The phenomena seem too elusive.

Monsters of the deep

For thousands of years, sightings of strange sea monsters have been reported around the world. Here, JANET and COLIN BORD argue that the ocean depths contain many creatures as yet unknown to science, and that these reports should not be discounted as wild imaginings

Below: a drawing of a 'most dreadful monster' seen off the coast of Greenland by Norwegian missionary Hans Egede in 1734. Known as the Apostle of Greenland, Hans Egede was a pious and honest man who took a keen interest in natural history

WITH MORE THAN 60 per cent of the Earth's surface covered with water, it is hardly surprising that sightings of giant underwater monsters have been reported since antiquity. Even today, marine biologists, who have long been aware of the vast unexplored depths of the Earth's oceans, cautiously accept that the numerous reports of sea monster sightings seem to provide evidence that many creatures, at present unknown and unclassified, may be living in the dark and hidden waters.

The Biblical beast of evil, the leviathan ('the twisting serpent . . . the dragon that is in the sea') is mentioned in the Old Testament five times, and from the Norsemen to the Aborigines in Australia, from the Chinese to the American Indians, ancient mythologies speak of giant sea serpents.

Many of the early reports of sea monsters were collected by Scandinavian ecclesiastics. Archbishop Olaf Mansson, now better known as Olaus Magnus, who was exiled to Rome after the Swedish Reformation in the early 16th century, published a natural history of the northern lands in 1555 that contained reports of sea serpents. He described a sea serpent 200 feet (60 metres) long and 20 feet (6 metres) thick that would eat calves, lambs and hogs, and would even pluck men from boats. Archbishop Magnus also stated that the monster's appearance foretold disasters such as wars.

Interestingly, Magnus described the sea serpent as being black, having hair hanging from its neck (or mane), shining eyes, and putting its 'head on high like a pillar'. These characteristics also appear in recent sighting reports, suggesting that Olaus Magnus was writing about originally factual reports that had become distorted and embroidered with much retelling.

Two hundred years later historians were still recording sightings of sea serpents, though the clergy still maintained that these were sightings of the beast of evil. On 6 July 1734 a sea monster appeared off the coast of Greenland, and was reported by a Norwegian missionary, Hans Egede. In 1741 he wrote that its body was as bulky as a ship and was three or four times as long, and that it leapt from the water and plunged back again.

Another 18th-century writer on the mystery of the sea serpent was the Bishop of Bergen, Erik Pontoppidan. After detailed enquiry he found that hardly a year went by without some sea serpent sightings along the Scandinavian coastline and he published his findings in 1752.

A year earlier Bishop Pontoppidan had arranged for a letter from Captain Lorenz von Ferry to be read to the Bergen Court of Justice, in which was described a sea serpent that the Captain and his crew had seen in 1746 while rowing ashore to Molde in Norway. He said it had a grey head like a

horse, large black eyes, a black mouth and a long white mane. Behind the head seven or eight coils could be seen above the water. Captain von Ferry fired at it and it sank below the water and did not reappear. Two of his seamen, who had also been witnesses, swore on oath that the contents of the report were true.

During the 18th century, the increasing importance attached to rational scientific analysis resulted in mariners' reports of monstrous sea beasts being discounted, then openly derided. A Norwegian scientist, Peter Ascanius, stated that sailors who saw a line of humps in the water were not viewing a huge water beast, but were in fact seeing a line of leaping dolphins. This doubtful explanation has since become a favourite standby for debunkers of sea monster reports.

However, perhaps surprisingly, naturalists who took the time to study the reports almost invariably pronounced in favour of the sea serpent's existence. These included Sir Joseph Banks, a leading British scientist in the early 19th century who sailed round the world with Captain Cook, and Thomas

Above: the eminent British naturalist, Sir Joseph Banks (1743–1820). In 1820 he affirmed his 'full faith in the existence of our Serpent in the Sea'

Right: when the crew of a French ship were saved from death at the hands of a frightful monster, they gave a painting of the event, in thanksgiving for their deliverance, to a church in St Malo. The original disappeared, but the French naturalist, Denys de Montfort, had a copy made in the 1790s (shown here), as he felt it confirmed the existence of giant sea monsters

Huxley, who in 1893 wrote that there was no reason why snake-like reptiles 50 feet (15 metres) or more in length should not be found in the sea.

American marine biologists of repute at this time agreed that the sea could very well contain unknown species of monstrous creatures and a curator of the London Zoological Gardens, A. D. Bartlett, wrote in 1877 that it was unwise to disregard the evidence from so many different sources.

Constantin Samuel Rafinesque was a brilliant and controversial naturalist, who made a tremendous contribution to the

knowledge of American flora and fauna. Born in 1783, he emigrated to America from Europe in 1815 where he became Professor of Natural Sciences at Transylvania University, in Kentucky. Among his wide range of interests was the sea serpent, of whose existence he was fully convinced.

During the first half of the 19th century there were a great many sightings of sea serpents along the north-east American coast, centred on the fishing port of Gloucester, in Massachusetts. Rafinesque examined the reports and decided that they fell into four groups, to which he gave the generic name of *Megophias*, or 'big snake'.

However, there were many opponents of scientists who were investigating the unexplained phenomenon of sea monsters. Among the more vociferous was Sir Richard Owen, an influential but conservative scientist of the 19th century, whom Darwin called 'one of my chief enemies'.

In 1848 Owen conducted a correspondence of some acerbity with Captain Peter M'Quhae, through the columns of *The Times*. Their debate concerned the 60-foot (18-metre) sea serpent that the Captain and his crew had seen in the southern Atlantic from the deck of HMS *Daedalus* on 6 August that year. Although Owen used the sceptic's customary ploy of interpreting the report to fit his own preconceptions (in this case his identification was a sealion), Captain M'Quhae would have none of it and firmly maintained that he had seen a sea serpent.

Antoon Cornelis Oudemans was a Dutch biologist who came from a family of scientists. Born in 1858, he studied biology at Utrecht and became an authority on mites and ticks. He also brought his scientific skills to bear on the problem of the sea monster.

Throughout his long life (he died in 1943) Oudemans collected many sighting reports and continued to speculate on the place of the sea monster in nature. His book, *The great sea serpent*, published in 1892, is based on 187 sighting reports and was a courageous work in the contemporary sceptical climate, but it is marred by his preconception that there is only one kind of unknown sea monster, closely related to the seal family.

As one would expect, sea monsters have long been a part of mariners' tales. Some reports have undoubtedly been exaggerated, but many others that made their way into ships' logs are strangely consistent.

In May 1901, when the officers on the bridge of the steamer *Grangense* in the western Atlantic saw a monstrous crocodile-like creature with 6-inch (15-centimetre) long teeth, splashing about on the surface, the Captain refused to note the encounter in the ship's log, saying: 'They will say we were all drunk, and I'll thank you, Mister, not to mention it to our agents at Para or Manaus.'

But there were others who were perhaps less careful of their reputation, such as

Left: Thomas Huxley (1825–1895) was another noted British scientist who pronounced in favour of giant sea serpents

Below: on 6 August 1848, Captain M'Quhae and six members of the crew of HMS *Daedalus* sighted a 60-foot (18-metre) serpent in the southern–Atlantic. When an illustrated report of the encounter appeared in the British press, it caused a fierce controversy

Bottom: one of the sea monsters described by Archbishop Olaus Magnus and illustrated in his history of Scandinavia, which was published in 1555

Despite scathing criticism from 19th-century scientists, sightings of sea monsters continued to be reported. The painting above shows a monster sinking a ship off the coast of Massachusetts in 1819, an area where giant sea creatures seemed to thrive

Lieutenant George Sandford who, as captain of the merchant ship *Lady Combermere*, in 1820 reported seeing in mid-Atlantic a serpent 60 to 100 feet (18 to 30 metres) long, spouting water like a whale. On 15 May 1833 four British Army officers and a military store-keeper were out for a day's fishing when they saw an 80-foot (24-metre) long serpent swim by, not more than 200 yards (180 metres) away. This was at Mahone Bay, 40 miles (65 kilometres) west of Halifax, Nova Scotia, and so convinced were they of the importance of their sighting that they all signed a statement and added:

> There could be no mistake, no delusion, and we were all perfectly satisfied that we had been favoured with a view of the 'true and veritable sea-serpent', which had been generally considered to have existed only in the brain of some Yankee skipper, and treated as a tale not much entitled to belief.

Another sighting of the crocodile-like type of sea monster was made by the captain and crew of the *Eagle* on 23 March 1830, a few hours before they docked at Charleston, South Carolina. Captain Deland sailed his schooner to within 25 yards (22 metres) of the basking creature and fired a musket at its head. When the bullet hit, the monster dived beneath the ship and struck it several times with its tail, blows strong enough to damage the craft if not to sink her.

Another military man who had a close-up view of an unknown monster from the depths was Major H. W. J. Senior of the Bengal Staff Corps. He was travelling on the *City of Baltimore* in the Gulf of Aden on 28 January 1879 and saw 500 yards (450 metres) from the ship a head with a 2-foot (60-centimetre) diameter neck protrude from the water to a height of 20 or 30 feet (6 or 9 metres). The creature was moving so rapidly he was unable to focus his field glasses upon it as it rose up, opened its mouth wide and closed it again before submerging, only to reappear a few moments later. No body was visible, but Major Senior described the head as of a bulldog-like appearance. His report was also signed by other witnesses.

In the 100 years since this sighting, sea monsters have continued to surface before startled onlookers. The intrepid trans–Atlantic rower Captain John Ridgway saw a monster just before midnight on 25 July 1966. His companion, Sergeant Chay Blyth, who has since became a world-famous yachtsman, was asleep. As Ridgway rowed he heard a swishing noise and a 35-foot (10-metre) long sea serpent outlined in phosphorescence, 'as if a string of neon lights were hanging from it', came swimming towards the boat. It dived underneath and did not reappear on the other side.

An ocean giant

Many zoologists believe the kraken – the legendary Norwegian sea monster – probably refers to the giant squids of the genus *Architeuthis*. These creatures inhabit the depths of the ocean and can grow to lengths of over 60 feet (18 metres). The sperm whale is the only animal brave enough to tackle these monsters and fierce battles take place between them.

The giant squid shown here was stranded at Ranheim, Norway, in 1954. Though not the largest specimen known to science, its overall length was 30 feet (9 metres).

From the sea serpent to the super-otter

Besides classic sightings of sea monsters there are 'classic' hoaxes, too. But this does not mean that we should discount the existence of unknown creatures. And, as JANET and COLIN BORD show, using the techniques pioneered by the Belgian zoologist Bernard Heuvelmans the whole subject can now be studied scientifically

MANY SCIENTISTS remain sceptical about the existence of underwater monsters, yet sightings of giant sea creatures, some extremely detailed, continue to be reported around the world.

An active monster of recent years, sighted off the coast of Cornwall, England, is known as Morgawr (Cornish for 'sea giant'). This was seen quite often during 1975 and 1976, in Falmouth Bay, and on 5 March 1976 two photographs of it were published in the *Falmouth Packet*. Although these were submitted anonymously, nevertheless they do appear very convincing, showing a long-necked creature similar to that reported to be in Loch Ness.

Another strange creature has been seen in the waters of Cardigan Bay off the west coast of Wales. On 2 March 1975, six local schoolgirls were walking along the beach at dusk when 200 yards (180 metres) away a creature moved across the beach towards the sea. They described it as being 10 feet (3 metres) long with a long neck and tail and large green eyes. They were quite terrified at this spectacle and ran away to report it to the coastguard. Later they described it to their art teacher, Colin Palmer, who drew the creature. When he showed his sketch to the crew of a fishing boat, who had seen a monster when they were fishing off Bardsey Sound,

The Cornish sea monster Morgawr was sighted several times during 1975 and 1976. 'Mary F' succeeded in photographing the creature, of which 15 to 18 feet (5 to 6 metres) were visible, in February 1976 at Rosemullion Head, near Falmouth

there was 'instant recognition'.

The consequences of the publicity attached to famous sightings are twofold: there is a sudden increase in similar reports, many of which turn out to be well-authenticated, and a subsequent crop of hoaxes. Researchers are, of course, keen to expose the latter. Spurious reports are intended to bring ridicule on those who believe them, so eventually they must be revealed to make their point.

A hoax report that contained, perhaps deliberately, a clue to its true nature was published by the *Globe* in 1848, scarcely a week after *The Times* had published an account of a sea serpent seen by Peter M'Quhae, Captain of HMS *Daedalus*.

The hoax was printed in the form of a

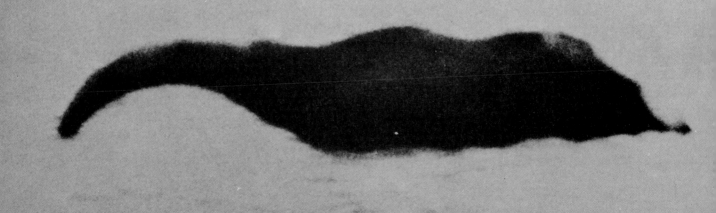

Above: until the Age of Enlightenment in the 18th century, people still thought of the oceans as full of fearsome monsters. In this 16th-century engraving, the whale is depicted as a huge creature with terrible fangs and claws

Right and below right: this strange-looking carcase with its huge head and duck-like beak was washed up on the rocks at Santa Cruz, California, in 1925. Decomposition made the specimen hard to identify but, after examining the skull, the Museum of the California Academy of Sciences showed that the carcase was that of an extremely rare beaked whale

subsequent enquiries revealed that the letter was a hoax.

Over 100 years later, in March 1965, an Australian magazine published an article on 'the Great Barrier Reef monster' by a Frenchman, Robert Le Serrec. He reported that he and his family had been camping on an island on the Great Barrier Reef where they had found a sea serpent, over 80 feet (24 metres) long and lying injured in the shallow lagoon water.

After cautiously circling around the creature in their boat and taking photographs, Le Serrec and his companion, Henk de Jong, entered the water armed with a rifle and a camera. As the two men approached to within 20 feet (6 metres) and took pictures, the creature turned its massive head towards them and opened its mouth threateningly. They quickly returned to their boat and the monster swam out to sea.

The story and photographs were also offered to an American magazine, whose

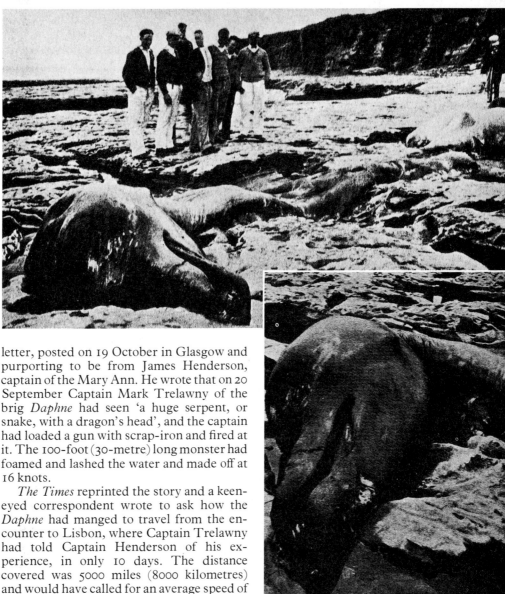

letter, posted on 19 October in Glasgow and purporting to be from James Henderson, captain of the Mary Ann. He wrote that on 20 September Captain Mark Trelawny of the brig *Daphne* had seen 'a huge serpent, or snake, with a dragon's head', and the captain had loaded a gun with scrap-iron and fired at it. The 100-foot (30-metre) long monster had foamed and lashed the water and made off at 16 knots.

The Times reprinted the story and a keen-eyed correspondent wrote to ask how the *Daphne* had manged to travel from the encounter to Lisbon, where Captain Trelawny had told Captain Henderson of his experience, in only 10 days. The distance covered was 5000 miles (8000 kilometres) and would have called for an average speed of 20 knots. The correspondent drily remarked: 'Probably the serpent took the brig in tow' –

An ancient Greek vase showing Heracles struggling with the river god Achelous to win Deianira. The god is represented with the torso of a man and the body of a sea serpent

editor asked Ivan T. Sanderson, the British biologist and investigator of the unexplained, his opinion of them. Le Serrec's background in France was also investigated. Here it was found that he had tried to finance his expedition by telling prospective financial backers that he would make a lot of money on the trip in a venture connected with a giant sea serpent.

Biologists who examined the photographs and descriptions were not satisfied that they portrayed a genuine animal. Its eyes were too far back on the top of its head and Le Serrec's story was not entirely consistent.

The various investigations all pointed to a hoax, probably achieved by filling a long plastic tube with air and sinking it with stones. Needless to say, the American magazine did not publish the story.

The sceptical scientist asks for physical remains to examine, and periodically, strange, large carcases are washed up on remote beaches. Owing to pressure of other work and the remoteness of the locations, these are usually ignored or identified at a distance as the remains of a known sea creature, often a basking shark.

The 55-foot (17-metre) long body that was washed up on the shore of the island of Stronsay in the Orkneys in 1808, was first seen by local fishermen and farmers but, before any informed examination could be made, storms had smashed the rotting carcase to pieces. The drawing that was made from the witnesses' descriptions showed an extraordinary animal with a long neck and undulating tail and three pairs of legs, a feature hitherto unknown in a vertebrate.

The corpse was finally identified as a shark by a British surgeon, Everard Home, who had made a study of shark anatomy and was able to obtain specimens of bones that had been removed from the beast. When shark carcases are washed up on shore, the rapid decomposition of certain parts of the anatomy, namely the lower jaw, the lower tail fluke and the fins, leaves what looks like a weird creature with a long thin neck and tail.

In 1925 an unidentified carcase was cast ashore at Santa Cruz, California. It appeared to have a 30-foot (9-metre) long neck and a huge beaked head, but was eventually identified as the remains of a very rare beaked whale from the North Pacific.

The large decomposing 'glob' that was washed up on a remote beach in western Tasmania in July 1960 received little official attention until March 1962. Then scientists from Hobart located the exact spot from the air and a group went to investigate. Helicopters were used to carry away samples, and the official statement said that the object was 'a large lump of decomposing blubber, probably torn off a whale'. However, the other

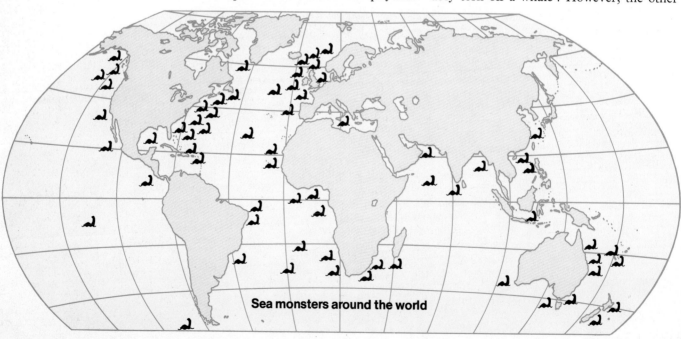

Sea monsters around the world

biologists who had been following the case thought that this was unlikely.

A more recent find occurred on 25 April 1977, when the Japanese trawler *Zuiyo Maru* hauled up a large, partially rotted carcase 28 miles (45 kilometres) east of Christchurch, New Zealand. Concerned that it might contaminate his catch, the captain, Akira Tanaka, had it photographed and drawn, then dropped it back in the sea. The incident intrigued the world's press and a television film crew flew from Japan to cover the story. Although the ship's crew were convinced that they had seen an unknown monster, the

Right: the long-necked sea serpent appears to be the most common of the nine specific types of sea monster classified by Belgian zoologist Dr Bernard Heuvelmans. Analysis of 48 certain sightings indicate that the creature is between 15 and 65 feet (5 and 20 metres) long and moves through the water with exceptional speed for an animal of this size

Long-necked

photographs suggest a decomposed shark.

Some of the most convincing evidence for the existence of sea monsters comes from those areas where they have been sighted repeatedly over decades or even centuries. In the Strait of Georgia between Vancouver Island and British Columbia, off the west coast of Canada, the creature known locally as Cadborosaurus or Caddy was sighted by the Indians long before the arrival of the white settlers.

In this century an early sighting of Caddy was made by F. W. Kemp, a local government official. On 10 August 1932, Mr Kemp was with his wife and son when they saw it swim at terrific speed through the water. Caddy was seen frequently during the 1930s and in 1950 was sighted by Judge James Brown and his family, when it appeared as a 45-foot (14-metre) long serpent that rose out of the water several times. Mrs. R. A. Stewart, who saw it in 1963 when fishing with her husband, was terrified by its wide-open jaws.

Further south on the American west coast is San Clemente Island, a favourite area for deep-sea angling and an area where water

Above and right: a recent find that attracted world-wide attention was the carcase hauled on board the Japanese trawler *Zuiyo Maru* in 1977. Concerned that the carcase might contaminate his catch, Captain Akira Tanaka had it photographed, then threw it back in the sea. Biologists believe that the photographs show a decomposed shark and not an unknown monster

monsters have been seen frequently throughout this century. When technical fishing writer J. Charles Davis interviewed numerous independent witnesses, he found their descriptions tallied to an amazing degree. Many of the witnesses were wealthy members of the big-game fishing clubs, who knew what to expect from the sea and had no desire to lay themselves open to ridicule.

Why does the sea serpent still remain comparatively unknown? One reason might be that although more than 60 per cent of the Earth's surface is covered by water, very little of it is travelled over by commercial

Many-humped

Super-otter

Left: the many-humped sea serpent and the super-otter are about the same size – 60-100 feet (18-20 metres) long. The many-humped category has been seen chiefly along the coast of New England, USA, though the number of sightings has diminished since the beginning of this century. As there has been no sighting of the super-otter since 1848, Dr Heuvelmans believes it may now be extinct

Right: the main characteristic of the many-finned sea serpent is breath blown out of the nostrils. It grows to a length of more than 60 feet (18 metres) and has been sighted only in tropical waters. The last mammal in Heuvelmans' classification is the merhorse, which has huge eyes and a reddish mane. It has been sighted in most waters of the world, apart from the Indian Ocean and the Polar seas

Many-finned

Merhorse

range from the most frequently seen 'long-necked' sea serpent, which has a cigar-shaped body, four webbed feet and is a fast swimmer, to the very infrequently seen marine saurians that look like crocodiles 50–60 feet (15–18 metres) long and have only been seen in mid-ocean tropical waters.

The other types Dr Heuvelmans names informally as merhorses, many-humped, super-otters, many-finned, super-eels, fathers-of-all-the-turtles and yellow-bellies. He has also found a group he calls 'ambiguous periscopes', which might be either long-necked monsters or super-eels. He

shipping, which follows fixed and narrow routes. The vibrations made by engines and bow waves are sufficient to keep timid sea creatures away from these areas, in contrast to the days of sail when the silent ships relied on wind and currents and were often driven well off their routes.

The cases cited above, and the hundreds of others that can be found in the various works on the subject, point to the fact that there is not just one type of sea monster. In 1965, Belgian zoologist Dr Bernard Heuvelmans completed the most detailed and exhaustive work on the subject in recent times – *In the wake of the sea-serpents*, a book that has been of great value to all modern writers on water monsters. In it, Dr Heuvelmans describes and analyses more than 500 reports, dating from 1639 to 1964. From these reports he draws certain conclusions and here we attempt a brief summary of them.

Of the 587 sightings that Heuvelmans collected, 56 of them he considered most likely to be hoaxes. Another group were known sea creatures mistakenly reported as unknown monsters – he found 52 of these. Another 121 reports were removed from his final analysis because the details given were too vague or ambiguous for any useful classification to be made.

This left 358 sightings with various characteristics of appearance and behaviour that could be divided into nine types. These

considers the long-necked serpent and the first four categories above to be mammals.

The super-eel is probably a fish whose normal habitat is the ocean depths and when seen on the surface is usually near death, while the marine saurian could well be a survivor from the Jurassic period that normally lives well below the surface and so has survived to the present. His yellow-belly group is somewhat more difficult to classify owing to a lack of detailed descriptions, but it could possibly be a fish, perhaps a shark.

Another interesting observation that Dr Heuvelmans has made is that the most frequent sightings during this century have been of the long-necked sea monster, which as a species may be on the increase. Conversely, there has been no sighting of the super-otter since 1848 and Heuvelmans suggests that these two are, or have been, in competition for the same ecological niche – the super-otter must be the loser and it may well now be extinct.

The world beneath the sea has still not been fully explored and, despite the sceptics, there appears to be abundant evidence for the existence of large, unknown sea creatures. Scientists believe that before long they will have a much more detailed knowledge of life in the ocean depths – indeed, new species are being discovered every year, so perhaps they will soon find the answer to the mystery of the underwater monster.

American Lake Monsters

Thousands of lakes are scattered across North America — and from many come tales of huge creatures, rivalling the legends of the Loch Ness monster and the sea serpents. PETER COSTELLO tells some of the stories of Nessie's North American cousins

THE LAKES OF NORTH AMERICA, both in the United States and in Canada, have produced more reports of monsters than any other continent. More than 90 lakes and rivers are credited with being haunts of 'unidentified swimming objects'. Few of these reports are backed up with anything as concrete as photographs or ciné film. Most of them remain unexplained, some of the most intriguing of modern zoological mysteries. If there are so many creatures at large in these lakes, what are they and how do they manage to remain so elusive?

Reports of American lake monsters have a very long history. Naturally enough, the original inhabitants of the continent, the Indians, had many legends of large water monsters. As with all folklore, their graphic details may well conceal something very real.

The Mic-Mac Indians of the Nova Scotia area believed in a 'fabulous snake', which was similar to one described by the Algonquin further west. The Iroquois of upper New York state had a monster called Onijore. In Indiana, the Potawatomi believed in a monster in Lake Manitou on the Wabash River; in the early 19th century they objected to the erection of a mill that would have disturbed the creature's way of life.

Lake Ontario, straddling the Canada/United States border, lies under a sheet of winter ice. Occasional sightings of monsters have been made here and in other Great Lakes. But the most frequently reported lake creature is Ogopogo, a denizen of Lake Okanagan in British Columbia. The model of Ogopogo (inset) is part of the lake shore dwellers' publicity

Lake monsters of the New World

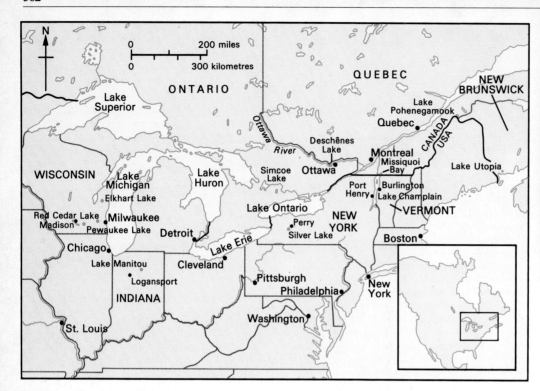

Above: the Lake Utopia monster pursues a canoe in this contemporary drawing from an issue of the *Canadian Illustrated News* of 1872. According to the highly coloured account of the witnesses, the monster had 'bloody jaws'

Left: north-eastern North America, a region once covered by glaciers, which gouged thousands of lakes out of the land. Have prehistoric aquatic animals escaped extinction in these sheltered waters?

Below: Lake Champlain, the reputed home of the Champ, who, whether he exists or not, enjoys legal protection from hunters

These Indian tribes were grouped around the area of the Great Lakes. Further west, in the Rocky Mountain states, there were other legends. Among the Shawnee there was a legend of a great reptile, which was killed by a magician with the aid of a young girl – like the legend of St George and the Dragon. The Kalapuya Indians of the Willamette River in Oregon believed in a monster called Aturki, which lived in the lakes, rivers and pools of that region. An anthropologist remarked that 'those who saw it described it as resembling a seal or a sea otter.' Were these mere myths? Or descriptions of extraordinary but real animals?

The earliest reports, as distinct from legends, come from the first decades of the 19th century. It is often said that the first report of an American lake monster was made by the great French explorer of Canada, Samuel de Champlain, in 1609, when he discovered the great lake in Vermont now named after him. But this is not so: this is one 'report' that can safely be ascribed to an error on the part of a journalist. The story has been taken up by every writer on Lake Champlain since the error was made in 1960. Champlain does indeed mention a frightful water monster, but that was supposed to haunt the sea coast of the St Lawrence estuary, which is far to the north-east.

One of the pioneers of sea serpent research, naturalist Constantin Samuel Rafinesque, noted that there was a tradition of 'a great Water Snake', which lived in a lake near Philadelphia. But he also collected reports of newer sightings:

On the 3rd of July, 1817, one was seen in Lake Erie, three miles [5 kilometres] from land, by the crew of a schooner, which was 35 or 40 feet [10.5 or 12 metres] long, and one foot [30 centimetres] in diameter; its colour was dark mahogany, nearly black. This account is very imperfect, and does not even notice if it had scales; therefore it must remain doubtful whether it was a snake or a fish. I am inclined to believe it was a fish.

In 1819 the animal was seen again, 'and described to be of a copper colour, with bright eyes, and 60 feet [18 metres] long'. Shooting at it seemed to have no effect: whether because it was protected by scales or because the marksmanship was poor.

At this time the New England sea serpent was taken very seriously. A report of a monster in Lake Ontario (with which Lake Erie connects) was even dignified by publication in a German scientific journal in 1835.

Monsters in limbo

Soon lake monsters joined sea serpents in that limbo to which 'respectable' journals consign them nowadays. No one was to take them so seriously again for a long time. They became a suitable topic for humorous journalism and for hoaxes.

During 1855 Silver Lake in New York state was the scene of a great sensation: a 'sea serpent' had been sighted in the lake. There were numerous reports of sightings and the local press took up the tale. Over the next couple of years the sightings faded away. Then there was a fire at the local hotel, and in the attic volunteer firemen discovered the remains of the 'sea serpent'. It was a dummy, kept afloat with compressed air, which the hotel owner had made to boost his business. Local people were angry at first; later the perpetrator of the hoax was forgiven. Today the town of Perry holds a periodic sea serpent

Below: the skyline of Buffalo, New York state, rises above the waters of Lake Erie. Sightings of monsters in the lake date from the early 19th century – but they occurred before the severe pollution of the lake

Bottom: Naitaka, the monster spirit of Lake Okanagan, depicted in a rock carving made by the Shushwap Indians. When Indians travelled on the lake, they would drop a chicken or pup into the waters as an offering to Naitaka: failure to do so would incur his wrath

written up in the *Canadian Illustrated News* with an astonishing woodcut of the creature curling through the water in pursuit of two men in a canoe. It had a head as large as a barrel, 'snapping its bloody jaws in a most horrible manner'. The monster was said to appear soon after the winter ice had broken up, which brought many visitors to the lake in March each year in the hope of seeing it.

One witness in the early 1950s was a Mrs Fred McKillop. Alone one day, she saw a large black shape churning up the water, and moving backwards and forwards at great speed.

For some scientists, anxious to explain away reports of lake monsters, this churning of the water holds a clue to what some 'monsters' might be. In Norway it was found that many reports came from mountain lakes

festival to commemorate the hoax.

Journalists in America were often responsible for creating instant folklore. In the 1830s, for instance, there came a series of reports from the lakes of Indiana in the Middle West. There had been, of course, earlier Indian legends. But then came reports, published in the Logansport newspaper, that white settlers had also been seeing monsters. These reports were investigated a century later by a professor of history at Indiana University. Donald Smalley discovered that they may well have been a journalistic 'joke'. As the last Indians were moved out of the state, the reports faded away.

In Canada, too, in areas then on the frontier, there were many reports. The most striking of these came from Lake Utopia, in New Brunswick, in 1867. Lumbermen employed at a mill on the lake were surprised to see some object splashing about in the water. The report that it was a large animal caused great excitement. In 1872 the monster was

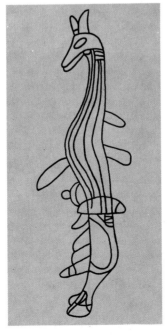

on the shores of which there were saw mills. On one famous occasion one of these 'monsters' was investigated by a policeman after it had surfaced in a patch of churning water. It turned out to be a great mass of sawdust and other vegetable rubbish, lifted to the surface of the water by the expanding gases created by its own rotting.

Were the Lake Utopia monster sightings caused by masses of decaying vegetation? But if so, what was it that chased the Indians? What of the reports from other lakes? What of the descriptions of long-necked creatures? Theories of this kind have to be seen in a wider context of reports from all over the North American continent, and especially from the Rocky Mountains and the Great Lakes region. There are no easy explanations that can cover *all* these sightings.

The reports of lake monsters in North America fall into a curious pattern. Nearly all are from mountain lakes, or from the rivers and lakes connected directly with them,

which include the Great Lakes.

An apparent exception to this was a series of reports of a monster in Alkali Lake (now Walgen Lake), which lies in the grasslands of Nebraska. The first reported sighting was in the summer of 1921, when a farmer saw a creature that spouted water 15 to 20 feet (4.5 to 6 metres) high. Several other reports followed. In one incident, five witnesses were said to have seen a brownish creature 'with the shape of a huge fish'. They could not see its head or tail, but the part they could see rose about 20 inches (50 centimetres) out of the water and was 12 to 15 feet (3.5 to 4.5 metres) long. They estimated that the total length of the beast must have been 20 feet (6 metres) or more.

Making the news

Unfortunately, these accounts all came through a journalist, John G. Maher. He was local correspondent for the *New York Herald* and, as he himself later confessed, was not above making up news when the real thing was in short supply. However, his imaginative accounts of the Alkali Lake monster created an interest that got out of hand. A local businessmen's association tried to mount an expedition to catch the monster, but were refused permission to use the lake. The monster even found its way into the material collected by a government agency, the Federal Writers' Folklore Project. Maher gave accounts of alleged sightings of the monster from earlier years. (But he did not mention that in 1889 the lake had dried up completely – without revealing any trace of a monster.)

Many of the sightings from the numerous American lakes are single reports, often from the 19th century. But a very few lakes have a long continuous history of sightings running up to the present. And after discounting journalistic invention, the accumulation of

Above: the remains of a water monster? In November 1970 this rotting carcass was washed ashore at Mann Hill Beach, Massachusetts. Long-necked and weighing between 15 and 20 tonnes, it was described as being like a camel without legs. However, it was later identified as a basking shark, which had acquired a serpent-like form when the cartilaginous parts of its body had rotted away. This, however, was a sea creature; no large animal living in the lakes is known that could give rise to the numerous reports of lake monsters

Right: the fictional monster inhabiting Lake La Metrie, about to meet its death at the hands of the US Cavalry. The saga of this relic of a prehistoric age appeared in *Pearson's Magazine* in 1899

evidence, though scattered and varied, is impressive and convincing in its totality.

One area with a long history of reports is the lake district of Wisconsin. There have been sightings in the four lakes that ring Madison, and in Waubeau, Red Cedar, Pewaukee and Elkhart Lakes. Though some of the sightings occurred in recent times it is difficult to know how much credence to place in them as they have not been properly investigated.

Of far greater interest are the reports of large water animals in the mountain states. Rumours of lake monsters in the Rockies were so common in the 19th century that they inspired sensational science fiction – such as *The monster of Lake La Metrie*, published in 1899. This story ends with a unit of the US Cavalry destroying a prehistoric plesiosaur in a remote mountain lake with a field gun.

This unlikely tale could have been based on fact, for there were many sightings of something very like a plesiosaur in several lakes. In Utah, such reports began after the Mormons had established themselves, though in the same region there had been earlier Indian legends of water creatures. The late 19th-century reports concerned Utah Lake and, especially, Bear Lake. A journalist writing in 1883 noted: 'There is abundant testimony on record of the actual existence at the present day of an immense aquatic animal of some species as yet unknown to science.'

In 1871 it was claimed that a young monster had been captured at Fish Haven, on Bear Lake – 'a creature some 20 feet [6 metres] long, which propelled itself through

the water by the action of its tail and legs.' Earlier reports spoke of a 3-foot [1-metre] neck, flippers and brown otter-like fur and a head that suggested a 'walrus without tusks'. The Shoshone Indians had said the animals used to come ashore.

These extraordinary reports faded away after the 1880s. From Payette Lake in the mountains of Idaho there were more reports in the 1930s – perhaps stimulated by the Loch Ness sensation. But in the summer of 1941 there was a sudden spate of reports. John McKay saw a large animal with a 'long dark body' and humps. A few months later a periscope-like head and neck were seen. These reports were not publicised. Then a local businessman described to the press his sighting of a 'snub-nosed crocodile' 50 feet (15 metres) long. This creature, nicknamed 'Slimy Slim', is still being reported. In June 1977 two people fishing in a boat in Cougar Bay noticed what looked like the wake of a boat – yet no boat had passed within the previous 10 minutes. Then they spotted a three-humped black object, 30 feet (9 metres) long, moving fairly fast.

Gary S. Mangiacopra, who has investigated these reports, suggests that the monster may well be some evolved form of elephant seal. This suggestion, however, scarcely accounts for the reports of humps that feature in so many of the sightings.

Reports of crocodile-like creatures have come from Folsom Lake in California, from lakes in the Trinity Alps, in the same state, and from many other places in the western states. However, Flathead Lake in Montana is the most interesting. In 1885 the captain of a lake steamer, the *U.S. Grant*, saw what he

A sturgeon (below) that came from Flathead Lake, Montana, lending colour to the theory that these fish give rise to monster reports. But this specimen was probably put into the lake (bottom right) to publicise it among local fishermen

Bottom left: the lakes of western North America. Mountain lakes seem to be the preferred haunts of giant water creatures

thought was another boat bearing down on him and then realised that it was a large whale-like animal. One of his passengers fired on it before it sank out of sight. In 1919 passengers on another boat, the *City of Polson*, saw what they thought was a log moving across the path of the ship: then they saw that it was an animal swimming away from the vessel.

During the following decades there were numerous reports, many of which were published by the editor of the *Flathead Courier*, Mr Paul Fugleberg. His enthusiasm kept the story fresh for a long while. He had a theory that the monster might be a giant sturgeon. This seems unlikely as there is no evidence that such fish have ever bred in the lake. Only *once* has a sturgeon been taken from the lake – and that may have been brought there as a stunt, to publicise the quality of the fishing.

Native peoples thought of the North American lakes as the homes of numerous divinities – including monsters. But flesh-and-blood water animals are the prizes sought by modern investigators

Coming u

CANADA AND ALASKA, lands scattered with innumerable lakes, do not lack for reports of monsters. Behind these modern reports there is a long legendary tradition among the native Eskimos and Indians.

In the late 1940s the Canadian writer Farley Mowat (then a naturalist in government service) was told about a monster called Angeoa, which had been seen in Tulemaliguak (Dubawnt Lake). His informant was an Eskimo friend, whose father and a companion had seen the creature at the end of the last century. The bones of a great beast had once been found on the shores of the lake: hence its Eskimo name, Lake of the Heaped-up Bones. As for the monster:

It was beyond the words of the people to tell you about, but my father who saw it said it was as long as twenty kayaks and broader than five. It had a fin which stood up from one end and that fin was as big as a tent. Neither my father nor Hekwaw saw its head and did not believe the beast had a head.

Terrified, the two Eskimos fled, but their kayak overturned. The informant's father survived, but his companion drowned.

This creature was doubtless related to the creature known in the Great Lakes area as Manitou Niba Nabais, the god of the waters and lakes. But these legends are scientifically relevant only as background to modern reports.

Take the case of Iliamna Lake in Alaska. This lake covers 1000 square miles (1600 square kilometres) and is said to be the seventh largest in the world. It is 90 miles (145 kilometres) long, whereas Loch Ness is only 22 miles (35 kilometres) long. In the scattered hamlets around the shores there are legends of the creature snatching children and caribou and biting through canoes.

In 1971 it was reported that the monster broke up the winter ice at Kokhanok, a small village on the south-eastern shore. Children sketched it before it disappeared. Susie Noatak drew it with 'an eye below his mouth'; John Nelson junior drew it as some kind of giant whale or sturgeon, trailing long tendrils. Some of the local game guards are convinced the creature is indeed a large sturgeon. A US Geological Survey worker saw two creatures together. In the mid 1960s some NASA astronauts flying an aircraft over the lake saw great shadows moving in the water. They swooped down over the lake and the shapes vanished. An old Indian told Reuben Gaines, a television personality and writer, that he saw someone shrivel up and die after seeing the lake monster. Some Indians refused to go out in red-bottomed boats, for red annoyed the monster.

Above: the Texas oil magnate Tom Slick, a keen monster hunter. He mounted an expedition to find the legendary monster of Iliamna Lake in Alaska, but failed in his quest. He is pictured here after a fruitless search for the Yeti in the Himalayas

Right: Simcoe Lake, Ontario, reputedly the home of a monster (inset) variously dubbed Igopogo and Kempenfelt Kelly. Reports of the monster go back to the 19th century

Centre right: the classic photograph of Manipogo, the monster of Lake Manitoba, taken on 12 August 1962. The two fishermen who took the picture saw what they 'believed to be a large black snake or eel . . . which was swimming with a ripple action'. They estimated that the hump was about 2 feet (60 centimetres) long. Their boat had an outboard motor, but they were unable to keep up with the creature and it escaped from them

Far right: the lakes north of Winnipeg, Manitoba. The best-known of the monsters reported from this area is Manipogo, reputed to dwell in Lake Manitoba

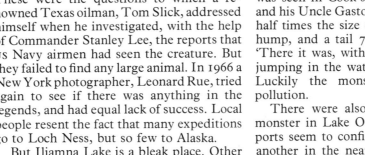

A giant sturgeon, or some type of whale? These were the questions to which a renowned Texas oilman, Tom Slick, addressed himself when he investigated, with the help of Commander Stanley Lee, the reports that US Navy airmen had seen the creature. But they failed to find any large animal. In 1966 a New York photographer, Leonard Rue, tried again to see if there was anything in the legends, and had equal lack of success. Local people resent the fact that many expeditions go to Loch Ness, but so few to Alaska.

But Iliamna Lake is a bleak place. Other more favoured lakes have received some

investigation. In Simcoe Lake, Ontario, which is near Toronto, a creature called Igopogo has been searched for by several expeditions. During the last century there were persistent reports, which were given greater plausibility by an Indian trapper's account in 1952. In 1963 a creature 'charcoal-coloured, 30 to 70 feet [9 to 21 metres] long and with dorsal fins' was seen by a minister, an undertaker and their families. It has been described by others as a dog-faced animal with a neck the diameter of a stove pipe.

Its supposed lair was in Kempenfelt Bay and it was dubbed 'Kempenfelt Kelly' for that reason. The bay was fouled by a million gallons (4.5 million litres) of raw sewage in

July 1980. But a few days later the creature was seen in Cook's Bay by John Bergeron and his Uncle Gaston. It had a head two and half times the size of a human's, a camel's hump, and a tail 7 feet (2.1 metres) long. 'There it was, with eyes as big as a cow's, jumping in the water for several minutes.' Luckily the monster had escaped the pollution.

There were also early reports about a monster in Lake Ontario. More recent reports seem to confirm this. And there was another in the nearby Deschênes Lake in 1880 part of its hairy hide was caught up in a propeller. A 'crocodile' stirred up New Hamburg, Ontario, in 1953. The local Mountie took a shot at it. Other monsters are said to live in some of the remote lakes further north.

Further west, beyond the Great Lakes, lie the numerous lakes of Manitoba. A series of connected lakes lies north of Winnipeg: Lakes Winnipeg, Manitoba, Winnipegosis and Dauphin. Lake Winnipeg alone covers 124 square miles (300 square kilometres).

The first report was from Lake Manitoba in 1908. A year later a trapper saw a huge creature swimming at about 2 miles per hour (3 km/h). It had a dark upper surface, which glistened, and its body projected 4 feet (1.2 metres) out of the water.

Other reports followed over the years. In

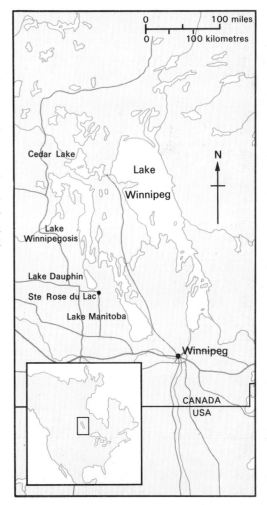

Left: Ogopogo, doyen of North American lake monsters. This rendering of the creature is a composite of many reports. The beast's name means 'remorseful one', for in Indian legend he was a murderer who had been changed into a water serpent in punishment for his crimes

Below: one of the pictures taken by Ed Fletcher on Okanagan Lake in summer of 1976. The creature, if such it was, remained visible for several hours and was pursued by Fletcher and his companions

1957 two men, Louis Belcher and Eddie Nipanik, saw a serpent-like monster in Lake Manitoba. Their reports and others that year – one witness spoke of hearing 'a bellow like a goods train whistle' – gave rise to a great deal of local concern. The provincial government sent in a team to search the lake for the monster, now dubbed 'Manipogo'. The Minister of Industry and Commerce said the safety and prosperity of Lake Manitoba might depend on the expedition. But the team failed to find any animal large enough to pose any kind of threat, to fishermen or to other lake users.

But still the reports came in. In the summer of 1960 a full-scale, if short-lived, scientific investigation was set up. On 12 August 1962 two fishermen, Richard Vincent and John Konefell, snapped what they reported was Manipogo. A Winnipeg zoologist, Dr James A. Macleod, said of the shallow-humped object in the picture: 'If that isn't the monster, I'd like to know what the deuce it is.'

These reports, though numerous, are far exceeded in volume by the evidence from Okanagan Lake concerning the monster there, the great Ogopogo. Already the subject of two books, Ogopogo has been called the Nessie of North America. But Nessie might better be called the Ogopogo of Scotland, because reports of the Canadian monster go back to 1850 – long before the notoriety of Nessie.

Okanagan is a long, deep mountain lake, running north to south in the pleasant fruit-growing territory of southern British Columbia. The details of innumerable reports give a picture of a large, dark-coloured creature with a long neck and humped back. Some sample reports show up the striking similarities.

In July 1890, Captain Thomas Shorts on the steamer *Jubilee* saw an animal off Squally Point, some 15 feet (5 metres) long, with a ram-like head and the Sun shining through its fins. This was one of the first reports;

there were another half dozen before 1925, when the rumour of the monster was taken up by a Vancouver paper and its modern history began. The idea, then popular, that the creature was a giant sturgeon was contradicted by many reports of a long-necked animal.

A classic case was the sighting in July 1959 by Dick Miller (the editor of the *Vernon Advertiser*) and his wife. Three days later he published his own account of the creature:

Returning from a cruise down the Okanagan Lake, travelling at 10 miles an hour [16 km/h], I noticed, about 250 feet [75 metres] in our wake, what appeared to be the serpent. On picking up the field glasses my thoughts were verified. It was Ogopogo and it was travelling a great deal faster than we were. I would judge around 15 to 17 miles an hour [24 to 27 km/h]. The head was about 9 inches [23 centimetres] above the water. The head was definitely snake-like with a blunt nose. . . . [They turned the boat round to approach the creature.] Our excitement was short-lived. We watched for

about three minutes, as Ogie did not appear to like the boat coming on him broadside, very gracefully reduced the five humps which were so plainly visible, lowered his head and gradually submerged. At no time was the tail visible. The family's version of the colour is very dark greenish. . . . This sea serpent glides gracefully in a smooth motion (without snake-like undulations sideways). This would lead one to believe that in between the humps it possibly has some type of fin, which it works together or possibly individually to control direction.

Ogopogo has been the subject of a much disputed ciné film, taken by Art Folden in August 1968. He and his wife were driving back to their home in Chase, along the shores of the lake. At a point on Highway 97, just

Above: Arlene B. Gaal, who has made Ogopogo her special study. In 1981 she photographed the monster, she believes

Right: Ogopogo, as filmed by Art Folden in August 1968. When the moving picture is viewed, three humps are apparent here

Above right: the creature leaves a wake as it moves off at high speed

Below: this plaque reflects the importance of Ogopogo to local tourism

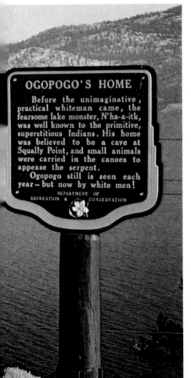

OGOPOGO'S HOME

Before the unimaginative, practical whiteman came, the fearsome lake monster, N'ha-a-itk, was well known to the primitive, superstitious Indians. His home was believed to be a cave at Squally Point, and small animals were carried in the canoes to appease the serpent.

Ogopogo still is seen each year – but now by white men!

DEPARTMENT OF
RECREATION & CONSERVATION

south of the town of Peachland, and about 300 yards (300 metres) from the lake, they saw something large moving through the water.

Art Folden, as luck would have it, was equipped with an 8-millimetre ciné camera, loaded with colour film and fitted with a telephoto lens. There was a short run of film left over from his coverage of the day's family outing. Focusing on the bay below he exposed a minute of film in short bursts, photographing the object only when it was visible on the surface.

Was Canada's most celebrated monster 'in the can' at last? Reluctant to expose himself to publicity, Folden kept quiet about the film, showing it only at home to his friends and relatives. A year later, in late 1969, his brother-in-law persuaded him to show the film publicly. When it was screened in February 1970 it caused a sensation. There then followed a spate of well-authenticated reports of sightings, but the film itself was disputed.

Pine trees in the foreground in some shots suggested that the object was about 60 feet (18 metres) long – the size of a canal barge. It

was some 3 feet (1 metre) across. It was clearly moving very fast with a definite wake. Some viewers thought they could make out a head and tail. Many local people were unconvinced, however. But Arlene Gaal, a local writer and author of a book dealing with the story of the Okanagan monster, investigated the site where the film was made, and became convinced that Art Folden's film showed some 'unusual form of life' in the deep waters of the lake.

In 1967 a black and white photograph, ostensibly showing Ogopogo, was discovered in the files of Kelowna Chamber of Commerce. The man who took it did not want any publicity for himself, even when the photograph was published in the local paper. He claimed to have seen the hump-backed creature in a small bay near Kelowna Bridge, but it had disappeared by the time he took the photograph. The picture probably shows 'windrows' – patterns on the surface created by the wind, and giving the appearance of humps.

Every year more reports came in. On 3 August 1976 a set of five photographs was taken by Ed Fletcher of Vancouver. For several hours that day he and his party chased Ogopogo back and forth while he took his series of colour photographs. These do indeed show a long, humped object moving through the water. Was it the monster? Or merely an effect of standing waves? (These are the stationary or slow-moving waves created where ordinary waves, travelling in different directions, overlap.) The witnesses had no doubts: they spoke of seeing a head and 'two things standing up from the head like the ears of a Dobermann pinscher'.

If any place provides ideal conditions for investigating reports of lake monsters it is Okanagan Lake. But, as we shall see, only a few intrepid scientists and laymen have taken up the challenge they present.

Explanations for the reported sightings of monsters in the North American lakes are nearly as numerous as the reports themselves. The theory that an unknown species of water animal is awaiting discovery is still a prime contender

WHILE MONSTER-HUNTING expeditions to Loch Ness have received enormous publicity, far less is heard of the research carried out on North American lakes. Predictably, 'official' zoologists and fisheries officials have tended to dismiss reports of monsters; but occasionally they have been more open-minded and have thrown resources into the search for unknown creatures.

Reports of strange animals in Lake Pohenegamook, in Quebec, started as long ago as 1874, and there was another spate of sightings in the 1920s. In 1957 Dr Vadim Vladikov, Director of the Quebec Department of Game and Fisheries, launched an investigation into the monster, which came to be called Ponik, or the Pohenegamook Sea Cow. According to descriptions given to Dr Vladikov, Ponik was:

> an animal between 12 and 18 feet [3.5 and 5.5 metres] long, brown or black in colour, with a round black back 2 or 3 feet [60 or 90 centimetres] wide, and a sawtooth fin down the centre. Any time anyone approaches close, the animal slithers away and sinks below the lake's surface.

Dr Vladikov, however, could find no tangible evidence of the creature. In the mid 1970s it was again investigated, this time by an expedition set up by an American organisation, the Society for the Investigation of the Unexplained. For 10 days three divers searched for the animal with the aid of sonar,

and they did obtain a trace of an object about 25 feet (7.5 metres) long underneath their boat, and on film they recorded a rather murky dark shape.

Other Canadian lake monsters have been investigated by qualified scientists. For many years the lakes north of Winnipeg have produced numerous sightings of unidentified animals. Lake Manitoba has been a particularly prolific source of reports since the first in 1908, but the sightings of 1960 were astounding. On 22 July 20 people

Above: the monster of Lake Champlain, on the border between Canada and the United States. The length of body seen above the water has been reported as about 20 feet (6 metres)

Below: Lake Champlain in the grip of winter ice

saw 'a large reptile'. Three weeks later on the same beach – now, naturally, named 'Manipogo Beach' – 17 people saw three monsters: two large ones and a smaller one.

These reports aroused the keen interest of Dr James A. Macleod, Chairman of the Zoological Department of the University of Manitoba. Dr Macleod was open-minded enough to take seriously the possibility that some prehistoric reptile did indeed survive in

The ones that got away

the northern end of the lake. But his research was short-lived because it was hard to find the finance to back the study of such ideas.

Lake Champlain, which straddles the Canadian-American border, has been the subject of much research in recent years, and possibly our best chance of finding out what these mysterious animals are lies here. The first reliable reports came from 1819, when pioneer settlers near Port Henry, New York state, saw the creature in Bulwagga Bay. After more than a half century of silence on the subject, there was a spate of sightings in the 1870s. The creature was reported by an excursion party in Horseshoe Bay, and during the summer of 1871 by the passengers of the steamer *Curlew*. The accounts spoke of a head raised on an erect neck, leaving a wake 30 to 40 feet (9 to 12 metres) long.

These reports came to the notice of the great P.T. Barnum, who in 1873 offered a reward of $50,000 for the hide of the 'sea serpent', which was to be sent to New York's State Hall in a copper boiler. On 30 October of that year the monster was given further celebrity by Thomas Nast, the crusading cartoonist of *Harper's Weekly* (best known for his part in bringing down the corrupt Tammany politician 'Boss' Tweed). Nast delighted the lecture audience with his baroque rendering of the creature.

This was all good fun, but even Barnum's tempting prize did not produce substantial evidence. However, in July 1880 a Dr Brigham and Mr Ashley Shelters saw the animal in Missiquoi Bay, in the Canadian waters of the lake. As they afterwards told the story:

portions of its body fully 20 feet [6 metres] in length appeared above the surface of the water. . . . [Its head was] as large as a flour barrel . . . of irregular shape . . . eyes being of greenish tinge.

Captain Mooney, sheriff of Clinton County, made a report of great interest. The animal he saw raised its head 4 or 5 feet (1.2 or 1.5 metres) out of the rough water; it was about 25 feet (7.5 metres) long and the exposed neck was 7 inches (18 centimetres) across. Mooney noted the muscles contracting in its neck, which was curved like that 'of a goose

Above: Lake Champlain's mystery creature, as photographed by Sandra Mansi in 1977. Sceptics suggest that what seem to be the head and neck are in reality the fin of a small whale, appearing above the water as the creature rolls on its side

Below: Ponik, the monster that supposedly inhabits Lake Pohenegamook in Quebec, is noteworthy for the sawtooth fin along its back. It is thought that sonar equipment detected it on one occasion

when about to take flight'.

Even more astonishing was a report of an animal hauling itself some 6 feet (2 metres) onto the shore at Cumberland Head in September 1899. It was said to be dark on top and lighter underneath – the camouflage colours one would expect for an aquatic animal.

By 1982 there were over 130 reports of the Lake Champlain monster. Of these 33 mention a long neck, the one feature that distinguishes reports of lake monsters from Loch Ness to Patagonia. It is hard to believe that any conventional explanation, such as a large fish, an otter or a seal, can account for all the details of the evidence.

Naturally, odd stories abound among the lake shore families. According to Carl Washburn – who had himself seen the monster while out fishing with his father in 1900 – 'another serpent had been caught and tied up near North Beach in Burlington'. Unfortunately, it escaped.

We owe the fact that so many reports have been preserved to the personal interest of a local journalist, Walter Hard, editor of *Vermont Life*. The part played by intelligent local editors in recording incidents such as the lake monster sightings cannot be overemphasised. One Scottish editor says her paper never publishes reports of water monsters, as a matter of policy. Fortunately, some others are more enlightened.

Extensive coverage of lake monster stories has the regrettable consequence that every possible oddity from the lake is twisted into a 'sea serpent' story. In 1945 a syndicated news

story was distributed under the headline 'Baby sea serpent taken in Vermont water – may be offspring of lake monster'. It reported that Erwin Bell of Burlington, an employee of the Champlain Transportation Company, captured a 14-inch (35-centimetre) 'reptile' in shallow water at Shelburne Bay. It resembled a small alligator, except that it had smaller jaws. Bell himself supposed that this 'baby sea serpent' was some kind of salamander – and he was probably correct.

The hero of Lake Champlain monster research is Joseph M. Zarzynski. In 1975 Zarzynski, then a 25-year-old social studies teacher, became 'almost obsessed' with the problem. From then on he and his friends made annual expeditions to the lake, following up old reports and discovering new ones. Exploration around Lake Champlain is difficult and costly. But his persistence has begun to pay off. Lacking the resources that have been expended on Loch Ness over the years, he has built up an immense dossier of reports, and has investigated the lake with great fortitude.

One thing disturbs him. He has noted that there seem to be fewer sightings of long-necked creatures in the years since 1920. The descriptions available from the early decades of this century and from the last century are also better than the later ones. The ever-increasing recreational use of the lake may be putting pressure on the monsters and gradually wiping them out, he surmises. In 1979 he appealed for protection of the creatures. In October 1980 the town trustees of Port Henry declared their waters off limits to anyone intent on harming the Champ, as the lake creature had been dubbed, and efforts were under way to get the legal protection of

Phineas T. Barnum, the great American showman, made his own contribution – of questionable value – to the study of unknown lake creatures by offering the huge sum of $50,000 for the Lake Champlain monster. He would have been content with the hide of the monster – which, fortunately, no hunter succeeded in providing

the New York state authorities.

The Zarzynski expeditions brought the Champ to the attention of newspapers and magazines all over the world, and made it almost as famous as Nessie. Then, at the end of June 1981, a colour photograph said to show the monster was published and aroused heated controversy. The photographer, Sandra Mansi, said she had taken the picture in July 1977 with a pocket camera. It showed the creature at the surface, its long neck curved back over a low humped body.

The Optical Sciences Center at the University of Arizona was asked to examine the print – the original negative had vanished. Professor B.R. Frieden, assisted by J.R. Greenwell, pronounced the print genuine. But Professor Paul Kurtz of the State University of New York, well-known as a debunker of all things mysterious and unexplained, said he thought the monster was as real as UFOs, the bigfoot – or the tooth fairy. However, another academic, Roy Mackal of Chicago University, speculated that the picture might show a zeuglodon – a primitive form of whale.

Sandra Mansi's inability to remember exactly where the photograph was taken has given ammunition to her critics. But the search for a monster in Lake Champlain goes on. Clifford Rollins of Rutland, Vermont, who considers all the fuss about monsters to be 'horse manure', has offered a reward of $500 on Champ – dead or alive. This is little enough reward for solving a centuries-old mystery – especially compared with Barnum's offer – and so far there have been no claimants.

Monsters have often been dismissed as myths, hoaxes or misperceptions. The small sample of cases briefly described in these

A touch of the sun

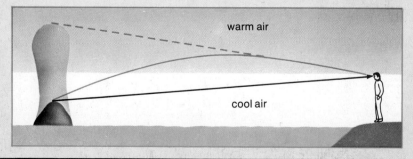

An atmospheric effect that could distort ordinary objects to give rise to monster reports has been described by W.H. Lehn, a Canadian scientist. It can occur when a layer of relatively warm air lies over cold air just above the water. Light rays travelling upwards from an object in the water, such as a boulder, are then deflected downward in the transition region between the two temperature zones (below). A person at an appropriate distance will see a composite of multiple images of the object – one

warm air

cool air

formed by light rays that have travelled in a straight line to his eye, and others formed by rays that have followed a curved path. This composite image of the object can be distorted in a vast number of different ways. One of the most common effects is to 'stretch' the image upwards, without making it correspondingly wider. The long thin shape resulting is very like many descriptions of sea serpents' necks. The object may be sufficiently distinctive to be recognisable – for example, it may be a ship. Or the atmospheric conditions may change, leaving the object in plain view. But in other cases the shifting layers of cold and warm air can create the illusion of a creature submerging and reappearing. The object may also have its own real motion: for example, a 'sea serpent' may be a killer whale, projecting its head from the water briefly – a hunting procedure that is called 'spy-hopping'. The phenomenon is, in fact, a mirage.

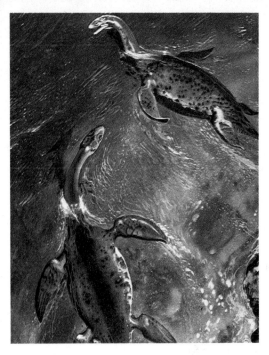

Left: two plesiosaurs of the Jurassic era. It is often suggested that some of them survived their supposed extinction and are the modern lake monsters

Below: the white whale, or beluga, which inhabits Arctic seas and rivers, and is often cited as the cause of monster sightings

therefore better able to cope with changes of water temperature.

Others have looked for less radical explanations. At Lake Flathead in Montana it has always been thought that the local monster might be a giant sturgeon. There are instances of Pacific sturgeon up to 18 feet (5.5 metres) in length; but in Russia they have been known to grow to about 26 feet (8 metres). Giant sticklebacks, manatees, white whales – these are other theories that have been proposed. And then there are the really radical theories: the suggestions that, because they have proved so elusive, like 'manimals' and giant flying creatures, they are psychic manifestations – perhaps a product of a particular witness's mind at a particular place and time.

But if the monsters exist and are of ordinary flesh and blood, then it is likely that the mystery will be solved one day, by the stranding of a carcase – or the capture of a large aquatic creature with distinctive eyes, a furry hide and a strange cry.

articles should make it clear that such wholesale dismissals are unjustified. Hoaxes and journalistic fabrication cover only a few incidents, which have been easily exposed. But we are still far from any solution to the mystery of what these creatures are.

Some reports of monsters may well have been optical illusions. Professor Waldemar H. Lehn of the University of Winnipeg has suggested that a distortion of the paths of light waves – a mirage – over the cold waters of a lake can cause ordinary objects and animals, such as a lake shore boulder, to appear greatly elongated, giving the long-necked appearance that is so typical of all monster photographs. But Dr Lehn insists that it is not the aim of his proposal 'to discredit the existence of yet unidentified animals or species, for there is impressive evidence to the contrary from sonar data and underwater photography'.

But while this may account for part of the evidence, it would be ridiculous as an explanation for the accounts of creatures 20 to 40 feet (6 to 12 metres) long, capable of hauling themselves onto the shore or making off at great speed. In many cases it is quite clear that the witnesses have seen something large, animate and terrifying.

Could it be that what they have seen is normal enough, but out of place? It has been suggested by the writer Loren Coleman that the monsters in the Californian Lake Folsom are errant crocodiles; however, a crocodile is unlikely to survive in the cold water of a mountain lake.

The same argument was brought against the suggestion that sea serpents and, by extension, lake monsters are surviving prehistoric reptiles, animals along the lines of long-necked plesiosaurs. But it has been suggested that some of the prehistoric reptiles may well have been 'warm-blooded' and

Right: a manatee, or sea cow – a plant-eating mammal confined to shallow tropical waters. If lake-dwelling cousins exist they may account for a few of the reports of monsters

Half human and half fish, mermaids and mermen have appeared many times over the centuries. But, asks PAUL BEGG, are the merfolk merely colourful figments of our imagination – or do they really exist?

ACCORDING TO THE South African *Pretoria News* of 20 December 1977, a mermaid had been found in a storm sewer in the Limbala Stage III township, Lusaka. The reports are garbled and it is difficult to tell who saw what – and what exactly it was they saw – but it seems that the 'mermaid' was first seen by some children and, as the news spread, so a crowd gathered. One reporter was told that the creature appeared to be a 'European woman from the waist up, whilst the rest of her body was shaped like the back end of a fish, and covered with scales.'

Legends about mermaids and mermen stretch back into antiquity and can be found in the folklore of almost every nation in the world. Merfolk have been seen and vouched for down the ages by witnesses of attested integrity – and they continue to be seen today.

The earliest merman in recorded history is the fish-tailed god Ea, more familiarly known as Oannes, one of the three great gods of the Babylonians. He had dominion over

A fishy tale

the sea and was also the god of light and wisdom, and the bringer of civilisation to his people. Originally Oannes was the god of the Akkadians, a Semitic people of the northern part of Babylonia from whom the Babylonians derived their culture, and was worshipped in Akkad as early as 5000 BC.

Almost all we know about the cult of Oannes is derived from the surviving fragments of a three-volume history of Babylonia written by Berossus, a Chaldean priest of Bel in Babylon, in the third century BC. In the 19th century, Paul Emil Botta, the French vice-consul in Mosul, Iraq, and an enthusiastic archaeologist – albeit one whose primary concern was loot – discovered a remarkable sculpture of Oannes dating from the eighth century BC, in the palace of the Assyrian king Sargon II at Khorabad, near Mosul. The sculpture, along with a rich collection of carved slabs and cuneiform inscriptions, is now held in the Louvre in Paris.

Another early fish-tailed god was Dagon of the Philistines who is mentioned in the Bible: I Samuel 5:1–4. The Ark of the Covenant was placed next to a statue of Dagon in a temple dedicated to Dagon in Ashod, one of the five great Philistine city states. The following day the statue was found to have 'fallen upon his face to the earth before the ark of the Lord'. Amid much consternation

and, no doubt, great fear, the people of Ashod set the statue of Dagon in its place again, but the following day it was again found fallen before the Ark of the Covenant, this time the head and the hands having broken off.

It is also probable that the wife and daughters of Oannes were fish-tailed, but the surviving representations of them are vague and it is impossible to be sure. However, no doubts surround Atargatis, sometimes known as Derceto, a Semitic Moon goddess. In his *De dea Syria* the Greek writer Lucian (*c.* AD 120–*c.* 180) described her: 'Of this Derceto likewise I saw in Phoenicia a drawing in which she is represented in a curious form; for in the upper half she is a woman, but from the waist to the lower extremities runs in the tail of a fish.'

Fish-tailed deities can be found in almost every culture of the ancient world but by medieval times they had become humanoid sea-dwellers. One of the most important scientific influences on the Middle Ages was Pliny the Elder (AD 23–79), a Roman administrator and encyclopedic writer who died in the eruption of Vesuvius that destroyed Pompeii (and whose 15th-century statue outside Como Cathedral looks disconcertingly like Harpo Marx). As far as medieval scholars were concerned, if Pliny said that something was so then it was

Top left: the 'Fejee mermaid' that was the star attraction of Phineas T. Barnum's touring show in 1842. Barnum, a cynical American showman who coined the phrase 'every crowd has a silver lining', advertised the creature with posters depicting voluptuous mermaids, similar to the painting by Waterhouse (top). The 'mermaid' was perhaps a freak fish

undeniably so. Of mermaids, Pliny wrote:

> I am able to bring forth for mine authors divers knights of Rome . . . who testifie that in the coast of the Spanish Ocean neere unto Gades, they have seen a Mere-man, in every respect resembling a man as perfectly in all parts of the bodie as might bee. . . .

Why, if the man so perfectly resembled a human, the 'divers knights of Rome' thought they had seen a *mer*man is not clear, but Pliny was convinced that merfolk were real and that they were seen regularly.

Tales of merfolk proliferated and were, oddly, encouraged by the Church, which found it politic to adapt ancient heathen legends to its own purpose. Mermaids were included in bestiaries, and carvings of them were featured in many churches and cathedrals. A fine example of a mermaid carving can

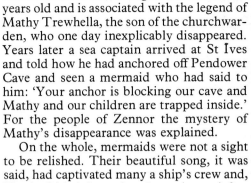

be seen in the church at Zennor, Cornwall, on a bench end. It is thought to be about 600 years old and is associated with the legend of Mathy Trewhella, the son of the churchwarden, who one day inexplicably disappeared. Years later a sea captain arrived at St Ives and told how he had anchored off Pendower Cave and seen a mermaid who had said to him: 'Your anchor is blocking our cave and Mathy and our children are trapped inside.' For the people of Zennor the mystery of Mathy's disappearance was explained.

On the whole, mermaids were not a sight to be relished. Their beautiful song, it was said, had captivated many a ship's crew and, like the fabled sirens, lured vessels to grief on dangerous rocks.

Above: the mermaid who is said to have abducted one Mathy Trewhella, carved for posterity on a pew in the church at Zennor, Cornwall. The carving is about 600 years old, but the legend may be considerably older

Left: mermaids, mermen and mer-children disport themselves in the turbulent sea

Below: the mermaid as erotic fantasy figure. She was widely believed to prey on drowning sailors, making them her sexual slaves

When mermaids surface

In the late Elizabethan, early Jacobean age belief in the mermaid waxed and waned. Men such as Frances Bacon and John Donne gave rational explanations for many natural phenomena, including the mermaid – yet it was also a time of blossoming maritime travel and some of the great seamen of the age told of personal encounters with merfolk. In 1608 Henry Hudson, the navigator and explorer (after whom the Hudson Bay territories are named), made the following matter-of-fact entry in his log:

> This morning, one of our companie looking over boord saw a Mermaid, and calling up some of the companie to see her, one more came up, and by that time she was come close to the ship's side, looking earnestly on the men: a little after, a Sea came and overturned her: From the Navill upward, her back and breasts were like a womans (as they say that saw her) her body as big as one of us; her skin very white; and long haire hanging down behinde, of colour blacke; in her going downe they saw her tayle, which was like the tayle of a Porposse, and speckled like a Macrell. Their names that saw her were Thomas Hilles and Robert Raynar.

Hudson was a very experienced seaman who surely knew the calibre of his men and presumably would not have bothered to record a blatant hoax. Also, the report itself shows that his men were familiar with the creatures of the sea and were of the opinion that this creature was exceptional – which, if their description is accurate, indeed it was.

But the great age for mermaids was the 19th century. More mermaids were faked and displayed to awed crowds at fairs and exhibitions than at any other time. It was also the period in which several remarkable sightings were reported, including two of the best authenticated on record.

On 8 September 1809 *The Times* published the following letter from one William Munro:

> About twelve years ago when I was Parochial Schoolmaster at Reay

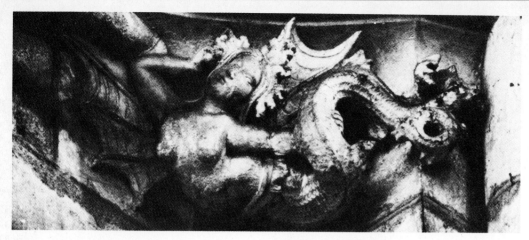

Left: a mermaid cornice decoration in Sens Cathedral, France

Below: the sirens attempt to lure Ulysses and his crew to their doom with their irresistible singing. Seen here as mermaids, they are more often thought of as half woman, half bird (below right)

Bottom: a predatory mermaid seizes a sailor and carries him off to her lair

[Scotland], in the course of my walking on the shore at Sandside Bay, being a fine warm day in summer, I was induced to extend my walk towards Sandside Head, when my attention was arrested by the appearance of a figure resembling an unclothed human female, sitting on a rock extending into the sea, and apparently in the action of combing its hair, which flowed around its shoulders, and of a light brown colour. The resemblance which the figure bore to its prototype in all its visible parts was so striking, that had not the rock on which it was sitting been dangerous for bathing, I would have been constrained to have regarded it as really a human form, and to an eye unaccustomed to the situation, it most undoubtedly appeared as such. The head was covered with hair of the colour above mentioned and shaded on the crown, the forehead round, the face plump, the cheeks ruddy, the eyes blue, the mouth and lips of natural form, resembling those of a man; the teeth I could not discover, as the mouth was shut; the breasts and abdomen, the arms and fingers of the size of a full-grown body of the human species, the fingers, from the action in which the hands were employed, did not appear to be webbed, but to this I am not positive. It remained on the rock three or four minutes after I observed it, and was exercised during that period in combing its hair, which was long and thick, and of which it appeared proud, and then dropped into the sea. . . .

Whatever it was that William Munro saw and described in such detail, he was not alone, for he adds that several people 'whose veracity I never heard disputed' had claimed to have seen the mermaid, but until he had seen it himself he 'was not disposed to credit their testimony'. But, as they say, seeing is believing.

In about 1830 inhabitants of Benbecula, in the Hebrides, saw a young mermaid playing happily in the sea. A few men tried to swim out and capture her, but she easily outswam

them. Then a little boy threw stones at her, one of which struck the mermaid and she swam away. A few days later, about 2 miles (3 kilometres) from where she was first seen, the corpse of the little mermaid was washed ashore. The tiny, forlorn body brought crowds to the beach and after the corpse had been subjected to a detailed examination it was said that:

the upper part of the creature was about the size of a well-fed child of three or four years of age; with an abnormally developed breast. The hair was long, dark and glossy; while the skin was white, soft and tender. The lower part of the body was like a salmon, but without scales.

Among the many people who viewed the tiny corpse was Duncan Shaw, factor (land agent) for Clanranald, baron-bailie and sheriff of the district. He ordered that a coffin and shroud be made for the mermaid and that she be peaceably laid to rest.

Of the many faked merfolk of this period, only one or two need be mentioned to

illustrate the ingenuity of the fakes and the
fakers. A famous example is recounted in *The
vicar of Morwenstow* by Sabine Baring-
Gould. The vicar in question was the eccentric Robert S. Hawker who, for reasons best
known to himself, in July 1825 or 1826
impersonated a mermaid off the shore of
Bude in Cornwall. When the Moon was full
he swam or rowed to a rock not far from the
shore and there donned a wig made from
plaited seaweed, wrapped oilskins around his
legs and, naked from the waist upwards, sang
– far from melodiously – until observed from
the shore. When the news of the mermaid
spread throughout Bude people flocked to
see it, and Hawker repeated his performance.

Mermaids have continued to be seen in
more recent years. One was seen in 1947 by a
fisherman on the Hebridean island of Muck.
She was sitting on a floating herring box
(used to preserve live lobsters) combing her
hair. As soon as she realised she was being
observed she plunged into the sea. Until his
death in the late 1950s the fisherman could
not be persuaded to believe that he had not
seen a mermaid.

In 1978, a Filipino fisherman, 41-year-old
Jacinto Fatalvero, not only saw a mermaid
one moonlit night but was helped by her to
secure a bountiful catch. Little more is
known, however, because having told his
story, Fatalvero became the butt of jokes, the

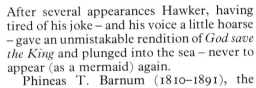

After several appearances Hawker, having
tired of his joke – and his voice a little hoarse
– gave an unmistakable rendition of *God save
the King* and plunged into the sea – never to
appear (as a mermaid) again.

Phineas T. Barnum (1810–1891), the
great American showman to whom are attributed two telling statements – 'There's one
[a sucker] born every minute' and 'Every
crowd has a silver lining' – bought a mermaid
that he had seen being shown at a shilling a
time in Watson's Coffee House in London. It
was a dreadful, shrivelled-up thing – probably a freak fish – but Barnum added it to the
curiosities he had gathered for his 'Greatest
Show on Earth'. His trick, however, was to
hang up outside his 'mermaid' sideshow an
eye-catching picture of three beautiful
women frolicking in an underwater cavern;
under this he had a notice that read: 'A
Mermaid is added to the museum – no extra
charge.' Drawn by the picture and the implication of what would be seen within, many
thousands of people paid their admission fee
and went to see this spectacle. As Barnum
said, if the shrivelled-up 'mermaid' did not
meet with their expectations, the rest of the
exhibits were worth the money.

object of derision – and, inevitably, hounded
by the media. Understandably he refused
to say another word.

It is widely accepted that the mermaid
legend sprang from the misidentification of
two aquatic mammals, the manatee and
dugong, and possibly seals. Obviously many
reports can be thus explained, but does this
explanation satisfactorily account for what
was seen by Henry Hudson's sailors in 1608
or for the mermaid seen by the schoolmaster
William Munro? Were these and other similar sightings sea-mammals or mermaids?

One suggestion, perhaps slightly tongue
in cheek, is that the merfolk are real, the
descendants of our distant ancestors who
came ashore from the sea. The merfolk, of
course, are descended from those ancestors
who either stayed in the sea or chose to return
to it. Human embryos have gills that usually
disappear before birth, but some babies are
born with them and they have to be removed
surgically.

But, whatever she is, the mermaid has a
long history of sightings and continues to be
seen. For this we should be thankful; the
romance and folklore of the sea would be all
the poorer without her.

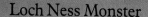

Local legends have long told of mysterious creatures living deep in the dark and brooding waters of Loch Ness. ADRIAN SHINE, director of a research project on Loch Ness, gives the background to the story

Rumours, legends and glimpses

THE WORLD has fewer and fewer unexplored regions – hostile or inaccessible regions such as jungles, mountain ranges, remote islands or the depths of seas or inland waters. But these are the places where any remaining unknown creatures of our Earth are likely to be found.

A scientist on the trail of an unknown animal must have a receptive ear to the observations of any people living nearby. Proof of its existence comes with verifiable sightings supported by scientific evidence. Although sceptics will dismiss out of hand local tales, folklore and legend, these can often only be exposed as true or false after painstaking research and documentation. In some cases this has been carried out successfully and 'monsters' have been identified as genuine living creatures.

Man's curiosity about the more inaccessible corners of the Earth has led to some startling discoveries. Only recently the impenetrable forests of the Congo revealed the mountain gorilla, the world's largest ape, and 'an antelope with the head of a giraffe and the hindquarters of a zebra' was identified as a species now known as the okapi. Another weird creature, also discovered this century, is the so-called Komodo dragon, which inhabits the remoter islands of Indonesia.

Situated in the Great Glen, a tear in the Earth's surface cutting across the centre of Scotland, Loch Ness is a relatively unexplored region, as impenetrable and hostile to man as any mountain or jungle. At its deepest point there is possibly more than

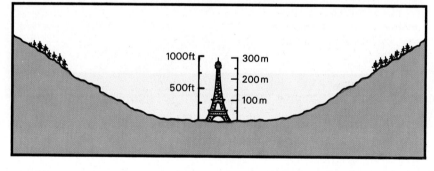

985 feet (3000 metres) of water; it stretches over a length of nearly 22 miles (35 kilometres); and because of the fine deposits of peat in the water, underwater visibility is very poor. Investigation of an area such as this requires more than human willpower or physical prowess: only the most sophisticated technological aids will – perhaps – finally unravel the mysteries of this, the largest body of fresh water in Britain.

Scientific interest in the dark depths of the sea was sparked off when commercial requirements of laying telegraph cable in the 1850s provided the stimulus and the means. Until a severed cable encrusted with animal life was raised from a depth of 6000 feet (1830 metres), it was commonly thought that all life ceased below 1800 feet (550 metres).

Britain, as the leading maritime nation, was quick to take the lead in oceanography with the dispatch of the *Challenger* expedition; this spent five years, between 1871 and 1876, dredging and sounding waters around the world. There was still, however, a

Top: the eerie beauty of Loch Ness at dawn

Above: in 1968 a submarine allegedly dived to a depth of 820 feet (250 metres) in Loch Ness; the official estimate of the phenomenal depth of the loch is 754 feet (230 metres), although other sources claim it is as much as 975 feet (297 metres) deep. The loch is less than 1 mile (1.6 kilometres) wide, and the sides plunge unusually steeply from the shore. But perhaps the most astounding feature of the loch is the sheer volume of water it contains – large enough to hold the population of the world, the loch has plenty of room for unknown creatures

Above: Komodo dragons, creatures so strange no one believed rumours of their existence until they were discovered earlier this century on a remote Indonesian island

Right: an ornate sea-dragon figurehead from a 9th-century Viking burial ship. Norse and Celtic mythologies are full of legends about the sea serpents of the seas of northern Europe

Below: a 'gigantic sea saurian' from a 19th-century English zoological work. The book contains a number of contemporary accounts of sightings of sea serpents

great reluctance to explore the freshwater world and the leader of that expedition, John Murray, had to launch a private venture to make the first study of British fresh water. This bathymetric survey of the Scottish lochs was mainly a sounding excercise that revealed the great depths of these land-locked waters.

The largest Scottish lochs are remarkable not only for their volume but for their depth, which often exceeds that of the sea surrounding our shores. Loch Morar, for example, is over 1000 feet (305 metres) deep – greater than the height of the Eiffel Tower in Paris.

The Scottish lochs all originate from the same period as the fjord-like lakes of Scandinavia and Ireland. Glaciers from successive Ice Ages deepened existing valleys, including the Great Glen fault line of Loch Ness, until about 10,000 years ago, when the ice retreated for the last time. For a while some of the lochs remained open to the sea, which had risen slightly owing to the water released by the melting ice. Then, relieved of the weight of the ice, the land rose steadily and the surface of Loch Ness, for example, now lies about 52 feet (16 metres) above sea level.

Because of the connection between these waters and the sea, it is interesting to recall some 'sea monster' tales that bear certain similarities to the 'monsters' mentioned in eyewitness accounts at Loch Ness.

Serpents of the sagas

Ever since the prows of the Vikings' longships bore the Sea Dragon as a figurehead, Norse and Celtic folklore has been full of references to a long-necked, hump-backed creature of the northern waters. Bishop Erik Pontoppidan of Bergen, in his *Natural history of Norway*, published in 1752, made reference to two sea monsters seen occasionally off the coast of Norway. The first was the great kraken, the subject of mythology and fisherman's tales – 'round, flat and full of arms'. The giant squid was not recognised by scientists as the origin of the kraken legend until the 1870s, when carcases of this species were washed ashore in Newfoundland.

This coincided with the dispatch of the *Challenger* expedition and an increasing awareness of the possibilities of discovery in the oceans of the world. In 1852 a French scientist had pronounced similar remains to be a vegetable – and the existence of such an animal to be 'a contradiction of the great laws of harmony and equilibrium that have sovereign rule over living nature as well as senseless and inert matter'. Science is often dogmatic when discussing subjects it is not equipped to investigate.

The second of Pontoppidan's 'mythical' creatures was the Soe-Orm – or sea snake. The most famous of the reports he collected was that of Lorenz von Ferry, Royal Commander and Pilot General of Bergen; this provided the classic 'sea serpent' impression

of a snake-like creature, but with vertical undulations. This creature was sighted near Molde, in Norway, as von Ferry's vessel was being rowed – probably due to lack of wind – on a very calm, hot day late in August 1746. Von Ferry was reading a book when he noticed the helmsman was off course; he was informed by members of the crew that they were attempting to avoid a sea serpent ahead. He ordered them to close in on it since, despite rumours, he had hitherto doubted its existence.

Sea-serpents ahead!

The grey-coloured head of the creature was held nearly a yard from the surface of the water and resembled that of a horse with a white mane. It had large eyes and mouth and seven or eight 'folds or coils' (possibly humps) were visible about 2 feet (60 centimetres) apart. When von Ferry fired at the creature it dived. For Pontoppidan's benefit, von Ferry later ordered two of his seamen to give sworn testimonies before a public court in Bergen. Pontoppidan would 'not entirely disbelieve what is related of the water snakes found in freshwater lakes'.

In Scandinavia many lakes have traditions of animals occasionally surfacing; these include Lake Suldal and Lake Storsjö, where implements made at the end of the 19th century to catch the 'animal' can still be seen. Similar stories involve Lake Okanagan in North America, the Lagerflot in Iceland and the Connemara loughs in Ireland which are inhabited by the pooka, kelpie or *each uisge* – 'water-horse' in Gaelic.

The kelpie and water-horse appear in the folklore of the Scottish Highlands. Strangely, however, although the first written account of a water monster in the River Ness concerns an incident in AD 565, no particular importance was given to reports from Loch Ness until quite recently. That first account

was drawn from St Adaman's *Life of St Columba*, which talked of 'the driving away of a certain water monster by the virtue of prayer of the holy man'.

Appearances of this kind were – and to some extent still are – regarded with superstitious reticence as ill omens. 'Who has not heard of the Mhorag?' wrote James MacDonald at the turn of this century. 'The Mhorag as a rule only shows herself on Loch Morar whenever a member of a certain clan is about to die . . . the Mhorag detaches herself upon the surface in three distinct portions, one portion representing death, another a coffin, and a third a grave.'

It was most unlikely that this sort of tale would be passed on in the 19th century by the local highlanders to the culturally and socially removed gentlemen from England, who visited during the shooting season; this makes the account in Lord Malmesbury's memoirs all the more significant.

Above: a sea-serpent from Konrad von Gerner's *Fischbuch* of 1598. At that time it was still commonly believed that monsters inhabiting the depths of the seas could be a hazard to shipping

Left: the kelpie, the malignant water-sprite of the Scottish lochs, which was said to lurk by the waterside, disguised as a horse, waiting for human victims. Some of the people who live near Loch Ness can remember, as children, being told not to bathe in the loch for fear of the kelpie

October 3rd 1857 – This morning my stalker and his boy gave me an account of a mysterious creature, which they say exists in Loch Arkaig, and which they call the Lake Horse. It is the same animal of which one has occasionally read accounts in newspapers as having been seen in the Highland lochs, and on the existence of which in Loch Assynt the late Lord Ellesmere wrote an interesting article. . . .

My stalker, John Stewart, at Achnacarry, has seen it twice, and both times at sunrise in summer on a bright sunny day, when there was not a ripple on the water. The creature was basking on the surface; he only saw the head and the hindquarters, proving that its back was hollow, which is not the shape of any fish or of a seal. Its head resembled that of a horse.

Lord Malmesbury commented that 'the Highlanders are very superstitious about this creature . . . and I believe they think it has something diabolical in its nature'.

Much more recently, the author Gavin Maxwell, who chose to exile himself on the west coast of Scotland, gave several accounts of similar creatures seen by friends and employees both in the sea and the sea lochs. These accounts come from skilled seamen with a lifetime's knowledge of the wildlife of the west coast.

Along with all the stories from other lochs, there have always been reports from Loch Ness. Some residents of the area can remember, as children, being told not to bathe in the loch for fear of the kelpie. But the loch really came to the public's notice only after 1933; in that year a road was blasted along the north shore and trees and undergrowth cut down to give a better view of the massive expanse of water. Among the more obvious effects of this development was the influx of visitors to the area – and so the 'sightings' of the Loch Ness 'monster' increased dramatically. The first widely publicised sighting was made on 14 April 1933 by Mr and Mrs Mackay and reported in the *Inverness Courier*. 'The creature disported itself for fully a minute, its body resembling that of a whale.' This sighting was swiftly followed by others – and so Loch Ness became a sensation throughout the world.

By now scientists had started to take an interest in freshwater biology, with the first British station beginning studies of microscopic animals and plants in Lake Windermere using primitive equipment. It was a decade before the development of sonar equipment and the aqualung would provide the means scientists needed to begin a systematic investigation of Loch Ness, and another three before advanced underwater camera techniques would make it possible to attempt to photograph the creature that is rumoured to live in the dark, peat-stained waters of the mysterious loch.

Below: a simplified distribution map of the recorded sightings of the Loch Ness monster. The monster is most often seen near the mouths of rivers

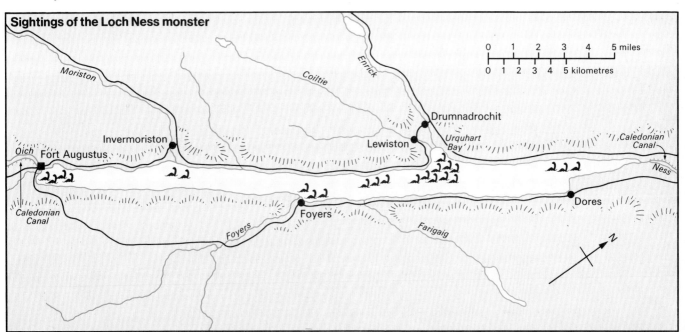

Sightings of the Loch Ness monster

Sounding out the sightings

Ever since the 1930s people have been attempting to capture the Loch Ness monster on film. The archives are full of alleged photographic evidence of the existence of the monster – but how much of it is genuine? And what does it tell us about the monster?

THE EXPLOSION of interest in what may or may not lurk in the dark depths of Loch Ness was sparked off by the Mackay sighting on 14 April 1933. Since then the volume of evidence has grown steadily – there were 50 other sightings in that year alone – and has been sustained ever since with many more sightings, photographs, films and other evidence as attempts have been made to investigate the 'monster'.

In addition to the better view afforded by tree-felling on the north side of the loch, press interest led to many sightings being documented; the two factors together could account for the apparent suddenness of the phenomenon. Once Loch Ness was publicly known to contain a mystery, people would obviously be on the lookout for any signs of the unusual and, by the same token, the interest would induce strong expectation and powerful suggestion.

The major difficulty in evaluating eyewitness accounts and evidence is one of subjectivity. An honest man may easily be mistaken or fooled; a dishonest one is quite likely to give a good impression; and an educated one may be imaginative. The fact is that without very specific experience, it is extremely difficult to judge time, size, distance or speed with any accuracy, especially over water. By pressing a witness to commit himself to just such details, the investigator is inadvertently contriving to make an honest man appear a liar or fool. So it is impossible to construct a particularly accurate picture of what has been seen by using this kind of material.

The loch itself presents problems because it plays tricks on the eyes. It is a large mass of water sometimes completely calm in a way that the sea, for example, rarely is, and its high shorelines cast deep shadows and reflections. In these conditions you can get a visual impression totally out of proportion to the actual cause – of small animals, water birds, boat wakes and wind. The wakes from boats passing through the loch, for example, can be reflected from the shores to form a standing wave in the centre of the loch after the particular boat has passed out of sight.

Despite these problems, thousands of

Above: is this the head of the Loch Ness monster? This photograph was taken, using an underwater camera, by Dr Robert Rines of the Academy of Applied Science, Massachusetts Institute of Technology, USA, on 20 June 1975. Although the peaty waters of the bottom of the loch make it difficult to identify what the photograph represents, it has been argued that the symmetry of the object shows it is animate; on the other hand, many experts hold that the photograph shows merely the bottom of the loch

Left: an artist's impression of the object in Dr Robert Rines's photograph. Some people believe the horns may be used by the monster as snorkel tubes to enable it to breathe without surfacing

Below: from the series of underwater photographs taken by Dr Robert Rines (see also page 190), an artist was able to build up this picture of what the Loch Ness monster might look like. It shows the long neck, small head and flippers mentioned in so many reports of sightings

Besides eyewitness evidence, there are the photographic records of surfacings. Although the photographic image may appear irrefutable, and may be seen to present measurable evidence that can be independently assessed, the limitations of the lens in fact make any such assessment very difficult. Photographs taken with ordinary equipment give far less information than the naked eye – and, sadly, the photographic print process is very easy to manipulate in order to produce fakes. Loch Ness is, naturally enough, fair game for hoaxers of all kinds.

The usual view of an object on the loch is that of a dark image on a light background. This makes the 'negative' fake simplicity itself since all that is needed is to draw a silhouette on the negative or print and then re-photograph the result, so producing an 'original' negative. One of the easiest and most frequently used ways of faking pictures

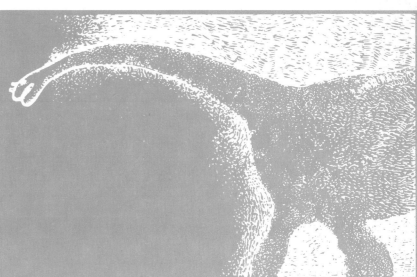

eyewitness sightings are now on record, thanks to the press, individual authors and investigative organisations such as the Loch Ness Investigation Bureau, which was active between 1962 and 1972. The descriptions are remarkably consistent, and describe a long-necked, hump-backed creature that sometimes moves at speed, both with neck raised and lowered, and at other times simply appears for a while and submerges quietly.

The first chronicler of the Loch Ness sightings was Lieutenant-Commander Rupert Gould who, in his book *The Loch Ness monster* (1934) described 42 sightings from 1923 to 1933 in a well-presented case. He felt that the creature was an isolated specimen that had become trapped in the loch. He was followed by Mrs Constance White, wife of the manager of the Caledonian Canal; her book *More than a legend*, published in 1957, contained references to over 60 sightings. She established that the phenomenon had not ceased after 1934 as some had believed and that sometimes more than one animal was seen at a time – suggesting a resident population. More recent authors include Tim Dinsdale, Ted Holliday, Peter Costello and Nick Witchell, all of whom have added more examples of eyewitness evidence; much of this evidence is drawn from the extensive files of the Loch Ness Investigation Bureau, which collected reports at the loch side.

The sheer volume of eyewitness evidence from Loch Ness and its intensity suggest there is a population of large animals in the water. This and some unexplained scientific findings, particularly through sonar, are all we can go by at present. Surface behaviour is so obviously uncharacteristic that no real pattern can be established. There are more sightings in the summer months, particularly at the mouth of rivers, and certainly more on calm, hot days. But weather conditions and the fact that summer marks the height of the tourist season must be taken into account.

is to photograph ordinary objects out of context. These range from the simple ruse of a pair of motor tyres, with a stone thrown in the water to cause disturbance, to quite sophisticated Loch Ness 'Muppets'. These photographs can, of course, be produced anywhere; background is generally absent since this tends to provide scale and make the object appear smaller and less significant. Where identifiable Loch Ness backgrounds are used, it is common to show existing features that have been slightly adapted, such as rocks in a line, logs or even a fence post adorned with a sock!

From time to time, however, photographs are produced that stimulate real interest. Those dating from 1933 to the present day may be divided into two main types – 'bad' ones that could well be genuine and 'good' ones that are probably not. The 'classic' pictures must be included in any discussion of the Loch Ness phenomenon, although very few are now considered significant evidence by the current Loch Ness and Morar Project. Not only do they differ markedly from one another, but none of the pictures taken during the comprehensive surface study by the Loch Ness Investigation Bureau over a 10-year period shows anything like the amount of body seen in the 'classic' photographs, although some show low-lying humps and wakes.

Ciné films are far harder to fake than still pictures; so, although their subject matter may still be open to debate, they do provide more valuable evidence. Two film sequences in particular are exceptional.

The first was shot on 23 April 1960 by Tim Dinsdale from the mouth of the River Foyers, which flows into Loch Ness from the south about a third of the way up from Fort Augustus. It shows a hump moving slowly away from him and then fast across his field of vision while submerging. The film was submitted to the Joint Air Reconnaissance Intelligence Centre (JARIC) by David James of the Loch Ness Investigation Bureau. In very broad terms, the analysts concluded the object was 'probably animate'. It was nearly $5\frac{1}{2}$ feet (1.7 metres) wide, moved through the water at a speed of about 10mph (16km/h) and appeared to submerge.

The second film, shot by Richard Raynor during the Loch Ness Expedition of 1967 on the morning of 13 June, is exceptional for its technical quality. The film, taken from opposite Dores at the north end of the loch, shows a wake, at the head of which a solid object appears from time to time; the object submerges as a boat enters the field of vision. Raynor is quite ready to entertain the possibility that the animal was an otter (the object was definitely animate); this is really the only possible candidate apart from an unknown animal. However JARIC – especially likely to be accurate in view of the photographic quality – estimates a possible length of 7 feet (2 metres) for the part that breaks the surface; an otter of this proportion would be, to say the least, remarkable.

This film seems to be the best we can expect from surface observation and photography. Although these better examples do suggest that a large animal is involved, they also demonstrate the limitations of this kind of evidence in terms of identification; aquatic creatures cannot be studied on the basis of what proportions of their body are by chance exposed above water.

It was not until 1970 that underwater photography was used as an investigative method. Its potential is enormous, since it should allow a complete profile view of the target to be obtained; in practice, however, the peaty water and limitations of normal underwater equipment reduce the range and coverage drastically. This makes interpretation of underwater pictures very difficult. The most interesting are two computer-enhanced pictures of a finlike object taken in 1972 by Dr Robert Rines of the Academy of Applied Science, Boston, Massachusetts, USA, with a time lapse camera fitted with a strobe flash. Whatever the biological discussions of this evidence, if the object is a fin it does not resemble that of any creature known to inhabit the loch.

Subsequent pictures taken by Rines in

Above: a still from Tim Dinsdale's famous film of 23 April 1960. It is very probably genuine – and, like most genuine photographs of the Loch Ness monster, it shows very little detail

Below: an example of just how misleading perfectly natural objects can sometimes be. The wake shown in this photograph is, experts agree, nothing more than a standing wave left by one of the heavy trawlers that regularly ply the Caledonian Canal, of which Loch Ness forms a part

1975 show six images other than the under-side of the boat from which the camera was slung; and it has been suggested that two of these are animate. Other upward shots show-ing the surface of the loch have brought suggestions of a 'major disturbance' and agitation of the camera. However the time lapse between these 'events' is 70 seconds and one sequence of these surface shots would actually imply that the camera was more or less at rest for at least two minutes rather than swinging. It has been argued that one object, the 'head', has sufficient sym-metry to suggest a living creature, with horns used for breathing without creating ripples, although this is obviously a matter of indi-vidual interpretation.

Unfortunately, this argument can be countered by the fact that two thirds of the images photographed in the same 24–hour period under the same conditions could by no stretch of the imagination be animate. Either the camera had touched the bottom

Photographs of the Loch Ness expedition of 1972–73: the team at Loch Ness (above); Dr Robert Rines examines one of the underwater cameras used in the search for the monster (left). Led by Dr Rines, the expedition team succeeded in taking the first ever underwater pictures of what was alleged to be the Loch Ness monster. A number of sophisticated techniques were used to obtain the pictures, including the use of sonar to trigger one of the cameras when large objects approached. A second expedition, mounted in 1975, also produced spectacular results, although some still think them controversial

through miscalculation of the depth or it had, in fact, come into contact with inanimate objects in midwater. With the shape of the camera frame and the fact that it would overbalance with the weight of the strobe light clamped above, the camera could tilt up or down if it touched the bottom.

But without doubt the most important class of evidence is that of the echo sounder and sonar. Developed during the Second World War as a submarine detection device, sonar relies on the reflection of transmitted sound waves by underwater targets. It is the only really effective instrument for 'seeing' underwater, particularly where the water is not clear, and by 1960 had been refined to a stage where it was used commercially in fishing – and in the Loch Ness investigations.

By far the most logical and relevant system of enquiry, sonar has also proved the most successful; most reasonably equipped teams have secured positive contacts with it. The 'hard evidence' that the system has provided is to some extent measurable. The problem, however, is that it requires some expertise to assess the results, and this ex-pertise is not generally found among zool-ogists. Also, the sonar at present likely to be used in Loch Ness cannot provide graphical representations.

The reflection of sound is caused mainly by the air cavities within a living creature and so an identification on sonar alone is not possible. At best a sonar record is a trace on a paper chart or a blip on a cathode ray tube. Fish shoals, temperature changes and rising gases are all possible causes of sonar contacts. On the positive side, with sonar it is possible to follow the movements of a target under water and to judge from this whether or not it is animate and even to gain some hints as to its identity.

So far teams from Oxford and Cambridge in 1962, Birmingham University in 1968–69, Vickers Oceanics in 1969, the Loch Ness Investigation Bureau between 1969 and 1970, Klein Associates and the Academy of Applied Sciences between 1970 and 1977 and the Partech Company in 1976–77 have all produced results that they consider indi-cate the presence of an animate contact larger than a salmon and displaying movement and diving rates different from those expected of fish. Some of the results are inconclusive, others positive.

For the most part the teams involved were experienced and in some cases expert; their evidence is not open to dispute, only to investigation. And, as with some of the photographs, attempts to discredit the evi-dence are as fruitless as overcredulous efforts to identify the type of animals seen.

A very strange fish?

What kind of creature is it that can survive in the cold, barren depths of Loch Ness? Where did it come from? Is it a mammal, a reptile or an amphibian? What does it look like?

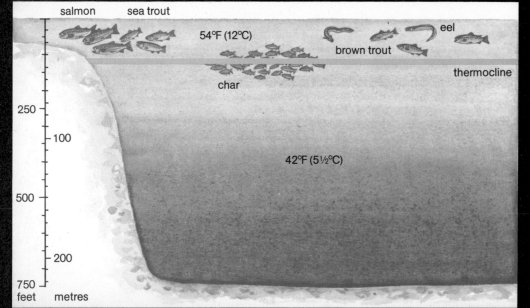

salmon   sea trout

54°F (12°C)

eel

brown trout

char

thermocline

250

100

42°F (5½°C)

500

200

750
feet   metres

Above: Loch Ness with Castle Urquhart on its lonely promontory in the background

Left: a section through Loch Ness in summer, showing its fish life, which is concentrated close to the surface. Here the temperature may rise as high as 54°F (12°C) in summer. Below a water layer known as the thermocline lies the main body of the loch. This cold, peaty water varies in temperature by no more than half a degree throughout the year and supports virtually no animal life

THERE ARE MANY QUESTIONS that have to be answered in considering Loch Ness as the possible home for one or more large creatures hitherto unidentified. For example, when could they have become established there, how could they exist and – most importantly – what could they possibly be?

Loch Ness, at the northern end of the Great Glen fault line that divides the Highlands of Scotland, is at least 700 feet (over 200 metres) deep and is connected by the River Ness to the sea, which is 52 feet (18 metres) below the level of water in the loch.

Ten thousand years ago, as the ice retreated from the north of Scotland for the last time, the Great Glen fault was opened up to the sea. At some time since then, the surrounding land rose, leaving Loch Ness connected to the sea only by the River Ness.

There is no question of Loch Ness being an evolutionary cul-de-sac, since any creatures that live in the loch must have arrived there after the retreat of the ice 10,000 years ago – a mere blink of the eye in the time-scale of evolution. And these creatures must have come from elsewhere – either from other freshwater areas, or from the sea.

It seems unlikely that any large creature could have entered the loch from freshwater areas – there are not, and never have been, any nearby, and travel to Loch Ness would have entailed considerable distances overland. Thus – and bearing in mind reports of a 'monster' sighted off the coast of Scotland – it seems reasonable to look to the sea for the origins of our creature.

All the larger aquatic species at present living in the loch are capable of migration via the river. The fish are mainly salmonids – salmon, sea trout, brown trout and char – and eels, which spend most of their adult life in fresh water before leaving to breed in the Sargasso Sea. The most likely explanation for the presence of any large unknown species is that it, too, entered from the sea via the River Ness. The salmonid fish, in fact, provide not only a parallel but also an incentive for an unknown species to remain in the loch, as further discussion will show.

Food for thought

As a habitat the loch is characterised not only by its great size but also by its stability. The majority of water in it does not alter in temperature by more than half a degree from $42°F$ ($5.5°C$). In summer the top 100 feet (or 30 metres) may warm up to $54°F$ ($12°C$), but this layer remains separated from the unchanged water underneath by what is known as the thermocline.

The potential food sources within the loch are plants, plankton, detritus (organic constituents of sediment) and fish. The dark, peaty water, steep sides and short summer restrict the growth of rooted plants, which are limited for the most part to the first 10 feet (3 metres) of water. Concentrations of bulky plants are close to the shore, so any

Above: a diver gathers material from the loch floor. Analysis of this matter provides an idea of the possible diet of a bottom-dwelling creature

Left: a salmon 'porpoising'. Salmon sometimes put on fantastic bursts of speed as they run up the fast-flowing rivers that lead into Loch Ness to spawn. Could it be that they are being chased by the Loch Ness monster?

creature feeding off these would be seen more often than recorded sightings suggest. All herbivorous animals require a very considerable volume of food to survive and the scarcity of aquatic vegetation in the loch rules out these species.

Some of the world's largest animals are plankton feeders – for instance, the largest mammal, the blue whale, and the largest fish, the basking and whale sharks – and it could be that the 'monster' also feeds on plankton. In general, however, the Scottish lochs are oligotrophic, which means they are very deep in relation to their surface area and are characterised by relative sterility. They also have sparse amounts of plankton compared to other lakes without 'monster' traditions, such as those in the Lake District. Plankton feeders exhibit physical adaptations for capturing and straining plankton from the water. Whales, for example, have baleen brushes and some fish have gills adapted as strainers. These feeders also possess large mouths to take in the greatest possible volume of water, which by all accounts does not seem to apply to our long-necked animal. They also display a great deal of surface activity, since it is near the surface that plankton is concentrated; this is also contrary to the evidence we have so far of our unknown species.

Detritus, as already mentioned, is the organic matter present in the deposits on the loch floor. Some coarse fish are detrital feeders, while others feed on the invertebrates and insect larvae found in or on the sides of the loch. In general the deposits on the floor of Loch Ness are not rich in organic material; samples taken from the loch floor show that organic material makes up 15 to 30 per cent of the total. Special observations were made at Loch Morar by divers briefed to look for signs of large animals feeding on the sediment to depths of up to 100 feet (or 30 metres). The divers were sent down in those areas found to have the greatest concentrations of organic matter, but they found no such traces. In themselves, however, these findings are not sufficient to rule out the possibility that unknown animals might find a suitable food source here, since a community

Left: the leatherback turtle, seen here returning to the sea off Malaya after laying its eggs. It has been argued that the Loch Ness monster could not possibly be a reptile, as a cold-blooded creature – one whose body temperature depends on its environment – could not survive in the loch. The leatherback turtle, however, can live in the chilliest seas, and has even been found off the coast of Scotland

Below: a ringed seal off the snowy coast of Greenland. Seals can survive in the coldest waters; this fact has been used to support the theory that the Loch Ness monster could be a mammal

of invertebrates was discovered living within the sediment at depths of 1,000 feet (300 metres) in Loch Morar. But the majority of evidence is against this theory.

By far the most likely food source for a large animal is the migratory salmonid fish. Although there is a good resident population of brown trout and eels that grow to maturity in Loch Ness, it remains true that the loch is a rather sterile place from a biological point of view. The productivity of any enclosed body of water involves a food chain beginning with the chemical nutrients entering the water and the amount of light available for photosynthesis. These, together with the degree of water circulation, set the limit for the phytoplankton (microscopic plants), which then limit the zooplankton (microscopic animals) that feed upon it. The zooplankton in turn, together with the insect

larvae and invertebrates in the mud on the bottom, become food for the fish population. Little in the way of nutrients enters the loch since the seven main rivers that flow into it – Oich, Tarff, Foyers, Farigaig, Enrick, Coiltie and Morriston – run rapidly over rocky terrain, picking up little from the smooth, stony river bed.

Chasing the salmon

It seems to rest with the salmon and sea trout to provide a solution to the food supply problem. The salmon hatch in rivers entering the loch and remain in fresh water for the first two years of their life, attaining a weight of up to 9 ounces (250 grams). They then leave for the sea for up to three years before returning to the same place to spawn. At this point in the cycle, they weigh anything up to 40 pounds (18 kilograms), all of the energy for this growth being derived from outside the loch's food chain. While in fresh water the salmon do not eat and do not therefore act as a drain on the loch's existing food resources; only in those first years must the young salmon (or parr) rely on the food chain. Mature salmon are present virtually all the year round, since they enter at different times – although mainly in spring and summer.

Some aspects of reported behaviour support the theory of a fish-predator. Sightings are frequently made off the mouths of rivers in spate, when the salmon are running up to spawn and recorded bursts of high speed would be consistent with an animal chasing the fish. If there is a large unknown animal species in the loch, it is reasonable to expect it to exploit this special bonus to the food chain – the salmonid fish.

One objection to the existence of a Loch Ness 'monster' has always been the absence of floating or beached remains. Animals are often recognised by science on the basis of their remains long before a living specimen is observed. Père David obtained the skin of a giant panda in 1869, but it was 50 years

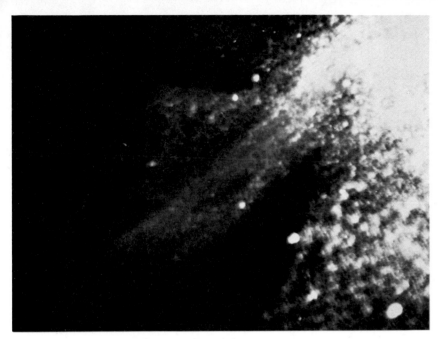

was an arm of the sea, an amphibian would seem a reasonable candidate. Amphibians do not need to breathe often and they hibernate and reproduce in water. The problem is that there are not, and palaeontology indicates that there never have been, any marine amphibians. Therefore if we are right in expecting to find the origins of our 'monster' at sea, we are probably not looking for an amphibian.

Reptile, mammal or fish?

Certainly the most popular theory is that the 'monster' is a reptile. However, the biological objections are strong. The temperature of the loch would seem too cold for a reptile to remain active. Also a reptile would have to surface in order to breathe and would be expected to come ashore to lay eggs. Of course there are always exceptions to prove the rule. Freshwater 'turtles', for example, can sometimes be seen swimming beneath the ice covering North American lakes (although Loch Ness itself does not freeze). The leatherback turtle, by virtue of its size, maintains its temperature above that of its surroundings and has been caught at sea off the west coast of Scotland. And sea snakes bear their young alive in the water.

The reptile most often suggested as fitting the 'descriptions' is the plesiosaur. On the precedent of the coelacanth, absent from

before the first one was seen alive by westerners (and promptly shot) in 1929. There are few records of strange carcases being found at Scottish lochs – and none of them recent. Loch Ness and Loch Morar are deep, steep-sided and cold, and it is particularly the depth that is relevant since the water pressure would slow down decomposition and allow time for eels to dispose of the remains. This probably accounts for Loch Ness's reputation for 'never giving up its dead'.

Many reptiles and mammals, both terrestrial and aquatic, have the curious habit of swallowing small stones. It seems that they use this additional weight as ballast, particularly when swimming near the surface where pressure due to water is insufficient to keep the animal submerged. Seals, for instance, have been found with up to 25 pounds (11 kilograms) of stones in their guts. This may also have some significance in the argument that the 'monster' is a reptile or a mammal – if it, too, swallows stones as ballast, these will cause its body to sink to the bottom of the loch after its death.

Exactly what the 'monster' is – if it exists at all – is the most interesting question of all. The presence of an adapted marine fish-predator within the loch is not, in itself, particularly remarkable. What is remarkable is that it seems to be an unknown animal. Furthermore, some of its 'characteristics' raise difficulties no matter what class of animal is considered. It is precisely these features, which make it hard for the zoologist to believe in the 'monster', that will make it such an interesting find.

The largest known invertebrate is the giant squid, until recently itself a 'mythical' animal. Very few of the sightings in Loch Ness could apply to the squid, quite apart from the fact that there are no known freshwater representatives of the family. Were it not for the fact that until recently Loch Ness

Above: Dr Robert Rines's famous 'monster flipper' photograph, taken in 1972. If this is indeed part of the Loch Ness monster, it provides some interesting information about what kind of creature it is. The photograph shows a rhomboid flipper with a clear central 'rib' – which, experts agree, is not an efficient design for swimming

Right: comparison with the fin of a fish (top left) and a sea-lion flipper (top right) reveals that the structure of the 'monster flipper' is entirely different. In fact, the nearest parallel is the fin of the Australian lungfish (bottom): this, too, has a clear central stiffening – but it is used mainly for crawling along the sea bed

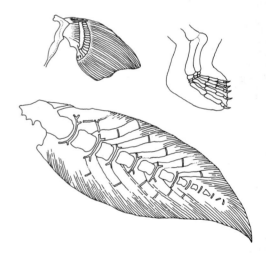

fossil records for 70 million years yet found alive and well in the Indian Ocean in 1938, the mere fact that the plesiosaur has been 'extinct' for a similar period does not deter its advocates. And it is conceivable that this type of animal could have adapted to cope with the difficulties of the loch already mentioned. Secondarily aquatic reptiles and mammals have waterproof skins and breathing apparatus – that is, lungs as opposed to gills. Their systems are therefore isolated from the water, which gives them some immunity from osmotic stress caused by moving from salt to fresh water, or vice versa; this makes long-term adaptation to fresh water easier. Creatures with permeable skins and using gills for breathing would normally suffer from the change, since the fresh water would cause an imbalance as it entered through the skin and gills into the existing body fluids.

From an environmental point of view, a mammal is a more probable bet. Most seals, for example, are perfectly at home in low temperatures, and a long-necked seal could account for some of the sightings. The problem of reproduction remains, however, since seals breed – and in general give birth – on land. And the need to breathe frequently – and therefore to surface – should not allow a population of this kind to remain so elusive.

The least unlikely solution would be a

Below: the Australian lungfish, whose fins provide the closest parallel to the 'monster flipper' of Dr Robert Rines's photograph that can be found among known living creatures

fish, which would certainly account for the rare surface appearances and take care of the reproduction as well. Unfortunately, most sighting reports do not seem to describe a fish, although there could be something in the opinion among locals that the 'monster' is a large eel of known or unknown species. Some of the sonar evidence suggests that contacts rise and return to the bottom, which is consistent with the behaviour of the eel or of the European catfish, both of which become active at night. The apparent tendency to surface in calm, hot weather, which was first noted by Pontoppidan of the 'sea serpent' in 1752 and is supported by testimonies at Loch Ness, is consistent with the behaviour of bottom-dwelling fish. At least they make rather 'extrovert' surface appearances in response to barometric pressure changes. This is true not only of the catfish but also of the European pond loach – or weather fish – which has, in fact, been used as a living barometer.

The 'flipper' picture taken in 1972 by Dr Robert Rines is interesting, if it is indeed part of an unknown animal. The flipper or fin is of a rhomboid shape, which led Rines and Sir Peter Scott, the naturalist, to suggest the scientific name *Nessiteras rhombopteryx* for the animal. It has been pointed out that the shape of this flipper makes it inefficient for aquatic propulsion. Efficient limbs, like those of the plesiosaur, sea lion and even the penguin, all have the rigid bones up at the leading edge, thus enabling the rest of the

Below: a model of the plesiosaur, the reptile that seems most nearly to fit the descriptions of the Loch Ness monster. The plesiosaur is thought to have been extinct for the past 70 million years – but that in itself does not automatically rule out the possibility that this *is* the monster. A rare fish, the coelacanth, was also thought to have been extinct for millions of years – until one was found in the Indian ocean in 1938

flipper to flex; this provides propulsion in precisely the same way as a diver's flipper. The 'flipper' picture shows a central 'rib', suggesting that propulsion would come from the flipper folding on the forward stroke and stiffening on the backward stroke, the mechanism for which is not apparent. Alternatively, the flipper would have to be rotated, or slewed, on the forward stroke, although again there is no obvious stiffening sufficient for this. This leads one to conclude that the flipper is not a prime source of propulsion, since power would be lost on one stroke rather than being gained on both as with a true flipper; this in turn would eliminate the plesiosaur as a candidate. The animal would therefore have to be propelled by its tail, with the flipper possibly functioning for steering – or even as a brake.

If the flipper is considered as part of a fish, in which case it would be appropriate to call it a fin, the position is different. Accepting the objection that the fin is inefficient for aquatic propulsion, fish are anyway almost always tail-propelled and many species have put their fins to other uses apart from swimming. The nearest parallel to the 'monster' flipper of Rines's photograph known in nature is, in fact, the fin of an Australian lungfish, which has a clear central stiffening and functions as a leg for crawling along the bottom. It could therefore be argued that the flipper is more likely to be the fin of a bottom-roving fish than the propulsive flipper of a reptile or mammal.

Whatever the Loch Ness 'monster' may turn out to be – and we do not at present have enough information to suggest any animal group with confidence – there will be some very interesting questions to be answered, far more interesting than the mere discovery of a 'monster'. If it is an amphibian, how did it invade the loch in the first place? If a reptile, how does it cope with the cold? If a mammal, how does it remain so elusive? And if it is a fish, it is indeed a very strange fish.

Creatures of the Irish lakes

The countless lakes and bogs of Ireland have yielded many sightings of large creatures of unknown species. JANET and COLIN BORD describe ancient legends and modern reports that tell of these monsters

THE BEST-KNOWN LAKE MONSTER in the world must surely be the one in Loch Ness, and many people suppose that 'Nessie' is unique. But if there really is a monster (or, more likely, a family of monsters) in Loch Ness, then why not in other lakes? According to reports by many reliable eyewitnesses, there are. Scottish lochs other than Loch Ness are reputed to hide monsters, for example 'Morag' of Loch Morar; and not far away across the Irish Sea many of Ireland's lakes, large and small, have over the years been the location of strange sightings. The reports have not come solely from 20th-century witnesses who might be jealous of Nessie's fame and hope to encourage tourists to visit Ireland's lakes. Stories of evil water monsters are part of Irish legend. Sometimes called *piast*, *peiste*, *payshtha*, *ollphiast* or *ullfish*, these water demons were said to be horse-like – hence another name still used today, horse-eel.

The 12th-century *Leabhar na h'Uidhre* ('Book of the dun cow') tells the story of a huge *piast* that lived in an unfathomable lakelet, Slieve Mis, in County Kerry. This beast was in the habit of emerging to make meals of the people and cattle living in a *cashel*, or stone-walled fort, on the shores of the lake. The Irish hero Cuchulain was close by one night when he heard it coming and, contrary to what one might expect of a hero, and indicating the terror that the *piast* aroused in him, he leapt over the wall into the cashel, out of reach of the monster. It was left to certain Irish saints to tangle with the water demons. St Mochua of Balla got the better of a monster in one of the loughs of Connaught, while St Senanus and St Kevin were successful in their struggles with the *piasts* of Scattery and Glendalough. St Patrick tricked

Right: lough monsters are today most commonly seen in County Kerry and the Connemara district of Galway

Bottom: Lough Ree, near Athlone, in which three priests watched a monster one day, in May 1960

the monster of a southern Irish lough into imprisoning itself beneath a large vat, while St Colman of Dromore rescued a girl who was swallowed by a monster while washing her nightdress in a pool. From the number of old legends and stories that mention lake monsters, it is clear that belief in them was widespread.

A description from the 10th-century *Book of Lismore* compares interestingly with recent sighting reports. The anonymous author has exaggerated his monster, but certain features are echoed in the 20th-century reports – a repulsive appearance, noticeable eyes, forked tail, existence on land or in the water, the inability of boats (and, of course, humans other than saints) to catch it, and a horse-like appearance. From both Ireland and Scotland come traditions of water horses, which look so much like real horses that people seeing them often mistook them for land horses. Legend tells that, in County Cavan, enchanted water horses would come out of Lough Ramor at night and graze on the oats in a farmer's field. He managed to catch a foal and trained it to work on his farm, but one evening as he rode it beside the lake, the water horses neighed and the foal plunged into the water, carrying the farmer with it. Neither was seen again. The same fate befell a boy working near Lough Caogh in County Leitrim, who captured what he thought was a stray horse and used it to harrow a field. After a while it ran back into the lake, taking harrow and boy with it.

Although such stories as these are farfetched and should not be considered as descriptions of actual events, they may indicate that people in past centuries saw monsters in the loughs just as people do

Above: Cuchulain, hero of Irish mythology. He is said to have encountered a huge lough monster in County Kerry, so terrifying that it frightened even him away

Above right: Patrick, the fifth-century missionary to Ireland who became the island's patron saint. Born in Britain, he was captured by Irish raiders at the age of 16 and was a slave until his escape six years later. He returned to Ireland and converted the country to Christianity. According to legend he not only captured a lough monster, but blessed the shamrock, banished snakes, and defeated the druids in feats of magical skill

Left: the *Book of Lismore*, dating from the 10th century. The manuscript has a detailed description of a lough monster, 'repulsive, outlandish, fierce and very terrifying'. It had the front end of a horse, iron claws, a fiery breath, and the tail fins of a whale, with iron nails on them. The sea would boil when this fearsome monster rushed into the water. Boats could not catch it and 'no-one escaped to tell the tale of it, from then till now . . .'

today and that, observing horse-like features, they wove tall tales around the facts. Some of the factual reports that follow liken the appearance of the monster's *head* to a horse's, but sometimes from a distance even today's monsters look entirely horse-like. Patrick Canning saw what he described as 'a lovely black foal' beside Lough Shanakeever in County Galway around 1955. He had gone to fetch his donkey out of the rain, and from about 200 yards (180 metres) he saw a black animal, the size of a foal, circling round the donkey. It had a long neck, and he also saw a head with ears. As he approached, it went into the water. Lough Shanakeever is the scene of many other sightings; these will be described later. Meanwhile, here are reports of some of the monsters that have been seen in the loughs around Ireland.

The monster of Lough Muck

Towards the end of the 19th century, a strange animal was occasionally seen in Lough Muck in County Donegal. Around 1885, a young woman had waded into the lough to pull bog-bean. Hearing a splash, she looked round and saw a big-eyed monster heading for her through the water. Not unnaturally, she got ashore as quickly as possible.

Lough Muck's monster was seen again in the following few years, its two humps above the water. One very strange fact is that Lough Muck is less than three-quarters of a mile (1 kilometre) long and half a mile (800 metres) across, and it is not the only small lake in Ireland where monsters have been seen. In such small areas of water, there is a very limited food supply, consisting mainly of fish such as brown trout. Later we shall return to this enigma – which initially seems to suggest that it would be impossible for large monsters to live in these loughs.

Lough Abisdealy in County Galway is another small lake, only 1 mile (1.6 kilometres) long by a quarter-mile (400 metres) wide. An Irish name for the lake translates as 'the lake of the monster', and there was a tradition that a water horse lived in it. A monster was reportedly seen during the Crimean War of 1854–56; then, in 1914, just before the outbreak of the First World War, it appeared again. Three people driving to church in a dogcart saw it as they passed close to the lake. It was long and black, long-necked and with a flat head held high, and two loops of its body moved in and out of the water as it travelled quickly across the lake, looking like a gigantic snake. On another occasion, at night, a man saw a huge eel-like creature crawling out of the lake.

It is always possible that a monster may attack witnesses – and this thought evidently went through the mind of Georgina Carberry, who with friends saw a monster in Lough Fadda, County Galway in 1954. Miss Carberry was the librarian at Clifden, and in the 1960s she told monster hunter F. W. Holiday about her frightening experience. She and her three friends were on a fishing expedition to the small lough – 1½ miles (2.4 kilometres) long and only 600 yards (550 metres) at its widest point – and by the time they pulled their boat on shore for a tea-break, they had caught several trout. Then one of the four noticed what looked at first like a man swimming in the water. But as it slowly got closer, they could see that it looked like nothing they knew. When it was only 20 yards (18 metres) away, they apprehensively moved back from the water's edge. Miss Carberry remembered the creature's open mouth quite clearly – 'a huge great mouth', which was white inside. The monster's body was 'wormy . . . creepy', and 'seemed to have movement all over it all the

Above: Lough Muck in County Donegal, one of the smaller Irish lakes, in which a two-humped monster was seen several times towards the end of the 19th century

Below: part of the Connemara district of County Galway. It is dotted with lakes hewn from the ice rock by ancient ice sheets, and is covered with peat bog. Most of the lakes are too small to support a large creature

time'. The head stood high above the water on a long neck, and as the watchers moved back the creature dived round a rock, showing a forked tail. When it surfaced further up the lake, they could see two humps out of the water behind its head. The shock of the sighting caused Miss Carberry to have nightmares for weeks afterwards. Such a reaction is not surprising, of course. Most of us could not easily cope with a sudden encounter with an unknown monster. Its horrible appearance, and its apparent intention, as it heads open-mouthed towards the witness, of grabbing a quick meal of tasty human flesh, are enough to give anyone nightmares. But the monster that swims towards lake-shore watchers may only be curious, like cows that wander across a field to stare at people. The

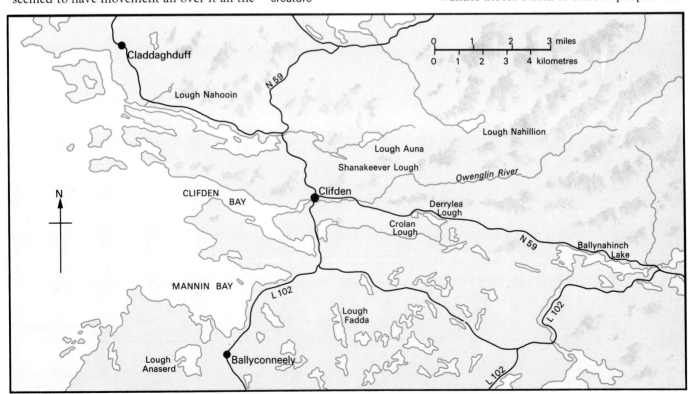

monsters are also likely to be harmless herbivores.

On 18 May 1960, three Dublin priests fishing in the waters of Lough Ree watched a long-necked, flat-headed animal swimming in the water only 100 yards (90 metres) away. It was a warm, calm evening, and the men saw the creature quite clearly. The head and neck, between 18 and 24 inches (45 and 60 centimetres) long, were separated by about 2 feet (60 centimetres) of water from another part of the body that could have been a hump on the back of a large creature beneath the water surface. They watched for two or three minutes as the creature swam slowly towards the shore. It then gradually submerged, reappearing a couple of minutes later and then disappearing again 30 yards (27 metres) from the shore.

A monster attacks

So far, we have described long-necked creatures with undulating bodies, but the creature seen in Lough Dubh near Glinsk, County Galway, by school-teacher Alphonsus Mullaney and his son does not fit this description at all. The lake was known to be a monster haunt. Three men had seen a strange animal there around 1956, while in 1960 three monsters were seen, one large and two smaller. It was in March 1962 that Mr Mullaney and his son had their encounter, and Mr Mullaney described to a newspaper reporter what happened:

> We were working on the bog after school and I had promised to take young Alphonsus fishing. We carried a twelve foot [4-metre] rod with a strong line and spoon bait for perch or pike, of which there are plenty in Lough Dubh.
>
> For a while I let the boy fish with the rod and used a shorter rod with worm bait. I got no 'answer'. After five minutes I decided that the fish were not there that evening, but I took the long rod and walked up and down the bank.
>
> Suddenly there was a tugging on the line. I thought it might be on a root, so I took it gently. It did not give. I hauled

Above: Georgina Carberry, an expert angler who encountered a lough monster

Below: the monster of Lough Fadda, as described by Miss Carberry and her companions

Bottom: Lough Fadda, County Galway, set in a wilderness of bogs

it slowly ashore, and the line snapped. I was examining the line when the lad screamed.

Then I saw the animal. It was not a seal or anything I had ever seen. It had for instance short thick legs, and a hippo face. It was as big as a cow or an ass, square faced, with small ears and a white pointed horn on its snout. It was dark grey in colour, and covered with bristles or short hair, like a pig.

Young Alphonsus screamed because the monster, apparently having taken the bait and in pain, had tried to get out of the lough and attack him. Father and son escaped, and Mr Mullaney alerted local men who took guns to the lake – but nothing was seen.

During the 1960s, the number of sighting reports increased, perhaps because of a generally growing interest in lake monsters. Some investigators visited the Irish loughs to carry out experiments, and they also talked to local people who had seen strange animals. Because so many of the loughs are small and remote, they are rarely visited, unlike Loch Ness, which has 40 miles (65 kilometres) of motor road around it, frequently patrolled by goggle-eyed tourists. It is usually local people or fishermen who see the Irish lough monsters – no one else visits the loughs.

W. J. Wood was fishing on Lough Attariff

in County Cork in June 1966 when a long, dark brown object suddenly surfaced about 100 yards (90 metres) away. It was facing him, and Mr Wood reported that 'it had the head of a well-grown calf and large glittering eyes almost at water-level.' After a couple of minutes it submerged. In 1967 the same witness saw a light, yellowish brown 'monster', about 7 feet (2 metres) long, which surfaced only a few yards from him when he was fishing in Lackagh Lake in County Kerry. When F. W. Holiday visited the area he found that a young man living nearby had seen a snake-like neck several feet long, topped by a small head with two stumpy horns, and the sight had scared the life out of him.

A more recent sighting has also come from a remote County Kerry lake, Lough Brin, which is 5 miles (8 kilometres) from a metalled road and approachable only along a rough

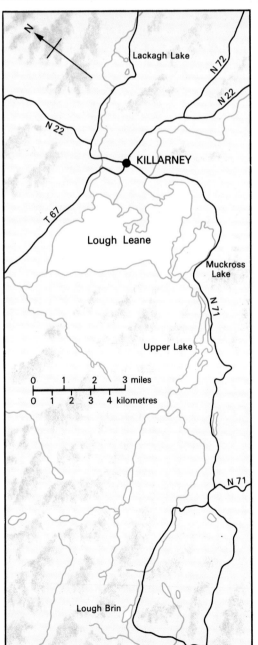

Above: Lough Dubh, scene of several monster sightings, which culminated in an attack on Alphonsus Mullaney

Right: the Lough Dubh creature, described as being covered with bristles and having a hippo-like face with a horn on its snout

Left: the area around Killarney, in County Kerry, scene of monster sightings

Right: the reptilian creature seen in Lough Brin, reconstructed from the accounts of two witnesses

Below: an invocation from this youthful witch at Lough Keane, County Kerry, in 1980 succeeded in attracting a photographer but failed to raise a water monster

track. Not surprisingly, its only visitors are local farmers. A monster has been seen there in past years, and in the summer of 1979 two farmers saw a reptilian creature something like a cross between a giant seal and the mythical dragon. It was as black as soot and about 10 feet (3 metres) long, and they watched it swim along the length of the 500-yard (450-metre) lough before submerging.

If lake monsters could be summoned up from their murky depths, the raging controversy as to whether they are real could be easily resolved.

The country folk of western Ireland tell of strange lake creatures – the 'water horses', 'water eels' or peistes – that are frequently seen there

THE IRISH LOUGHS where lake monsters have been seen are very small – too small, it might seem, to support large mysterious creatures. But would-be monster catchers face fewer problems in searching one of these than in confronting Loch Ness, a huge body of water, 22 miles (35 kilometres) long.

In the 1960s a researcher into the lake monsters of Connemara in County Galway, Captain Lionel Leslie, tried some experiments in monster raising. His first was in October 1965 at Lough Fadda, where Georgina Carberry had a clear sighting of a 'creepy' monster while fishing in 1954. Captain Leslie got permission to detonate gelignite at Lough Fadda. His intention was to create a large shock-wave that would disturb the monster and cause it to surface. He set 5 pounds (2 kilograms) of explosive against the rock where Miss Carberry had seen the monster at close range. Ten seconds after it exploded, the Captain and his companions saw a large, blackish object surface amid much splashing about 50 yards (45 metres) away. Unfortunately not much detail could be seen because of the splashing, but they saw enough to convince them that there

Above: the monster of Lough Nahooin, in an artist's impression based on descriptions given by the seven members of the Coyne family

Below: Lough Nahooin, a tiny peat tarn in County Galway. Stephen Coyne (inset) was the first to see the mysterious creature on that memorable evening in February 1968

was a monster in the lake, still very much alive.

Captain Leslie's next plan was to net Lough Fadda, and he was able to do this in October 1967. The net was in place for a couple of weeks, but nothing was caught. Storms prevented Leslie from dragging the lake for the monster.

Nothing daunted, in 1968 Captain Leslie laid plans to search other Irish loughs where monsters had been seen. This time he worked with a large team of monster hunters. The lough finally chosen for netting was Lough Nahooin, near Claddaghduff in County Galway. It was a tiny lake, only about 100 yards (90 metres) long and 80 yards (73 metres) wide, and the chances of catching the monster seemed very high. They were certain that there was a monster

The perplexing Irish peiste

Left: setting nets across Lough Nahooin in the second hunt for the monster. The heavy polystyrene net, with its 12-inch (30-centimetre) mesh, was intended to reach the bottom, but the lough had risen since the first attempt to net it, and a gap remained beneath the net in several places. Nets were placed in two other loughs at the same time, but none yielded a monster. Yet in this small area of Ireland, F. W. Holiday found that over half the local people had stories about strange aquatic creatures they had seen

in the lake because a local farmer, Stephen Coyne, had seen it on 22 February 1968, only five months before the netting operation. Mr Coyne was out gathering peat at the lakeside in the early evening, accompanied by his eight-year-old son and their dog. Seeing a black object in the water, Mr Coyne whistled to it, thinking it was his dog. To his surprise the dog came running along from behind him, stopped on seeing the creature in the water, and began to bark. The creature swam towards the shore, mouth open, apparently responding to the dog's barking (and perhaps thinking of supper?), but when Mr Coyne went over to join the dog, the monster changed direction and swam around the lake.

Mr Coyne sent his son to fetch the rest of the family, and soon he was joined by his wife and four other children. They watched the monster for a while, and before the light failed they were able to see it clearly enough to describe it in some detail. Its closest approach to them was between 5 and 10 yards (4.5 and 9 metres). It was about 12 feet (3.5 metres) long, black and hairless, with an eel-like texture to the skin. They caught glimpses of a tail, and when the monster put its head underwater two humps appeared. The neck was pole-like and about 12 inches (30 centimetres) in diameter. The interior of the mouth was pale, and the creature had two 'horns' on top of its head. Neither Mr nor Mrs Coyne noticed any eyes. The monster seen by Georgina Carberry in Lough Fadda had a pale mouth; one seen in Lackagh Lake had two stumpy horns; and humps are often reported. Stephen Coyne told the monster hunters that he had also seen a monster in the lake 20 years earlier. It had rolled over and he had seen its pale underbelly.

The netting operation began at Lough

Left: Tommy Joyce at his house overlooking Shanakeever Lough, where he saw a mysterious creature

Below: the disturbance of these reeds, seen here from Tommy Joyce's position during the sighting, gave him an impression of the bulk of the creature

Nahooin on 15 July 1968, and by 17 July a line of nets stretched across the entire width of the lake. Only 23 feet (7 metres) deep at its deepest part, where Mr Coyne had seen the monster appear on both occasions, the lake proved much easier to net than would Loch Ness, 800 to 900 feet (240 to 275 metres) deep. The only similarity between the lakes, apart from their reputation as monster haunts, is the peat in the water, which makes it dark and visually impenetrable.

David James had an electronic fish-attracting device with him, but neither that nor the 'monster rousers' (empty petrol tins containing pebbles, pulled through the water on a rope) succeeded in raising a monster. The nets remained empty and Professor Mackal did not need his harpoon gun, which he was hoping to use to obtain a tissue sample from the monster. The team members could

spare only a few days in Ireland and so the experiment unfortunately ended in failure.

However, in 1969 Captain Leslie, Ivor Newby, F. W. Holiday and others decided to try again. This time they netted three loughs – Nahooin once again, Shanakeever, and Auna. Auna and Shanakeever were inter-connected, and both of them had been reported to contain monsters.

About the turn of the century, a woman saw a 'horse-eel' come out of Lough Auna and on to the turf bank very close to where she was working. She did not wait to see what happened next!

Some years later, a man stacking peat by the lough saw a humped creature with a length of 30 to 40 feet (9 to 12 metres) rolling in the water. It seemed to have a mane or fin along its neck.

Patrick Canning's 1950s sighting of a

The thing in Lough Auna

A sighting of a lough monster crowned a summer barbecue party held in 1980 by Air Commodore Kort, a retired officer of the Royal Netherlands Air Force, now resident in County Galway. The party took place at Mr Kort's cottage in County Limerick. He and his guests had just retired indoors when he saw an odd shape moving through the waters of nearby Lough Auna. With a guest,

Right: the form seen by Air Commodore Kort and Mr Adrian O'Connell gliding through the waters of Lough Auna one May evening

Below: the westward motion of the creature carried it into the reeds. It had been seen by at least three watchers

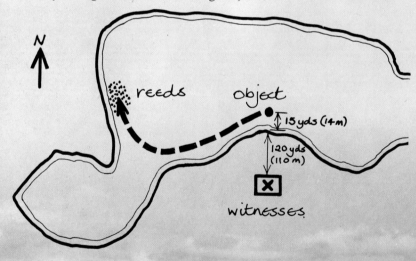

Adrian O'Connell, he watched it for several minutes as it moved at no more than walking pace towards the western end of the lake. One other guest glimpsed it as it disappeared in the reeds. Although the size of the strange object was difficult to estimate, he judged it to be 5 feet (1.5 metres) long and to rise about 1 foot (30 centimetres) above the water. Some guests suggested that it was a very large fish, others that it was an otter with three young on its back. But Mr Kort believes that either of these creatures would have left a v-shaped wake, clearly visible on the lake, which was now calm and without so much as a ripple; whereas, as he recalls, 'the uncanny thing about it was the gliding movement without any disturbance of the water on the surface.'

Below: F. W. Holiday, life-long monster hunter. He studied the Loch Ness monster intensively, as well as attempting to snare some of the creatures reported in the Irish loughs. He believed that the lake creatures, and perhaps other large serpents, now extinct, were the basis of the age-old legends of dragons, the cornerstone of many ancient cults. They died out wherever Man disturbed the lakes

black creature on the shore of Shanakeever Lough was described as 'a lovely black foal'. In either 1963 or 1964 Tommy Joyce, an alert local farmer, saw a dark grey object about 7½ feet (2.5 metres) long in the water among the reeds of the same lough.

These sightings were all reported to the monster-hunting team, who were able to meet and talk to most of the witnesses. The investigators had no doubts about the witnesses' veracity and became convinced that they had seen something strange. So, despite the failure of earlier netting attempts, they began their 1969 experiments with confidence. Even at Lough Nahooin, where they had found no trace of a monster in 1968, they were keen to try again, since they had heard of a sighting there that took place only a month before. On 8 September a sheep farmer, Thomas Connelly, saw a black creature, bigger than a young donkey, on the lake shore a few yards from the water's edge. It seemed to have four stumpy legs, and was slithering towards the lake. As Connelly watched, the monster moved into the water and sank. This sighting has strong echoes of Patrick Canning's beside Shanakeever Lough, where he saw a creature resembling a black foal.

Unfortunately, an attempt to drag Lough Nahooin with chains failed because they kept getting caught in the thick water lilies. The nets stretched across all three loughs remained in place and the monsters shyly remained hidden. The persistent but unlucky hunters, assailed by wind and rain,

Above: the loughs and bogs of Connemara. Seen from the air, the countryside is a patchwork of small lakes set in broad areas of peat. The lake creatures may be amphibious, moving from lough to lough at night and feeding on the land as well as in the water

Right: two generations ago, children were kept away from Lough Crolan, in Connemara, because of the 'horse-eels' that had been seen in it. In 1961 Tom Connelly, a local man, watched an eel-like creature with a 'velvety' skin, at least 12 feet (4 metres) long, rising and sinking repeatedly in one spot for over half an hour.

realised that they were not going to catch their monster.

From all the evidence, it seems clear that the so-called 'lake monsters' are amphibious and can live as well on land as in water. The Loch Ness monster has been seen on land several times, and so have the monsters in a number of the Irish sightings. The monsters are obviously happier in water, as it conceals them so well. But when disturbed, as by hunters, they appear to slip out of the lough and make their way across the bog to another stretch of water. This would not be too

difficult a feat in Connemara where there are vast areas of uninhabited bogs and many small lakes.

That the monsters do leave the loughs is also suggested by two reports from Connemara, dating from the end of the 19th century. The first described an 'oversized eel' that got jammed in the culvert connecting Crolan Lough with Derrylea Lough, and died there, its corpse being left to rot away. At Ballynahinch, a spear was made to kill a 30-foot (9-metre) monster trapped under a bridge. But before the men could kill it, a flood occurred one night and carried the lucky creature away with it.

Such tales as these are frustrating to monster hunters, whose attempts to catch, or even glimpse, a monster invariably meet with failure. Even more frustrating are recent reports of close sightings of monsters on land. Why is it that monsters are almost always seen by people who are not expecting them, who react by running away, and who never have a ciné camera to hand? For example, in 1968 the monster of Sraheens Lough on Achill Island, County Mayo, was very active. The lake was known as a monster haunt, sightings having been made there in the 1930s and in 1966. Yet again the lake is small, only about 1200 feet (365 metres) in circumference, and therefore unlikely to be

Below: the monster of Sraheens Lough was seen three times in 10 days in May 1968. Twice it appeared on land, and was terrifying enough to scare the witnesses away

able to supply a monster with food for very long. Two local men, Michael McNulty and John Cooney, came upon the monster at night on 1 May 1968, while driving home. As they passed the lough, a strange creature ran across the road only a few yards ahead of the car and then disappeared into the thick undergrowth. They could see it clearly in the car's headlights, and what they saw made the driver step on the accelerator, with no thought of stopping to investigate! Eight to ten feet (2½ to 3 metres) long and about 2½ feet (75 centimetres) tall, the animal had a long thick tail, a long neck, and a head like a sheep or greyhound. It was a shiny dark brown in

colour, and as it ran it rocked from side to side.

Only a week later, 15-year-old Gay Dever saw the monster in daylight. He was cycling by Sraheens Lough when he heard a splashing noise on the shore. Stopping to look, he was amazed to see a large black animal crawling out of the water. It was much bigger than a horse, and had a long neck, a sheeplike head, a tail and four legs, the hind ones being the biggest. Gay Dever's reaction was to leave the scene without delay.

Two days later, the monster was allegedly seen yet again, by two girls trying to hitchhike home to Achill Sound. They were waiting near the lough and as a car stopped for them, one of the girls turned back towards the lough. By the light of the full Moon she and the driver saw a monster.

F. W. Holiday, who researched deeply into lake monsters, wrote that there are 'at least 50 credible accounts' of monsters seen on land. But there is a lack of food for so many monsters in small Irish loughs, and the failure of determined hunters to prove conclusively the existence of even one lake monster after years of concentrated effort made him wonder whether these monsters are not just large aquatic animals, but might also have a paranormal aspect. On numerous occasions monsters appeared immediately after observers had put their cameras away, or else the cameras jammed. The comment he made in 1976 is still relevant: 'Monsters are certainly a fact; but they are not the sort of fact we first supposed.'

Above: John Cooney who, with a companion, saw the Sraheens monster in the headlights of his car

Left: nearly a century ago, a large eel-like creature was trapped in a culvert leading from Lough Crolan into Lough Derrylea. The carcase was so loathsome that no one would remove it and it was left to decompose

Delusions and transformations

History abounds with stories of people who claim to be werewolves, and behave in a savage and bestial way – and yet keep their human shape. This form of madness still occurs today. IAN WOODWARD seeks an explanation

MOST PEOPLE'S CONCEPTION of a werewolf is of an excessively hairy and ferocious man-beast that walks upright on two legs, growls and foams at the mouth, and displays large, dirty-looking lupine teeth. This, of course, is the now familiar portrait represented by late-night television movies like *Curse of the werewolf*, *The wolf man* and *Legend of the werewolf* – and it is inaccurate in all essentials.

History and mythology are quite clear in describing a man transformed into a were-wolf as being little different from a natural wolf, except perhaps slightly larger than the wild species.

Those unfamiliar with the subject also tend to bracket werewolves with lycan-thropes and talk about them as if they were one and the same thing. They are not.

A *lycanthrope* is a mentally sick person who believes that he has assumed the shape, voice and behaviour of a wolf, although he has not actually undergone any physical transformation. In the 15th and 16th centuries it was believed that the werewolf's fur grew on the inside of his skin; and many a lycanthrope has given this explanation when asked why, if he is a wolf, he still looks exactly like a person.

A *werewolf*, on the other hand, is tradi-tionally a man who, by the agency of magic or by natural inclination, possesses an ability to change his shape to that of a wolf. All the characteristics associated with that animal – the ferocity, strength, cunning and swiftness – are readily displayed, to the dumbfounded

Above: Oliver Reed stars in the Hammer film *The curse of the werewolf*, made in 1960. Typically, this movie werewolf is quite unlike its traditional original; it remains clothed and walks upright

Below: 'the gleaming eyes of the classic werewolf dream', in a 1930s illustration by Peter Coccogna for the American magazine *Fantasy Fiction*. Some writers have suggested that werewolves are astral projections from lycanthropic dreams

horror of all whose path he crosses. He may remain in his animal form for a few hours or even permanently.

When Peter Stump, a notorious German 'werewolf' who died a terrible death near Cologne in 1589, confessed to magical self-transformation, we may be inclined to think him as fanatical as his judges were credulous. But having killed, mutilated and devoured hundreds of human and animal victims – though he admitted to only 16 people – while convinced he was to all intents and purposes a wolf, we can be in no doubt at all that he was suffering from the madness called lycanthropy.

'Lycanthropy' and 'lycanthrope' derive directly from the Greek words *lycos*, mean-ing 'wolf', and *anthropos*, meaning 'man'. Although lycanthropy originally referred to the ancient phenomenon of men capable of undergoing animal metamorphosis, a pheno-menon fervently believed in by such ancient Greek physicians as Cribasios and Aetios, it gradually became a term applied exclusively to men who *imagined* they had effected transformation into wild beasts of prey. For this reason, lycanthropy is looked upon by psychiatrists as a fundamental delusion.

As for the werewolf proper, two qualities were said to remain when a man was trans-formed into a wolf: his human voice and his eyes. But in all other respects the meta-morphosed werewolf was entirely animal: he had the hairy skin and claws of a wild wolf.

In his human form, however, a number of physical characteristics distinguished the werewolf from his fellow men. His eyebrows were said to meet on the bridge of the nose, and his long, almond-shaped fingernails were of a 'sickening' blood-red tinge; the third finger, in particular, was always very long. The ears, which were positioned rather

Right: the life of Peter
Stump, Germany's infamous
werewolf, in a 16th-century
woodcut. While in wolf
form, he would seek out
young women working in
the fields and, changing
back into his human shape,
would rape them, then
murder and devour them. It
was alleged that he tore
unborn babies from their
mothers' wombs, gulping
down the hearts 'panting hot
and raw'. He was eventually
brought to justice in 1589,
and confessed to having
made a pact with the Devil,
who had taught him the art
of shape-changing and
provided him with a wolf's
skin for the purpose. The
final pictures show his
torture, and execution with
his wife and daughter

low down and to the back of the head, and a
tendency towards hairiness of the hands and
feet, were also clear identifying marks.

There are traditionally three principal
types of werewolf. The first was the *heredi-
tary werewolf*. His involuntary malady was
passed down from one generation to another
as a consequence of some terrible family
curse. The second was the *voluntary werewolf*. His depravity of mind led him by choice
to the realms of black-magic ritual, and to the
use of all manner of terrible charms, potions,
ointments, girdles, animal skins and Devil-
worship incantations to bring about the
desired metamorphosis. And the third was
the *benevolent werewolf*. This gentle, protective scion of the werewolf family is almost
a contradiction in terms. He felt nothing but
shame for his brutal appearance and wished
that no harm should befall man or animal.
Two of the most familiar benevolent werewolves are depicted in a fine pair of 12th-
century romances, *William and the werewolf*

Below: the benevolent
werewolf of the late-12th-
century Breton *Lay of the
bisclaveret*, by Marie de
France, in an illustration from
Frank Hamel's *Human
animals* of 1915. The poem
tells the story of one of
Brittany's finest knights, who
spends three days of every
week as a werewolf – but
has no savage instincts,
except against his unfaithful
wife and her lover. In the
end, the wife outwits her
husband by persuading her
lover to steal his clothes –
without which the werewolf
cannot regain human form

by Guillaume de Palerne and Marie de
France's *Lay of the bisclavaret* (*bisclavaret* is
the Breton term for the Norman *varulf*, or
werewolf), about one of Brittany's most
gallant knights.

The medieval theory was that, while the
werewolf kept his human form, his hair grew
inwards; when he wished to become a wolf,
he simply turned himself inside out. An
examination of the many verbatim trial documents reveals that the prisoners – undoubtedly lycanthropes – were painstakingly
questioned in a bid to discover the 'secrets' of
animal metamorphosis. When such interrogation failed and the patience of the judges
ran out, some wretched victim would invariably have his arms and legs cut off, or be
partly flayed, in an attempt to find the
reputed inward-growing hair.

Haunters of shadowy woods

Another theory was that the possessed person had merely to put on a wolf's skin in
order to assume instantly the lupine form
and character. There is a vague similarity
here with the alleged fact that the berserker –
the Scandinavian bear-man or *werebear* –
haunted the shadowy woods at night clothed
in the hides of wolves or bears to acquire
superhuman strength by transformation.

Such a skin was kept by a half-witted wolf-
boy called Jean Grenier. Jacques Rollet, a
sixteenth-century lycanthrope, confessed to
using a magic salve or ointment, as he
admitted in court on 8 August 1598.

'What are you accused of having done?'
asked the judge.

'Of having offended God,' replied the 35-
year-old accused werewolf. 'My parents
gave me an ointment; I do not know its
composition.'

Then the judge asked, 'When rubbed with

A change for the worse

Why is it that so many werewolf stories stem from medieval times? One theory suggests that the fact cannot be explained away by pointing to the superstitious nature of the medieval mind: biochemically-induced hallucinations may have been almost everyday experiences for many people.

Extracts from the skins of toads, and plants such as mandrake, henbane and deadly nightshade, or belladonna, were frequently used by practitioners of the secret arts to induce sensations of flying or the delusion of growing claws and nails and turning into an animal.

But such hallucinations were not available only to people who *chose* to take these drugs. In medieval mills, grain was sorted into two heaps: clean grain for the aristocracy and clergy, and *ergotised* grain for the peasants. Ergotised grain carries a fungus that produces lysergic acid diethylamide – a drug similar to LSD that also produces the illusion of being turned into an animal. Thus almost anyone, at any time, could suddenly feel himself turning into – a werewolf.

Below: Charles Leadbeater, an early Theosophist, who made a study of astral projection in his book *The astral plane* (1895), and believed that the idea of the astral body was of central importance in understanding the werewolf phenomenon

---

this ointment, do you become a wolf?'

'No,' Rollet replied, 'but for all that, I killed and ate the child Cornier: I was a wolf.'

'Were you dressed as a wolf?'

'I was dressed as I am now. I had my hands and my face bloody, because I had been eating the flesh of the said child.'

'Do your hands and feet become the paws of a wolf?'

'Yes, they do.'

'Does your head become like that of a wolf – your head become larger?'

'I do not know how my head was at the time; I used my teeth; my head was as it is today. I have wounded and eaten many other little children.'

A further method of becoming a werewolf was to obtain a girdle, usually of animal origin, but occasionally made from the skin of a hanged man. Such a girdle was fastened with a buckle having seven tongues. When the buckle was unclasped, or the girdle cut, the charm was dissolved.

One account tells of a 16th-century sorcerer who possessed such a girdle. One day he went away from the house for a few hours without remembering to lock up the girdle. His young son subsequently climbed up to the cupboard to get it, and, as he was buckling it around his waist, he was instantly transformed into a 'strange-looking beast'. At this point, his father returned home and, on seizing the girdle, restored the child to his former natural shape.

It is said that the boy confessed that no

Below: the famous 19th-century French occultist Eliphas Levi, who suggested that, in certain cases, while people lay in bed having nightmares about being wolves, their 'sidereal bodies' would wander the countryside in the form of werewolves

sooner had he buckled the girdle than he was tormented with a fierce hunger and a bestial rage. But it seems more likely that, being of a susceptible age, he had heard his father boast of the girdle's magical qualities and was determined to 'experience' them for himself.

Eliphas Levi, the leading French occultist of the 19th century, who once collapsed in terror as a result of his own remarkable 'transcendental' magic, has explained the process of werewolfic transformation as a 'sympathetic condition between man and his animal presentment [form]'. He rightly notes in *History of magic* (1860) that werewolves, though tracked down, hunted and even maimed, have never been killed on the spot; and that people suspected of these atrocious self-transformations have always been found at home, after the pursuit of the werewolf, more or less wounded, sometimes dying, but in their natural form.

Savage and sanguinary instincts

Levi then goes on to discuss the phenomenon of man's 'sidereal body' – 'the mediator between the soul and the material organism' – and uses it as the basis of an explanation of werewolfism:

This body remains awake very often while the other is asleep, and by thought transports itself through all space which universal magnetism opens to it. It thus lengthens, without breaking, the sympathetic chain attaching it to the heart and brain. The form of our sidereal body is conformable to the habitual condition of our thoughts, and in the long run it is bound to modify the features of the material organism.

Levi proceeds to suggest that the werewolf is nothing more than the sidereal body of a man whose savage and sanguinary instincts are represented by the wolf, who, while his phantom is wandering abroad, dreams that he is nothing less than a savage wolf.

Certainly Theosophists today believe that during the Middle Ages, when public execution was common, many people sank so low morally that their astral bodies, the human spirits that we are said to use after death, actually linked with an animal. This explains why, if the astral body were to manifest itself in the form of a wolf, and it were subsequently wounded – its paw cut off, say, by a hunter – that wound would be duplicated on the werewolf's physical body in its human form: that is, one of the hands would be badly wounded or missing when the werewolf reverted to its human state.

Charles Webster Leadbeater, an Anglican

Above: Rose Gladden, a British clairvoyant and healer who has dealt with many cases of werewolfism. She believes that the werewolf is an astral projection that has been transformed by evil into the shape of a wolf

certainly a theory that is gaining considerable ground among many of today's spiritual thinkers. Rose Gladden, one of Britain's most experienced exorcists and a renowned clairvoyant healer, has no doubt that the diabolical application of astral projection played a key role in the lives of many accused werewolves. She explains:

Suppose I was a cruel person who enjoyed the horrible things in life – well, as I projected my astral body out of my physical body, all the surrounding evil could grasp me. And it would be the evil grasping my astral projection, or grasping my 'double', which would transform me into an animal, into a wolf.

The atmosphere is always full of evil forces, and these evil forces find it much easier to exist within mankind – within an evil man, say – than in a nebulous vacuum. People addicted to werewolfery were – indeed, still are – the most evil manifestations of humanity. I can well understand why there are so many instances on record of 'wound-doubling'.

A strange restlessness

Among the countless number of wound-doubling reports on historical record is one concerning a German farmer and his wife who were hay-making near Caasburg in the summer of 1721. After a while the wife said that she felt an unconquerable restlessness: she could not remain there a minute longer; she would have to go away.

After making her husband promise that if any wild animal came near he would throw his hat at it and run away, she quickly disappeared. But she had not been gone many seconds when a wolf was seen to be swimming across the nearby stream and heading for the hay-makers. The farmer threw his hat at the beast, which tore it to bits; but before he could make a hasty retreat, a man stole round with a pitchfork and stabbed the wolf to death. The beast's form changed instantly . . . and everyone was horrified to see that the man had slain the farmer's wife.

Whether fact or fancy, killing a werewolf in this way has always, by tradition, been the most favoured means by which to force him (or her) to resume his natural form on the spot, or lead to his speedy detection. But the bizarre episodes of wound-doubling often reported in werewolf cases are also common in out-of-the-body experiences. Could it be that this remarkable fact points towards a possible explanation of the werewolf superstition – astral projection? Is a werewolf no more than a manifestation of the 'sidereal body' spoken of by Eliphas Levi – a man's projected phantom?

clergyman who lived at the turn of the century and became one of the principal figures of the Theosophical Society, substantiates with great enthusiasm the theory of wound-doubling in his book *The astral plane* (1895):

As so often with ordinary materialisation, any wound inflicted upon that animal will be reproduced upon the human physical body by the extraordinary phenomenon of repercussion; though after the death of that physical body, the astral (which will probably continue to appear in the same form) will be less vulnerable. It will then, however, be also less dangerous, as unless it can find a suitable medium it will be unable to materialise fully.

The phenomenon of wound-doubling, through the agency of astral projection, is

Above: a werewolf attacks a man while his friend looks on, horrified and powerless to help, in a 16th-century woodcut from *Die Emeis* by Johann Geiler von Kaiserberg

PART 6
OPEN FILES

Introduction

MOST OF US enjoy a good mystery: knowing that something is out of joint, a crime has been committed, someone has disappeared, and take pleasure from watching the pieces of the broken jigsaw put slowly and carefully back together again. The classic kind of mystery that works like this is the detective thriller, for not only is the plot tantalisingly unravelled, clue by clue, but in the end justice is seen to be done. And yet the curious thing about mysteries like this is that we go back for more, time and time again. Because it's not really the solution of the plot that we find absorbing: it's the thrill of the chase, the suspense that comes of unsatisfied curiousity. How often do we actually feel a sense of anti-climax when the hero finally catches the villain?

A whole industry has grown up around this realisation that, secretly, we want the mystery to go on for ever. But its products are not to be found under the headings of fiction in the book stores. More often these books masquerade as fact, with titles like *Atlantis rediscovered*, or *More about the Bermuda Triangle*. What the people who write these (often lurid) volumes fail to understand, though, is that it is terribly easy to pull the rug out from underneath such spurious mysteries and tell the world how unlikely they are. And once someone does that, it's very simple to see that the writer in question has not just tried to play a confidence trick on his readers, he's also made it plain that he despised them all along. Not a good way, one would have thought, to remain a popular author.

It's a particularly curious activity to indulge in, too, for the simple reason that there are a vast number of *genuine* unsolved mysteries crying out for serious treatment and a fair hearing – we have gathered some of the most interesting for inclusion in this book.

They range from the eerie story of Joan Norkot who, having been given the chance by being lifted from her grave, pointed out her murderers, dead though she undoubtedly was, by a sign as casual yet as eloquent as a wink. They move through the scarcely less chilling story of the well-to-do Barbados family whose coffins refused to keep still, although they were sealed in the family mausoleum, to the peculiar case of the clergyman who found himself, to all intents and purposes, in contact with the long-dead King Henry VIII. They include straightforward material mysteries such as the unexplained yet enormously elaborate pit built hundreds of feet deep on Oak Island off the coast of Canada, and questions that go to the heart of every human being – as in the strange story of the North African Dogon tribe, who seem to know an extraordinary amount about what goes on in the region of the star Sirius B: so have we, after all, been visited by beings from outer space? Does this mean we are *not* alone in the Universe?

Then we have stories about people whose existence raises more questions than anyone – occasionally including themselves – can answer. Spring-heeled Jack could certainly have told much about himself had he ever been caught in his escapades, which were considerably less grisly than his later namesake, the Ripper. Some of these bear all the hallmarks of a somewhat over-enthusiastic practical joker, though others were less amusing to the victims. And despite some strong suspicions as to his identity, the prankster has never been conclusively identified.

Kaspar Hauser, on the other hand, acquired a respectable enough name – but absolutely nothing can be said for sure about his actual origins. He simply wandered out of nowhere into a German town – and straight into a controversy about his origins that lasts until today. Was he the illegitimate son of a wealthy noble – someone even of royal blood? An amnesiac? Whatever the answer, and despite the resources of modern scholarship, it looks as if we shall never know the answers – nor the true reason for his death, which was as mysterious as his life.

Then there are animals that have perplexed everyone who has come across their tracks – or, on occasion, had the privilege of seeing them. The most mysterious animal in England is given an outing in these pages – the elusive Surrey puma, still seen from time to time today, but whose heyday was in the 1960s. Quite what an animal better suited to the Rocky Mountains and other inhospitable climes was doing wandering about in populous and leafy southern England is not at all clear. What does seem to have been clearly established, however, is that the animal had not escaped from a zoo, wasn't someone's exotic pet, and had absolutely no intention of being caught. Unlike unexplained or unknown animals of other varieties – bigfeet in particular – the Surrey puma does not seem to have attracted weird phenomena of other kinds, such as UFO sightings. It does seem to be a fairly straightforward kind of creature – except that it has a genius for keeping out of the clutches of even the most elaborate hunting parties.

Britain's other odd animal was not thought of at first as an animal at all – at least not by many of those who found its tracks, one cold morning in Devon in the 19th century. As tracks, they weren't especially unusual: what was odd was that they carried on for mile after mile across the countryside, deviating occasionally, and unnervingly, to pay a visit to the doors of churches. The rustics promptly said that the Devil had been abroad that night, and doubtless fled home in terror. Learned naturalists tended to believe that a less netherworldly agency had been at work, despite the possibility that Satan in his overweening pride almost certainly would have chosen a snowy night to stalk the earth, if only to ensure maximum publicity. The professors however, were hard put to say just what the creature might have been, so there, more or less, the matter rests.

Possibly the weirdest animals ever reported in the annals

of science were those that disturbed the peace of electrical pioneer Andrew Crosse. While conducting a fairly unremarkable experiment he was suitably astonished to discover that tiny bugs – which he called *acari* – were emerging from the crystalline substance he had concocted. No less a scientist than Michael Faraday was convinced that Crosse had somehow stumbled on a means of creating life – and a fairly complex form of life at that. The possibility that the tiny creatures had already been present in Crosse's equipment was fairly readily dismissed when another experimenter managed to reproduce the results. The world has since steered very clear of this extremely thorny issue, and at the time was reduced to making rude noises about Crosse – as if he had somehow plotted to embarrass and flummox the learned men of the day. In doing so, science actually retreated from the chance to discover, as far as was possible, what had actually occurred in his laboratory that day.

Having opened with the suggestion that when it comes to a mystery we prefer to travel on our journey than to arrive at a solution, it may seem paradoxical that some of the cases in this book do have distinct and definite conclusions. One of the most notorious animals in the history of psychical research, for example, is Gef the talking mongoose. The companion – not to say familiar – of an intelligent teenage girl, Gef caused headlines in the 1930s with the claim that he could speak. That was all very well, but hardly anyone actually clapped eyes on the beast. Few people, for some reason, seem to have been inspired to ask what a mongoose, which likes to live in the tropics and enjoys eating snakes, was doing on a dank island off the coast of England in the first place, but that has not stopped the tale being repeated in sensationalist books and magazine articles for decades. And when one knows the facts as they are detailed here, that is something of a mystery in itself.

Another such tale is the so-called 'haunting' of Lord Dufferin by a spectre who seemed to herald his death. The true story of this oft-repeated legend is rather different, but has rarely seen the light of day. And it seemed only fair to close some of the traditional 'open files', lest it be thought we had missed some really inexplicable cases.

Hence, too, our inclusion of the present, accurate version of the story of the man in the iron mask. This has often been taken to be a mystery as intriguing as the fate of the Dauphin of France at the time of the Revolution, with all kinds of surreal and unlikely characters being suggested as the mysterious masked prisoner. The true story is quite intriguing enough, however, without any embroidery or fantastic additions.

But of all the unexplained feats of story-telling, perhaps the prize goes to the legend of the Indian rope trick. The main features of this astounding display are familiar to almost everyone: the rope that mysteriously stands on end by itself, the boy who climbs up it and whose limbs in due course come tumbling gruesomely from the sky. Of the various theories suggested to account for the rope trick perhaps the most plausible was that some form of mass suggestion was worked by the fakir. But such authentic photographs as did exist of the trick would not bear this out. The rope trick became part of that magic and romantic place, the 'mysterious East', populated by 'inscrutable Orientals' who were capable of working the most powerful spells and performing impossible feats. This is not the place to give away the secret of the rope trick, but it is a mystery whose solution is so stunningly simple that, once more, one is left amazed that anyone was taken in the first time around.

There remains just one more class of 'open file' that we've so far left unmentioned. That is the mysterious place. The moving stones of Racetrack Playa in Death Valley, California, have long attracted attention – and bemusement – for leaving long tracks behind them as they shift about. The only problem is that no-one has ever seen one of these stones move, and though there are a number of plausible theories as to how they do it, no-one is sure that any of them is correct.

Even more peculiar are the events in England's Clapham Wood, where people disappear, strange rites are performed, and UFOs habitually pass by. This is one of those instances of a site of very ancient significance that seems to attract both peculiar phenomena and unusual behaviour, as if the very age of the place itself exerted some power. Or, perhaps, the prehistoric people who first noticed the place were better able than we are to judge that it held some secret, and accordingly made it a sacred place. Whatever the reason, the power of the site seems undiminished even today.

Here then are mystery stories, most of them without heroes or villains – or dramatic endings. Perhaps one day we shall find the answers. But do we really want to?

PETER BROOKESMITH

Joan Norkot

With a nod or a wink

The old belief that a corpse will react to the presence of its murderer seems to have found horrific expression in the strange case of Joan Norkot. GRAHAM FULLER and IAN KNIGHT investigate the 'impossible' story of the rotting corpse that winked

ONCE DEAD AND BURIED few people have shown signs of life, but those that have, or are rumoured to have been reanimated, have naturally enough inspired the witnesses with awe and fear. In the case of Joan Norkot, who died in 1629, her brief moment of posthumous glory did more; it was enough to point the finger of accusation – almost literally – at her murderers, and subsequently to secure their conviction.

Such was the course of justice in 17th-century England. In those days of widespread superstition it was firmly believed that the body of a murder victim would bleed at the touch of the assassin, and considered binding legal evidence if it did so.

The strange case of Joan Norkot was rediscovered in 1851, when it was one of the legal and historical occurrences selected from the day books of Dr Henry Sampson for inclusion in the July edition of *The Gentleman's Magazine and Historical Review*. In 1851 pragmatism, fact and scientific evidence were the order of the day, as this Victorian journal's prefatory remarks on the case show:

The next extract contains a narrative of a very singular legal case, which comes down to us upon the most unquestionable authority – that of the old Serjeant who, after having been an original member of the Long Parliament of Charles I, lived as father of the bar to congratulate King William on his accession in 1688. . . . It would be difficult to parallel the following relation of superstition and miserable insufficiency of legal proof. . . .

Top: the Long Parliament of 1640, in which John Mainard (above) had sat, living long enough to see William III come to the throne in 1688. Yet his intellect remained as sharp as ever and he was considered an impeccable witness to the bizarre case of Joan Norkot

Left: the resuscitation of Margaret Dickson, a murderer who was hanged in 1728. But Joan Norkot had actually decomposed – how could she have revived?

The 'old Serjeant' in question was one Sir John Mainard, 'a person of great note and judgment in the law', whose version of the Norkot incident was recorded in a manuscript 'fair written with his own hands' and discovered among his papers after his death at the age of 88 in 1690; a copy of it was taken by a Mr Hunt of the Temple, who gave it to Dr Sampson for his records.

Joan Norkot lived in Hertfordshire – it is not known exactly where – with her husband Arthur, her infant son, her sister Agnes and brother-in-law John Okeman, and her mother-in-law Mary Norkot. By all accounts a cheerful, good-looking woman, happily married and a good mother, Joan was well-known to the locals, who expressed surprise and horror when it was revealed that one morning she had been found with her throat cut, apparently the victim of a violent attack, still clutching her child in her arms. Her family claimed that it was suicide.

So had Joan committed suicide? On the night of her death, said Mary Norkot and the Okemans, Joan's husband had been away, visiting friends. They further claimed that there had been 'a deal of trouble' between Arthur and Joan of late, and that on her last

evening alive she had been 'in a sour temper, and some despondency'. So maybe, in a fit of despair, she had plunged the knife into her throat. But this was not good enough for Joan's friends and neighbours. In the weeks following the inquest rumour grew to such an extent in the village that it directly challenged the legal verdict. With new evidence coming to light from investigations at the Norkot cottage, it was widely believed that Joan could not have killed herself. Acting on popular opinion,

the jury, whose verdict was not drawn into form by the coroner, desired the coroner that the body, which was buried, might be taken up out of the grave, which the coroner assented to, and thirty days after her death she was taken up, in presence of the jury and a great number of the people.

The touch test

It was at the exhumation, according to the testimony later given in court by the local clergyman, that the test of touch decreed by superstitious custom was made. Mainard takes up the story:

. . . the four defendants present, they were required, each of them, to touch the dead body. Okeman's wife fell on her knees and prayed God to show token of their innocency, or to some such purpose. . . . The appellers did touch the dead body, whereupon the brow of the dead, which was of a livid or carrion colour (that was the verbal expression in the terms of the witness) began to have a dew or gentle sweat [which] ran down in drops on the face, and the brow turned and changed to a lively and fresh colour, and the dead

Left: a portrait said to be of Sir Nicholas Hyde, the Lord Chief Justice at Hertford Assizes (below) in 1629 when Joan Norkot's family were tried for her murder. At first it was thought that Joan had committed suicide, but the local people suspected foul play and her body was exhumed. Each member of Joan's family was compelled to touch the grisly remains, which then winked and raised a finger – damning evidence against them in those days. Once the case was brought to court other, more conventional, evidence came to light, and the accused were convicted of Joan's murder and duly hanged – except for her sister-in-law Agnes, who was reprieved because she was pregnant. The motive for the murder remains obscure

opened one of her eyes and shut it again, and this opening the eye was done three several times. She likewise thrust out the ring or marriage finger three times and pulled it in again, and the finger dropt blood from it on the grass.

This, in 1629, was irrefutable proof of homicide, and once the furore that necessarily accompanied Joan Norkot's sudden return to the land of the living (and equally abrupt return to eternal sleep) had died down, the jury altered its verdict.

Although it was now declared that Joan Norkot had been 'murdered, by person or persons unknown', the eye of suspicion had come to rest firmly on Arthur, Mary, Agnes and John, and they were subsequently tried at Hertford Assizes – and at first acquitted.

'The evidence' weighed so heavily against them, however, that presiding Judge Harvy suggested 'that it were better an appeal were brought than so foul a murder should escape unpunished.' Joan Norkot's orphaned son became the plaintiff in the appeal, which was duly lodged against his father, grandmother, aunt and uncle. Said Mainard himself, '. . . because the evidence was so strange I took exact and particular notice of it.' In the trial the events at the graveside were soberly recounted by the local parish minister, described by the chronicler as a 'grave person' but one whose name has not survived.

Not surprisingly, the officiating judge, Chief Justice Nicholas Hyde, doubted the old cleric's evidence. 'Who saw this beside yourself?' he asked the witness. 'I cannot swear that others saw it,' replied the minister, 'but my Lord, I believe the whole company saw it, and if it had been thought a doubt, proof would have been made of it, and many would have attested with me . . . .'

Further, less fantastic evidence was then brought against Mrs Norkot senior and the Okemans, adding to the argument that if no

Below: an altar tomb. There are many legends of 'mysterious' rappings coming from such tombs, and of skeletons found bent and twisted inside them. Premature burial was common – comatose or cataleptic people were often thought to be dead and were duly buried, only to die of asphyxiation, thirst or horror. Yet it seems that Joan Norkot was well and truly dead when her body was exhumed, so premature burial can be ruled out as an explanation for her brief reanimation

one had gone into the cottage between the time when Joan retired for the night and when she was found dead, then they must be her murderers. Joan had been found lying in her bed with the bedclothes undisturbed, and her child with her – indicating that suicide had not taken place in the bed, in fact not at all. Her throat was cut from ear to ear and her neck broken, and if she first cut her throat, she could not break her neck while lying in the bed, or vice versa.

Murder most foul

Clearly the dead body had been moved and there had been a half-hearted attempt to conceal the evidence. Moreover, the bloody knife had been firmly embedded in the floor some distance from the bed, point towards the bed, haft towards the door. However violent her death throes, there is no way that Joan Norkot – had she actually taken her own life – could have thrown the blade into that position. Lastly, there was the bloody print of a left hand on top of Joan's own left hand, an item of evidence that Chief Justice Hyde questioned but eventually accepted.

The four prisoners were then brought forward but had no defence to offer. Arthur Norkot's alibi collapsed when it was revealed that he had not visited the friends he had claimed to be staying with for several years. The jury retired and when it returned found Norkot, his mother and Agnes guilty of murder. Okeman was acquitted. The three guilty persons each cried out, 'I did not do it! I did not do it!' but, nevertheless, judgement was passed. Norkot and his mother were sentenced to death and duly hanged, but Agnes Norkot was reprieved when it was discovered she was pregnant.

In his reconstruction and discussion of the case in *Unsolved mysteries* (1952), Valentine Dyall suggests a possible – though speculative – reason for the murder:

> The motive for the crime remained obscure, though it was generally supposed that Arthur Norkot had believed his wife unfaithful. The other two women of the family, known to be jealous of Joan's good looks and position as mistress of the house, probably made willing accomplices – while John Okeman, a simple fellow, was bullied into silence.

But there is no logical explanation for the incredible scene that took place when Joan was disinterred. We can toy with the notion of premature burial, but there can be no doubt that Joan Norkot was well and truly deceased when she was laid to rest. Perhaps exposure to the elements had an immediate chemical effect on her decaying flesh, explaining the 'lively and fresh colour' of her brow, but how did Joan's eye wink, and her finger move and yield fresh blood?

Maybe it was just that Joan Norkot, in the course of divine retribution, awoke fleetingly from death to ensure that justice was done.

Memories of a distant star?

The Dogon people of West Africa have a detailed knowledge of the Universe that is astonishingly accurate. But, asks FRANCIS HITCHING, how did they obtain this knowledge? Was it, as the Dogon claim, passed on by ancient astronauts?

LIKE MANY AFRICAN TRIBES, the Dogon people of the Republic of Mali have a shadowed past. They settled on the Bandiagara Plateau, where they now live, some time between the 13th and 16th centuries. It is about 300 miles south of Timbuktu, for most of the year a desolate, arid, rocky terrain of cliffs and gorges dotted with small villages built from mud and straw.

Although most anthropologists would class them as 'primitive', the 2 million people who make up the Dogon and surrounding tribes would not agree with this epithet. Nor do they deserve it, except in the sense that their way of life has changed little over the centuries. Indifferent though they are to

Below: a Dogon settlement at the foot of the Bandiagara cliffs. The Dogon are a primitive people, yet they have a profound belief that they were originally taught and 'civilised' by beings from outer space – from the star system Sirius

Right: Sirius lies in the constellation Canis Major, near the foot of Orion. It can be readily identified as it sits in a line with the three bright stars of Orion's belt

Western technology, their philosophy and religion is both rich and complex. Outsiders who have lived with them, and learned to accept the simplicity of their lives, speak of them as a happy, contented, fulfilled people whose attitude to the essential values of life dates back millennia.

Unremarkable enough so far – but the Dogon make one astounding claim. They believe, with absolute certainty, that they were originally taught and 'civilised' by creatures from outer space: specifically, from the star system Sirius, 8.7 light years away.

And they back up this claim with what seems to be extraordinarily detailed knowledge of astronomy for such a 'primitive' and isolated tribe. Notably, they know that Sirius, the brightest star in the sky, has a companion star, invisible to the naked eye, which is small, dense, and extremely heavy. This is perfectly accurate. But its existence was not even suspected by Western astronomers until the middle of the 19th century; it was not described in detail until the 1920s, and not photographed (so dim is this star, called Sirius B) until 1970.

Yet this curious astronomical fact forms the central tenet of Dogon mythology. It is enshrined in their most secret rituals, portrayed in sand drawings, built into their sacred architecture, and can be seen in carvings, and patterns woven into their blankets, whose designs almost certainly date back hundreds, if not thousands, of years.

It has been held as the most persuasive evidence yet that Earth had, in its fairly recent past, an interplanetary connection – a close encounter of the educational kind. The extent of Dogon knowledge has also been looked at extremely sceptically, to establish whether all that they say is true, and if true, whether their information may not have

Above left: Sirius, the brightest star in the sky, and its white dwarf companion Sirius B. This tiny star is so dim that it was not photographed until 1970 – yet the Dogon have always made sand drawings portraying Sirius accompanied by another star

Above: Marcel Griaule and Germaine Dieterlen (top), the two French anthropologists who lived with the Dogon tribe for over 20 years, and to whose careful study we owe much of our knowledge of Dogon mythology

Right: cave paintings depicting the myths of the Dogon people

come from an Earthbound source – a passing missionary, say.

So first, how did we in the West come to know of the Dogon beliefs? There is just one basic source, which fortunately is a very thorough one. In 1931 two of France's most respected anthropologists, Marcel Griaule and Germaine Dieterlen, decided to make the Dogon the subject of extended study. For the next 21 years they lived almost constantly with the tribe. In 1946 Griaule was invited by the Dogon priests to share their innermost sacred secrets. He attended their rituals and their ceremonies, and learned, so far as it was possible for any Westerner to do so, the enormously complex symbolism that stemmed from their central belief in the amphibious creatures, which they called Nommo, that had come from outer space to civilise the world. Griaule himself came to be revered by the Dogon as much as their priests. At his funeral in Mali in 1956, a quarter of a million tribesmen gathered to pay him homage.

The findings of the two anthropologists were published first in 1950, in a cautious and scholarly paper entitled 'A Sudanese Sirius System' in the *Journal de la Société des Africainistes*. After Griaule's death, Germaine Dieterlen remained in Paris, where she was appointed Secretary General of the Société des Africainistes at the Musée de

Right: the entrance to a Dogon shrine

Far right: members of the tribe performing a ritual dance. The designs on the masks worn by the dancers are said to represent the descent of a Nommo 'ark'

Below: carved wooden figure of a Dogon ancestor. Such carvings are essential to the tribe's many rituals

l'Homme. She wrote up their joint studies in a massive volume entitled *Le renard pâle*, the first of a planned series, published in 1965 by the French national Institute of Ethnology.

The two works make it overwhelmingly clear that the Dogon belief system is indeed based on a surprisingly accurate knowledge of astronomy, mingled with a form of astrology. Lying at the heart of it is Sirius, and the various stars and planets that they believe to orbit around it. They say that its main companion star, which they call *po tolo*, is made of matter heavier than anything on Earth, and moves in a 50-year elliptical orbit.

All these things are true. Western astronomers first deduced that something curious was happening around Sirius about 150 years ago. They noted certain irregularities in its motion which they could explain only by postulating the existence of another star close to it, which was disturbing Sirius's movements through the force of gravity. In 1862 the American astronomer Alvan Graham Clark actually spotted the star when testing a new telescope, and he called it Sirius B.

However, it took another half-century from the first observation of Sirius's peculiarities until a mathematical and physical explanation could be found for why such a small object was exerting such massive force. Sir Arthur Eddington, in the 1920s, formulated the theory of certain stars being 'white dwarfs' – stars near the end of their life that have collapsed in on themselves and become superdense.

The description fitted the Dogon version precisely. But how could they have learned about it in the three years between Eddington's announcement of the theory in a popular book in 1928, and the arrival of Griaule and Dieterlen in 1931? The two anthropologists were baffled: 'The problem of knowing how, with no instruments at their disposal, men could know of the movements and certain characteristics of virtually invisible stars has not been settled.'

At this point another researcher entered the scene: Robert Temple, an American scholar of Sanskrit and Oriental Studies living in Europe, who became deeply fascinated by the two questions raised by the Dogon enigma.

First, was the evidence of the Dogon understanding of astronomy to be believed? And second, if the answer to the first question was positive, how could they conceivably have come by this knowledge?

A careful reading of the source material, and discussions with Germaine Dieterlen in Paris, convinced him after a time that the Dogon were indeed the possessors of an ancient wisdom that concerned not just Sirius B, but the solar system in general. They said the Moon was 'dry and dead like dry dead blood'. Their drawing of the planet Saturn had a ring round it (two other exceptional cases of primitive tribes privy to this information are known). They knew that planets revolved round the sun, and recorded the movements of Venus in their sacred architecture. They knew of the four 'major moons' of Jupiter first seen by Galileo (there are now known to be at least 14). They knew correctly that the Earth spins on its axis. They believed there was an infinite number of stars, and that there was a spiral force involved in the Milky Way, to which Earth was connected.

Since much of this came down in myth and symbolism, in which objects on Earth were said to represent what went on in the skies, and in which a concept of 'twinning' made many of the calculations obscure, it could not be said that the evidence was totally unambiguous. But with Sirius B in particular the central facts seemed unarguable. The Dogon deliberately chose the smallest yet most significant object they could find – a grain of their essential food crop – to symbolise Sirius B: *po tolo* means literally a star made of *fonio* seed. They stretched their imaginations to describe how massively heavy its mineral content was: 'All earthly beings combined cannot lift it.'

Temple found the sand drawings particularly compelling. The egg-shaped ellipse might perhaps be explained away as representing the 'egg of life', or some such symbolic

Below: grain stores in a Dogon settlement. The doors to the granaries (right) are decorated with painted figures depicting the tribe's heavenly ancestors

meaning. But the Dogon were insistent that it meant an orbit – a fact discovered by the great astronomer Johannes Kepler in the 16th century, but certainly not known to untutored African tribes. And they also put the position of Sirius within the orbit exactly where it ought to be rather than where someone might naturally guess it: that is, at a focal point near the edge of the ellipse, rather than in the centre.

So how did the Dogon come to have this unearthly knowledge? Here, so far as the priests were concerned, there was no ambiguity whatsoever in the answer: they believe profoundly that amphibious creatures from a planet within the Sirius system landed on Earth in distant times and passed on the information to the initiates, who in turn handed it down over the centuries. They call the creatures Nommos, and worship them as 'the monitor of the universe, the father of mankind, guardian of its spiritual principles, dispenser of rain and master of the water'.

Temple found that the Dogon drew sand diagrams to portray the spinning, whirling descent of a Nommo 'ark', which he takes to mean a spaceship:

The descriptions of the landing of the ark are extremely precise. The ark is said to have landed on the earth to the north-east of the Dogon country, which is where the Dogon claim to have come from originally.

The Dogon describe the sound of the landing of the ark. They say the 'word' of Nommo was cast down by him in the four directions as he descended, and it sounded like the echoing of the four large stone blocks being struck with stones by the children, according to special rhythms, in a very

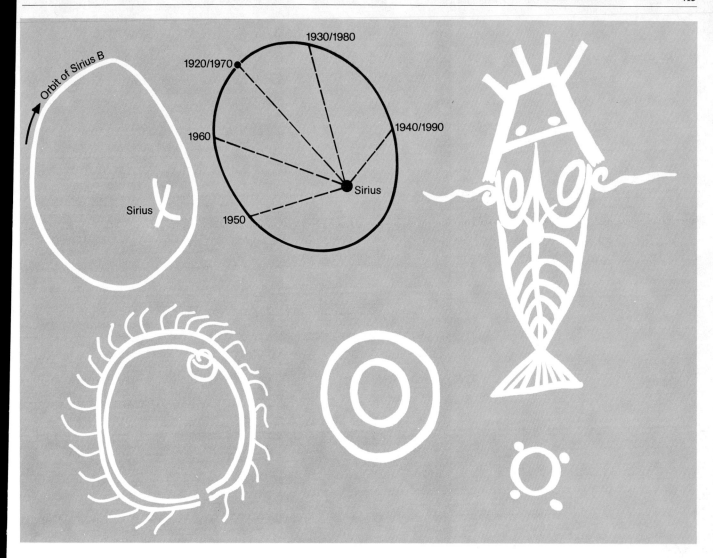

Tribal drawings of the Nommo (top right), the amphibious creatures said to have given the Dogon information about the solar system, and of the descent of the ark (above), the 'spaceship' in which the Nommo travelled. The Dogon's knowledge of astronomy is illustrated in their drawings: their portrayal of the orbit of Sirius B around Sirius (top left) is remarkably similar to a modern astronomical diagram (top centre); they show Saturn with its ring (above centre), and depict the four 'major moons' of Jupiter discovered by Galileo (above right)

small cave near Lake Debo. Presumably a thunderous vibrating sound is what the Dogon are trying to convey. One can imagine standing in the cave and holding one's ears at the noise. The descent of the ark must have sounded like a jet runway at close range.

Other descriptions that the Dogon priests used to refer to the landing of the 'ark' tell how it came down on dry land and 'displaced a pile of dust raised by the whirlwind it caused. The violence of the impact roughened the ground . . . it skidded.'

Robert Temple's conclusions, first published in 1976 in his book *The Sirius mystery*, are at once highly provocative and extensively researched. As such, his findings have been used as ammunition both by those who believe in extra-terrestrial visitations in Earth's formative past, and by those (including the majority of scientists and historians) who believe the idea is bunkum.

Erich von Däniken, for instance, whose best-selling books on the subject have now been shown to be based, in the main, on distorted evidence, has welcomed the Dogon beliefs, calling them 'conclusive proof . . . of ancient astronauts'. Against him range a number of science writers – among them Carl

Sagan and Ian Ridpath – who believe the case is by no means proved, and that Temple has read too much into Dogon mythology.

Robert Temple himself, 10 years after first becoming interested in the subject, found nothing to retract from the answer he gave to his publisher, who expressed his central doubt about the manuscript thus: 'Mr Temple, do you believe it? Do you believe it *yourself*?'

Temple answered: 'Yes, I do. I have become convinced by my own research. In the beginning I was just investigating. I was sceptical. I was looking for hoaxes, thinking it couldn't be true. But then I began to discover more and more pieces which fit. And the answer is *yes, I believe it.*'

The crucial question is whether the Dogon's knowledge could have been obtained in any ordinary, mundane way. Was this apparently arcane, obscure and detailed astronomical information given to them by the Nommo – or was it simply obtained from Westerners and rapidly absorbed into their mythology?

The amphibians from outer space

Did ancient astronauts civilise the Earth? And could they have come from a third star in the Sirius system, a star not yet discovered by Western astronomers?

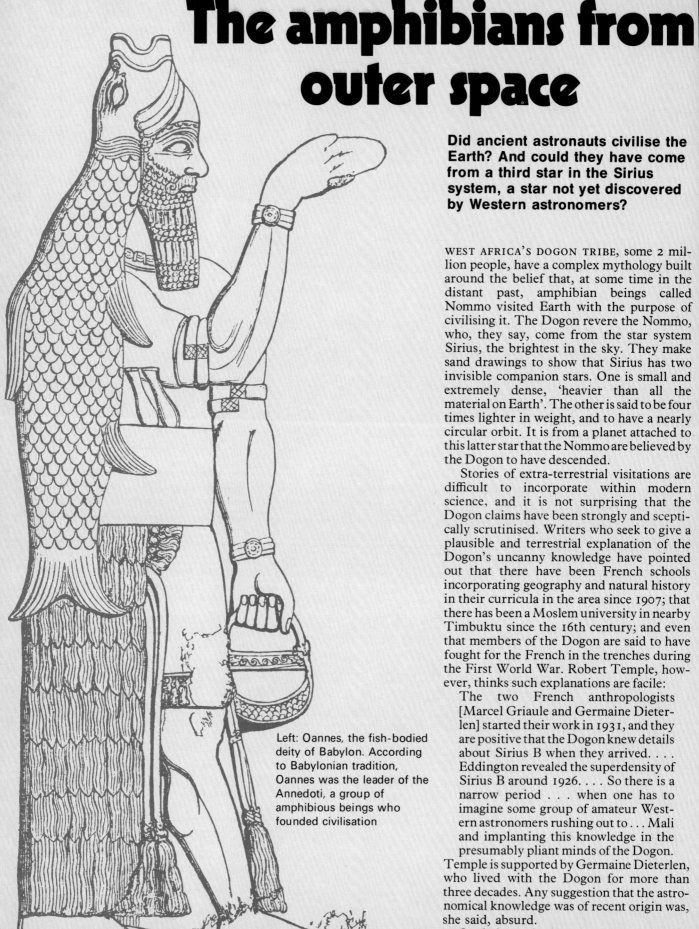

Left: Oannes, the fish-bodied deity of Babylon. According to Babylonian tradition, Oannes was the leader of the Annedoti, a group of amphibious beings who founded civilisation

WEST AFRICA'S DOGON TRIBE, some 2 million people, have a complex mythology built around the belief that, at some time in the distant past, amphibian beings called Nommo visited Earth with the purpose of civilising it. The Dogon revere the Nommo, who, they say, come from the star system Sirius, the brightest in the sky. They make sand drawings to show that Sirius has two invisible companion stars. One is small and extremely dense, 'heavier than all the material on Earth'. The other is said to be four times lighter in weight, and to have a nearly circular orbit. It is from a planet attached to this latter star that the Nommo are believed by the Dogon to have descended.

Stories of extra-terrestrial visitations are difficult to incorporate within modern science, and it is not surprising that the Dogon claims have been strongly and sceptically scrutinised. Writers who seek to give a plausible and terrestrial explanation of the Dogon's uncanny knowledge have pointed out that there have been French schools incorporating geography and natural history in their curricula in the area since 1907; that there has been a Moslem university in nearby Timbuktu since the 16th century; and even that members of the Dogon are said to have fought for the French in the trenches during the First World War. Robert Temple, however, thinks such explanations are facile:

> The two French anthropologists [Marcel Griaule and Germaine Dieterlen] started their work in 1931, and they are positive that the Dogon knew details about Sirius B when they arrived. . . . Eddington revealed the superdensity of Sirius B around 1926. . . . So there is a narrow period . . . when one has to imagine some group of amateur Western astronomers rushing out to . . . Mali and implanting this knowledge in the presumably pliant minds of the Dogon.

Temple is supported by Germaine Dieterlen, who lived with the Dogon for more than three decades. Any suggestion that the astronomical knowledge was of recent origin was, she said, absurd.

On balance it does not seem as if the

Dogon information came from modern Western sources – at least according to the researchers who have lived in and studied the area. But the evidence is by no means unambiguous, and there are only two ways of reaching a sound judgement about the extraordinary Dogon beliefs: first, to see if there is any supportive evidence in other legends from other places; and second, to see if there is any claim made by the Dogon that can be scientifically tested.

We are in the fortunate position of being able to make both approaches. The Dogon description of the Nommo is quite clear – they were amphibians, and they had a civilising, life-giving role. And their description of two invisible stars orbiting Sirius is intensely interesting, for although one (a so-called white dwarf) has already been discovered by Western astronomers, the other has not yet been. If the Dogon turned out to be correct in this, it would be powerful confirmation of the rest of their mythology.

In antiquity, the Dogon were almost certainly neighbours of the Egyptians, living in North Africa on the shores of the Mediterranean. So it is the classical mythologies – Egyptian, Mesopotamian and Greek – that must be examined to see if there are parallel legends speaking of Sirius as something special in the sky, and of being the home of amphibian visitors from outer space.

It is a difficult task even for classical scholars. In his book *The Sirius mystery*, Robert Temple points out that the Dogon knowledge, until unearthed by two trusted French anthropologists, was sacred and secret to the priesthood. Similarly with classical legends.

> Secret doctrines are not scribbled down too frequently and left for posterity. The most secret doctrine of the

Above: the two medallions worn by this Dogon woman are said to signify the 'twinning' concept of Dogon mythology – the notion that each element of nature is one of a pair of opposites

> Dogon was only revealed with great reluctance after many, many years, and following upon a conference by the initiates. The Egyptians were no fools, and we can hardly expect them to have left papyri or texts specifically revealing in so many words what they were not supposed to reveal. We can only try to piece together clues.

In Temple's view, the clues 'turn into a veritable avalanche'. But about the star system Sirius itself the myths tell us disappointingly little. Peter James, a classical historian at London University, points out that it is hardly surprising that the ancients regarded Sirius as an important star and attached to it a number of mythological motifs. Sirius was not only the brightest star in the sky, but for many centuries its heliacal rising coincided with the inundation of the Nile, giving it a special calendrical importance. 'None of the myths as they stand obviously describe the kind of knowledge about Sirius' invisible astronomy such as the Dogon appear to possess – nothing suggests extraordinary knowledge of Sirius B.'

As an example of how far one has to stretch interpretation of myths in order to read into them an occult knowledge of Sirius's companion star, Peter James quotes the Isis/Osiris relationship as the best of Robert Temple's 'clues'. It is, to say the least, obscure:

> Isis, the goddess of Sirius, had a husband called Osiris, who was considered dark, or black. One of his aspects was Anubis, a Jackal-headed god. There is not much to go on here, but it at least suggests the possibility that the Egyptians knew about an invisible companion to Sirius A.

However, the parallels between Greek and

Left: in ancient Egyptian mythology, the dog god Anubis is often identified with Osiris, companion of the goddess Isis. Historian Robert Temple considers that as Isis herself was identified with Sirius, it is reasonable to suppose that her companion was identified with the companion of Sirius – suggesting that the ancient Egyptians knew of the existence of Sirius B

Dogon legends about civilising amphibian creatures are much more promising. Fish-bodied aliens abound in Greek mythology, notably in the island of Rhodes, with its culture-bearing inhabitants the Telchines.

Diodorus Siculus, the Greek historian, wrote of them that they were 'the discoverers of certain arts and introduced other things which are useful for the life of mankind.' Other texts speak of them being 'submarine magic spirits' and 'demons of the depths of the sea'; they 'had dog's heads and flippers for hands'.

From Berossus, a Babylonian priest, there is a very similar description of creatures called Annedoti ('Repulsive Ones'), fish-men who introduced civilisation. The first and most famous was called Oannes or Oe, who was thought to have come from a great egg, and who instructed the Babylonians 'in

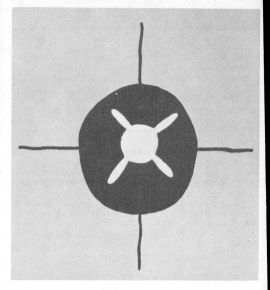

every thing which could tend to soften manners and humanize mankind'.

Peter James's cautious conclusion is 'there does seem to be a substratum of Greek myth that connects fish-deities with the introduction of civilisation and the oracles, that has parallels in the traditions of the Dogon and the Babylonians.'

None of this, of course, is as conclusive as would be the discovery of a third star in the Sirius system, as predicted by the Dogon. For the time being, once again the signs are not promising, but within the bounds of possibility. Indeed, the matter has been the subject of considerable astronomical debate.

In the 1920s, a number of astronomers repeatedly said they had observed a third star, and named it Sirius C. It was perceived as being red, so it could be what is known as a red dwarf, which is much less dense than a white dwarf. This would be consistent with the Dogon description of the third star being four times lighter (in weight) than Sirius B.

Subsequently, it has not been possible to observe the star. Also, perturbations in the

Above right: a Dogon drawing portraying the heliacal rising of Sirius. The Dogon claim their knowledge of such astronomical events came from the Nommo; but the ancient Egyptians knew of the rising of the star and based their calendar on it – could they have given the information to the Dogon?

Above: an altar object, depicting seven Nommo figures, from a Dogon shrine

Left: the hounds of Actaeon. According to Greek legend these were the survivors of the Telchines, amphibian, life-giving gods of Rhodes

movement of Sirius A, which were thought to be linked to a possible third star, have now been shown to be unconnected. The astronomer who provided this 'disproof', Irving W. Lindenblad at the US Naval Observatory in Washington, DC, thinks the existence of a third star highly unlikely: 'The possibility of a *very distant* third body cannot be ruled out theoretically as being physically impossible but there is absolutely no evidence for such a body.' Two astronomers at London University, writing in the technical journal *Astrophysics and space science*, were slightly more optimistic: they had produced on a computer near-circular orbits (as described by the Dogon) lasting from 275 to 425 years for a third star that would be consistent with the motion of Sirius A.

So where does this argument and counter-argument leave us? Are the Dogon traditions good evidence of extra-terrestrial visitors?

It is fair to conclude that, somehow or another, they are privy to astronomical information, which by right they should not be. This is the considered opinion of Germaine Dieterlen, and it seems preferable to accept her first-hand judgement than that of her (and Temple's) critics who re-interpret the myths at second hand.

But where did the knowledge derive? Is the misty link between the amphibians of Greek and Babylonian legend and the Dogon Nommo enough to make us sure that Earth has been visited in the past? It is so unlikely a possibility that before embracing it we might also consider other unlikely explanations: that the priesthoods of classical times formed their knowledge of the Universe through extra-sensory perception, using secret oracular methods that we have long forgotten, but that percolated into the mythology of the Dogon priesthood. Perhaps, against all the astronomical odds, the third star in the Sirius system, a supposed red dwarf, flared so violently that it could be seen and its orbit calculated. It is, you might say, a balance of improbabilities.

From a remote hilltop on the Isle of Man there came, in the 1930s, news of an amazing talking animal – a mongoose that was often heard but seldom seen. MELVIN HARRIS investigates the story of 'Gef' and the family he haunted

THE AFFAIR of the talking mongoose caused a great deal of excitement in the early 1930s. Initially called the 'talking weasel', this amazing creature lived in a remote place on the Isle of Man and, so the newspaper accounts said, did not just repeat words like a parrot. It used words with an understanding of their meaning. Indeed, according to the family with whom the creature lived, it gave direct answers to questions and made spontaneous comments – some of them quite witty and knowledgeable.

The animal haunted a place called Doarlish Cashen, an isolated farmstead perched over 700 feet (215 metres) up on the west coast of the island. It was a cheerless terrain without trees or shrubs. Even the nearest neighbours were out of view, over a mile (1.6 kilometres) away. Ordinarily there would be little to attract anyone to Doarlish Cashen. But, in September 1931, the rumours of the talking weasel sent the journalists scrambling up the forbidding hill to meet the Irving family who lived at the farm.

A rare picture of Gef, the talking mongoose – centre of a media sensation in the early 1930s. Usually Gef would not show himself even to the family with whom he lived – or whom he haunted – on the Isle of Man. But, so the family said, he allowed this photograph to be taken by Voirrey Irving, the daughter of the house. The wonderful talking animal, often witty and as often insulting, managed to elude all his many investigators

The head of the family was James Irving, a retired commercial traveller approaching 60. An intelligent man with mild, benign features, he was known as an engaging talker and raconteur. He seemed to keep his cheerfulness and good humour despite the fact that his farmstead production had steadily declined, reducing his income to a mere 15 shillings a week.

His wife Margaret was a few years younger than he. She was said to be tallish with a 'dignified bearing, upright and square of carriage'. Her grey hair rose primly above her forehead '. . . to frame her most compelling feature – two magnetic eyes that haunt the visitor with their almost uncanny power'. It was all too easy to draw the conclusion that Margaret Irving was the dominant personality in the household.

The Irvings' daughter Voirrey was 13 but old for her years. She seemed a reserved and undemonstrative child, hardly a scholar but obviously intelligent. And she took an intelligent and eager interest in anything to do with animals, reading any article or book she could get that dealt with them. By contrast, she was also fascinated by mechanical devices such as motor cars, aeroplanes and cameras.

Voirrey's knowledge of animals was not just theoretical but also practical. She was

The mongoose that talked

fully experienced in handling sheep and goats. And she had devised a successful way to catch rabbits. She would roam the hills with her sheepdog Mona until a rabbit was sighted. While Mona 'pointed' the prey and put it in a frozen mesmerised state, Voirrey would slowly creep up behind and kill the rabbit with a sharp blow to the head. The significance of her skills in this regard came out later.

Of the many newspaper reporters who met the Irvings, the luckiest came from the Manchester *Daily Dispatch*, for he was the only one to hear the talking weasel. He wrote of his successful mission:

Right: the Irving family in their ill-lit home, known as Doarlish Cashen. From the left are Voirrey, her mother Margaret and her father Jim

> The mysterious 'man-weasel' . . . has spoken to me today. Investigation of the most remarkable animal story that has ever been given publicity . . . leaves me in a state of considerable perplexity. Had I heard a weasel speak? I do not know, but I do know that I've heard today a voice which I should never have imagined could issue from a human throat.

He left the house puzzled and impressed but fully convinced that the Irvings were honest and responsible – unlikely to be the initiators

Below: Voirrey and her dog Mona. Some investigators hinted that Gef might be the creation of this lonely and intelligent girl, but this was not proved conclusively

of an elaborate and sustained practical joke. His next report, however, was more guarded:

> Does the solution of the mystery of the 'man-weasel' of Doarlish Cashen lie in the dual personality of the 13-year-old girl, Voirrey Irving? That is the question that leaps to my mind after hearing the piercing and uncanny voice attributed to the elusive little yellow beast with a weasel's body. . . . Yesterday I heard several spoken sentences. . . . The conversation was between the 'weasel-voice' and Mrs Irving, who was unseen to me in another room, while the girl sat motionless in a chair at the table. I could see her reflection, although not very clearly, in a mirror on the other side of the room. She had her fingers to her lips. . . . The lips did not move, so far as I could see, but they were partly hidden by her fingers. When I edged my way into the room the voice ceased. The little girl continued to sit motionless, without taking any notice of us. She was sucking a piece of string, I now saw.

Remarkably, none of the eager visitors ever caught sight of the talking animal. They all had to rely on Jim Irving's description to picture it. He judged it to be about the size of 'a three-parts grown rat, without the tail' and thin enough to pass through a 1½-inch (4-centimetre) diameter hole. Its body was yellow like a ferret's, its long bushy tail was tinged with brown, and its face was shaped somewhat like a hedgehog's but with a flattened, pig-like snout. This description was based on the pooled information of the three

Irvings, for each of them claimed to have seen the animal on separate occasions.

According to Jim Irving, their tiny lodger had first made itself known by barking, growling and spitting – all purely animal sounds. Irving took the sudden notion to try to teach the creature other kinds of noises. So he began to imitate animal and bird sounds and to name each creature as he made its sound. Within days, he claimed, the weasel would repeat the sounds as soon as the relevant animal or bird name was called out. The most astounding part of his experiment soon followed. 'My daughter then tried it with nursery rhymes, and no trouble was experienced in having them repeated.'

From then on there was no stopping the wily weasel. By February 1932 it was freely demonstrating its remarkable cleverness to the Irvings. Jim Irving wrote:

> It announces its presence by calling either myself or my wife by our Christian names. . . . It apparently can see in the dark and described the movements of my hand. Its hearing powers are phenomenal. It is no use whispering: it detects the whisper 15 to 20 feet [4.5 to 6 metres] away, tells you that you are whispering, and repeats exactly what one has said.

When the ghost hunter Harry Price learned of the talking weasel, he acted swiftly by asking a colleague to visit the Irvings and file a report. Price called this investigator 'Captain Macdonald' to protect him from any unwanted publicity. Macdonald obliged

and turned up at the farmhouse on the evening of 26 February 1932. There he sat around for almost five hours – and heard and saw nothing. But as he left the place, he heard a shrill scream from inside the house – 'Go away. Who is that man?' The words were quite clear at first, then they tailed away into unintelligible squeals. When Macdonald hurried back into the house, the voice ceased. So he arranged to return early the next day.

The next day's vigil started with the Captain being shown some water trickling from a hole in the wall. He was solemnly assured that this was 'the animal performing its natural functions'. The vigil proved more fruitful later. In the evening, Voirrey and her mother went into the bedroom above the living room and within minutes a shrill voice started talking to Margaret Irving. This went on for a quarter of an hour. Then Macdonald appealed to the animal to show itself. 'I believe in you!' he shouted, hoping to charm the evasive weasel. But the squealed reply was final. 'No, I don't mean to stay long as I don't like you!' Macdonald then tried to creep up the stairs but slipped, making a deafening clatter. With that the creature screamed, 'He's coming!' So ended Macdonald's hoped-for ambush.

Ten days later, Charles Northwood –

Doarlish Cashen, high on a cheerless hilltop with the nearest neighbour more than a mile (1.6 kilometres) away. The ramshackle house gave Gef plenty of scope for playing hide and seek

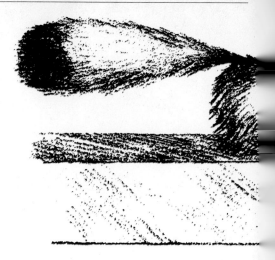

again, not his real name – turned up at Doarlish Cashen. An old friend of Jim Irving, he came out of concern for the Irvings, and later he sent a favourable report to Price. By now, the family had christened the talking animal 'Gef' and had discovered that he was an Indian mongoose born in Delhi on 7 June 1852. These details 'came from Gef himself'.

Once Northwood had settled in, Irving called out, 'Come on Gef, Mr Northwood's here. You promised to speak you know!' But not a squeak was heard – until Voirrey went into the kitchen to prepare lunch. Then in a mild voice Gef said, 'Go away Voirrey, go away.' Two minutes later Gef began to speak again. Then, when Irving asked him to bark,

Right: Jim Irving points to Gef's fingers appearing through the slats on the bedroom wall. All the pictures of the talking mongoose were uniformly poor and indistinct, leaving as much to the imagination as to the eye

Below: the wooden box-like structure known as 'Gef's Sanctum', located in Voirrey's room. On top is a chair that, according to the Irvings, the mongoose pushed around for exercise

he promptly did so. But he refused to sing his favourite song *Carolina moon*, even though the gramophone record was played to inspire him. Later still, Gef shouted, 'Charlie, Charlie, Chuck, Chuck . . . Charlie my old sport! . . . Clear to the Devil if you don't believe!'

Gef's mood changed when he heard that Northwood's son, Arthur, was due to arrive at the Irving farm. He grew threatening. 'Tell Arthur not to come. He doesn't believe. I won't speak if he does come. I'll blow his brains out with a thruppenny cartridge!'

Then he softened a little and returned to domestic small talk. 'Have you ordered the rooster, James, from Simon Hunter? Mind you do so. Have you posted that letter?' But a short while later his vicious side took over again. As Northwood put it:

> . . . from behind the boards in the sitting room, possibly some 25 to 30 feet [8 to 9 metres] away, I heard a very loud voice penetrating, and with some malice in it: 'You don't believe. You are a doubter,' etc. This was very startling, and for the first time put a bit of a shiver through me. Equal to a couple of irascible women's voices put together! I said: 'I do believe.' I had to shout this.

Then came the probing query, 'Charlie. . .is Arthur coming?' followed by a screech and a loud thump.

By this time Northwood had to leave, which meant the end of the encounter. But on his way down the hill he heard some screeches behind him and each of these was identified by Irving as having been made by Gef.

Northwood made a second visit a few days afterwards, bringing his sister-in-law and niece. This time, he claimed, his sister-in-law and her little girl heard the talking mongoose as well. 'Gef said the name of my sister-in-law's child and said that she had a powder puff in her bag.' He conceded that this was not very telling because both these facts were well-known to Voirrey. Despite that, he remained convinced that Gef was not Voirrey, but 'some extraordinary animal which has developed the power of speech by

some extraordinary process.'

The Northwood visits were the last productive ones for the next three years. But that long timegap did not mean that Gef had gone to earth. On the contrary, the Irvings stated that he became more entertaining and more adventurous during those years. And Jim Irving was able to produce a diary that recorded many of the mongoose's new sayings and antics.

From this account we learn that Gef began killing rabbits to help the family budget. After killing them he would leave them near the house and report the exact position to the family. Then he started bringing home other useful things: a paintbrush one day, then a pair of pincers, then a pair of gloves.

Top: a drawing of Gef from Harry Price's book on the talking mongoose affair. Irving said that he had got the description he gave to the artist from Gef himself, since the mongoose so shyly stayed out of sight

Above: two mongooses in their natural habitat. The Indian species, of which Gef claimed to be one, is famous for its snake-killing skill. But the mongoose is a predator of small mammals as well, and Gef concentrated on killing rabbits

In the house itself, he grew increasingly playful. He would bounce a rubber ball up and down in time with gramophone records and push a lightweight chair around to get exercise. According to the diary, all these events were staged on top of a wooden box-like structure in Voirrey's room, known as 'Gef's Sanctum'.

As a return for his services and entertainment he expected, in fact demanded, choice titbits. For him the orthodox mongoose diet was out. Gef insisted on offerings of lean bacon, sausages, bananas, biscuits, sweets and chocolates. These were carefully placed on one of the crossbeams of the roof so that he could sneak up and grab them when he chose. For Gef continued to be abnormally shy and hated being watched. The family had only brief glimpses of him on rare occasions.

During this period, Gef demonstrated both that he could speak in other languages, even if he used only the odd word and short phrase, and that he could perform some elementary arithmetic. He showed that he could read by yelling out some of the items printed in the newspapers left around the house. He also increased his repertoire of

songs and delighted the family with his renderings of *Home on the range*, *The Isle of Capri* and the Manx national anthem, as well as some Spanish and Welsh ditties.

More surprisingly, Gef allowed himself to be handled – though he still refused to show himself in full. Margaret Irving was permitted to place her finger in his mouth and feel his teeth. She was also graciously allowed to shake one of Gef's paws – which, she said, had 'three long fingers and a thumb'. These paws were obviously extremely versatile, since Irving claimed that Gef had opened drawers with them, struck matches and operated an electric torch.

The irascible Gef grew very free with his insults. When Irving was slow at opening his mail, Gef shouted, 'Read it out you fat-headed gnome!' When a visitor said she was returning to South Africa, he screamed, 'Tell her I hope the propeller drops off!'

A fascinating mystery

The formerly shy and retiring talking mongoose finally even agreed to pose for some photographs taken by Voirrey. But these were of poor quality and revealed almost no details. Then boldness prompted Gef to leave samples of his fur for examination. These samples were forwarded to Captain Macdonald who passed them on to Harry Price. In turn, Price sent them for examination to F. Martin Duncan, an authority on fur and hair at the Zoological Society of London.

While Price waited for the expert's opinion, Captain Macdonald visited Doarlish Cashen once more. Yet again, he heard Gef's voice but saw nothing of the elusive creature. This helped Price to decide to make an inspection of the house himself.

What sealed Price's decision to visit Doarlish Cashen was a revealing report from Duncan on the alleged mongoose hairs. Duncan's letter of 23 April 1935 read:

I have carefully examined them microscopically and compared them with hairs of known origin in my collection. As a result I can definitely state that the specimen hairs never grew upon a mongoose, nor are they those of a rat, rabbit, hare, squirrel or other rodent, or from a sheep, goat or cow. . . . I am inclined to think that these hairs have probably been taken from a longish-haired dog or dogs. . . . When you visit the farm keep a look-out for any dog . . . with a slight curly hair and a fawn and dark colour.

On 30 July 1935 Harry Price trudged up the hill to the Irving home on the trail of the talking mongoose. With him went R.S. Lambert, editor of the *Listener*. The two hoped to solve a fascinating mystery. And they bore Duncan's final words well in mind.

Lost for words

Were Voirrey Irving and Gef, the talking mongoose, one and the same? Were she and her family in a game of deception together? If so, what did they hope to gain?

THE INVESTIGATION BY Harry Price and R.S. Lambert of the talking mongoose of Doarlish Cashen ended after three days, for the amazing Gef failed to speak or display himself. Jim Irving, whose home the creature 'haunted', explained this away by saying that Gef had 'gone missing' some weeks before. So the investigators departed, feeling thwarted and baffled – for the Irvings had seemed to live up to their reputation as level-headed and sincere people.

They left behind a new camera for Irving's daughter Voirrey, but they took away some hairs from the collie dog Mona – samples they had secretly snipped off.

As soon as the two researchers had left the island, Gef reappeared – or so Irving said. And to make up for his temperamental vanishing act, Gef now promised to provide imprints of his paws. Price took up the offer and received three 'paw impressions' made in plasticine. These welcome exhibits were photographed and the prints, marked A, B and C, were given to R.I. Pocock, FRS, at the Natural History Museum in London.

Pocock's opinion of 5 October 1935 was that impression A did not represent the footprint of any animal known to him 'except possibly a raccoon, an American animal'. Impression B had no connection with A, but 'conceivably it was made by a dog'. Impression C had no possible connection with B, for: 'There is no mammal in which there is such disparity in the size of the fore and hind foot.' He concluded: 'I must add that I do not believe these photographs represent foot tracks at all. Most certainly none of them was made by a mongoose.'

Meanwhile, Mona's hair had been given to F. Martin Duncan, who had examined specimens of 'Gef's fur' earlier and had suggested that Price get samples from Voirrey's dog. Duncan's conclusion was unequivocal. He wrote '. . .your sample on examination is absolutely identical with the alleged "mongoose hairs". . .they all came from the same animal – the dog – and not from any "mongoose".' Along with his report, he sent photomicrographs and detailed drawings showing the unmistakable identity of the two batches of hair. So much for the only tangible evidence.

One last visit by Captain Macdonald, who was investigating at Harry Price's request, also failed to provide anything substantially new. Even fresh snapshots by Voirrey were

Right: three paw prints and some teeth marks (bottom right) said to belong to Gef, the talking mongoose of the Isle of Man. A scientist at London's Natural History Museum discredited them

Below right: some of the myriad documents in the file on Gef at the Society for Psychical Research. Gef's antics enlivened the media for several years in the early 1930s

Left: Voirrey and Jim Irving with R.S. Lambert, who investigated their claims about the talking mongoose with Harry Price. Lambert got into trouble with his employer, the BBC, over his part in the matter

Below: the desolate hilltop where the affair of the talking mongoose was played out

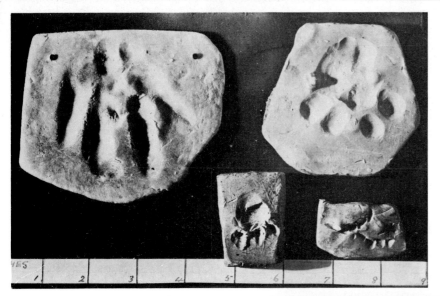

In the end the case just petered out, and the Irvings moved away.

So what lay behind the strange and colourful antics of the talking mongoose? Some of the earliest explanations considered Gef as a psychic phenomenon. The most curious psychical interpretation was advanced by the medium Florence Hodgkin in *Light* magazine of 3 June 1937. She claimed to have received an astonishing communication from a Lama about 'a race of people, actually in existence and living on the Earth at this moment, of whom the world has never heard. They are highly developed, cultured and so advanced that their animals have attained speech.' Gef apparently was an advance emissary, for Florence Hodgkin insisted:

> The Irving family 'know'. . . . That action fought so recently in our Courts of Law [see box] was a means of

of no value, since they simply showed something that could have been an out-of-focus fur collar.

Dr Nandor Fodor was another psychical researcher who looked into the 'Gef' phenomenon thoroughly. At the end of his extensive research on the Isle of Man, he could not come to any conclusion as to what Gef was.

There were four possibilities, as he saw it. One was that Gef was a poltergeist, centring on Voirrey. The second was that Gef was a ghost, haunting the house itself and unconnected to the Irvings. The third was that the elusive animal was a sort of 'familiar', a survival from the days of witchcraft. The final proposition was that Gef was indeed an animal. Fodor reluctantly decided in favour of the animal theory, remarking that 'All the evidence is in favour of Gef being a talking animal. I cannot prove he is an animal. I have not seen him. He did not talk to me. He claimed to be an animal. I cannot disprove that claim.'

Gef permitted Voirrey to take some pictures of him on a five-barred gate, about 300 yards (275 metres) from the house. None of these pictures was of even passable quality though, as Fodor records, 'some of them are distinct enough to show a small animal very much like a mongoose'. The pictures are shadowy and blurred, but a case can be made for Fodor's opinion.

However, the saddest part of the story is that Fodor was given the opportunity to photograph Gef, but he bungled it. What he did was to set up a kitchen scale and train Voirrey's camera at it, with a flashlight so fixed that if Gef could be persuaded to climb on the scale, he would take his own picture. Eventually the mongoose did agree to explode the flash in this way – but the image did not develop properly because of the inexpert way in which the apparatus had been set up. By using make-shift equipment for such an important experiment, Fodor muffed one of the finest opportunities given to a psychic investigator.

Richard Stanton Lambert was the editor of the BBC publication the *Listener* at the time that he helped Harry Price to investigate Gef, the talking mongoose – and he came to some grief over his part in the affair. For, after writing about Gef, he found himself under attack by Sir Cecil Levita, a former chairman of the London County Council.

Thought, word and deed

Sir Cecil went to the Assistant Programme Controller at the BBC, Gladstone Murray, and complained about Lambert's involvement in the occult. Words like 'unstable' and 'hysterical' were bandied about with regard to Lambert's character.

Fearing that his job was in jeopardy, Lambert brought a libel action against Sir Cecil. The trial came up on 4 November 1936 and Lambert was represented by the eminent barrister, Sir Patrick Hastings, KC. In summing up the case, Sir Patrick declared, 'Sir Cecil was saying in terms: this man is cracked. He has got to go, and if you, Mr Gladstone Murray, do not yourself go to the BBC and get Mr Lambert removed, I will go to them myself.'

The court found in Lambert's favour and awarded him what were then record damages. But it did not end there. The case caused a sensation and led to questions in Parliament and the setting up of a Parliamentary Board of Enquiry into relationships between the BBC and its staff. This in turn led to reforms within the BBC.

Not bad going for a mongoose – real or imaginary, talking or not.

broadcasting in a very real sense this stupendous and unbelievable fact. Irrefutable proof will be forthcoming shortly, because, as the Lama says, 'The time is coming for such a revelation.'

Such a revelation not having come, the talking mongoose affair makes sense only when viewed as a family fantasy.

To understand the background to this case, imagine what it was like living in that sombre, windswept farmhouse. There was no electricity, no television, no radio – not even a next-door neighbour. So the family was thrown in on itself, spending every evening together in gloomy rooms. This probably exaggerated their character traits.

Now, every child lives in a wonderland at times. Many create imaginary playmates who are talked to as if they were flesh and blood. In Voirrey's case, she seems to have created an exotic animal playmate with human capabilities, a mischievous schoolgirl wit, and a moody personality.

But why a mongoose? Well, it so happens that mongooses were once found in the very area that the Irvings lived in. In 1912, a farmer imported dozens of them and let them loose to cut down the rabbit population. That farmer's name was Irvine.

Voirrey could hardly have escaped hearing of *Irvine's* mongooses. And from there it was only one step to thinking about *Irving's* mongoose. Her very own unusual pet. A chatty little creature that would prowl the

deadly-dull farmhouse and bring it to life. An exhaustive examination of the documents in this case leads logically to the conclusion that Voirrey and Gef were one and the same. Indeed, one of the earliest newspaper accounts already proposed that the solution to the mystery lay in 'the dual personality' of Voirrey.

Gef never had a personality or existence independent of Voirrey. He brought home rabbits, as did Voirrey. His favourite foods were also Voirrey's favourites. He shared her strong interests in mechanical things. Moreover, Gef was never heard unless Voirrey was out of the room or so placed that her mouth could not be watched. The voice itself was described by one observer, who believed in Gef, as 'like a girl's voice of about 15 or 16 – a striking penetrating voice.' In other words, just the sort of voice Voirrey could easily assume.

It is true that some visitors had difficulty in spotting where Gef's voice came from, but that is not surprising. For the inside walls of the house were covered in boarding to keep out the cold, and these boards were fixed so that they stood some 5 inches (13 centimetres) away from the stone walls. As one reporter observed, 'It cannot be emphasised too much that the interior of the house resembles, in a way, a wooden drum.' Price similarly described the walls as acting like a 'vast speaking tube, with panels like drumheads'. By speaking against these panels, or into one of the many cracks and knotholes, it

Below: Rikki-Tikki-Tavi, the clever and engaging mongoose of Kipling's *The jungle book*. Voirrey Irving was known to be an avid reader of books about animals. If she was Gef's creator, as suspected, maybe she read about, and was inspired by, the storybook mongoose

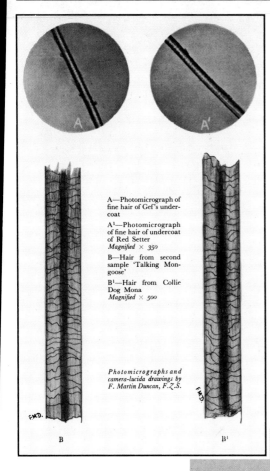

A—Photomicrograph of fine hair of Gef's under-coat

A¹—Photomicrograph of fine hair of undercoat of Red Setter *Magnified × 350*

B—Hair from second sample 'Talking Mongoose'

B¹—Hair from Collie Dog Mona *Magnified × 500*

Photomicrographs and camera-lucida drawings by F. Martin Duncan, F.Z.S.

B   B¹

Enlarged photographs (top) and detailed drawings (above) showed the sample of 'Gef's fur' (right) to be that of Mona (above right), Voirrey's pet dog. The analysis was made by an expert at the Zoological Society of London

was easy to project the voice and conceal its true point of origin.

But if Voirrey was indeed Gef, why did her parents go along with the deception? It is not unreasonable to assume that they were caught up in the masquerade and became accomplices. Indeed, Jim Irving became so involved that he 'became obsessed with the thing'. He would speak for hours, telling and retelling the saga to anyone who would listen. Price said that Irving spoke about Gef for two hours in his presence and, in that time, his recital 'invariably coincided (almost word for word) with what had been recorded in the letters [he] sent'.

It may well be that Irving came to need the

diversion more than Voirrey – to the point of forcing it to continue beyond its natural life. For, as Nandor Fodor noted, appearances in the Irving household were deceptive. Margaret Irving was not the dominant partner she seemed to be. The kingpin of the household was Jim Irving, under whose bland personality Fodor spotted that 'a tyrannical personality arose. . .the family never dared to challenge his autocratic rule.' Fodor summed Irving up as 'a man who failed in life. . . whose passions were too strong to bear this failure with resignation.'

So Irving was a man desperately needing fame of some kind – and promoting Gef made him notorious in his twilight years. Perhaps it was even the high point of his whole life. The publicity, the collecting of anecdotes, the storytelling: all these were Irving's responsibility – and his pride. He constantly interpreted Gef's speech for visitors. Half the time they weren't sure if they had heard the words for themselves or had picked up Irving's translation.

Surprise appearance

His role as an interpreter is clearly shown in the account written for the *Listener* by J. Radcliffe of the *Isle of Man Examiner*. He visited Doarlish Cashen with his father and some friends, but when Gef stayed silent, they left. On the doorstep they chatted for a while. Then:

> Suddenly there was a shrill squeak from the corner of the room where Voirrey, the daughter, was sitting, and Mr Irving in great excitement gripped my arm and pointing to the opposite side of the room whispered: 'He's there! Did you hear him?' Evans and I gazed at each other in sheer amazement. . . . We were again conducted to the door and the squeaks at intermittent intervals continued. Each squeak was kindly translated by Mr Irving to mean: 'They don't believe' or 'I want to back a horse', etc. The squeak in every case was of particularly short duration. . . . On our way down I noticed Voirrey had a tendency to hang behind, and once again we heard a piping squeak with Mr Irving again wildly gesticulating and pointing to the hedge and whispering: 'He's there, I tell you. He's there.' This was really too much, for my hearing is very good, and the squeak without doubt was human and came from immediately behind us. We laughed over the whole incident for days. . .because it was so badly done that it was extremely funny.

And laughter is surely the best response to the 'talking mongoose mystery' – for it was never a malicious affair and it provided a good deal of amusement and excitement. For those who cannot accept this verdict, perhaps Gef himself had the answer when he shrieked: 'Nuts! Put a sock in it! Chew coke!'

The terror of London

Who was the frightening figure – a man known only as Spring-heeled Jack – who terrorised the people of London for decades in the 19th century? In an attempt to unravel the mystery PAUL BEGG examines the legend that has built up around this bizarre character

THE LONELY LANES AND COMMONS of 19th-century suburban London were haunted by the weird and terrifying figure of Spring-heeled Jack, who pounced upon passers-by, sometimes wounded them severely, and bounded away in enormous leaps. Today the antics of Spring-heeled Jack are almost forgotten, or dismissed as a figment of the imagination – a mere character in Victorian horror literature, or a bogeyman used by mothers to warn errant children: 'Be good or Spring-heeled Jack will get you!' Some writers believe that Jack is a figure of popular folklore. Kellow Chesney in his book *The Victorian underworld* says that Jack is 'pure legend' – perhaps the invention of servants reluctant to admit negligence when thieves robbed their master's home.

But Jack was not a character in fiction, folklore or legend. He was real, and his appearances were widely reported in the local and national press.

Nobody seems certain when Jack first appeared. Many sources say that reports of a peculiar leaping man were in circulation as

On the tombstone, with upraised arms and rage in every feature, towered the terrific form of Spring-Heeled Jack. Freezer and Links stood transfixed; their ghastly burden slipped slowly to the grass, but they remained gaping, terror-struck. Vengeance had fallen!

early as 1817, but it was not until 1838 that Spring-heeled Jack became a figure of considerable and widespread interest and speculation. On 9 January 1838 the Lord Mayor of London, Alderman Sir John Cowan, revealed, at a public session held in the Mansion House, the contents of a letter he had received several days earlier. He had withheld it, he said, in the hope of obtaining further information. The correspondent, who signed the letter 'a resident of Peckham', wrote that, as the result of a wager, a person of the highest rank had adopted several frightening guises and set out to scare 30 people to death. He had 'already succeeded in depriving seven ladies of their senses', two of whom 'were not likely to recover, but likely to become burdens to their families.' The resident of Peckham continued:

The affair has now been going on for some time, and, strange to say, the papers are still silent on the subject. The writer has reason to believe that they have the whole history at their finger-ends but, through interested motives, are induced to remain silent.

We do not know why the Lord Mayor made

the contents of this letter public, nor can we judge the truth of the letter's allegation of a press 'cover-up', but from the quantity of letters that poured into the Mansion House it is clear that the activities of Spring-heeled Jack were common knowledge in suburban London.

Spring-heeled Jack had appeared as a milk-white bull, a white bear, and an enormous baboon; he had been seen dressed in a suit of shining brass armour, and on another occasion in one of burnished steel; once, in Hackney, he appeared as a lamplighter – who walked upon his hands and carried his ladder between his feet. His ability to make prodigious leaps was popularly ascribed to springs attached to his boots.

On Wednesday, 18 February 1838, 18-year-old Lucy Scales and her sister Margaret were returning home after visiting their brother, a butcher who lived in a respectable part of the district of Limehouse. Lucy, slightly ahead of her sister, was passing the

Above: Tod Slaughter as Spring-heeled Jack in the spine-chilling film *The curse of the Wraydons*, which was made in 1946

Left: 'Spring-heeled Jack parts the lovers', an illustration from a 19th-century 'penny dreadful'. Jack was the inspiration for several of these weekly serials: although usually portrayed as the villain of the piece, often terrorising young women (far left), he occasionally appeared as the hero, an avenger of crime and a punisher of wrongdoers (below left)

entrance to Green Dragon Alley when a figure leapt upon her from the shadows. The apparition breathed fire into Lucy's face and then bounded away as the girl fell to the ground, seized by violent fits.

Two days later, 18-year-old Jane Alsop replied to a violent ringing of the bell at the front gate of her parents' home in east London. Outside was an extremely agitated man who identified himself as a policeman. 'For God's sake bring me a light,' he cried, 'for we have caught Spring-heeled Jack in the lane!'

Blinded by fire

Jane fetched a candle, but when she handed it to the 'policeman', the man discarded his all-enveloping cloak. On his head was a large helmet, he wore a skin-tight suit of what looked like white oilskin, and in the light of the candle his protuberant eyes burned like coals. Without uttering a word, he vomited blue and white flames into Jane's face and grabbed the temporarily blinded and very frightened girl with talon-like fingers, which tore her dress and raked her skin. Attracted by her screams, Jane's sisters, Mary and Sarah, came to the girl's assistance. Somehow Sarah pulled Jane from the fiend's grasp, thrust her indoors and slammed the door in Jack's face.

A week later Jack tried the same deception but for some reason his intended victim was suspicious and Jack was forced to flee. A witness claimed that under his cloak Jack had been wearing an ornate crest and, in gold filigree, the letter 'w'.

After these attacks Jack's infamy grew. His exploits were reported in many newspapers and became the subject of no less than four 'penny dreadfuls' and melodramas performed in the cheap theatres that abounded at that time. But, perhaps as a result of the publicity, Jack's appearances became less frequent and occurred over a large area. It was not until 1843 that terror of Spring-heeled Jack again swept the country. Then he appeared in Northamptonshire, in Hampshire – where he was described as 'the very image of the Devil himself, with horns and eyes of flame' – and in East Anglia, where he took particular delight in frightening the drivers of mail coaches.

In 1845 reports came from Ealing and Hanwell, in west London, of a weird figure, leaping over hedges and walls and shrieking and groaning as it went. The perpetrator turned out to be a practical joker, a butcher from Brentford.

Later that year Jack was seen at Jacob's Island, Bermondsey, a disease-ridden slum of decaying houses linked by wooden galleries across stinking ditches. This area had been immortalised by Charles Dickens seven years earlier as the lair of Fagin and his motley band in *Oliver Twist*. Jack cornered a 13-year-old prostitute named Maria Davis on a bridge over Folly Ditch. He breathed fire into her face and hurled her into the stinking, muddy ditch below. The girl screamed terribly as the muddy waters claimed her. Witnesses reported the affair to the police, who dragged the ditch and recovered the poor girl's body. The verdict at the subsequent inquest was one of death by misadventure, but the inhabitants of the area branded Jack as a murderer.

There were isolated reports of Spring-heeled Jack over the next 27 years, none of them well-attested. Then, in November 1872, the *News of the World* reported that London was 'in a state of commotion owing to what is known as the Peckham Ghost . . . a mysterious figure, quite as alarming in appearance' as Spring-heeled Jack, 'who terrified a past generation.'

In 1877 Jack gave a virtuoso performance

at Aldershot Barracks. The terror began one night in early March. A sentry on duty at the North Camp peered into the darkness, his attention attracted by a peculiar figure bounding across the common towards him. The soldier issued a challenge, which went unheeded or unheard, and the figure disappeared from sight for a few moments. Then it was beside the guard and delivered several slaps to his face with a hand as cold and clammy as a corpse.

There were several more attacks on guards at Aldershot. Once a soldier shot at Jack; afterwards a rumour that Jack was invulnerable to bullets spread like wildfire. In fact the soldier had fired blanks at him.

Various theories were advanced at the time, but no real clues ever emerged. The identity of the miscreant and the purpose of his attacks remains unknown.

The final bow

It was 10 years before Jack's activities made further headlines, this time in Cheshire, where he frightened several young ladies. One was playing the piano in the drawing-room of her father's house in Oxton when a black-clad figure rushed into the room, swept every ornament off the mantelpiece and vanished as suddenly as he had appeared. According to a rather satirical article in the *Liverpool Citizen*, it was widely rumoured that a number of young 'swells . . . sons of well-known men and bearing historic names' had wagered £1000 that none of their number could impersonate the original Jack. The wager was accepted, and presumably won.

Spring-heeled Jack made his final bow in a sensational appearance in Everton, Liverpool, in 1904. According to the *News of the World* of 25 September, crowds of people gathered to watch Jack scampering up and down William Henry Street, where he executed tremendous leaps, some of which are

Left: Jacob's Island in east London, the scene of the murder of young Maria Davis. Witnesses stated that Spring-heeled Jack was the culprit, but that he bounded away before he could be apprehended. A verdict of death by misadventure was recorded at the inquest

Right: Jack outwits the peelers with one enormous leap – another illustration from a 'penny dreadful'

said to have exceeded 25 feet (7.5 metres). Finally he leaped clean over the houses and vanished forever.

Although this story of Spring-heeled Jack's final bow has been widely told and might seem to be one of the best-attested examples of his prowess, investigation has proved it to be untrue. Only four days before the report quoted above, the *Liverpool Echo* contained an article about a house in William Henry Street that was said to be haunted by a poltergeist. 'The story,' said the *Echo*, 'as it passed from mouth to mouth, reached sensational dimensions.' At about the same time further excitement was caused by a man suffering from religious mania who would climb upon the roof of his house and cry out that his wife was a devil or witch. The police or a fire-engine would attempt to bring the man down, but he would escape them by jumping from one roof to the next. From these incidents the spurious story of Spring-heeled Jack was born.

But who or what was the original Spring-heeled Jack? One suggestion is that he was an insane circus fire-eater or acrobat; other theories range from a kangaroo dressed up by a demented animal trainer to, more recently, the inevitable UFO occupant. But Jack was almost certainly a human being – or to be more precise more than one, for it is unlikely that the apparition that appeared at Aldershot in 1877 was the same as the one that spread terror in suburban London some 40 years earlier. And Jack is known to have had his imitators, such as the Brentford butcher

and, perhaps, the perpetrators of the Cheshire scare of 1887.

A very plausible candidate for the title of the Spring-heeled Jack behind the terror of 1837 to 1838 is Henry de la Poer Beresford, Marquis of Waterford. He had already been an inveterate and notorious prankster during his days at Eton and Oxford, where he was also an outstanding boxer and oarsman. He once proposed to a railway company that they should arrange for two locomotives to crash, at his expense, so that he could witness the spectacle. One night in 1837, having been to the races, he painted the town red – literally. His decorative activities included doors, windows and one of the town watchmen. He and his associates were each fined £100 for this escapade.

Later in that year the *Herald*, of Fife in Scotland, reported:

> The Marquis of Waterford passed through this town the other day, on the top of a coach, with a few of his associates. In the course of the journey they amused themselves with the noble occupation of popping eggs from a basket at any individual who happened to be standing at the wayside.

The Times commented on this incident: 'This vivacious person is a long time sowing his "wild oats". He is nearly 27 years old.'

The activities of the Marquis were not always so entertaining. Once he evicted more than 30 tenant families from their homes on his estate at a moment's notice. He habitually treated people and animals with cruelty.

A brutal attack

The young Lord Waterford visited Blackheath Fair in October, 1837; on the same day Polly Adams, a 17-year-old serving-girl, was brutally attacked as she left the fair. Earlier she had been accosted by someone with 'pop eyes', whom she believed to be a nobleman. Waterford's eyes had always been noticeably protruberant. His family emblem fitted the description of a crest seen on the clothes of Jack in one attack. The whereabouts of the Marquis during this period are consistent with the locations of Jack's appearances.

Waterford's cruel and bullying exploits gradually ceased after this time, and he became a model of respectability after his marriage in 1842. He was killed in a fall from his horse in 1859. The idea that Waterford was Spring-heeled Jack was being treated virtually as established fact by newspapers later in the century.

Never caught, never positively identified, Spring-heeled Jack, together with his escapades, is all but forgotten today. Nobody remembers the 'penny dreadfuls', the melodramas, or the only film about Jack – *The curse of the Wraydons*, made in 1946 and starring Tod Slaughter. And the names of new bogeymen come to the lips of mothers who a century ago would have cried: 'Be good or Spring-heeled Jack will get you!'

The man who created life

Frankenstein about to bring his monster to life (left) in the spoof film *Young Frankenstein* (1974). Andrew Crosse (below), an eccentric 19th-century gentleman-scientist, has been likened to Frankenstein because he may have created life during his electrical experiments

Out of his test tubes and retorts, Andrew Crosse is said to have created living creatures – and so threw his 19th-century world into a frenzy. PAUL BEGG asks if this English gentleman-scientist was a real-life Frankenstein

FEAR HANGS OVER the village as heavy and black as the threatening storm-clouds. In the distance a sprawling mansion stands gaunt against the hills. A dim yellow light from a ground floor window shows that the scientist is at home and at work. A roll of thunder echoes around the hills. A flash of lightning rends the sky. Suddenly the mansion window is ablaze with stark, almost incandescent light. The fear tightens as the villagers imagine the demonic activities that could be going on inside the grey, forbidding walls of the mansion.

This description could fit the popular image of Baron Victor Frankenstein at work, but it could be applied equally to a real-life gentleman-scientist named Andrew Crosse. He too had a compulsion towards unorthodox laboratory experiments and is said to have actually created life from inanimate matter.

Andrew Crosse was born into a wealthy English family on 17 June 1784. In 1793 he was sent to Dr Seyer's School in The Fort in Bristol, and it was here that he was introduced to science.

Later described by his second wife as one who 'delighted in whatever was strange and

Benjamin Franklin, American political leader and diplomat, writer and scientist. Crosse probably heard about Franklin's own electrical experiments through his father, who was a personal acquaintance

marvellous', Crosse was obsessed with the new science of electricity from about the age of 12. It is possible that his interest was inspired by his father, among whose acquaintances were Benjamin Franklin and Joseph Priestley, two pioneers of the new science. Crosse himself attributed it to a lecture on the subject. In any event, he spent much of his time thereafter conducting experiments.

In June 1802 he went to Brasenose College, Oxford. Here he was encouraged to lead a profligate life and he virtually abandoned his experiments.

Crosse inherited the family estates and fortune in 1805 on the death of his mother and teetered on the brink of becoming a typical wealthy wastrel, until he met George John Singer at a party. Singer's great passion for electrical experiments rekindled Crosse's own enthusiasm and in 1807 he began a series of experiments into electro-crystallisation at Fyne Court, his family seat.

In 1837 one of Crosse's experiments resulted in something that has puzzled scientists to this day. From inanimate matter Andrew Crosse created life. He tells how it happened:

In the course of my endeavours to form artificial minerals by a long continued electric action on fluids holding in solution such substances as were necessary to my purpose, I had recourse to every variety of contrivance that I could think of; amongst others I constructed a wooden frame, which supported a Wedgewood funnel, within which rested a quart basin on a circular piece of mahogany. When this basin was filled with a fluid, a strip of flannel wetted with the same was suspended over the side of the basin and inside the funnel, which, acting as a syphon, conveyed the fluid out of the basin through the funnel in successive drops: these drops fell into a smaller funnel of glass placed beneath the other, and which contained a piece of somewhat porous red oxide iron from Vesuvius. This stone was kept constantly electrified. . . .

On the fourteenth day from the commencement of this experiment I observed through a lens a few small whitish excrescences or nipples, projecting from about the middle of the electrified stone. On the eighteenth day these projections enlarged, and stuck out seven or eight filaments, each of them longer than the hemisphere on which they grew. On the twenty-sixth day these appearances assumed the form of a perfect insect, standing erect on a few bristles which formed its tail. . . . On the twenty-eighth day these little creatures moved their legs. . . . After a few days they detached themselves from the stone, and moved about at pleasure.

Crosse was baffled by this totally unexpected development. He anxiously sought a rational explanation but none seemed available. Over the succeeding months he repeated the experiment. He then wrote:

After many months' action and consequent formation of certain crystalline matters, I observed similar excrescences with those before described at the edge of the fluid in every one of the cylinders except two which contained the carbonate of potassa and the metallic arsenic; and in due time the whitish

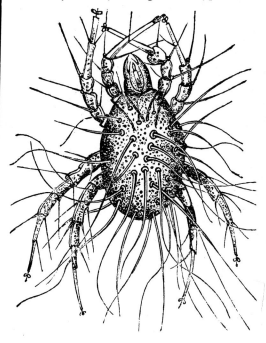

The strange insect that came to life in the bottom of a basin during Crosse's experiments with electricity. Crosse was reviled by the religious community for meddling in God's work when the existence of the 'acari' came to light

Fyne Court, the family seat of Andrew Crosse. Here he carried out his many experiments – for a long time in secret – and gave rise to the local opinion that he was probably an evil wizard

appearances were developed into insects. In my first experiment I had made use of flannel, wood, and a volcanic stone. In the last, none of these substances were present.

Again no solution presented itself for the appearance of these acari, or tiny mites, and he repeated the experiment a third time. On this occasion Crosse made an error that, far from shedding any light on the mystery, merely served to intensify it:

I had omitted to insert within the bulb of the retort a resting place for these acari (they are always destroyed if they fall back into the fluid from which they have emerged). It is strange that, in a solution eminently caustic and under an atmosphere of oxihydrogen gas, one single acarus should have made its appearance.

The discovery made public

Andrew Crosse now wrote a report on his 'discovery' and dispatched it to the Electrical Society in London. It was received with some scepticism but sufficient interest to invite another electrical experimenter to repeat Crosse's work. The man chosen for the task was W.H. Weeks of Sandwich in Kent. The results were published in the *Annals of Electricity* (October 1836–1837) and in the *Transactions* of the London Electrical Society (1838).

Weeks published only a summary of the results of his experiments, but it seems clear that he took a number of precautions to ensure that no extraneous matter, such as the ova of insects, had in some manner gained entry into his equipment. Weeks worked slowly and methodically. While he was still experimenting, the story of Crosse's discovery became public knowledge.

Had the matter been confined to the

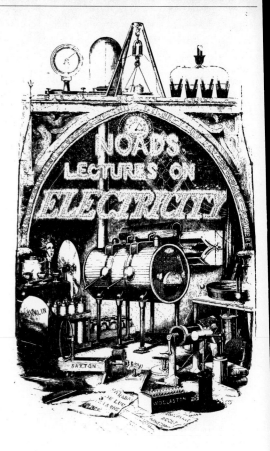

Right: the frontispiece of *Noad's lectures on electricity*, in which detailed descriptions of Crosse's experiments were published. Crosse's name appears on the top left of the arch above the title, along with other illustrious scientists

Below: the scientist Michael Faraday at work in his laboratory. This respected physicist and chemist was a defender of Crosse during the controversy surrounding his experiments

scientific community, it is probable that it would not have caused the storm that it did. But Crosse discussed the acari, to which he had apparently given life, with a number of friends. One of these was the editor of the *Western Gazette*. Crosse's second wife, Cornelia, recorded the result:

. . . the editor of a West of England paper . . . immediately, unauthorised, but in a very friendly spirit, published an account of the experiment; which account quickly flew over England, and indeed Europe, satisfying at once the credulity of those who love the marvellous, and raising up a host of bitter and equally unreasoning assailants, whose personal attacks on Mr Crosse, and their misrepresentations of his views, were at once ridiculous and annoying.

As the storm broke and whirled around Andrew Crosse, many people came to his defence. Among them was the respected scientist Michael Faraday who, in an impassioned lecture at the Royal Institution in 1837, condemned those who attacked Crosse. Faraday also claimed to have conducted Crosse's experiment himself and to have confirmed Crosse's findings. However, this did nothing to lessen the controversy and neither did Mr Weeks, who confirmed that Crosse's experiment did indeed 'give birth' to the acari. In fact, it could be argued that Faraday and Weeks unintentionally intensified the widespread opinion that Crosse was a meddler in the act of creation, a man who set himself up as a rival of God.

Andrew Crosse was angered, hurt,

possibly mystified by the outburst, and he retired to the seclusion of Fyne Court. Here he found himself reviled and shunned by his neighbours. On one occasion a local clergyman, the Reverend Philip Smith, conducted a service of exorcism on the hills above Crosse's country estate.

In 1846 Crosse's first wife and his brother Richard died within four days of each other. Bereaved, Crosse returned to his experiments. In his journal and in letters to friends he wrote of his hopes and aspirations. He said that he wanted to construct 'a battery at once cheap, powerful and durable' – perhaps a vision of the dry-cell battery that was patented by Georges Leclanché in 1868. He also experimented with the preservation of food and the purification of sea water and other liquids through the use of electricity.

A new lease of life

In the late 1840s Andrew Crosse emerged from his self-imposed seclusion at Fyne Court. In 1849 he met Cornelia Burns, still in her twenties, and romance blossomed. Crosse took on a new lease of life and even began attending a few social gatherings. On 22 July 1850 the two were married.

Over the next five years Crosse's health began to deteriorate and on 26 May 1855 he suffered a paralytic seizure. He never recovered. On 6 July he awoke in terrible pain. Holding his young wife's hand just before dying, he said, 'My dear, the utmost extent of human knowledge is but comparative ignorance.'

Today Andrew Crosse is all but forgotten, just one of the many amateur scientists who in some small way contributed to the widening of scientific knowledge. Where his name is remembered, it is not in scientific textbooks but in books about mysteries.

The question remains: what were the acari? Nobody in recent years has been known to repeat Crosse's experiment, and no solution to the mystery seems to be generally accepted. Several theories have, however, been proposed.

Dr A.C. Oudemans in 1934 suggested that

Right: a giant insect is about to attack in the story *The electric vampire*, which appeared in the *London Magazine* in 1910. It was inspired by the tales about how Crosse had created life in his laboratory in an insect-like form

Below: Mary Shelley, author of *Frankenstein*. Crosse in many ways lived up to the popular image of the man she made famous in one of the best-known horror tales in all literature

Left: Crosse's grave stone. The inscription refers to him as 'the electrician' – a modest designation for a man whose intricate experiments and slightly odd character made him a storm centre

the acari were *Glyophagus domesticus*, a commonplace insect that has an amazing power to hold onto life no matter what the conditions. It also manages to get into equipment despite precautions to keep it out.

Another idea is that the chemical constituents in Crosse's tests took on a form and gave the appearance of living things.

Perhaps one of these theories could be correct. But it is difficult to credit that the ova of *Glyophagus domesticus* were present in all the experiments conducted by Crosse, Weeks and possibly Faraday. It is likewise hard to believe that the experimenters did not consider and test the possibility that the acarus was not a living creature.

In the final analysis, we do not know what Andrew Crosse's acari were – and the man himself remains strange and extraordinary.

In his book *The man who was Frankenstein*, Peter Haining suggests that Crosse was the model for Mary Shelley's Baron Frankenstein. He points out that, in the autumn of 1814, the Shelleys were visited by the poet Robert Southey, who knew Crosse and had stayed at Fyne Court. The three apparently discussed Crosse's electrical experiments and on 28 December, Mary and Percy Shelley attended a lecture given by Crosse.

The evidence that Andrew Crosse and his experiments with the new science of electricity fuelled Mary Shelley's imagination is at best circumstantial. But this slightly eccentric gentleman-scientist, experimenting in his remote mansion in the wilds of the hazy Quantocks, certainly fits the popular picture of Baron Victor Frankenstein.

Turning in the grave

The mysterious movement of lead-cased coffins in a sealed tomb in Barbados in the 19th century was believed by many to be the work of some supernatural force. What really happened? GRAHAM FULLER and IAN KNIGHT report

THEY SAY the dead tell no tales. And since the corpses interred in a Barbadian graveyard vault early last century were, apparently, the only human agencies present when the actual coffins they were laid in moved, there naturally exists no immediate first-hand account of this eeriest of mysteries.

The so-called 'creeping coffins of Barbados' crept, with some alacrity, into West Indian folklore between 1812 and 1820. Indeed, this was no isolated incident, but a phenomenon that repeated itself with chilling regularity until the nerve of the vault's owners and the local dignitaries finally ran out. At the time the tomb in question, situated near the entrance of the graveyard of Christ Church, overlooking the bay at Oistins on the south coast of the island, belonged to the Chase family. It was a solid affair, built of large, cemented blocks of coral, 12 feet long by 6 feet wide (4 metres by 2 metres), sunk halfway into the ground and sealed off by a great marble slab. Anyone trying secretly to get in (or out) of the vault would have found it an arduous task.

Two burials took place before anything happened. On 31 July 1807 Mrs Thomasina Goddard's funeral was held, and on 22 February 1808 that of the infant Mary Anna Maria Chase. Then, on 6 July 1812, pallbearers and mourners arrived to lay to rest Dorcas Chase, the elder sister of Mary Anna Maria. Several of the men heaved the door open – struggling with its great weight – and the coffin was lifted down to the portals of the tomb. Peering into the darkness from the few first steps, the leading pallbearers were greeted by a truly sepulchral sight. Mary Anna Maria's coffin had moved to the corner opposite the one in which it had been placed; Mrs Goddard's had been flung aside against

a wall. Something more than a draught had moved them – both coffins were cased in lead. Without pausing to ask questions the labourers lifted them back into position, placed Dorcas's among them and sealed the vault up again. But who or what had tampered with the dead – and why? Amazed and frightened, the mourners chose to put the blame on the Negro slaves who had assisted at the funeral of the first Chase sister.

So were the Negroes to blame? There was reputedly little love lost between the patriarch Thomas Chase and the black slaves he employed. Chase was by all accounts a cruel man whose tyrannical behaviour had driven his daughter Dorcas to kill herself. It seems improbable though that anyone bearing a grudge against him would have gone to such lengths to inflict such trivial damage.

The work of malign spirits?

As it was, Chase himself died within the month; and on 9 August 1812 his coffin was placed among the other three, which this time had remained undisturbed. A few years slipped by with no reason for anyone to believe that anything untoward was taking place in the Oistins churchyard. On 25 September 1816 the vault was reopened for the burial of a little boy, Samuel Brewster Ames. Once again the coffins lay in disarray – and the accusing eye was again turned on the Negro labourers, who promptly denied all charges and shrank in fear from what they considered the work of malign spirits: Negroes regarded the dead with superstition and were in fact the most unlikely of suspects. There was little the mourners could do, however, but return the coffins to their rightful places, leave Master Ames among them and block up the doorway with the great slab – which they did, hastily. It was opened again on 17 November for the interment of Samuel Brewster, whose coffin was being transferred to the Chase vault from its original home in a St Philip graveyard. The mystery surrounding the vault was now so

well-known that a crowd gathered in anticipation of fresh disturbances.

It was not to be disappointed. All of the coffins had shifted ground. That of Mrs Goddard, who had been lying in 'rest' now for nearly a decade, had finally given up under the strain and fallen apart. An exhaustive search of the vault proved futile – the walls, floor and roof were as solid and unyielding as ever. And yet for the third time there were unmistakable signs of violent activity within. Would it happen again? One wonders with what sense of dreadful, resigned foreboding the mourners repositioned the coffins (tying and bundling the remnants of Mrs Goddard's against the wall) and cemented the great door back into place.

Nearly three years passed before the vault was opened again – during which time it received thousands of curious visitors. On 17 July 1819 the funeral of Thomasina Clarke took place. It seems that the mystery was now a major national issue, for Viscount Combermere, the Governor of Barbados, and two of his officials attended the funeral. In front of hundreds of hushed spectators the marble slab was cut free by masons and dragged aside by a team of slaves. Inside, all was chaos; every coffin had moved save only the shattered fragments of Mrs Goddard's, which had remained in their little pile. The vault was searched again. Nothing. Not one clue. Undeterred, the labourers lugged the coffins back. Sand was then sent for and sprinkled over the floor of the tomb so that it formed a smooth, thick carpet that would surely show the traces of the mysterious coffin mover. Once the door was replaced

The bay at Oistins on the south coast of Barbados received thousands of visitors in the years between 1812 and 1820. The tourists flocked to Christ Church graveyard to see at first hand the vault of the Chase family where, it was rumoured, someone – or something – was tampering with the dead

Combermere left the impression of his seal in the cement and others did the same.

No recently deceased Barbadian was brought to the vault when it was opened again on 18 April 1820. Public speculation and excitement about the strange goings-on had mounted to such a degree that no one had the patience to wait for someone to pass on before the mystery could be finally solved or abandoned. After prolonged debate that could lead to only one conclusion, Viscount Combermere, the Honourable Nathan Lucas, Major J. Finch (secretary to the Governor), Mr R. Bowcher Clarke and Mr Rowland Cotton journeyed to Christ Church, collected the Reverend Thomas Orderson and repaired to the graveyard with a band of quaking Negro labourers.

The seals on the cement were intact – no one had therefore since removed the door and entered that way. And from the outside the vault was as solid as ever. Combermere ordered the cement to be chipped away and the huge slab was dragged aside, causing a strange, grating noise. This was the result of one of the larger lead coffins having been thrown up against the door, against which it now lay. Mary Anna Maria's tinier coffin, meanwhile, had been sent flying to the far end of the vault with such violence that it had damaged the coral wall. The other coffins

were scattered about, but there were no tell-tale marks in the sand to suggest what might have moved them. The Honourable Nathan Lucas, reporting the incident, had this to say:

I examined the walls, the arch, and every part of the vault, and found every part old and similar; and a mason in my presence struck every part of the bottom with his hammer, and all was solid. I confess myself at a loss to account for the movements of these leaden coffins. Thieves certainly had no hand in it; and as for any practical wit or hoax, too many were requisite to be trusted with the secret for it to remain unknown; and as for negroes having anything to do with it, their superstitious fear of the dead and everything belonging to them precludes any idea of the kind. All I know is that it happened and that I was an eye-witness of the fact!!!

Whatever, or whoever, it was that caused the coffins in the Chase vault to wander between those four walls was given no further opportunity to do so. All of the coffins were lugged out and given more peaceful resting places elsewhere in the churchyard. The vault remains open and unused to this day.

'Werewolves and vampires'

There have been other cases of coffins refusing to stay put. Discussing the Barbados mystery in his book *West Indian tales of old*, Sir Algernon E. Aspinall makes reference to the *European Magazine* of September 1815, which cites a vault at Stanton in Suffolk, England, where on at least three separate occasions, and, as at Oistins, behind a sealed door, coffins had moved off their raised biers; during one of these 'manoeuvres' the heaviest coffin – another eight-pallbearer affair – had climbed onto the fourth step of the vault. 'Whence arose this operation, in which it was certain that no-one had a hand?' asked the *European Magazine* writer. Needless to say, the people of Stanton were as shocked as the Barbadians. In 1867 Mr F. C. Paley, son of the rector of Gretford, near Stamford in Lincolnshire, England, wrote to *Notes and Queries* concerning the repeated movement of heavy lead coffins (also cased in wood) in a local vault; his letter was corroborated by a witness who commented that some of the coffins had moved to a leaning position against the wall.

The superstitious people of Arensburg on the Baltic island of Oesel immediately blamed vampires and werewolves when similar trouble occurred in the town cemetery in 1844. The crisis started in June with the 'spooking' of horses belonging to visitors to the graveyard. Some of these horses bolted, others fainted or dropped dead; many, so the story goes, went mad. The fault was laid at the door of the Buxhoewden family vault. When a funeral service in the family chapel was interrupted by eerie sounds from the

The entrance to the Chase vault in Christ Church graveyard, Oistins. The vault has stood open and empty since 1820, when all the coffins it contained were removed and buried in another, more peaceful, place

Viscount Combermere, the Governor of Barbados, supervised the sealing of the Chase vault after the funeral of Thomasina Clarke on 17 July 1819. When he returned nine months later to check on the state of the tomb he found the coffins in total disarray – and yet the seals on the door had remained intact

adjacent burial chamber, the bravest of the Buxhoewdens entered the tomb to find that the coffins of their late relatives had been thrown around. Rumours of 'devilry' spread and there was great fear and consternation in Arensburg. The president of the local ecclesiastical court, the Baron de Guldenstabbé, headed an official enquiry and personally visited the vault, which had been put back in order and locked. The coffins had moved again.

Determined to get to the bottom of the mystery, the Baron set up a committee to investigate it. They went further than their Barbadian cousins and had the floor of the vault ripped up, hoping, in vain, to find a secret passage. They suspected ghouls, though none of the coffins had in fact been robbed. Forced to give up their fruitless search, the committee laid not sand but ash throughout the vault and chapel and, as at Oistins, left secret seals that would break if the door were opened by any means. For three days and nights the place was guarded by soldiers. Then the committee returned: the seals were unbroken, the ashes were untouched and the coffins were everywhere they shouldn't have been – some standing on their heads, one so badly cracked that a bony arm protruded from it. Lacking the patience of the Barbadians who had put up with this sort of thing for eight years, the Arensburg committee and the Buxhoewdens immediately had the coffins moved elsewhere and put an end to the vault's activities.

What causes coffins to move about, whether they are in vaults in Barbados, in England or on an island in the Baltic Sea? There is no ready explanation. The 'traps' set up by the various investigators – the secret seals and the sand or ash covered floors – strongly indicate that no human villains are involved. That in Barbados it was malevolent Negro slaves – or the malevolent spirits suspected by the Negroes themselves – seems implausible. Among those who have considered the supernatural and paranormal possibilities are Sir Arthur Conan Doyle, who believed that the Oistins coffins moved because of the strange physical powers that are supposed to reside in the bodies of the prematurely dead – like the young Chase girls and Samuel Brewster Ames. There is more credence in the theory proffered by George Hunte, author of *Barbados*, who suggests that 'gas from decomposing bodies and not malevolent spirits was responsible for the violent separations and disarray of the sober arrangements which were made by undertakers'.

What about water in the vaults? Could the coffins have floated? The Chase vault was not only watertight but high and dry too; underground currents can be ruled out. The man who confirmed Mr Paley's letter about the Gretford coffins believed they floated into their strange positions when the vault was

Below: drawings made by eyewitness Nathan Lucas to show how the coffins were originally placed in the vault (left) and how they were found in April 1820 (right). However, there are discrepancies between the account given by Lucas and those of other witnesses, and a second set of drawings (bottom) – also said to have been made on the spot and at the time the tomb was opened – is generally accepted to be a more accurate portrayal of the arrangement of the coffins

Frank Russell compared the drawings in his chapter on the coffin phenomenon in *Great world mysteries* (published in 1957):

As first placed, three large coffins were put in a neat row with the middle one set slightly further away from the vault's door. Three smaller coffins sat tidily on top of the big ones. All had their feet towards the door, their heads towards the back of the vault, their longitudinal axes parallel to the side walls.

When found out of place all coffins were in varying but fairly regular stages of reversal, their heads now being more or less towards the door, their feet more or less towards the back wall. They look exactly as if caught when rotating at snail's pace around their own centres of gravity, some having twisted farther than others, their axes now cutting through an arc of about 120 degrees. The picture they present is that of a swirl, or a spiral effect, like so many metal shapes, heavier at one end than the other, spun around by some force gravitational, gyroscopic, electromagnetic or goodness knows what.

However inconclusive, Russell's suggestion seems the most plausible. Superstition and fear though – slamming the door shut on the case of the creeping coffins of Barbados and abandoning the vault (as at Arensburg) – precluded further scientific research into the whole weird business, which remains wreathed in mystery. All that is known for sure is that for eight macabre years in the Chase vault at Oistins there were, to adapt the words of Emily Brontë, 'unquiet slumbers for the sleepers in that quiet earth'.

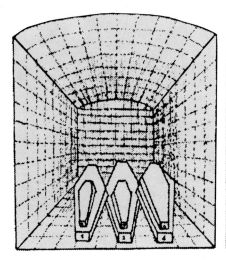

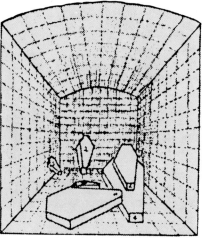

flooded – but there is no evidence that it ever was. Since the events at Arensburg all took place within a few weeks, any sign of flooding would have been noticed; none was. Lead coffins *can* float – they need something to float on, however.

The movements of the Oistins coffins could be ascribed to earth tremors. Barbados lies on a seismic belt and is framed by fracture zones; moreover there is a volcano on the nearby island of St Vincent. The slightest underground tremor could have displaced the coffins – but why only those in the Chase vault? The theory is dubious. Stanton, Gretford and Arensburg are not known for seismic activity.

Most of the coffins in the vault at Barbados were made of lead, so ordinary magnetic forces did not cause the mischief. And yet some such force may provide the answer to the mystery. One vital clue has emerged from the investigations of the Barbadians. At the time of the last burial there in 1819 someone saw fit to make a drawing of the vault in a state of orderliness; and another of its supposedly chaotic appearance when it was opened for the final time in April 1820. Eric

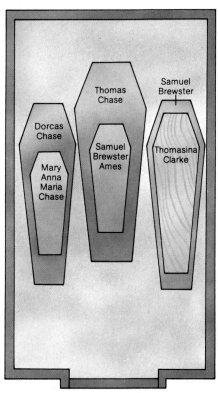

Stalking the Surrey puma

Surrey is one of the most English of counties, a patchwork of commuter towns and rich, rolling countryside. Yet in the 1960s, as CHRIS HALL recounts, a wild, American 'big cat' frightened people and attacked farm animals there

ERNEST JELLETT WILL NEVER forget one Monday morning in 1962. His work for the Mid Wessex Water Board took him to inspect Heathy Park Reservoir, in the North Downs near Farnham, Surrey, early on the morning of 16 July. It is reached by a long track through dense woodland. As a countryman, Mr Jellett is very familiar with the local wildlife – so it was not the rabbit beside the track that surprised him but the big cat-like animal stalking it.

Before he had had time to take this in, things began to happen rather quickly. The rabbit sensed him and fled towards the 'cat', which pounced but missed. Both animals ran up the track towards Mr Jellett. The rabbit made off into the undergrowth, but the other animal bounded straight at him. Having no weapon, he shouted loudly, and fortunately frightened it off.

He later described what he had seen as sandy coloured and resembling a small lion. 'It had a sort of round, flat face, like a big cat, and its tail was long and thin, not bushy. It had big paws.' He was sure it was not a fox.

Later, police searched the area, but found only flattened bracken where 'a good sized animal' had rested. A few days later cattle on a nearby farm were unusually restless,

Bottom: did the lush woods and farmland of Surrey conceal a mysterious big cat during the 1960s? Something resembling a puma (inset) was often seen – but never caught – and such an animal could easily have adapted to the local climate and terrain

Below: Mr A. Burningham, who saw 'an enormous great cat' in late August 1959 while driving past Godsfield Copse, south of Preston Candover. The creature had a cat-like head, mangy looking coat, pointed ears and a tail that curled up – and was, perhaps, a puma

milling about in their field until midnight, as if something unfamiliar were about. Then a woman walking near the village of Crondall saw an animal in a field that she later – having consulted a wildlife book – thought might be a jaguarundi, a South American member of the cat family.

And so began a legend that, after infrequent and isolated reports over the next two years, was to grow to a scale comparable with the Loch Ness monster: the legend of the Surrey puma.

The first account of a strange cat-like animal in Surrey seems to be that recorded by William Cobbett in his *Rural rides*. He recalled seeing it in a tree near Waverley Abbey in his childhood, which would date it around 1770. However, the description he gives could be of a wild cat; these were known in Surrey until at least the 1920s.

New research has revealed several reports from the 1950s that may be related to the puma saga. The most detailed of these occurred at harvest time in 1959, near Preston Candover, 5 miles (8 kilometres) north-east of Winchester.

Another local man, Mr A. Burningham, was driving along a country road in the early evening when 'an enormous great cat' crossed the lane about 40 yards (40 metres) ahead of him. It was the size of a labrador dog, but its head and walk were distinctly feline. He stopped his car and saw the animal, screened by trees, watching lambs in a field, but did not think it wise to leave his

car for a closer look. He was unable to make anything of what he had seen until he noticed the report of Mr Jellett's experience in a local newspaper.

But it was in 1964 that things really began to happen. During the summer, strange cat-like animals were seen around Farnham and near Bordon. A frightful howling kept people awake, likened by one to 'the sound of a hundred cats being murdered.' Then, almost simultaneously, two events brought the mystery to the nation's attention.

Farmer Edward Blanks was manager of Bushylease Farm in Crondall, near Farnham. For two years he had been seeing and hearing a strange cat-like creature that all his countryman's knowledge could not identify. Then in August 1964, a herd of cattle broke out of their field – which they would not have done unless alarmed. One of them was later found bitten and mauled in nearby woods. A vet who examined it was of the opinion that the injuries were not caused by 'any animal found in this country' – though not everyone agreed, and some tried to play down the whole affair.

All the same, by the end of August the hunt was on for the 'Crondall cougar', with Bushylease Farm as hunt headquarters and armed farmers patrolling the woods. They were joined by Billy Davidson, a Canadian ranger with experience of puma tracking who was on holiday in Britain. He did not catch the Surrey puma, but he did find 'definite evidence' of a big cat, including a lair.

In early September there were so many sightings that a mass break-out from a zoo seemed the most likely explanation. A puma was seen at Crondall, and on Farnham Common, and the howling continued. The next

Above: Mr Edward Blanks and his son (left) with a steer apparently mauled by the puma in August 1964. Mr Blanks says the puma was in the area for six or seven years between 1962 and 1969, returning to his farm during March each year. The family got used to it, though it had 'an awful stench'. The big cat seems to have been little trouble, killing only what it needed to survive – and the steer soon recovered

sighting was made by George Wisdom, who had decided to spend his lunch hour gathering blackberries on Munstead Heath, near Godalming. He did not pick many. Whatever it was that snarled at him from the bushes had no wish for his company.

He gave one of the best descriptions of a puma of the whole affair, which is interesting because at this point puma descriptions had not been publicised. Three days later a half-mile (800-metre) trail of footprints appeared overnight in freshly raked sand used for practice gallops by nearby riding stables. Each was 6 inches (15 centimetres) across, and they were identified as possible puma prints by experts at London Zoo.

The many footprints that have been found after sightings of the 'puma' would seem to

Sightings of the Surrey puma

offer the best hope of evidence for positive identification of the creature. But in fact most of them turn out to have been made by dogs or foxes, and others are too indistinct to be of any help at all. Only two were pronounced puma by the experts: a single print from Hurtwood Common – and the Munstead trail.

Most experts agreed the Munstead prints were of a large cat, probably puma. But naturalist Dr Maurice Burton, who lived nearby and was closely involved in (and sceptical of) the puma affair, found that large dogs could leave similar prints in some circumstances. A St Bernard was missing in the area on the night the footprints appeared, and bloodhounds were kept near the stables.

It is true that some people have claimed that the Munstead print looks more like that of a bloodhound than a puma; but if it was a dog that snarled at Mr Wisdom from the blackberry bushes, it was a very strange dog indeed. He visited a zoo shortly afterwards, and found an identical 'dog' on show. It was in an enclosure marked 'puma'.

After Mr Wisdom's spectacular sighting, the puma became weekly news. A special cage was kept at Godalming police station where an emergency plan to capture the beast, called the 'Munstead monster', was prepared. The public were asked to notify the police promptly, and local papers kept everyone informed. Zoo and RSPCA experts were at hand.

A log of all reports investigated, including unusual attacks on farm animals, was kept by police. When it was finally closed in 1968, it had 362 entries, but there were many more that were either not reported, or that the police for various reasons were unable to investigate.

On safari in Surrey

The most determined efforts to catch the puma took place in 1966, and quite a few serious and not-so-serious 'safaris' were made into the wilds of Surrey in the mid 1960s. These projects ranged from teams of experienced big-game hunters to a local pub selling 'game permits' to would-be puma hunters, with proceeds being donated to charity. But all, whether naturalists or youth clubs, had one thing in common: they failed to find their quarry.

Then, in 1968, it all ended. To this day local lore says that the puma was shot by a farmer, but there is no agreement on where, what became of the body, or why the event received no publicity at the time.

Whatever the truth, the legend lives on, still widely remembered; people still believe they saw the puma. And from time to time its ghost still walks: a few big cats are reported every year in south-east England – for instance, one near Guildford in September 1980, and another at Hastings in December of the same year.

So much at least is legend, but could there

Mr George Wisdom was picking blackberries from these bushes one day in September 1964 when something large and feline snarled at him from amid the foliage. Three days later strange animal footprints appeared nearby – one of only two sets pronounced by experts to be authentic puma tracks

Below: police took this plaster cast of 'puma' footprints from tracks at Bramley Golf Club in 1969

really have been a puma in Surrey? And could it have survived to the present day? Well, it might be improbable, but is not impossible. The climate is milder than much of the puma's natural American habitat. There is no shortage of food: a puma could live on the equivalent of 10 rabbits a day, and the region has tens of thousands of them. Surrey is England's most wooded county; its heaths can be very lonely places where a largely nocturnal animal could roam for weeks unseen.

But where might the puma have come from? In 1964 there were officially just 23 pumas in Britain, all securely behind bars. If it existed, the Surrey puma must have been imported illegally; then it either escaped, or was deliberately freed. If this is correct, it was probably smuggled in as a cub, possibly around 1958.

To support this theory four early sightings were of small big cats, described as 'young puma' in August 1959, 'small lion' and 'jaguarundi' in July 1962, and 'lynx' in January 1963 – but we are left with a 'huge lion' near Fleet in 1959. At a puma exhibition at the Guildford Show in 1966, a young boy was overheard to say he knew a family who had released three puma cubs. Perhaps inevitably he vanished, leaving his story unconfirmed. If it was not a hoax, it would explain everything – but as such proof is lacking, our enquiry must depend on more controversial evidence.

The puma, also known as the cougar or mountain lion, is a shy, mainly nocturnal animal, native to the Americas. It is very adaptable to terrain, being at home in forest or mountains. A full-grown puma would be about 5 feet (1.5 metres) long and 3 feet (0.9 metres) high. Its colour is normally sandy to ginger.

There is no shortage of its alleged sightings, but comparison of their details with the descriptions of a puma is not very encouraging. A shy nocturnal animal should not be seen so often in or near towns in broad daylight. The reported animals are usually too small. Only in colour do we find reasonable agreement, but a number of the creatures are described as black. Black pumas are very rare, and to accept these reports is to accept a double improbability: that there are two pumas in Surrey, one of them a rare type – or that there are both a puma and a panther.

Yet a lot people saw something that they could not identify. Unfortunately, many of the vague descriptions could just as well fit domestic cats or dogs, foxes or deer. Some sightings are very definitely *not* puma.

Others are at considerable distance, very brief, or brief and at night. A significant number are by townspeople, who have little need to know the wildlife in the way a farmer does, and usually take little real notice of it until puma stories appear all over the local paper. It is then a small step to glimpsing next door's ginger tom one night and creating another puma report. Sadly, over three-quarters of the reports must be regarded as suspect.

A camera shy cat

Photographs could solve this problem, but there are few in existence. One, said to show the puma in a garden in Farnham in 1966, cannot be traced. Those taken on a misty autumn morning at Reigate in 1977 are indistinct. The photograph taken at Worplesdon in August 1966 by two ex-police photographers looks suspiciously like a large domestic cat, although one zoologist said its size was like that of a female puma.

To find an animal killed in a way typical of big cats would be good supporting evidence. Pumas generally bring their prey to the ground by hurling themselves against it, and then attack the throat and breast. Some writers on the puma mystery have tended to

Though the Surrey puma saga reached its height in the mid 1960s – and the animal itself was reputedly shot in 1968 – large cat-like animals are still seen in the area and unusual tracks still found. Here 17-year-old Gwen Fraser of Farnborough prepares to measure footprints found in her garden in December 1970

Photographs of the Surrey puma are few and far between, and none of those available are satisfactory. This, taken at Worplesdon in 1966, is supposed to be of the big cat but bears a rather stronger rememblance to a small one of the domestic variety

point to *all* the attacks on farm animals in the region at the time as suggesting puma, an approach that draws justified criticism from sceptics. There are 6000 attacks on farmstock each year, mostly the work of dogs. A dog can inflict terrible injuries, even tearing off whole limbs.

In one case a deer found at Cranleigh could have been killed by a puma. A number of other reports checked by Ministry of Agriculture experts involved injuries 'outside the previous experience' of the officers.

But what of the frightful howling? It could have been made by foxes, badgers or even owls. All the recordings made were identified as fox calls: mating vixen can make perhaps the most terrifying sound of all British wildlife. That leaves us with the sounds reported by farmers – who know the sounds of the countryside – that they had not heard anything like before.

So far we have assumed that either there was no puma at all, or that an ordinary flesh-and-blood puma was loose. Other theories have been put forward to explain how an animal that, by all the rules, should not be there was reported so often.

Some people have claimed that UFOs may be in some way responsible; many have been seen over Surrey, some in places where the puma has also been seen, but many more do not tie into the pattern so conveniently. Timeslips, thought-forms and Bermuda triangle-like vortices have all been suggested. Or is the Surrey puma somehow connected with leys? In 1973 a survey of sightings of mystery cats around Bournemouth showed them all to lie close to leys.

It cannot now be conclusively proven that a puma once prowled the Surrey hills. But it does seem very likely that, at least in the mid 1960s, one did, with remarkably little risk to either human life or farm economy. And it will live on, a blend of reality and imagination, in the folklore of our land.

Dufferin: the fatal flaw

A brilliant diplomat saved from death by the intervention of supernatural forces – this spectacular story, in various guises, travelled the world in the late Victorian period. But how do the facts stand up to scrutiny? MELVIN HARRIS investigates

FATE WAS KIND to the first Marquis of Dufferin and Ava: in 1893 he was saved – so his chroniclers tell us – by supernatural intervention from a violent death.

The story begins some 10 years earlier, when Lord Dufferin was enjoying a welcome break from the incessant bustle of diplomatic life. His distinguished career had already included six years as Governor General of Canada, and in 1883 he was completing a report on British government reorganisation in Egypt. A great house near Tullamore in County Offaly, Ireland, seemed to provide an ideal refuge for anyone seeking tranquillity. But one night, this peaceful idyll was shattered by a terrifying apparition.

Lord Dufferin was in bed when he suddenly found himself wide awake, sick with terror. He had been awoken by strange sounds from the grounds outside – terrifying sounds. However, Lord Dufferin was no coward; he climbed out of bed to investigate. Trembling in every limb and heart racing, he went to the French windows and peered out.

He could see the trim lawns, bathed in moonlight. Almost every section was in plain view, except for one spot, where tall trees cast long black shadows. And from these shadows came the sounds that had woken him – heartrending sobs, more animal than human.

Lord Dufferin began to fumble with the window latches – and, as he did so, a man staggered out of the shadows into the moonlight. He was bent double under the weight of a load on his back. At first sight it looked like a long linen-chest – but, as the man came closer, Dufferin suddenly became aware that the chest was, in fact, a coffin.

Lord Dufferin threw open the windows, ran across the lawn and shouted at the man to halt. Until then the man's face had been held down and hidden, but on hearing the shout

he lifted his head and turned it towards Lord Dufferin. And the moonlight fell on a face that was unforgettably loathsome – so contorted with hate that Lord Dufferin stopped dead in his tracks. Then, he drew on his reserves of courage, advanced on the man and walked – right through him!

At the same time the man disappeared – coffin and all. And with his disappearance the gloom lifted and the house and grounds became as calm and restful as ever.

Lord Dufferin returned to his bedroom shaken and puzzled. Then, after writing a complete account of the event in his diary, he managed to snatch some sleep.

At breakfast next morning he read out his account and appealed to his host and fellow guests for an explanation. But no one could help. The description of the man matched no one in the area, past or present. There wasn't even a local ghost to blame – and so the event remained an inexplicable mystery.

Over the years, the memory of that night stayed with Lord Dufferin – but it no longer troubled him. He grew to believe that it really might have been nothing more than an extraordinarily vivid nightmare. And that is how things stood for the next 10 years. Then, in 1893, the vision took on a new significance.

At the time, Lord Dufferin was the British Ambassador to France, and was obliged to attend a diplomatic reception at the Grand Hotel in Paris. When he entered the hotel foyer he found it jam-packed with impatient guests, for the elevator was taking ages to get to the reception area on the top floor. Together with his secretary, he joined the queue for the elevator. Eventually he reached the head of the queue; the elevator arrived, its door squealed open and the attendant waved the guests in.

A hideous double

Lord Dufferin turned pale, stood fast and refused to enter. He mumbled an excuse to the officials with him, then stepped backwards, pulling his secretary after him. Nothing would persuade him to use that elevator, for the attendant was, in every feature, the double of that hideous man he had seen 10 years earlier in Ireland.

The other officials ignored the eccentric Englishman. They crowded into the elevator and it began its laborious climb. Lord Dufferin, meanwhile, went hunting for the manager's office. He had to know who the attendant was and where he came from. But, before the Marquis reached the office there came a disaster. The elevator's cable snapped and it plunged down the shaft to destruction. The passengers were killed outright – as was the ghastly attendant.

No one ever came forward to claim or identify the attendant's body. The hotel manager could answer no questions either, for the attendant was a casual worker taken on for the day. A man without documents or records. Lord Dufferin was baffled. But not

even his money and influence could turn up a single fact about the man. The one certainty was that his strange vision at Tullamore had saved Dufferin's life.

That, in its essentials, is the remarkable story of Lord Dufferin's escape. Published accounts often vary in detail, but no one ever questions the basic truth of the tale. On the contrary, it is always asserted that the facts have been fully researched and investigated. One writer, for example, states that 'The evidence is incontrovertible . . . the details of this story have been carefully investigated by the well-known French psychologist de Maratray, who brought them to the attention of the British Society for Psychical Research.' Another writer adds, 'the accident was reported in the Press . . . but neither the management of the hotel, nor the accident investigators could find any record of the man's name or background.' So, here we seem to have a case that cannot be challenged.

But in fact, the facts are not as watertight as they seem. To begin with, the case was never investigated by the Society for Psychical Research. The society was certainly in existence at the time of the alleged event, but its files prove that it had no record of the Dufferin case. And no newspaper carried reports of the accident – for very good reasons. In fact, the first written account of the Dufferin case did not emerge until 1920 – that is, 18 years after the death of Lord Dufferin and 26 years after the alleged elevator crash.

This primary account was written by the French pyschologist Monsieur R. de Maratray on 18 July 1920. He gave it to the

French astronomer Flammarion, who included it in his book *Death and its mystery*. De Maratray added force to his account by claiming that his wife was related to Lord Dufferin and his family had been kept informed of the events at the time. Flammarion made no attempt to check the story for himself. He even neglected to ask why de Maratray had kept quiet for so long. Instead, he simply took de Maratray's word for everything.

In fact, the fatal accident in the elevator of the Grand Hotel took place in 1878 – some five years before the vision in Ireland, and 15 years before the date of Lord Dufferin's 'miraculous escape'. At the time of that genuine accident there was not a diplomatic reception at the hotel. In any case, Lord Dufferin was not even in Paris – but was serving in Canada as Governor-General. On top of that, in the real accident only one person, a young lady, died – not an elevator full of people, certainly no unknown attendant!

Jettisoning logic

All the facts were established shortly after the publication of Flammarion's book. The intrepid investigator who nailed the story as a lie was Paul Heuze, a journalist with the Paris magazine *L'Opinion*. Heuze proved that, when it came to psychical research, Flammarion jettisoned all the logic and care that went into his astronomical work. As a result his books were crammed full of unsubstantiated stories and hearsay. To his discredit, Flammarion made no attempt to revise these books and the Dufferin story was given wide circulation and picked up by author after author.

But how did such a tale become linked with Lord Dufferin? The files of the Society for Psychical Research provide the answer. They show that in November 1949, a Mr Louis Wolfe of New York wrote to the SPR and asked for details of the society's 'Dufferin investigation'. The SPR replied that it had never been asked to check on the case. But, prompted by this enquiry, the society's secretary then wrote to Lord Dufferin's grand-daughter and asked for her help. In her reply Lady Dufferin stated that the tale did not apply to her grandfather. It was a new version of an old story he used to tell about *someone else*! In the original version, though, an unnamed man had taken his holiday in Scotland, at Glamis Castle. And the vision itself had involved a hearse driven by a man with an ugly and hateful face.

Further research showed that the yarn first appeared as an anonymous second-hand account in the spiritualist paper *Light* of 16 April 1892. *Light*'s editor at the time was the Reverend Stainton Moses and his behaviour paralleled that of Flammarion: he took the tale completely on trust. He wrote this about it: 'It has been communicated to me by a personal friend, and is both authentic and trustworthy.' The account by the Reverend

Moses's personal friend ran as follows: I have just heard from a friend of a remarkable dream. She thought she heard a loud knock on the door, and on looking out she saw that a hearse had stopped at the house. Being greatly surprised, she rushed downstairs and herself opened the hall door. A strange-looking man was on top of the hearse; on seeing her, he said, 'Are you not ready yet?' She said, 'Oh, no; certainly not.' And slammed the door. The sound seemed to have caused her to wake.

She was much puzzled to know what could be the significance of such a very unusual dream. The face of the man haunted her, and for weeks she could not get the remembrance out of her head. All her family and friends were told about the dream, and all the circumstances of it had been discussed.

Some weeks had passed when one day the young lady happened to be in a

Top: Lady Dufferin, grand-daughter of the first Marquis, pictured in 1958. It was she who finally cleared up the origin of the escape story: it was a version of a tale her grandfather used to tell about someone else – a man who had taken his holiday at Glamis Castle in Scotland (above). In Lord Dufferin's original version, however, the apparition had been of a man driving a hearse

large warehouse in the City, and was just going to step into the elevator, when she looked at the man who had charge of it, and immediately drew back, having recognised the face of the man she had seen in her dream. When she drew back her consternation was added to by the exclamation from the man of the very words she had heard in her dream, 'What are you not ready yet, Miss?' Her determination not to ascend in the elevator was confirmed, and she declined to go into it. It only reached to the next floor, when the machinery gave way, the elevator being smashed to pieces and the man killed.

The elevator tale travelled to the United States and Europe, being constantly altered

The face of death

The weird blend of fact and fantasy that characterises the Dufferin tale reached another level of confusion with the release of the classic Ealing movie *Dead of night* in 1945. It was based on a short story by E.F. Benson, *The room in the tower* – itself based on a hearsay version of the Dufferin legend.

The film concerns a group of people at a party, each of whom tells a story about a mysterious happening – and one of the stories is strangely similar to the Dufferin tale. A racing driver dreams, not of a man carrying a coffin, but of the driver of a hearse. And later, the racing driver refuses to get into a bus when he recognises its conductor as the driver of the hearse. The bus subsequently plunges over an embankment.

and added to in its passage. Nine years later, it returned to England in a new guise, now posing as an authentic American event! Ironically enough, it was promptly picked up and reprinted in the pages of *Light*. It seems the new editor and his staff had completely forgotten their earlier account furnished by a 'personal friend' of the Rev. Moses. And on 9 February 1907, it ran the following story under the heading 'Saved by a vision':

The Progressive Thinker gives an instance of a warning dream, as related by Miss Gray, 'A young woman prominent in educational work' in Washington State. While staying in Chicago, where she had planned to visit 'a new department store which had just been opened, whose elevators were death-traps,' she woke up in the middle of the night and saw an unknown face at the window, twenty feet [6 metres] above the ground. On going to the window she saw a hearse standing in the street below, with her nocturnal visitant occupying the driver's box; he looked her squarely in the face and beckoned to her. The next day she visited the store, and on going to one of the crowded elevators the man in charge beckoned to her and said that there was room for one more. His features were those of the man on the hearse in her dream or vision of the night before. She refused to enter the elevator, which 'started down, stuck, and dropped four storeys, killing two of its passengers and injuring everyone else in the car'.

In the meantime, another variation of the story had been incorporated in Lord Dufferin's bag of after-dinner yarns. One day he related it to a young impressionable nephew and gave it special treatment. Adult wiles were not fully appreciated. The twinkle

in Dufferin's eyes was missed. And when he spun out the tale as his very own real-life adventure, the boy was awe-struck and convinced. The boy grew up to become a distinguished diplomat and writer. Out of conviction he retold this 'true story' frequently to his friends – once, unfortunately, to the de Maratrays, who proved as gullible as he himself had been. The innocent culprit, the unwitting father of this tenacious myth was none other than Harold Nicolson.

Right: Harold Nicolson, diplomat and writer – and nephew of Lord Dufferin. Lord Dufferin told the schoolboy Nicolson of his 'escape' – and Nicolson believed it. In adult life he used often to retell the story, so beginning the extraordinarily tenacious myth that, in various guises, was soon known all over the world

Riddle of Racetrack Playa

The stones move – and no one sees them do it. Yet thousands have seen their tracks in the dry lake beds that dot the Sierra Nevada mountains in the western United States. BOB RICKARD tells how the moving stones make their mysterious journeys

HIGH IN THE Sierra Nevada mountains, in the remote region of California's border with Nevada, there are places where stones move at night. Once, a band of pioneers was trapped in these rough, deeply channelled hills and unexpected dried-up lake beds, on their way to prospect or to settle in more hospitable places. Now it is part of the vast Death Valley National Park, of which the moving stones are a great attraction.

Perhaps the most famous of these dry lake beds, or playas, is Racetrack Playa, about 1¼ miles (2 kilometres) wide by 3 miles (5 kilometres) long and nearly 4000 feet (1200 metres) above sea level. The visitor's eye is immediately drawn to the scattered boulders and stones that litter this plain of hard, cracked mud. The quality of light at this altitude adds to the surreal effect, so that the rocks, with their snaking furrows behind them, give the impression of being both stationary and stirring. No one has ever seen the stones move – but move they do.

Over the years it was noticed that the rocks that moved had not rolled along but were pushed, leaving a groove the same size as their width behind them. Then in 1955 a geologist called George M. Stanley wrote in the *Bulletin* of the Geological Society of America (GSA) that he believed wind and ice were involved. Stanley was intrigued by the fact that groups of rocks often moved together. He suggested that sheets of ice formed around a group of rocks and that the wind raised the whole sheet slightly and propelled it along. This sounds plausible and was accepted for many years, especially after ice sheets embedded with rocks had been seen moving on other Californian playas. However, the ice layers on the Death Valley playas are extremely thin, and while they may be capable of moving smaller stones, even Stanley did not suggest they could shift the 300- to 600-pound (135- to 270-kilogram) boulders that had made tracks.

The mystery of Racetrack Playa became world-famous in the 1960s, and in 1969 it attracted the attention of Dr Robert P. Sharp, of the California Institute of Technology's geology department, who began a study of the moving stones that lasted seven years. He selected 25 stones of a variety of shapes and weights, up to about 1000 pounds (455 kilograms), named them, and used a metal stake to mark their position. Later he included five more rocks. When he was able to make the arduous journey to the playa over more than 30 miles (50 kilometres)

Opposite: the trail of a moving stone is marked by clear tracks behind it in the arid landscape of Racetrack Playa – one of the dried-up lakes of the Sierra Nevada mountains. The moving stones are a tourist attraction of the Death Valley National Park

These two sets of tracks show how far some of the moving stones travel (right) and how they can change direction (below)

of rough dirt road, he looked for any tagged rocks that had moved, staked their new position and measured the distance travelled.

During the seven-year study period, 28 of the 30 rocks moved. The longest track measured 860 feet (262 metres) but, as in all cases, this distance was reached by a number of smaller moves rather than all at once. The longest single movement was 659 feet (201 metres) by a 9-ounce (250-gram) cobble called Nancy. The direction of these movements was north-north-easterly, with a few deviations to the east and south-east, which matched the direction of the prevailing winds in the playa.

Sharp soon noticed that there was a ridge on the edges of the furrow and that a small heap of debris was pushed up at the front of the rock by its movement. This indicated that the rocks must have moved when the playa surface was soft, not during its hard-baked or frozen state. Sharp found that most of the recorded movements occurred in three periods: the particularly wet or stormy winters of 1968 to 1969, 1972 to 1973 and 1973 to 1974. Although only some of the stones moved during all three periods, Sharp could infer that rain was as important a factor as wind. The playas get very little rain – about 0 to 3 inches (0 to 8 centimetres) annually – but they are surrounded by about 70 square miles (180 square kilometres) of hills, which make a fine catchment area. Even a light rain in the area could result in a thin layer of water over most of the playa.

Because the surface of the playa is made of fine clay, the action of the rain creates a sheet of water with clay particles in suspension. If the water soaks the surface deeply enough or for long enough, the rocks get bogged down in soft, sticky clay. But when about a quarter of an inch (0.6 centimetres) of water collects, the surface is firm enough to support the rocks. 'The secret,' Sharp wrote in the GSA *Bulletin* in 1976, 'is to catch the play of wind and water at precisely the right moment.' He thinks that movement probably occurs within one to three days of wet or stormy weather when the surface is 'as slick as a whistle'. A powerful gust of wind is all that is needed to make the rock slide, and a slighter wind afterwards will keep it going. Sharp maintains that the surrounding hills scoop

and channel the winds into the playa at sufficient speeds to start the rocks moving – and the smoother the bottom of a stone, the farther it will skid. He has also calculated the maximum velocity of a moving stone as about 3 feet (1 metre) per second.

The phenomenon of moving rocks is not unique to Racetrack Playa. Tracks have been observed on at least 10 other playas in California and Nevada, and from time to time, in the literature of geology, similar anomalies have been reported. In an article written in 1879 for the periodical *Nineteenth Century*, Lord Dunraven told of a strange sight on the shore of a lake in Nova Scotia the previous year:

One day my Indian told me that in a lake close by all the rocks were moving out of the water, a circumstance I thought not a little strange. However, I went to look at the unheard of spectacle and, sure enough, there were the rocks apparently all moving out of the water on to dry land. The lake is of considerable extent, but shallow and full of great masses of rock. Many of these masses appear to have travelled right out of the lake and are now high and dry some 15 yards [14 metres] above the margin of the water. You may see them of all sizes, from blocks of, say, 6 or 8 feet [1.8 or 2.4 metres] in diameter, down to stones which a man could lift. Moreover, you find them in various stages of progress, some 100 yards [90 metres] or more from the shore and apparently just beginning to move; others halfway to their destination; and others again. . . high and dry above the water. In all cases there is a distinct groove or furrow, which the rock has clearly plowed for itself.

One of the 'walled lakes' in the state of Iowa, USA. According to Professor Charles A. White in a *Scientific American* article (1884), these walls were formed by deposits of compacted gravel, earth and boulders through the action of ice expansion in the shallow lakes. An early theory about the moving stones of the playas maintained that ice formation had caused their movement

Lord Dunraven noticed one enormous specimen some distance from the water's edge; earth and stones were heaped up in front of it to over 3 feet (1 metre) in height. A furrow the exact width of the rock extended down the shore and into the water until it was lost from sight in the depths.

This weird scene, remarkably similar to that on the playas, was explained in a letter to the *Scientific American* later in 1879. The writer, who signed the letter 'J.W.A.', claimed to have seen identical effects in other Canadian lakes. The effect is most prominent in shallow lakes that are partly bounded by steep banks or cliffs, according to the explanation. As ice forms it expands and pushes outwards in all directions. The cliffs form an immovable obstacle on one shore, however, doubling the thrust on the opposite, open shore. In shallow water the ice extends to the lake bottom and embeds the rocks there. As the ice expands, it takes the rocks and any other debris with it, depositing them farther along when expansion stops and a thaw sets in. As the lake ice expands and melts each winter, cumulative movements would be enough to drive the rocks onto the land. A similar explanation was proposed by Professor Charles A. White (*Scientific American* 1884) to account for the mystery of the so-called 'walled lakes' of Iowa, which were originally thought to be 'the work of an extinct race'. He said that successive expansions of ice in shallow prairie lakes gradually deposited substantial ridges of compacted earth, gravel and boulders around the perimeter of the lakes.

So we may know how the rocks move. But the surrealistic scene of playas, rocks and their snaking track marks can still awaken a keen appreciation of the wonder and mystery of the natural world.

Indian rope trick

The rise and fall of the rope trick

The one conjuring trick that has fired the imagination for centuries – and caused endless speculation – is the Indian rope trick. Is it, as some claim, just a myth? Or an hypnotic illusion? And why is it no longer staged? MARC CRAMER explains how the trick might have been performed

FOR CENTURIES EUROPEAN travellers in India have brought back tales of incredible conjuring tricks of Hindu street magicians, but one trick in particular has seized the imagination: the famous Indian rope trick. Many rumours have grown up around it, including the assertion that it is mere myth, and that one could never find anyone who had seen it themselves, but only heard about it at second, or even third, hand. One thing is sure: the Indian rope trick has prompted more heated debate than any other single conjuring trick. So did it ever happen? If so, how?

Perhaps the answer lies partly in the training of those who performed the trick. Many Indian magicians (or *fakirs*, an Arabic

The conjurer 'Karachi' – an Englishman called Arthur Claud Derby – practises his version of the rope trick in Sussex in 1935. The dummy head on the mat is known as a 'vent head' among stage magicians

word meaning 'the humble ones') are quite capable of achieving genuinely remarkable feats, such as controlling their nervous systems at will, a faculty due to their Yogic training. But fakirs tend also to be excellent showmen with a gift for creating illusions and performing conjuring tricks. Much of their repertoire has been dismissed by Westerners as 'mass hallucination' or 'mass hypnosis', and the legendary rope trick seems obviously to belong to this rather arbitrary category. And it is likely to remain there in popular imagination for there is said to be no one left who knows the real trick and no one living who remembers seeing it performed. Doomed to extinction, the Indian rope trick will be remembered – if at all – as a mass delusion or merely a highly colourful myth.

It is neither. But one may be forgiven for thinking it a myth for it has a long and sensational history. It is unlikely that the West would have heard of the rope trick, let

slight kick and there was the child, who got up and stood quite straight, completely whole.

Since there is no rational explanation for such outrageous deeds as levitating ropes and miraculous resurrections, succeeding generations looked upon Ibn Batutah's report and subsequent accounts as tall tales or blatant chicanery to extract a few coins from the purses of the credulous. It is small wonder that medieval scholars dismissed the rope trick as a complete tissue of lies, and that the Victorians sought to explain it in terms of the new, fashionable science of hypnosis. During the 1890s the British public enjoyed a flirtation with all things psychical and mysterious. Laymen and scientists soon began to argue over the rope trick, often quite bitterly.

The enterprising American newspaper, the *Chicago Daily Tribune*, suffering at the time from a decline in sales, threw its hat into the ring of debate by sending one S. Ellmore, a writer, and a painter called Lessing to distant India with a bold mission to fulfil. They were to photograph, sketch, and ultimately disprove, the infamous Hindu hoax.

Although it was common knowledge that the Indian rope trick was seldom performed, the two Americans soon managed to return

alone taken it seriously, if it were not for the writings of a respected Moroccan explorer and geographer named Ibn Batutah. One evening in the year 1360 he dined with Akbah Khan and a number of honoured guests at the Royal Court in Hang-Tcheou in China. After an enormous meal, the Khan invited his sated guests to join him in the palace gardens where he had arranged a special surprise entertainment. Ibn Batutah noted in his journal that:

> When the feast was over, one of the entertainers took a ball of wood in which there were several holes. Through these he passed a rope. He threw it into the air and it went up to a point where we could no longer see it, finally to be held there without visible support. When there was only a little end of the rope in his hand, the entertainer told one of his assistants to hang on to the rope and climb into the air, which he did, until we could no longer see him. The entertainer called him three times with no response. Then he took his knife in hand, as if he were angry, grabbed the cord and disappeared also.
>
> Next, the magician threw on the ground the hand of the child who had climbed the rope, then a foot, after that the other hand, then the other foot, the body and (finally) the head. He came down out of breath, his clothes tinged with blood . . . the entertainer took the limbs of the young boy and put them on the ground in their original position. He then gave the mutilated body a

Far left: this photograph, said to be of the famous rope trick, was taken by an anonymous English soldier in India. It seems, however, that this was merely one of the many rope 'suspension tricks' common in the East

Left: the apparently instant growth of a mango tree. The seed was planted, watered, and covered with a cloth, while the conjurer and his assistants performed their professional patter. The plant was uncovered from time to time, revealing it steadily sprouting – and finally bearing fruit. A clever mixture of sleight of hand and suggestion, this act once rivalled the rope trick in travellers' tales

Below left: an engraving showing a Chinese suspension trick in which performers climbed up ropes, fell down apparently dismembered, and were reassembled by 'magic'

Right: the secret of the classic rope trick:
1 At dusk, the audience are seated around a circle of lanterns, half blinded by the light. Meanwhile the rope has been thrown into the air and invisibly hooked onto a wire out of sight of the spectators. A hidden confederate hoists another, stabilising, wire over the main one.
2 A small, lithe boy begins to climb the erect rope – and disappears.
3 When he insolently refuses to come down, the fakir, apparently seething with rage, climbs the rope himself, with a dagger clenched in his teeth. Then suddenly the horrified audience see the boy's limbs drop one by one to the ground.
4 The fakir then descends the rope, while his assistants stand lamenting around the boy's remains. In fact, the 'limbs' are those of a monkey – and the boy has also descended the rope with the fakir, strapped inside his robes. A few magic words and the boy is whole again

to Chicago with several sketches and photographs that, it seemed, put the death blow to the trick by 'proving' that it was, as suspected, a grand 'mass hallucination'. When their film was developed, the photograph showed only a baggy-trousered Hindu surrounded by an apparently hypnotised crowd. There was no sign of an erect rope, let alone a boy clinging to its top. It was therefore concluded that it was all caused by collective suggestion. The article was printed in August 1890 and it was clear that yet another triumphant debunking had been achieved by the *Tribune*'s sagacious journalists.

A few months passed and another 'daring trick' came to light, but this time one that the *Tribune* had not bargained for. The Lessing-Ellmore illustrations were exposed for the outright fakes they were. Lessing had never set foot on Asian soil and had certainly never witnessed the much-maligned Indian rope trick. What was worse, journalist 'S. Ellmore' *did not exist*. Under pressure, the newspaper's publisher was forced to print a retraction, confessing the elaborate hoax, the object of which was to increase sales.

Thirty years on, the rope trick became news again as a certain Colonel Elliot addressed the London Magic Circle in an attempt to settle the matter once and for all. In March 1919 the Colonel put up a prize of £500 to anyone who could perform the trick under carefully controlled scientific conditions. Because of the marked absence of London-based fakirs, an advertisement was placed in the *Times of India* offering the fabulous prize to any rope-climbing Hindu able to perform the elusive feat. But the worthy challenge went unanswered.

Much to their frustration, the poor Colonel and his band of eager dilettantes concluded that the trick must therefore be, as rumoured, a myth. It had never occurred to their naïve, ethnocentric minds that fakirs are not the sort of chaps who pass a quiet afternoon at the local gentlemen's club reading English-language newspapers. The fakirs of the 1920s were, for the most part, illiterate even in their own language and could not speak, let alone read, English. The dour gentlemen of the Magic Circle grudgingly agreed with the supporters of parapsychology and came to the tidy conclusion that the Indian rope trick was the product of 'collective hallucination'.

However, some years after the attempts of the Magic Circle to investigate the rope trick, a group of Irish and English soldiers

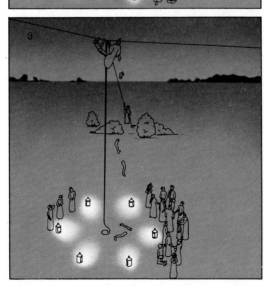
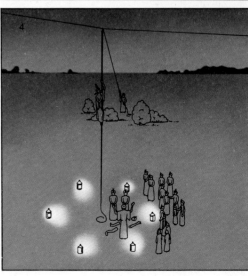
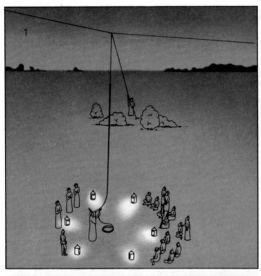

454

stationed in Upsala, India, witnessed a performance that was almost identical to the feats reported by Ibn Batutah in China in the 14th century – the account of which may be found in the *Journal* of the Society for Psychical Research.

If, for the moment, we imagine the situation reversed and assume that you are a hypnotist touring India and giving demonstrations of your skill to native audiences, it is logical to assume the following. Your audience comprises (say) 50 Hindus from New Delhi (who almost always speak English) and 50 lamas from Sikkim (who rarely ever speak English). Unable to speak either Hindu or Tibetan, you begin to make hypnotic suggestions in English to your audience, and your skills soon take effect. You instruct them to fall into a deep sleep and to 'see' a dragon with gold wings. You are bound to notice that your English-speaking Delhites are busily looking at mythical beasts while there are 50 wide-awake lamas sitting in front of you waiting for something to happen.

The magic of words
The principle seems clear enough. Hypnotic suggestion is, as far as we know, always a verbal procedure and if the subject cannot understand the language of the hypnotist's suggestions, then that person cannot be hypnotised at all.

If mass hypnosis is not the answer, how can we explain the rope trick and the reason why it is so seldom seen?

The secret of the trick has been a closely guarded secret that was handed, like a family heirloom, from father to son. At any given time, the number of people who knew how to perform the trick could be counted on one hand since very few fakirs had the skill or the courage to stage the trick successfully, especially when failure would have inevitably resulted in a broken neck. It is said that by the mid 1940s all the old-time performers

Stills from a film purporting to show the classic rope trick, taken in the 1920s by a European in India. The fakir shows the crowd that the rope is just an ordinary length of hemp (bottom) then throws it into the air where it remains rigid (below). The boy begins to climb up it (below right) and is clearly seen at the top (right). But was this a tame version of the fabled trick or just another clever balancing act?

were far too ancient, or too unsure of their audiences, to bother with the Indian rope trick. But if it was not a myth, how was it actually done?

One might reasonably suspect that the secret is in the rope itself and that joints of metal or bone hold it erect, or that the magician works some sort of hidden device on the ground. But the true secret is literally up in the air.

When the trick was first planned – long before the advent of invisible wires used by today's stage magicians – a long, fine and remarkably strong wire or line was skilfully woven from black hairs. Since this was not completely invisible, the trick was always performed at dusk when the wire would be concealed against a darkening sky. Moreover, it was necessary to perform this version of the trick against a carefully chosen background: never, for example, in a desert or an open space. The only way to avoid

detection was to perform in a valley between two hillocks or knolls. The wire was stretched from one hill to another, spanning the valley so that the fine cord was concealed by the foliage in the background in the same way that modern telephone wires are obscured by a woody countryside but visible against a clear sky. Ever careful to avert the suspicious eye and to win the confidence of his audience, the fakir always began the magic show at dusk and 'warmed up' the crowd with juggling, story-telling and a few banal tricks until the sky was black.

It was at this point that his assistants would come forth with several lanterns and place them at specific points around the seated performer. As this was being done, the magician performed a routine 'patter', deliberately inducing a state of mild boredom and distraction in his audience.

Imagine the scene: as he is chattering to the audience – who are seated some 12 feet

(3.5 metres) in front of him – the fakir removes a length of hemp from a wicker basket and throws it up in the air many times to show that it is just an ordinary rope. Most fakirs will not attempt to slip the wooden ball into the rope in front of their audience but will have concealed it in the rope beforehand. Still chattering, he throws the rope once more into the air. The spectators are now bored, so they fail to notice that on the final handling the magician has slipped a sturdy metal hook into a special hole in the wooden ball. This hook is attached to an extremely fine hair wire, which cannot be seen against the inky sky. The wire leads up to, and over, the main horizontal cord suspended some 60 feet (18 metres) in the air. And as the audience looks up to watch the rope rising into the air by some seemingly magical force they are compelled to stare into the bright lanterns. This creates a partial night-blindness so that the rope appears to be

levitating, reaching up 200 to 300 feet (60 to 90 metres) into the heavens – given that the perspective is cunningly faked. What the audience does not know is that the rope is being hoisted up by a hidden assistant.

From where the audience is sitting it is impossible to see the top of the rope, and when the magician's young assistant refuses his command to climb the rope they can quite see why. The small boy – usually a lad of eight or nine – protests fearfully. Of course, he eventually gives in and climbs up the rope, which begins to sway dramatically. Then suddenly he appears to vanish into thin air. The 'miracle', however is the result of natural camouflage, since the boy is no longer within the range of the lanterns after he has climbed as far as 30 feet (10 metres) or so. When he reaches the top he takes another hook from his dark robes and adds further support to the rope by slipping it in the wooden ball and over the main wire.

Suddenly the fakir shouts out something to the boy, who gives an insolent answer. Apparently seething with anger, the fakir takes up a cruel-looking knife and, placing it between his teeth, he proceeds to climb the rope. In a few moments, he also vanishes. The audience below then hears a bitter argument, followed by screams of mortal agony. And, horribly, one by one the poor lad's limbs fall to the ground with sickening thuds. But these are really only the shaved limbs of a large freshly slaughtered monkey wrapped up in cloth to match the boy's clothing and hidden in the fakir's commodious robes. The conjurer merely removes them and sprinkles them with a little blood he keeps in a glass phial. Finally the boy's severed head – a carefully painted wooden model in a turban – falls to the ground. The audience is in no mood to inspect it.

Four assistants rush to the butchered body, noisily lamenting. Meanwhile, at the top of the rope, the boy slips into a harness inside the fakir's loose clothing, pressing himself against the trickster's stomach while his legs and arms fit into four well-concealed loops. The magician then climbs down the rope with the boy hidden in his robes, and with a noticeably bloodied blade between his teeth. On the ground the magician feigns sorrow as he stares at the hacked-up remains of the lad that are laid out before him. The assistants gather around the grief-stricken fakir and attempt to console him. While this is being staged, the boy slips out of his master's robes and the confederates hide the butchered monkey limbs in their costumes. The assistants' backs form an effective screen that prevents the audience seeing the boy as he lies down on the ground in place of the gory pile. The fakir's confederates step back as the magician utters words of power and gives the little fellow a good, swift kick that – lo and behold! – brings the butchered boy back to life.

A hint of hidden treasure

Since rumours of buried treasure on Oak Island began in 1795, speculators have spent a small fortune trying to find it. EDWARD HORTON describes their attempts – and explains why the treasure remains as elusive as ever

ON A SUMMER'S DAY in 1795 a 16-year-old lad named Daniel McGinnis beached his canoe on the south-eastern shore of a small island in Mahone Bay, which makes a deep indentation in the southern coast of Nova Scotia. Why McGinnis chose this particular island for his excursion is unknown. Perhaps he was attracted by the feature that distinguishes the island from its neighbours – a thick covering of red oak, which had given rise to its unofficial name, Oak Island.

McGinnis set off for the interior of the island, following an old path through the trees. Presently he found himself in a clearing, where the oak trees had been cut down and a second growth was springing up to take their place. Curiously, however, there stood in the centre of the clearing a single, ancient oak. McGinnis noticed that one of its branches had been lopped off and that the stump overhung a depression in the earth from a height of about 15 feet (5 metres). The depression, and the fact that he could plainly see lacerations on the stump, which he took to be scoring from a rope, suggested to McGinnis that he had stumbled upon the site of buried treasure. He hurried back to his home town of Chester, 4 miles (6 kilometres) distant on the eastern shore of Mahone Bay, to enlist the aid of friends.

The following day McGinnis returned to Oak Island, accompanied by 20-year-old John Smith and 13-year-old Anthony Vaughn. With picks and shovels the boys set to work beneath the tree.

No sooner had they begun shovelling out the loose earth than they discovered that they were indeed following in someone's footsteps. For they found themselves in a clearly defined circular shaft, 13 feet in diameter, with walls of hard clay that bore the marks of

As the units of measurement used in early records of excavations at the Money Pit were Imperial, in this article the original measurements have not been converted into metric equivalents. The following conversion chart may be helpful.

1 inch=2.5 centimetres
10 inches=25 centimetres
1 foot=30 centimetres
10 feet=3 metres
100 feet=30 metres
1 mile=1.6 kilometres

Right: this diagram shows the various levels of the Oak Island Money Pit found by successive treasure-seeking expeditions from 1795 to 1850. The ingenious system of tunnels that ensured the flooding of the pit each time it was excavated beyond a certain depth can clearly be seen

Left: Oak Island lies off the coast of Nova Scotia, sheltered by the wide sweep of Mahone Bay. The aerial view (far right) shows how successive excavations have eaten away at the coastline close to the Money Pit, which is situated in the foreground of the photograph, to the right

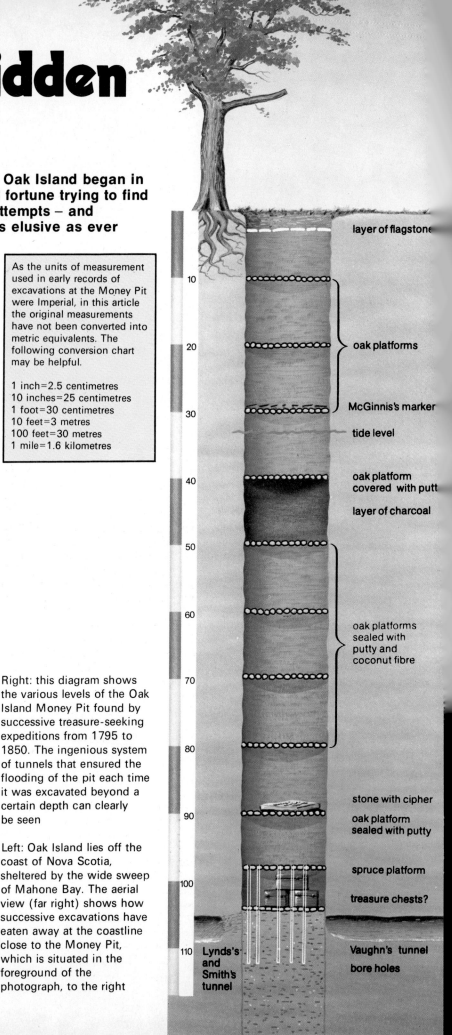

layer of flagstone

oak platforms

McGinnis's marker

tide level

oak platform covered with putt

layer of charcoal

oak platforms sealed with putty and coconut fibre

stone with cipher

oak platform sealed with putty

spruce platform

treasure chests?

Vaughn's tunnel

bore holes

Lynds's and Smith's tunnel

Prince Edward Island

NOVA SCOTIA

Oak Island

ATLANTIC OCEAN

picks. Four feet down they encountered a layer of flagstones, which could not have come from Oak Island. They hauled them out and kept digging. At 10 feet they ran into a platform of solid oak logs extending right across the shaft and firmly embedded in its clay walls. They managed to remove the logs and dug on. At 20 feet there was a similar platform, and at 30 feet yet another. With such limited equipment the lads could go no further – indeed, it was a prodigious feat for them to have got as far as they did. They returned to Chester to drum up more support, having first driven in stakes to indicate the depth they had reached.

Surprisingly, in view of the obvious allure of buried wealth and the intriguing nature of their discovery, the boys found no takers. Apparently Oak Island had a shady reputation. It was haunted – dangerously so. A Chester woman, whose mother had been one of the first settlers in the area, recalled that fires and strange lights had once been observed on the island. A boatload of men had set off to investigate these goings-on and had disappeared without trace. Clearly, the place should be given a wide berth.

It was nine years later, when the boys had grown into men, that help finally came forth in the shape of one Simeon Lynds, a well-heeled 30-year-old who became interested in the story as told him by Vaughn and who formed a syndicate to assist the original three in their quest. John Smith at least had not been idle all this time. He had managed to buy the land surrounding the excavation, and indeed over the next three decades would add to his holding, lot by lot, until he was in possession of the whole eastern end of the island. So it was that in 1804 a group of determined men, well-equipped for the task in hand and confident of success, descended on the mysterious Oak Island.

First they had to clear out the mud that had settled in the pit, but once they came to the sticks left nine years before, they were satisfied that their site had been unmolested during the intervening years. They now set to work in earnest. Reports of what they encountered between 30 feet and 90 feet down vary both in detail and in sequence, but the following account is accurate in its essence and does not sensationalise the discoveries made by the syndicate of 1804. At the 40-foot level they found another oak platform, this time covered in putty; at 50 feet, having dug through charcoal, they came upon yet another oak platform, this one sealed with coconut fibre. Then at regular 10-foot intervals there were more platforms, all of oak, either unadorned or covered with putty or coconut fibre.

Indecipherable inscription

At a depth of 90 feet they hit a flat stone, 3 feet long and 1 foot wide. It was not native stone and, of more significance, it bore an indecipherable inscription on the underside. This stone, with its strange markings, was surely a most valuable clue, but it was apparently treated in an off-hand manner. John Smith installed it at the back of the fireplace in the house he had built on the island, a move that was hardly calculated to preserve any message the stone was intended to convey. Half a century later the stone was exhibited in Halifax, as a lure for the recruitment of further funds for exploring the pit. At that time a professor of languages claimed to have cracked the code: 'Ten feet below two million pounds.' Someone who saw the stone in the early years of this century recalled in 1935 that whatever inscription there was had faded completely by the time he saw it, and his must be the final word – literally; no one has been able to trace the stone since then.

The treasure hunters pressed on, now with a crowbar. The earth was so sodden that they had to haul up one cask of water to every two casks of earth. At 98 feet they struck

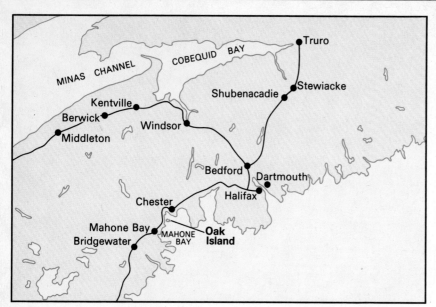

A map of Mahone Bay and Oak Island. It was here that the search for buried treasure began when, one summer's day in 1795, 16-year-old Daniel McGinnis paddled his canoe across Mahone Bay to explore Oak Island – and stumbled on the Money Pit

something solid, stretching across the entire width of the shaft. They reckoned that it was wood – and it required only a small leap of faith to conclude that it must be a chest. It was nearly nightfall on Saturday, and the men returned to their homes, confident that Monday morning would bring them riches beyond the dreams of avarice.

In fact, Monday morning brought nothing but disappointment. To their chagrin, they found the pit filled with water to within 33 feet of the surface. They tried to bale it out with buckets, but the level remained stubbornly unchanged. They rigged up a pump and lowered it to the 90-foot level. The pump burst, and the syndicate abandoned work for the year.

In the spring of 1805 they returned to the site and tried to drain the pit by digging another, deeper one alongside. At 110 feet, still dry, they tunnelled sideways towards the original shaft – to be greeted by a veritable Niagara. They were lucky to escape with their lives (as some of their dogged successors did not). By the following morning the débâcle was complete. Having once been only inches from their goal, so they had believed, they now stared glumly at two muddy pits, both filled with water to within 33 feet of the surface. They had exhausted their capital and now admitted defeat, blaming their misfortune on a caprice of nature. They would not be the last to mistake the identity of their unseen adversary.

For 44 years the Money Pit, as it was to become known, lay undisturbed, but then in 1849 a new syndicate was formed, with an ageing Anthony Vaughn acting in an advisory capacity. The Truro syndicate (named after the town in which it was formed) found both shafts caved in, but 12 days' hard labouring took them 86 feet down the original shaft. As had happened half a century before, the diggers left for home on a Saturday evening, light of heart. An inspection on Sunday morning showed nothing

amiss, and the men set off for church in Chester, doubtless to render heartfelt thanks. If so, their gratitude was premature. When they returned at 2 p.m., 'to their great surprise [they] found water standing in the Pit, to a depth of 60 feet, being on a level with that in the Bay.' Their attempts to bail it out were described in an account a few years later as being 'as unsatisfactory as taking soup with a fork'.

Undismayed, the Truro men decided to employ a pod auger (a horse-driven drill that could bring to the surface samples of what it penetrated) in order to determine precisely what it was that the pit contained below the 98-foot level. They erected a platform above the water and bored five holes, the first of them to the west of centre of the pit, the others progressively eastward across the pit. The first two revealed only mud and stones.

The third, however, was a different matter. In a written report, the man in charge of the drilling operations commented as follows:

The platform was struck at 98 feet just as the old diggers found it, when sounding with the iron bar [in 1804]. After going through the platform, which was 5 inches thick, and proved to be spruce, the auger dropped 12 inches and then went through 4 inches of oak; then it went through 22 inches of metal in pieces; but the auger failed to bring up anything in the nature of treasure, except three links resembling the links of an ancient watch chain. It then went through 8 inches of oak, which was thought to be the bottom of the first box and the top of the next; then 22 inches of metal, the same as before; then 4 inches of oak and 6 inches of spruce, then into clay 7 feet without striking anything.

This was certainly exciting, and the fourth bore was no anticlimax. Eighteen inches below the platform the drill appeared to scrape the side of a chest (so they surmised), and in fact splinters of oak were brought to the surface, along with what they took to be coconut fibre.

Double dealing

The fifth and final bore took a bizarre turn. The foreman, James Pitblado, was under instructions to remove every speck of material clinging to the drill when it was brought to the surface, so that it could be examined under a microscope. This he did, but not quite in the spirit intended. He was seen by one of the syndicate members to take something out of the auger, wash it, study it closely and slip it into his pocket. When challenged, he blithely retorted that he would display his findings at the next meeting of the syndicate directors. Incredibly enough, he was taken at his word. Instead of attending the board meeting, Pitblado found himself a backer, who promptly made an unsuccessful attempt to buy the eastern end of Oak Island. It was commonly believed that what Pitblado found was a jewel.

The Truro syndicate was now convinced to a man – and not without good reason – that two oak chests filled with loot lay, stacked one on top of the other, immediately below the 98-foot level. It remained merely to conquer nature's obstinacy over the matter of the water. In the spring of 1850 a new shaft was sunk some 10 feet to the west of the Money Pit: hard clay to a depth of 109 feet, and no flooding. Then another shaft was bored sideways into the Money Pit, just as in 1805, and with the same result: water burst in, half-filling it within minutes.

It is hard to credit, but it seems that it was only at this stage in the saga that anyone got round to questioning the source of all the water that was so bedevilling things. The story goes that someone tumbled into one of the pits, swallowed a mouthful and pronounced the water *salt*! In any case, it is a fact that only at this juncture was a connection made between the water in the shaft and the sea surrounding Oak Island. The association between the two was easily confirmed by noting that the water in the shafts rose and fell with the tides.

The composition of the soil ruled out any possibility of natural seepage (which would have made it impossible to dig the Money Pit in the first place anyway), so there was only one conceivable explanation. The Money Pit was in some way or other connected with the sea by a subterranean passage. How?

The answer was not difficult to find. A quick search on the nearest beach, 500 feet from the Money Pit at Smith's Cove, revealed all. When the tide ebbed, the sand 'gulched water like a sponge being squeezed'. A bit of spadework showed why. At a depth of 3 feet the workmen turned up a 2-inch layer of the now familiar coconut fibre. Beneath this was a 5-inch layer of kelp, or seaweed, then carefully arranged flat stones, criss-crossing one another. This 'sponge' extended for 145 feet along the beach, between low and high water marks. Next the searchers uncovered five box drains, skilfully constructed of flat stones, 8 inches apart, at a depth of 5 feet. These drains converged, fan-like, on a funnel-shaped sump hole, just above high-water mark. (When one of the drains was uncovered it was completely free of silt – a comment on the high quality of the original workmanship.) From the sump a tunnel ran inland and steadily downwards to the Money Pit, finishing its 500-foot course somewhere below the 98-foot mark.

The present-day observer, like the men from Truro, is driven to accept a remarkable conclusion – a conclusion that, were it not for incontrovertible evidence, he would be inclined to laugh out of court. Someone, at some time prior to 1795, had badly wanted to conceal something. Either by chance or by design, he set about his business on an obscure island in a Nova Scotia bay. He started by digging a shaft to a depth of over 100 feet. Then he constructed a 500-foot tunnel between the shaft and the beach at Smith's Cove, where he constructed a fiendishly clever bit of 'plumbing' that booby-trapped the approach to his hiding place. He then filled in the shaft, having rendered it inaccessible in its lower reaches, not haphazardly but in a most deliberate manner. Finally, having switched on the burglar alarm, as it were, he sailed off into the sunset, leaving behind the tell-tale oak tree.

The men from Truro were awed, as well they might be, but not overawed. What 17th- or 18th-century Man could ravel, 19-century Man could unravel. Or so he thought.

Smith's Cove on Oak Island. Here treasure hunters discovered the secret of why the Pit flooded each time they reached a certain level in their excavations

Over the years scores of prospectors made their way to Oak Island, each one convinced that he would recover the fabulous treasure from the ingenious Money Pit.

IF THE TREASURE SEEKERS of the Truro group had ever wavered in their belief in the existence of a fabulous hoard at the bottom of the Money Pit, the discovery of the ingenious flood tunnel enabled them to cast off any doubts. Quite apart from the sheer brilliance of the tunnel arrangement, the task of building the pit had been nothing short of Herculean. It was inconceivable that someone would go to such lengths to protect run-of-the-mill booty. The Money Pit must harbour a fortune, and it was well worth any amount of effort to reach it.

Accordingly, the workmen built a coffer dam 150 feet long across Smith's Cove, between the low-water mark and the catchment, hoping thereby to cut off the water supply. It would then remain only to pump the Money Pit dry once and for all. Unfortunately, a particularly high tide swept the dam away before it was completed. The Truro men then compounded their misfortune by misjudgement.

It should have been plain to them that it was possible to build a dam successfully, for how, without making one himself, could their mysterious predecessor have dug his tunnel in the first place? Yet instead of persevering with their original plan, they opted for a quicker, cheaper solution. They decided to intercept the tunnel between the shore and the Money Pit and to block it off. The reports are confused about how many fresh shafts they sank, and where, in an attempt to locate the tunnel. At one point they thought they had it, when they dislodged a boulder at a depth of 35 feet and were greeted by a surge of water. In fact, they

As the units of measurement used in early records of excavations at the Money Pit were Imperial, in this article the original measurements have not been converted into metric equivalents. The following conversion chart may be helpful.

1 inch=2.5 centimetres
10 inches=25 centimetres
1 foot=30 centimetres
10 feet=3 metres
100 feet=30 metres
1 mile=1.6 kilometres

Oak Island, which takes its name from the thick growth of red oaks that covers both its ends, seen here from the coast of Nova Scotia. A tiny, uninhabited island, it became a hive of activity after the discovery of the Money Pit in 1795. Through the years men and equipment were taken to the island by boat, but in 1963 Robert Dunfield, an American petroleum geologist, built a causeway from the mainland (this can be seen at the right of the photograph) to facilitate the transportation of heavy machinery

were far too close to the Money Pit for the flood tunnel to be so near the surface, and when they attempted to seal off the supposed tunnel by driving stakes and timbers into it, the water level in the Money Pit remained undisturbed. Thwarted, they resorted to an expedient that had been tried before. Fifty feet from the Money Pit, they dug down to a depth of 118 feet and then tunnelled sideways towards their goal. They were even more unlucky than their predecessors had been: the pit collapsed into the tunnel.

This was worse than anything that had happened before, and the Truro men believed that in the subterranean turmoil their treasure 'chests' had tumbled deeper into the shaft, perhaps to a depth of 150 feet. Whether or not that bleak conclusion was justified, this latest development was more than a minor setback. Where before there had been 'chests' lodged securely around the 100-foot mark, there was now chaos, a dreary sea of mud in which their dreams of wealth lay trapped. Their funds were exhausted, and they called a halt.

In 1859 the group re-formed, and the following year there emerged a new Truro syndicate, which nevertheless numbered some of the original members. More shafts were sunk, all with the purpose of blocking off or diverting the flow of water from the flood tunnel, and all with the same conspicuous lack of success. As many as 33 horses and 63 men were employed at the pumps at one time, and then in 1861 steam power was harnessed to the seemingly insuperable task of draining the Money Pit. The boiler burst, scalding one of the workmen to death. By 1865 the men from Truro had had enough and quit for good, making way for a new syndicate from Halifax, which was formed the following year.

Like the original Truro syndicate, the Halifax group set about things the sensible

Sinking into the quagmire

way. They tried to cut off the water at source by building a dam. As before, the tide demolished their handiwork before it was completed, and, as before, this single failure deflected the treasure seekers from their sound strategy. Instead of buckling down to the arduous business of building a *better* dam, they returned to the Money Pit. They pumped and they dug; they bored holes and dug some more, running branch tunnels laterally in an attempt to intercept the flood tunnel. This they finally accomplished, although it did them no good. They discovered that the flood tunnel, some 4 feet high and $2\frac{1}{2}$ feet wide, entered the Money Pit at a depth of 110 feet (that is, 10 feet below the supposed original location of the treasure). But finding the flood tunnel and cutting off the flow of water from the sea were two different matters, and in 1867 the syndicate gave up the unequal struggle. Before his death in 1938, one of the syndicate members, Isaac Blair, told his nephew Frederick Blair (who would himself be closely involved with many attempts to solve the Oak Island mystery during his long life): 'I saw enough to convince me that there was treasure buried there and enough to convince me that they will never get it.' Prophetic words.

A sound analysis

By now the pattern of failure was pretty clearly defined, and a quarter of a century was to elapse before the next brave attempt. Then in 1894 the Oak Island Treasure Company was established, with $60,000 capital. The young Blair drew up the prospectus, which was certainly sound enough in its historical analysis. Eager investors were told: 'It is perfectly obvious that the great mistake thus far has been in attempting to "bail out" the ocean.' The answer, it suggested, was 'to use the best modern appliances for cutting off the flow of water

Above: the head of the Money Pit at the time of the excavations by Frederick Blair's Oak Island Treasure Company. Over a period of about five years Blair and his associates made repeated attempts to drain the pit – but without success

Below: a group of eager prospectors at work at the Money Pit in about 1915. Blair's own funds had long since run out, but he continued to act as an adviser to other syndicates that arrived on the island. Right up to his death in 1954, Blair remained convinced that the elusive treasure would be found

through the tunnel at some point near the shore, before attempting to pump out the water'.

As so often before, an attempt to intercept the flood tunnel was made close to the Money Pit rather than near the shore (where it must lie nearer the surface), and with the usual inconclusive results. Then, again as before, the Money Pit itself was attacked – with added difficulty now because the century-long depredations had obscured its precise location. Blair and his associates found it, however, by working their way upwards from one of the side tunnels leading off an earlier shaft. (By this time a cross-section of the area would have resembled a rabbit warren.) They discovered the flood tunnel too, where it entered the Money Pit at the 110-foot mark. But the tidal water pressure was far too great to stem at that point.

It was 1897 by the time Blair and his colleagues belatedly turned their attention to the beach at Smith's Cove. They had no intention of building a dam, but they launched a determined assault on the flood tunnel, near its source. They bored five holes in a line running across the supposed path of the flood tunnel, and one of them yielded salt water, which rose and fell with the tides. They lowered 160 pounds (73 kilograms) of dynamite to a depth of 80 feet, and when they set it off, they observed considerable turbulence in the Money Pit. Assuming that they had finally destroyed the flood tunnel, they returned to the Money Pit and the pumps, but still the water poured in.

According to the traditional sequence of events, it was now time to start drilling. First they sank a 3-inch pipe, which came to rest against iron at 126 feet. Inside the pipe they lowered a drill, which went past the obstruction and struck what was identified as cement at 151 feet. Twenty inches further on the drill struck oak 5 inches thick. Then it hit what 'felt like' large metal objects, which persistent twisting and turning of the auger

Left: in 1971 the Triton Alliance Company lowered a submarine television camera into the Money Pit, which they had drilled to a depth of over 200 feet, and claimed that it revealed the presence of three chests – and a severed hand

Right: details of some of the major excavations of the Money Pit between 1850 and 1970. Despite the use of increasingly sophisticated machinery, which enabled successive expeditions to dig deeper and deeper into the ground, the pit still refused to give up its secret

Below: one of the shafts leading to the seemingly bottomless Money Pit. Since its discovery in 1795, hundreds of thousands of dollars have been poured into the pit and the lives of five men have been lost

dislodged, so that the drill could, apparently, slip between them. Then it struck loose metal, which was even more difficult for the drill to force its way through, then more of the large metal objects.

This was the first evidence of a buried hoard since the original Truro syndicate had bored through wood and metal in 1849. The drillers concluded that a layer of loose coin lay wedged between two stacks of metal bars – and they did not think the bars were iron.

They followed up this discovery with the application of sound technique, and only the most maddening bad luck prevented them from bringing samples to the surface. They tried to secure the drill hole by piping below 126 feet, and to that end they sent down a pipe of the same diameter as the drill ($1\frac{1}{2}$ inches) inside the 3-inch pipe. But at 126 feet the pipe was deflected by metal and struck what appeared to be the wall of the pit. They removed the pipe and sent the drill down again – but it followed the new, sterile path made by the pipe. The original hole down to the cement and the metal beyond was lost! Nor could other drills, sent down immediately afterwards, find that elusive hole. In one of these later drillings it was thought that the auger glanced off the outer edge of a chest. Finally, this particular avenue of attack had to be abandoned when at 126 feet the drill struck a channel of water, which spouted up the pipe at the rate of 400 gallons (1800 litres) per minute. This, of course, suggested that there were *two* flood tunnels, the second, deeper one providing back-up cover for the first.

A simple test proved that this was in fact the case. Blair poured red dye into the Money Pit when the water level was at its highest (that is, at high tide) and scanned the shore as the tide receded. The red dye surfaced in three separate places, 600 feet from the Money Pit, only this time on the south shore.

In a futile attempt to intercept this second tunnel, Blair sank six shafts, and by the time he was finished – when the syndicate ran out of money – the only result was that the quagmire around the Money Pit was so bad that its precise location had become uncertain again. In the course of this series of persistent failures, however, Blair did uncover a mysterious object that served to convince his syndicate – and many later searchers – that beyond a shadow of a doubt, there was a cache of something buried in the Money Pit. In one of the drillings the auger brought to the surface a small ball of parchment that, when smoothed flat, revealed the letters 'v.i.'. What they stood for remains a mystery, but a scrap of parchment retrieved from such a depth is hard to dismiss. It was clearly evidence of some kind – but evidence of what?

Next came Captain Harry L. Bowdoin, a New York mining and marine engineer. He started well, clearing the Money Pit to a depth of 113 feet. From there he put down a core drill, which struck what was presumed to be cement at 149 feet. This caused great excitement. Were they finally on the threshold of a watertight treasure chamber? Alas, no. Nothing but yellow clay and stones for the next 18 feet. Then bedrock. A further 25 borings yielded no more, while experts at Columbia University pronounced the 'cement' to be 'natural limestone pitted by the action of water'. Bowdoin departed, declaring that the treasure was a myth.

Others came and went without adding anything to the considerable but infuriatingly inconclusive body of knowledge about the Money Pit. Then in 1931 William Chappell, who had operated the drill that had

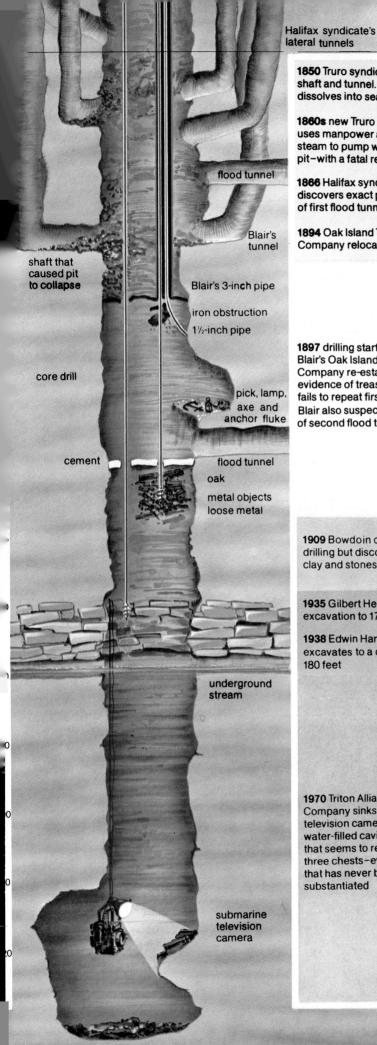

1850 Truro syndicate digs shaft and tunnel. Pit dissolves into sea of mud

1860s new Truro syndicate uses manpower and, later, steam to pump water from pit–with a fatal result

1866 Halifax syndicate discovers exact position of first flood tunnel

1894 Oak Island Treasure Company relocates site of pit

1897 drilling starts and Blair's Oak Island Treasure Company re-establishes evidence of treasure but fails to repeat first success. Blair also suspects possibility of second flood tunnel

1909 Bowdoin continues the drilling but discovers only clay and stones

1935 Gilbert Hedden extends excavation to 170 feet

1938 Edwin Hamilton excavates to a depth of 180 feet

1970 Triton Alliance Company sinks submarine television camera into water-filled cavity that seems to reveal three chests–evidence that has never been substantiated

Labels on illustration:
flood tunnel
Blair's tunnel
shaft that caused pit to collapse
Blair's 3-inch pipe
iron obstruction
1½-inch pipe
core drill
pick, lamp, axe and anchor fluke
cement
flood tunnel
oak
metal objects
loose metal
underground stream
submarine television camera

brought up the piece of parchment more than 30 years before, returned for another attempt. Digging either in or near the Money Pit (he and his old colleague Blair could not agree on the location), Chappell uncovered, at depths of between 116 and 150 feet, plenty of evidence of earlier work – a pick, an oil lamp, an anchor fluke, an axe head estimated to be 250 years old. The only way such objects could have been trapped at that depth, Blair reasoned, was by a natural cavity somewhere below the 100-foot mark (the original location of the 'chests'), into which all had fallen at some point in the siege.

Whether or not Blair had drawn the right conclusion, he had certainly touched upon the central irony of the quest. Each failure had rendered subsequent attempts less likely to succeed, despite the fact that as the years rolled by, increasingly sophisticated techniques and equipment were available to the searchers. During the middle 1930s Gilbert Hedden, a New Jersey businessman, cleared Chappell's shaft and lowered it to a depth of 170 feet. After two seasons' labour, he too gave up and sold his equipment to Edwin Hamilton, a machinery engineer. Hamilton reached 180 feet, and while he found no treasure, he at least found the place where the second flood tunnel entered the Money Pit, at a depth of 150 feet. He also proved that this second tunnel, like the first, led from Smith's Cove. The reason Blair's red dye had surfaced on the south shore was that at 180 feet there was a natural stream flowing across the pit in that direction.

An unsolved riddle

The catalogue of failures continued after the Second World War, and in 1963 defeat was accompanied by tragedy. A retired circus stunt rider, Robert Restall, was overcome by exhaust fumes from the pump that he was using as he worked in the shaft. His son and two other men died with him when they went to his rescue. Then, two years later, a mighty attempt was made by Robert Dunfield, an American petroleum geologist. He even built a causeway from the mainland to enable him to get a 70-foot-high clam digger onto the site. With this he dug a massive hole 80 feet wide and 130 feet deep on the site of the Money Pit. No luck.

In 1970 a group calling itself the Triton Alliance Company took over Dunfield's concession. A year later, Triton announced that it had discovered a water-filled cavity at a depth of 212 feet, and that a submarine television camera had revealed what looked like three chests and, gruesomely, a severed hand, flesh intact. Divers were subsequently lowered into the cavern at a depth of 235 feet. They found neither chests nor hand. At this stage it seemed unlikely that anyone would ever solve the riddle of the Money Pit.

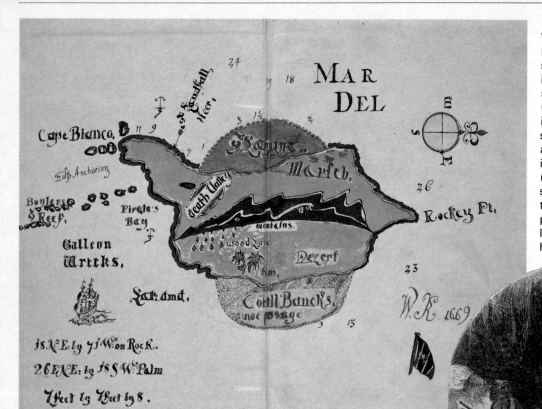

Left: one of Harold Wilkins's alleged Kidd-Palmer charts, dated 1669, showing an unidentified island that is remarkably similar to Oak Island. Captain Kidd was hanged in 1701 (right), and subsequently became the arch-pirate of popular imagination; this illustration (below) depicts him supervising the burial of treasure in a cave. Many people believed it was Kidd's legendary hoard that lay hidden in the Money Pit

So near, yet so far

Who was the engineering genius behind the Money Pit? What did he bury there – and why? After years of investigation all hope of solving the mystery was abandoned. But there was one vital clue that everyone had overlooked

FROM THE MOMENT that Daniel McGinnis chanced upon the Money Pit in 1795 to the present day, attempts to salvage the supposed treasure have naturally gone hand in hand with speculation about the identity of those who buried it. There has been no shortage of candidates, from a tribe of Incas to a party of Norsemen. Dottiest of all, surely, is the theory that the Money Pit conceals manuscripts of Francis Bacon's that reveal his authorship of Shakespeare's plays. All along, however, the popular favourites for the role have been pirates – either pirates unknown or one particularly well-known pirate, Captain William Kidd.

This is hardly surprising, given the romantic association between pirates and buried treasure. And while, generally speaking, the pirate connection has been regarded as self-evident, there is at least one small piece of circumstantial evidence that appears to confirm such a suspicion. The oft-mentioned coconut fibre (if it was correctly identified) presumably came from the West or East Indies, notorious haunts of pirates and buccaneers. Nova Scotia is far from the beaten track of piracy, but there is certainly no reason why some of the English maurauders who preyed so successfully on Spanish ships and towns in the Caribbean during the middle part of the 17th century, the notorious 'brethren of the coast', should not have made their way up the Atlantic coast.

It is an attractive theory that conjures up visions of pieces of eight, a frenzy of moonlit activity by desperate men with the sea at their backs, blood on their hands and avarice in their hearts. But it founders on the question of dates. It will be recalled that McGinnis found a clearing with young oaks springing up to replace those that had been felled. The red oaks of the North American and Canadian coast grow quickly, and McGinnis would have found mature trees towering above him, not saplings, had the Money Pit been dug a century and more before.

The identification of the pirate in question as Captain Kidd presents difficulties too. He

---

As the units of measurement used in early records of excavations at the Money Pit were Imperial, in this article the original measurements have not been converted into metric equivalents. The following conversion chart may be helpful.

1 inch=2.5 centimetres
10 inches=25 centimetres
1 foot=30 centimetres
10 feet=3 metres
100 feet=30 metres
1 mile=1.6 kilometres

was hanged for piracy at Wapping in 1701 and has subsequently been popularly associated with practically every tale of buried treasure that has ever been told. Nevertheless, Kidd and the mysterious Oak Island brush against each other in a strange way.

In 1935 a book entitled *Captain Kidd and his Skeleton Island* appeared in England. It included a map of an island and a set of directions. The map was based, according to the author of the book, Harold T. Wilkins, on the famous Kidd charts, which had recently come into the hands of a collector of pirate relics, Hubert Palmer. The charts, four of them, had been found hidden in three sea chests and an oak bureau – apparently genuine Kidd relics. All depict an unidentified island in greater or lesser detail, and they contain various markings and inscriptions (not all of them identical, although the island is always the same), including the initials w.k., the location 'China Sea' and the date 1669. These Kidd-Palmer charts, as they are known, were accepted by experts as being genuine 17th-century documents.

There are striking similarities between the island depicted in these charts and Oak Island, despite the 'China Sea' location. It has been suggested, incidentally, that the latter is both a red herring and, rather whimsically, a pun on *la chêne*, French for 'oak'. These similarities almost leaped off the page at Gilbert Hedden, who came across Wilkins's book as he was mounting his campaign on Oak Island in 1937. And Wilkins's drawing, apparently based on the original charts, contained these clear directions:

18 w and by 7 E on Rock
30 sw 14 N Tree
7 by 8 by 4

Hedden set out on a determined exploration of the area around the Money Pit with Wilkins's book open in his hands. Fifty feet

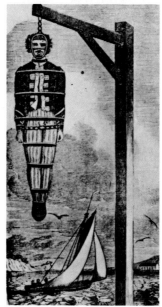

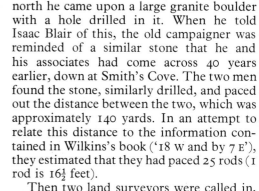

Below: this map, from Harold Wilkins's book *Captain Kidd and his Skeleton Island*, convinced prospector Gilbert Hedden that Skeleton Island was in fact Oak Island, and that there was indeed an immense treasure buried there. But the map came from Wilkins's imagination, and it bears little resemblance to any of the genuine Kidd-Palmer charts

north he came upon a large granite boulder with a hole drilled in it. When he told Isaac Blair of this, the old campaigner was reminded of a similar stone that he and his associates had come across 40 years earlier, down at Smith's Cove. The two men found the stone, similarly drilled, and paced out the distance between the two, which was approximately 140 yards. In an attempt to relate this distance to the information contained in Wilkins's book ('18 w and by 7 E'), they estimated that they had paced 25 rods (1 rod is $16\frac{1}{2}$ feet).

Then two land surveyors were called in, who calculated a position 18 rods from the rock by the Money Pit and 7 rods from the one at Smith's Cove. From that point they measured 30 rods south-west, following the directions in the chart. And there, beneath tangled undergrowth, they found a triangle of beach stones, each side of which was 10 feet long; its base was enclosed in an arc, giving the appearance of a rough sextant. An arrow of stones ran 14 feet from the curved base of the triangle to its apex. The arrow pointed north, straight at the Money Pit. Hedden and Blair could make no sense of the third line of instructions, but they had seen enough to convince them that Captain Kidd's island and Oak Island were undoubtedly one and the same.

A mythical island

So persuaded was Hedden by this discovery that he journeyed to England to discuss it with Wilkins. Wilkins was flabbergasted. He explained that he had drawn the map from memory, that it was a composite of the four Kidd-Palmer charts that Palmer had only allowed him to glimpse, that he had had no chance to make a note of the directions that two of the charts contained. So where had Wilkins got those directions he published with his drawing – directions that had led Hedden to his discovery on Oak Island? The author was adamant: he had simply made them up. When pressed further by Hedden, Wilkins confessed that the *map itself* had come straight from his imagination too – that Palmer had refused his request for a sight of the original charts. As for Oak Island, he had never heard of it, had never seen its outline, had never in fact crossed the Atlantic. Yet he had to concede that his mythical island did indeed look like Oak Island, and that Hedden had proved that those fanciful directions did indeed correspond to something very real. By the time Hedden left England to return to Oak Island, Wilkins appeared to have convinced himself that he was no less than the reincarnation of Captain Kidd.

Hedden went away shaking his head in bewilderment, which is all anyone could do about this aspect of the Oak Island mystery until the answer to the Wilkins enigma was provided by Rupert Furneaux, in his book *Money Pit, the mystery of Oak Island* (1972). Furneaux discovered that Wilkins had lied to

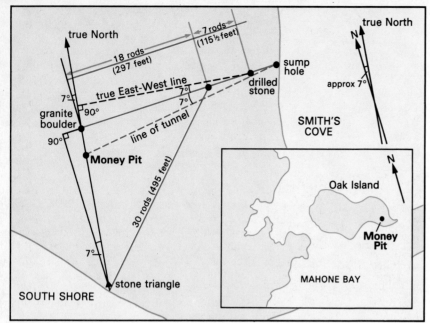

Hedden. Wilkins had in fact been corresponding with a Nova Scotian, who in 1912 had chanced upon a box containing charts among a pile of stones on an island 15 miles (24 kilometres) north of Mahone Bay. Those charts are now lost or hidden, but someone who had seen them was able to draw for Furneaux, from memory, the mystery island depicted in the charts, complete with directions. Moreover, in the charts the island was named Gloucester Isle, which, Furneaux had already discovered, was the name given to Oak Island when Mahone Bay was charted by the British Admiralty hydrographer, Joseph Frederick Wallet Des Barres, in 1773. The Des Barres charts of various parts of the Atlantic coast were not printed until later that decade, by which time the war raging between Britain and the American colonies would certainly have ensured that they were closely guarded documents. Hence, according to Furneaux, the inescapable conclusion is that whoever buried the charts that were discovered in 1912 had access to the Des Barres chart of Mahone Bay and merely added his own directions to mark the location of the Money Pit (*his* Money Pit, it follows). Wilkins had blithely reproduced these directions and the island shaped like Oak Island in his book on Captain Kidd, thereby adding confusion to genuine mystery – the mystery of who buried what on Oak Island. (There is a further mystery: the island in the Kidd-Palmer charts bears an unnerving resemblance to Oak Island; this is inexplicable.)

In his book Furneaux claimed to have worked out a plausible solution to the mystery, and he reasons his case carefully, sifting the known from the speculative, weighing the likely against the improbable. As he sees it, everything points in one direction.

Furneaux ridiculed the commonly held notion that the Money Pit and its elaborate defences were the work of pirates – the

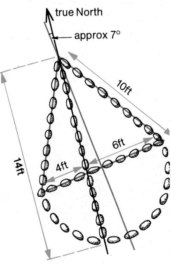

Top: the course plotted by Gilbert Hedden and Frederick Blair (who was still acting as unofficial adviser to operations on Oak Island), following the directions on Harold Wilkins's map. This led to the discovery of a triangle of stones (above) embedded in the soil beneath a dense tangle of undergrowth, and within the triangle was an arrow – pointing directly at the Money Pit

redoubtable Kidd or any of his ilk. First, the idea that pirates went around burying treasure chests is largely a fiction; it runs counter to the 'live for today' mentality of thieves in general and pirates in particular. Crews of pirate ships were paid on a share basis and on the nail, since, like all seamen, they demanded the right to squander their hard-earned money in time-honoured pursuits at the end of the voyage. Why would they help their captain to hide the spoils on some remote island to which they would, in all likelihood, never return?

This argument is mere conjecture, but it makes a great deal of sense. Even more telling is Furneaux's contention that to ascribe to pirate riff-raff a scheme so brilliant in conception and so masterful in execution is simply ludicrous. According to one authority whom Furneaux consulted, the tunnelling operation would have taken 100 disciplined men, working in three shifts, six months to accomplish. Whoever it was who directed them in this back-breaking enterprise, he was a trained engineer of outstanding quality.

Finally, there is the date of construction, which has already been mentioned in connection with the sapling oaks. If Furneaux was right that whoever did the job must have access to the Des Barres chart (which means that the work was undertaken some time after the mid 1770s), then pirates are ruled out virtually on that score alone, since their halcyon days in the Caribbean and along the Atlantic coast were long gone by that time.

A most important clue

So, if pirates were not responsible for the Money Pit, then who did built it? And how? And why? According to Furneaux, the date of construction provides the most important clue; he worked out an ingenious method for pinpointing that date. He reasoned that one of the many problems facing the mysterious mastermind was how to ensure that his tunnellers, working inland from Smith's Cove, kept on a straight line so as to run smack into the Money Pit. That line is 14° south of the true east-west line. Surely, according to Furneaux, he would have given his men, who were presumably working in dim light deep underground, one of the clearly marked cardinal points of the compass (west). If so, the magnetic variation west of north at the time must have been 14°. The magnetic values for Nova Scotia go back to 1750 and can be estimated for much earlier periods. It is thought that Oak Island would have recorded that particular variation in about 1611. It seems pretty certain that it did so in 1780.

Who would have wanted to conceal something of great value on Oak Island in 1780? The answer lies in the world around Oak Island in that year. General Sir Henry Clinton, commander-in-chief of the British forces in America, had been installed in his headquarters at New York for two years. The year of his appointment, 1778, witnessed France's entry into the war on the side of the colonists, and the combined threat to New York from the French fleet and Washington's army was very real. Clinton's fall-back position, should he have had to evacuate New York, was Halifax, about 40 miles (64 kilometres) north of Oak Island. Is it not reasonable to suppose, asked Furneaux, that at some point during these perilous years Clinton may have seized on the idea of removing to a safe place some of the huge quantities of specie (money for the conduct of the war) in his keeping? If so, an island in Mahone Bay, which was en route should he have had to fall back on Halifax, would make sense. Moreover, a friend and colleague of Clinton's, John Montrésor, had surveyed Mahone Bay some years earlier. Perhaps Montrésor suggested the site.

So, according to this theory, some time around 1780 a contingent of British sappers,

led by an unknown engineer of rare genius, descended on Oak Island and performed their great work. The shattering implication of this for generations of treasure seekers is that the money, if it was actually deposited there (the hiding place could have formed part of a contingency plan that was not put into operation), must have been recovered by those who had hidden it, since there is no record of Clinton's having to explain away a few missing millions when he returned to England.

How could such a recovery have been effected, given the Money Pit's fool-proof system of flooding? For years searchers had tried in vain to locate flood gates, which they reckoned the designer must have installed to enable him to shut off the water when he returned. A blind alley, according to Furneaux – and so, in effect, was the Money Pit itself. Furneaux suggests that after the Money Pit and the tunnels had been dug (but not connected), one or more branch tunnels were run outwards and upwards from the Money Pit; at the end of those upward-reaching tunnels, probably not far beneath the surface of the ground, the treasure was concealed. Then the Money pit was filled in, the flood tunnels were connected to it, and the treasure was thereby completely safe-guarded. Only he who knew its precise location could find it (and perhaps he could do so without bothering to excavate the Money Pit). All others would flounder in the watery swamp of the Money Pit forever.

It must be admitted that this solution to the puzzle has a weightiness about it that is alien to the old skull-and-crossbones tradition. But before assenting to it too quickly, it is appropriate to ask whether it accounts for all the evidence. How, for example, does it make sense of the metal objects encountered by the drilling operations of 1849 and 1897? And what about that piece of parchment with the tantalising inscription 'v.i.'?

Top: Sir Henry Clinton, commander-in-chief of the British forces in America from 1778 to 1782, who may have been responsible for the Money Pit. According to one theory, Clinton ordered his miners and engineers (above) to build the pit as a hiding place for some of the war funds in his keeping

Right: tourists listen to the story of the Money Pit, of the generations of hopeful prospectors who searched for what they believed to be a fortune at the bottom of the pit – and of the mystery that still surrounds it

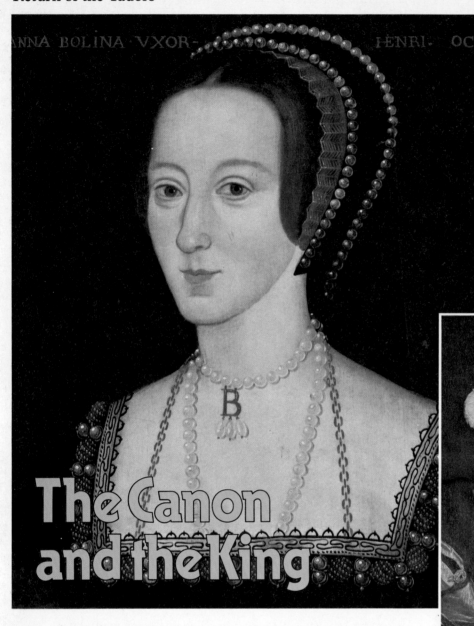

ANNA BOLINA VXOR-   HENRI· OCTA

The Canon and the King

Left: Anne Boleyn found a champion in Canon William Pakenham-Walsh, according to her supposed psychic communications. He believed her innocent of the adultery for which she was executed. Her real offence in the eyes of Henry VIII may have been to fail to provide a male heir

Below: Henry VIII's progress in the afterlife was allegedly hindered by the weight of his past offences. Canon Pakenham-Walsh regarded it as his life's work to help him move beyond the 'dark place' in which he found himself

Henry VIII died in 1547 at the end of a career darkened by many acts of greed and cruelty. LYNN PICKNETT recounts the story of a 20th-century churchman who believed he had brought Henry's spirit to repentance

IN 1917 A BRITISH MISSIONARY in China happened to read a biography of Anne Boleyn, second wife of Henry VIII, who was executed for adultery in 1536. The missionary was William Pakenham-Walsh, later a canon of Peterborough Cathedral. He was at first merely interested in Anne's life but gradually became immersed in the subject, which soon became a life-long passion. On his return to England, he determined to rescue the reputation of 'a Queen who has been much misunderstood'. But he soon found himself drawn into the afterlife agonies of Henry VIII himself, as communicated to well-known mediums and often in the presence of the clergyman.

The experiences of Pakenham-Walsh were related in *A Tudor story*, which was

published in 1963, three years after his death at the age of 92. It is a bizarre yet poignant story. The author's sincerity, integrity and simplicity are strongly evident throughout. He himself had no psychic powers. He was a good-hearted, uncomplicated man who enjoyed cycling and brisk country walks. At seances, however, he broke almost every rule possible, divulging information in advance, and 'leading' the medium in obvious ways. Nevertheless, because of inner consistencies, certain circumstantial evidence and the clergyman's sense of purpose, the book is an intriguing and important contribution to psychical literature.

In August 1921 Pakenham-Walsh met a certain Mrs Clegg, a medium, at his sister's house. The first sitting set the pattern for many that followed over the next 12 years, involving several other mediums: a mixture of ingenuous 'leading' and reading between the lines by the Canon – and genuine but obscure 'evidence'. The spirit of a white-haired old man who appeared to Mrs Clegg was assumed by the Canon to be Anne Boleyn's father; a vague description of his daughter – 'with good hands, rather plump' – was, said the Canon, 'of course a perfect description of the Lady Anne' (despite the fact that Anne had six fingers on one hand).

Yet some of the information was confirmed later, after research. Queen Anne Boleyn did indeed have five brothers, whose names were correctly given by Mrs Clegg; and Anne had seriously quarrelled with her sister Mary, as the medium said. But Pakenham-Walsh then committed a major blunder by telling the medium who the spirit was – and had further meetings after that. One ended with Mrs Clegg saying that Anne foresaw how 'you will be offered a parish with the snowdrops and you will go to it with the daffodils.' Pakenham-Walsh was soon after appointed to the parish of Sulgrave in Northamptonshire, carpeted with snowdrops on his first visit and ablaze with daffodils when he took up residence. The gardener said he had 'never seen the like' in 40 years.

A need for forgiveness

If Anne Boleyn had restricted her 'visits' to Mrs Clegg the story might never have developed further. In December 1922, however, Pakenham-Walsh received a letter from Miss Eleanor Kelly, a Christian psychic. In her daily session of automatic writing, she said, she had received a message in which were mentioned both the Canon and Mr Frederick Bligh Bond, the eminent architect and 'psychic archaeologist'. She added: 'I

The chapel of St Peter ad Vincula (St Peter in chains), at the Tower of London, is Anne Boleyn's burial place. Her remains lie beneath the left-hand end of the altar. William Pakenham-Walsh prayed here that Anne, by whom he had become fascinated, 'might be to me a guardian angel'. He decided that he would write a play about her tragic life. It was not long afterwards that she first communicated with him – as he believed – at a seance

William Pakenham-Walsh was still a parson when he first received messages that he believed to come from Anne Boleyn. In due course he became a canon of Peterborough Cathedral – where, he noted, there was a shrine to Henry VIII's first wife, Katherine of Aragon. Did his devotion to the memory of Anne Boleyn cause him to misinterpret the evidence that came out of the sittings? Or did it mark him as the ideal recipient for the dead queen's urgent appeal for help?

have had some communication now and again with souls who have died in the same period as Henry VIII, and I am very much interested in the reference [in her script] to him and the Lady Anne and the need . . . for forgiveness on her part and reparation on his.'

She later received another message, this time from 'Alwyn, once a Thane of Sussex'. It spelled out the task at hand:

As all who touch the lives of others intimately must at least remove *all* that obstructs their unity, so must these two souls be cleared each alone, and each in unison, before they too take their places in the great structure of the Body of Christ. Anne has even still some shadows to let fall before her vision is clear; he, Henry, is but now beginning to be vaguely conscious of his need of cleansing.

To this end Mr Bond arranged for the Canon to meet one of the most famous mediums of the day, Mrs Hester Dowden, at her home in Chelsea, London. The seance took the form of automatic writing with the word Katherine repeated several times. The pencil then wrote: 'I want you to help someone who needs help from your world.' They obeyed instructions to move to a nearby house so that better 'contact' could be made. There, Mrs Dowden's pencil flew violently across her writing pad: 'I am here – HENRY REX.' They had, the Canon believed, made contact with the King through Katherine of Aragon, his first wife.

Using Mrs Dowden as amanuensis, Mr Bond and Miss Kelly talked to the monarch. Asked if he knew he was dead, Henry replied: 'Yes, I know. It has been but a nightmare. . . . I want to be told exactly what has happened and why I am still in a dark place. I feel as if I was back again in the earth.' He said that his daughter Elizabeth (whose mother was Anne Boleyn) meant nothing to him. When told she had become a great ruler, he answered acidly: 'I did not expect it from her mother's child.' Reminded that the divine right of kings would carry no weight on Judgement Day, Henry erupted: 'I shall not listen to *you*. You are a fool. I would have had you executed in my time.' And the information that England's current king was George V caused a further outburst: 'I care not. You are a varlet; some knave from a tavern who is making sport of me because I lie at your mercy.' Veering from self-reproach to self-pity to outbursts of rage, he finally agreed to pray for forgiveness, but added: 'I will not pray here. A king prays alone.'

Henry, it appeared, was in the grip of great inner conflict caused by his actions as king. It seemed that he would need to forgive and be forgiven by other souls from his lifetime, such as Cardinal Thomas Wolsey and Henry's third Queen, Jane Seymour. Historians generally believe that she was his favourite wife, yet the King's spirit ranted that he detested her. This hatred seemed to be the main obstacle to his own spiritual

Katherine of Aragon, the first wife of Henry VIII, had many children by him, but only one, the future Mary I, survived. Henry's anxiety to divorce Katherine in order to marry Anne Boleyn and secure the succession led to England's break with Rome and the establishment of the Anglican Church. Katherine refused to recognise the annulment enacted by Thomas Cranmer, the new Archbishop of Canterbury – and was allegedly still obdurate 400 years after her death

progress. The Canon felt particularly pleased, therefore, when he and the mediums effected a reconciliation between the spirits of Henry and Jane.

Of Henry's six wives it was his first, Katherine of Aragon, who claimed him as husband and who wrote, through Miss Kelly: 'Love is guiding him along the upward, rugged path.' It is clear, however, that Henry's desire to be helped began in earnest when Pakenham-Walsh told him that if he repented his sins he would be reunited with his sons – Henry, who died after six weeks (but who, it was claimed, had since grown up in the afterlife), and Edward, who had reigned from 1547 to 1553.

The Canon's greatest day was 24 June 1933 when, in the company of two mediums, Mrs Heber-Percy and Mrs Theo Monson, he was told that he was in the presence not

Edward VI was Henry's son by Jane Seymour and succeeded to the throne on his father's death. He was nine years old at the time he began his reign: by the age of 16 he had died of consumption. Henry's desire to be reunited with Edward and with his other son, also called Henry, seemed to be a strong motive for his ultimate repentance

only of Henry and his Queens, Wolsey, Sir Thomas More, Elizabeth I and others, but also the spirits of his own daughter Helen and his son Willy. Henry wished it to be made public that he repented of his misdeeds. Anne Boleyn said that 'the manuscript [of *A Tudor story*] is one of the ladders from here to you and from you to us, by which many may climb to true knowledge.' The Canon pronounced a blessing on the gathering, seen and unseen, and then the visitors were gone.

A prayer answered

If one believes that the soul can survive death and that even the most evil man can be helped to progress in the afterlife, then the child-like honest Canon would seem eminently suitable to 'rescue' the arrogant Henry.

Critics, however, would find it all too easy to tear the story apart. Although none of the mediums knew Pakenham-Walsh before they met, they would almost certainly have heard of his obsession with the Tudors. A sensitive could, even if unconsciously, have picked up telepathic impressions of his desire to be Anne Boleyn's champion and of his exalted image of Anne. It is natural, too, that Pakenham-Walsh should have wanted to help Henry, a tortured soul in search of redemption. It is significant that Henry's first wife, Katherine, sought earthly help for him. In the Canon's eyes, she was probably Henry's only legal wife. Although a number of 'tests' set by Anne were seized upon by Pakenham-Walsh as evidence of her survival, it could also be said that they proved only that he was ignorant of the modern theory of general (super) ESP.

Anne Boleyn had said on the scaffold in 1536: 'I pray God to save the King.' Could, perhaps, a gentle ex-missionary have been chosen to answer her prayer 400 years later?

Prisoner without a face

For over 200 years the European imagination has been haunted by the legend of a prisoner condemned by Louis XIV to spend his life masked and in solitude. SIMON INNES reveals the true history of the man behind the mask

AT THREE O'CLOCK IN THE AFTERNOON of Thursday 18 September 1698, a new governor of the Bastille prison, Monsieur de Saint-Mars, arrived in Paris. In his litter he brought with him a man known only as the 'ancient prisoner', whose face was hidden by a black velvet mask fastened at the neck by iron clasps. He had been in the custody of Saint-Mars for no less than 29 years.

When the prisoner died five years later, he was buried in the night, under a false name.

Above: the myth of the man in the iron mask – doomed perpetually to wear a heavy helmet and manacles. In reality he was not kept in fetters, and his mask was of velvet, with iron clasps

Below: Pinerolo, the citadel where the man in the mask was first imprisoned

For 34 years no one around him had mentioned his true name, he had been kept from the sight of anyone who might recognise him, and he had been strictly prevented from speaking to his gaolers.

Not one of these afflictions was remarkable in itself. Many prisoners of Louis XIV were kept incommunicado – some were even required to wear masks. All were buried anonymously. Ministers who had been dismissed from their posts in the government, royal envoys who had for some reason failed to bring negotiations to a successful conclusion, courtiers who had killed a man in a duel – anyone could find himself in a royal prison and, unless he was returned to favour, die there.

But there were strange rumours about this particular prisoner. Eight years after his death Madame Palatine, sister-in-law of Louis XIV, wrote to the Electress Sophia of Hanover, mother of the future George I of England:

He was an English lord who had been mixed up in the Duke of Berwick's affair against King William. He was treated thus so that the king might never know what became of him.

This could not be true. William of Orange did not accede to the English throne until 1689, when the prisoner had been in Saint-Mars's custody for some 20 years. This rumour had clearly been encouraged by Louis to obscure the true identity of the man in the mask.

The philosopher and writer Voltaire thought that he had come nearer the truth. He was twice imprisoned in the Bastille, in 1717 and 1726, and could have spoken to prisoners and gaolers who knew the 'ancient prisoner'. In 1738 he wrote to the Abbé Dubois: 'I am fairly well informed on the adventure of the man in the iron mask.'

This is the first mention of an *iron* mask; the legend took root firmly. In 1771 Voltaire alleged that the mysterious prisoner was a half-brother of Louis XIV, imprisoned because he threatened Louis's Crown.

From that time, the myth grew apace – especially after the publication of Alexandre

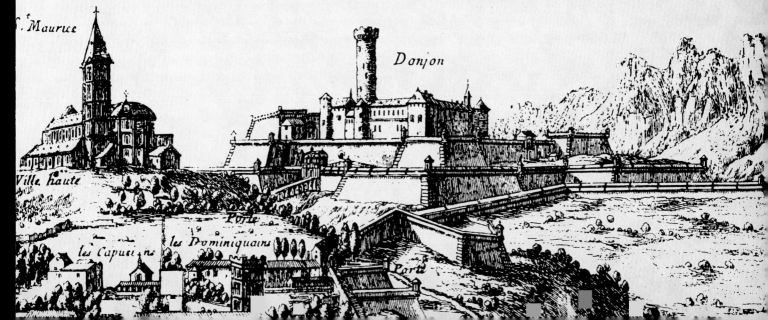

have the man named Eustache Dauger sent to Pignerol. It is of the utmost importance to His service that he should be most securely guarded and that he should in no way give information about himself nor send letters to anyone at all. I am informing you of this in advance so that you can have a cell prepared in which you will place him securely, taking care that the windows of the place in which he is put do not give on to any place that can be approached by anyone, and that there are double doors to be shut, for your guards not to hear anything. You must yourself take to him, once a day, the day's necessities, and you must never listen, under any pretext whatever, to what he may want to reveal to you, always threatening to kill him if he ever opens his mouth to speak of anything but his day-to-day needs.

This letter was dated 19 July 1669. On the same day Louvois wrote to de Vauroy, military governor of the town of Dunkirk, which was temporarily an English possession. The letter called de Vauroy away from

Above: the fortress of the Bastille, in Paris, as it was in the 18th century. The prisoner in the mask died here in 1703. The governor of the Bastille, Saint-Mars (inset), had been the custodian of the man in the mask for some 34 years. Whenever Saint-Mars was appointed to a new post, he would take his prisoner along with him

Left: Louis XIV, portrayed as the commander of the French army, trampling down the enemies of France. Among these, presumably, was counted the unfortunate prisoner in the mask – but his offence is still not known with certainty

Dumas's world-famous novel on which many romances and films were to be based. Only after the fall of the French monarchy in 1789 and the gradual disclosure of the state archives did it become possible to trace the history of the 'ancient prisoner'.

In 1664 Saint-Mars, a former under-officer of the Musketeers, was appointed governor of the prison in the fortress at Pinerolo (or Pignerol), in Piedmont, north-western Italy. Pinerolo was then in the kingdom of Savoy, but the French occupied the fortress under the terms of the Treaty of Cherasco of 1631.

Some five years after his appointment, Saint-Mars received a letter from the French Minister of War, the Marquis de Louvois:

The King has commanded that I am to

Left: Voltaire – dramatist, poet, philosopher and wit – was one of the first writers to elaborate on the story of the prisoner in the mask. His fanciful account, full of inconsistencies and errors, proposed the idea that the prisoner was an illegitimate half-brother of Louis XIV, the result of infidelity by Louis XIII's queen

the duties that normally occupied him:

I am informed that officers of the Spanish troops are pursuing deserters on the King's territory. . . . His Majesty desires that you are to attack these officers who come into conflict with our troops when they are seizing their deserters.

And to the civil governor of Dunkirk he wrote: 'As M. de Vauroy has business which requires him to absent himself, I beg you very kindly to give him leave.'

But a very different mission was intended for de Vauroy. It seems likely that at this date news had been received that Dauger was about to arrive in Dunkirk on a ship from England, and that arrangements were being made well in advance for his arrest and imprisonment.

This is indicated by the date of the letter of authorisation instructing de Vauroy to

Above: de Louvois, Louis XIV's ruthless Minister of War, who issued a stream of harsh orders concerning the 'ancient prisoner'

Left: the popular notion of the man in the iron mask has found its way into novels, plays, films and music. This affecting scene embellished the cover of a 19th-century song sheet

Below: Nicolas Fouquet was a fellow-prisoner of the man in the mask. This portrait shows him while still a powerful statesman

Below right: d'Artagnan, who escorted Nicolas Fouquet to Pinerolo, was linked forever with the masked prisoner by Dumas in one of his romances of the three musketeers

convey Eustache Dauger to Pinerolo. It was issued on 28 July, only nine days after de Vauroy was supposedly assigned to deal with intruding Spanish troops. A smokescreen had been laid down over Dauger's arrest – even before it had occurred.

The arrival of the prisoner at Pinerolo was confirmed by a letter from Saint-Mars to Louvois, dated 21 August:

M. de Vauroy has handed over to me the man named Eustache d'Auger. As soon as I had put him in a very secure place, while waiting for the cell I am having prepared for him to be completed, I told him in the presence of M. de Vauroy that if he should speak to me or anyone else of anything other than his day-to-day needs, I would run him

through with my sword. On my life, I shall not fail to observe, very punctiliously, your commands.

There is no doubt whatsoever, then, that a man of considerable importance named Eustache Dauger was arrested in the vicinity of Dunkirk some time between 19 and 28 July 1669, and by 21 August was safely incarcerated in the dungeon of the fortress of Pinerolo.

The most important of the prisoners who were already in captivity at Pinerolo was Nicolas Fouquet, the disgraced Minister of Finance. He had been an extremely powerful statesman during the troubled years between the death of Louis XIII in 1643 and the assumption of active government by Louis XIV at the age of 21, in 1660. He was a member of a secret society – the Company of the Holy Sacrament, known usually as *la Compagnie* – which exercised incalculable influence during this time. He was very close to Cardinal Mazarin, who shaped the destiny of France at the beginning of the new reign.

Committed for life

Fouquet became Minister of Finance in 1653 and had hoped to become prime minister, but his former friend Jean-Baptiste Colbert rapidly destroyed his reputation with the King by drawing attention to all sorts of irregularities in the accounts. On 20 December 1664, Fouquet was committed for life into the custody of Saint-Mars. Four weeks later, guarded by 100 musketeers under the command of d'Artagnan – destined to be the hero of a succession of Dumas novels – he arrived at Pinerolo. The King had written to Saint-Mars:

With respect to the form and manner according to which the said Captain de Saint-Mars will have to guard the said Fouquet, His Majesty does not prescribe any, relying entirely on his prudent and wise conduct and on what he saw practised by M. d'Artagnan during all the time he guarded him both at the Bois de Vincennes and at the Bastille; His Majesty only recommends

very expressly to Captain de Saint-Mars not to allow the said Fouquet to communicate with anyone by word or by writing or to be visited by anyone or to leave his apartment for any cause or under any pretext whatever, not even to take a walk.

Fouquet was to be allowed a confessor, but he was to be chosen by Saint-Mars and his visits were restricted to four per year.

When Dauger was admitted to the prison nearly five years later, Louvois wrote:

> You can give a prayer book to your new prisoner, and if he asks you for any other give it him also. You can let him hear on Sundays and Feast Days the mass that is said for M. Fouquet, without, however, being at the same place, and you will see that he is so well guarded during that time that he cannot escape or speak to anyone; you can even let him have confession three or four times a year, if he so wishes, and no more unless he should contract some mortal illness.

It is easy to deduce from this that, as a prisoner, Dauger was equal in importance to Fouquet. The insistence on his total isolation

Right: the masked prisoner tries to send a message to the outside world. According to Voltaire, he scratched a message on a silver plate with a knife, and flung the plate from a window. But it was found by an illiterate fisherman, who obligingly returned it to the prison governor

Below: the mysterious prisoner dines with his custodian on the journey to his last prison, the Bastille. Only the governor's pistol, lying within easy reach, reveals that this is no ordinary social occasion

suggests that he was a direct threat to the security of the realm, or that he knew something so dangerous that he had to be kept from all contact with others.

If Saint-Mars had any difficulty in maintaining sufficient secrecy concerning his prisoner, his problems must have increased in November 1671, when he took charge of another important prisoner. This was the Comte de Lauzun, formerly Captain of the King's Bodyguard. Louvois ordered that Lauzun was to be imprisoned with a single valet and was never to be allowed to leave the prison or communicate with anybody. On 9 December 1671, Saint-Mars wrote:

> I will lodge him in the two vaulted chambers that are over those of M. Fouquet: these are the ones with the barred windows that you yourself examined. . . . The place is so constructed that I can have holes made, through which I can spy into the apartment. I shall also know all that he does and says through the valet whom I will furnish as you have ordered. I have found one with much trouble, for the clever ones do not wish to pass their lives in prison. . . .

In 1675 Fouquet's valet, La Rivière, became seriously ill with dropsy and was not always able to serve his master. In reply to a request from Saint-Mars, Louvois wrote:

> His Majesty approves that you give, as valet to M. Fouquet, the prisoner whom M. de Vauroy brought to you; but whatever may happen, you must refrain from placing him with M. de Lauzun, or with anyone else. . . .

The implication of this is that Fouquet

would already be in possession of whatever secrets Dauger knew. It also suggests that Dauger was of nowhere near the same social standing as Fouquet – unless he was being deliberately humiliated.

Louvois wrote directly to Fouquet on several subsequent occasions, stressing that Dauger must not be allowed to converse with La Rivière, his other valet. However, when Fouquet died in 1680 this prohibition must have been forgotten, for the two valets were locked up together.

Lauzun, the other important prisoner, was aware of Dauger's existence: he had contrived to make a hole through a fireplace into Fouquet's cell. But after his release from Pinerolo in 1682 he seems never to have spoken or written of Eustache Dauger, with whom he had been incarcerated for 10 years.

In 1681 Saint-Mars received a promotion: he was appointed to the governorship of the fortress of Exiles, a prison some 30 miles (50 kilometres) distant from Pinerolo. Two particularly important prisoners accompanied Saint-Mars, their safe custody being of the utmost importance to the King – and from the correspondence of the time it is clear that they were Dauger and La Rivière.

The two prisoners were placed under even greater security than at Pinerolo: their rooms were watched over by sentries day and night, and for confessor they were allowed only a very old priest who lived some distance away.

In January 1687 Saint-Mars wrote to Louvois to inform him that the prisoner who had been sick – La Rivière – had died. In his reply Louvois informed Saint-Mars of his appointment to the prison on the island of Ste Marguerite in the Bay of Cannes and instructed him to convey the 'ancient prisoner' there in secrecy.

It was while Dauger was in the prison at Ste Marguerite, if we are to believe Voltaire, that he scratched a message with a knife on a silver plate and flung it from a window. It was picked up by a fisherman – who took it to Saint-Mars. The prison governor asked him if he had read what was on the plate. When the fisherman replied that he could not read, Saint-Mars remarked that it was lucky for him that he could not, and dismissed him.

On 1 March 1698 Saint-Mars was again promoted, this time to the governorship of the Bastille. He was to come with his ancient prisoner, 'taking all precautions to prevent his being seen or recognised by anyone'.

It was on the journey from Ste Marguerite to Paris that the mask made its first recorded appearance: from that time on the prisoner wore it continually until he died.

Above: the prison on the island of Sainte Marguerite, where the man in the mask spent 11 years. The window of his cell is the third from the right. It was from here that he threw the plate bearing a message

Right: the legend of the iron mask has been heavily embroidered in fiction. In this scene from a London theatre production of 1899, the cell has become rather crowded: the prisoner has the company of a gaoler, a beautiful girl, a noble visitor – and a corpse

Many identities have been proposed for the prisoner in the mask. Many reasons for his long imprisonment have been suggested. Historical evidence disposes of most of them, but the most perplexing mysteries remain

Left: Louis XIII is often linked with the masked prisoner. Was the prisoner the bastard son of the King, and therefore a grave threat to the legitimate son, Louis XIV?

Below: Anne of Austria who, after 14 childless years, bore a son to Louis XIII. One theory suggests that Louis was not the father of the child, who was to become Louis XIV. Years later, one of the illegitimate King's half-brothers had to be kept quiet – and became the prisoner in the mask

Poisoner, priest or pretender?

THE 'ANCIENT PRISONER' who died in the Bastille in 1703 was undoubtedly called Eustache Dauger. This was established in 1890 by Jules Lair, who traced the prisoner's career back to his arrest in 1669. Lair's work put paid to what had until then been the most plausible of the theories concerning the man in the iron mask.

This theory hinged on the false name under which the prisoner's burial was recorded: de Marchiel, or Marchioly. It was known that one Ercole Mattioli, secretary to the Duke of Mantua, had been imprisoned in Pinerolo in 1679 and there was no other record that could be interpreted as referring to his death. It seemed logical, then, to identify Mattioli with the man in the mask –

Above: the masked prisoner, dressed in the finest clothes, and heavily guarded even in his cell. This picture is as fanciful as the story it illustrates – *The man in the iron mask*, by Alexandre Dumas, which did so much to shape the legend

even though there was no secret about Mattioli's imprisonment. However, now that it is known that the prisoner was Dauger, who was imprisoned in 1669, and since we can now follow his movements up to his death, it is clear that he was not Mattioli.

Another suspect had been James de la Roche, who represented himself to the Jesuits in Rome as an illegitimate son of Charles II. He was supposedly sent on a secret mission to London in the spring of 1669, under the name of the Abbé Pregnani. However, he died in the summer of that year – just when the man in the mask was beginning his long imprisonment.

There was indeed a real Abbé Pregnani, and he was himself in London at this time:

Eustache Dauger was one Martin, valet of Paul Roux de Marsilly, a man who was involved in a Protestant intrigue and executed in Paris in June 1669. The Foreign Minister had written to the French ambassador in London, asking him to persuade Martin to return to France for the trial of his master. However, there is also in existence a letter from Louvois, the Minister of War, dated 13 July 1669, stating that the valet's evidence is no longer needed, and that he is therefore not required to return.

It was in 1930 that a historian, Maurice Duvivier, searching the Bibliothèque Nationale in Paris, uncovered a real Eustache Dauger. He had been born in 1637, the third son of François Auger de Cavoye and Marie de Lort de Sérignan. The father, captain of the guard to Cardinal Richelieu, came from a minor landowning family in Picardy; his wife was from the Languedoc and had been a young widow when he married her.

There were 11 children altogether – six boys and five girls. Four of the sons had been killed in the service of the King by the time of Dauger's arrest in 1669, but Eustache's younger brother Louis lived until 1715, becoming Marquis de Cavoye and Grand Maréchal des Logis de la Maison du Roi (superintendent of the king's household).

Eustache was a year older than Louis XIV, and as children the two knew one another well in the inner circles of the court. His other playmates included Philip Mancini, the nephew of Cardinal Mazarin, who was a friend of the family, and the future Duc de Lauzun, who was later to be incarcerated with him in the prison at Pinerolo.

By the year 1654, when he was still only 17, Eustache had become the eldest surviving son, with the death in battle of both his elder brothers. But as soon as he reached his majority, Eustache seems to have become involved in a succession of unsavoury episodes, including a black mass and the killing

an astrologer and intriguer, he had been sent there to spy on Charles II. He arrived in February and met the King a few days later, but he failed to impress him. As Charles wrote to his sister:

> I came from Newmarket the day before yesterday. . . . L'Abbé Pregnani was there most of the time and I believe will give you some account of it, but not that he lost his money upon confidence that the stars could tell which horse would win, for he had the bad luck to foretell three times wrong and Monmouth had such faith in him that he lost his money.

The Abbé was recalled to France on 17 July, but any possibility that he was the man arrested in Dunkirk a few days later is disposed of by the fact that he died in Rome in 1678 or 1679.

In his book *The valet's tragedy* the English folklorist Andrew Lang suggested that

Above: Louis XIII and his foremost subject, Cardinal Richelieu, kneel at the feet of Christ. Among the Cardinal's services to his king were strenuous efforts to ensure that France was provided with an heir to the throne. The masked prisoner may have met his fate because he knew a state secret – the identity of Louis XIV's true father

Right: the young Louis XIV. One of his playmates was Eustache Dauger, son of Richelieu's captain of the guard. Louis became absolute monarch: Dauger may have been his victim, the prisoner in the mask

of a court page. In 1664 his mother disinherited him, and in 1665 he was forced to sell his commission.

We now have an outline portrait of the man in the mask: a young man of good family, a childhood friend of the King, who has grown increasingly dissolute and spendthrift and by the age of 30 has fallen on hard times. But this does not explain the long punishment that he was subsequently to endure. When his younger brother Louis, later to become a distinguished member of the court, was sent to the Bastille for killing a man in a duel, he served only four years. What could Eustache have done that could merit not only 34 years in prison, but also exceedingly stringent measures to conceal his identity?

There is reason to suspect that he was engaged in espionage. He was probably returning from England when he was arrested in Dunkirk. Charles II was engaged in secret and tortuous negotiations with Louis XIV, hoping to obtain French money to support the re-establishment of a Catholic monarchy in England. Clandestine agents regularly went back and forth between the two courts.

In December 1667 Charles had written to his sister Minette, the sister-in-law of Louis:

> You know how much secrecy is necessary for the carrying out of the business and I assure you that nobody does or shall know anything of it but myself and *that one person more*, till it be fit to be public.

A year later, in January 1669, he wrote:

Above: the English king, Charles II, engaged in intrigues with Louis XIV in an attempt to get French money. Eustache Dauger may have been used as an agent in the negotiations between the two monarchs

> I had written thus far when I received yours by the Italian whose name and capacity you do not know, and he delivered your letter to me in a passage where it was so dark as I should not know his face again if I saw him.

Could this 'Italian' have been Dauger? It is strange, but not impossible, that Charles should have thought him to be an Italian. A mission of such delicacy could have suited Eustache Dauger well. Known to everyone at court as a personable, swashbuckling ex-officer, his movements between the French and English courts would not arouse suspicion. Being desperately in need of funds, he was just the sort of man likely to be recruited as an agent.

Doctor of death

However, at about this time there was a certain 'surgeon d'Auger' who has been identified – by Maurice Duvivier, who carried out so much of the investigation into Eustache's life – with the man in the mask. This d'Auger was involved with a gang of poisoners around 1670. If the man in the mask had once been a poisoner, an obscure postscript in a letter written by Louvois gains in interest. Louvois had written to Saint-Mars, governor of the prison at Pinerolo, shortly after the sudden death of Fouquet. Aged 65, Fouquet had been expecting a pardon from the King. Louvois wrote:

> Send me word how it happened that the man named Eustache has been able to

Recipe for evil

Maurice Duvivier, who identified the masked prisoner as Eustache Dauger, believed that he was the same man as a surgeon called d'Auger, who was named in a great poisoning scandal involving the nobility. The most eminent person to be implicated was Madame de Montespan, who, while a lady-in-waiting, had engaged in black masses in order to become Louis XIV's mistress – and had obtained her wish. She plunged deeper into blasphemous practices designed to retain the King's favour. When at last he tired of her in 1679 she tried to kill him by black magic. Her activities were exposed by Nicolas de la Reynie, chief of the Paris police, who had been investigating the widespread use of love charms and poisons by the nobility. Madame de Montespan was allowed to live: 36 other people were executed. One of these was Catherine Monvoisin (right), who became the most notorious magician arrested by La Reynie. D'Auger's name was cited in the trials of 1679 and 1680 – but he had disappeared 10 years before.

do what you sent me word of, and where he got the drugs necessary for the purpose. . . .

What had Dauger been doing with these drugs? Had he been trying to heal Fouquet? Or helping him on his way out of this life? As we shall see, there may have been a connection between Dauger and Fouquet that antedated their shared imprisonment in Pinerolo, and may have led to enmity between them.

Whatever the truth about the death of Fouquet, the question remains: why should a failed secret agent, or a convicted poisoner, have been treated with such severity and regarded as so important that no unauthorised person should be able to speak with him or catch a sight of his face? Could there be substance in the original rumour, retailed by Voltaire, that the prisoner was a half-brother of Louis XIV?

Most commentators have considered the possibility that Eustache Dauger was the

Below: the true end of the 'ancient prisoner': the certificate of his burial, under the name Marchioly, at the Bastille in 1703

Bottom: 'the skeleton in the iron mask' – supposedly found at the fall of the Bastille in 1789. This is yet another wholly fanciful detail in the legend

Richelieu prevailed on the captain of his personal guard to perform the act of which Louis XIII proved incapable.

The secret may have been known to Eustache and his brother Louis – and it was one that could topple the throne of France. Is the solution of the mystery of Eustache's incarceration simply that, penniless and increasingly dissolute, he had begun to talk? Had he tried to add substance to his insinuations by drawing attention to his family resemblance to the King? It is possible. Louis XIV, although determined to be an absolute monarch, may have drawn the line at ordering the execution of his half-brother.

But there is an additional fascinating possibility. It is suspected that Nicolas Fouquet, together with the priest who was later to be canonised as St Vincent de Paul and other members of *la Compagnie*, was conspiring to restore the Merovingian line, the dynasty that had been deposed from the French throne by the Carolingians in the seventh century. If Louis XIV's illegitimacy could be proved, and Eustache Dauger was prepared to bear witness, a Merovingian pretender stood a good chance of succeeding to the throne. Is this why Dauger, half-brother of the King, was shut away from converse with others, his face sometimes hidden in a mask, until, after 34 years, he died – and became a legend?

illegitimate son of Louis XIII. But the suggestion does not seem consistent with Madame de Cavoye's renowned fidelity. There is another intriguing possibility, however: that Louis XIV was himself the illegitimate son – of Dauger's father, François.

The birth of Louis XIV was 'unexpected, almost miraculous' (in the words of the *Cambridge modern history*). In 1637 Louis XIII and his queen, Anne of Austria, had been married for 22 years, but had lived apart for 14. They had no children and it was rumoured that the King was impotent.

Nevertheless, it was essential that an heir to the throne of France should be born, and Cardinal Richelieu, who was effectively the real ruler of France, began to arrange a reconciliation between the King and Queen. They met at one of Richelieu's houses in the country, and soon afterwards it was announced that the Queen was pregnant. The King's younger brother, the Duke of Orleans, who had hoped to succeed to the throne, was so sceptical of the news that he remarked that Richelieu must be the father.

The child that was born was a fine physical specimen, quite unlike Louis XIII. But we know that it was often remarked, a half-century later, how alike Louis XIV was to the Marquis de Cavoye, Eustache's younger brother Louis. It seems quite probable that

Clapham Wood

Under the greenwood tree

The greenwood has always been a place where strange things happen – a doorway from the real world into the beyond. And weird things still happen in woods – as in Clapham Wood on England's South Downs. HAMISH HOWARD and TOYNE NEWTON report

A hollow oak stands sentry to the village of Clapham – and to the forbidding Clapham Wood (inset), for hundreds of years the scene of weird incidents

CLAPHAM WOOD is a small densely-treed area nestling in the shelter of the South Downs in West Sussex, England. Travelling south-wards, a sharp left turn off the busy road known as Long Furlong at Findon leads into this area of mystery and intrigue, of strange disappearances and UFO sightings. There is even an ancient hollow oak, which signposts the way to the village, adding to the general air of mystery. That there is 'something weird' in the woods has always been rumoured. But what that something is, no one seems to know.

On a hill above the village, as if protecting its parishioners from the dark woods beyond, stands the 13th-century Church of the Blessed Virgin Mary. The strange atmosphere of the woods themselves is felt immediately. Stunted trees twist and writhe as if in pain; there is a larger crater, believed to

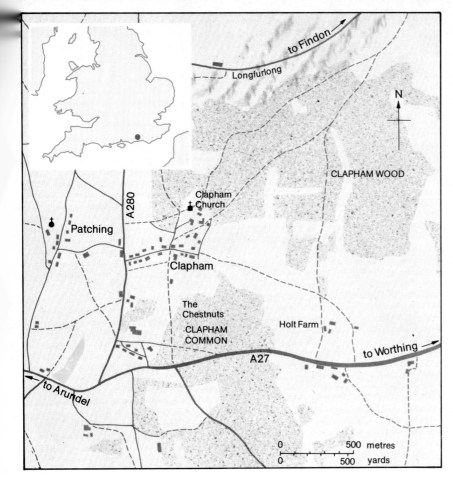

One such sighting concerns a telephone engineer who was driving home alone along the Findon Road after night duty when he saw a large saucer-shaped object in the sky above the woods. It hovered for some time before making a circle of the area, then veered off. That was in October 1972, when other sightings were independently reported in that area. One report came from a couple out walking near Long Furlong who thought they saw Jupiter or Venus low in the western sky – until it started to move very quickly due north, keeping in line with a ridge of the downs, as it came towards them. Suddenly, when the object was over Clapham Wood, a beam of light descended vertically from it, and then rapidly withdrew, and the object shot away north-eastwards at great speed. The beam was visible for about 10 seconds.

In fact the brief time the Clapham Wood UFOs are visible makes their verification almost impossible, as one inhabitant of the village found in 1968. It was 2 a.m. and, being unable to sleep, he was making himself a hot drink; glancing out of the kitchen window, he saw a saucer-shaped object hovering directly over the nearby woods. He promptly made an emergency call to the police; although the call was answered speedily, by the time the police arrived the UFO had disappeared.

By far the most significant sightings in this area are those reported by Paul Glover of the British Phenomenon Research Group, who was walking with a friend along the downs towards Clapham Wood one clear starlit night in the summer of 1967. At about 10 p.m. both suddenly became aware of a 'huge black mass' low in the sky blotting out the stars as it moved very quickly towards them.

The object was boomerang-shaped and made no sound. As it passed overhead the displacement of air was so great they ducked into the bushes for safety.

have been caused by a wartime bomb – although some maintain it was a meteorite and yet others say it is merely an ancient lime pit – where nothing grows; and there are mysterious little clearings containing ruins of old cottages.

Perhaps it was from one of these, a couple of centuries ago, that an old woman saw what would today be recognised as a UFO. She told villagers that one dark night she had seen a 'bright round shape like the full Moon' float down into the woods and disappear in the bushes.

The outcome of this event seems to have been that 'the woods were filled with fumes that stinketh of burning matter' and that many local folk thereafter were 'affeared to go there'. As for the old woman of the woods, she appears to have been immediately 'smitten of the palsy', and was given a wide berth by the locals; this may have been because of her sighting, but it seems more reasonable to suppose she was the victim of one of the witch hunts so prevalent in England at that time.

Since those far off days there have been many more UFO sightings – and some say landings – in the small area of Clapham Wood, and although several witnesses have given reports to the police there must be many people who are too afraid of ridicule to do so. The fact that these sightings often occur at night when few witnesses are about makes them very difficult to prove.

Above: the location of Clapham Wood

Below: Mr R. D. Bennett, warden of Clapham church, whose rector disappeared in Clapham Wood in 1979. Mr Bennett comments that the villagers think the wood is 'extremely weird'

had landed recently to fetch supplies of sulphur and other chemicals.

No one believed the boys, of course, but nearly 10 years later an investigation was carried out when soil samples were taken from the woods. From the report given in BBC-TV's *Nationwide* programme at the time it seems there was more than a grain of truth at least in the boys' sulphur story.

The investigation had actually been triggered off by reports of dogs disappearing in the woods in 1975. According to a local newspaper, the *Worthing Herald*, Wallace, a three-year-old chow belonging to Mr and Mrs Peter Love of Clapham, disappeared, as did a two-year-old collie belonging to Mr John Cornford. Apparently the collie, although normally obedient, suddenly rushed off into a small copse between two trees in an area known locally as the Chestnuts, and was never seen again – although its mystified owner searched the place thoroughly.

Mrs H. T. Wells, who lives at nearby Durrington, said that when her collie gets near the woods it 'becomes desperate', and a golden retriever belonging to Mr E. F. Rawlins of Worthing ran into the woods one day and returned 'very distressed'. Shortly afterwards it became paralysed and the vet had to destroy it.

Another dog owner, who wishes to remain anonymous, reported that when she took her dog to this area it ran round in circles foaming at the mouth, with its eyes bulging

They vehemently denied it could have been a cloud, for it retained its shape, was on a definite course, and there was no wind to drive it – certainly not at the tremendous speed at which it was travelling. Somewhat shaken they continued their walk, and minutes later saw two bright objects high in the sky, which they watched for several minutes. One of the UFOs released a smaller object that travelled across to the second object, seemed to enter it, and then re-emerged and veered off, disappearing from sight.

There was no denying that that night there was increased UFO activity in the area for some reason, but it was when Paul Glover and his companion were approaching Clapham Wood about an hour later that the most spectacular sighting occurred. Two yellow lights descended in the region of the woods, followed just a few seconds later by two more, and then a final pair, making a total of three groups of two. Then at the point where they seemed to have dipped down into the woods, two white beams of light shot out horizontally – quite unimpeded by the contours of the downlands – followed by the next two beams and then the final two, all travelling very fast, before disappearing into the night sky. No craft of any kind could be seen behind the lights.

Messages from a ouija board

During that same year, in the village of Rustington a few miles westwards along the coast, two schoolboys, Toyne Newton and John Arnold, who had never even heard of Clapham Wood, had a strange story spelled out to them on a ouija board: that Clapham Wood was a base for spacecraft, and that one

Paul Glover saw UFOs in Clapham Wood – a huge black boomerang (above) followed by small lights moving at speed (below)

out of its head as if in great pain, and only with difficulty did she manage to entice it back into her car and drive home, where the dog eventually calmed down.

This part of the woods is easily accessible to the public, being on the A27 dual carriageway, and it is regularly used for exercising dogs. It is also used by horse riders. One young horseman (who wishes to remain anonymous) tethered his mount firmly to a tree stump while he relieved himself in the woods, and was amazed to find the animal had disappeared during his brief absence. Although he searched the area extensively and made exhaustive enquiries, the horse was never found.

Animals are not alone in being affected by the peculiar atmosphere in this particular part of the woods, for several people have described how they have felt 'pushed over by invisible forces', while others have felt faint for no apparent reason.

Two men walking together in the woods told how they were both suddenly afflicted at the same time – one doubling over in agony and staggering, the other clutching at his head and saying that he felt as if his eardrums 'were being pulled from the inside outwards'. These painful effects disappeared simultaneously when the two men had gone about 50 yards (45 metres) further.

It seems beyond doubt that this small area encapsulates a source of electrical charge, or ray, or unknown force, which, when released into the atmosphere in small bursts, seems to affect anyone in the vicinity at the time with some kind of abnormal pressure or even mild apoplexy. But what the force is, no one seems to know.

Its strange and disturbing effects seem to be metamorphic, for – according to the local press – the body of a man who went missing in the woods was found only two weeks later in such an advanced state of decomposition

Above: Clapham Wood's mysterious crater. Nothing will grow there; no one knows its cause

Over: the strange black shape seen in Clapham Wood by Dave Stringer in 1977. He later found a footprint at the site (above right) – similar to one he had seen at the meeting place of a black coven in Brighton

Below: Mr John Cornford, a local farmer, whose two-year-old collie dog went missing in Clapham Wood and was never seen again

that only when the body was positively identified could the short time lapse be pinpointed. Forensic evidence showed that the normally accepted rate of a decomposing corpse had, in this particular case, been greatly accelerated due to some unknown factor.

Mystifying reports such as these have a double effect in that, while keeping apprehensive people away, those given to seeking the truth of such situations are particularly drawn to the area. Among these is Dave Stringer of the Southern Paranormal Investigation Group, who, while not disbelieving the reports of so many independent witnesses, nevertheless visited the woods in August of 1977 'with an open mind' – and his Geiger counter.

He was aware of a strange silence, but the woods were beautiful and the air still as he came to the part called the Chestnuts. Everything appeared normal, but as he walked through the heavy undergrowth he had to raise the Geiger counter above his head. It was then that it began to register at an alarming rate before returning to normal.

Wonderingly, Stringer looked back at the area through which he had just passed, and saw a dark shape about 12 feet (3.5 metres) in height; while not being distinctive in outline, it was very definitely not smoke, or a smoke-enshrouded bush, but he could describe it only as a 'black mass'. Seconds later a large white disc shot out from behind nearby trees at an angle of about 45° and disappeared into the sky, and simultaneously the dark form disappeared also.

Stringer retraced his steps, not using the Geiger counter this time but looking down at the ground, which was part grass and part muddy footpath, for some evidence of a solid shape to back up what he thought he had witnessed. At the spot where the form had appeared he came upon a faint imprint of a four-toed foot, twice the width of a man's foot but very narrow at the heel.

Only on one other occasion had he seen such a mysterious footprint, and that had been at Devil's Dyke near Brighton, where there was known to be a black magic coven. Could there be a connection?

Devil's footprint?

Part of a black coven's ritual involves the burning of sulphur, which could account for the acrid smell and fumes reported in the woods, and one particular branch of their rumoured experimentation concerns the dematerialisation of small creatures. This, it is claimed, releases the creatures' 'life spark', which escapes without form or shape.

Stringer made a quick sketch of the single footprint, which, although unknown to him at the time, coincides significantly with the footprint of the demon Amduscias, illustrated in the 1863 edition of Collin de Plancy's *Dictionnaire infernal*.

The consistency of UFO sightings over

Clapham Wood continued during 1978 and 1979, one being reported by a man standing on nearby Highdown Hill, which is higher than Clapham and overlooks the woods. The witness says he saw a large orange ball about twice the size of an aircraft, which manoeuvred above the woods for some 20 minutes before disappearing. And several independent witnesses from different vantage points reported seeing a huge light in the sky above Clapham Wood one summer's night in 1979. It descended vertically into the woods and glowed among the trees.

Could it be explained away as mere coincidence? It seems unlikely with so many people coming forward with similar stories of sightings all made at the same time.

The spate of strange reports that year concluded with the disappearance of the Reverend Neil Snelling, vicar of Clapham church. One fine morning after shopping at Worthing he decided to walk back to his Steyning home through Clapham Wood. Almost certainly he would have taken the 'Chestnuts' route. He has not been heard of since, and an exhaustive search of the area revealed nothing.

What happened to him? Why did the dogs

Right: a photograph taken by Paul Glover. He saw nothing at the time, although he felt intense cold – but when the photograph was developed, it showed a goat's head, age-old symbol of satanism

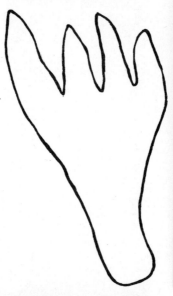

disappear so completely within only a few yards of their unsuspecting owners? How can solid bodies vanish into thin air without leaving a trace? Is there a deadly chemical in the soil, or some unknown force that disrupts the molecular structure of organic creatures? Did a meteorite – or some unknown object from space – once fall in the area, and if so, is it giving off harmful rays or acting as a beacon for UFOs?

So many independent reports cannot be ignored, but real proof of the phenomena is not easy to come by. It was in the hope of obtaining some form of proof that Paul Glover armed himself with a camera and, accompanied by Dave Stringer and another friend, made for Clapham Wood.

It was a dark, clear evening, but there was no UFO activity. Eventually they decided to make their way homewards via the Chestnuts route, and it was as they were walking through this area that all three of them, simultaneously, had a feeling of intense cold. They hurried on, and the feeling ceased. So they walked back over the same area – three times in fact – and each time experienced this sudden and unnatural drop in temperature.

Glover decided to point the camera at what he thought was the source of this strange condition, seeing nothing, but firing the shutter purely on speculation.

When the photograph was developed, however, it showed an uncanny white mass revealing the unmistakable image of a goat's head, the age-old symbol of satanic rites. Was this confirmation of the past – or present – activities of a black coven? Or was it quite separate, adding yet another phenomenon to the enigma of Clapham Wood?

INDEX

...ed by AGIP, ATV Network, Aberdeen Journals, Acorn Photographics, ..., Aldus/Field Museum of Natural History, Aldus/Warburg ...ia/Zdenek Burian (c), Ashmoleum, Associated Press, Atlantic ...dio Ltd, BBC Hulton Picture Library, BTA, Herbert Ballard, ... Tourist Board, Bettman Archive, Bildarchiv Preussischer ...Colin Bord, Fred Bost, Boston University Library, Paul ...eum, Richard Burgess, Cambridge University ...ge University Dept. of Engineering, Canada Press, ...alian TV, G Chapman, Jean-Loup Charmet, John ...Coleman Ltd, Colorific!, Contemporary Films, ... George E Crouther, Culver Pictures, John ...Rene Dazy, Dept. of Environment, Devon ...y/York Archaeological Trust, E-T ...Estall, Mary Evans Picture Library, ...el Finler Collection, Ed Fletcher, ...Archive, Fortean Picture ...Albertus/Paracelsus College/Salt ...nn Frost Historical Newspaper ...eif Geiges, Gent y la Actualidad, ...dliffe, Colin Goodman, Granada ...ruber, Sonia Halliday, Robert Harding, ..., Hertford Museum, Hertfordshire Echo & ... Michael Holford, Michael Holford Library, ...nn Hughes, Robert Hunt Picture Library, Anwar Hussein, Alan Hutchison Library, Image Bank, Imperial War Museum, Inter-Photo, Alix Jeffrey, Kadima Productions Inc., Keystone, Keystone Press Agency, L. Allen Klope, Kobal Collection, Larry Kusche, Laing Art Gallery, Frank W. Lane, Laphina, Beverley Lebarrow, Lisbon Academy of Science, London Express, W.G. Lucas, William MacQuitty, Macmillan Publishers, Dr. J.A. Macrae, Mansell Collection, P.R. Marsh, Marshall Cavendish, Martin Aircraft Co., Roger Mayne, McDonnell Douglas, Meteorological Office/J.H. Golden, F. Millar, R.B. Minton, Musées des Beaux-Arts de Belgique, NASA, National Archives, National Gallery of Ireland, National Maritime Museum, National Monuments Record, National Portrait Gallery, Natural Science Photos, New English Library, Newark Museum, Peter Newark, Peter Newark's Western Americana, North Carolina Museum of History, Nostra, Nova Scotia Dept. of Government Services, Novosti, Pan Books, Peabody Museum, Photri, Picturepoint, Guy Lyon Playfair, Axel Poignant, Coral Polge, Popperfoto, Press Association, Psychic News, Psycho Physical Research Foundation, Henry Puharich, Radio Times, Review, Rex Features, Rochester Museum, Roger-Viollet, Routledge & Kegan Paul, Royal Academy, Royal Collection, Royal Commission on Ancient & Historical Monuments of Scotland, Royal Geographical Society, Royal Irish Academy, Robert Runge, SITU, Scala, Ronald Sheridan Photo Library, Adrian Shine, Paul Snelgrove, Brian Snellgrove, Society for Psychical Research, Souvenir Press, Space Frontiers, Neville Spearman Ltd, Spectrum Colour Library, Sphere Books, Frank Spooner, Sri Sathya Sai Baba Trust, Roy Stemman, John Massey Stewart, A.F. Stubbs, Suddeutscher-Verlag, Mai Sullivan, Sunn Classic Productions, Syndication International, Tate Gallery, Michael Taylor, Theosophical Society, John Topham Library, John Topham Picture Library, David Towersey, Tyne Tees TV, UPI, US National Archives, USAF, Udreasfeavifen, Ullstein, Van Duren Publishers, Frances Vargo, Roger Viollet, P. Warrington, Washington Post, Harold Wilkins, Woodward Picture Library, J. Worsley, George Wright, ZEFA, Zenka.